# Psychological Science

FOURTH EDITION

# Psychological Science

FOURTH EDITION

Michael S. Gazzaniga
UNIVERSITY OF CALIFORNIA, SANTA BARBARA

Todd F. Heatherton
DARTMOUTH COLLEGE

Diane F. Halpern
CLAREMONT MCKENNA COLLEGE

W. W. NORTON & COMPANY
NEW YORK • LONDON

**W. W. NORTON & COMPANY** has been independent since its founding in 1923, when William Warder Norton and Mary D. Herter Norton first published lectures delivered at the People's Institute, the adult education division of New York City's Cooper Union. The Nortons soon expanded their program beyond the Institute, publishing books by celebrated academics from America and abroad. By mid-century, the two major pillars of Norton's publishing program—trade books and college texts—were firmly established. In the 1950s, the Norton family transferred control of the company to its employees, and today—with a staff of four hundred and a comparable number of trade, college, and professional titles published each year—W. W. Norton & Company stands as the largest and oldest publishing house owned wholly by its employees.

Editor: Sheri L. Snavely
Developmental Editor and Project Editor: Kurt Wildermuth
Managing Editor, College: Marian Johnson
Manuscript Editor: Janet Greenblatt
Editorial Assistants: Mary Dudley, Catherine Rice, and Carson Russell
Production Manager: Chris Granville
Art Director: Rubina Yeh
Book Designer: Lissi Sigillo
Photo Editors: Stephanie Romeo and Michael Fodera
Photo Researcher: Julie Tesser
Marketing Manager: Andrea Matter
Emedia Editor: Patrick Shriner
Associate Editors: Callinda Taylor and Matthew Freeman
Illustrators: Dragonfly Media Group
Compositor: Prepare, Emilcomp Inc.
Manufacturer: Transcontinental, Inc.


Printed in Canada

Library of Congress Cataloging-in-Publication Data

Gazzaniga, Michael S.
Psychological science / Michael S. Gazzaniga, Todd F. Heatherton, Diane F. Halpern. — 4th ed.
p. cm.
Includes bibliographical references and index.

**ISBN 978-0-393-91157-2 (hardcover)**

1. Psychology. I. Heatherton, Todd F. II. Halpern, Diane F. III. Title.
BF121.G393 2013
150—dc23

2011043532

W. W. Norton & Company, Inc., 500 Fifth Avenue, New York, N.Y. 10110
www.wwnorton.com

W. W. Norton & Company Ltd., Castle House, 75/76 Wells Street, London W1T 3QT

6 7 8 9 0

*We dedicate this book to*
Lilly, Emmy, and Garth Tretheway
Sarah Heatherton and James Heatherton
Sheldon, Evan, Karen, Amanda, and Jason Halpern
and Jaye, Danny, and Belle Halpern-Duncan.

# Contents in Brief

# About the Authors

**MICHAEL S. GAZZANIGA** (Ph.D., California Institute of Technology) is Distinguished Professor and Director of the Sage Center for the Study of the Mind at the University of California, Santa Barbara. He founded and presides over the Cognitive Neuroscience Institute and is founding editor-in-chief of the *Journal of Cognitive Neuroscience.* He is past president of the American Psychological Society and a member of the American Academy of Arts and Sciences, the Institute of Medicine, and the National Academy of Sciences. He has held positions at the University of California, Santa Barbara; New York University; the State University of New York, Stony Brook; Cornell University Medical College; and the University of California, Davis. In his career, he has introduced thousands of students to psychology and cognitive neuroscience. He has written many notable books, including, most recently, *Who's in Charge?: Free Will and the Science of the Brain.*

**TODD F. HEATHERTON** (Ph.D., University of Toronto) is the Lincoln Filene Professor in Human Relations in the Department of Psychological and Brain Sciences at Dartmouth College. His recent research takes a social brain sciences approach, which combines theories and methods of evolutionary psychology, social cognition, and cognitive neuroscience to examine the neural underpinnings of social behavior. He is associate editor of the *Journal of Cognitive Neuroscience* and serves on many editorial boards and grant review panels. He was elected president of the Society of Personality and Social Psychology in 2011 and has served on the executive committees of the Association of Researchers in Personality and the International Society of Self and Identity. He received the Award for Distinguished Service on Behalf of Social-Personality Psychology in 2005, was named to Thompson Reuters' ISI HighlyCited for Social Sciences in 2010, and received the Carol and Ed Diener Award for Outstanding Mid-Career Contributions to Personality Psychology in 2011. He received the Petra Shattuck Award for Teaching Excellence from the Harvard Extension School in 1994, the McLane Fellowship from Dartmouth College in 1997, and the Friedman Family Fellowship from Dartmouth College in 2001. He is a fellow of the American Psychological Association, the Association for Psychological Science, the Society of Experimental Social Psychology, and the Society for Personality and Social Psychology. He teaches introductory psychology every year.

**DIANE F. HALPERN** (Ph.D., University of Cincinnati) is the Trustee Professor of Psychology and Roberts Fellow at Claremont McKenna College. She is past president of the American Psychological Association, the Western Psychological Association, the Society for General Psychology, and the Society for the Teaching of Psychology. She has won many awards for her teaching and research, including the 2002 Outstanding Professor Award from the Western Psychological Association, the 1999 American Psychological Foundation Award for Distinguished Teaching, the 1996 Distinguished Career Award for Contributions to Education from the American Psychological Association, and the California State University's State-Wide Outstanding Professor Award. She has written many books, including *Thought and Knowledge: An Introduction to Critical Thinking and Sex Differences in Cognitive Abilities*. Her edited book, *Undergraduate Education in Psychology: A Blueprint for the Future of the Discipline* (APA Books), was published in 2009. She teaches introductory psychology every year.

# Preface

## Why Teach with *Psychological Science*?

### Our Book Delivers What Students Need to Know

From the moment the original author team, Mike Gazzaniga and Todd Heatherton, conceived the first edition of *Psychological Science,* our primary motivation was to create a textbook that captured ongoing revolutionary changes in the field. Instead of an encyclopedic and homogenized compendium that dutifully covered worn themes and tired topics, we wanted to create a readable book that captured the excitement of contemporary research and yet respected the rich tradition of scientific research accumulated by the field. We sought and received excellent advice from countless colleagues about what was most important to them in introductory psychology courses and what they believed was of greatest value to students. It became clear that most instructors wanted a textbook that focused on material that students really needed to know at the introductory level. They did not want a book that burdened readers with unnecessary details.

In revising the book for each subsequent edition, we have kept students foremost in mind. We worked hard on hitting the right level of detail and also on keeping the material accessible, relevant, and interesting. We retained our ask and answer thematic approach, which captures the reader's interest, and our declarative prose style, which focuses on the answers to current scientific questions.

### Our Book Crosses Levels of Analysis and Embraces Diverse Approaches

Although Mike came to the book with a strong background in cognitive neuroscience and Todd in social and personality psychology, our early goal was to feature research that crossed levels of analysis, from cultural and social context to genes and neurons. To really understand basic cognitive and perceptual processes, researchers need to appreciate that social contexts shape what people think about and how they perceive the world around them. Moreover, important differences in personality mean that people have unique interactions with those social environments.

Our focus on contemporary research extends well beyond brain science to include new thinking in social, personality, and developmental psychology as well as contemporary approaches to understanding psychological disorders and their treatment. Each subfield has made great progress over the last decade, and our goal in each edition has been to highlight how contemporary research is providing new insights into the brain, behavior, and psychological disorders. The unified approach to each topic has been to concentrate on what we have learned from scientific study, such as research over the past decade on the empirical basis of psychological treatment.

## Students Will Succeed with Our Science of Learning Approach

For the third edition, the renowned critical thinking expert Diane Halpern joined the team. Diane shared our interest and vision in creating a highly accessible, scientifically grounded textbook. What she added, and we very much desired, was her expertise on the science of learning. Although we (Mike and Todd) had spent considerable time in the classroom and received awards for our teaching, Diane's empirical approach to the science of learning resonated for us. That, after all, is the point of our book: We learn how things work through careful scientific study.

Our book seeks to be the perfect union between the science of psychology and the science of learning. Through careful empirical research into the cognitive, individual, and environmental factors that influence active learning, psychologists have discovered the best practices for teaching. Researchers have studied the way people think, learn, and remember, yet this knowledge is not often applied to student learning. Our pedagogical framework is based on what researchers have learned about how students learn. Thanks to Diane's expertise, we incorporated many new science-based learning features into the third edition: an enhanced ask and answer approach; Learning Objectives, which focus students on the central questions they should be able to answer after reading a chapter; Summing Up/Measuring Up interim assessments, which are explicitly tied to the Learning Objectives and give students take-home messages as well as questions to test their understanding; Practice Tests, at the end of the chapters and on the student Web site, which help students consolidate their learning; and Critical Thinking sections, which show students how to put critical thinking into action. These features provide students with many opportunities to practice retrieval and use higher-order thinking, both of which increase the building of durable, transferable knowledge.

We also used a science of learning approach to design the visual art program. Because we value a scientific approach, we consulted with one of the world's leading educational psychologists, Richard Mayer, whose research focuses on how people can learn more effectively using visual materials. Rich helped us conceptualize new presentations of visual information that encourage active learning. For instance, we sought to help visual learners with clear, attractive graphics that stimulated students' thinking skills and drove home their understanding of key concepts. We introduced the "Try for Yourself" features, which encourage students to engage in demonstrations on their own. We introduced the "Scientific Method" illustrations, which carefully and consistently lead students through the steps of some of the most interesting experiments and studies in psychological science. In the chapter on sensation and perception, we created "How We" figures, which help students understand the complex processes involved in sensing and perceiving the world. These step-by-step figures enable students to see processes in action and to view the material from both micro perspectives and macro perspectives.

In this new edition, we continued our innovation by adding questions at the end of at least two captions in each chapter. These caption questions facilitate deeper understanding by encouraging students to connect the photos and figures to the concepts presented in the text.

## New to This Edition: SmartWork Takes the Science of Learning Online

An exciting new development for the fourth edition is the creation of SmartWork, a sophisticated, flexible online homework system developed by W. W. Norton. For

*Psychological Science,* SmartWork is integrated with the fourth-edition art program and pedagogy, using interactive questions and activities to reinforce core concepts. We are very fortunate to have Sarah Grison and her team of psychologists authoring SmartWork for our book. Sarah has 17 years of teaching experience and has taught introductory psychology to thousands of students at the University of Illinois at Urbana-Champaign. Sarah's research examines how psychological research can be applied to teaching and learning.

## Students Care about What They Learn in Our Book

A major goal of the fourth edition is encouraging students to care about psychology. As engaged readers, students will learn more deeply, understand themselves and others more fully, and become better critical thinkers and decision makers. And by acquiring skills and knowledge that they remember long after the course is finished, these engaged readers will come away with a richer appreciation of our field. As noted, Diane Halpern's vast experience has led to our popular Critical Thinking Skills sections, which address topics such as regression to the mean and drug bias in research. New to the fourth edition are "Psychology: Knowledge You Can Use" features, which keep students engaged and thinking. One per chapter, these applications address the question of what students might immediately do with the information they learn. "Psychology: Knowledge You Can Use" topics include the relationship between sleep and study habits, how psychology can help a person navigate in his or her romantic life, and how to help a friend who seems suicidal. By making clear how psychological concepts can have real-time usefulness, these applications provide additional motivation for students to engage with the material.

## Have You Read It Lately?

Our adopters regularly praise our clear and inviting writing style. This feedback warms our hearts and makes the effort of writing a textbook worthwhile. However, instructors who have not adopted *Psychological Science* often indicate that they respect our book but think it is "too high-level" for their students. For the fourth edition, we decided to face this challenge head-on. After all, students should be focusing on the concepts, not the reading. With the help of reviewers, advisors, and our developmental editor, we found ways to maintain the integrity of content but make the explanations even clearer and more accessible. We cut unnecessary terms, examples, and digressions, shortening some chapters by as much as 10 percent. We reworked complex sentences and long paragraphs to maximize student understanding. We revised even the shortest sentences to engage introductory readers more colloquially. In addition, we further enhanced the already strong relationship between the art and the narrative to help students form lasting associations.

Throughout the book, we scrutinized the discussions of neuroscience to make their connections with the chapters' major concepts as meaningful as possible. Consider Chapter 7, "Attention and Memory." In the third edition, readers encountered the section "What Brain Processes Are Involved in Memory?" in the middle of the chapter, between discussions of long-term memory and forgetting. In the fourth edition, that material has been reduced to essentials, titled "Memory Is the Result of Brain Activity," and incorporated into "What Is Memory?", a brand-new, reader-friendly opening section that establishes the major themes of the chapter.

## The Content Reflects Our Global, Multicultural Society

For the third edition, we reached our goal of increasing the inclusivity of our discussions. In every chapter, we added more material related to gender, culture, and international issues. For the fourth edition, we have continued our efforts to represent the world in its diversity: the young and the middle-aged and the elderly, blacks and whites, Asians and Middle Easterners, southerners and northerners, gays and straights, women and men and people in between. For example, the third-edition's discussion of Mary Whiton Calkins and Margaret Flay Washburn has been expanded to a subsection, "Women Have Helped Shape the Field," which acknowledges the historical and modern roles of women in countless areas of psychology. And for the first time, our human development chapter discusses the concept of *transgender.*

Meanwhile, it is unfortunate that many psychology textbooks focus almost completely on research from North America, because a tremendous amount of exciting psychological research takes place around the world. After all, the rich history of psychological science reflects contributions from scholars around the globe, such as Wundt's original work in Germany. Students should learn about the best psychological science, no matter where it originates. Our goal has always been to present the best psychological research regardless of country, and in the fourth edition each chapter includes new important research from many corners of the globe. For example, we discuss the fascinating work of researchers in Belgium and England who have been able to communicate with people who are in comas. We describe research from Australia that provides an elegant description of how working memory is updated to take into account new information. We describe cross-cultural work on self-perception. Such research from outside North America will not only help students learn more about psychology. It will also bring them new perspectives, encouraging a sense of themselves as global citizens.

## The Content Reflects Our Colleagues and Our Students

The three of us hope that the revisions we have made to our textbook will greatly appeal to students and instructors. We conducted focus sessions of adopters, friends, and potential users to canvass their thoughts, and the text has been greatly improved because of their advice and experience in the classroom. In making major changes to every chapter, we feel that we have hit the perfect balance between fundamentals and the excitement that drives our science. As we have noted in previous editions, the present is an exciting time to work in psychological science, and we hope that our excitement is contagious to our readers and our students. We are energized and inspired by the many undergraduate and graduate students we have the pleasure to interact with each day. This book is written for them, with our respect for their intelligence and our admiration for their inquisitiveness.

# Acknowledgments

We begin as always by acknowledging the unwavering support we have received from our families. Writing a textbook is a time-consuming endeavor, and our family members have been generous in allowing us the time to focus on writing. We are also extremely grateful to the many colleagues who gave us constructive feedback and advice. Some individuals deserve special recognition. First and foremost is our good friend Margaret Lynch, who read every sentence of the revised edition and made valuable comments throughout. Margaret is an amazing advocate for students and reminds us never to take them for granted or underestimate them. She has been a valuable partner throughout. Debra Mashek, recent recipient of an APA teaching award, has been an invaluable member of the team for two editions. For the third edition, Debra helped us create parts of the pedagogical system. For the fourth edition, Debra wrote the "Psychology: Knowledge You Can Use" features. Thanks in large part to Debra's engaging, insightful voice, students will love applying the findings of psychological science to their own lives. Also for the fourth edition, Sarah Grison and her talented team of psychologists—Angela Isaacs, Genevieve Hendricks, and Crystal Carlson—joined the team to guide the development of our SmartWork program. Sarah's teaching experience and her empirical research on the science of learning provide unparalleled expertise in how students best learn, and we are delighted that she has shared her expertise with us.

Sunaina Assanand graciously read each chapter, provided valuable critiques, and guided us in revising the chapter pedagogy to reflect the revision. Sunaina was especially valuable for making sure the details were accurate, and her insights often helped us frame the material to maximize student understanding. Insightful teacher/researcher Tasha R. Howe helped us revise the development chapter substantially, adding a new section on adolescence and bringing a more contemporary approach.

Throughout the planning process, we sought expert advice on many aspects of the textbook and the ancillary package. A talented group of individuals gave us tough-minded, thoughtful critiques that helped shape the ancillaries, helped launch SmartWork, and provided wisdom for the fourth edition revision. We would like to give special recognition to the following:

George Alder, *Simon Fraser University*
Sunaina Assanand, *University of British Columbia–Vancouver*
Karen Brebner, *St. Francis Xavier University*
Kathleen H. Briggs, *University of Minnesota*
Michele R. Brumley, *Idaho State University*
Patrick Carroll, *University of Texas*
Sarah P. Cerny, *Rutgers University–Newark*
Heidi L. Dempsey, *Jacksonville State University*
Renee Engeln-Maddox, *Northwestern University*
Clifford D. Evans, *Miami University of Ohio*
Kimberly Fenn, *Michigan State University*
Sarah Grison, *University of Illinois at Urbana-Champaign*
Jeffrey Henriques, *University of Wisconsin*
Tasha R. Howe, *Humboldt State University*
Howard C. Hughes, *Dartmouth College*
Sheila M. Kennison, *Oklahoma State University*
Lisa Kolbuss, *Lane Community College*
Dianne Leader, *Georgia Institute of Technology*
Jeff Love, *Pennsylvania State University*
Margaret F. Lynch, *San Francisco State University*
Corrine L. McNamara, *Kennesaw State University*
Kevin E. Moore, *DePauw University*
David Payne, *Wallace County Community College*
Steve Prentice-Dunn, *University of Alabama*
Gabriel Radvansky, *Notre Dame University*
Alan C. Roberts, *Indiana University–Bloomington*
David A. Schroeder, *University of Arkansas*
John W. Wright, *Washington State University*

Producing a textbook requires a small army of people who are crucial at each step of the way. Our ancillary team was instrumental in producing first-rate materials that will assist students and instructors in having a rich experience with the material. David Payne wrote the new Visual Summaries and authored a brand-new Study Guide with our longtime friends and colleagues from Bloomsburg University: Brett Beck, Eileen Astor-Stetson, and Jennifer Johnson. Brett, Eileen, and Jennifer also authored superb new content for the student StudySpace Web site, and Christa Padovano lent her creativity to design the Visual Summaries. Pat Carroll once again assembled wonderful video offerings that contribute so much to classroom instruction. Sue Franz wrote a spectacular Instructor's Manual, which is adapted to the new Interactive Instructor's Guide online format. For each chapter, Kimberly Fenn wrote a terrific set of class-tested "clicker questions" that will make instructors look like superstars. We are so grateful to all these individuals, who lent their talent and time to create a strong support package for the fourth edition.

We need to make special mention of the Test Bank, which, as every instructor knows, is crucial to a successful course. Inadequate test banks with uneven or ambiguous items can frustrate students and instructors alike. For the fourth edition, the Test Bank was again compiled using the science of learning approach to assessment designed by Valerie Shute and Diego Zapata-Rivera. The highly accomplished team of Nikole Diane Huffman, Matthew Isaak, Natasha Tokowicz, Todd McKerchar, and Roxana Conroy authored the new fourth edition Test Bank, aided by reviews from Joseph Etherton, Emily Stark, and Rachel Messer. We cannot express the depth of our appreciation for their efforts.

## The Norton Team

In the modern publishing world, where most books are produced by large multinational corporations, W. W. Norton stands out as a beacon to academics and authors. Its employees own the company, and therefore every individual who worked on our book has a vested personal interest in its success; it shows in the great enthusiasm they bring to their work. Two individuals deserve special recognition for this new edition. Sheri Snavely took over as editor during the third edition and played a central role in shaping this new edition. Sheri is an amazingly talented and insightful editor who brought not only many years of expertise in science editing, but also a profound dedication to getting the word out on how we have revised the book and making sure the marketing message clearly articulated the strengths of our book. She has been a rock for us and has also become our good friend. There is not a better editor in psychology, and we are grateful for the attention she has given our book even as she has built one of the best overall lists in psychology today. Roby Harrington was a genius for hiring her, and we also express our gratitude to Roby for his support of the book.

There will always be a special place in our hearts for Kurt Wildermuth. In the third edition, we noted that Kurt is a wordsmith of the highest order. For the fourth edition, we capitalized on his talents by having him help us consider every single sentence in the book to make sure the writing was crisp and accessible. Kurt threw himself into this project and was crucial for every step of the revision, from overseeing the schedule to helping craft the chapter opening vignettes. Words fail to fully capture our admiration for his contributions to this revision and for his loyalty to the textbook.

Many others also provided crucial support. Mary Dudley was an extraordinary editorial assistant until she was promoted to traveler, where she will use her talents to help market the book in her new Texas territory. Catherine Rice has stepped into the editorial assistant role and helped us keep organized as all the final details came together. Our associate editor, Callinda Taylor, efficiently and creatively brought the best authors to our ancillaries program. Patrick Shriner, our media editor and a veteran when it comes to science media, has worked tirelessly to pull together our groundbreaking media program for the new edition and the SmartWork online homework system for psychology. Photo editors Stephanie Romeo and Michael Fodera did a wonderful job of researching and editing all the photos in our book and finding the captivating faces that begin each chapter.

We are grateful for our marketing manager, Andrea Matter, who has created a cutting-edge and informative marketing campaign. She truly understands "better learning through science" and is doing a marvelous job of making sure our message reaches travelers and professors. A big thank you to the psychological science specialists Peter Ruscitti and Heidi Shadix, who travel across North America and have probably racked up enough frequent flier points traveling for our book that they could fly to the moon and back. Indeed, the entire sales force at W. W. Norton, led by Michael Wright and his legendary team of managers, has supported our book, and they continue to get the word out and develop key relationships in psychology departments. The Norton travelers are distinguished by the time they take to learn about the psychology in our book so that they can present it in the best way to professors. A special thank you to the senior travelers who have represented several editions of the book and know it almost as well as we do. They are Scott Cook, John Darger, John Kelly, Doris Oliver, Yovanny Pulcini, and Mary Helen Willett.

Finally, we acknowledge the president of Norton, Drake McFeely, for inspiring a workforce that cares so deeply about publishing and for having continuing faith in us.

## *Psychological Science* Reviewers and Consultants

George Alder, *Simon Fraser University*
Rahan Ali, *Pennsylvania State University*
Gordon A. Allen, *Miami University of Ohio*
Mary J. Allen, *California State University, Bakersfield*
Ron Apland, *Malaspina College*
Christopher T. Arra, *Northern Virginia Community College*
Sunaina Assanand, *University of British Columbia, Vancouver*
Alan Baddelay, *Bristol University*
Lori Badura, *State University of New York, Buffalo*
Mahzarin Banaji, *Harvard University*
David H. Barlow, *Boston University*
Carolyn Barry, *Loyola College*
Scott Bates, *Utah State University*
Holly Beard, *Midlands Technical College*
Bernard C. Beins, *Ithaca College*
Lisa Best, *University of New Brunswick*
Joan Bihm, *University of Colorado Denver*
Joe Bilotta, *Western Kentucky University*
Colin Blakemore, *Oxford University*
Karen Brebner, *St. Francis Xavier University*
Kathleen H. Briggs, *University of Minnesota*
John P. Broida, *University of Southern Maine*
Michele R. Brumley, *Idaho State University*
Randy Buckner, *Washington University*
William Buskist, *Auburn University*
Tara Callaghan, *St. Francis Xavier University*
Elisabeth Leslie Cameron, *Carthage College*
Katherine Cameron, *Washington College*
Jennifer Campbell, *University of British Columbia*
Timothy Cannon, *University of Scranton*
Tom Capo, *University of Maryland*
Charles Carver, *University of Miami*
Michelle L. Caya, *Trident Technical College*
Sarah P. Cerny, *Rutgers University, Newark*
Jonathan Cheek, *Wellesley College*
Stephen Clark, *Keene State College*
Dennis Cogan, *Texas Tech University*
Martin Conway, *Bristol University*
Michael Corballis, *University of Auckland*
Brent Foster Costleigh, *Brookdale Community College*

Graham Cousens, *Macalester College*
Dale Dagenbach, *Wake Forest University*
Haydn Davis, *Palomar College*
Suzanne Delaney, *University of Arizona*
Heidi L. Dempsey, *Jacksonville State University*
Joseph Dien, *Tulane University*
Michael Domjan, *University of Texas at Austin*
Wendy Domjan, *University of Texas at Austin*
Jack Dovidio, *Colgate University*
Dana S. Dunn, *Moravian College*
Howard Eichenbaum, *Boston University*
Naomi Eisenberger, *University of California, Los Angeles*
Renee Engeln-Maddox, *Northwestern University*
James Enns, *University of British Columbia*
Clifford D. Evans, *Miami University of Ohio*
Raymond Fancher, *York University*
Valerie Farmer-Dougan, *Illinois State University*
Greg Feist, *University of California, Davis*
Kimberly M. Fenn, *Michigan State University*
Fernanda Ferreira, *University of South Carolina*
Vic Ferreira, *University of California, San Diego*
Holly Filcheck, *Louisiana State University*
Joseph Fitzgerald, *Wayne State University*
Trisha Folds-Bennett, *College of Charleston*
Margaret Forgie, *University of Lethbridge*
Howard Friedman, *University of California, Riverside*
David C. Funder, *University of California, Riverside*
Christopher Gade, *University of California, Berkeley*
Christine Gancarz, *Southern Methodist University*
Wendi Gardner, *Northwestern University*
Preston E. Garraghty, *Indiana University*
Margaret Gatz, *University of Southern California*
Caroline Gee, *Saddleback College*
Peter Gerhardstein, *Binghamton University*
Katherine Gibbs, *University of California, Davis*
Bryan Gibson, *Central Michigan University*
Rick O. Gilmore, *Pennsylvania State University*
Jamie Goldenberg, *University of South Florida*
Laura Gonnerman, *Lehigh University*
Peter Graf, *University of British Columbia*
Leonard Green, *Washington University*
Raymond Green, *Texas A&M–Commerce*
Sarah Grison, *University of Illinois at Urbana-Champaign*
James Gross, *Stanford University*
Tom Guilmette, *Providence College*
John Hallonquist, *University of the Caribou*
Thomas W. Hancock, *University of Central Oklahoma*
Erin E. Hardin, *Texas Tech University*
Brad Hastings, *Mount Aloysius College*
Linda Hatt, *University of British Columbia Okanagan*
Mikki Hebl, *Rice University*
Steven Heine, *University of British Columbia*
John Henderson, *Michigan State University*
Norman Henderson, *Oberlin College*
Mark Henn, *University of New Hampshire*
Terence Hines, *Pace University*
Sarah Hodges, *University of Oregon*
Cynthia Hoffman, *Indiana University*
Don Hoffman, *University of California, Irvine*
James Hoffman, *University of Delaware*
Mark Holder, *University of British Columbia Okanagan*
Tasha R. Howe, *Humboldt State University*
Howard C. Hughes, *Dartmouth College*
Jay Hull, *Dartmouth College*
Jake Jacobs, *University of Arizona*
Thomas Joiner, *Florida State University*
Steve Joordens, *University of Toronto–Scarborough*
William Kelley, *Dartmouth College*
Dacher Keltner, *University of California, Berkeley*
Lindsay A. Kennedy, *University of North Carolina–Chapel Hill*
Sheila M. Kennison, *Oklahoma State University–Stillwater*
Mike Kerchner, *Washington College*
Rondall Khoo, *Western Connecticut State University*
Lisa Kolbuss, *Lane Community College*
Gabriel Kreiman, *Harvard University*
Gert Kruger, *University of Johannesburg*
Gerard La Morte, *Rutgers University, Newark*
Lori Lange, *University of North Florida*
Mark Laumakis, *San Diego State University*
Natalie Kerr Lawrence, *James Madison University*
Steven R. Lawyer, *Idaho State University*
Benjamin Le, *Haverford College*
Dianne Leader, *Georgia Institute of Technology*
Mark Leary, *Wake Forest University*
Ting Lei, *Borough of Manhattan Community College*
Charles Leith, *Northern Michigan University*
Carol Lemley, *Elizabethtown College*
Gary W. Lewandowski Jr., *Monmouth University*
Christine Lofgren, *University of California, Irvine*
Liang Lou, *Grand Valley State University*
Jeff Love, *Pennsylvania State University*
Monica Luciana, *University of Minnesota*
Margaret F. Lynch, *San Francisco State University*
Neil Macrae, *University of Aberdeen*
Karl Maier, *Salisbury University*
Mike Mangan, *University of New Hampshire*

Gary Marcus, *New York University*
Leonard Mark, *Miami University (Ohio)*
Debra Mashek, *Harvey Mudd College*
Tim Maxwell, *Hendrix College*
Ashley E. Maynard, *University of Hawaii*
Dan McAdams, *Northwestern University*
Doug McCann, *York University*
Paul McCormack, *St. Francis Xavier University*
David McDonald, *University of Missouri–Columbia*
Bill McKeachie, *University of Michigan*
Patricia McMullen, *Dalhousie University*
Corrine L. McNamara, *Kennesaw State University*
Paul Merritt, *George Washington University*
Peter Metzner, *Vance Granville Community College*
Dennis K. Miller, *University of Missouri*
Hal Miller, *Brigham Young University*
Judy Miller, *Oberlin College*
Douglas G. Mook, *University of Virginia, Emeritus*
Kevin E. Moore, *DePauw University*
Joe Morrisey, *State University of New York, Binghamton*
Todd Nelson, *California State University–Stanislaus*
Julie Norem, *Wellesley College*
Maria Minda Oriña, *University of Minnesota–Twin Cities*
Dominic J. Parrott, *Georgia State University*
Lois Pasapane, *Palm Beach State College*
David Payne, *Wallace Community College*
James Pennebaker, *University of Texas at Austin*
Zehra Peynircioglu, *American University*
Brady Phelps, *South Dakota State University*
Elizabeth Phelps, *New York University*
Jackie Pope-Tarrance, *Western Kentucky University*
Steve Prentice-Dunn, *University of Alabama*
Gabriel Radvansky, *Notre Dame University*
Patty Randolph, *Western Kentucky University*
Catherine Reed, *Claremont McKenna College*
Lauretta Reeves, *University of Texas at Austin*
Jennifer Richeson, *Northwestern University*
Alan C. Roberts, *Indiana University–Bloomington*
Caton Roberts, *University of Wisconsin–Madison*
William Rogers, *Grand Valley State University*
Alex Rothman, *University of Minnesota*
Paul Rozin, *University of Pennsylvania*
Sharleen Sakai, *Michigan State University*
Juan Salinas, *University of Texas at Austin*
Laura Saslow, *University of California, Berkeley*
Heather Schellink, *Dalhousie University*
Richard Schiffman, *Rutgers University*
Lynne Schmetter-Davis, *Brookdale Community College*
David A. Schroeder, *University of Arkansas*
Constantine Sedikedes, *University of Southampton*
Ines Segert, *University of Missouri*
Allison Sekuler, *McMaster University*
Margaret Sereno, *University of Oregon*
Andrew Shatte, *University of Pennsylvania*
J. Nicole Shelton, *Princeton University*
Arthur Shimamura, *University of California, Berkeley*
Rebecca Shiner, *Colgate University*
Jennifer Siciliani-Pride, *University of Missouri–St. Louis*
Scott Sinnett, *University of Hawaii at Manoa*
Reid Skeel, *Central Michigan University*
John J. Skowronski, *Northern Illinois University*
Andra Smith, *University of Ottawa*
Dennison Smith, *Oberlin College*
Ashley Smyth, *South Africa College of Applied Psychology*
Mark Snyder, *University of Minnesota*
Sheldon Solomon, *Skidmore College*
Sue Spaulding, *University of North Carolina, Charlotte*
Faye Steur, *College of Charleston*
Dawn L. Strongin, *California State University–Stanislaus*
James Sullivan, *Florida State University*
Lorey K. Takahashi, *University of Hawaii at Manoa*
George Taylor, *University of Missouri–St. Louis*
Lee Thompson, *Case Western Reserve University*
Diane Tice, *Case Western Reserve University*
Rob Tigner, *Truman State College*
Peter Tse, *Dartmouth College*
David Uttal, *Northwestern University*
Robin R. Vallacher, *Florida Atlantic University*
Kristy L. vanMarle, *University of Missouri–Columbia*
Simine Vazire, *Washington University*
Shaun Vecera, *University of Iowa*
Athena Vouloumanos, *New York University*
Benjamin Walker, *Georgetown University*
Elaine Walker, *Emory University*
Brian Wandell, *Stanford University*
Kenneth A. Weaver, *Emporia State University*
Kevin Weinfurt, *Duke University*
Rajkumari Wesley, *Brookdale Community College*
Doug Whitman, *Wayne State University*
Gordon Whitman, *Tidewater Community College*
Nicole L. Wilson, *University of California, Santa Cruz*
Maxine Gallander Wintre, *York University*
Clare Wiseman, *Trinity College*
Al Witkofsky, *Salisbury University*
Vanessa Woods, *Santa Barbara City College*
John W. Wright, *Washington State University*
Jill A. Yamashita, *Saint Xavier University*
Dahlia Zaidel, *University of California, Los Angeles*

# Instructor Resources

## Lecture Presentation Resources

Presentation Resources come in four varieties designed to help you build your lecture in the way that best suits your course needs:

- **Art:** Every figure, photo, and table from the textbook in JPEG and PowerPoint files enhanced for optimal viewing when projected.
- **Lecture Slides:** PowerPoint slides for each chapter with lecture outlines, key figures, and ideas and teaching suggestions in the notes field.
- **Beyond the Textbook Material:** PowerPoint slides that present research studies and applications for each chapter that are not included in the textbook.
- **Clicker Questions:** Authored by Kimberly Fenn, Michigan State University. Each chapter offers at least ten questions in PowerPoint that will engage your students by actively involving them in your lectures.

Lecture Presentation Resources are available on the Instructor's Resource Disc and downloadable on the Interactive Instructor's Guide.

## Norton Psychology Video Resources

**Patrick Carroll,** *University of Texas, Austin*

Norton's popular video clips series has been updated and revitalized both with additional clips and by a new system of streaming video delivery.

The *Norton Psychology in the News DVD* features nearly 200 clips profiling recent psychological research.

Norton now offers instructors streaming video through its new **Interactive Instructor's Manual.** Patrick Carroll has selected a mix of classical and contemporary research studies, as well as videos that show applications of psychological concepts in the real world. New clips will be added through the academic year.

## Test Bank

**Nikole Diane Huffman,** *Ohio State University*
**Matthew Isaak,** *University of Louisiana at Lafayette*
**Natasha Tokowicz,** *University of Pittsburgh*
**Todd McKerchar,** *Jacksonville State University*
**Roxana Conroy,** *Jacksonville State University*

With the goals of promoting a higher level of understanding for the student and a more targeted system of assessment for the professor, the *Psychological Science* test questions have been completely revised using an evidence-centered approach designed by Valerie Shute of Florida State University and Diego Zapata-Rivera from the Educational Testing Service. Using the chapter Learning Objectives and Bloom's taxonomy of cognitive skills, question creation has been fully integrated with the elements of the student study package, including SmartWork and the Study Guide.

The Test Bank is available in print, on disc in the ExamView Assessment Suite, and downloadable on the Interactive Instructor's Guide.

## Instructor's Resource Manual

**Sue Frantz,** *Highline Community College*

The IRM is a rich resource for enhancing lectures and adapting *Psychological Science* for your course. It includes sample lectures, discussion questions, demonstrations, handouts, and suggested film/video, printed, and Web resources—all designed to make lectures more active, engaging, and informative.

## Coursepacks

Available at no cost to professors or students, Norton coursepacks for online or hybrid courses are available in a variety of formats, including all versions of Blackboard and WebCT. With just a simple download from our instructor's Web site, an adopter can bring high-quality Norton digital media into a new or existing online course (no extra student passwords required), and it's theirs to keep forever. Coursepacks for *Psychological Science* draw on content from StudySpace, but go beyond it. Features include test bank, StudySpace quizzes, animations, Critical Thinking exercises, Studying the Mind videos, discussion questions, Learning Objectives exercises, and video exercises. Available in Blackboard, WebCT, ANGEL, Desire2Learn, and Moodle.

### NEW—Interactive Instructor's Guide ties it all together online

The new IIG Web site makes it easy for instructors to integrate all the resources from the IRM, PowerPoint files, and video clips into their courses. Flexible searching and browsing tools help instructors find just the right resources to enhance their lectures and serve as a central hub for finding introductory psychology materials.

# Integrated Study Package Helps Students Focus

The integration of the *Psychological Science* study package means that students will hear a single voice regardless of where they go to study—in the book, online, or beyond.

**Study support starts in the textbook:**

Like the Summing Up/Measuring Up boxes for chapter sections, the **Summary** and **Practice Test** features at the end of each chapter boil down the key ideas and then test student comprehension of them.

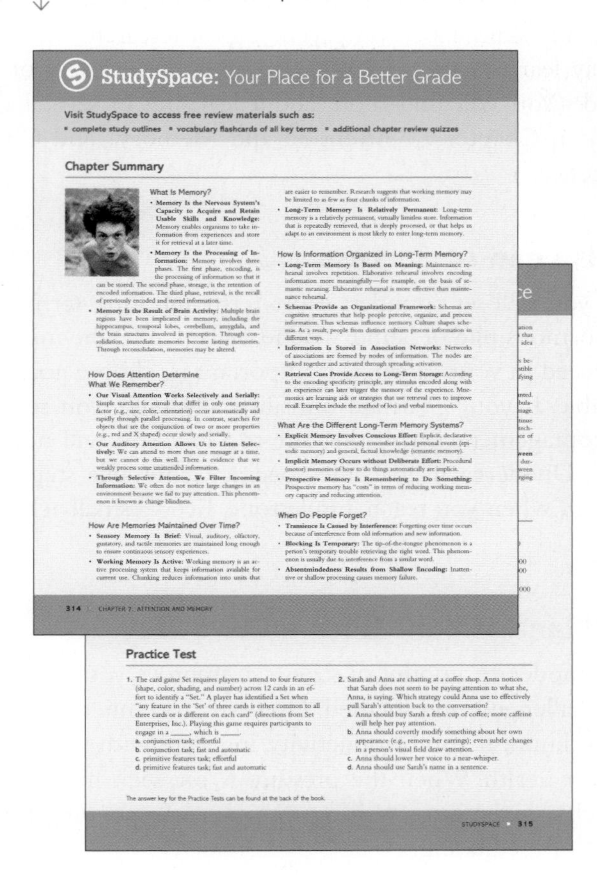
StudySpace: Your Place for a Better Grade

Visit StudySpace to access free review materials such as:
• complete study outlines • vocabulary flashcards of all key terms • additional chapter review quizzes

Chapter Summary

What Is Memory?

How Does Attention Determine What We Remember?

How Are Memories Maintained Over Time?

How Is Information Organized in Long-Term Memory?

What Are the Different Long-Term Memory Systems?

When Do People Forget?

314 CHAPTER 7: ATTENTION AND MEMORY

Practice Test

The answer key for the Practice Tests can be found at the back of the book.

STUDYSPACE 315

**Student review continues online with our free (no password or registration code) StudySpace Web site.**

Our new **Visual Summaries** tie it all together and expand students' understanding of concepts by helping them see how core ideas relate to one another.

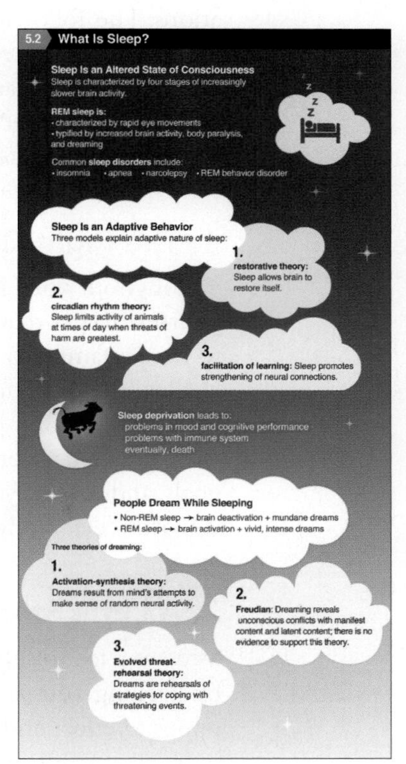


Other **StudySpace** features include chapter **Study Plans** to help students get organized, **Flashcards** to aid in their mastery of key terms, and **Quiz+** chapter review quizzes that guide student learning. **Video Exercises** help students connect concepts to the world beyond the classroom.

## Study Guide

**David Payne,** *Wallace Community College*
with Brett Beck, Eileen Astor Stetson, and Jennifer Johnson, *Bloomsburg University*

Our print Study Guide offers students a "guided approach" through the chapter content. Each section presents a reading schedule, priming questions, sets of quiz questions with hints and suggestions of where in the textbook to learn about particular concepts, and study-skills "best practices."

# Student Preface

## How Can Psychology Help You Learn?

In this increasingly fast-paced world, we are constantly bombarded with information: News stories reach us in minutes from around the globe, new technologies replace old ones, and groundbreaking scientific studies alter long-held beliefs about the physical world. To succeed in college and in your career, you will need to develop powerful learning strategies that produce durable and flexible learning—learning that lasts well into the future and that you can transfer to new situations. The following study skills, based on psychological research, will help you work more productively, learn more efficiently, and apply in a variety of settings what you have learned. (You will find more about learning in several chapters in this book, especially in Chapter 7, "Attention and Memory," and Chapter 8, "Thinking and Intelligence.")

### 1. The Right Goals Lead to Success

Throughout your life, you will set countless short-term and long-term goals for yourself: to get that enormous pile of laundry done, to run an eight-minute mile, to have a family, to succeed in your career. It is important to choose goals that are challenging yet attainable. If your goals are unrealistically high, you set yourself up for failure and discouragement, but if they are too low, you will not achieve your greatest potential. Divide each goal into specific, achievable steps, or subgoals, and reward yourself when you reach a milestone. Even a small achievement is worth celebrating!

### 2. A Little Stress Management Goes a Long Way

Stress is a fact of life. A moderate amount of stress can improve your performance by keeping you alert, challenged, and focused. However, too much stress has the opposite effect and can diminish your productivity, interfere with your sleep, and even take a toll on your health. When the pressure is on, seek healthy ways to manage your stress, such as exercising, writing in a journal, spending time with friends, practicing yoga, or meditating.

### 3. Cramming Is a Crummy Way to Learn

You have a busy life, and it is always tempting to postpone studying until the night or two before an exam. But in all of your classes, there is too much to learn to cram your learning into a few days or late nights. You might be able to remember enough information to get a passing grade on an exam the following day, but plenty of research has shown that cramming does not produce learning that lasts. To make learning stick, you need to space out your study sessions over the semester and build in plenty of time for active reviews.

## 4. Learning Is Not a Spectator Sport

The more effort you put into your studying, the more benefit you will receive. Merely rereading a chapter or your class notes is not as effective as actively trying to remember what you have learned. Every time you learn something, you create "memory traces" in your brain. By retrieving the information that was learned, you strengthen the memory traces so that you will be more likely to recall the memory in the future. In this book, to encourage active studying, every major section heading is in the form of a question. When you go back to study each section, begin by writing out an answer to the question in the heading without looking at the book. Then check the accuracy and completeness of what you wrote.

## 5. Explaining Enhances Understanding and Memory

As you learn, focus on trying to explain and describe complicated topics in your own words, as opposed to just memorizing terms and definitions. For example, simply using flashcards to learn about visual perception may help you memorize individual parts of the eye and their functions, but doing so will not help you put the pieces together to understand the incredible process of how we see and recognize objects in the world. Memorizing isolated bits of information is also likely to result in shallow learning that is easily forgotten. A deeper level of learning based on explanation and description would give you a more holistic understanding and a greater ability to generalize the information.

## 6. There Is More Than One Way to Learn

As you will read in Chapter 7, people process information in two channels—visual and verbal. Another strategy for creating durable learning is to use both of these information formats. Try to supplement the notes you take with visual and spatial displays such as concept maps, graphs, flowcharts, and other types of diagrams. Doing so not only makes you more likely to remember the information but also helps you gain a better understanding of the big picture by emphasizing the connections among important ideas.

A knowledge of psychology can be useful to you in many ways, even if you do not pursue a career in the field. For this reason, we have tried to make all the material in *Psychological Science* accessible and interesting for you as well as directly applicable to your life. As you gain an integrated grounding in traditional and new approaches within psychological science, we hope that this book spurs your curiosity about psychological phenomena. We hope that, by thinking critically about issues and themes in psychological science and in aspects of your life, you will develop a greater understanding of yourself and others.

*Mike, Todd, and Diane*

# Contents



## Chapter 1 The Science of Psychology 1

*This chapter provides a broad introduction to psychology. The authors review the primary schools of thought and latest developments in psychology. They attempt to make the content personally relevant to the reader.*

## Chapter 2 Research Methodology 29

*This chapter reviews research methods in psychology. The authors discuss descriptive, correlational, and experimental studies; describe methods of data collection; and introduce the reader to basic statistical concepts.*

## Chapter 3 Biology and Behavior 73

*This chapter reviews contemporary theory and research related to the brain and behavior. The authors discuss neurophysiology, neurotransmitters, neuroanatomy, the endocrine system, and neurodevelopment.*

## Chapter 4 Sensation and Perception 131

*This chapter discusses taste, smell, touch, hearing, and vision. For each of these phenomena, the authors review the processes associated with sensation and perception. At the end of the chapter, a section on visual perception illustrates the complexity of human perceptual processes.*

## Chapter 5 Consciousness 181

*This chapter reviews theory and research related to consciousness. The authors discuss our contemporary understanding of consciousness and variations in consciousness, sleep, methods of altering consciousness, and drugs that influence consciousness.*

## Chapter 6 Learning 223

*This chapter reviews classic and contemporary theory and research on learning. The authors discuss operant and classical conditioning; the roles that cultural transmission, observation, and imitation can play in learning; and the biological basis of learning.*

## Chapter 7 Attention and Memory 267

*This chapter reviews theory and research on attention and memory. The authors provide an overview of varied theoretical perspectives on memory.*

## Chapter 8 Thinking and Intelligence 317

*This chapter reviews theory and research on thinking and intelligence. The authors discuss mental representations, reasoning, decision making, problem solving, and aspects of intelligence such as assessment and group differences.*

## Chapter 9 Human Development ........ 365

*This chapter presents the major stages and series of changes that constitute the human life span, from conception through childhood and adolescence to adulthood and old age. The authors discuss topics such as attachment, language acquisition, the sense of self, and the need to belong.*

## Chapter 10 Emotion and Motivation ........ 421

*This chapter presents classic theories of emotion, together with contemporary work on the neurological basis of emotional experience, emotional expression, and the functions of emotion. It then presents classic research on motivation, eating, and sexual behavior, together with contemporary work on each of these topics.*

## Chapter 11 Health and Well-Being 469

*This chapter reviews a substantial body of work related to health and well-being. The authors begin by discussing classic work on stress and coping, then progress to contemporary ideas from positive psychology.*

# Chapter 12 Social Psychology 513

*This chapter reviews research related to social psychology. The authors consider topics such as conformity, compliance, obedience, aggression, and love.*

## Chapter 13 Personality 567

*This chapter presents theory and research in personality psychology. The authors discuss psychological perspectives on personality, the assessment and significance of personality, biological bases of personality, and personality in relation to the sense of self.*

## Chapter 14 Psychological Disorders ..... 617

*This chapter reviews psychological disorders identified by the* DSM-IV-TR. *The authors also present contemporary research and controversies associated with a number of these disorders.*

## Chapter 15 Treatment of Psychological Disorders 673

*This chapter reviews contemporary treatments for a wide array of psychological disorders. The authors discuss the comparative effectiveness of treatments.*

# Psychological Science

FOURTH EDITION

## Key Terms

adaptations, p. 10
behaviorism, p. 14
cognitive neuroscience, p. 16
cognitive psychology, p. 15
critical thinking, p. 4
culture, p. 7
evolutionary theory, p. 10
functionalism, p. 10
Gestalt theory, p. 11
introspection, p. 9
mind/body problem, p. 7
natural selection, p. 10
nature/nurture debate, p. 7
psychoanalysis, p. 14
psychological science, p. 2
social psychology, p. 16
stream of consciousness, p. 10
structuralism, p. 9
unconscious, p. 14

## Practice Test

1. When you mention to your family that you enrolled in a psychology course, your family members share their understanding of the field. Which comment best reflects the nature of psychological science?
   a. "You're going to learn how to get in touch with your feelings."
   b. "The concept of 'psychological science' is such an oxymoron. It is impossible to measure and study what goes on in people's heads."
   c. "I think you'll be surprised by the range of questions psychologists ask about the mind, the brain, and behavior, not to mention the methods they use to answer these questions."
   d. "By the end of the class, you'll be able to tell me why I am the way I am."

2. Match each definition with one of the following ideas from evolutionary theory: adaptations, natural selection, survival of the fittest.
   a. Gene mutations that endow physical characteristics, skills, and abilities can increase an organism's chances of survival and of reproduction.
   b. Individuals better adapted to their environment will leave more offspring.
   c. Organisms' adaptive random mutations are passed along, and mutations that hinder both survival and reproduction are not.

3. Titles of recent research articles appear below. Indicate which of the four levels of analysis—cultural, social, individual, or biological—each article likely addresses.
   a. Achievement motivation in adolescents: The role of peer climate and best friends (Nelson & DeBacker, 2008)
   b. Circadian affective, cardiopulmonary, and cortisol variability in depressed and nondepressed individuals at risk for cardiovascular disease (Conrad, Wilhelm, Roth, Spiegel, & Taylor, 2008)
   c. Schooling in Western culture promotes context-free processing (Ventura, Pattamadilok, & Fernandes, 2008)
   d. Severity of physical aggression reported by university students: A test of the interaction between trait aggression and alcohol consumption (Tremblay, Graham, & Wells, 2008)

4. Indicate which school or schools of thought each of the following scholars is associated with: John Dewey, William James, Wolfgang Köhler, Kurt Lewin, George Miller, B. F. Skinner, Edward Titchener, Edward Tolman, John B. Watson, Max Wertheimer, Wilhelm Wundt.
   a. Structuralism
   b. Functionalism
   c. Gestalt psychology
   d. Behaviorism
   e. Cognitive psychology
   f. Social psychology

5. Match each description with one of the following theoretical ideas: dualism, information processing theory, introspection, localization, stream of consciousness.
   a. A systematic examination of subjective mental experience that requires people to inspect and report on the contents of their thoughts
   b. The notion that the mind and the body are separate and distinct
   c. Some psychological processes are located in specific parts of the brain
   d. A continuous series of ever-changing thoughts
   e. The view that the brain takes in information as a code, processes it, stores relevant bits, and retrieves stored information as required

6. Imagine you have decided to seek mental health counseling. You mention this to a few of your friends. Each friend shares an opinion with you. Based on your understanding of psychological science, which friend offers the strongest advice?
   a. "I wouldn't bother if I were you. All therapy is a bunch of psychobabble."
   b. "I know a therapist who uses this really cool method that can fix any problem. Seriously, she knows the secret!"
   c. "That's great! Psychologists do research to figure out which interventions are most helpful for people with different concerns."
   d. "Well, I guess if you like relaxing on couches and talking, you might get a lot out of therapy."

The answer key for the Practice Tests can be found at the back of the book. It also includes answers to the green caption questions.

# 2

# Research Methodology

VIONIQUE VALNORD-KASSIME WAS 32 YEARS OLD when she was killed by a drunk driver (**Figure 2.1a**). This tragedy happened at 1 AM on a Sunday in late September 2009. Having just left a friend's wedding reception in Brooklyn, New York, Valnord-Kassime was in the street trying to hail a cab. It was rainy and foggy. Andrew Kelly, a 30-year-old off-duty police officer, was driving his sport utility vehicle on that street (**Figure 2.1b**). Another off-duty cop was among the passengers in the vehicle, which struck Valnord-Kassime and threw her body several feet away. She died on the scene.

Andrew Kelly pled guilty to vehicular manslaughter and driving while intoxicated. His guilty plea helped him avoid the maximum prison sentence of seven years, but it ended his eight-year career in the police department. His official punishment? Kelly's driver's license was suspended for a year. He was ordered to complete an alcohol treatment program and install an ignition lock on

(a)

(b)

**FIGURE 2.1 Avoidable Tragedy (a)** Vionique Valnord-Kassime lost her life because she was standing in the street at the wrong time. Here she is shown in a photo held by her father. **(b)** Andrew Kelly accidentally killed Valnord-Kassime because he got behind the wheel when he was drunk.

his car. And he was sentenced to 90 days in jail. In a courtroom, Valnord-Kassime's father, a pastor, accepted an apology from Kelly. Still, her family filed a wrongful-death civil lawsuit against Kelly and the NYPD. The woman died for nothing, and lives connected with hers have been changed for the worse. Her family members and friends are left to deal with their loss.

What will it take to convince people not to drive after drinking? Will news stories like this one do the trick?

You know the facts. We all know the facts. Alcohol is a potent drug that slows down the nervous system. It changes how the brain operates. It can keep us from being able to think straight, speak properly, or even walk a straight line. It certainly can keep us from having the perceptual abilities, coordination, and motor skills necessary to operate machinery safely. People should not be drinking and then driving cars, riding motorcycles, piloting boats, flying planes, using power tools, or attempting any other activity that endangers their lives or the lives of others.

What if those facts are not enough to stop the problem? What if you read yet another story about someone injured or killed by a drunk driver, about a family ruined by a drunk driver's selfishness, and you become fed up? You happen to be a psychologist. For you, facts are not facts—they are simply *theories*—until they are supported empirically. Perhaps, you hope, by providing scientific evidence about the effects of alcohol on driving skills, you might be able to convince some people not to drink and drive. You might help prevent at least one tragedy.

How do you start? You begin with an idea: Alcohol probably impairs motor skills and coordination. This idea might seem obvious. In fact, it might seem so obvious that it would not need to be shown scientifically. If you are really going to understand how alcohol impairs driving, however, you need to move beyond a simple commonsense view. Think of a scientific understanding as being like a scale on which an increasing amount of evidence tips the balance in one direction.

To build up evidence around your particular idea, you need to test a specific way that alcohol affects behavior. And to begin this investigation, you set up a research study in which you give people alcohol and measure some behavioral response that you believe is related to driving skill. For example, you might want to see how well a person under the influence can see something in her or his visual field or how quickly the person can respond to a command to press a brake pedal. Basically, you are designing an *experiment* in which you alter, or *manipulate,* the situation to see how the change affects mental state or behavior. To see if the manipulation changes behavior, you must also measure the same behavior when your research participants have not been drinking. Alternatively, you could compare your group's behavior after drinking with that of another group of people who did not consume alcohol. You are measuring the effects seen in your experiment against a baseline, a condition that does not involve your manipulation.

Once you have collected the performance information, you evaluate it. You sift through it, draw conclusions from it, and put it into a form that you can share with other people. You need to share it with other psychologists for review. Ultimately, you want to see it published, so that your research becomes part of the scientific literature on drinking and driving. Only then can the facts, as developed scientifically, make their way into the public's consciousness.

Of course, an idea is not true just because you think it is. What if your research indicates that alcohol probably does *not* impair motor skills and coordination? Welcome to the world of scientific inquiry. ■

**scientific method** A systematic procedure of observing and measuring phenomena (observable things) to answer questions about *what* happens, *when* it happens, *what causes* it, and *why;* involves a dynamic interaction between theories, hypotheses, and research.

## 2.1 What Is Scientific Inquiry?

**Learning Objectives**

- Describe the scientific method.
- Differentiate between theories, hypotheses, and research.

This chapter will introduce you to the science and the art of psychological research methods. You will learn the basics of collecting, analyzing, and interpreting the data of psychological science. In this way, you will come to understand how psychologists study behavior and mental processes: describing *what* happens, predicting *when* it happens, controlling *what causes* it to happen, and explaining *why* it happens. Using these same research methods, you can test your own best guesses about people's thoughts and actions. With some practice, you can even contribute to the field of psychological science.

Contributions of this kind are collectively known as *scientific inquiry*. That term boils down to careful scientific research, nothing more and nothing less. Careful scientific research is a way of finding answers to empirical questions, meaning questions that can be answered by observing the world and measuring aspects of it. To be confident in the conclusions drawn from their observations, researchers in the various fields of science use a general approach known as the **scientific method.** This method is more objective than casual observations. It is more objective, in part, because it is *systematic*. To answer research questions, scientists use objective procedures in orderly steps that are carefully planned. An objective procedure is free from bias. If another researcher uses the same procedure with the same sample of people, he or she would expect to receive the same results.

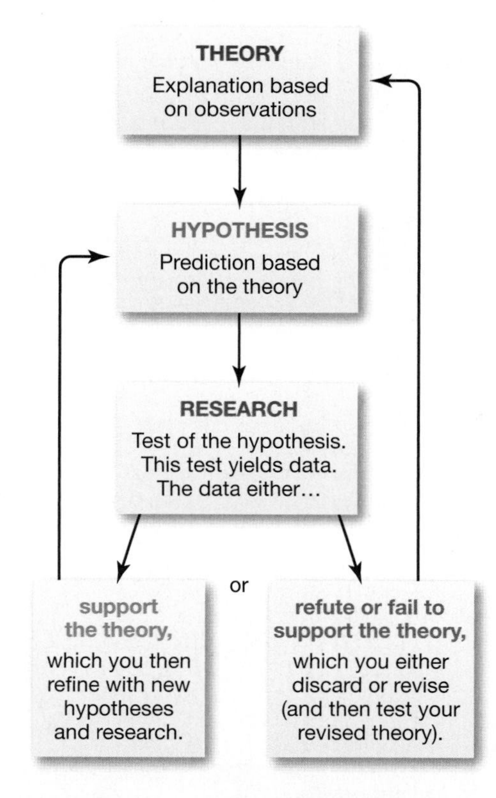


**FIGURE 2.2 The Scientific Method** The scientific method reflects a cyclical relationship: First the scientist formulates a theory. From the theory, the scientist derives one or more testable hypotheses. The scientist then conducts research to test the hypothesis. Findings from the research might prompt the scientist to reevaluate and adjust the theory. A good theory evolves over time, and the result is an increasingly accurate model of some observable thing.

### The Scientific Method Depends on Theories, Hypotheses, and Research

The scientific method reflects a dynamic interaction between three essential elements: theories, hypotheses, and research (**Figure 2.2**). A **theory** is an explanation or model of how a *phenomenon*—an observable thing—works. The theory consists of interconnected ideas or concepts. It is used to explain prior observations and to make predictions about future events.

A good theory should generate a **hypothesis** (or multiple hypotheses). A hypothesis is a specific, testable prediction about the outcome that would best support the theory. If the theory is reasonably accurate, the prediction framed in the hypothesis should be supported. To see how theories lead to testable hypotheses, imagine you have begun your study of alcohol intoxication. You have spent some time observing people as they drank alcohol, and your observations indicate that people who drink alcohol tend to stumble, drop things, have impaired language, and show poor social judgment. What theory might you derive from these observations? Because you want to limit your research so that you can easily control its conditions, you probably would focus your theory on only some of those behaviors. For example, you might theorize that drinking alcohol impairs driving ability. What hypothesis might you derive from that theory? You might hypothesize that people who consume alcohol will tend to display poorer coordination and poorer motor control than will people who do not consume alcohol.

Once you have developed hypotheses to test your theory, you must do **research.** The research process involves the systematic and careful collection of **data.** The data consist of objective information that indicates whether the hypothesis—and ultimately the theory—is likely to be supported. In other words, the data provide a way to test the hypothesis, just as the hypothesis provides a way to test the theory. To test the hypothesis about alcohol's effects on coordination and motor skills, you would arrange for research participants to work with you. You might have some of

**theory** A model of interconnected ideas or concepts that explains what is observed and makes predictions about future events.

**hypothesis** A specific prediction of what should be observed if a theory is correct.

**research** A scientific process that involves the systematic and careful collection of data.

**data** Objective observations or measurements.

**replication** Repetition of an experiment to confirm the results.

the participants drink enough alcohol to bring their blood alcohol levels to the legal definition of drunkenness. You might have others drink tonic water. Or you might have all the participants drink tonic water as part of the first phase of the research, then have them drink alcohol as part of the second phase. You would systematically record the participants' behavior as they performed specific, carefully defined tasks.

Once the research findings are in, you would return to the original theory to evaluate the implications of the data you collected. The findings either support your theory or require that your theory be modified or discarded. Then the process starts all over again. Yes, the same sort of work needs to be performed repeatedly. You might consider the repetition unfortunate, but it is necessary. Good research reflects the cyclical process shown in Figure 2.2. In other words, a theory is continually refined by new hypotheses and tested by new research methods (**Figure 2.3**).

Often, more than one theory can explain human behavior. For this reason, no single study can provide a definitive answer about any phenomenon. In general, we can have more confidence in scientific findings when research outcomes are replicated. **Replication** involves repeating a study and getting the same (or similar) results. When the results from two or more studies are the same, or at least support the same conclusion, confidence in the findings increases.

**THEORIES SHOULD GENERATE HYPOTHESES** How can we decide whether a theory is good? When we talk about a good theory, we do not mean that it is likely to be supported by research findings. Instead, a good theory produces a wide variety of *testable* hypotheses. For instance, in the early twentieth century, the developmental psychologist Jean Piaget proposed a theory of infant and child development (see Chapter 9, "Human Development"). According to Piaget's theory, cognitive development occurs in a fixed series of "stages," from birth to adolescence. From a scientific standpoint, this theory was good because it led to a number of hypotheses. These hypotheses concerned the specific kinds of behaviors that should be observed at each stage of development. In the decades since its proposal, the theory has generated thousands of scientific papers. Our understanding of child development

**FIGURE 2.3 The Scientific Method in Action**

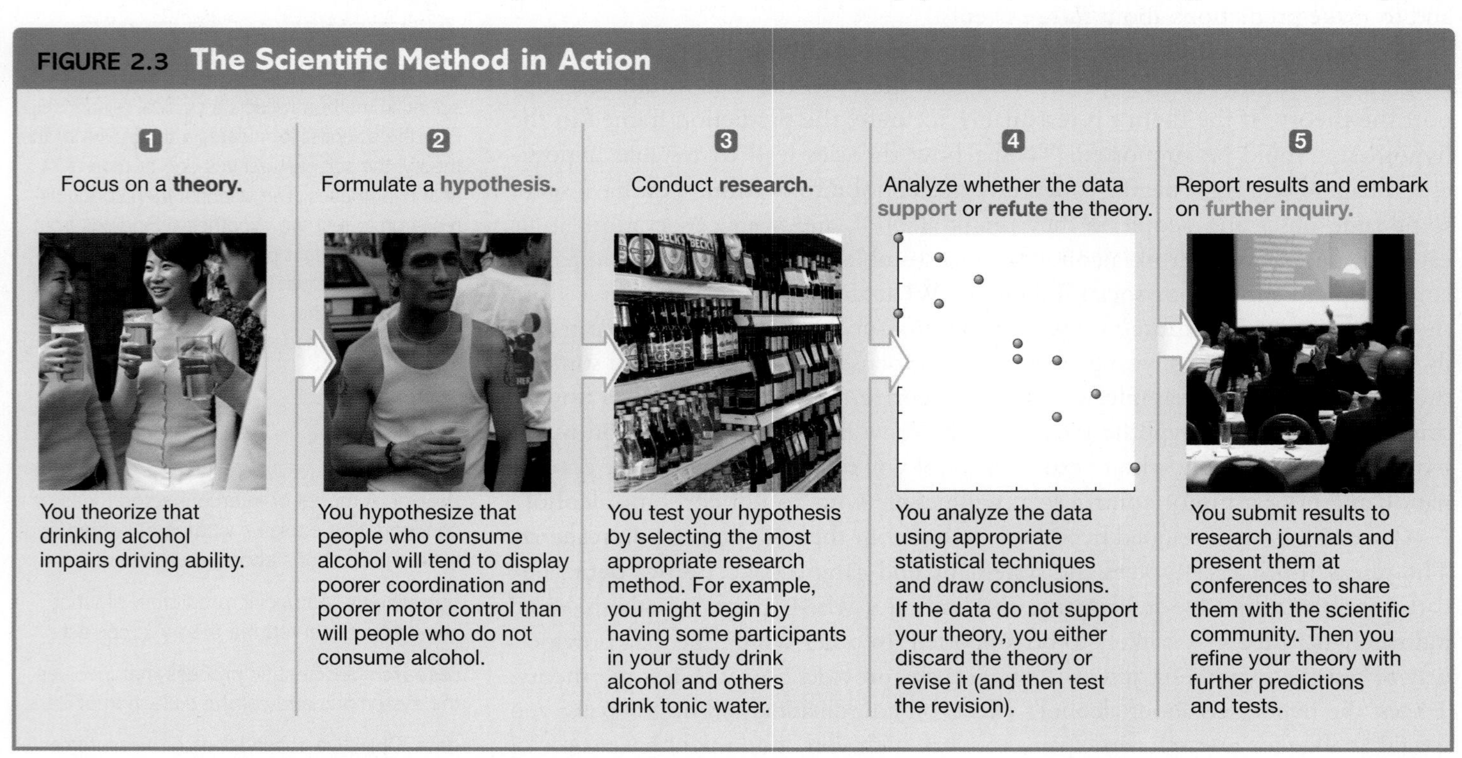

has been enhanced both by studies that supported Piaget's stage theory and by those that failed to support it.

In contrast, Piaget's contemporary Sigmund Freud, in his famous treatise *The Interpretation of Dreams,* outlined the theory that all dreams represent the fulfillment of an unconscious wish. From a scientific perspective, Freud's theory was not good, because it generated few testable hypotheses regarding the actual function of dreams. Researchers were left with no way to evaluate whether the wish fulfillment theory was either reasonable or accurate. After all, unconscious wishes are, by definition, not known to anyone, including the person having the dreams. Indeed, on being presented with a patient's dream that clearly contained no hint of wish fulfillment, Freud went so far as to claim that the dreamer's unconscious wish was to prove his theory wrong!

## Unexpected Findings Can Be Valuable

Research does not always proceed in a neat and orderly fashion. On the contrary, many significant findings are the result of *serendipity*. In its general sense, serendipity means unexpectedly finding things that are valuable or agreeable. In science, it means unexpectedly discovering something important.

For example, in the late 1950s, the physiologists Torsten Wiesel and David Hubel recorded the activity of nerve cells in cats' brains. Specifically, they were measuring the activity of cells in brain areas associated with vision. Wiesel and Hubel were studying how information travels from the eye to the brain (a process explored extensively in Chapter 4, "Sensation and Perception"). They had hypothesized that certain cells in the visual portion of the brain would respond when the cats looked at dots. To test that hypothesis, they showed slides of dot patterns to the cats. After much disappointing work that produced no significant activity in the brain cells being observed, the projector suddenly jammed between slides. The cells in question began to fire at an astonishing rate! What had caused this firing? Wiesel and Hubel realized that the jammed slide had produced a visual "edge" on the screen. Because of this little accident, they discovered that the cells do not respond to simple dots. Wiesel and Hubel eventually received a Nobel Prize for the serendipitous finding that these brain cells respond to lines and edges. Although their discovery is an example of serendipity, these researchers were not just lucky. They did not stumble onto a groundbreaking discovery that led straight to a Nobel Prize. Rather, they followed up on their unexpected finding. After a lifetime of hard work, they understood the implications of the rapid firing of brain cells in response to straight lines but not to other types of visual stimuli.

### Summing Up

#### What Is Scientific Inquiry?

Our subjective beliefs, such as intuitions, can be useful in suggesting research questions. They are often biased, however, or based on limited information. To explain behavior, researchers use the scientific method. That is, researchers use objective, systematic procedures to measure behavior. The empirical process is based on the use of theories to generate hypotheses that can be tested by collecting objective data through research. Theories, in turn, must be adjusted and refined as new findings confirm or disconfirm the hypotheses. Good theories will generate several testable hypotheses. Unexpected findings can suggest new theories.

## Measuring Up

1. How are theories, hypotheses, and research different?
   a. Theories ask questions about possible causes of thoughts, emotions, and behaviors; hypotheses provide the empirical answers; and research is used to examine whether theories are correct.
   b. Theories are broad conceptual frameworks; hypotheses are derived from theories and are used to design research that will support or fail to support a theory; and research is a test of the hypotheses.
   c. Theories are assumed to be true; hypotheses need to be tested with appropriate experiments; and research is the final step.
   d. Theories do not require data for their verification because they are abstract; hypotheses depend on experimental findings; and research uses human participants to test theories and hypotheses.

2. How does psychological research differ from relying on personal experience or intuition as a way of understanding thoughts, emotions, and behaviors?
   a. Personal experience is the most objective method for understanding thoughts, emotions, and behaviors.
   b. Carefully designed research is the most objective method for understanding thoughts, emotions, and behaviors.
   c. Research provides theoretical answers that are best verified through individual experience.

**Answers:** 1. b. Theories are broad conceptual frameworks; hypotheses are derived from theories and are used to design research that will support or fail to support a theory; and research is a test of the hypotheses.
2. b. Carefully designed research is the most objective method for understanding thoughts, emotions, and behaviors.

### Learning Objectives

- Distinguish between descriptive studies, correlational studies, and experiments.
- List the advantages and disadvantages of different research methods.
- Explain why random sampling and random assignment are important when conducting research studies.

# 2.2 What Types of Studies Are Used in Psychological Research?

Once a researcher has defined a hypothesis, the next issue to be addressed is the type of study design to be used. There are three main types of designs: *descriptive, correlational,* and *experimental.* These designs differ in the extent to which the researcher has control over the variables in the study. The amount of control over the variables, in turn, determines the type of conclusions the researcher can draw from the data.

All research involves variables. A **variable** is something in the world that can vary and that the researcher can measure. The term can refer to something that the researcher manipulates, something the researcher measures, or both. For instance, some of the variables you might use in your study of alcohol and driving would be: amount of alcohol consumed, level of intoxication, coordination, motor control, and balance.

Researchers must define variables precisely and in ways that reflect the methods used to assess them. They do this by using *operational definitions.* This phrase might seem intimidating, but it simply means identifying variables and *quantifying* them so they can be measured. In other words, each variable is specified in a way that makes it possible to record its *quantity.* For example, if you choose to study how coordination is affected by alcohol, how will you quantify "coordination" so you can judge whether it is affected by alcohol? One option might be to measure how easily people can touch their fingers to their noses with their eyes

**variable** Something in the world that can vary and that a researcher can measure.

closed. In this case, the operational definition could be the number of inches by which people miss their noses. The concrete definition would help other scientists know precisely what you measured. That knowledge would make it possible for them to replicate your research.

**descriptive studies** A research method that involves observing and noting the behavior of people or other animals to provide a systematic and objective analysis of the behavior.

**naturalistic observation** A type of descriptive study in which the researcher is a passive observer, making no attempt to change or alter ongoing behavior.

**participant observation** A type of descriptive study in which the researcher is actively involved in the situation.

## Descriptive Studies Involve Observing and Classifying Behavior

**Descriptive studies** are sometimes called *observational studies*. They involve observing and noting behavior to analyze that behavior objectively (**Figure 2.4**). For instance, an observer might take notes on the types of foods that people eat in cafeterias, measure the time that people spend talking during an average conversation, count the number and types of mating behaviors that penguins engage in during their mating season, or tally the number of times poverty or mental illness is mentioned during a presidential debate. Some researchers observe behavior at regular time intervals. These intervals span durations from as short as seconds to as long as entire lifetimes and across generations. In this manner, the researchers can keep track of what research participants do at particular points in time. They can study behaviors that may take years to unfold, as in tracking the job histories of college graduates.

There are two basic types of descriptive studies. In **naturalistic observation,** the observer remains separated from the situation and makes no attempt to change it. By contrast, in **participant observation,** the researcher is involved in the situation. An example of the latter was conducted by social psychologists who joined a doomsday cult to see how the cult members would respond when the world did not end on the date that was predicted by the cult. (The members made sense of this nonevent by deciding that their faith saved the world; Festinger, Riecken, & Schachter, 1956.) One possible problem with participant observation is that the observer might lose objectivity. Another is that the participants might change

**Descriptive studies** involve observing and classifying behavior, either with no intervention by the observer (naturalistic observation) or with intervention by the observer (participant observation).

**Advantages** Especially valuable in the early stages of research, when trying to determine whether a phenomenon exists. Takes place in a real-world setting.

**Disadvantages** Errors in observation can occur because of an observer's expectations (observer bias). Observer's presence can change the behavior being witnessed (reactivity).

Naturalistic observation

Participant observation

**FIGURE 2.4 Descriptive Studies**
**(left)** Employing naturalistic observation, the primatologist Jane Goodall observes a family of chimpanzees. Animals are more likely to act naturally in their native habitats than in captivity. **(right)** The evolutionary psychologist and human behavioral ecologist Lawrence Sugiyama has conducted fieldwork in Ecuadorian Amazonia among the Shiwiar, Achuar, Shuar, and Zaparo peoples. Here, hunting with a bow and arrow, he is conducting a particularly active form of participant observation.

**Longitudinal studies** involve observing and classifying developmental changes that occur in the same people over time, either with no intervention by the observer or with intervention by the observer.

**Advantages** Provide information about the effects of age on the same people, allowing researchers to see developmental changes.

**Disadvantages** Expensive, take a long time, and may lose participants over time.

**FIGURE 2.5 Longitudinal Studies** The *Up* series of documentary films is an ongoing longitudinal study that since 1964 has traced the development of 14 British people from various socioeconomic backgrounds. New material has been collected every seven years, starting when the participants were 7 years old. Here, three participants—Jackie, Sue, and Lynn—are pictured from the latest film, *49 Up*.

their behavior if they know they are being observed. You can imagine how bar patrons would respond if researchers entered the bar and announced they were studying the behavior of people who go to bars to meet potential dates. Such an announcement would interfere with the normal interactions that occur in bars. It might even eliminate those interactions. Thus observers need to keep their objectivity and minimize their impact on a situation.

Descriptive techniques are especially valuable in the early stages of research. At that point, researchers are trying to see whether a phenomenon exists. They can learn a great deal about behavior by just watching and taking careful notes. Even the simplest observations can prove valuable. Imagine you are observing seating patterns during lunch at two high schools. You find that at one school the lunch tables are racially segregated but at the other school students sit in mixed-race groups. With this finding, you have learned something valuable about racial behaviors at these two schools. You would need different types of research designs to understand what causes student groups to be segregated or integrated, but description would have proved a good first step in documenting this phenomenon.

Researchers sometimes design studies to examine developmental changes that occur over time. Sometimes the researchers want to watch changes unfold naturally, as in a descriptive design. Other times they want to see how different interventions affect future development. **Longitudinal studies** are one type of developmental design (**Figure 2.5**). If you wanted to know how intellectual abilities change over the adult years, you could begin by assessing the abilities of a group of young adults. You would then reassess the same participants every five years, as they progressed toward old age. Alternatively, you could assess the intellectual abilities of young adults and old adults and compare their scores on various measures of intellectual ability. Research designs of this type, comparing different groups to make inferences about both, are known as **cross-sectional studies** (**Figure 2.6**).

Like all research design choices, each of these methods has advantages and disadvantages. Longitudinal designs provide information about the effects of age on the same people, but they are expensive, they take a long time, and they can be jeopardized when (not if) some participants drop out of the experiment over time. By contrast, cross-sectional designs are faster and less expensive, but they include the possibility that some unidentified variable is responsible for any difference between the groups. In the example just given, the older people might not have received the same amount or type of education as the younger people, or differences between the age groups might be due to changes in societal norms. This potential difference is known as a *cohort effect*.

**OBSERVER BIAS** In conducting observational research, scientists must guard against **observer bias.** This flaw consists of systematic errors in observation that occur because of an observer's expectations. Observer bias can especially be a problem if cultural norms favor inhibiting or expressing certain behaviors. For instance, in many societies women are freer to express sadness than men are. If observers are coding men's and women's facial expressions, they may be more likely to rate female expressions as indicating sadness because they believe that men are less likely to show sadness. Men's expressions of sadness might be rated as annoyance or some other emotion. Likewise, in many societies women are generally expected to be less assertive than men. Observers therefore might rate women as more assertive when exhibiting the same behavior as men. Cultural norms can affect both the participants' actions and the way observers perceive those actions.

**longitudinal studies** A research method that studies the same participants multiple times over a period of time.

**cross-sectional studies** A research method that compares participants in different groups (e.g., young and old) at the same time.

**observer bias** Systematic errors in observation that occur because of an observer's expectations.

There is evidence that observer expectations can even change the behavior being observed. This phenomenon is known as the **experimenter expectancy effect.** In a classic study conducted in the 1960s by the social psychologist Robert Rosenthal, college students trained rats to run a maze (Rosenthal & Fode, 1963). Half the students were told their rats were bred to be very good at running mazes. The other half were told their rats were bred to be poor performers. In reality, there were no genetic differences between the groups of rats. Nonetheless, when students believed they were training rats that were bred to be fast maze learners, their rats learned the task more quickly! Thus these students' expectations altered how they treated their rats. This treatment in turn influenced the speed at which the rats learned. The students were not aware of their biased treatment, but it existed. Perhaps they supplied extra food when the rats reached the goal box. Or perhaps they gave the rats inadvertent cues as to which way to turn in the maze. They might simply have stroked the rats more often. This study exemplifies the idea that some aspects of our own behavior are not under our conscious control. We are not always aware of the many factors that affect how we think, feel, and act (**Figure 2.7**).

**Cross-sectional studies** involve observing and classifying developmental changes that occur in different groups of people at the same time.

**Advantages** Faster and less expensive than longitudinal studies.

**Disadvantages** Unidentified variables may be involved (cohort effect).

**FIGURE 2.6 Cross-Sectional Studies**
Together, the young adults on the top and the older adults on the bottom might participate in a cross-sectional study.

*As discussed extensively in this chapter, different types of research methods play important roles in the stories of psychological science. In each chapter of the book,* ***Scientific Method*** *features will lead you through the steps of some of the most interesting experiments and studies discussed in the text.*

**FIGURE 2.7 Scientific Method: Rosenthal's Study of Observer Bias**

**Hypothesis:** Research participants' behavior will be affected by experimenters' biases.

**Research Method:**

1. One group of college students was given a group of rats and told to train them to run a maze. These students were told their rats were bred to be very poor at running mazes.
2. A second group of college students was given a group of rats to train that were genetically the same as the first group of rats. These students were told their rats were bred to be very good at running mazes.

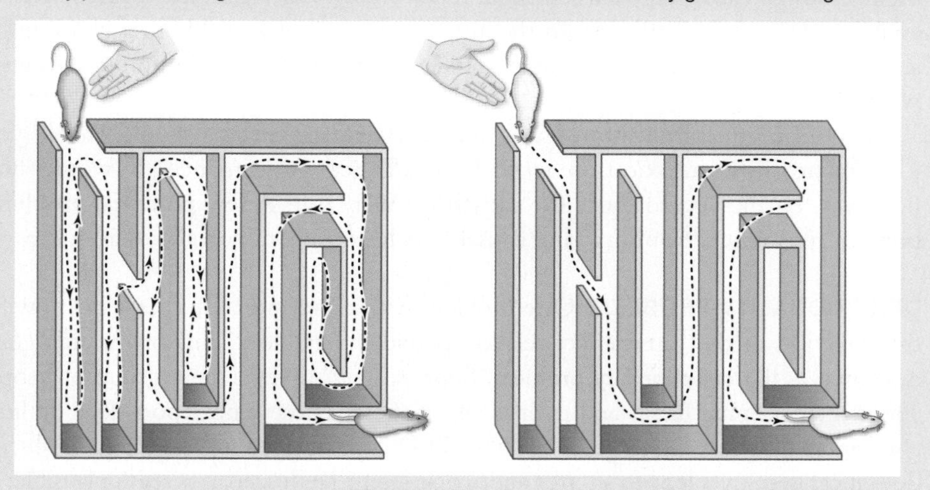

**Results:** The rats trained by the students who believed their rats were bred to be fast maze learners did learn the task more quickly.

**Conclusion:** The results for the two groups of rats differed because the students' expectations caused them to give off subtle cues that changed the rats' behavior.

**Source:** Rosenthal, R., & Fode, K. L. (1963). The effect of experimenter bias on the performance of the albino rat. *Behavioral Science, 8*, 183–189.

**experimenter expectancy effect** Actual change in the behavior of the people or nonhuman animals being observed that is due to the expectations of the observer.

**Correlational studies** examine how variables are related, with no intervention by the observer.

**Advantages** Rely on naturally occurring relationships. May take place in a real-world setting.

**Disadvantages** Cannot be used to support causal relationships (that one thing happened because of the other). Cannot show the direction of the cause/effect relationship between variables (directionality problem). An unidentified variable may be involved (third variable problem).

**FIGURE 2.8 Correlational Studies** There may be a correlation between the extent to which parents are overweight and the extent to which their children are overweight. A correlational study cannot demonstrate the cause of this relationship, which may include biological propensities to gain weight, lack of exercise, and high-fat diets.

How do researchers protect against experimenter expectancy effects? It is best if the person running the study is *blind* to, or unaware of, the study's hypotheses. For example, the study just described seemed to be about rats' speed in learning to run through a maze. Instead, it was designed to study experimenter expectancy effects. The students believed they were "experimenters" in the study, but they were actually the participants. Their work with the rats was the subject of the study, not the method. Thus the students were led to expect certain results so that the researchers could determine whether the students' expectations affected the results of the rats' training. For these reasons, the researchers would not have told the person running the test (i.e., the true experimenter) that all the rats in the study were more or less the same genetically. That way, the person did not have knowledge that might have influenced the behavior of the students.

## Correlational Studies Examine How Variables Are Related

There is a rather unfortunate twist to the case discussed at the opening of this chapter. According to news reports, Andrew Kelly reeked of booze at the scene of the fatal accident. He refused a Breathalyzer test. The off-duty cop in the SUV with him and the cop who arrived on the scene gave him chewing gum and water. By the time he underwent a blood alcohol test, seven hours later, Kelly's body was alcohol free. This drunk driver seems to have understood very well the connection between his physiological state and his actions behind the wheel. He understood the connection well enough to try to hide it.

Other drunk drivers do not have Kelly's options, however, so records exist of their physiological states. To study the effects of alcohol intoxication on behavior, you might sift through police records of alcohol-related accidents. Your goal would be to match the reported intoxication levels of drunk drivers with some measure of their driving performance, such as the severity of the drivers' accidents. Research of this kind consists of **correlational studies.** These studies examine how variables are naturally related in the real world, without any attempt by the researcher to alter them or assign causation between them (**Figure 2.8**). For example, researchers have established a correlation between the amount of alcohol available in a community and the likeliness of late-night, single-vehicle accidents in that community (Gruenewald et al., 1996).

Your data on intoxication levels and driving performance would enable you to compare how intoxication *might* have affected performance. It would not, however, enable you to show the causation. Why not? A few potential problems prevent researchers from drawing causal conclusions from correlational studies.

**DIRECTIONALITY PROBLEM** One problem with correlational studies is in knowing the direction of the cause/effect relation between variables. This sort of ambiguity is known as the **directionality problem.** Suppose you survey a large group of people about their sleeping habits and their levels of stress. Those who report sleeping little also report having a higher level of stress. Does lack of sleep increase stress levels, or does increased stress lead to shorter and worse sleep? Both scenarios seem plausible:

The Directionality Problem

Sleep (A) and stress (B) are correlated.

- Does less sleep cause more stress? (A → B)

*or*

- Does more stress cause less sleep? (B → A)

**correlational studies** A research method that examines how variables are naturally related in the real world, without any attempt by the researcher to alter them or assign causation between them.

**directionality problem** A problem encountered in correlational studies; the researchers find a relationship between two variables, but they cannot determine which variable may have caused changes in the other variable.

**THIRD VARIABLE PROBLEM** Another drawback with all correlational studies is the **third variable problem.** Instead of variable A causing variable B, as a researcher might assume, it is possible that a third variable, C, causes both A and B. Consider the relationship between drinking and driving. It is possible that people who are really stressed in their daily lives are more likely to drink before driving. It is also possible that they are likely to be distracted while driving. Thus the cause of both drinking and bad driving is the third variable, stress:

**third variable problem** A problem that occurs when the researcher cannot directly manipulate variables; as a result, the researcher cannot be confident that another, unmeasured variable is not the actual cause of differences in the variables of interest.

The Third Variable Problem

Drinking before driving (A) is correlated with being distracted while driving (B).

- Stress (C) causes some people to drink before driving. (C → A)

*and*

- Stress (C) causes some people to be distracted while driving. (C → B)

Sometimes the third variable is obvious. Suppose you were told that the more churches there are in a town, the greater the rate of crime. Would you conclude that churches cause crime? In looking for a third variable, you would realize that the population size of the town affects the number of churches and the frequency of crime. But sometimes third variables are not so obvious and may not even be identifiable. For instance, we have all heard that smoking causes cancer. Is the connection that simple for everyone? Evidence indicates that a particular gene predisposes some smokers to develop lung cancer (Paz-Elizur et al., 2003). In addition, a genetic predisposition—a built-in vulnerability to smoking—combines with environmental factors to increase the probability that some people will smoke *and* that they will develop lung cancer (Thorgeirsson et al., 2008). This connection is one of the countless ways that nature and nurture work together inseparably.

Sometimes, however, people mistakenly believe there is a causal relationship between two variables when there is a correlation. Suppose the newspaper reports that children who attend preschool are better readers in first grade than those who do not. It is tempting to conclude that children are better readers in first grade *because* they learned prereading skills in preschool. This explanation of the data might be true. Another explanation might also be true: Children who attend preschool have parents who are concerned with their academic success. Such parents probably read to their children and monitor their schoolwork more than parents who are less concerned with academic success.

**ETHICAL REASONS FOR USING CORRELATIONAL DESIGNS** Despite such potentially serious problems, correlational studies are widely used in psychological science. Some research questions require correlational research designs for ethical reasons. For example, suppose you want to know if soldiers who experience severe trauma during combat have more difficulty learning new tasks after they return home than soldiers who have experienced less-severe trauma during combat. Even if you theorize that severely traumatic combat experiences *cause* later problems with learning, it would be unethical to induce trauma in some soldiers so that you could compare soldiers who had experienced different degrees of trauma. (Likewise, most research on psychopathology uses the correlational method, because it is unethical to induce mental disorders in people to study the effects.) For this research question, you would need to study the soldiers' ability to learn a new task after they had returned home. You might, for example, observe soldiers who were attempting to learn computer programming. The participants in your study would have to include some soldiers who had experienced severe trauma during combat and some who had experienced less-severe trauma during combat. You would want to see which group, on average, performed less well when learning the task.

**MAKING PREDICTIONS** Correlational studies can be used to determine that two variables are associated with each other. In the example just discussed, the variables would be trauma during combat and learning difficulties later in life. By establishing such connections, researchers are able to make predictions. If you found the association you expected between severe trauma during combat and learning difficulties, you could predict that soldiers who experience severe trauma during combat will—again, on average—have more difficulty learning new tasks when they return than soldiers who do not experience severe trauma during combat. Because your study drew on but did not control the soldiers' wartime experiences, however, you have not established a causal connection.

By providing important information about the natural relationships between variables, researchers are able to make valuable predictions. For example, correlational research has identified a strong relationship between depression and suicide. For this reason, clinical psychologists often assess symptoms of depression to determine suicide risk. Typically, researchers who use the correlational method use other statistical procedures to rule out potential third variables and problems with the direction of the effect. Once they have shown that a relationship between two variables holds even when potential third variables are taken into account, researchers can be more confident that the relationship is meaningful.

## An Experiment Involves Manipulating Conditions

In experimental research, the investigator has maximal control over the situation. An **experiment** is a study in which the researcher manipulates one variable to examine that variable's effect on a second variable. In studying how alcohol intoxication affects people's ability to drive, you could manipulate the extent to which participants were intoxicated and then measure their driving performance using a driving simulator. You might also incorporate a **control group** (a comparison group). This group might consist of participants who did not consume alcohol or participants who drank tonic water instead of alcohol. This way, you could compare two or more **experimental groups** (treatment groups) with the control condition. In this example, one experimental group might consist of participants who had just reached the legal measure of intoxication. Another group might consist of participants whose blood alcohol levels were double the legal measure of intoxication (**Table 2.1**). Two experimental groups and one control group is just one possible research design for this question. The variable that is manipulated (the amount of intoxication) is the **independent variable.** The variable that is measured (driving performance) is the **dependent variable.**

The benefit of an experiment is that the researcher can study the causal relationship between the two variables. If the independent variable (such as intoxication state) consistently influences the dependent variable (such as driving performance), then the independent variable is assumed to cause the change in the dependent variable.

**ESTABLISHING CAUSALITY** A properly performed experiment depends on rigorous control. Here *control* means the steps taken by the researcher to minimize the possibility that anything other than the independent variable will affect the experiment's outcome. A **confound** is anything that affects a dependent variable and that may unintentionally vary between the study's different experimental

**experiment** A study that tests causal hypotheses by measuring and manipulating variables.

**control group** A comparison group; the participants in a study that receive no intervention or receive an intervention that is unrelated to the independent variable being investigated.

**experimental groups** Treatment groups; the participants in a study that receive the intervention.

**independent variable** In an experiment, the variable that is manipulated by the experimenter to examine its impact on the dependent variable.

**dependent variable** In an experiment, the variable that is affected by the manipulation of the independent variable.

**confound** Anything that affects a dependent variable and may unintentionally vary between the experimental conditions of a study.

**TABLE 2.1 Blood Alcohol Content and Its Effects**

In the United States, blood alcohol content is measured by taking a sample of a person's breath or blood and determining the amount of alcohol in that sample. The result is then converted to a percentage. For example, in many states the legal limit is .08 percent. To reach this level, a person's bloodstream needs to have 8 grams of alcohol for every 100 milliliters of blood.

Different blood alcohol levels produce different physical and mental effects. These effects also vary from person to person. This table shows typical effects.

| BAC Level | Effects |
|---|---|
| .01–.06 | Feeling of relaxation<br>Sense of well-being<br>Thought, judgment, and coordination are impaired. |
| .06–.10 | Loss of inhibitions<br>Extroversion<br>Reflexes, depth perception, peripheral vision, and reasoning are impaired. |
| .11–.20 | Emotional swings<br>Sense of sadness or anger<br>Reaction time and speech are impaired. |
| .21–.29 | Stupor<br>Blackouts<br>Motor skills are impaired. |
| .30–.39 | Severe depression<br>Unconsciousness<br>Breathing and heart rate are impaired. |
| >.40 | Breathing and heart rate are impaired.<br>Death is possible. |

SOURCE: BloodAlcoholContent.Org (2007–2010).

conditions. When conducting an experiment, a researcher needs to ensure that the only thing that varies is the independent variable. Control thus represents the foundation of the experimental approach, in that it allows the researcher to rule out alternative explanations for the observed data (**Figure 2.9**). For example, in

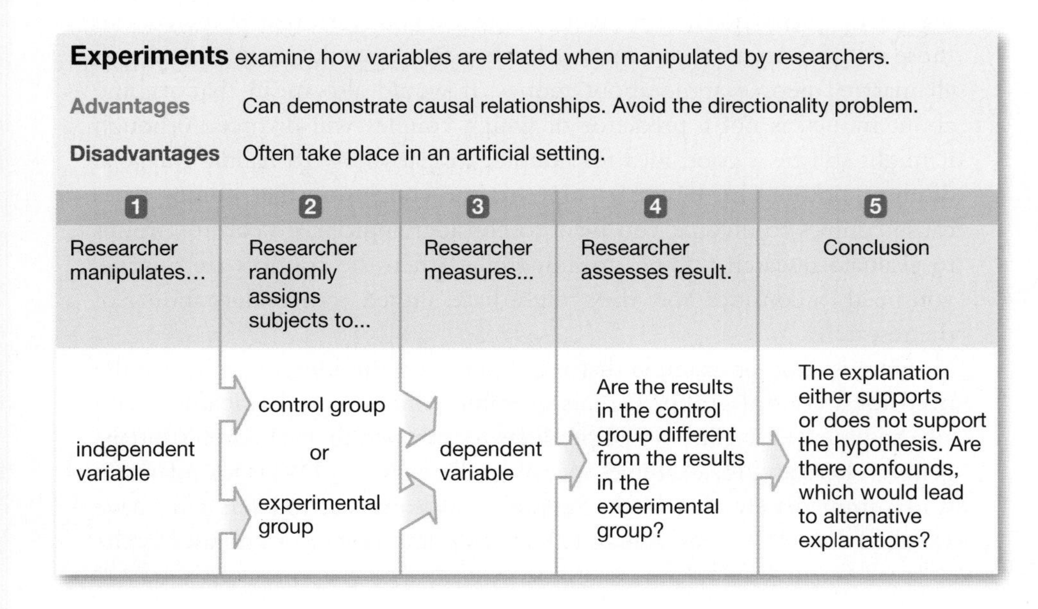


**FIGURE 2.9** Experiments

CRITICAL THINKING SKILL

## Identifying the Need for Control Groups

The two critical thinking skills for this chapter—identifying the need for control groups and recognizing that large samples provide more reliable data than small samples (see p. 46)—are essentially applications of research methods to everyday life. The idea that the principles of research methods can inform critical thinking was expressed by George (Pinky) Nelson, a leading U.S. astronaut who is deeply concerned with enhancing the critical thinking abilities of students as a way of preparing them for their future in the information age. Nelson said:

> Most people seem to believe that there is a difference between scientific thinking and everyday thinking. Clearly, most people haven't developed the capacity to think [scientifically]. Otherwise, they wouldn't buy lottery tickets that they can't afford. They wouldn't consistently fall for cheap promises and easy answers from politicians. They wouldn't become victims of medical quackery or misinformation from tobacco companies. They wouldn't keep employing the same failed strategies, both in their personal lives and in society at large, just because that's what they've always done.... But, the fact is, these same scientific thinking skills can be used to improve the chances of success in virtually any endeavor. (1998, April 29, p. A 14)

When designing an experiment, a researcher needs to include a control group that does not receive the treatment or experience being investigated. It is usually easy to recognize the need for such a comparison when planning a research project. It can be difficult to spot the need for control groups, however, when thinking about the many research results that we are bombarded with in newspapers, on the Web, in everyday conversation, and in advertisements.

Suppose you read in the newspaper that 75 percent of couples who are going through a divorce argue about money. You might conclude that disputes about money are a major cause of divorce. You might even conclude that more marriages would be saved if couples learned how to handle financial disputes. Missing from this analysis is a comparison figure for couples who do not divorce. Suppose you learn that 80 percent of those couples argue about money. Such a result would mean that almost all married people argue about money. It would also mean that arguing about money is not a predictor of which couples will divorce. Although it might still be a good idea for couples to learn how to handle financial disputes, nothing in these data supports the conclusion that money woes cause couples to divorce. You need to consider appropriate control groups to evaluate research findings meaningfully. When the controls are missing, you need to consider how they might have altered your understanding of the research.

Here is another example that requires critical thinking to recognize the need for a control group. Parents of young children are bombarded with advertisements for educational products to enhance their children's intelligence. There are, for example, special (and expensive) DVDs for infants to watch immediately after birth. Suppose you learn that toddlers who have watched these DVDs are able to talk in two- and three-word phrases by the time they are 18 months old. You might infer that the toddlers are communicating at such a young age because of the DVDs. However, you are missing data about toddlers who do not watch this material. At what age do they talk in two- and three-word phrases? In fact, studies show that the age at which toddlers begin talking does not depend on the use of specific learning programs. The National Academy of Pediatricians recommends that toddlers younger than 2 watch *no* DVDs, videos, or television. Without a control group, it would not be possible for you—as a researcher, concerned citizen, or parent—to know if particular programs had an effect on children's language development or any aspect of development.

your hypothetical study of alcohol and driving performance, what if a car with an automatic transmission is simulated to assess driving when participants are sober, but a car with a manual transmission is simulated to assess performance when participants are intoxicated? Given that manual transmissions require greater dexterity to operate than automatic transmissions, any apparent effect of intoxication on driving performance might actually be caused by the type of car. In this example, the drivers' skills might be *confounded* with the type of transmission, making it impossible to determine the true effect of the alcohol.

Other potential confounds include changes in the sensitivity of the measuring instruments, such as a systematic change in a scale so that it weighs things more heavily in one condition than in another. Changes in the time of day or the season when the experiment is conducted can also confound the results. The more confounds and thus alternative explanations that can be eliminated, the more confident a researcher can be that the change in the independent variable is causing the change (or effect) in the dependent variable. For this reason, researchers have to watch vigilantly for potential confounds. As consumers of research, we all need to think about confounds that could be causing particular results.

## Random Sampling and Random Assignment Are Important for Research

An important issue for any research method is how to select participants for the study. Psychologists typically want to know that their findings *generalize,* or apply, to people beyond the individuals in the study. In studying the effects of alcohol on motor skills and coordination, you ultimately would not focus on the behavior of the specific participants. Instead, you would seek to discover general laws about human behavior. If your results generalized to all people, they would enable you, other psychologists, and the rest of humanity to predict, in general, how intoxication would affect driving performance. Other results, depending on the nature of the study, might generalize to all college students, to students who belong to sororities and fraternities, to women, to men over the age of 45, and so on.

The group you want to know about is the **population.** To learn about the population, you study a subset from it. That subset, the people you actually study, is the **sample.** *Sampling* is the process by which you select people from the population to be in the sample. The sample should represent the population, and the best method for making this happen is *random sampling.* This method gives each member of the population an equal chance of being chosen to participate.

**population** Everyone in the group the experimenter is interested in.

**sample** A subset of a population.

Most of the time, a researcher will use a *convenience sample*. As the term implies, this sample consists of people who are conveniently available for the study. Even if you wanted your results to generalize to all students in your country or in the world, you would, realistically, probably use a sample from your own college or university and hope that this sample represented all students in your country and beyond. It is important for researchers to assess how well their results generalize to other samples (Henrich, Heine, & Norenzayan, 2010). For many topics studied in psychology—for example, sex differences in some mating preferences (discussed in Chapter 10) and the structure of personality (in Chapter 13)—the findings appear highly similar regardless of the sample studied. For many other topics studied—for example, the Mueller-Lyer illusion (in Chapter 4) and the self-concept (in Chapter 13)—the results obtained from samples of North American university students do not apply to other populations. Indeed, they often look quite different from population to population.

Even with random sampling, one likely confound in a study is preexisting differences between groups that are assigned to different conditions. For example, in your study of drinking and driving, what happens to the results if the people assigned to have many drinks just happen to be heavier drinkers and therefore are less affected by alcohol? Some heavy drinkers develop such a tolerance to alcohol that they show few outward signs of intoxication even when they have blood alcohol levels that would knock out or even kill a typical person (Chesher & Greeley, 1992; tolerance to drugs such as alcohol, especially tolerance as a component of addiction, is discussed in Chapter 5, "Consciousness"). Alternatively, some participants might become intoxicated on very small amounts of alcohol. Unless you have assigned participants randomly to the various conditions, the possibility always exists that any difference you find derives from preexisting differences between the groups. Research design often involves a series of choices: It means balancing the problems of taking people as they come with the problems of creating an artificial environment for the experiment. In fact, although experiments allow us to infer cause, they are often criticized for being artificial. In real life, for example, people decide for themselves how much alcohol they can drink and still drive safely. Assigning different levels of impairment may be so artificial that you end up studying something you had not intended, such as how people react when they are told how many drinks they can have. If the experiment creates a greatly artificial situation, the experiment is said to be low in **external validity.** This term refers to the degree to which the findings of an experiment can be generalized outside the laboratory. (*Internal validity* is discussed later in this chapter.)

**SELECTION BIAS** When the groups are not equivalent because participants in different groups differ in unexpected ways, the condition is known as **selection bias.** Suppose you have two of the experimental conditions described earlier: a group assigned to drink tonic water and a group assigned to reach a blood alcohol level twice the legal definition of intoxication. What happens if the group assigned to drink tonic water includes many small-bodied young women with little drinking experience and the other group includes many overweight older men with strong tolerances for alcohol? How would you know if the people in the different conditions of the study are equivalent? You could match each group for age, sex, weight, drinking habits, and so on, but you can never be sure that you have assessed all possible factors that may differ between the groups.

**external validity** The degree to which the findings of an experiment can be generalized outside the laboratory.

**selection bias** In an experiment, unintended differences between the participants in different groups.

**RANDOM ASSIGNMENT** The only way to make it more likely that the groups are equivalent is to use **random assignment.** This method gives each potential research participant an equal chance of being assigned to any level of the independent variable. For your study, there might be three levels: drinking tonic water, reaching the blood alcohol level that is the legal definition of intoxication, and reaching the blood alcohol level that is double the legal definition of intoxication. First, you would gather participants by taking either a random sample or a convenience sample from the population. Then, to randomly assign those participants, you might have them draw numbers from a hat to determine who was assigned to the control group (tonic water) and to each experimental group (legal definition of intoxication and double the legal definition). Of course, individual differences are bound to exist among participants. For example, any of your groups might include some people with low tolerance for alcohol and some people with high tolerance, some people with excellent coordination and some people with comparably poor coordination. But these differences will tend to average out when participants are assigned to either the control or experimental groups randomly, so that the groups are equivalent *on average.* Random assignment balances out known and unknown factors (**Figure 2.10**).

**random assignment** Placing research participants into the conditions of an experiment in such a way that each participant has an equal chance of being assigned to any level of the independent variable.

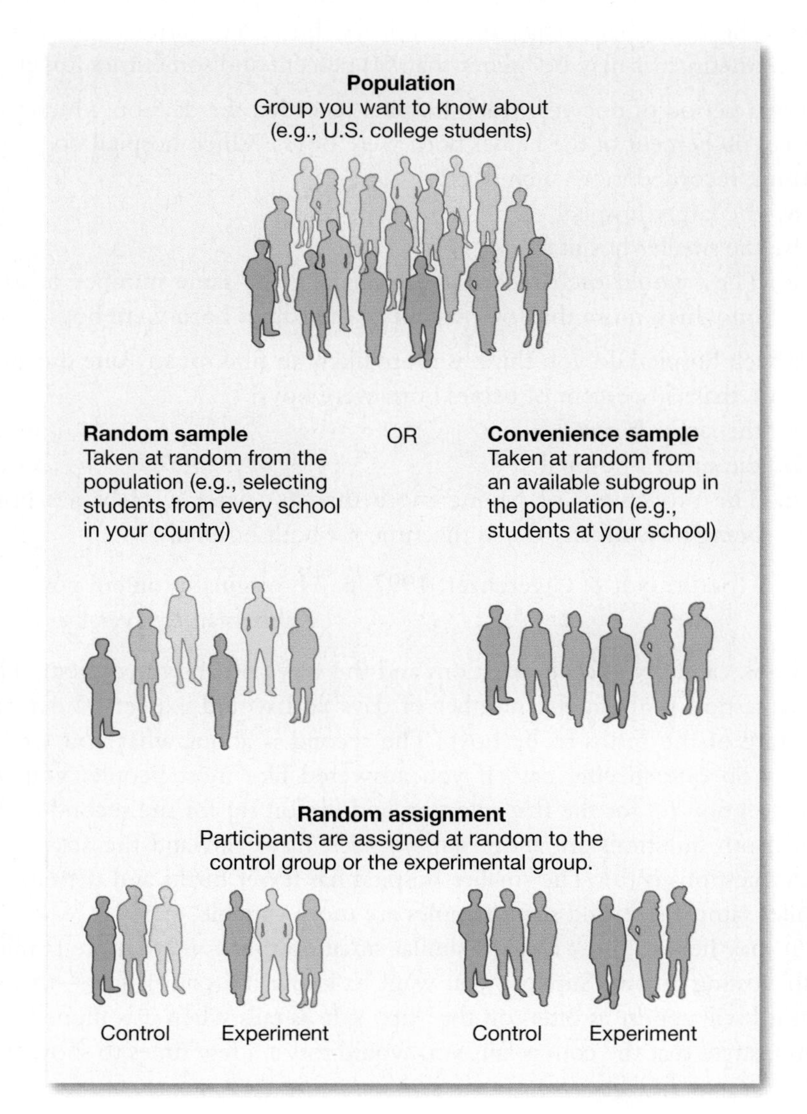


**FIGURE 2.10 Sampling** For the results of an experiment to be considered useful, the participants should be representative of the population. The best method for making this happen is random sampling, but most of the time researchers are forced to use a convenience sample. Random assignment is used when the experimenter wants to test a *causal* hypothesis.

CRITICAL THINKING SKILL

## Recognizing That Large Samples Generate More Reliable Results Than Small Samples

*Given a thimbleful of facts, we rush to make generalizations as large as a tub.*
*—Gordon Allport (1954, p. 8)*

A general critical thinking skill related to sampling from populations is considering the size of the sample, or the number of participants in the study. As consumers of research, we need to understand which studies provide strong evidence and which are poor science. The number of participants in a sample is one critical difference between the two types of studies. The importance of sample size can be difficult to understand when you think about it one way, but it can be easy to understand when you think about it a different way. First, read the following information and answer the questions:

A certain town is served by two hospitals. In the larger hospital, about 45 babies are born each day, and in the smaller hospital, about 15 babies are born each day. As you know, about 50 percent of all babies are boys. The exact percentage of baby boys, however, varies from day to day. Sometimes it may be higher than 50 percent and sometimes lower.

**1.** For a period of one year, each hospital recorded the days on which more than 60 percent of the babies born were boys. Which hospital do you think recorded more such days?
  **a.** the larger hospital
  **b.** the smaller hospital
  **c.** They would each record approximately the same number of days on which more than 60 percent of the babies born were boys.

**2.** Which hospital do you think is more likely to find on any one day that more than 60 percent of babies born were boys?
  **a.** the larger hospital
  **b.** the smaller hospital
  **c.** The probability of having more than 60 percent of babies born being boys on any day is the same for both hospitals.

(Sedlmeier & Gigerenzer, 1997, p. 34; original problem posed by Kahneman & Tversky, 1972)

Look carefully at both questions and the way you answered them. The first question is about the number of days you would expect 60 percent or more of the births to be boys. The second is about what you would expect on one specific day. If you answered like most people, you selected option (c) for the first question and option (b) for the second question. Both questions are about sample sizes, however, and the answer to both questions is (b). The smaller hospital has fewer births and therefore a smaller sample size, and small samples are more variable.

It may help to think about a similar situation that you are more familiar with: tossing a coin. Suppose you want to know if a coin is fair—that is, if heads will appear as often on the "up" side as tails when it is flipped. To demonstrate that the coin is fair, you would toss it a few times to show that heads and tails each come up about half the time. Suppose you flip it 4 times. Might you get 3 heads and 1 tail in 4 flips of a fair coin when there is an equal chance of getting a head or tail on each flip? It is not hard to see how heads and tails might not appear equally if you flip a coin a few times. Now suppose you flip the same coin 100 times. You probably would not get exactly 50 heads and 50 tails, but just by chance you would get close to 50 for each. With only 4 flips, it is quite possible that 75 percent of the flips could be all heads or all tails just by chance. With 100 flips, that same 75 percent is very unlikely.

Can you see how this is the same problem as in the hospital scenario? The smaller hospital is more likely to have some days when the percentage of boys (or girls) is higher than 60 percent, even when the true number of girl and boy babies in the population is approximately equal. It is easier to understand this principle when thinking about any single day (question 2) than about the number of days (question 1), although the reasoning is the same. Variability is discussed in more detail later in this chapter, but for now, just remember that small samples are more variable than large samples.

**FIGURE 2.11 Large Samples or Small Samples?** Suppose you want to compare how many women go to the beach versus how many men do. Why might your results be more accurate if you use a large sample (such as the big picture here) rather than a small sample (such as the detail)?

The *law of large numbers* states that you get more accurate estimates of a population from a large sample than from a small one. To apply this law in an everyday context, suppose you are deciding which of two colleges to attend. To help make this decision, you spend one day at each college and attend one class at each. You like the professor you meet at one of the colleges much better than the professor you meet at the other. Should this small sample of classes and professors influence your decision about which college to attend? Can you see how results from such a small sample could be very misleading? In planning a research project, as in deciding how you feel about a place, you must consider the size of the sample you are generalizing from (**Figure 2.11**).

### Summing Up

## What Types of Studies Are Used in Psychological Research?

There are three main types of studies in psychological research: descriptive, correlational, and experimental. In descriptive and correlational designs, researchers examine behavior as it naturally occurs. These types of studies are useful for describing and predicting behavior, but they do not allow researchers to assess causality. Correlational designs have limitations, which include directionality problems (knowing whether variable A caused variable B or the reverse) and the third variable problem (the possibility that a third variable is responsible for variables A and B). In an experiment, a researcher manipulates the independent variable to study how it affects the dependent variable. An experiment enables a researcher to establish a causal relationship between the independent and dependent variables. It also enables the researcher to avoid the directionality problem when trying to understand how one variable might affect another. An experiment gives the researcher the greatest control, so that the only thing that changes is the independent variable. If the goal is to conclude that changes in one variable cause changes in another variable, the researcher must assign participants at random to different groups to make the groups as equal as possible (on average) on all variables except the one being studied. The researcher wants to know about a population. Because it is usually impossible for everyone in the population to be a research participant, the researcher uses a representative sample of the population and then generalizes the findings to the population. Random sampling, in which everyone in the population has an equal chance of being a research participant, is the best way to sample. Since this is usually not possible, most researchers use a convenience sample. Among the most important factors in whether the results from a particular sample can be generalized back to the population is sample size. In general, large samples provide more accurate results than small ones.

## Measuring Up

1. The main reason researchers randomly assign participants to different groups in an experiment is that ________________.
   a. it is easier to assign participants to different conditions than it is to find people who naturally fit into different conditions
   b. random assignment controls for any intuitions the participants may have at the start of the experiment
   c. random assignment is used when there are ethical reasons for not using observational or correlational research designs
   d. random assignment is the only way to ensure that the experimental groups are (on average) equal and that any difference in the dependent variable is due to the participants' being in different experimental groups

2. Match each of the main methods of conducting research with the advantages and disadvantages listed below. Write in "descriptive," "correlational," "experimental," "longitudinal," or "cross-sectional" next to its advantage or disadvantage.
   a. ________ Allows the researcher to conclude that one variable causes a change in another variable.
   b. ________ Allows for a detailed description in a real-world setting.
   c. ________ Allows the researcher to understand if two or more variables are related, without demonstrating a causal relationship.
   d. ________ Measures people of different ages to learn about developmental changes.
   e. ________ Data are most likely to be biased (reflect the thoughts and beliefs of the person collecting the data).
   f. ________ The same people are repeatedly measured over time to understand developmental changes.
   g. ________ The research conditions are most likely to be artificial (because this method is often used in a laboratory).
   h. ________ It is always possible that a third variable not considered by the researcher causes the results.

**Answers:** 1. d. random assignment is the only way to ensure that the experimental groups are (on average) equal and that any difference in the dependent variable is due to the participants' being in different experimental groups.
2. a. experimental; b. descriptive; c. correlational; d. cross-sectional; e. descriptive; f. longitudinal; g. experimental; h. correlational.

## 2.3 What Are the Data Collection Methods of Psychological Science?

**Learning Objectives**

- Distinguish between five methods of data collection.
- List the advantages and disadvantages of different methods of data collection.
- Discuss the use of animal models in psychological research.
- Identify ethical issues associated with psychological research.

Once the researcher has established the best design for a particular study, the next task is to choose a method for collecting the data. The researcher's ultimate goal for the study, of course, is to answer an empirical question by observing and measuring some aspects of the world. A fundamental principle of psychological research is that the question the researcher wants to answer dictates the appropriate method for doing the observing and the measuring. In short, you start with a theory, derive a hypothesis from your theory, and phrase your hypothesis in the form of a question. Then you ask yourself: What sort of data will best answer my question? What collection method will best provide that data?

Recall from Chapter 1 the four major research categories that span the levels of analysis: biological, individual, social, and cultural. The first step in selecting a data collection method is determining the level of analysis a particular question is addressing. The data collection method used in the study must be appropriate for questions at that level of analysis.

When the research question is aimed at the biological level of analysis, researchers measure things such as brain processes and changes in body chemistry. For instance, they might record how the brain responds when people look at pictures of scary faces, or they might compare whether people secrete more testosterone when their favorite team wins than when the team loses. At the individual level of analysis, researchers are looking for individual differences among participants' responses. To find those differences, researchers might question participants directly. They might also use indirect assessments, such as observing how quickly participants respond to a particular question or whether they accurately discriminate between stimuli. At the social level of analysis, researchers often collect data by observing people within a single culture and seeing how they interact. Most work at the cultural level of analysis compares groups of people from different cultures as a way of studying the effect of culture on some variable. For example, cross-cultural studies might examine beliefs about appropriate roles for women and men or attitudes toward pornography. The various methods for studying this latter topic might include attitudinal measures, such as noting cultural differences in defining pornography; behavioral measures, such as observing who buys pornographic materials in different countries; and archival measures, such as examining legislative summary documents that collect differences in the laws regarding pornography.

One difficulty in comparing people from different cultures is that some ideas and practices do not translate easily across cultures, just as some words do not translate easily into other languages. Apparent differences between cultures may reflect such differences in language, or they may reflect participants' relative willingness to report things about themselves publicly. A central challenge for cross-cultural researchers is to refine their measurements to rule out these kinds of alternative explanations (**Figure 2.12**).

Some psychological traits are the same across all cultures (e.g., care for the young). Others differ widely across cultures (e.g., behaviors

**Cross-cultural studies** compare groups of people from different cultures.

**Advantages** Examine the effect of culture on some variable of interest. In this way, they help make psychology more applicable around the world.

**Disadvantages** Some situations and some specific words do not convey the same meaning when translated across cultures. These cultural differences can leave room for alternate explanations (other than culture per se). For example, misunderstandings can occur during the research process.

**FIGURE 2.12 Cross-Cultural Studies (top)** The living space and treasured possessions of a family in Japan, for example, differ from **(bottom)** those of a family in Mali. Cross-cultural researchers might study how either family would react to crowding or to the loss of its possessions.

**culturally sensitive research** Studies that take into account the role that culture plays in determining thoughts, feelings, and actions.

**observational techniques** A research method of careful and systematic assessment and coding of overt behavior.

expected of adolescents). **Culturally sensitive research** takes into account the significant role that culture plays in how we think, feel, and act (Adair & Kagitcibasi, 1995; Zebian, Alamuddin, Mallouf, & Chatila, 2007). Scientists use culturally sensitive practices so that their research respects—and perhaps reflects—the "shared system of meaning" that each culture transmits from one generation to the next (Betancourt & Lopez, 1993, p. 630). In cities with diverse populations, such as Toronto, London, and Los Angeles, cultural differences exist among different groups of people living in the same neighborhoods and having close daily contact. Researchers therefore need to be sensitive to cultural differences even when they are studying people in the same neighborhood or the same school. Researchers must also guard against applying a psychological concept from one culture to another without considering whether the concept is the same in both cultures. For example, Japanese children's attachment to their parents looks quite different from the attachment styles common among North American children (Miyake, 1993).

## Observing Is an Unobtrusive Strategy

**Observational techniques** (see Figure 2.4) involve the systematic assessment and coding of overt behavior. Coding involves determining what previously defined category the behavior fits into. For example, researchers might watch and note people's gestures during social interactions, or they might code the behavior of nonhuman animals that have been injected with drugs that affect brain function.

Using observational techniques to collect data requires researchers to make at least three decisions. First, should the study be conducted in the laboratory or in a natural environment? The answer to that question will depend on the behavior being studied. Must it occur as it would in the real world? Might the laboratory setting lead to artificial behavior? For example, suppose you hypothesize that people greet friends and family more effusively at airports than at train stations (perhaps because people think of air travel as more dangerous than rail travel, or perhaps because travelers tend to make longer trips by air and so are likely to have been apart longer from the people greeting them). To begin your study, you most likely would decide that it is very important for your participants to exhibit such behavior naturally. Therefore, you would observe the behavior at airport gates and train platforms. It would not make sense for you to re-create the experience of arrival and greeting in a laboratory.

Second, how should the data be collected? Observers can write descriptions of what they see, or they can keep running tallies of prespecified categories of behavior. For your study of arrival and greeting, you would need to operationally define different categories of effusive greetings. You might rate hugging and kissing as more effusive than hand shaking or head nodding. Then, while observing each episode of greeting at the airport gate or train platform, you could check off the appropriate category on a tally sheet. Researchers generally prefer preestablished categories as being more objective. However, badly chosen categories can lead observers to miss important behavior. For example, how would you classify the two-cheek air kiss, a more popular greeting in some countries than in others? The extent to which such a greeting is "effusive" depends on the cultural context. Likewise, a kiss on the mouth is a standard greeting between men in some parts of the world, but it suggests a romantic relationship in other parts of the world. Any greeting would need to be rated and interpreted in its cultural context.

Third, should the observer be visible? The concern here is that the presence of the observer might alter the behavior being observed. Such an alteration is called **reactivity.** People may feel compelled to make a positive impression on an observer, so they may act differently when they believe they are being observed. An example of this happened in a series of studies on workplace conditions and productivity. Specifically, the researchers manipulated working conditions and then observed workers' behavior at the Hawthorne Plant, a Western Electric manufacturing plant in Cicero, Illinois, between 1924 and 1933 (Olson, Hogan, & Santos, 2006; Roethlisberger & Dickson, 1939). The conditions included different levels of lighting, different pay incentives, and different break schedules. The main dependent variable was how long the workers took to complete certain tasks. Throughout the studies, the workers knew they were being observed. Because of this awareness, they responded to changes in their working conditions by increasing productivity. The workers did not speed up continuously throughout the various studies, however. Instead, they worked faster at the start of each new manipulation, regardless of the nature of the manipulation (longer break, shorter break, one of various changes to the pay system, and so on). The *Hawthorne effect* refers to changes in behavior that occur when people know that others are observing them (**Figure 2.13**).

**reactivity** When the knowledge that one is being observed alters the behavior being observed.

How might the Hawthorne effect operate in other studies? Consider a study of the effectiveness of a new reading program in elementary schools. Say that the teachers know they have been selected to try out a new program. They also

**FIGURE 2.13 Scientific Method: The Hawthorne Effect**

**Hypothesis:** Being observed can lead participants to change their behavior.

**Research Method:**

1. During studies of the effects of workplace conditions, the researchers manipulated several **independent variables,** such as the levels of lighting, pay incentives, and break schedules.
2. The researchers then measured the **dependent variable,** the speed at which workers did their jobs.

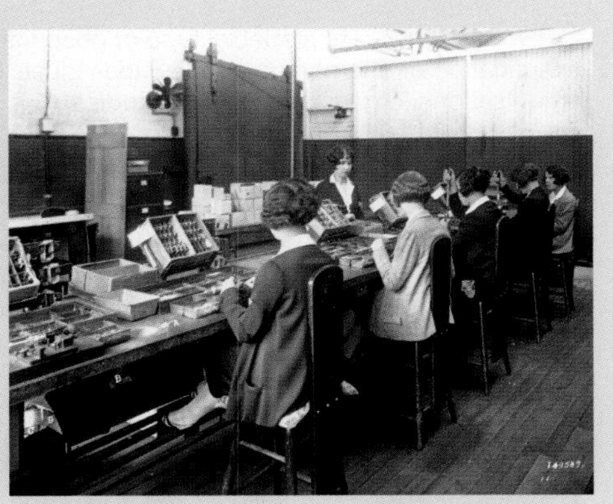

**Results:** The workers' productivity increased when they were being observed, regardless of the change to the independent variable.

**Conclusion:** Being observed can lead participants to change their behavior because people often act in particular ways to make positive impressions.

**Source:** Roethlisberger, F. J., & Dickson, W. J. (1939). *Management and the worker: An account of a research program conducted by the Western Electric Company, Hawthorne Works, Chicago*. Cambridge, MA: Harvard University Press.

**case studies** A research method that involves the intensive examination of unusual people or organizations.

know that their students' reading progress will be reported to the schools' superintendent. It is easy to see how these teachers might teach more enthusiastically or pay more attention to each child's reading progress than would teachers using the old program. One likely outcome is that the students receiving the new program of instruction would show reading gains caused by the teachers' increased attention and not by the new program. In general, observation should be as unobtrusive as possible.

## Case Studies Examine Individual Lives and Organizations

**Case studies** involve the intensive examination of unusual people or organizations (**Figure 2.14**). An organization might be selected for intensive study because it is doing something very well (such as making a lot of money) or very poorly (such as losing a lot of money). The goal of an organizational case study is to determine which practices led to success or failure. Did the employees have flexible work schedules, or was an exercise program offered at work? As discussed in Chapter 1, many psychologists work in organizations, employed to study the variables that influence human behavior at work.

In psychology, case studies are frequently conducted with people who have brain injuries or psychological disorders. Case studies of people with brain injuries have provided a wealth of evidence about which parts of the brain are involved in various psychological processes. In one case, a man who was accidentally stabbed through the middle part of the brain with a fencing foil lost the ability to store new memories (Squire & Moore, 1979). Case studies of people with psychological disorders, or clinical case studies, are the type used most frequently in psychology. The major problem with these studies is that it is difficult to know whether the researcher's theory about the cause of the psychological disorder is correct. The researcher has no control over the person's life and is forced to make assumptions about the effects of various life events. The same problem applies to organizational case studies. The researcher cannot know why different work practices can have different outcomes for different organizations.

**Case studies** are a special type of observational/descriptive study that involves intensive examination of one person or a few individuals (clinical case studies) or one or a few organizations (organizational case studies).

**Advantages** Can provide extensive data about one or a few individuals or organizations.

**Disadvantages** Can be very subjective: If a researcher has a preexisting theory (for example, people who are loners are dangerous), this theory can bias what is observed and recorded. The results cannot be generalized from a single case study to the population.

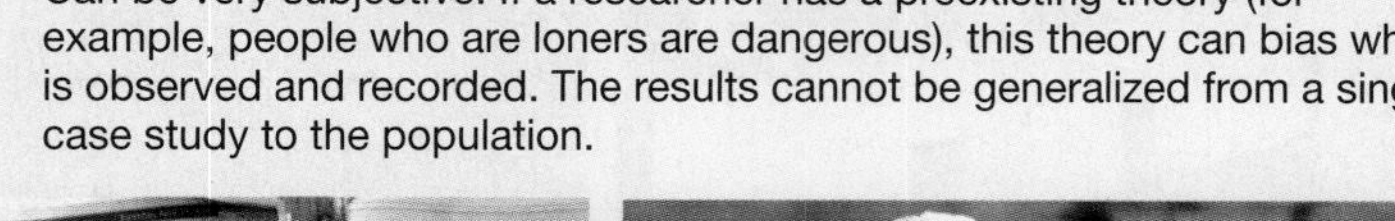

**FIGURE 2.14 Case Studies** The tragic story of Virginia Tech student Seung-Hui Cho provides a case study of a severely disturbed individual. Cho sent photos of himself to news organizations right before he went on a deadly campus shooting spree in April 2007, and he left in his wake a devastated campus that had lost 27 students and 5 teachers.

Thus the interpretation of case studies is often very subjective. Another big problem with case studies is the sample size, which equals one.

Consider an event that provides a snapshot into the mind of a severely disturbed individual. In April 2007, Seung-Hui Cho, a student at Virginia Tech University, went on a campus shooting spree. On the day of the shooting, Cho first shot two students in their dorm, then returned to his room to write about his extreme loneliness and anger. Finally, he went to a nearby classroom building, where he shot at everyone within his range before killing himself. Ultimately, he killed 32 people and wounded many others. The horror of these events led many people to ask what had been known about Cho's mental health. In fact, campus officials knew that Cho was deeply troubled. His professors had been concerned about him because of the violent themes in his writing, especially a 10-page play that was filled with anger and extreme violence.

In hindsight, it is easy to see that Cho should have been put in a locked facility where he could not harm others and could get treatment. Before his rampage, however, there was not enough evidence to allow his involuntary commitment to an institution. No one could have predicted his actions with certainty. Fortunately, murderous outbursts like this one are extremely rare. Unfortunately, that rarity makes them almost impossible to predict. Cho's writing might make him seem like a typical character in a horror novel or Hollywood thriller. But because Cho is not representative of disturbed individuals in general, psychologists and law enforcement officials cannot use the data from this unique case to identify other people who might erupt in similar ways. Some lonely people write violent stories, but very few of those people commit violent crimes. In this way, a case study can reveal a lot about the person being examined, but it does not allow generalization to all similar people (lonely ones, violent ones, what have you). Thus its use as a research tool is limited.

## Asking Takes a More Active Approach

Ideally, observation is an unobtrusive approach for studying behavior. By contrast, asking people about themselves, their thoughts, their actions, and their feelings is a much more interactive way of collecting data. Methods of posing questions to participants include surveys, interviews, and questionnaires. The type of information sought ranges from demographic facts (e.g., ethnicity, age, religious affiliation) to past behaviors, personal attitudes, beliefs, and so on. "Have you ever used an illegal drug?" "Should people who drink and drive be jailed for a first offense?" "Are you comfortable sending food back to the kitchen in a restaurant when there is a problem?" Questions such as these require people to recall certain events from their lives or reflect on their mental or emotional states.

A critical issue in question-based research is how to frame the questions. *Open-ended questions* allow respondents to provide any answers they think of and to answer in as much detail as they feel is appropriate. In contrast, *closed-ended questions* require respondents to select from a fixed number of options, as in a multiple-choice exam. Ultimately, the researcher decides what style of question will provide the most appropriate information for the hypothesis being investigated.

Like all methods of data collection, methods that require participants to answer questions have strengths and weaknesses. Consider the differences between asking respondents to fill out a survey and actually interviewing each person

**self-report methods** Methods of data collection in which people are asked to provide information about themselves, such as in questionnaires or surveys.

with open-ended questions. **Self-report methods,** such as questionnaires or surveys, can be used to gather data from a large number of people in a short time (**Figure 2.15**). They can be mailed out to a sample drawn from the population of interest or handed out in appropriate locations. They are easy to administer and cost-efficient. Interviews, another type of interactive method, can be used successfully with groups that cannot be studied through questionnaires or surveys, such as young children. Interviews are also helpful in gaining a more in-depth view of a respondent's opinions, experiences, and attidudes. Thus the answers from interviewees sometimes inspire avenues of inquiry that the researchers had not planned. The interview setting can give researchers handy opportunities to explore new lines of questioning.

What if researchers want to understand how thoughts, feelings, and behaviors vary throughout the day, week, or longer? They turn to a relatively new method of data collection, *experience sampling.* As the name implies, researchers take several samples of the participants' experiences over time. By repeatedly getting answers to set questions, researchers can determine how the responses vary over time. Suppose you want to know what a typical day is like for a high school student. You might give each student-participant a notebook with labeled categories in which to fill in what is happening and how the participant feels about it. Or you might give each student-participant a personal digital assistant (PDA) to carry at all times. At random or predetermined times, the PDA would signal the participants to record what they are doing, thinking, or feeling at that moment. Studies with experience sampling have shown, by the way, that high school students are frequently bored in class; most likely not paying attention; and generally thinking about lunch, friends, or other topics unrelated to the course content (Schneider & Csikszentmihalyi, 2000).

SELF-REPORT BIAS A problem common to all asking-based methods of data collection is that people often introduce biases into their answers. These biases make it difficult to discern an honest or true response. In particular, people may not reveal personal information that casts them in a negative light. Consider the question *How many times have you lied to get something you wanted?* Although most of us have lied at some points in our lives to obtain desired outcomes or objects, few of us want to admit this, especially to strangers. Researchers therefore have to consider the extent to which their questions produce *socially desirable responding,* or *faking good,* in which the person responds in a way that is most socially acceptable. Imagine having an interviewer around your parents' age—or, if you are an older student, perhaps a 20-something interviewer—ask you to describe intimate aspects of your sex life. Would you be embarrassed and therefore not very forthcoming? Might you even lie to the interviewer?

Even when respondents do not purposely answer incorrectly, their answers may reflect less-than-accurate self-perceptions. Research has shown that, at least in some cultures, people tend to describe themselves in especially positive ways, often because people believe things about themselves that are not necessarily true. This tendency is called the *better-than-average effect.* For instance, most people believe they are better-than-average drivers. The tendency to express positive things about oneself is especially common in Western cultures, such as those of North America and Europe, but is less pronounced in Eastern cultures, such as those in Korea and Japan (as discussed in Chapter 13, "Personality"). Although East Asians tend to rate themselves as better than average on a wide range of variables, they do so less consistently than people from Canada and the United States (Heine & Hamamura, 2007).

**Interactive methods** involve asking questions of participants. The participants then respond in any way they feel is appropriate (open-ended questions) or select from among a fixed number of options (closed-ended questions).

**Advantages** Self-report methods such as questionnaires can be used to gather data from a large number of people. They are easy to administer, cost-efficient, and a relatively fast way to collect data. Interviewing people face-to-face gives the researcher the opportunity to explore new lines of questioning. Experience sampling allows researchers to determine how responses vary over time.

**Disadvantages** People can introduce biases into their answers (self-report bias). They may not recall information accurately.

Surveys and questionnaires

Interviews

Experience sampling

**FIGURE 2.15 Interactive Methods**

## Response Performance Measures the Processing of Information

As noted in Chapter 1, Wilhelm Wundt established the first psychology laboratory in 1879. Wundt and his students pioneered many of the methods for studying how the mind works. For example, they examined how participants responded to psychological tasks such as deciding whether two stimuli were the same or whether words flashed on a screen were the names of animals. Such tests represent a research method called **response performance.**

**response performance** A research method in which researchers quantify perceptual or cognitive processes in response to a specific stimulus.

This method has three basic forms (**Figure 2.16**). First, the researcher can measure and interpret *reaction times.* The interpretation of reaction times is the most useful and dependable research method of cognitive psychology. It is based on the idea that the brain takes time to process information. The more processing a stimulus requires, the longer the reaction time to that stimulus. So research participants will make an easy decision, such as whether a figure flashed on a screen is red or blue, faster than a more difficult decision, such as whether that figure is red or blue *and* round or square. By manipulating what a participant must do with a stimulus and measuring reaction times, the researcher can gain much information about how the participant's brain processes information.

Reaction times for responding to simple stimuli are often measured in hundredths or thousandths of a second. For example, think of the time it takes to press one key on a computer keyboard if a red shape appears or a different key if a blue

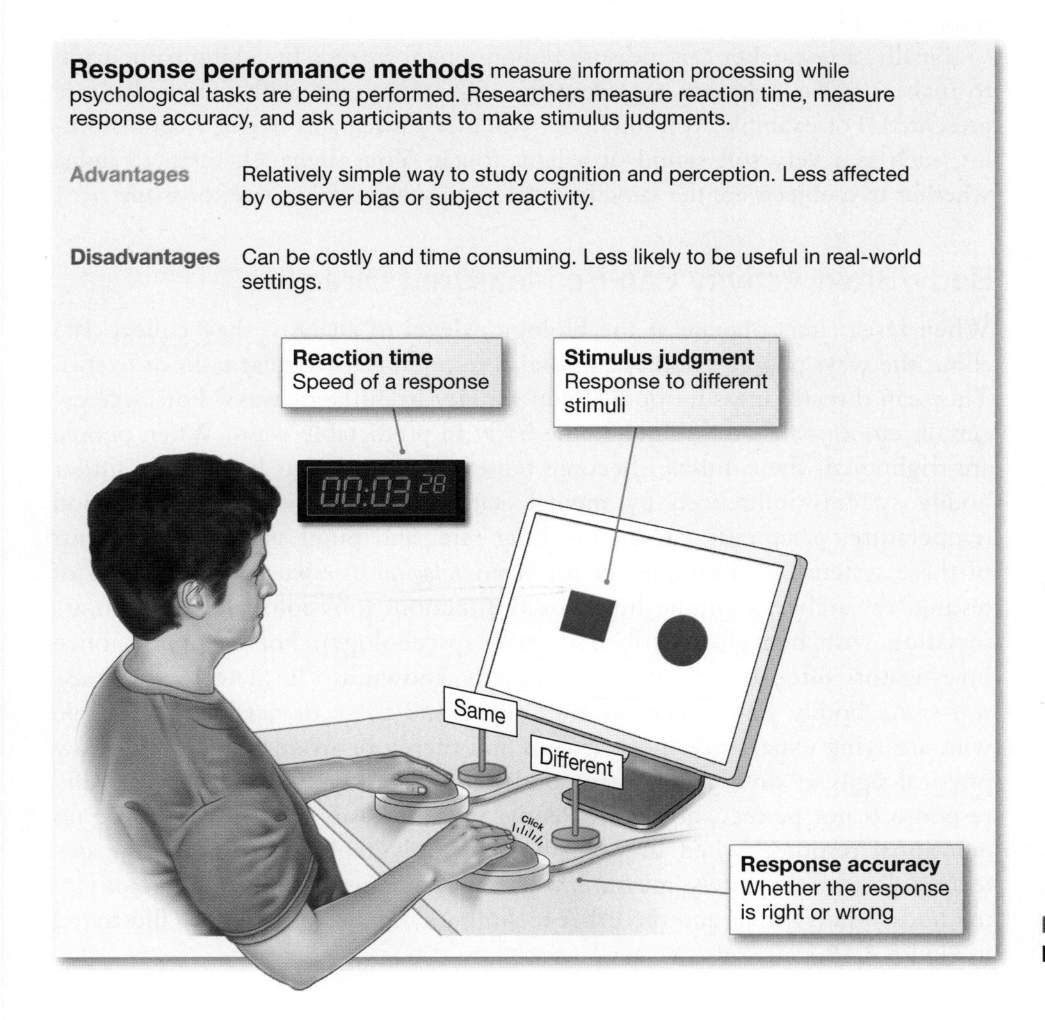


**FIGURE 2.16 Response Performance Methods**

**FIGURE 2.17 Try for Yourself: The Stroop Effect**

As quickly as you can, name the color of the ink each word is printed in. Do not read the words.

red blue green red blue yellow red blue

blue red green yellow red blue green red

yellow blue green red blue yellow red green

green yellow red yellow blue red green blue

If you are like most people, your reaction time for naming the ink colors in the bottom two rows was slower than your reaction time for naming the top two rows.

**Explanation:** The Stroop effect, named after the psychologist John Ridley Stroop, accounts for this phenomenon. Simply put, it takes longer to name the colors of words for colors when they are printed in conflicting colors. The tendency to automatically read the words interferes with the process of naming the ink colors.

shape appears. One reason psychologists use reaction times as dependent measures is that reaction times cannot be faked. If a participant tries to respond more slowly, for example, the reaction time will be much longer than what is expected (maybe two or three seconds instead of a fraction of a second). The experimenter will know immediately that the response was not a measure of actual processing time. Because people have very limited control over their reaction times, these measures again illustrate the idea that some psychological processes happen unconsciously. We have no conscious knowledge about what is happening in our brains as we use information, but measures of reaction time indirectly reflect brain processing (**Figure 2.17**).

A researcher can also measure *response accuracy*. For example, does paying attention to a visual stimulus improve a person's perception of that stimulus? To study this question, you might ask participants to pay attention to one side of a computer screen while keeping their eyes focused on the center of the screen. You would present a stimulus, such as by flashing a shape on either side of the screen. Then you would ask the participants whether the shape was a hexagon or an octagon. Suppose the participants answer more accurately when the stimulus appears on the side of the screen they are paying attention to than when it appears on the side they are ignoring. These results would indicate that attention improves perception of the stimulus.

Finally, a researcher can measure response performance by asking participants to make *stimulus judgments* regarding the different stimuli with which they are presented. For example, you might ask whether participants notice a faint stimulus, such as a very soft sound or a light touch. You might ask them to judge whether two objects are the same in some way, such as color, size, or shape.

## Body/Brain Activity Can Be Measured Directly

When researchers operate at the biological level of analysis, they collect data about the ways people's bodies and brains respond to particular tasks or events. They can directly measure body/brain activity in different ways. For instance, certain emotional states influence the body in predictable ways. When people are frightened, their muscles become tense and their hearts beat faster. Other bodily systems influenced by mental states include blood pressure, blood temperature, perspiration rate, breathing rate, and pupil size. Measurements of these systems are examples of *psychophysiological assessment*. In this type of testing, researchers examine how bodily functions (physiology) change in association with behaviors or mental states (psychology). For example, police investigators often use *polygraphs*, popularly known as "lie detectors," to assess some bodily states. The assumption behind these devices is that people who are lying experience more arousal and therefore are more likely to show physical signs of stress. The correspondence between mental state and bodily response is not perfect, however. People who lie easily can show little or no emotional response when they lie during a polygraph recording, so lie detectors do not accurately measure whether someone is lying. (Brain activity methods—polygraphs and the other techniques discussed here—are illustrated in **Figure 2.18**.)

**Body/brain activity methods** measure body/brain responses to tasks or events.

**Advantages** Identify physical responses to external events. Polygraphs record changes in bodily activity. EEG measures electrical activity in the brain. PET, fMRI, and TMS identify brain regions involved in various tasks. MRI shows brain structure.

**Disadvantages** Deemphasize brain localization. Some methods are better for assessing how quickly the body or brain responds (polygraph, EEG) but not as good for identifying the brain regions that are active. Other methods (PET, fMRI, TMS) are better for localizing brain activity but not as good for examining the time course of that activity. All these data are correlational and thus have the disadvantage of the third variable problem; directionality problem.

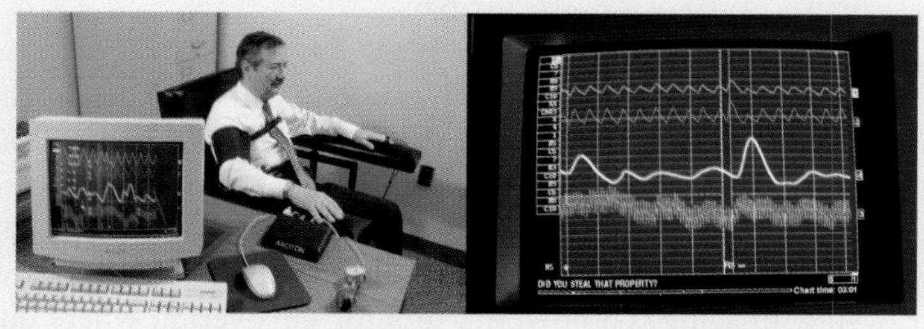

A polygraph (lie detector) measures changes in bodily functions (e.g., heart rate, perspiration rate, blood pressure) related to behaviors or mental states. These changes are *not* reliable measures of lying.

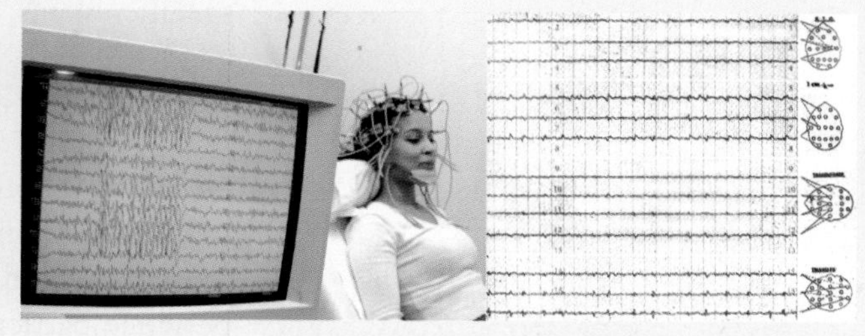

An electroencephalograph (EEG) measures the brain's electrical activity.

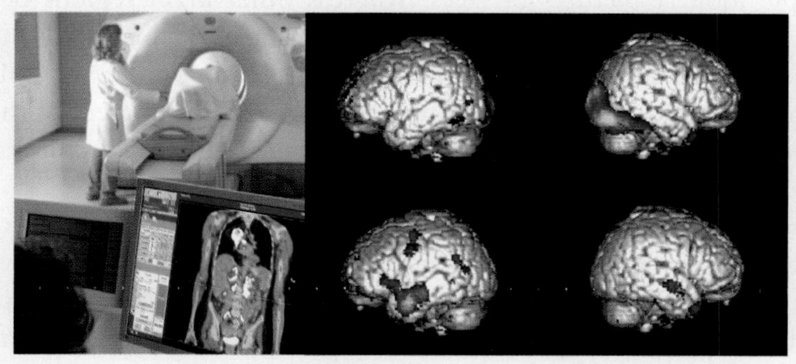

Positron emission tomography (PET) scans the brain's metabolic activity.

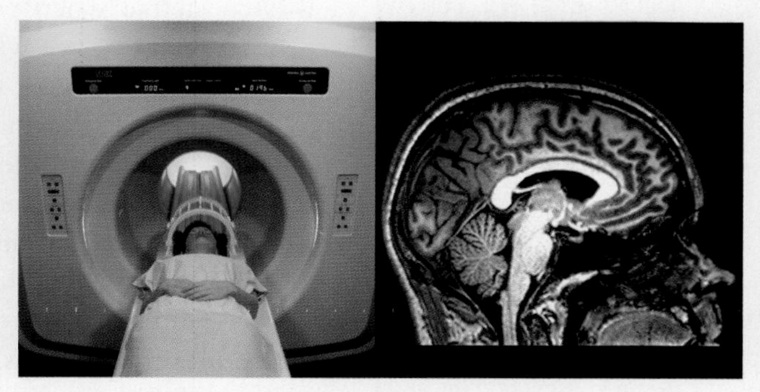

Magnetic resonance imaging (MRI) produces a high-resolution image of the brain.

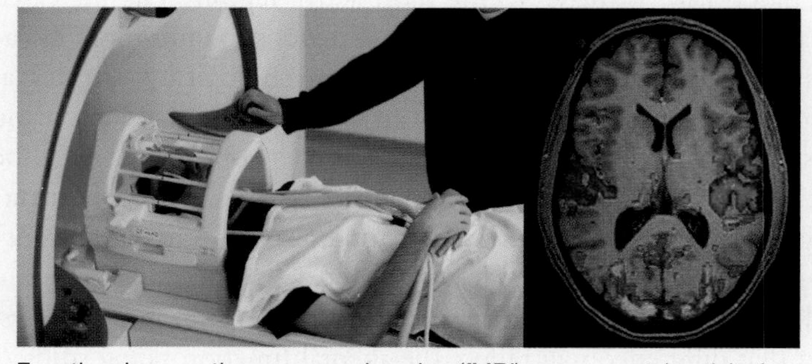

Functional magnetic resonance imaging (fMRI) maps mental activity by assessing the blood's oxygen level in the brain.

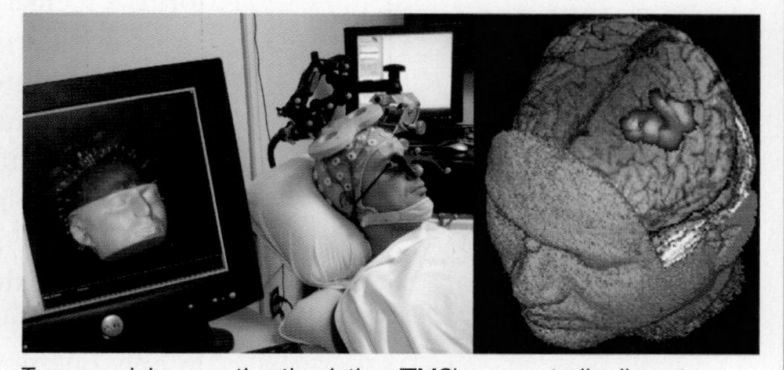

Transcranial magnetic stimulation (TMS) momentarily disrupts brain activity in a specific brain region.

**FIGURE 2.18 Body/Brain Activity Methods**

**ELECTROPHYSIOLOGY** *Electrophysiology* is a data collection method that measures electrical activity in the brain. A researcher fits electrodes onto the participant's scalp. The electrodes act like small microphones that pick up the brain's electrical activity instead of sounds. The device that measures brain activity is an **electroencephalograph (EEG).** This measurement is useful because different behavioral states produce different and predictable EEG patterns. As Chapter 5 discusses further, the EEG shows specific, consistent patterns as people fall asleep.

**electroencephalograph (EEG)** A device that measures electrical activity in the brain.

It also reveals that the brain is very active even when the body is at rest, especially during dreams. As a measure of specific cognitive states, however, the EEG is limited. Because the recordings (*electroencephalograms*) reflect all brain activity, they are too "noisy" or imprecise to isolate specific responses to particular stimuli. A more powerful way of examining how brain activity changes in response to a specific stimulus involves conducting many trials and averaging across the trials. Because this method enables researchers to observe patterns associated with specific events, it is called *event-related potential (ERP).*

**BRAIN IMAGING** The brain's electrical activity is associated with changes in the flow of blood carrying oxygen and nutrients to the active brain regions. *Brain imaging* methods measure changes in the rate, or speed, of the flow of blood to different regions of the brain. By keeping track of these changes, researchers can monitor which brain areas are active when people perform particular tasks or experience particular events. Imaging is a powerful tool for uncovering where different systems reside in the brain and how different brain areas interact to process information. For example, research has shown that certain brain regions become active when people look at pictures of faces, whereas other brain regions become active when people try to understand what other people are thinking. One brain imaging study—directly related to the impact of drinking on driving ability—found that alcohol leads to a one-third reduction in activity in areas of the brain concerned with vision (Levin et al., 1998). The major imaging technologies are *positron emission tomography* and *magnetic resonance imaging*.

**Positron emission tomography (PET)** is the computer-aided reconstruction of the brain's metabolic activity. After the injection of a relatively harmless radioactive substance into the bloodstream, a PET scan enables researchers to find the most active brain areas. The research participant lies in a special scanner that, by detecting the injected radiation, produces a three-dimensional map of the density of radioactivity inside the participant's brain. This map is useful because as the brain performs a mental task, blood flow increases to the most active regions. The increased blood flow carrying the radioactive material leads these regions to emit more radiation. The researchers have the participant perform some psychological task (such as looking at pictures of faces expressing fear). They scan the participant's brain during each phase of the task. By collating those scans, the researchers obtain a map of the brain's metabolic activity during the task. Since the entire brain is extremely metabolically active all the time, however, the researchers must also scan the participant's brain during the performance of another, closely related task (such as looking at pictures of faces with neutral expressions). The second task will differ from the first in only one way, and that difference will reflect the mental function being studied. Researchers are thus able to correlate brain regions with specific mental activities. One downside of PET is the need to inject a radioactive substance into the body. For safety reasons, researchers limit the use of this technology.

**Magnetic resonance imaging (MRI)** is the most powerful imaging technique. In MRI, a research participant lies in a scanner that produces a powerful magnetic field. Amazingly, this field is as strong as the kind used to pick up scrap metal at junkyards. The researchers momentarily disrupt the magnetic forces. During this process, energy is released from brain tissue in a form that can be measured by detectors surrounding the head. Because different types of brain tissue release energy differently, the researchers can produce a high-resolution image of the brain. (The amount of energy released is very small, so having an MRI is not dangerous. Nor is there any danger in being exposed to the magnetic field at the levels used in research.) MRI is extremely valuable for providing

**positron emission tomography (PET)**
A method of brain imaging that assesses metabolic activity by using a radioactive substance injected into the bloodstream.

**magnetic resonance imaging (MRI)**
A method of brain imaging that produces high-quality images of the brain.

information about the structure of the brain. It can be used to determine the location of brain damage or of a brain tumor. It can also be used to create images of other body parts, such as in determining hip and knee injuries.

Like a PET scan, **functional magnetic resonance imaging (fMRI)** makes use of the brain's blood flow to map the working brain. Again, the researchers have the participant perform a task (such as deciding whether a face looks happy or sad). During that task, the researchers scan the participant's brain. Whereas PET measures blood flow directly by tracking a radioactive substance, fMRI measures blood flow indirectly by assessing changes in the blood's oxygen level. As in all brain imaging methods, the participant then performs a task that differs from the first one in only one way and that reflects the particular mental function of interest. The researchers then compare images to examine differences in blood flow and therefore brain activity.

**functional magnetic resonance imaging (fMRI)** An imaging technique used to examine changes in the activity of the working human brain.

**transcranial magnetic stimulation (TMS)** The use of strong magnets to briefly interrupt normal brain activity as a way to study brain regions.

**TRANSCRANIAL MAGNETIC STIMULATION** One limitation of brain imaging is that the findings are necessarily correlational. We know that certain brain regions are active while a task is performed. We do not know whether each brain region is necessary for the task. As a correlational method, brain imaging has the conceptual problems, such as the third variable and directionality problems, discussed earlier. To see whether a brain region is important for a task, researchers ideally want to compare performances when that area is working effectively and when it is not. **Transcranial magnetic stimulation (TMS)** uses a very fast but powerful magnetic field to disrupt brain activity momentarily in a specific brain region. For example, placing the TMS coil over areas of the brain involved in language will disrupt a person's ability to speak. This technique has its limitations, particularly that it can be used only for short durations to examine brain areas close to the scalp. When used along with imaging, however, it is a powerful method for examining which brain regions are necessary for specific psychological functions.

## Research with Animals Provides Important Data

Throughout the history of psychological science, many of the most important research findings have been obtained by studying the behavior of nonhuman animals. For instance, watching animals—usually rats—run through mazes or press levers to earn rewards led to the development of many principles about learning. Indeed, Ivan Pavlov's observation of a salivating dog inspired John B. Watson to launch the behaviorist movement (these topics are discussed further in Chapter 6, "Learning"). A central assumption underlying Watson's behaviorism was that humans are subject to the same laws of nature as other animals. Humans' behavior might seem more complex than that of rats or dogs. But the forces that control the behaviors of rats, dogs, and humans are in many ways the same. Indeed, those forces tend to control the behaviors of all animals—human and nonhuman—in very similar ways.

As our knowledge of the human genome increases, our interest increases in the way genes affect behaviors, physical illnesses, psychological disorders, and well-being. Psychologists working at the biological level of analysis manipulate genes directly to examine their effects on behavior. Of course, for ethical reasons, much of the genetic research cannot be conducted with humans, so researchers use other animals for this important work.

As Chapter 3 discusses in greater detail, specific genes can be targeted for manipulation. Researchers can delete genes to eliminate their effects or move genes to other locations to enhance their effects. For research purposes, *transgenic mice* are produced by manipulating the genes in developing mouse embryos—for

"WHAT IT COMES DOWN TO IS YOU HAVE TO FIND OUT WHAT REACTION THEY'RE LOOKING FOR, AND YOU GIVE THEM THAT REACTION."

**institutional review boards (IRBs)** Groups of people responsible for reviewing proposed research to ensure that it meets the accepted standards of science and provides for the physical and emotional well-being of research participants.

example, by inserting strands of foreign DNA into the genes. The new genes are integrated into every cell of each mouse's body. This sort of research is providing new hope for curing and preventing many diseases (**Figure 2.19**).

## There Are Ethical Issues to Consider

When scientists select a research method, they must make decisions with full knowledge of the ethical issues involved. They must also adhere strictly to the relevant ethical guidelines. Are they asking the participants to do something unreasonable? Are the participants risking physical or emotional harm from the study? Some ethical concerns are specific to the kind of method used, while others apply across all methods. Therefore, to ensure the participants' well-being, all colleges, universities, and research institutes have strict guidelines in place regarding research. **Institutional review boards (IRBs)** are the guardians of those guidelines. Convened at schools and other institutions where research is done, IRBs consist of administrators, legal advisers, trained scholars, and members of the community. They review all proposed research to ensure that it meets scientific standards. The research design must also put to rest any ethical concerns for the safety and well-being of participants.

**PRIVACY** One of the more prominent ethical concerns about research is participants' reasonable expectation of privacy. If behaviors are going to be observed, is it okay to observe people without their knowledge? This question obviously depends on what sorts of behaviors researchers might be observing. If the behaviors tend to occur in public rather than in private, researchers might be less concerned about observing people without their knowledge. For example, even without their knowledge, it would be okay to observe couples saying good-bye in a public place such as an airport. Without the couples' knowledge, it would be inappropriate to observe their private sexual behaviors. The concern over privacy is compounded by the ever-increasing technology for monitoring people remotely. Although it might be useful to compare men's and women's behaviors in public bathrooms, would it be acceptable to install discreet video cameras to monitor people in restrooms? (The answer is no!)

When people are asked for information, should some topics not be raised because they may be too personal or otherwise inappropriate? Say that researchers would like to understand how a physically and emotionally traumatic event affects people in the months and years after it occurs. Such issues must be explored to develop strategies for overcoming physical pain and emotional anguish. Still, researchers must consider how their lines of questioning will affect the individuals they are studying. They must also monitor the effects on the participants during the questioning.

**FIGURE 2.19 Animal Research** Researchers observe the behaviors of transgenic mice to understand how certain genes affect behavior.

**ACCESS TO DATA** No matter what research method they use, researchers must also consider who will have access to the data they collect. Participant confidentiality should always be guarded carefully so that personal information is not linked publicly to the study's findings. When participants are told that their information will remain confidential, the implicit promise is that their information will be kept secret or made available to only the few people who need to know it. Often the quality and accuracy of data depend on the participants' certainty that their responses will be kept confidential. When emotionally or legally sensitive topics are involved, people are especially likely to provide valid data after they are promised confidentiality.

For studies concerning extremely sensitive topics, the participants' responses should remain anonymous. *Anonymity* is not the same as *confidentiality,* although these terms are often confused. Anonymity means that the researchers collect no personal information, so responses can never be traced to any individual. If you wanted to know how many college students in your sample had ever cheated on an exam, the students would have to be assured of anonymity so that they would be comfortable about responding honestly. An anonymous study might be conducted in the form of a written questionnaire that asked about cheating but did not ask for any identifying information. Participants would return the completed questionnaires to a large box so that no questionnaire could be linked to any individual.

**INFORMED CONSENT** Research involving human participants is a partnership based on mutual respect and trust. People who volunteer for psychological research have the right to know what will happen to them during the course of the study. Compensating people for their participation in research does not alter this fundamental right. Ethical standards require giving people all relevant information that might affect their willingness to become participants. *Informed consent* means that participants make a knowledgeable decision to participate. Typically, researchers obtain informed consent in writing. In observational studies of public behavior, the observed individuals remain anonymous to the researchers to protect their privacy, so informed consent is not required. Minors, the intellectually incapacitated, and the mentally ill cannot legally provide informed consent. If such an individual is to participate in a study, a legal guardian must grant permission.

It is not always possible to inform participants fully about a study's details. If knowing the study's specific goals may alter the participants' behavior, thereby rendering the results meaningless, researchers may need to use deception. That is, they might mislead the participants about the study's goals or not fully reveal what will take place. Researchers use deception only when other methods are not appropriate and when the deception does not involve situations that would strongly affect people's willingness to participate. If deception is used, a careful *debriefing* must take place after the study's completion. Here, the researchers inform the participants of the study's goals. They also explain the need for deception, to eliminate or counteract any negative effects produced by the deception.

**RELATIVE RISKS OF PARTICIPATION** Another ethical issue is the relative risk to participants' mental or physical health. Researchers must always remain conscious of what they are asking of participants. They cannot ask people to endure unreasonable amounts of pain or of discomfort, either from stimuli or from the manner in which data measurements are taken. Fortunately, in the vast majority of research being conducted, these types of concerns are not an issue. However, although risk is low, researchers have to think carefully about the potential for risk to specific participants. Again, any research conducted at a college, university, or research institute must be approved by an IRB familiar with the rules and regulations that protect participants from harm. Most IRBs look at the relative trade-off between risk and benefit. Potential gains from the scientific enterprise sometimes require asking participants to expose themselves to some risk to obtain important findings. The *risk/benefit ratio* is an analysis of whether the research is important enough to warrant placing participants at risk.

Psychology: Knowledge You Can Use

# Should I Participate in Psychological Research?

Someday, perhaps even this term, you will be invited to participate in a psychological research study (**Figure 2.20**). Participating is a good idea for two reasons: It will help you contribute to scientific knowledge, and it will give you an insider's view of how psychological research works. Students in introductory psychology may worry that researchers will manipulate or trick them into doing something they do not want to do. Others may feel anxious because they have no idea what to expect once they walk through the doors of a psychology laboratory. Understanding the ethical principles that guide psychological research arms potential research participants, such as yourself, with insight about what to expect when participating in a study.

The research in which you participate might be conducted by professors or students at your college, or it might be conducted by researchers at another institution. Regardless of where the research takes place, psychologists in the United States conduct their studies according to a specific set of ethical principles, collectively known as the Belmont Report (http://www.hhs.gov/ohrp/policy/belmont.html). Psychologists outside the United States follow similar guidelines. The principles of the Belmont Report, a few of which are described below, guide many aspects of participants' experiences in research studies.

First, your participation is voluntary. No one can force you to participate in a study. Many psychology departments "require" students to participate in research as part of the students' course work, but the departments usually offer alternatives for fulfilling this requirement. For example, in some departments, students can read and write about articles published in journals in lieu of participating in research. Even once you agree to participate in a study, you have the right to discontinue your participation at any time, for any reason, and without penalty. And you can skip any questions you do not care to answer, perhaps because you find them intrusive or offensive. These freedoms mean that *you* are in the driver's seat when it comes to choosing if, and to what extent, you participate in a study.

**FIGURE 2.20 Student Participation in Psychological Research** These students are enjoying the opportunity to contribute to scientific knowledge. Join them by participating in a study!

Second, you are legally and ethically entitled to know what you are getting into so you can make an informed decision about participating. Researchers cannot reveal their exact research questions and hypotheses, because knowing that information might change the way you behave in the study. Researchers will be able to tell you, however, the general purpose of the study and the kinds of activities you will be asked to complete. You might, for example, be asked to answer questionnaires, solve math problems, or engage in moderate physical activity. Importantly, researchers must tell you about the risks and potential benefits faced by participants. A researcher studying eating disorders would inform volunteers about a possible risk: that some participants might experience psychological distress as a result of thinking about their health behaviors. A researcher studying the effectiveness of a new technique that might be used in psychological treatment would inform volunteers about a possible benefit: that participation might result in improved self-esteem. The point here is that you will actually know a good deal about the research study before the study even begins.

Third, after you complete the study, you can expect the researchers to provide a thorough explanation of the study, called a *debriefing*. During the debriefing, the researchers will tell you if they used deception in the study and why it was necessary. For example, if you participated in a study about first impressions, you might learn during the debriefing that the "person" you interacted with was actually a member of the research team chosen because he or she was very attractive and the researchers were interested in how physical attractiveness affects how people are judged. If you had known in advance that the researchers were studying this idea, it might have affected how you evaluated the person you were judging. In addition, the researcher will likely describe the questions and hypotheses driving the study and will invite you to leave your contact information if you would like to learn the results of the investigation.

Finally, you can expect that the data you provide will remain confidential. Researchers take great pains to protect your confidentiality. For example, they remove all identifying information, such as your name, from any data submitted. They store consent forms separately from data, password-protect electronic files that contain sensitive information, and keep all files in a secured location. Then, when it comes time for researchers to share their results with others, they will do so while maintaining your privacy. For example, they will not show conference attendees a video clip of you discussing a problem in your romantic relationship (unless you provided consent for them to do so).

Just as researchers are governed by formal ethical guidelines (in addition to their own moral compasses), good study participants also engage in the research process respectfully. When you sign up to participate in a study, record the date, time, and location in your calendar. Jot down the researcher's contact information in case an emergency arises and you are unable to fulfill your commitment to attend the study session. Out of respect for the time of the researcher and any other participants, arrive at your session on time, and bring with you any paperwork your institution might require for you to receive class credit for your participation. Whether you are completing a study online or in a laboratory, make every effort to minimize potential distractions. Turn off your cell phone, iPod, and other devices that might divert your attention from the task at hand. And, importantly, ask questions! One of the benefits of volunteering in research is learning firsthand about the research process. Getting answers to your questions helps you fully derive this benefit.

Study participants are essential to the research enterprise, and researchers are grateful for the time and effort participants devote. The principles described here emerged out of concern for the well-being of these participants and in response to violations of human rights in early research studies. Understanding your rights prepares you to contribute meaningfully and confidently, without fear of trickery or unknown risks, to psychologists' efforts to understand and improve the human condition. On behalf of psychologists everywhere, thank you for joining us in this endeavor.

For a list of opportunities to participate in online research studies, see http://psych.hanover.edu/research/exponnet.html.

## Summing Up

### What Are the Data Collection Methods of Psychological Science?

In psychological science, there are five basic data collection methods. These methods operate at different levels of analysis. The choice of which to use is generally dictated by the research question. First, researchers can observe behaviors as they take place. They can either write down general descriptions of the behaviors or check off a tally sheet of prespecified behavior categories. Second, researchers may use case studies to examine unusual people or organizations. Third, researchers can ask people for information about their thoughts, feelings, and behaviors by using surveys, questionnaires, and interviews. Fourth, researchers can measure how quickly and accurately people respond to a stimulus. Fifth, researchers can directly measure the body's activity (e.g., psychophysiological reactions) and the brain's activity (e.g., electrical activity, blood flow), or they can disrupt ongoing brain processes. Psychological research has benefited from the use of animal models. Regardless of the method chosen, researchers must consider the ethical consequences of their data collection. They must carefully consider the use of deception and weigh the study's relative risks against its potential benefits.

## Measuring Up

**For each example below, indicate which data collection method would work best. Fill in the blank with one of the following: description/observation, case study, survey, interview, experience sampling, response performance (which includes accuracy and reaction time), EEG, brain imaging, or transcranial magnetic stimulation.**

1. A researcher is investigating Adolf Hitler's childhood and teenage years to see if there are ways of recognizing the experiences that made Hitler evil as an adult. What data collection method is he using? ________
2. As discussed in Chapter 10, "Emotion and Motivation," Alfred Kinsey studied the sexual behaviors of large numbers of people from every walk of life. What data collection method or methods would you have suggested he use? ________

3. Fascinating new data reveal that the social lives of the great apes are surprisingly similar to human social systems. What method was probably used to obtain these data? ____________

4. In a study of families, the researchers want to know when children and their parents feel stressed, happy, relaxed, and bored throughout the day. What data collection method should the researchers use? ____________

5. If you wanted to study which parts of their brains longtime soccer players use when they perform spatial tasks, what method would you use? ____________

6. Researchers are often interested in the similarities and differences between men's and women's brain processes. If you believed that women use both sides of their brains more equally when using language than men do, you could interrupt the brain processes and see what happens. What research method would be best for this proposed study? ____________

**Answers:** 1. case study; 2. survey or interview; 3. description/observation [in the wild is best]; 4. experience sampling; 5. brain imaging; 6. transcranial magnetic stimulation.

**Learning Objectives**

- Identify three characteristics that reflect the quality of data.
- Describe measures of central tendency and variability.
- Describe the correlation coefficient.
- Discuss the rationale for inferential statistics.

## 2.4 How Are Data Analyzed and Evaluated?

So far, this chapter has presented the essential elements of scientific inquiry in psychology: how to frame an empirical question using theories, hypotheses, and research; how to decide what type of study to run; and how to collect data. This section focuses on the data. Specifically, it examines the characteristics that make for good data and the statistical procedures that researchers use to analyze data.

### Good Research Requires Valid, Reliable, and Accurate Data

If you collect data to answer a research question, the data must address that question. **Internal validity** refers to whether the data you collect address your question. For data to be internally valid, they must measure what you want to measure. By doing so, they provide clear information you can use to evaluate your theory or hypothesis. Suppose you hypothesize that people in their 20s are more likely to channel surf (rapidly switch among television channels) than are people in their 50s. To test your hypothesis, you would need to study television-watching behavior and, in particular, the average length of time people stay tuned to each station they watch. To be internally valid, your data would need to reflect the independent variable (age) and the dependent variable (time spent watching stations). Say, for example, that participants in their 20s tended to do other things, such as sleeping or checking their Facebook status, while watching television. Because these participants were not paying attention during the study, the data would not reflect television watching and would not be internally valid. Likewise, say that a participant in his 50s was watching with children and trying to find programs that would appeal to those children. That participant's behavior would not reflect the television-watching experience of people in their 50s.

Another important aspect of data is **reliability,** the stability and consistency of a measure over time. If the measurement is reliable, the data collected will not vary substantially over time. One option for measuring the duration of each channel stay would be to have an observer use a stopwatch. There is likely to be some variability,

**internal validity** The extent to which the data collected in a study address the research hypothesis in the way intended.

**reliability** The extent to which a measure is stable and consistent over time in similar conditions.

however, in when the observer starts and stops the watch relative to when the surfer actually changes channels. As a consequence, the data in this scenario would be less reliable than data collected by a computer linked to each viewer's television remote.

The third and final characteristic of good data is **accuracy,** the extent to which the measure is error free. A measure may be valid and reliable but still not be accurate. Psychologists think about this problem by turning it on its head and asking, How do errors creep into a measure? Suppose that for the channel surfing study you use a stopwatch to measure the duration of each channel stay. The problem with this method is that each measurement will tend to overestimate or underestimate the duration (because of human error or variability in recording times). This is known as a *random error,* because although an error is introduced into each measurement, the value of the error differs each time. But suppose the stopwatch has a glitch, such that it always overstates the time measured by 2 seconds. This is known as a *systematic error,* because the amount of error introduced into each measurement is constant (**Figure 2.21**). Generally, systematic error is more problematic than random error because the latter tends to average out over time and therefore is less likely to produce inaccurate results.

**accuracy** The extent to which an experimental measure is free from error.

**descriptive statistics** Statistics that summarize the data collected in a study.

**central tendency** A measure that represents the typical response or the behavior of a group as a whole.

## Descriptive Statistics Provide a Summary of the Data

The first step in evaluating data is to inspect the *raw values.* This term refers to data that are as close as possible to the form in which they were collected. In examining raw data, researchers look for errors in data recording. For instance, they assess whether any of the responses seem especially unlikely (e.g., blood alcohol content of 50 percent or a 113-year-old participant). Once the researchers are satisfied that the data make sense, they summarize the basic patterns using **descriptive statistics.** These mathematical forms provide an overall summary of the study's results. For example, they might show how the participants, on average, performed in one condition compared with another.

The simplest descriptive statistics are measures of **central tendency.** This single value describes a typical response or the behavior of the group as a whole. The

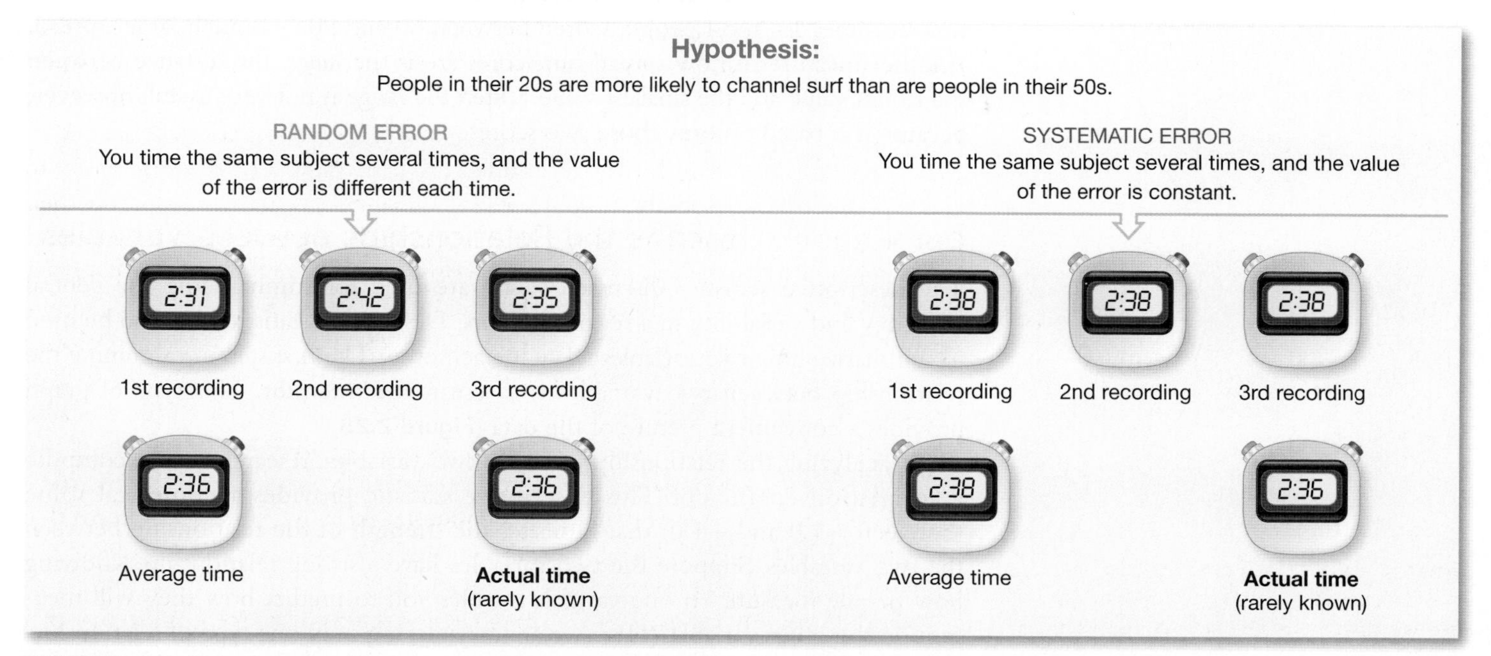


**FIGURE 2.21 Data Accuracy** Good data should be accurate (free from error). These examples illustrate how errors can creep into a measure. Random error occurs when the degree of error varies each time. Systematic error occurs when the measurement has the same degree of error each time.

**mean** A measure of central tendency that is the arithmetic average of a set of numbers.

**median** A measure of central tendency that is the value in a set of numbers that falls exactly halfway between the lowest and highest values.

**mode** A measure of central tendency that is the most frequent score or value in a set of numbers.

**variability** In a set of numbers, how widely dispersed the values are from each other and from the mean.

**standard deviation** A statistical measure of how far away each value is, on average, from the mean.

**scatterplot** A graphical depiction of the relationship between two variables.

most intuitive measure of central tendency is the **mean,** the arithmetic average of a set of numbers. The class average on an exam is an example of a mean score. Consider the hypothetical study of alcohol and driving performance. A basic way to summarize the data would be to calculate the means for driving performances: You would calculate one mean for when participants were sober and a second mean for when they were intoxicated. If alcohol affects driving, you would expect to see a difference in the means between sober and intoxicated driving performances.

A second measure of central tendency is the **median,** the value in a set of numbers that falls exactly halfway between the lowest and highest values. For instance, if you received the median score on a test, half the people who took the test scored lower than you and half the people scored higher. Sometimes researchers will summarize data using a median instead of a mean because if one or two numbers in the set are dramatically larger or smaller than all the others, the mean will give either an inflated or a deflated summary of the average. This effect occurs in studies of average incomes. Perhaps approximately 50 percent of Americans make more than $45,000 per year, but a small percentage of people make so much more (multiple millions or billions for the richest) that the mean income is much higher than the median and is not an accurate measure of what most people earn. The median provides a better estimate of how much money the average person makes.

A third measure of central tendency is the **mode,** the most frequent score or value in a set of numbers. For instance, the modal number of children in an American family is two, which means that more American families have two children than any other number of children. (For examples of how to calculate all three central tendency measures, see **Figure 2.22.**)

In addition to measures of central tendency, another important characteristic of data is the **variability** in a set of numbers. This term refers to how widely dispersed the values are about the mean. The most common measure of variability—how spread out the scores are—is the **standard deviation.** This measure reflects how far away each value is, on average, from the mean. For instance, if the mean score for an exam is 75 percent and the standard deviation is 5, most people scored between 70 percent and 80 percent. If the mean remains the same but the standard deviation becomes 15, most people scored between 60 and 90—a much larger spread. Another measure of how spread out scores are is the *range,* the distance between the largest value and the smallest value. Often the range is not very useful, however, because it is based on only those two scores.

## Correlations Describe the Relationships between Variables

The descriptive statistics discussed so far are used for summarizing the central tendency and variability in a set of numbers. Descriptive statistics can also be used to summarize how two variables relate to each other. The first step in examining the relationship between two variables is to create a **scatterplot.** This type of graph provides a convenient picture of the data (**Figure 2.23**).

In analyzing the relationship between two variables, researchers can compute a correlation coefficient. This descriptive statistic provides a numerical value (between −1.0 and +1.0) that indicates the strength of the relationship between the two variables. Suppose the two variables have a strong relationship. Knowing how people measure on one variable enables you to predict how they will measure on the other variable. (Here we are considering only one type of relationship: a linear relationship, in which an increase or decrease in one variable is associated with an increase or decrease in the other variable.) What signifies a strong relationship? Consider the different scatterplots in **Figure 2.24.** If two variables

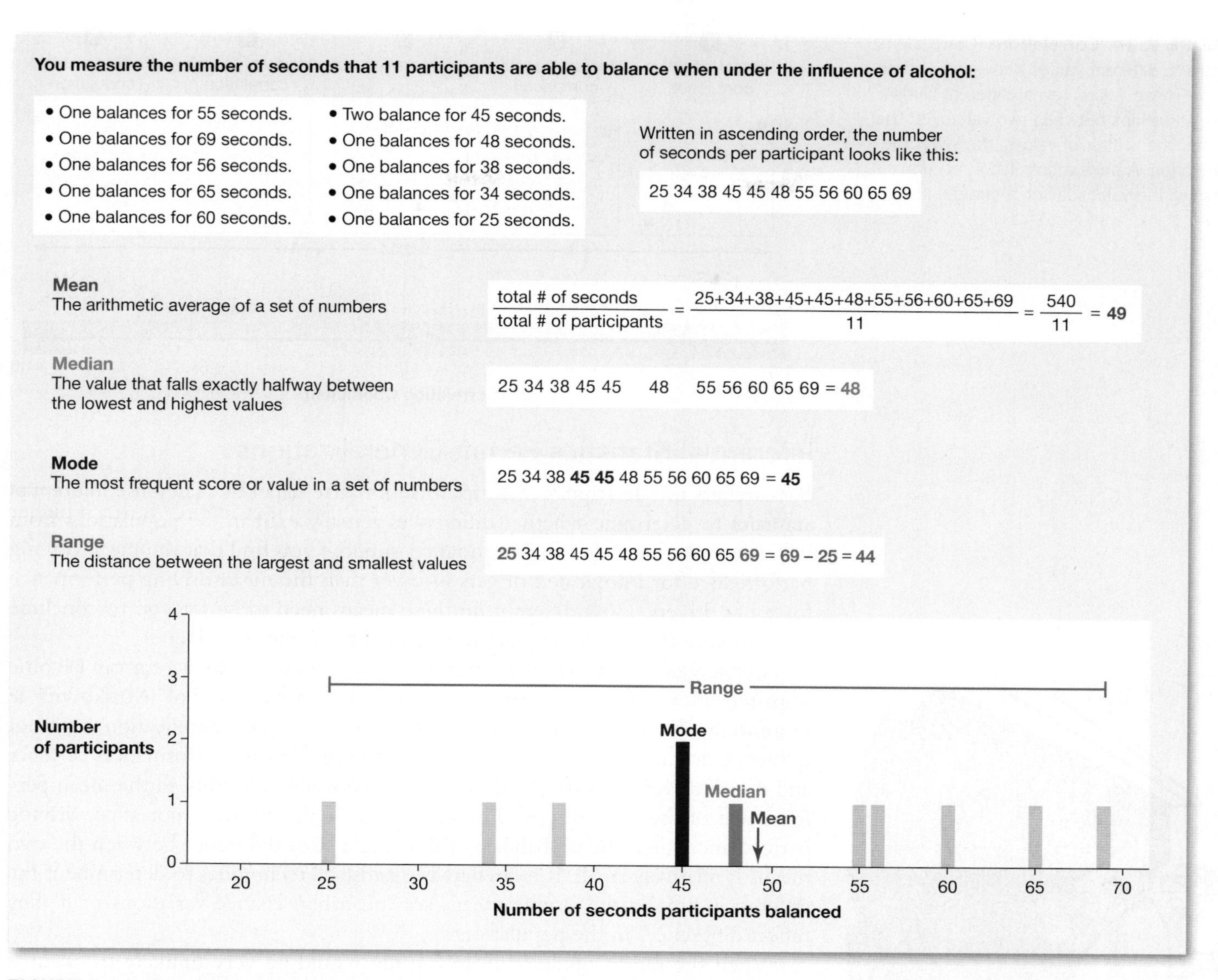


**FIGURE 2.22 Descriptive Statistics** Descriptive statistics are used to summarize a data set and to measure the central tendency and variability in a set of numbers. The mean, median, and mode are different measures of central tendency. The range is a measure of variability. **Which measure of central tendency provides the best summary for the data in this figure? Why is that measure more useful than the range?**

have a positive correlation, they increase or decrease together. For example, the more people drink, the more likely they are to engage in risky behavior. This correlation is positive because the two parts increase together, not because either one is good or bad. A perfect positive correlation is indicated by a value of +1.0. If two variables have a *negative correlation,* as one increases in value, the other decreases in value. For example, as people become more intoxicated, they become less able to balance on one foot, so intoxication and balance have a negative correlation. A perfect negative correlation is indicated by a value of −1.0. If two variables show no apparent relationship, the value of the correlation will be a number close to zero (assuming a linear relationship for the purposes of this discussion).

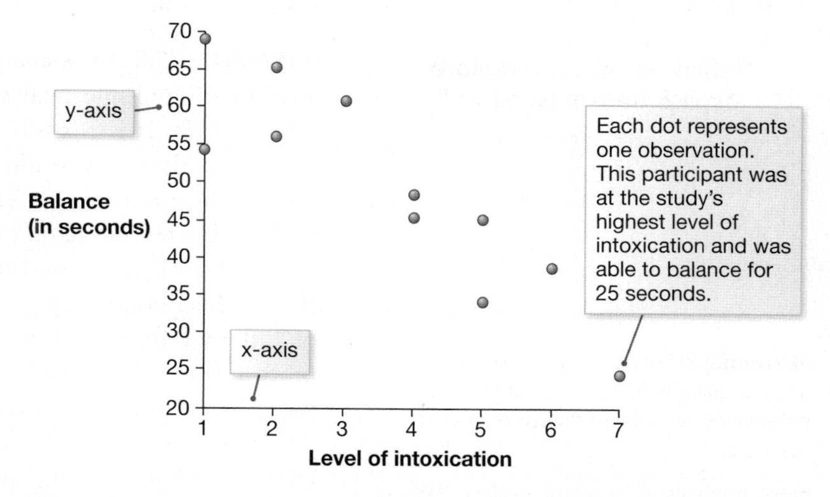


**FIGURE 2.23 Scatterplots** Scatterplots are graphs that illustrate the relationship between two variables. **In general, according to this scatter plot, how was the ability to balance related to the level of intoxication?**

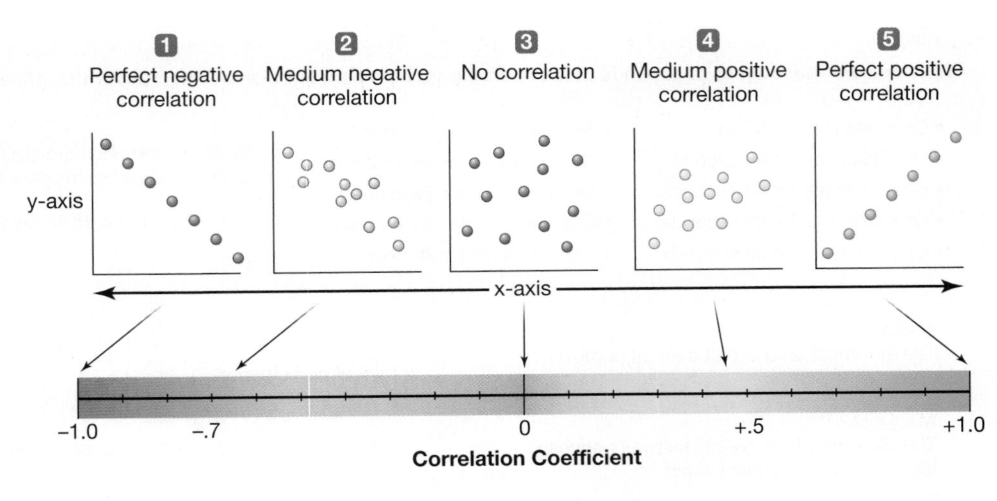


**FIGURE 2.24 Correlations** Correlations can have different values between −1.0 and +1.0. These values reveal different kinds of relationships between two variables. The greater the scatter of values, the lower the correlation. A perfect correlation occurs when all the values fall on a straight line.

## Inferential Statistics Permit Generalizations

Researchers use descriptive statistics to summarize data sets. They use **inferential statistics** to determine whether differences actually exist in the populations from which samples were drawn. For instance, suppose you find that the mean driving performance for intoxicated drivers is lower than the mean driving performance for sober drivers. How different do these means need to be for you to conclude that drinking alcohol does in fact reduce people's ability to drive?

A review of 112 studies found that the skills necessary to drive a car can become impaired after people consume even small amounts of alcohol (Moskowitz & Fiorentino, 2000). Pretend for a moment, however, that intoxication does not influence driving performance. If you measure the driving performances of sober and drunk drivers, just by chance there will be some variability in the mean performance of the two groups. The key is that if alcohol does not affect driving performance, then the probability of showing a large difference between the two means is relatively small. Researchers use statistical techniques to determine if the differences among the sample means are (probably) chance variations or if they reflect differences in the populations.

When the results obtained from a study would be very unlikely to occur if there really were no differences between the groups of subjects, the researchers conclude that the results are *statistically significant*. According to generally accepted standards, researchers typically conclude there is a significant effect only if the obtained results would occur by chance less than 5 percent of the time.

**"I think you should be more explicit here in step two."**

META-ANALYSIS **Meta-analysis** is a type of study that, as its name implies, is an analysis of multiple analyses. (The plural of *meta-analysis* is *meta-analyses.*) In other words, it is a study of studies that have already been conducted. With meta-analysis, many studies that have addressed the same issue are combined and summarized in one "study of studies." Suppose, for example, that 10 studies have been conducted on men's and women's effectiveness as leaders. Among these 10 studies, 5 found no differences, 2 favored women, and 3 favored men. Researchers conducting a meta-analysis would not just count up the numbers of different findings from the research literature. Instead, they would weight more heavily those studies that had larger samples. After all, large samples are more likely to provide more accurate reflections of what is true in populations. The researchers would also consider the size of each effect. That is, they would factor in whether each study found a large difference, a small difference, or no difference between the groups being compared—in this case, between women and men. (The researchers who conducted such a meta-analysis on men's and

**inferential statistics** A set of procedures used to make judgments about whether differences actually exist between sets of numbers.

**meta-analysis** A "study of studies" that combines the findings of multiple studies to arrive at a conclusion.

women's effectiveness found no overall differences; Eagly, Karau, & Makhijani, 1995.) Because meta-analysis combines the results of separate studies, many researchers believe that meta-analysis provides stronger evidence than the results of any single study. As discussed earlier in this chapter, we can be more confident about results when the research findings are replicated. Meta-analysis has the concept of replication built into it.

## Summing Up

### How Are Data Analyzed and Evaluated?

Data analysis begins with descriptive statistics, which summarize the data. Measures of central tendency indicate the typical response or the behavior of a group as a whole. Measures of variability indicate how widely numbers are distributed about the mean or average score. A correlation coefficient describes the relationship between two variables: positive, negative, or none. Inferential statistics indicate whether the results of a study reflect a true difference between groups or are likely to be due to chance. Meta-analysis combines the results of several studies to arrive at a conclusion.

## Measuring Up

1. When researchers want to summarize in a single number all the data they collect, they compute a measure of central tendency. Here are hypothetical data for a study in which 10 people in a sample consumed alcohol. The researchers measured the number of glasses of alcohol each person consumed and assessed her or his motor control after consuming the alcohol. The scores on motor control ranged from 1 (poor motor control) to 10 (good motor control). Compute the mean, median, and mode for the amount of alcohol consumed and the ratings of motor control.

| Amount of Alcohol Consumed | Rating of Motor Control |
|---|---|
| 3 | 4 |
| 1 | 9 |
| 5 | 1 |
| 2 | 7 |
| 3 | 5 |
| 3 | 3 |
| 1 | 8 |
| 4 | 2 |
| 5 | 1 |
| 2 | 6 |

2. Which is an accurate description of the rationale for inferential statistics?
   a. When the means of two sample groups are significantly different, we still need to compute a mean value for each population before we can conclude that the groups really are different.
   b. When the means of two sample groups are significantly different, we can be fairly certain that we did not make any mistakes in our research.
   c. When the means of two sample groups are significantly different, we can be certain that the data are not correlated.
   d. When the means of two sample groups are significantly different, we can infer that the populations the groups were selected from are different.

**Answers:** 1. Amount of alcohol consumed: mean = 2.9, median = 3, and mode = 3; rating of motor control: mean = 4.6, median = 4.5, and mode = 1.
2. d. When the means of two sample groups are significantly different, we can infer that the populations the groups were selected from are different.

# StudySpace: Your Place for a Better Grade

**Visit StudySpace to access free review materials, such as:**

- complete study outlines
- vocabulary flashcards of all key terms
- additional chapter review quizzes

## Chapter Summary

### 2.1 What Is Scientific Inquiry?

- **The Scientific Method Depends on Theories, Hypotheses, and Research:** Scientific inquiry relies on objective methods and empirical evidence to answer testable questions. Interconnected ideas or models of behavior (theories) yield testable predictions (hypotheses), which are tested in a systematic way (research) by collecting and evaluating evidence (data).
- **Unexpected Findings Can Be Valuable:** Unexpected (serendipitous) discoveries sometimes occur, but only researchers who are prepared to recognize their importance will benefit from them.

### 2.2 What Types of Studies Are Used in Psychological Research?

- **Descriptive Studies Involve Observing and Classifying Behavior:** Researchers observe and describe naturally occurring behaviors to provide a systematic and objective analysis.
- **Correlational Studies Examine How Variables Are Related:** Correlational studies are used to examine how variables are naturally related in the real world, but cannot be used to establish causality or the direction of a relationship (which variable caused changes in another variable). Correlational reasoning occurs in many contexts, so readers need to be able to recognize correlational designs in everyday contexts, not just when reading research reports.
- **An Experiment Involves Manipulating Conditions:** In an experiment, researchers control the variations in the conditions that the participants experience (independent variables) and measure the outcomes (dependent variables) to gain an understanding of causality. Researchers need a control group to know if the experiment has had an effect.
- **Random Sampling and Random Assignment Are Important for Research:** Researchers sample participants from the population they want to study (e.g., drivers). They use random sampling when everyone in the population is equally likely to participate in the study, a condition that rarely occurs. To establish causality between an intervention and an outcome, random assignment must be used. When random assignment is used, all participants have an equal chance of being assigned to any level of the independent variable, and preexisting differences between the groups are controlled.

### 2.3 What Are the Data Collection Methods of Psychological Science?

- **Observing Is an Unobtrusive Strategy:** Data collected by observation must be defined clearly and collected systematically. Bias may occur in the data because the participants are aware they are being observed or because of the observer's expectations.
- **Case Studies Examine Individual Lives and Organizations:** A case study, one kind of descriptive study, examines an individual or an organization. An intensive study of an individual or organization can be useful for examining an unusual participant or unusual research question. Interpretation of a case study, however, can be subjective.
- **Asking Takes a More Active Approach:** Surveys, questionnaires, and interviews can be used to directly ask people about their thoughts and behaviors. Self-report data may be biased by the respondents' desire to present themselves in a particular way (e.g., smart, honest). Culturally sensitive research recognizes the differences among people from different cultural groups and from different language backgrounds.
- **Response Performance Measures the Processing of Information:** Measuring reaction times and response accuracy and asking people to make stimulus judgments are methods used to examine how people respond to psychological tasks.
- **Body/Brain Activity Can Be Measured Directly:** Electrophysiology (often using an electroencephalograph, or EEG) measures the brain's electrical activity. Brain imaging is done using positron emission tomography (PET), magnetic resonance imaging (MRI), and functional magnetic resonance imaging (fMRI). Transcranial magnetic stimulation (TMS) disrupts normal brain activity, allowing researchers to infer the brain processing involved in particular thoughts, feelings, and behaviors.
- **Research with Animals Provides Important Data:** Research involving nonhuman animals provides useful, although simpler, models of behavior and of genetics. The purpose of such research may be to learn about animals' behavior or to make inferences about human behavior.
- **There Are Ethical Issues to Consider:** Ethical research is governed by a variety of principles that ensure fair and informed treatment of participants.

### 2.4 How Are Data Analyzed and Evaluated?

- **Good Research Requires Valid, Reliable, and Accurate Data:** Data must be meaningful (valid) and their measurement reliable (i.e., consistent and stable) and accurate.
- **Descriptive Statistics Provide a Summary of the Data:** Measures of central tendency and variability are used to describe data.

- **Correlations Describe the Relationships between Variables:** A correlation is a descriptive statistic that describes the strength and direction of the relationship between two variables. Correlations close to zero signify weak relationships; correlations near +1.0 or –1.0 signify strong relationships.

- **Inferential Statistics Permit Generalizations:** Inferential statistics allow us to decide whether differences between two or more groups are probably just chance variations (suggesting that the populations the groups were drawn from are the same) or whether they reflect true differences in the populations being compared. Meta-analysis combines the results of several studies to arrive at a conclusion.

## Key Terms

accuracy, p. 65
case studies, p. 52
central tendency, p. 65
confound, p. 40
control group, p. 40
correlational studies, p. 38
cross-sectional studies, p. 36
culturally sensitive research, p. 50
data, p. 31
dependent variable, p. 40
descriptive statistics, p. 65
descriptive studies, p. 35
directionality problem, p. 38
electroencephalograph (EEG), p. 57
experiment, p. 40
experimental groups, p. 40
experimenter expectancy effect, p. 37
external validity, p. 44
functional magnetic resonance imaging (fMRI), p. 59
hypothesis, p. 31
independent variable, p. 40
inferential statistics, p. 68
institutional review boards (IRBs), p. 60
internal validity, p. 64
longitudinal studies, p. 36
magnetic resonance imaging (MRI), p. 58
mean, p. 66
median, p. 66
meta-analysis, p. 68
mode, p. 66
naturalistic observation, p. 35
observational techniques, p. 50
observer bias, p. 36
participant observation, p. 35
population, p. 43
positron emission tomography (PET), p. 58
random assignment, p. 45
reactivity, p. 51
reliability, p. 64
replication, p. 32
research, p. 31
response performance, p. 55
sample, p. 43
scatterplot, p. 66
scientific method, p. 31
selection bias, p. 44
self-report methods, p. 54
standard deviation, p. 66
theory, p. 31
third variable problem, p. 39
transcranial magnetic stimulation (TMS), p. 59
variability, p. 66
variable, p. 34

## Practice Test

1. Which of the following is a technique that increases scientists' confidence in the findings from a given research study?
   a. amiable skepticism
   b. operationalization of variables
   c. replication
   d. serendipity

*For the following five questions, imagine you are designing a study to investigate whether deep breathing causes students to feel less stressed. Because you are investigating a causal question, you will need to employ experimental research. For each step in the design process, indicate the most scientifically sound decision.*

2. Which hypothesis is stronger? Why?
   a. Stress levels will differ between students who engage in deep breathing and those who do not.
   b. Students who engage in deep breathing will report less stress than those who do not engage in deep breathing.

3. Which sampling method is strongest? Why?
   a. Obtain an alphabetical list of all students enrolled at the college. Invite every fifth person on the list to participate in the study.
   b. Post a note to your Facebook and MySpace accounts letting friends know you would like their help with the study. Ask your friends to let their friends know about the study, too.
   c. Post fliers around local gyms and yoga studios inviting people to participate in your study.

4. Which set of conditions should be included in the study? Why?
   a. All participants should be given written directions for a deep-breathing exercise.
   b. Some participants should be given written directions for a deep-breathing exercise; some participants should be given a DVD with demonstrations of deep-breathing exercises.
   c. Some participants should be given written directions for a deep-breathing exercise; some participants should be given no instructions regarding their breathing.

5. How should participants be chosen for each condition? Why?
   a. Once people agree to participate in the study, flip a coin to decide if each will be in the experimental or control condition.
   b. Let participants select which condition they would like to be in.

The answer key for the Practice Tests can be found at the back of the book. It also includes answers to the green caption questions.

# 3

# Biology and Behavior

LENORE WEXLER HAD SO LITTLE CONTROL OVER HER MOVEMENTS that she stumbled across the street. A policeman watched her. Then he asked her why she was drinking so early in the day. Wexler was not drinking, however. She was showing the first symptoms of Huntingon's disease. This genetic disorder affects the nervous system, specifically damaging parts of the brain (**Figure 3.1**). The damage results in mental deterioration, abnormal body movements, loss of control over all movement, dementia, and eventually death.

(a)

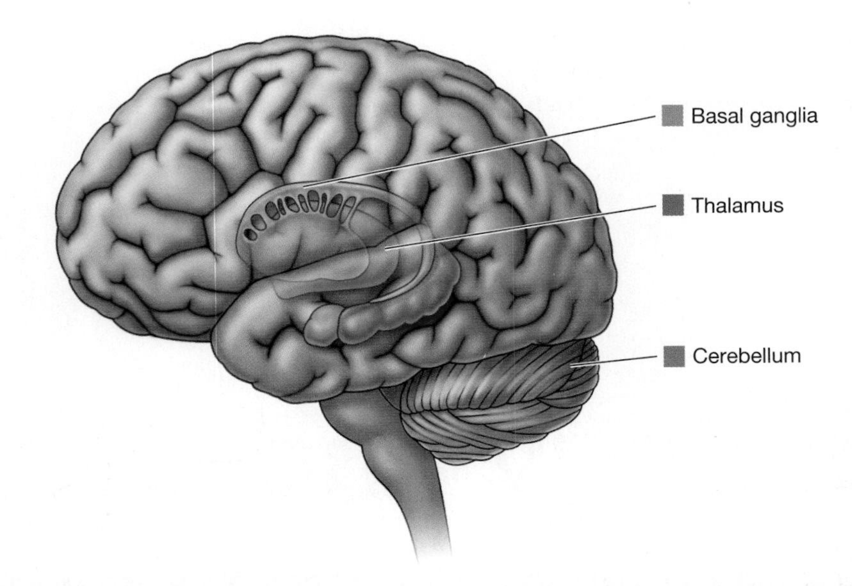


**FIGURE 3.1 Huntington's Disease as a Brain Disorder** This diagram shows the areas of the brain damaged by Huntington's disease.

(b)

**FIGURE 3.2 Huntington's Disease as an Inheritable Condition (a)** One of the most famous people to have suffered from Huntington's disease is the folksinger Woody Guthrie, the writer and performer of classic songs such as "This Land Is Your Land." Guthrie died of Huntington's at age 55, in 1967. **(b)** Woody Guthrie fathered eight children. His most famous child is the folksinger Arlo Guthrie, the writer and performer of classic songs such as "Alice's Restaurant." Like his siblings, Arlo Guthrie has a 50/50 chance of inheriting Huntington's. Two of his siblings have inherited the disease, but he has not exhibited symptoms of it.

The first symptoms of Huntington's typically appear when people are middle-aged, but they can occur much earlier. The afflicted person develops a jerky walk and eventually loses the ability to walk, write, or speak. Emotional and personality changes occur, such as extreme anxiety and depression. Many people in the early stages of the disease commit suicide. No cure has been found.

Lenore Wexler was the mother of Nancy Wexler. At the time of her mother's illness, Wexler was a clinical psychologist. After her mother's death—from Huntington's, in 1978—she changed the nature of her scientific research. Moving from the clinical area of the field to the biological area, Wexler dedicated herself to finding the genetic marker for the progressive, degenerative disorder that had killed her mother. This dedication and love for her mother were rewarded when Wexler found the genetic marker for Huntington's.

If a parent has Huntington's, a biological child has a 50/50 chance of developing the disorder. Because symptoms often do not appear before the afflicted person is around 40, many of those with Huntington's have children before they realize they have a genetic disorder. Those who have relatives with Huntington's spend a good part of their lives wondering whether they will develop symptoms and whether it is safe for them to have children (**Figure 3.2**).

Thanks to the work of Nancy Wexler and her colleagues, people can now take a genetic test to determine whether they are going to develop the disease. But Wexler decided not to take the genetic test that she played an integral role in developing. Now in her early 60s, she shows no signs of the disease, and her chances of developing it are dropping each year.

If one of your immediate relatives showed symptoms of Huntington's, would you take the test? Suppose you tested positive for Huntington's—or any fatal illness. How might that knowledge affect your future? Would you live the rest of your life with the same goals? Would you stay in school, aim for the same career, keep working if you are already working? How might your personal relationships be affected? Would you remain hopeful?

To know what makes us who we are, we need to understand how physiological processes affect our thoughts, feelings, and behavior. We need to understand the genetic underpinnings of those physiological processes. We also need to understand how these aspects of our biology interact with the environment: How does nurture influence nature, and how does nature influence nurture? ■

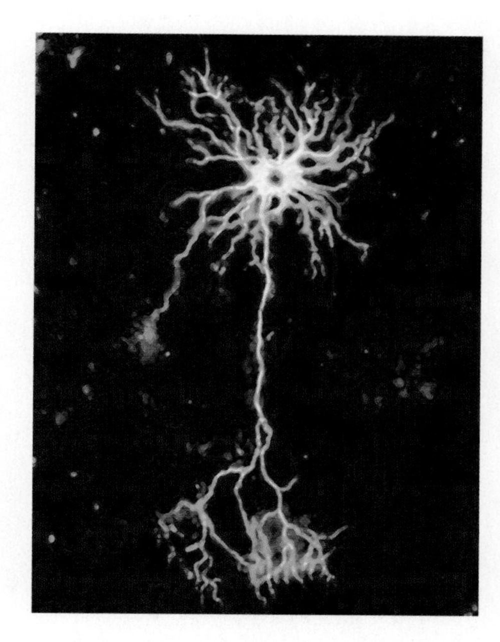

**FIGURE 3.3 Human Nerve Cell** Nerve cells, or neurons, like this one are the basic units of the human nervous system.

## 3.1 How Does the Nervous System Operate?

Over the past three decades, scientific understanding of the physiological foundations of psychological activity has increased dramatically. As technology has advanced, scientists have developed sophisticated tools to explore the biological bases of who we are. Researchers have learned a great deal about the biological basis of brain activity. For example, they have been able to study why particular drugs affect thoughts and emotions in specific ways. And as noted in the previous chapters, brain imaging has enabled psychologists to better understand the functions of different brain regions. In addition to examining people's genetic makeup—predicting who will develop specific disorders and understanding how certain diseases are passed from one generation to the next—researchers have also identified the functions of specific genes. For example, they know which combination of genes predisposes people to be outgoing or to be intelligent. In presenting such intimate yet far-ranging developments, this chapter will introduce you to the basics of some human biological systems. You are about to learn how psychological activity is related to the nervous system, the endocrine system, and genetics.

### Learning Objectives

- Distinguish between the functions of distinct types of neurons.
- Describe the structure of the neuron.
- Describe the electrical and chemical changes that occur when neurons communicate.
- Identify the major neurotransmitters and their primary functions.

The nervous system is an amazing network, responsible for everything we think, feel, or do. Essentially, each of us *is* a nervous system. The basic units of this system are nerve cells, called **neurons** (**Figure 3.3**). These cells receive, integrate, and transmit information in the nervous system. Complex networks of neurons sending and receiving signals are the functional basis of all psychological activity. Although the actions of single neurons are simple to describe, human complexity results from billions of neurons. Each of these billions makes contact with tens of thousands of other neurons. Neurons do not communicate randomly or arbitrarily, however. They communicate selectively with other neurons to form circuits, or *neural networks*. These networks develop through maturation and experience. In other words, permanent alliances form among groups of neurons.

The entire nervous system is divided into two functional units: The **central nervous system (CNS)** consists of the brain and the spinal cord, both of which contain massive numbers of nerve cells. The **peripheral nervous system (PNS)** consists of all the other nerve cells in the rest of the body. These two units are anatomically separate, but their functions are highly interdependent. The peripheral nervous system transmits a variety of information to the central nervous system. The central nervous system organizes and evaluates that information and then directs the peripheral nervous system to perform specific behaviors or make bodily adjustments.

**neurons** The basic units of the nervous system; cells that receive, integrate, and transmit information in the nervous system. They operate through electrical impulses, communicate with other neurons through chemical signals, and form neural networks.

**central nervous system (CNS)** The brain and the spinal cord.

**peripheral nervous system (PNS)** All nerve cells in the body that are not part of the central nervous system. The peripheral nervous system includes the somatic and autonomic nervous systems (discussed later in this chapter).

### Neurons Are Specialized for Communication

Neurons are specialized for communication. That is, unlike other cells, nerve cells are excitable: They are powered by electrical impulses and communicate with other nerve cells through chemical signals. During the reception phase, they

**sensory neurons** One of the three types of neurons; these afferent neurons detect information from the physical world and pass that information to the brain.

**motor neurons** One of the three types of neurons; these efferent neurons direct muscles to contract or relax, thereby producing movement.

**interneurons** One of the three types of neurons; these neurons communicate only with other neurons.

take in the chemical signals from neighboring neurons. During integration, they assess the incoming signals. During transmission, they pass their own signals to yet other receiving neurons.

**TYPES OF NEURONS** The three basic types of neurons are *sensory neurons, motor neurons,* and *interneurons* (**Figure 3.4**). **Sensory neurons** detect information from the physical world and pass that information along to the brain, usually via the spinal cord. Sensory neurons are often called *afferent* neurons. This term means that they carry information to the brain. To get a sense of how fast that process can work, think of the last time you touched something hot or accidentally pricked yourself with a sharp object, such as a tack. Those signals triggered your body's nearly instantaneous response and sensory experience of the impact. The sensory nerves that provide information from the skin and muscles are referred to as *somatosensory nerves.* (This term comes from the Greek for "body sense." It means sensations experienced from within the body.)

**Motor neurons** direct muscles to contract or relax, thereby producing movement. Motor neurons are therefore *efferent* neurons. This term means that they transmit signals from the brain to the muscles throughout the body. **Interneurons** communicate within local or short-distance circuits. That is, interneurons integrate neural activity within a single area rather than transmitting information to other brain structures or to the body organs.

Together, sensory and motor neurons control movement. For instance, if you are using a pen to take notes as you read these words, you are contracting and relaxing your hand muscles and finger muscles to adjust your fingers' pressure on the pen. When you want to use the pen, your brain sends a message via motor neurons to your finger muscles so they move in specific ways. Receptors in both your skin and your muscles send back messages through sensory neurons to help determine how much pressure is needed to hold the pen. This symphony of neural communication for a task as simple as using a pen is remarkable, and yet most of us employ motor control so easily that we rarely think about it. In fact, our *reflexes,* automatic motor responses, occur before we even think about those responses. For each reflex action, a handful of neurons simply converts sensation into action.

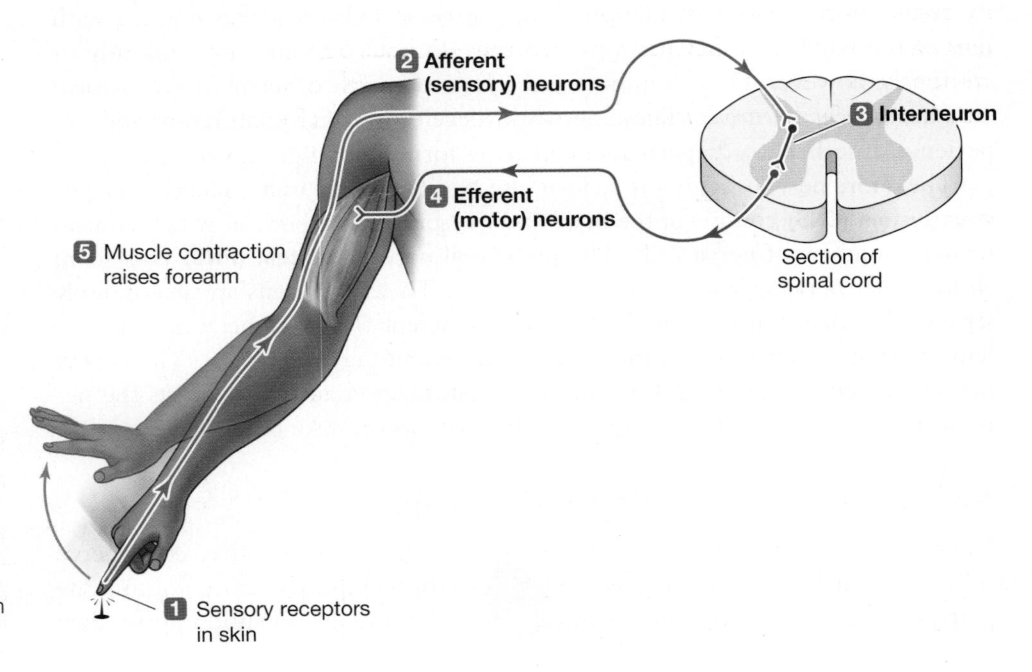


**FIGURE 3.4 The Three Types of Neurons** Receptors send afferent signals to the brain for processing. To produce a response, an efferent signal is then sent from the brain to the body via the spinal cord.

**NEURON STRUCTURE** In addition to performing different functions, neurons have a wide assortment of shapes and sizes. A typical neuron has four structural regions that participate in communication functions: the *dendrites,* the *cell body,* the *axon,* and the *terminal buttons* (**Figure 3.5**). The **dendrites** are short, branchlike appendages that increase the neuron's receptive field and detect chemical signals from neighboring neurons. In the **cell body,** also known as the *soma* (Greek for "body"), the information received from thousands of other neurons is collected and integrated.

Once the incoming information from many other neurons has been integrated in the cell body, electrical impulses are transmitted along a long, narrow outgrowth known as the **axon.** Axons vary tremendously in length, from a few millimeters to more than a meter. The longest axons stretch from the spinal cord to the big toe. You probably have heard the term *nerve,* as in "a pinched nerve." In this context, a nerve is a bundle of axons that carry information between the brain and other specific locations in the body. At the end of the axon are knoblike structures called **terminal buttons.** The site where chemical communication occurs between neurons is called the **synapse.** Because neurons do not touch each other, they communicate by sending chemicals into the **synaptic cleft,** a tiny gap between the axon of the "sending" neuron and the dendrites of the "receiving" neurons. Chemicals leave one neuron, cross the synapse, and pass signals along to other neurons' dendrites. Thus neurons in the chain of communication are referred to as *presynaptic* or *postsynaptic.*

The neuron's membrane plays an important role in communication between neurons: It regulates the concentration of electrically charged molecules that are the basis of the neuron's electrical activity. These electrical signals travel quickly down the axon because of the fatty **myelin sheath** that encases and insulates it like the plastic tubing around wires in an electrical cord. The myelin sheath is made up of *glial cells,* commonly called *neuroglia* or simply *glia* (Greek for "glue"). It grows along an axon in short segments. Between these segments are small gaps of exposed axon called the **nodes of Ranvier** (after the researcher who first described them). Located at these gaps are *ion channels.* These specialized pores allow negatively and positively charged molecules called *ions* to pass in and out of the cell when the neuron transmits signals down the axon.

**THE RESTING MEMBRANE POTENTIAL IS NEGATIVELY CHARGED** When a neuron is resting, not active, the inside and outside are different electrically. This phenomenon is called the **resting membrane potential.** The difference occurs because the ratio of negative to positive ions is greater inside the neuron than outside it. Therefore, the electrical charge inside the neuron is slightly more negative

**dendrites** Branchlike extensions of the neuron that detect information from other neurons.

**cell body** Site, in the neuron, where information from thousands of other neurons is collected and integrated.

**axon** A long narrow outgrowth of a neuron by which information is transmitted to other neurons.

**terminal buttons** Small nodules, at the ends of axons, that release chemical signals from the neuron into the synapse.

**synapse** The site at which chemical communication occurs between neurons.

**synaptic cleft** The gap between the axon of a "sending" neuron and the dendrites of a "receiving" neuron; it contains extracellular fluid.

**myelin sheath** A fatty material, made up of glial cells, that insulates the axon and allows for the rapid movement of electrical impulses along the axon.

**nodes of Ranvier** Small gaps of exposed axon, between the segments of myelin sheath, where action potentials are transmitted.

**resting membrane potential** The electrical charge of a neuron when it is not active.

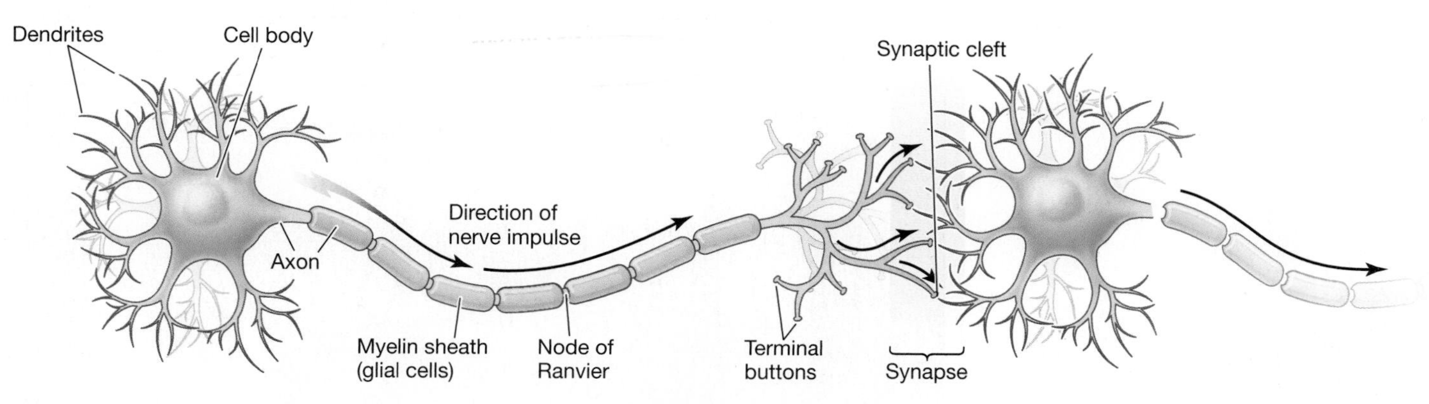


**FIGURE 3.5 Neuron Structure** Messages are received by the dendrites, processed in the cell body, transmitted along the axon, and sent to other neurons via chemical substances released from the terminal buttons across the synaptic cleft.

than the electrical charge outside. When the electrical charge inside a neuron is different from the electrical charge outside the neuron, this condition is known as *polarization*. Thus, when a neuron has more negative ions inside it than outside it, the neuron is described as being *polarized*. The polarized state of the resting neuron creates the electrical energy necessary to power the firing of the neuron.

**THE ROLES OF SODIUM AND POTASSIUM IONS** Two types of ions that contribute to a neuron's resting membrane potential are *sodium ions* and *potassium ions*. Although other ions are involved in neural activity, sodium and potassium are most important for this discussion. Ions pass through the cell membrane at the ion channels (**Figure 3.6**). Each channel matches a specific type of ion: Sodium channels allow sodium ions but not potassium ions to pass through the membrane, and potassium channels allow potassium ions but not sodium ions to pass through the membrane. The flow of ions through each channel is controlled by a gating mechanism. When a gate is open, ions flow in and out of the cell membrane. A closed gate will prevent their passage. Ion flow is also affected by the cell membrane's selective permeability. That is, much like a bouncer at an exclusive nightclub, the membrane allows some types of ions to cross more easily than others. Partially as a result of this selective permeability of the cell

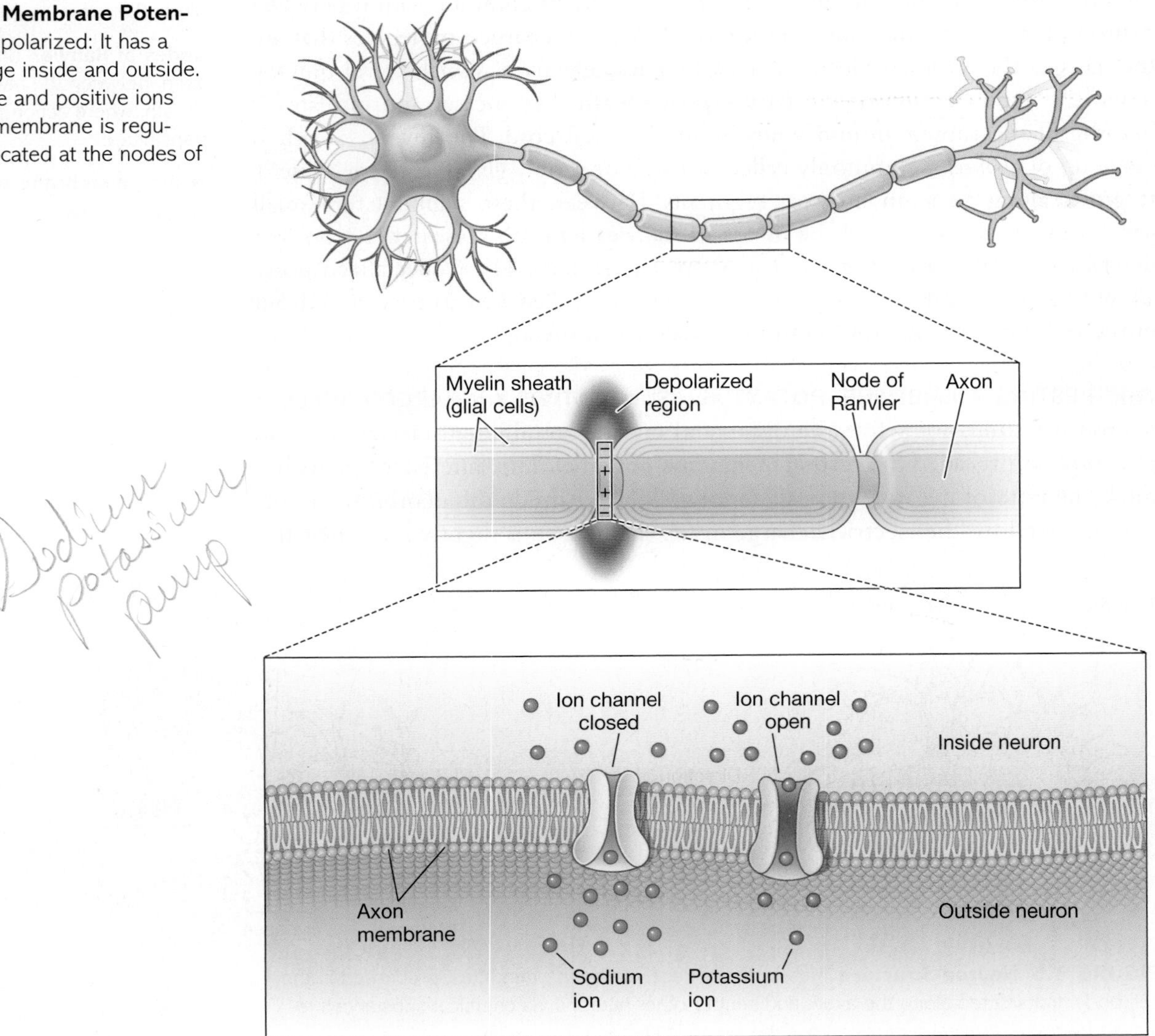


**FIGURE 3.6 Resting Membrane Potential** A neuron at rest is polarized: It has a different electrical charge inside and outside. The passage of negative and positive ions inside and outside the membrane is regulated by ion channels located at the nodes of Ranvier.

Sodium potassium pump

membrane, more potassium than sodium is inside the neuron. This imbalance contributes to polarization. Another mechanism in the membrane that contributes to polarization is called the *sodium-potassium pump.* This pump works to increase potassium and decrease sodium inside the neuron.

**action potential** The neural impulse that passes along the axon and subsequently causes the release of chemicals from the terminal buttons.

## Action Potentials Cause Neural Communication

Neural communication depends on a neuron's ability to respond to incoming stimulation. The neuron responds by changing electrically and then passing along signals to other neurons. An **action potential,** also called *neural firing,* is the electrical signal that passes along the axon and causes the release of chemicals that transmit signals to other neurons. The following sections examine some factors that contribute to the firing of an action potential.

**CHANGES IN ELECTRICAL POTENTIAL LEAD TO ACTION** A neuron receives chemical signals from nearby neurons through its dendrites. By affecting polarization, these signals tell the neuron whether to fire. The signals arrive at the dendrites by the thousands and are of two types: *excitatory* and *inhibitory.* Excitatory signals depolarize the cell membrane (i.e., reduce polarization), increasing the likelihood that the neuron will fire. Inhibitory signals hyperpolarize the cell (i.e., increase polarization), decreasing the likelihood that the neuron will fire. Excitatory and inhibitory signals received by the dendrites are integrated within the neuron. If the total amount of excitatory input surpasses the neuron's threshold, an action potential is generated.

When a neuron fires, the sodium gates in the cell membrane open. The open gates allow sodium ions to rush into the neuron. This influx of sodium causes the inside of the neuron to become slightly more positively charged than the outside. A fraction of a second later, potassium channels open to allow the potassium ions inside the cell membrane to rush out. This change from a negative charge to a positive one inside the neuron is the basis of the action potential. As the sodium ion channels close, the sodium ions stop entering the cell. Similarly, as the potassium ion channels close, potassium ions stop exiting the cell. Thus, during this process, the electrical charge inside the cell starts out slightly negative in its initial resting state. As the cell fires and allows more positive ions inside, the charge becomes positive. Through natural restoration, the charge then returns to its slightly negative resting state (**Figure 3.7**).

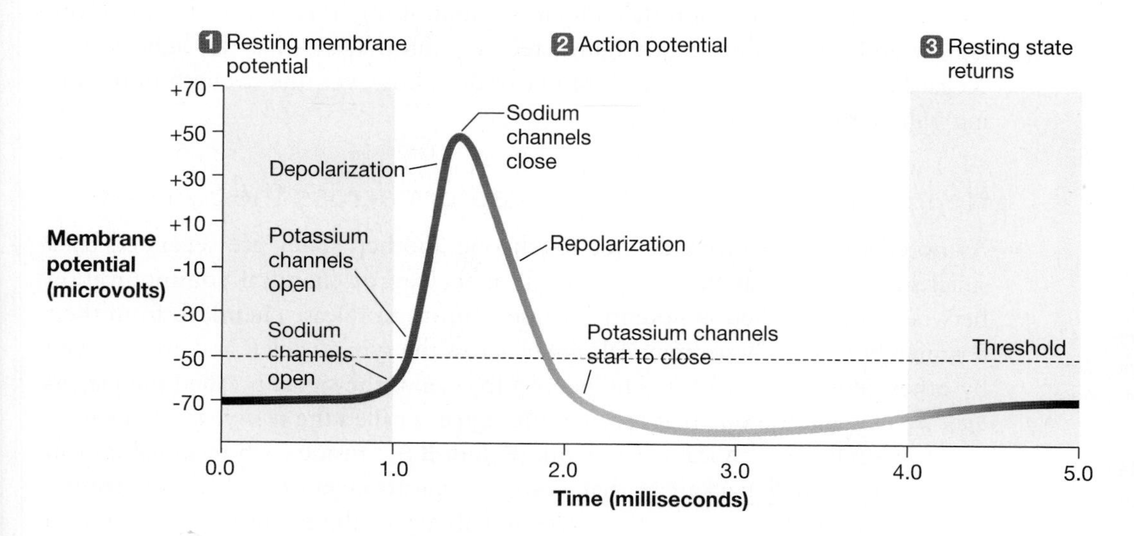


**FIGURE 3.7 Action Potential** The electrical charge inside the neuron starts out slightly negative (resting membrane potential). As the neuron fires, it allows more positive ions inside the cell (depolarization). Through natural restoration (repolarization), it then returns to its slightly negative resting state. This three-part process repeats at every node of Ranvier along the axon.

**ACTION POTENTIALS SPREAD ALONG THE AXON** When the neuron fires, the cell membrane's depolarization moves along the axon like a wave. This movement is called *propagation*. Sodium ions rush through their ion channels, causing adjacent sodium channels to open. Thus, like toppling dominoes, sodium ion channels open successively. The action potential always moves down the axon away from the cell body to the terminal buttons. Because of the insulation provided by the myelin sheath, the action potential skips quickly along the axon. It pauses briefly to be recharged at each node of Ranvier on the axon. The entire process takes about $^{1}/_{1,000}$ of a second, permitting the fast and frequent adjustments required for coordinating motor activity.

To understand the importance of neural insulation, consider the disease multiple sclerosis (MS). The earliest symptoms can begin in young adulthood and often include numbness in the limbs and blurry vision. This especially tragic neurological disorder is characterized by deterioration of the myelin sheath. Because the myelin insulation helps messages move quickly along axons, demyelination slows down neural impulses. The axons essentially short-circuit, and normal neural communication is interrupted. Motor actions become jerky, as those afflicted lose the ability to coordinate motor movements. Over time, movement, sensation, and coordination are severely impaired. As the myelin sheath disintegrates, axons are exposed and may start to break down. The life expectancy of people with MS is 5 to 10 years less than that of people who are not afflicted.

**ALL-OR-NONE PRINCIPLE** Any one signal received by the neuron has little influence on whether the neuron fires. Normally, the neuron is barraged by thousands of excitatory and inhibitory signals, and its firing is determined by the number and frequency of those signals. If the sum of excitatory and inhibitory signals leads to a positive change in voltage that exceeds the neuron's firing threshold, an action potential is generated.

A neuron either fires or it does not. It cannot partially fire. The **all-or-none principle** dictates that a neuron fires with the same potency each time. In other words, it does not fire in a way that can be described as weak or strong. How often the neuron fires depends on the strength of stimulation.

For the sake of comparison, suppose you are playing a video game in which you fire missiles by pressing a button. Every time you press the button, a missile is launched at the same velocity as the previous one. It makes no difference how hard you press the button. If you keep your finger on the button, additional missiles fire in rapid succession. Likewise, if a neuron in the visual system, for example, receives information that a light is bright, it might respond by firing more rapidly and more often than when it receives information that the light is dim. Regardless of whether the light is bright or dim, however, the strength of the firing will be the same every time.

## Neurotransmitters Bind to Receptors across the Synapse

As noted earlier, neurons do not touch one another. They are separated by a small space known as the synaptic cleft, at the site of chemical communication between neurons. Action potentials cause neurons to release chemicals from their terminal buttons. These chemicals travel across the synaptic cleft and are received by other neurons' dendrites. The neuron that sends the signal is called the *presynaptic neuron,* and the one that receives the signal is called the *postsynaptic neuron.*

How do these chemical signals work (**Figure 3.8**)? Inside each terminal button are vesicles (small packages) that contain **neurotransmitters.** Neurotransmitters are chemical substances that carry signals across the synaptic cleft. After an

**all-or-none principle** The principle whereby a neuron fires with the same potency each time, although frequency can vary; a neuron either fires or not—it cannot partially fire.

**neurotransmitters** Chemical substances that carry signals from one neuron to another.

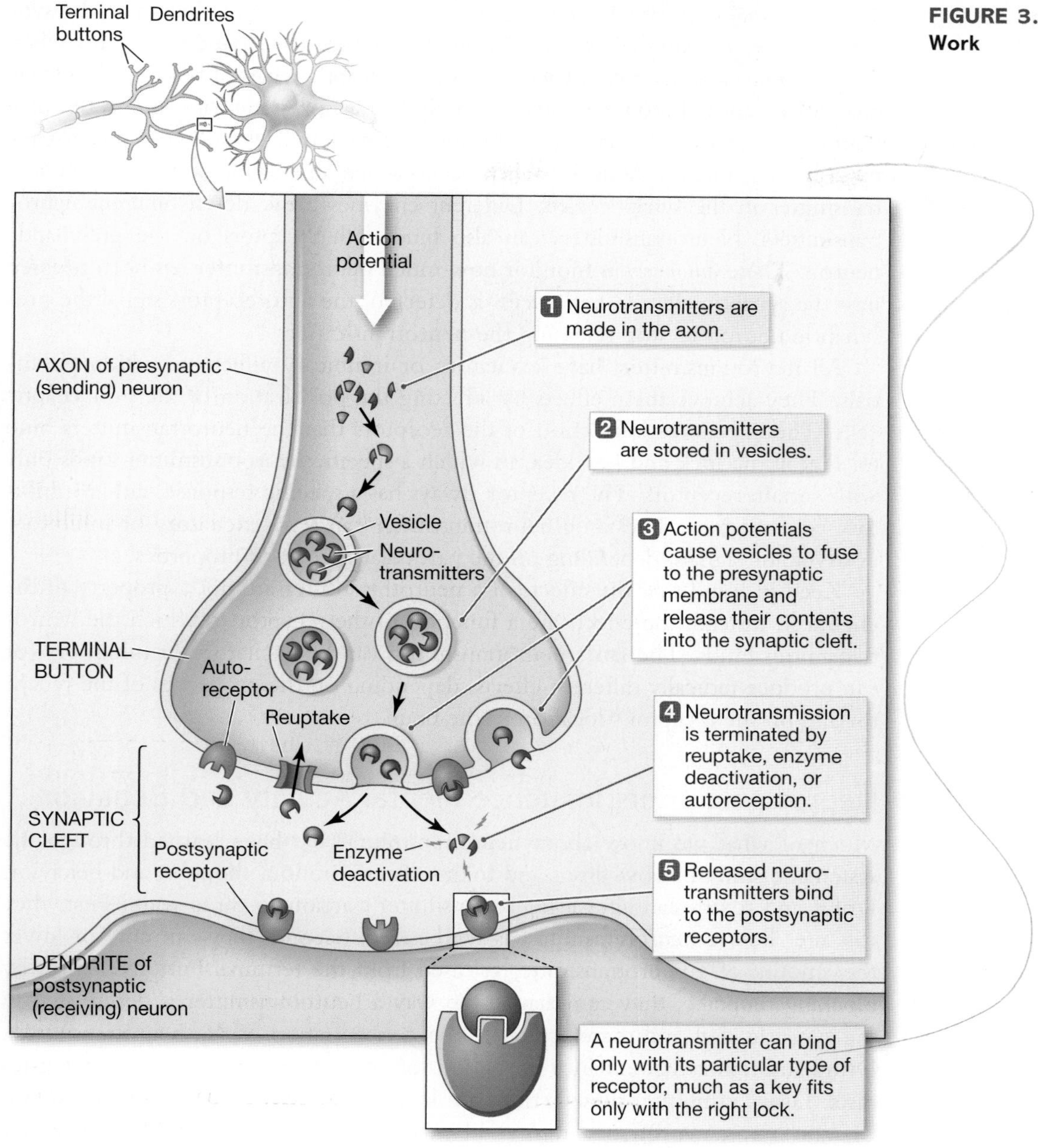


**FIGURE 3.8 How Neurotransmitters Work**

action potential travels to the terminal button, it causes the vesicles to attach to the presynaptic membrane and release their neurotransmitters into the synaptic cleft. These neurotransmitters then spread across the synaptic cleft and attach themselves, or *bind,* to receptors on the postsynaptic neuron. **Receptors** are specialized protein molecules located on the postsynaptic membrane that specifically respond to the chemical structure of the neurotransmitter available in the synapse. The binding of a neurotransmitter with a receptor produces an excitatory or inhibitory signal for the postsynaptic neuron. An excitatory signal encourages the neuron to fire, whereas an inhibitory signal discourages it from firing.

**NEUROTRANSMITTERS BIND WITH SPECIFIC RECEPTORS** More than 60 chemicals convey information in the nervous system. Different neurotransmitters influence either emotion, thought, or behavior. In much the same way as a lock opens only with the correct key, each receptor can be influenced by only one type of neurotransmitter.

Once a neurotransmitter is released into the synaptic cleft, it continues to fill and stimulate that receptor. It also blocks new signals until its influence is terminated.

**receptors** In neurons, specialized protein molecules on the postsynaptic membrane; neurotransmitters bind to these molecules after passing across the synaptic cleft.

**reuptake** The process whereby a neurotransmitter is taken back into the presynaptic terminal buttons, thereby stopping its activity.

**agonists** Drugs that enhance the actions of neurotransmitters.

**antagonists** Drugs that inhibit the actions of neurotransmitters.

The three major events that terminate the neurotransmitter's influence in the synaptic cleft are *reuptake, enzyme deactivation,* and *autoreception.* **Reuptake** occurs when the neurotransmitter is taken back into the presynaptic terminal buttons. The cycle of reuptake and release repeats continuously. An action potential prompts terminal buttons to release the neurotransmitter into the synaptic cleft and then take it back for recycling. *Enzyme deactivation* then occurs when an enzyme destroys the neurotransmitter in the synaptic cleft. Different enzymes break down different neurotransmitters. Neurotransmitters can also bind with receptors on the presynaptic neuron. These *autoreceptors* monitor how much neurotransmitter has been released into the synaptic cleft. When excess is detected, the autoreceptors signal the presynaptic neuron to stop releasing the neurotransmitter.

All neurotransmitters have excitatory or inhibitory effects on action potentials. They achieve these effects by affecting the polarization of the postsynaptic cells. The effects are a function of the receptors that the neurotransmitters bind to. Recall the lock and key idea, in which a specific neurotransmitter binds only with certain receptors. The receptor always has a specific response, either inhibitory or excitatory. The same neurotransmitter can send excitatory or inhibitory postsynaptic signals, depending on the particular receptor's properties.

Keep in mind that the effects of a neurotransmitter are not a property of the chemical. Instead, the effects are a function of the receptor to which the neurotransmitter binds. The same neurotransmitter can be excitatory or inhibitory, or can produce radically different effects, depending on the properties of the receptor and on the receptor's location in the brain.

## Neurotransmitters Influence Mental Activity and Behavior

Much of what we know about neurotransmitters has been learned through the systematic study of how drugs and toxins affect emotion, thought, and behavior. Drugs and toxins can alter a neurotransmitter's action in three ways: First, they can alter how a neurotransmitter is synthesized. Second, they can raise or lower the amount of a neurotransmitter released from the terminal buttons. Third, by blocking reuptake, they can change the way a neurotransmitter is deactivated in the synaptic cleft and therefore affect the concentration of the neurotransmitter. Drugs and toxins that enhance the actions of neurotransmitters are known as **agonists.** Drugs inhibiting these actions are known as **antagonists.** Drugs and toxins can also mimic neurotransmitters and bind with their receptors as if they were the real thing (**Figure 3.9**). Addictive drugs such as heroin and cocaine, for example, have their effects because they are chemically similar to naturally occurring neurotransmitters. The receptors cannot differentiate between the ingested drug and the real neurotransmitter released from a presynaptic neuron. That is, although a neurotransmitter fits a receptor the way a key fits a lock, the receptor-lock cannot tell a real neurotransmitter-key from a forgery—either will open it.

Researchers often inject agonists or antagonists into animals' brains to assess how neurotransmitters affect behavior. The goal is to develop drug treatments for many psychological and medical disorders. For instance, researchers can test the hypothesis that a certain neurotransmitter in a specific brain region leads to increased eating. Injecting an agonist into that brain region should increase eating. Injecting an antagonist should decrease eating.

**TYPES OF NEUROTRANSMITTERS** There are many kinds of neurotransmitters. Nine of them have been the focus of research in psychological science. These nine neurotransmitters are particularly important in understanding how we think, feel, and behave (**Table 3.1**).

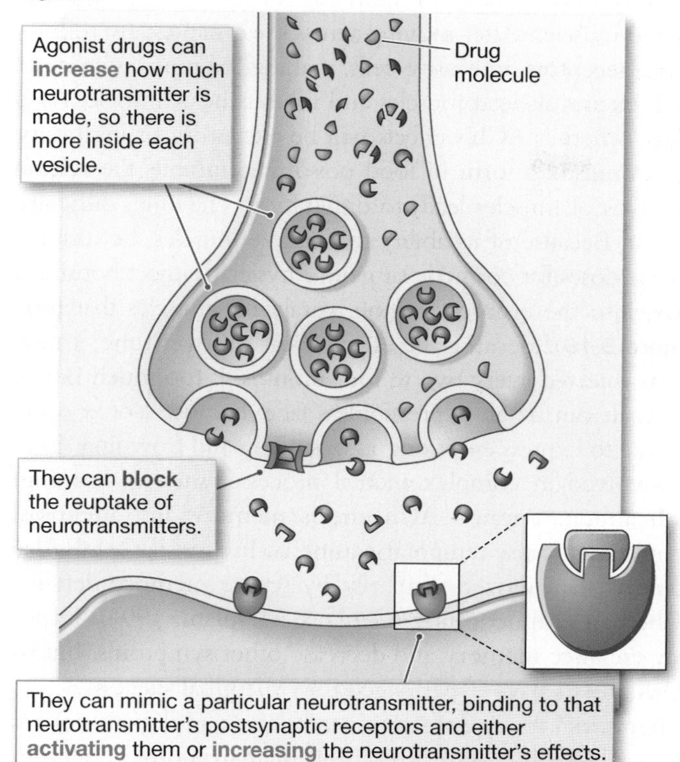


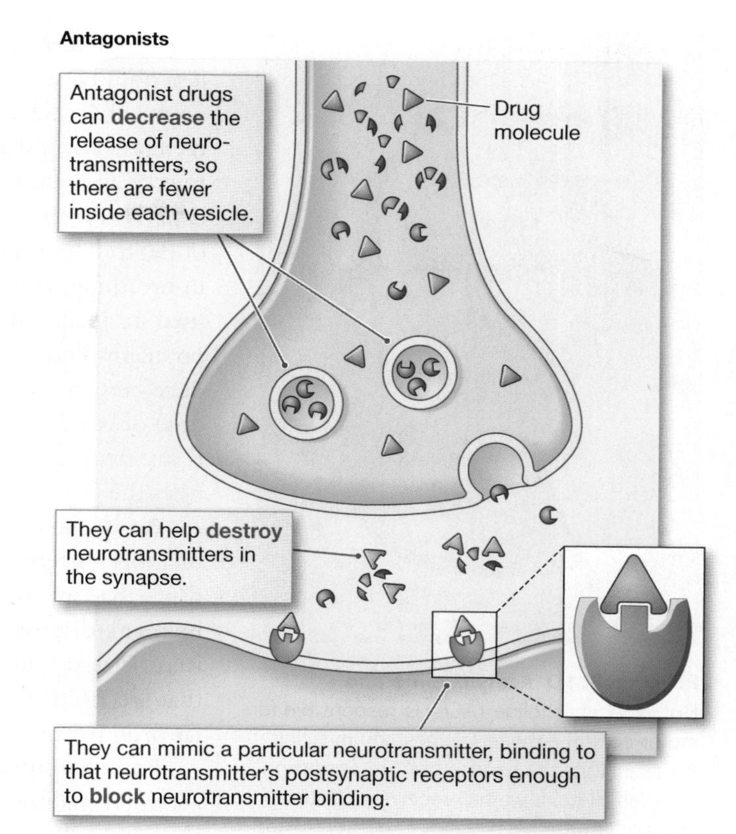


**FIGURE 3.9 How Drugs Work**

**TABLE 3.1 Common Neurotransmitters and Their Major Functions**

| Neurotransmitter | Functions |
|---|---|
| Acetylcholine | Motor control over muscles<br>Learning, memory, sleeping, and dreaming |
| Epinephrine | Energy |
| Norepinephrine | Arousal and vigilance |
| Serotonin | Emotional states and impulsiveness<br>Dreaming |
| Dopamine | Reward and motivation<br>Motor control over voluntary movement |
| GABA (gamma-aminobutyric acid) | Inhibition of action potentials<br>Anxiety reduction<br>Intoxication (through alcohol) |
| Glutamate | Enhancement of action potentials<br>Learning and memory |
| Endorphins | Pain reduction<br>Reward |
| substance P | Pain perception<br>Mood and anxiety |

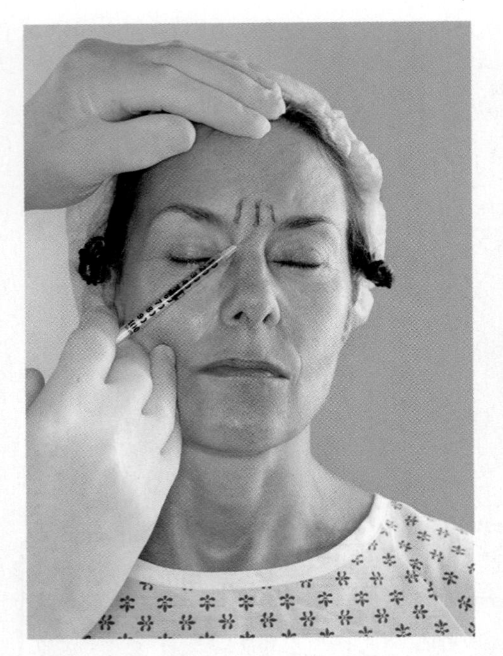

**FIGURE 3.10 Acetylcholine and Botox** Acetylcholine (ACh) is responsible for motor control between nerves and muscles. Botox inhibits the release of ACh, paralyzing muscles. Here, a woman receives a Botox injection to remove wrinkles in her forehead. **How do you feel about the practice of paralyzing muscles to change appearance? Why do you feel this way?**

The neurotransmitter **acetylcholine (ACh)** is responsible for motor control at the junctions between nerves and muscles. After moving across the synapses, ACh (pronounced A-C-H) binds with receptors on muscle cells, making the muscles contract or relax. For instance, ACh excites skeletal muscles and inhibits heart muscle. As is true of all neurotransmitters, whether ACh's effects will be excitatory or inhibitory depends on the receptors. Botulism, a form of food poisoning, inhibits the release of ACh. The resulting paralysis of muscles leads to difficulty in chewing, difficulty in breathing, and often death. Because of its ability to paralyze muscles, botulism is used in small, much less toxic doses for cosmetic surgery. Physicians inject botulism, popularly known as Botox, into the eyebrow region, paralyzing muscles that produce certain wrinkles (**Figure 3.10**). Because the effects wear off over time, a new dose of botulism needs to be injected every two to four months. If too much Botox is injected, however, the result can be an expressionless face, because Botox paralyzes the facial muscles we use to express emotions, as in smiling and frowning.

Acetylcholine is also involved in complex mental processes such as learning, memory, sleeping, and dreaming. Because ACh affects memory and attention, drugs that are ACh antagonists can cause temporary amnesia. In a similar way, Alzheimer's disease, a condition characterized primarily by severe memory deficits, is associated with diminished ACh functioning (Geula & Mesulam, 1994). Drugs that are ACh agonists may enhance memory and decrease other symptoms, but so far drug treatments for Alzheimer's have experienced only marginal success.

Four transmitters (epinephrine, norepinephrine, serotonin, and dopamine) are grouped together because each has the same basic molecular structure. Together they are called *monoamines*. Their major functions are to regulate arousal, regulate feelings, and motivate behavior.

The neurotransmitter **epinephrine** was initially called *adrenaline*. This name is the basis for the phrase *adrenaline rush*, a burst of energy caused by the release of epinephrine that binds to receptors throughout the body. This adrenaline rush is part of a system that prepares the body for dealing with threats from an environment (this fight-or-flight response is discussed in Chapter 11, "Health and Well-Being"). **Norepinephrine** is involved in states of arousal and alertness. It is especially important for vigilance, a heightened sensitivity to what is going on around you. Norepinephrine appears useful for fine-tuning the clarity of attention.

**Serotonin** is involved in a wide range of psychological activity. It is especially important for emotional states, impulse control, and dreaming. Low levels of serotonin are associated with sad and anxious moods, food cravings, and aggressive behavior. Drugs that block serotonin reuptake and thus leave more serotonin at the synapse to bind with the postsynaptic neurons are used to treat a wide array of mental and behavioral disorders, including depression, obsessive-compulsive disorders, eating disorders, and obesity (Tollesfson, 1995). One class of drugs that specifically target serotonin is prescribed widely to treat depression. These drugs, which include Prozac, are referred to as *selective serotonin reuptake inhibitors*, or *SSRIs*.

**Dopamine** serves many significant brain functions, especially motivation and reward. Many theorists believe dopamine is the primary neurotransmitter that communicates which activities may be rewarding. Eating when hungry, drinking when thirsty, and having sex when aroused, for example, activate dopamine receptors and therefore are experienced as pleasurable. At the same time, dopamine activation is involved in motor control and planning. It helps guide our behavior toward things—objects and experiences—that will lead to additional reward.

A lack of dopamine may be involved in problems with movement, and dopamine depletion is implicated in Parkinson's disease (PD). First identified by the physician James Parkinson in 1917, Parkinson's is a degenerative and fatal neurological

**acetylcholine (ACh)** The neurotransmitter responsible for motor control at the junction between nerves and muscles; also involved in mental processes such as learning, memory, sleeping, and dreaming.

**epinephrine** A monoamine neurotransmitter responsible for bursts of energy after an event that is exciting or threatening.

**norepinephrine** A monoamine neurotransmitter involved in states of arousal and awareness.

**serotonin** A monoamine neurotransmitter important for a wide range of psychological activity, including emotional states, impulse control, and dreaming.

**dopamine** A monoamine neurotransmitter involved in motivation, reward, and motor control over voluntary movement.

disorder marked by muscular rigidity, tremors, and difficulty initiating voluntary action. It affects about 1 in every 200 older adults and occurs in all known cultures. The actor Michael J. Fox is one of the many famous people who have developed this disease. Most people with Parkinson's do not experience symptoms until after age 50, but as Fox's case makes clear, the disease can occur earlier in life. With Parkinson's disease, the dopamine-producing neurons slowly die off. In the later stages of the disorder, people suffer from cognitive and mood disturbances. Injections of one of the chief building blocks of dopamine, *L-DOPA,* help the surviving neurons produce more dopamine. When used to treat Parkinson's disease, L-DOPA often produces a remarkable, though temporary, recovery.

A promising development in Parkinson's research is the transplantation of fetal tissue into human brains in the hope that the new fetal cells will produce dopamine. The first American to undergo fetal neural transplantation, Donald Wilson, regained the ability to walk and returned to his hobby of woodworking. Research in Canada has found that transplanted dopamine neurons thrive and can last as long as 14 years (Mendez et al., 2008; **Figure 3.11**). At the same time, other clinical studies using random assignment have not found large differences between patients receiving fetal cell transplants and those undergoing sham surgery, which mimics the real surgery but does not involve transplantation (Olanow et al., 2003). These methods are still being developed, though, and researchers continue to explore how fetal cell transplants might be used to treat brain disorders.

A more promising approach is *deep brain stimulation.* The physician Alim Louis Benabid pioneered this method, in 1987. It involves surgically implanting electrodes deep within the brain and then using mild electrical stimulation in the regions affected by the disorder, much the way a pacemaker stimulates the heart. Deep brain stimulation of motor regions of the brains of Parkinson's patients reverses many of the movement problems associated with the disease (DeLong & Wichmann, 2008). Researchers have reported successful long-term results from this treatment, lasting as long as six years (Lozano et al., 2010).

**GABA** (gamma-aminobutyric acid) is the primary inhibitory neurotransmitter in the nervous system. It is more widely distributed throughout the brain than most other neurotransmitters. Without the inhibitory effect of GABA, synaptic excitation might get out of control and spread through the brain chaotically.

**GABA** Gamma-aminobutyric acid; the primary inhibitory transmitter in the nervous system.

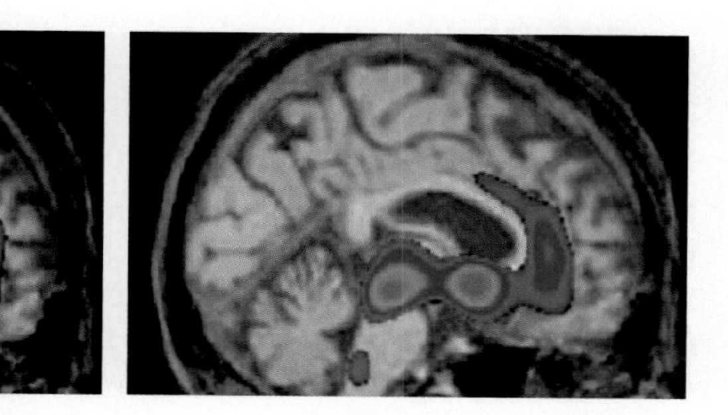

**FIGURE 3.11 Hope for Parkinson's Patients** In this study, neurosurgeons transplanted fetal tissue into two brain regions of a 48-year-old male. A brain scan using PET imaging indicates the survival and functioning of the transplanted dopamine neurons. (The areas in color show increased dopamine.)

**glutamate** The primary excitatory transmitter in the nervous system.

**endorphins** Neurotransmitters involved in natural pain reduction and reward.

**substance P** A neurotransmitter involved in pain perception.

Epileptic seizures may be caused by low levels of GABA (Upton, 1994). Drugs that are GABA agonists are widely used to treat anxiety disorders. For instance, people with nervous disorders commonly use benzodiazepines, which include drugs such as Valium, to relax. Ethyl alcohol—the type people drink—has similar effects on GABA receptors, which is why alcohol typically is experienced as relaxing. GABA reception also may be the primary mechanism by which alcohol interferes with motor coordination.

In contrast, **glutamate** is the primary excitatory transmitter in the nervous system and is involved in fast-acting neural transmission throughout the brain. Glutamate receptors aid learning and memory by strengthening synaptic connections.

**Endorphins** are involved in both natural pain reduction and reward (**Figure 3.12**). In the early 1970s, the pharmacology researchers Candace Pert and Solomon Snyder established that opiate drugs such as heroin and morphine bind to receptors in the brain, and this finding led to the discovery of naturally occurring substances that bind to those sites. Called *endorphins* (short for *endogenous morphine*), these substances are part of the body's natural defense against pain. Pain is useful because it signals to animals, human and nonhuman, that they are hurt or in danger and therefore should try to escape or withdraw. Pain can also interfere with adaptive functioning, however. If pain prevents animals from engaging in behaviors such as eating, competing, and mating, the animals fail to pass along their genes. Endorphins' painkilling, or analgesic, effects help animals perform these behaviors even when they are in pain. In humans, the administration of drugs, such as morphine, that bind with endorphin receptors reduces the subjective experience of pain. Apparently, morphine alters the way pain is experienced rather than blocking the nerves that transmit pain signals: People still feel pain, but they report detachment and do not care about the pain (Foley, 1993).

**Substance P** is another neurotransmitter involved in pain perception as well as mood states and anxiety. This mysterious-sounding substance was first identified in 1931 by the pharmacology researchers Ulf von Euler and John Gaddum, who referred to it in their notes simply by the initial *P*. Substance P helps transmit signals about pain to the brain. Probably the best evidence for it can be found at your local Mexican restaurant, where you can conduct your own experiment. Chili peppers such as jalapeños contain the substance capsaicin, which activates sensory neurons and leads to the release of substance P in the brain. This neural activity makes you feel your tongue and mouth burn, makes your eyes water, and makes your hand reach for the nearest pitcher of water. Water spreads capsaicin around, however, and causes the release of more substance P, which only intensifies the pain.

**FIGURE 3.12 Exercise and Endorphins** Endorphins are involved in both pain reduction and reward, and scientists think that endorphin production can be stimulated by strenuous exercise. An endurance event, such as a marathon or a speed skating competition, will yield an enormous endorphin rush. Here, the final leg runner in the Saudi men's 4 × 400 relay team, Yousef Ahmed Masrahi, celebrates after finishing first in the men's 4 × 400 relay final at the 16th Asian Games in Guangzhou on November 26, 2010.

### Summing Up

## How Does the Nervous System Operate?

Neurons are the nervous system's basic units. Their primary task is to take in information, integrate that information, and pass signals to other neurons. A neuron receives information at the dendrites and processes that information in its cell body. By firing, it passes signals down its axon and then to other neurons' dendrites. The insulating myelin sheath surrounding the axon allows the firing, or action potential, to travel, or propagate, rapidly. When a neuron is in a resting state, it is (slightly) negatively charged. Whether a neuron fires depends on the combination of excitatory and inhibitory signals the dendrites receive. Excitatory neurotransmitters make the postsynaptic neuron more likely to fire, and inhibitory neurotransmitters make the postsynaptic neuron less likely to fire. This firing results from the changes in the electrical charge across the cell membrane: Sodium ions rush in when the sodium channels open, and potassium ions rush out when the potassium channels open. When the channels close, sodium ions stop entering and potassium ions stop exiting, allowing the neuron to return to its resting state. The intensity of the excitatory signal affects the frequency of neural firing but not its strength—neurons fire on an all-or-none basis.

Action potentials cause vesicles to fuse to the presynaptic membrane and release neurotransmitters into the synaptic cleft. Neurotransmitters diffuse across the synaptic cleft and bind with specific postsynaptic receptors. These signals are terminated through reuptake, enzyme deactivation, or the actions of autoreceptors. Substances that enhance the actions of neurotransmitters are agonists. Substances that inhibit the actions of neurotransmitters are antagonists. The number of known substances that act as neurotransmitters is now more than 60 and growing, but certain neurotransmitters are especially important for psychological research: Acetylcholine is involved in motor control and several complex mental processes; epinephrine and norepinephrine are associated with energy, arousal, and attention; serotonin is important for emotional states, impulse control, and dreaming; dopamine is involved in reward, motivation, and motor control; GABA and glutamate are related to general inhibition and excitation; endorphins are important in pain reduction; and substance P is related to pain perception.

## Measuring Up

1. Neurons communicate by firing. Put the following steps in the correct order so they describe this process.
   a. The presynaptic neuron "reuptakes" the neurotransmitter from the synapse.
   b. If the postsynaptic neuron receives a sufficient amount of excitatory input, it will respond by opening its sodium and potassium channels.
   c. Neurotransmitters bind with receptors on the postsynaptic neuron's dendrites.
   d. Excitatory and inhibitory messages are compared in the cell body of the postsynaptic neuron.
   e. Neurotransmitters are released into the synaptic cleft by a presynaptic neuron.
   f. The charge inside the cell goes from negative to positive.
   g. The channels open in succession as the information is passed along the axon away from the cell body and toward the terminal buttons.
   h. The sodium and potassium channels close, and the neuron returns to its resting potential.

2. Match each major neurotransmitter with its major functions.

| **Neurotransmitter** | **Major Functions** |
|---|---|
| a. substance P | 1. emotional states, impulse control, dreaming |
| b. glutamate | 2. reward, motivation, voluntary muscle control |
| c. acetylcholine | 3. enhancing action potentials, facilitating learning and memory |
| d. serotonin | 4. pain perception, mood, and anxiety |
| e. endorphins | 5. motor control, learning, memory, sleeping, dreaming |
| f. dopamine | 6. reward, pain reduction |
| g. GABA | 7. inhibiting action potentials, reducing anxiety, intoxication (through alcohol) |

**Answers:** 1. e, c, d, b, f, g, h, a.
2. a. 4; b. 3; c. 5; d. 1; e. 6; f. 2; g. 7.

Learning Objective

- Identify the basic structures of the brain and their primary functions.

## 3.2 What Are the Basic Brain Structures and Their Functions?

The first animals' nervous systems were probably little more than a few specialized cells with the capacity for electrical signaling. Today, an adult human brain weighs approximately 3 pounds (1.4 kilograms) and is considerably more complex. The brain is best viewed as a collection of interacting neural circuits that have accumulated and developed throughout human evolution. Through the process of adapting to the environments in which humans have lived, the brain has evolved specialized mechanisms to regulate breathing, food intake, sexual behavior, and body fluids, as well as sensory systems to aid in navigation and assist in recognizing friends and foes. Everything we are and do is accomplished by the brain and, for more rudimentary actions, the spinal cord (**Figure 3.13**). Early in life, overabundant connections form among the brain's neurons. Subsequently, life experiences help "prune" some of these connections to strengthen the rest, much as pruning weak or nonproductive branches will strengthen a fruit tree.

The brain's basic structures and their functions enable us to accomplish feats such as seeing, hearing, remembering, and interacting with others. Understanding these relationships also helps us understand psychological disorders.

By the beginning of the nineteenth century, anatomists understood the brain's basic structure reasonably well. But debates raged over how the brain produced mental activity. Did different parts do different things? Or were all areas of the brain equally important in cognitive activities such as problem solving and memory? (This idea is called *equipotentiality*.) In the early nineteenth century, the neuroscientist Franz Gall and his assistant, the physician Johann Spurzheim, proposed their theory of phrenology, based on the idea that the brain operates through functional localization. *Phrenology* is the practice of assessing personality traits and mental abilities by measuring bumps on the human skull. The theory of phrenology was so popular that in the 1930s an enterprising company manufactured 33 Psychographs. Psychographs were devices used to tell about participants' personalities based on the locations and sizes of bumps on their heads. The popularity of these machines at state fairs and amusement parks suggests that few people, if any, took the personality readings seriously (**Figure 3.14**). Phrenology was influential, however, because it was based on the seemingly scientific principle that brain functions were localized. At the time, the technology was not available to test this theory scientifically.

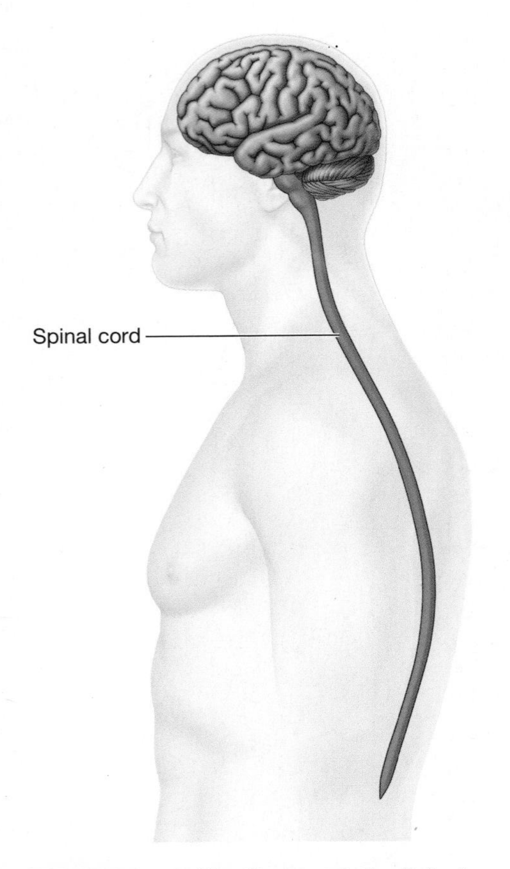


**FIGURE 3.13 The Brain and the Spinal Cord** This drawing illustrates the brain exterior and the brain's connection with the spinal cord. The view is from the left side of the body.

In the early decades of the twentieth century, the behavioral psychologist Karl Lashley built his research on the general idea of equipotentiality. Lashley believed that specific brain regions were involved in motor control and sensory experiences, whereas all other parts of the brain contributed equally to mental abilities. Today, Lashley's theory has been largely discredited. We now know that the brain consists of a patchwork of highly specialized areas.

The first strong evidence that brain regions perform specialized functions came from the work of the physician and anatomist Paul Broca (Finger, 1994). In 1861, Broca performed an autopsy on his patient Monsieur Leborgne. Before his death, Leborgne had lost the ability to say anything other than the word *tan* but could still understand language. When he examined Leborgne's brain, Broca found a large lesion (substantially damaged tissue) in a section of the front left side. This observation led him to conclude that this particular

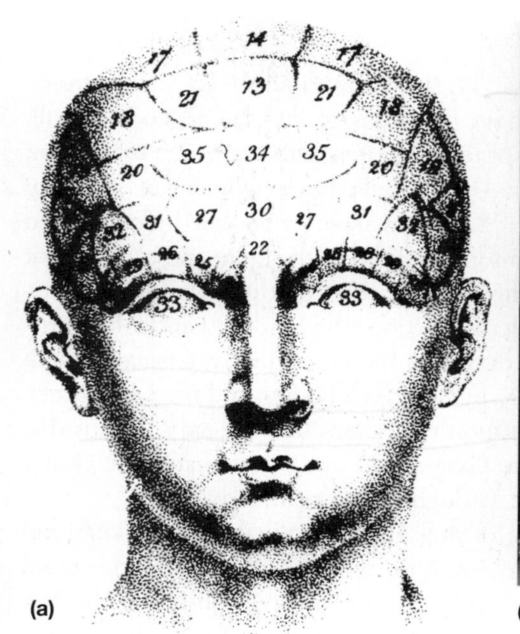

(a)

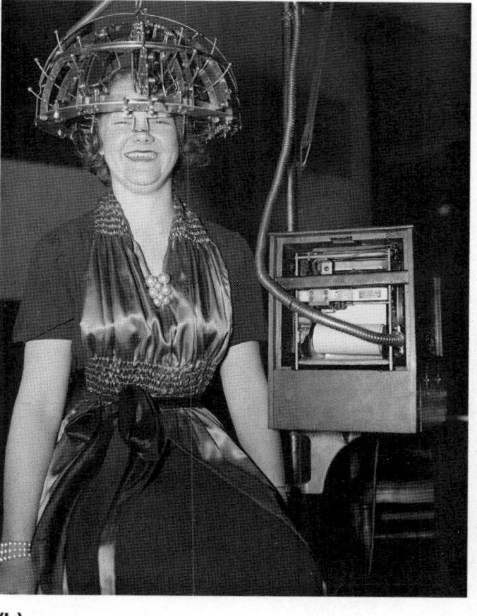

(b)

**FIGURE 3.14 Phrenology and the Psychograph (a)** In the early nineteenth century, Johann Spurzheim created phrenological maps of the skull. In this one, each numbered region corresponds to a different characteristic. **(b)** Psychographs, such as the one depicted here, were marketed as being able to "do the work of a psychoanalyst" by showing "your talents, abilities, strong and weak traits, without prejudice or flattery."

region was important for speech. Broca's theory has survived the test of time. This left frontal region, crucial for the production of language, became known as **Broca's area** (**Figure 3.15**).

**Broca's area** A small portion of the left frontal region of the brain, crucial for the production of language.

For most of human history, of course, theorists and researchers have not had methods for studying ongoing mental activity in the working brain. In the late 1980s, the invention of brain imaging methods changed that situation swiftly and dramatically. The new imaging techniques have advanced our understanding of the human brain the way the development of telescopes advanced our understanding of astronomy—and the brain's structures and functions may be as complex as distant galaxies. The following sections discuss specific brain areas. They explore how each area is linked with particular mental processes and particular behaviors.

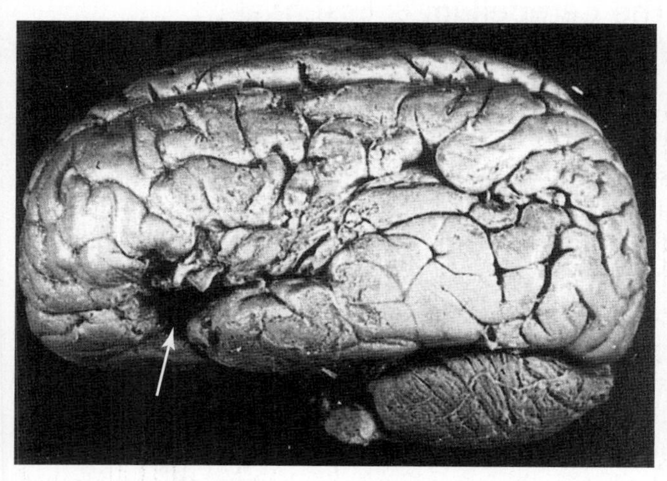

(a)

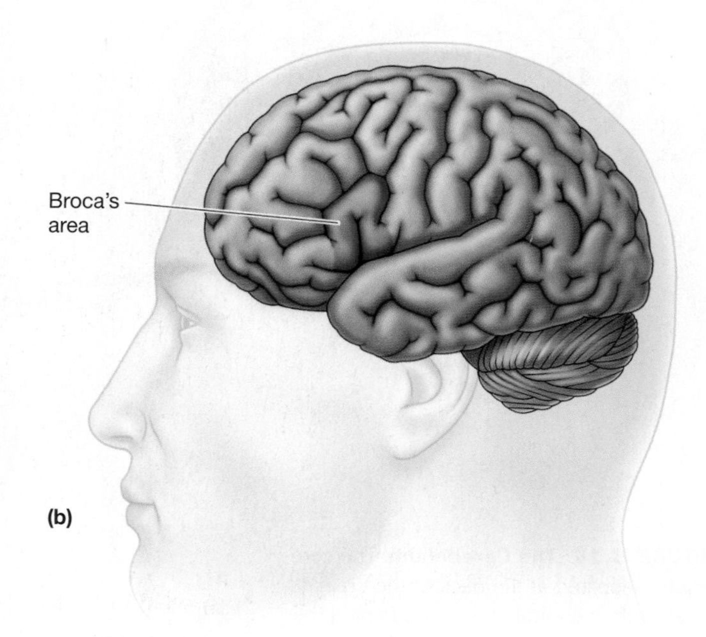


(b)

**FIGURE 3.15 Broca's Area (a)** Paul Broca studied Monsieur Leborgne's brain and identified the lesioned area as crucial for speech production. **(b)** This illustration shows the location of Broca's area.

**brain stem** An extension of the spinal cord; it houses structures that control functions associated with survival, such as breathing, swallowing, vomiting, urination, and orgasm.

**cerebellum** A large, convoluted protuberance at the back of the brain stem; it is essential for coordinated movement and balance.

## The Brain Stem Houses the Basic Programs of Survival

The spinal cord is a rope of neural tissue. As shown in Figure 3.13, it runs inside the hollows of the vertebrae from just above the pelvis up into the base of the skull. One of its functions is the coordination of reflexes, such as the reflexive movement of your leg when a doctor taps your knee or the reflexive movement of your arm when you jerk your hand away from a flame. Its most important function is to carry sensory information up to the brain and carry motor signals from the brain to the body parts below to initiate action. In cross section, the cord is seen to be composed of two distinct tissue types: the *gray matter*, which is dominated by neurons' cell bodies, and the *white matter*, which consists mostly of axons and the fatty sheaths that surround them. Gray matter and white matter are clearly distinguishable throughout the brain as well.

In the base of the skull, the spinal cord thickens and becomes more complex as it transforms into the **brain stem** (**Figure 3.16**). The brain stem consists of the *medulla oblongata,* the *pons,* and the *midbrain*. It houses the nerves that control the most basic functions of survival, such as heart rate, breathing, swallowing, vomiting, urination, and orgasm. Thus a significant blow to this region can cause death. As a continuous extension of the spinal cord, the brain stem also performs functions for the head similar to those that the spinal cord performs for the rest of the body. Many reflexes emerge from here, analogous to the spinal reflexes; gagging is one example.

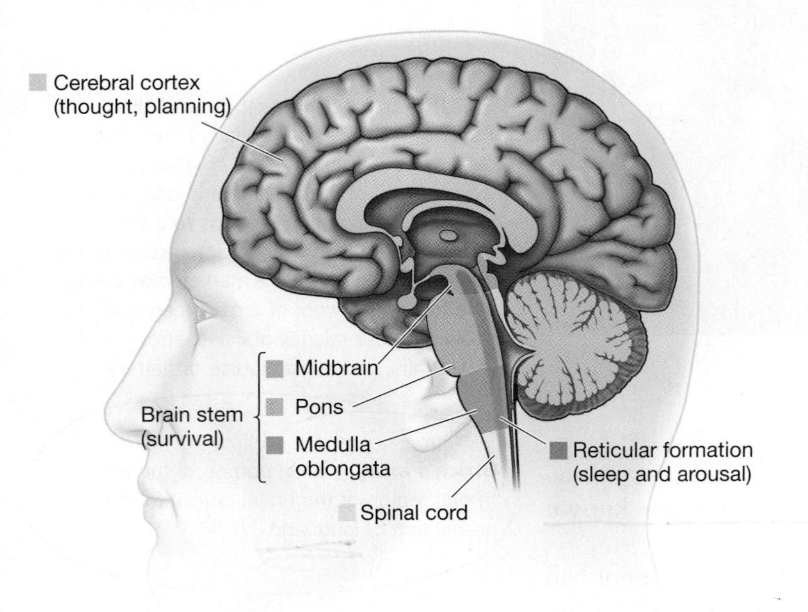


**FIGURE 3.16 The Brain Stem** This drawing shows the brain stem, and its parts, in relation to the cerebral cortex.

The brain stem also contains a network of neurons, known collectively as the *reticular formation*. The reticular formation projects up into the *cerebral cortex* (outer portion of the brain—discussed shortly) and affects general alertness. It is also involved in inducing and terminating the different stages of sleep (as discussed in Chapter 5, "Consciousness").

## The Cerebellum Is Essential for Movement

The **cerebellum** (Latin, "little brain") is a large protuberance connected to the back of the brain stem (**Figure 3.17**). Its size and convoluted surface make it look like an extra brain. The cerebellum is extremely important for proper motor function, and damage to its different parts produces very different effects. Damage to the little nodes at the very bottom causes head tilt, balance problems, and a loss of smooth compensation of eye position for head movement. Try turning your head while looking at this book and notice that your eyes remain focused on the material. Your eyes would not be able to do that if an injury affected the bottom of your cerebellum. Damage to the ridge that runs up its back would affect your walking. Damage to the bulging lobes on either side would cause a loss of limb coordination, so you would not be able to perform tasks such as reaching smoothly to pick up a pen.

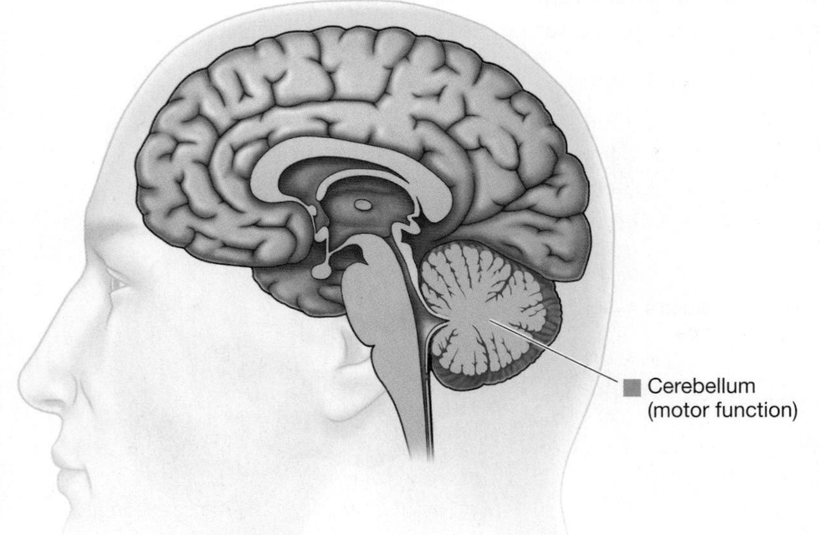


**FIGURE 3.17 The Cerebellum** The cerebellum is located at the back of the brain: It is below the cerebral cortex and behind the brain stem.

The cerebellum's most obvious role is in motor learning and motor memory. It seems to be "trained" by the rest of the nervous system and operates independently and unconsciously. For example, the cerebellum allows you to ride a bicycle effortlessly while planning your next meal. In fact, the cerebellum may be involved in cognitive processes such as making plans, remembering events, using language, and experiencing emotion. Researchers have observed the cerebellum's activation when a person experiences a painful stimulus or observes a loved one receiving that stimulus, so the cerebellum may be involved in the experience of empathy (Lamm, Batson, & Decety, 2007; Singer et al., 2004).

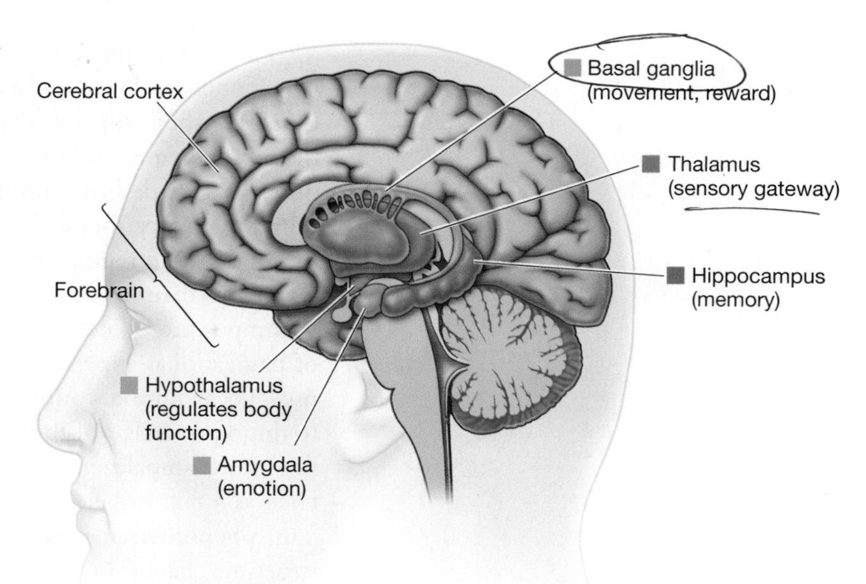


**FIGURE 3.18 The Forebrain and the Subcortical Regions** The subcortical regions are below the forebrain. They are responsible for many aspects of motivation and emotion.

## Subcortical Structures Control Emotions and Appetitive Behaviors

Above the brain stem and cerebellum is the *forebrain*, which consists of the two cerebral hemispheres (left and right; **Figure 3.18**). From the outside, the most noticeable feature of the forebrain is the cerebral cortex. Below this are the *subcortical* regions, so named because they lie under the cortex. Subcortical structures that are important for understanding psychological functions include the *hypothalamus*, the *thalamus*, the *hippocampus*, the *amygdala*, and the *basal ganglia*. Some of these structures belong to the *limbic system*. *Limbic* is the Latin word for "border," and this system serves as the border between the evolutionarily older parts of the brain (the brain stem and the cerebellum) and the evolutionarily newer part (the cerebral cortex). The brain structures in the limbic system are especially important for controlling appetitive behaviors, such as eating and drinking, and emotions (as discussed in Chapter 10, "Emotion and Motivation").

HYPOTHALAMUS The **hypothalamus** is the brain's master regulatory structure. It is indispensable to the organism's survival. Located just above the roof of the mouth, it receives input from almost everywhere in the body and brain, and it projects its influence to almost everywhere in the body and brain. It affects the functions of many internal organs, regulating body temperature, body rhythms, blood pressure, and blood glucose levels. It is also involved in many motivated behaviors, including thirst, hunger, aggression, and lust.

THALAMUS The **thalamus** is the gateway to the cortex: It receives almost all incoming sensory information, organizes it, and relays it to the cortex. The only exception to this rule is the sense of smell. The oldest and most fundamental sense, smell has a direct route to the cortex. During sleep, the thalamus partially shuts the gate on incoming sensations while the brain rests. (The thalamus is discussed further in Chapter 4, "Sensation and Perception.")

HIPPOCAMPUS AND AMYGDALA The **hippocampus** (Greek, "sea horse," for its sea horse shape) plays an important role in the storage of new memories. It seems to do this important work by creating new interconnections within the cerebral cortex with each new experience. Karl Lashley, in his research discussed earlier, failed to find the location of memory by removing parts of rats' cerebral cortices (plural of *cortex*). Had he damaged their hippocampal formations as well, his results would have been quite different.

**hypothalamus** A brain structure that is involved in the regulation of bodily functions, including body temperature, blood pressure, and blood glucose levels; it also influences our basic motivated behaviors.

**thalamus** The gateway to the brain; it receives almost all incoming sensory information before that information reaches the cortex.

**hippocampus** A brain structure that is associated with the formation of memories.

The hippocampus has recently been shown to grow larger with increased use. This finding is consistent with the role of the hippocampus in memory formation. One hypothesis suggests that this structure may be involved in how we remember the arrangements of both places and objects in space, such as how streets are laid out in a city or how furniture is positioned in a room. The best study to support this theory focused on London taxi drivers. Maguire and colleagues (2003) found that one region of the hippocampus was much larger in London taxi drivers' brains than in most other London drivers' brains. Is a person with a large hippocampus more likely to drive a taxi? Or does the hippocampus grow as the result of navigational experience? London taxi drivers are well known for their expertise. To acquire a commercial license, a London taxi driver must take an exam testing knowledge of the city's streets. In this study, the volume of gray matter in the hippocampal region was highly correlated with the number of years of experience as a taxi driver. In other words, the hippocampus changes with experience. This phenomenon is just one of many examples of the way the brain's size and structure change in response to experiences. More examples are discussed at the end of this chapter.

The **amygdala** (Latin, "almond," for its almond shape) is located immediately in front of the hippocampus. It serves a vital role in our learning to associate things in the world with emotional responses, such as an unpleasant food with disgust. The amygdala thus enables us to overcome instinctive responses. It also intensifies the function of memory during times of emotional arousal. For example, a frightening experience can be seared into your memory for life, although (as discussed further in Chapter 7, "Attention and Memory") your memory of the event may not be completely accurate. Research also shows that emotional arousal can influence what people attend to in their environments (Schmitz, De Rosa, & Anderson, 2009).

The amygdala plays a special role in our responding to stimuli that elicit fear. The emotional processing of frightening stimuli in the amygdala is a hardwired circuit that has developed over the course of evolution to protect animals from danger. The amygdala is also involved in evaluating a facial expression's emotional significance (Adolphs et al., 2005). Imaging studies have found that the amygdala activates especially strongly in response to a fearful face (Whalen et al., 2001).

In addition, the amygdala is involved in the processing of more-positive emotions, including sexual arousal. Hamann and colleagues (2004) have found that activity within the amygdala increases when people view sexually arousing stimuli, such as nude photos or videos of sexual activity, and that the amygdala activates markedly higher in men. This finding suggests that the amygdala may be involved when men respond more strongly to visual sexual stimuli than women do.

THE BASAL GANGLIA The **basal ganglia** are a system of subcortical structures crucial for planning and producing movement. These structures receive input from the entire cerebral cortex. They project that input to the motor centers of the brain stem. Via the thalamus, they also project the input back to the motor planning area of the cerebral cortex. Damage to the basal ganglia can produce symptoms that range from the tremors and rigidity of Parkinson's disease to the uncontrollable jerky movements of Huntington's disease. In addition, there is evidence that damage to the basal ganglia can impair the learning of movements and habits, such as automatically looking for cars before you cross the street.

One structure in the basal ganglia, the *nucleus accumbens,* is important for experiencing reward and motivating behavior. As discussed in Chapter 6, nearly every pleasurable experience, from eating food you like to looking at a person you find attractive, activates dopamine neurons in the nucleus accumbens and

**amygdala** A brain structure that serves a vital role in our learning to associate things with emotional responses and in processing emotional information.

**basal ganglia** A system of subcortical structures that are important for the production of planned movement.

**cerebral cortex** The outer layer of brain tissue, which forms the convoluted surface of the brain.

**occipital lobes** Regions of the cerebral cortex—at the back of the brain—important for vision.

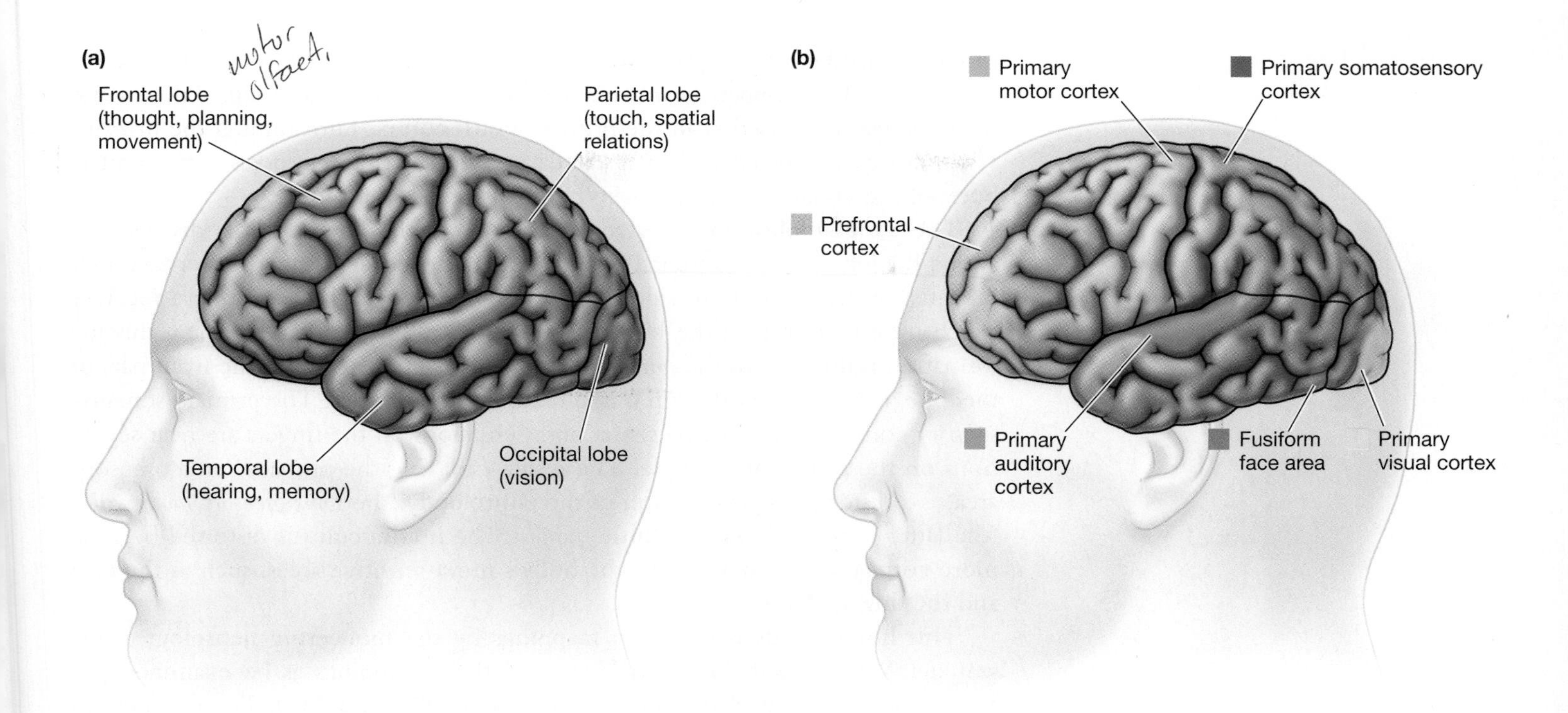


**FIGURE 3.19 The Cerebral Cortex (a)** This diagram identifies the lobes of the cerebral cortex. **(b)** The colored areas mark important regions within those lobes.

makes you want the thing or person you are experiencing. One brain imaging study found that viewing expensive sports cars led to greater activation of the nucleus accumbens in men than did viewing less expensive economy cars (Erk, Spitzer, Wunderlich, Galley, & Walter, 2002). The more desirable objects are, the more they activate basic reward circuitry in our brains.

## The Cerebral Cortex Underlies Complex Mental Activity

The **cerebral cortex** is the outer layer of the cerebral hemispheres and gives the brain its distinctive wrinkled appearance. (*Cortex* is Latin for "bark"—the kind on trees. The cerebral cortex does not feel like bark, however. It has the consistency of a soft-boiled egg.) In humans, the cortex is relatively enormous—the size of a large sheet of newspaper—and folded in against itself many times so as to fit within the skull. It is the site of all thoughts, detailed perceptions, and complex behaviors. It enables us to comprehend ourselves, other people, and the outside world. By extending our inner selves into the world, it is also the source of culture and communication. Each cerebral hemisphere has four "lobes": the *occipital, parietal, temporal,* and *frontal* lobes (**Figure 3.19**). The *corpus callosum,* a massive bridge of millions of axons, connects the hemispheres and allows information to flow between them (**Figure 3.20**).

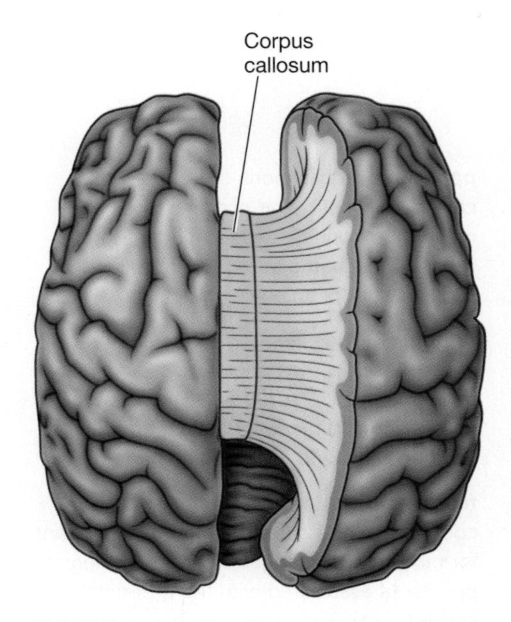


**FIGURE 3.20 The Corpus Callosum** In this top view of the brain, the right cerebral hemisphere has been pulled away to expose the corpus callosum. This fibrous structure connects the two hemispheres of the cerebral cortex.

The **occipital lobes** are at the back portion of the head. Devoted almost exclusively to vision, they include many visual areas. By far, the largest of these areas is the *primary visual cortex,* the major destination for visual information. As discussed further in Chapter 4, visual information is typically organized for the cerebral cortex in a way that preserves spatial relationships. That is, the image relayed from the eye is "projected" more or less faithfully onto the primary visual cortex. Two objects near one another in a visual image, then, will activate neurons near one another in the primary visual cortex. Surrounding the primary visual cortex is a patchwork of secondary visual areas that process various attributes of the visual image, such as its colors, forms, and motions.

The **parietal lobes** are devoted partially to touch. Their labor is divided between the left and right cerebral hemispheres. The left hemisphere receives touch information from the right side of the body, and the right hemisphere receives touch information from the left side of the body. In each parietal lobe, this information is directed to the *primary somatosensory cortex,* a strip in the front part of the lobe, running from the top of the brain down the sides. The primary somatosensory cortex groups nearby sensations: Sensations on the fingers are near sensations on the palm, for example. The result, covering the primary somatosensory area, is a distorted representation of the entire body: the *somatosensory homunculus* (the latter term is Greek for "little man"). The homunculus is distorted because more cortical area is devoted to the body's more sensitive areas, such as the face and the fingers (**Figure 3.21a**).

This homunculus is based on mappings by the pioneering neurological researcher Wilder Penfield. Penfield created these mappings as he examined patients who were to undergo surgery for epilepsy (**Figure 3.21b**). The idea behind this work was to perform the surgery without damaging brain areas vital for functions such as speech. After a local anesthetic was applied to the scalp and while the patient was awake, Penfield would electrically stimulate regions of the brain and ask the patient to report what he or she was experiencing (**Figure 3.21c**). Penfield's studies provided important evidence about the amount of brain tissue devoted to each sensory experience.

A stroke or other damage to the right parietal region can result in the neurological disorder *hemineglect.* Patients with this syndrome fail to notice anything on their left sides. Looking in a mirror, they will shave or put makeup on only the right sides of their faces. If two objects are held up before them, they will see only the one on the right. Asked to draw a simple object, they will draw only its right half (**Figure 3.22**).

The **temporal lobes** hold the *primary auditory cortex,* the brain region responsible for hearing. Also within the temporal lobes are specialized visual areas (for recognizing detailed objects such as faces), plus the hippocampus and the amygdala (both critical for memory, as discussed above). At the intersection of the temporal and occipital lobes is the *fusiform face area.* Its name comes from the fact that this area is much more active when people look at faces than when they look at other things. In contrast, other regions of the temporal lobe are more activated by objects, such as houses or cars, than by faces. Damage to the fusiform face area can cause specific impairments in recognizing people but not in recognizing objects.

The **frontal lobes** are essential for planning and movement. The rearmost portion of the frontal lobes is the *primary motor cortex.* The primary motor cortex includes neurons that project directly to the spinal cord to move the body's muscles. Its responsibilities are divided down the middle of the body, like those of the sensory areas: The left hemisphere controls the right arm, for example, whereas the right hemisphere controls the left arm. The rest of the frontal lobes consists of the **prefrontal cortex,** which occupies about 30 percent of the brain in humans. Scientists have long thought that what makes humans unique in the animal kingdom is our extraordinarily large prefrontal cortex. Recent evidence, however, indicates that what separates humans from other animals is not how much of the brain the prefrontal cortex occupies but rather the complexity and

**parietal lobes** Regions of the cerebral cortex—in front of the occipital lobes and behind the frontal lobes—important for the sense of touch and for conceptualizing the spatial layout of an environment.

**temporal lobes** Regions of the cerebral cortex—below the parietal lobes and in front of the occipital lobes—important for processing auditory information, for memory, and for object and face perception.

**frontal lobes** Regions of the cerebral cortex—at the front of the brain—important for movement and higher-level psychological processes associated with the prefrontal cortex.

**prefrontal cortex** The frontmost portion of the frontal lobes, especially prominent in humans; important for attention, working memory, decision making, appropriate social behavior, and personality.

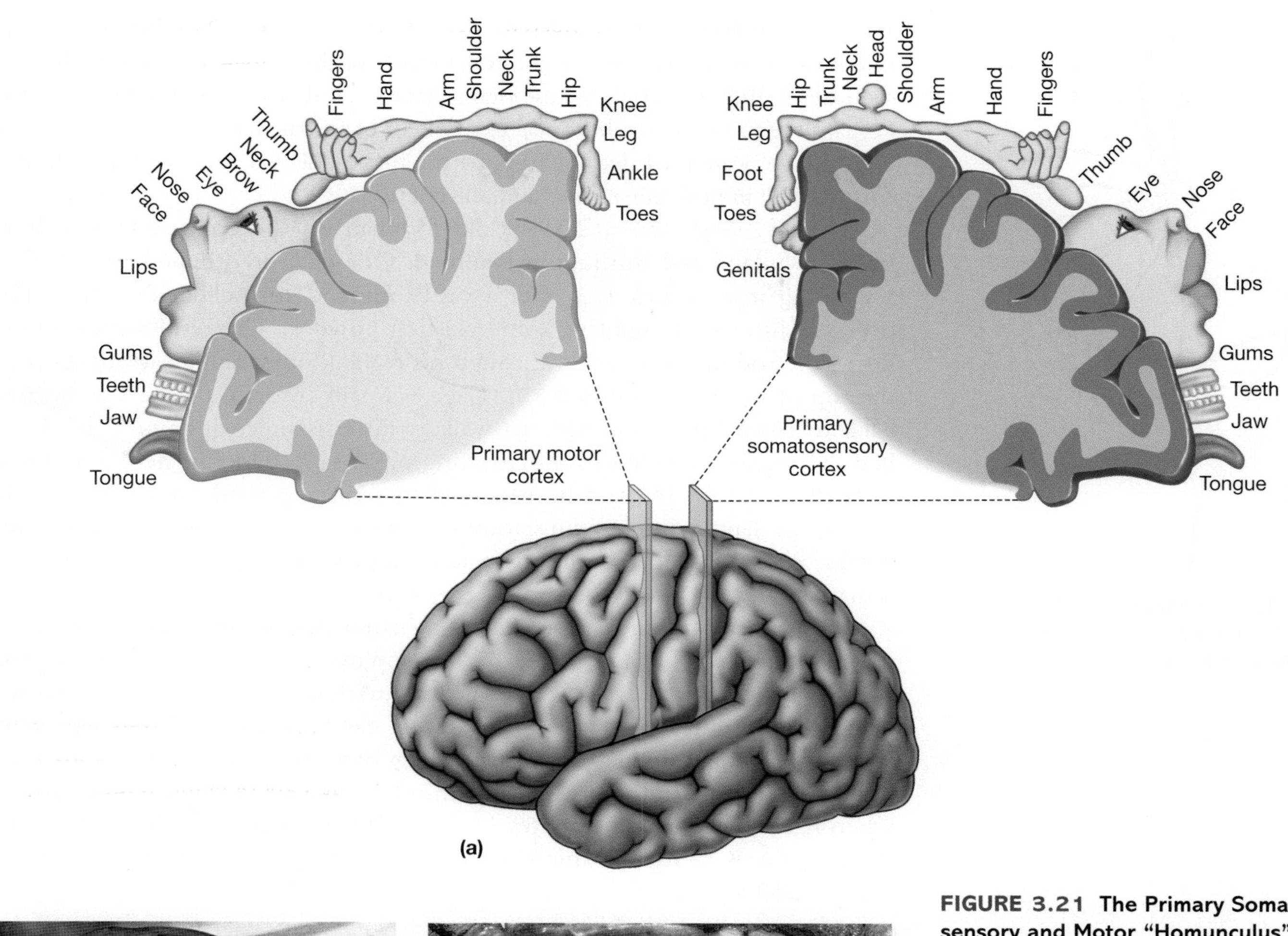


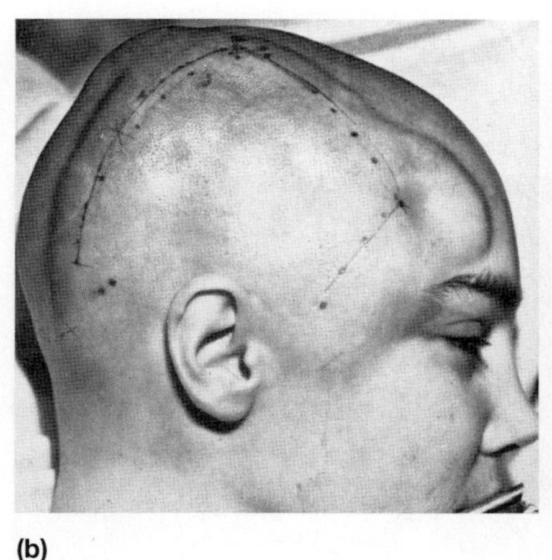
(b)

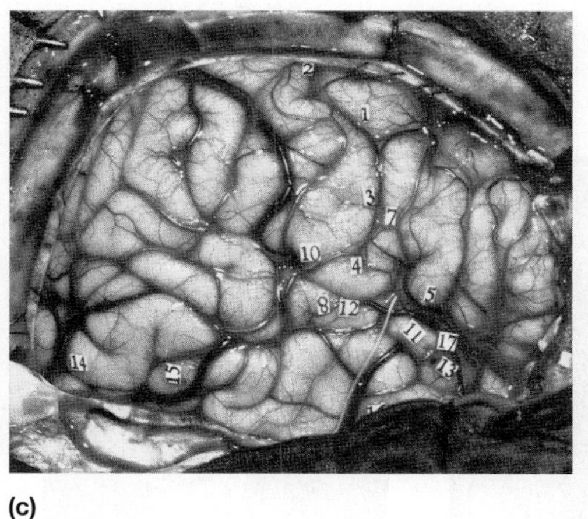
(c)

**FIGURE 3.21 The Primary Somatosensory and Motor "Homunculus"**
**(a)** The cortical representation of the body surface is organized in strips that run down the side of the brain. Connected areas of the body tend to be represented next to each other in the cortex, and more-sensitive skin regions have more cortical area devoted to them. **(b)** Wilder Penfield's mappings of the brain provided the basis for our knowledge of the homunculus. This photograph shows one of Penfield's patients immediately before direct stimulation of the brain. **(c)** Here you can see the exposed surface of the patient's cortex. The numbered tags denote locations that were electrically stimulated.

organization of its neural circuits—the way it is put together (Bush & Allman, 2004; Schoenemann, Sheehan, & Glotzer, 2005).

Parts of the prefrontal cortex are responsible for directing and maintaining attention, keeping ideas in mind while distractions bombard us from the outside world, and developing and acting on plans. The entire prefrontal cortex is indispensable for rational activity. It is also especially important for many aspects of human social life, such as understanding what other people are thinking, behaving according to cultural norms, and contemplating our own existence. It provides both our sense of self and our capacity to empathize with others or feel guilty about harming them.

**FIGURE 3.22 Hemineglect** This drawing, made by a hemineglect patient, omits much of the flower's left side.

**THE PREFRONTAL CORTEX IN CLOSE-UP** Psychologists have learned a great deal of what they know about the functioning of different brain regions through the careful study of people whose brains have been damaged by disease or injury. Perhaps the most famous historical example of brain damage is the case of Phineas Gage. Gage's case provided the basis for the first modern theories of the prefrontal cortex's role in both personality and self-control.

In 1848, Gage was a 25-year-old foreman on the construction of Vermont's Rutland and Burlington Railroad. One day, he dropped a tool called a tamping iron, which was over a yard long and an inch in diameter. The iron rod hit a rock, igniting some blasting powder. The resulting explosion drove the rod into his cheek, through his frontal lobes, and clear out through the top of his head (**Figure 3.23**). Gage was still conscious as he was hurried back to town on a cart. Able to walk, with assistance, upstairs to his hotel bed, he wryly remarked to the awaiting physician, "Doctor, here is business enough for you." He said he expected to return to work in a few days. In fact, Gage lapsed into unconsciousness and remained unconscious for two weeks. Afterward, his condition steadily improved. Physically, he recovered remarkably well.

Unfortunately, Gage's accident led to major personality changes. Whereas the old Gage had been regarded by his employers as "the most efficient and capable" of workers, the new Gage was not. As one of his doctors later wrote, "The equilibrium or balance, so to speak, between his intellectual faculties and animal propensities seems to have been destroyed. He is fitful, irreverent, indulging at times in the grossest profanity . . . impatient of restraint or advice when it conflicts with his desires. . . . A child in his intellectual capacity and manifestations, he has the animal passions of a strong man." In summary, Gage was "no longer Gage."

(a)

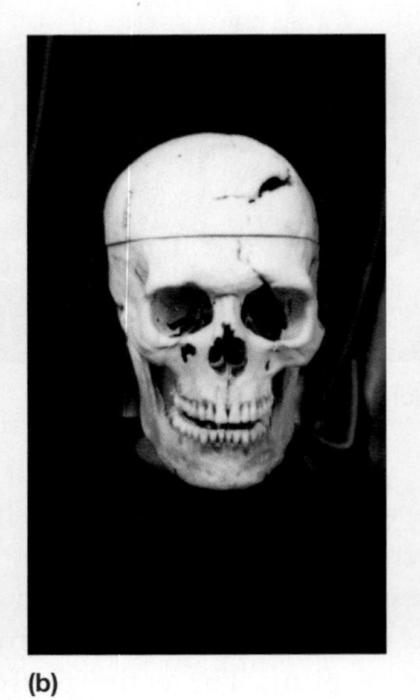

(b)

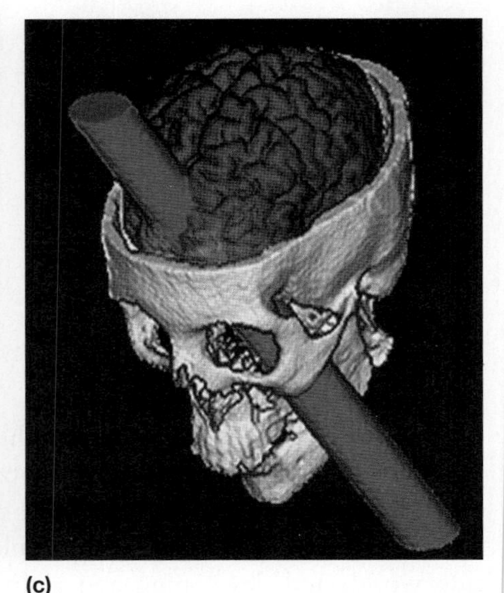

(c)

**FIGURE 3.23 Phineas Gage** Analysis of Gage's damaged skull provided the basis for the first modern theories about the role of the prefrontal cortex in both personality and self-control. **(a)** This recently discovered photo shows Gage holding the rod that passed through his skull. **(b)** Here you can see the hole in the top of Gage's skull. **(c)** This computer-generated image reconstructs the rod's probable path through the skull.

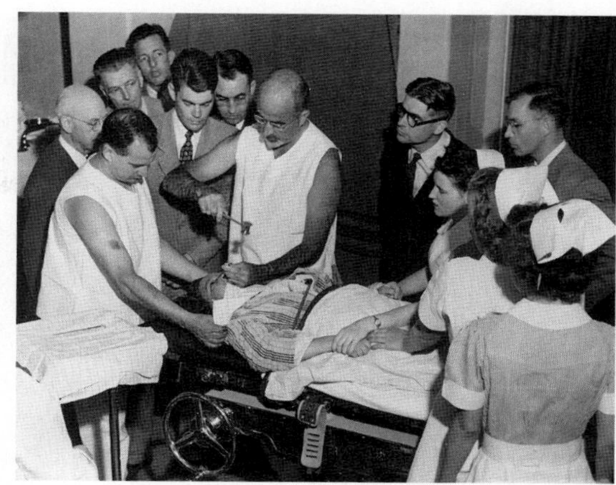

**FIGURE 3.24 Lobotomy** This photo shows Dr. Walter Freeman performing a lobotomy in 1949. Freeman is inserting an ice pick–like instrument under the upper eyelid of his patient to cut the nerve connections in the front part of the brain.

Unable to get his foreman's job back, Gage exhibited himself in various New England towns and at the New York Museum (owned by the circus showman P. T. Barnum). He worked at the stables of the Hanover Inn at Dartmouth College. In Chile, he drove coaches and tended horses. After a decade, his health began to decline, and in 1860 he started having epileptic seizures and died within a few months. Gage's recovery was initially used to argue that the entire brain works uniformly and that the healthy parts of Gage's brain had taken over the work of the damaged parts. However, the medical community eventually recognized that Gage's psychological impairments had been severe and that some areas of the brain in fact have specific functions.

Reconstruction of Gage's injury through examination of his skull has made it clear that the prefrontal cortex was the area most damaged by the tamping rod (Damasio, Grabowski, Frank, Galaburda, & Damasio, 1994). Recent studies of patients with similar injuries reveal that this brain region is particularly concerned with social phenomena, such as following social norms, understanding what other people are thinking, and feeling emotionally connected to others. People with damage to this region do not typically have problems with memory or general knowledge, but they often have profound disturbances in their ability to get along with others.

Beginning in the late 1930s, mental health professionals treated many patients by performing a procedure called *lobotomy,* a deliberate damaging of the prefrontal cortex (**Figure 3.24**). This form of brain surgery generally left patients lethargic and emotionally flat, and therefore much easier to manage in mental hospitals, but it also left them disconnected from their social surroundings. Most lobotomies were performed in the late 1940s and early 1950s. In 1949, António Egas Moniz received the Nobel prize for developing the procedure, which was phased out with the arrival of drugs to treat psychological disorders.

## Summing Up

### What Are the Basic Brain Structures and Their Functions?

Distinct functions are associated with the structures of the nervous system. The spinal cord carries sensory information from the body to the brain and motor information from the brain to the body. It also produces reflexes. The brain stem serves survival functions, such as breathing, swallowing, and urination. At the back of the brain stem is the cerebellum. This structure is associated with coordinated movement, balance, and motor learning. Beneath the cerebral cortex are a number of structures that serve unique functions: The hypothalamus regulates bodily functions; the thalamus serves as a way station through which sensory information travels to the cortex; the hippocampus is involved in memory formation; the amygdala influences our emotional states; and the structures of the basal ganglia are involved in the planning and production of movement. The cerebral cortex is the outer surface of the brain and is divided into lobes: The occipital lobes are associated with vision; the parietal lobes are associated with touch; the temporal lobes are associated with hearing, memory, facial perception, and object perception; and the frontal lobes, which contain the prefrontal cortex, are associated with movement, higher-level psychological processes, and personality.

## Measuring Up

1. Match each of the following brain structures with its role or function. (You will need to remember these terms and facts to understand later discussions of learning, memory, loving, mental illness, anxiety, and other aspects of mind and behavior.)

| Brain Structure | Role/Function |
|---|---|
| a. brain stem | 1. primary structure for memory |
| b. cerebellum | 2. sensory relay station |
| c. basal ganglia | 3. important for emotions |
| d. hypothalamus | 4. divided into four lobes |
| e. thalamus | 5. regulates vital functions such as body temperature |
| f. hippocampus | 6. regulates planned movement |
| g. amygdala | 7. regulates breathing and swallowing |
| h. cerebral cortex | 8. "little brain," involved in movement |

2. Match each lobe of the brain with its function.

| Lobe | Function |
|---|---|
| a. frontal | 1. hearing |
| b. occipital | 2. thought |
| c. parietal | 3. touch |
| d. temporal | 4. vision |

**Answers:** 1. a. 7; b. 8; c. 6; d. 5; e. 2; f. 1; g. 3; h. 4.
2. a. 2; b. 4; c. 3; d. 1.

### Learning Objectives

- Differentiate between the divisions of the nervous system.
- Identify the primary structures of the endocrine system.
- Explain how the nervous system and the endocrine system communicate to control thought, feeling, and behavior.

# 3.3 How Does the Brain Communicate with the Body?

Recall that the nervous system consists of the central nervous system (the brain and the spinal cord) and the peripheral nervous system (all the other nerves in the rest of the body). The peripheral nervous system transmits a variety of information to the central nervous system. It also responds to messages from the central nervous system to perform specific behaviors or make bodily adjustments. In the production of psychological activity, however, both of these systems interact with a different mode of communication within the body, the *endocrine system*.

## The Peripheral Nervous System Includes the Somatic and Autonomic Systems

The peripheral nervous system has two primary components: the *somatic nervous system* and the *autonomic nervous system* (**Figure 3.25**). The **somatic nervous system** transmits sensory signals to the central nervous system via nerves. Specialized receptors in the skin, muscles, and joints send sensory information to the spinal cord, which relays it to the brain. In addition, the central nervous system sends signals through the somatic nervous system to muscles, joints, and skin to initiate, modulate, or inhibit movement. The second major component of the peripheral nervous system, the **autonomic nervous system (ANS)** regulates the body's internal environment by stimulating glands (such as sweat glands) and by maintaining internal organs (such as the heart). Nerves in the autonomic nervous system also

**somatic nervous system** A component of the peripheral nervous system; it transmits sensory signals and motor signals between the central nervous system and the skin, muscles, and joints.

**autonomic nervous system (ANS)** A component of the peripheral nervous system; it transmits sensory signals and motor signals between the central nervous system and the body's glands and internal organs.

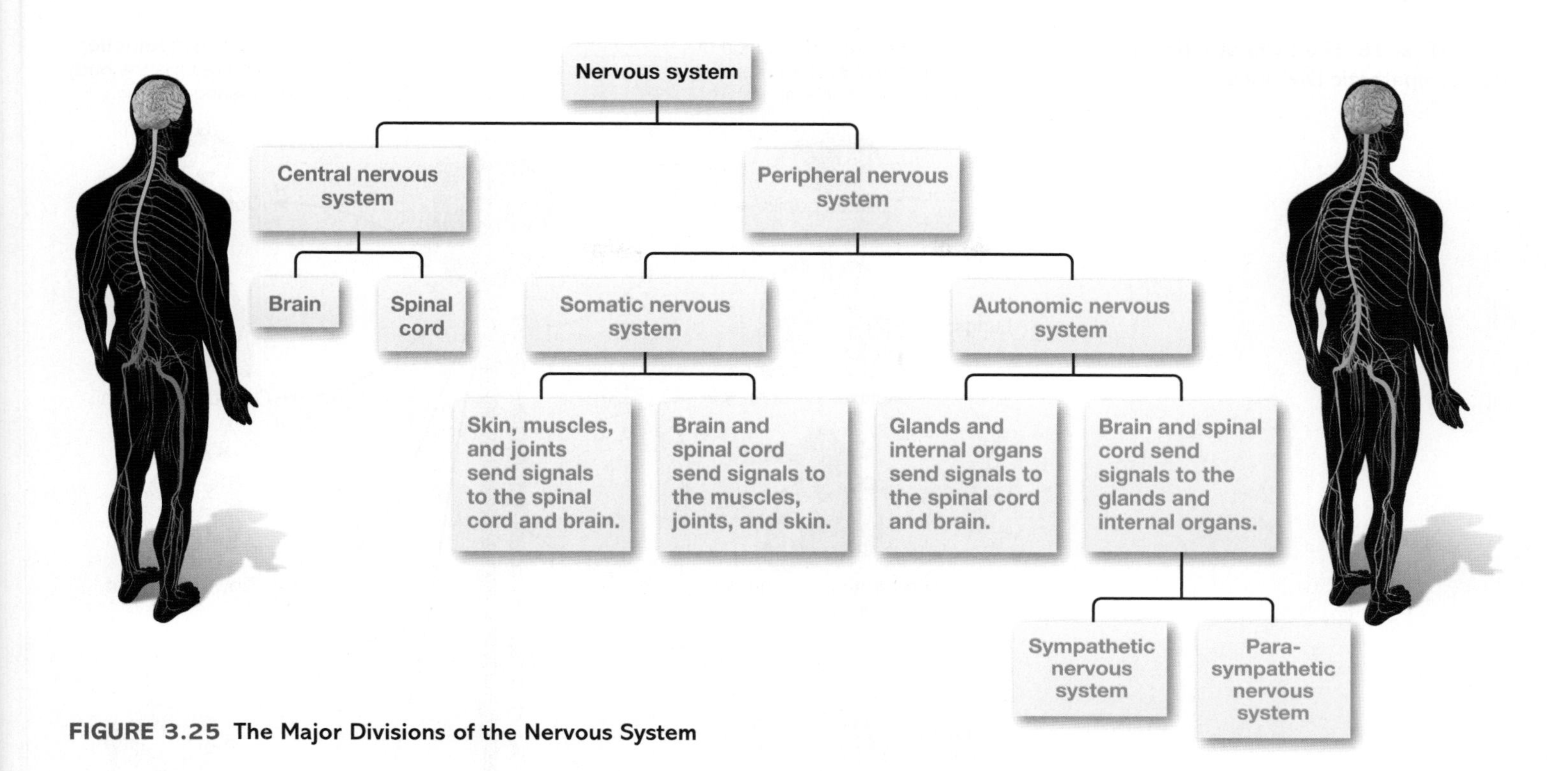


**FIGURE 3.25 The Major Divisions of the Nervous System**

carry somatosensory signals from the glands and internal organs to the central nervous system. These signals provide information about, for example, the fullness of your stomach or how anxious you feel.

SYMPATHETIC AND PARASYMPATHETIC DIVISIONS Two types of signals, *sympathetic* and *parasympathetic*, travel from the central nervous system to organs and glands, controlling their activity (**Figure 3.26**). To understand these signals, imagine you hear a fire alarm. In the second after you hear the alarm, signals go out to parts of your body that tell those parts to prepare for action. As a result, blood flows to skeletal muscles; epinephrine is released, increasing your heart rate and blood sugar; your lungs take in more oxygen; your digestive system suspends activity as a way of conserving energy; your pupils dilate to maximize visual sensitivity; and you perspire to keep cool. These preparatory actions are prompted by the autonomic nervous system's **sympathetic division.** Should there be a fire, you will be physically prepared to flee. If the alarm turns out to be false, your heart will return to its normal steady beat, your breathing will slow, you will resume digesting food, and you will stop perspiring. This return to a normal state will be prompted by the ANS's **parasympathetic division.** Most of your internal organs are controlled by inputs from sympathetic and parasympathetic systems. The more aroused you are, the greater the sympathetic system's dominance.

It does not take a fire alarm to activate your sympathetic nervous system. When you meet someone you find attractive, for example, your heart beats quickly, you perspire, you might start breathing heavily, and your pupils widen. Such signs of sexual arousal provide nonverbal cues during social interaction. These signs occur because sexual arousal has activated the ANS's sympathetic division. The sympathetic nervous system is also activated by psychological states such as anxiety or unhappiness. Certain people worry a great deal or do not cope well with stress. Their bodies are in a constant state of arousal. Important research

**sympathetic division** A division of the autonomic nervous system; it prepares the body for action.

**parasympathetic division** A division of the autonomic nervous system; it returns the body to its resting state.

**FIGURE 3.26 The Sympathetic and Parasympathetic Divisions**

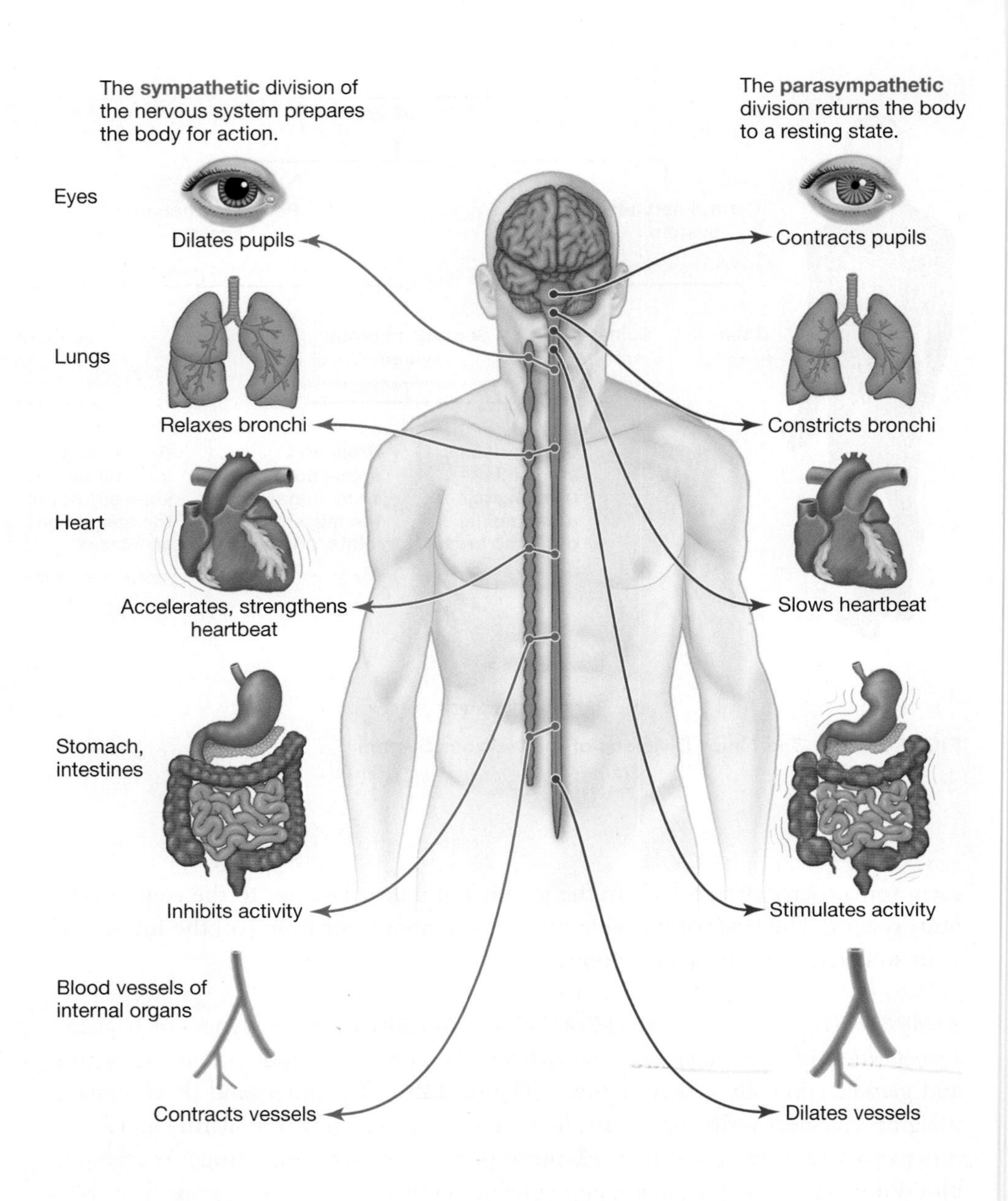


in the 1930s and 1940s by Hans Selye demonstrated that chronic activation of the sympathetic nervous system is associated with medical problems that include ulcers, heart disease, and asthma. Selye's work is discussed further in Chapter 11, "Health and Well-Being."

## The Endocrine System Communicates through Hormones

Like the nervous system, the **endocrine system** is a communication network that influences thoughts, behaviors, and actions. Both systems work together to regulate psychological activity. For instance, from the nervous system the brain receives information about potential threats to the organism. The brain communicates with the endocrine system to prepare the organism to deal with those threats. (The threats could involve physical injury or be psychological, such as nervousness at having to talk in front of a group.) The main difference between the two systems is in their modes of communication: Whereas the nervous system uses electrochemical signals, the endocrine system uses *hormones*.

**endocrine system** A communication system that uses hormones to influence thoughts, behaviors, and actions.

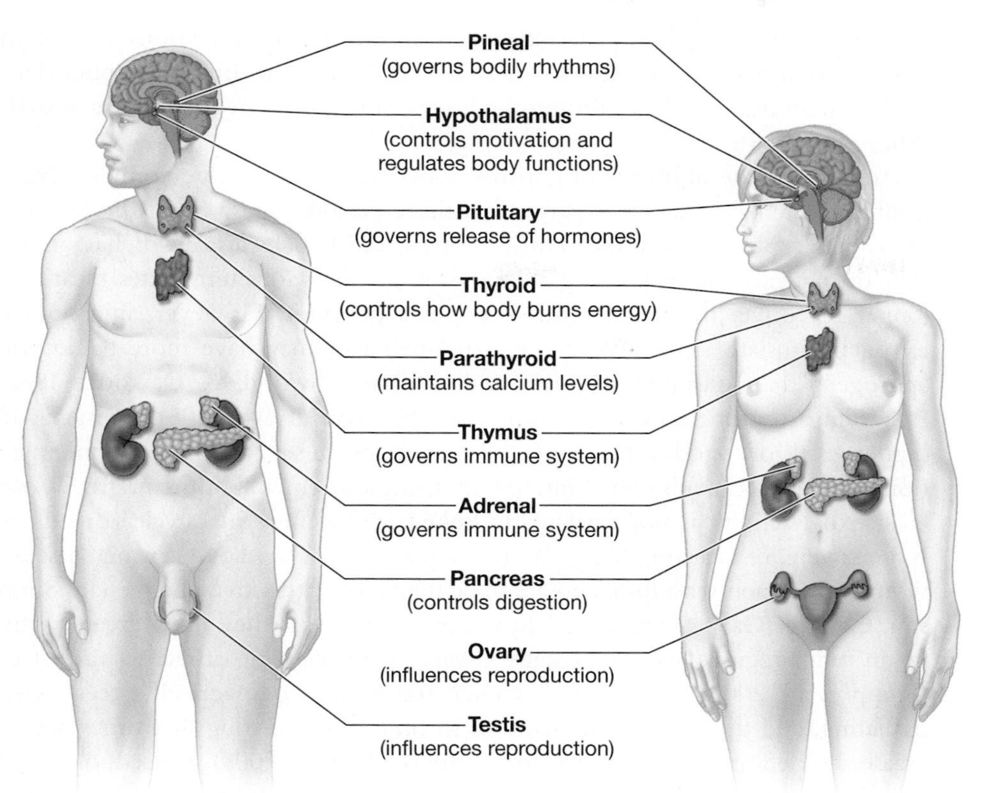


**FIGURE 3.27 The Major Endocrine Glands**

**Hormones** are chemical substances released into the bloodstream by the ductless *endocrine glands,* such as the pancreas, thyroid, and testes or ovaries (**Figure 3.27**). Once released, hormones travel through the bloodstream until they reach their target tissues, where they bind to receptor sites and influence the tissues. Because they travel through the bloodstream, hormones can take from seconds to hours to exert their effects. Once hormones are in the bloodstream, their effects can last for a long time and affect multiple targets.

*"You've been charged with driving under the influence of testosterone."*

**HORMONES' EFFECTS ON SEXUAL BEHAVIOR** An example of hormonal influence is in sexual behavior. The main endocrine glands influencing sexual behavior are the **gonads:** the testes, in males, and the ovaries, in females. Although many people talk about "male" and "female" hormones, the two major gonadal hormones are identical in males and females. What differs is the quantity: *Androgens* such as testosterone are more prevalent in males, whereas *estrogens* such as estradiol and progesterone are more prevalent in females. Gonadal hormones influence the development of secondary sex characteristics (e.g., breast development in females, growth of facial hair in males). Gonadal hormones also influence adult sexual behavior.

For males, successful sexual behavior depends on having at least a minimum amount of testosterone. Prior to puberty, surgical removal of the testes, or *castration,* diminishes the capacity for developing an erection and lowers sexual interest. Yet a man castrated after puberty will be able to perform sexually

**hormones** Chemical substances, released from endocrine glands, that travel through the bloodstream to targeted tissues; the tissues are subsequently influenced by the hormones.

**gonads** The main endocrine glands involved in sexual behavior: in males, the testes; in females, the ovaries.

if he receives an injection of testosterone. Testosterone injections do not increase sexual behavior in healthy men, however, and this finding implies that a healthy man needs only a minimum amount of testosterone to perform sexually (Sherwin, 1988).

In females, the influence of gonadal hormones is much more complex. Many nonhuman female animals experience a finite period, *estrus,* when the female is sexually receptive and fertile. During estrus, the female displays behaviors designed to attract the male. Surgical removal of the ovaries terminates estrus: No longer receptive, the female ends her sexual behavior. However, injections of estrogen reinstate estrus. Women's sexual behavior may have more to do with androgens than estrogens (Morris, Udry, Khan-Dawood, & Dawood, 1987). According to pioneering work by Barbara Sherwin (1994, 2008), women with higher levels of testosterone report greater interest in sex, and testosterone injections increase women's sexual interest after surgical removal of the uterus. Women's sexual activity is not particularly linked to the menstrual cycle (Breedlove, Rosenzweig, & Watson, 2007). When they are ovulating, however, heterosexual women find men who look and act masculine more attractive (Gangestad, Simpson, Cousins, Garver-Apgar, & Christensen, 2004), and they show greater activity in brain regions associated with reward while viewing attractive male faces (Rupp et al., 2009). In addition, women report having lower self-esteem when ovulating, and their greater motivation to find a mate during that time may increase their efforts to appear attractive (Hill & Durante, 2009). Indeed, one study found that when their fertility was highest, women showed up for a laboratory study wearing more-revealing clothing than they normally wore (Durante, Li, & Haselton, 2008).

## Actions of the Nervous System and Endocrine System Are Coordinated

All the communication systems described in this chapter link neurochemical and physiological processes to behaviors, thoughts, and feelings. These systems are fully integrated and interact to facilitate survival. They use information from the organism's environment to direct adaptive behavioral responses. Ultimately, the endocrine system is under the central nervous system's control. The brain interprets external and internal stimuli, then sends signals to the endocrine system, which responds by initiating various effects on the body and on behavior.

Most of the central control of the endocrine system is accomplished by the hypothalamus (for the location of this gland, see Figure 3.27; for a more detailed look, see Figure 3.18). How does this central control work? At the base of the hypothalamus is the **pituitary gland,** which governs the release of hormones from the rest of the endocrine glands. Neural activation causes the hypothalamus to secrete a particular *releasing factor.* The releasing factor causes the pituitary to release a hormone specific to that factor, and the hormone then travels through the bloodstream to endocrine sites throughout the body. Once the hormone reaches the target sites, it touches off the release of other hormones, which subsequently affect bodily reactions or behavior. The pituitary is often referred to as the "master gland" of the body: By releasing hormones into the bloodstream, it controls all other glands and governs major processes such as development, ovulation, and lactation. This integration can be extremely finely tuned.

**pituitary gland** A gland located at the base of the hypothalamus; it sends hormonal signals to other endocrine glands, controlling their release of hormones.

Consider physical growth. *Growth hormone (GH),* a hormone released from the pituitary gland, prompts bone, cartilage, and muscle tissue to grow or helps them regenerate after injury. Since the 1930s, many people have administered or self-administered GH to increase body size and strength. Many athletes have sought a competitive advantage through GH. For example, the legendary baseball pitcher Roger Clemens has been accused of injecting GH to improve his performance. Clemens has long denied the accusation. In August 2010, however, a U.S. federal grand jury indicted him for lying to Congress during its 2008 hearings about the use of performance-enhancing drugs in major league baseball (**Figure 3.28**).

Similarly, GH has helped make the current generation of young adults in Japan considerably taller than their parents' generation (Murata, 2000). This increase has resulted from the increased availability and consumption of dietary protein in Japan after World War II. How is GH related to protein intake? *Growth hormone releasing factor (GRF)* stimulates the release of GH, which relies on protein to build bones and muscles. GRF also selectively stimulates the eating of protein but not of fats or carbohydrates, perhaps by making protein especially enjoyable (Dickson & Vaccarino, 1994). The area of the hypothalamus connected to GRF neurons is involved in sleep/wake cycles. Thus the bursts of GH, the need for protein, and the consumption of protein are controlled by the body's internal clock. All these connections illustrate how the CNS, the PNS, and the endocrine system work together to ensure the organism's survival: These systems prompt the behaviors that provide the body with the substances it needs when it needs them.

**FIGURE 3.28 Growth Hormone and Baseball** Growth hormone (GH) helps bone, cartilage, and muscle tissues to grow or to regenerate after injury. In February 2008, a bipartisan committee of the U.S. House of Representatives held hearings on the use of performance-enhancing drugs in major league baseball. The committee particularly addressed accusations that Roger Clemens **(lower left corner, in the blue suit, with his back to the camera)** had injected GH and steroids to improve his competitive advantage.

## Summing Up

### How Does the Brain Communicate with the Body?

The central nervous system, consisting of the brain and spinal cord, attends to the body and its environment, initiates actions, and directs the peripheral nervous system and endocrine system to respond appropriately. The peripheral nervous system is made up of the somatic nervous system and autonomic nervous system; the autonomic nervous system controls sympathetic and parasympathetic activity. The endocrine system consists of a number of endocrine glands. The central nervous system, peripheral nervous system, and endocrine system use chemicals to transmit their signals. Transmission in the nervous system occurs across synapses, whereas transmission in the endocrine system uses hormones that travel through the bloodstream. Gonadal hormones (estrogen, progesterone, and testosterone) are important in the development of secondary sex characteristics and in sexual behavior. The hypothalamus controls the endocrine system by directing the pituitary to release hormones that affect other endocrine glands. The various communication systems are integrated and promote behavior that is adaptive to the organism's environment.

## Measuring Up

1. Complete each statement by choosing one or more of the following terms: peripheral nervous system (PNS); somatic nervous system; autonomic nervous system (ANS); sympathetic division; parasympathetic division.
   - **a.** You are studying quietly in the library when a friend jumps out from behind a partition and scares you, making your heart race. Your ________________ has been affected.
   - **b.** When you calm down and return to your former (not scared) state, your ________________ is affected.
   - **c.** The ________________ controls movement by carrying signals from the central nervous system to the muscles.
   - **d.** The ________________ has two primary components: the somatic nervous system and the autonomic nervous system.
   - **e.** The ________________ consists of two main divisions that regulate the body's internal environment.
2. Which of the following statements are true? Choose as many as apply.
   - **a.** Only gays and lesbians secrete testosterone and estrogen.
   - **b.** All (normal) people of both sexes secrete testosterone and estrogen.
   - **c.** Men have gonads, and women have ovaries.
   - **d.** The endocrine system acts more slowly than the nervous system.
   - **e.** Hormones are secreted from several places in the body, including the brain.
   - **f.** The pituitary gland is called the master gland.
   - **g.** The central nervous system and the peripheral nervous system work together, whereas the endocrine system works independently.
   - **h.** Women's sexual responsiveness is related more to androgens (such as testosterone) than to estrogen.

**Answers:** 1. a. sympathetic division; b. parasympathetic division; c. somatic nervous system; d. peripheral nervous system (PNS); e. autonomic nervous system (ANS).
2. Choices b, d, e, f, and h are true.

# 3.4 What Is the Genetic Basis of Psychological Science?

**Learning Objectives**

- Explain how genes are transmitted from parent to offspring.
- Discuss the goals and methods of behavioral genetics.
- Explain how both environmental factors and experience influence genetic expression.

So far, this chapter has presented the basic biological processes underlying psychological functions. The following section considers how genes and environment affect psychological functions. From the moment of conception, we receive the genes we will possess for the remainder of our lives, but do those genes determine our thoughts and behaviors? How do environmental influences, such as the cultures in which we are raised, alter how our brains develop and change?

Until the last few years, genetic research focused almost entirely on whether people possessed certain types of genes, such as genes for psychological disorders or for intelligence. Although it is important for us to discover the effects of individual genes, this approach misses the critical role of environmental factors in shaping who we are. While the term *genetics* is typically used to describe how characteristics such as height, hair color, and eye color are passed along to offspring through inheritance, it also refers to the processes involved in turning genes "on" and "off." This research reflects and reveals that environment affects our genes: how they are expressed and therefore how they influence our thoughts, feelings, and behavior. Genetic predispositions are often important in determining the environments we select for ourselves, so biology and environment mutually influence each other. All the while, biology and environment—in other words, our genes and every experience we ever have—influence the development of our brains.

## All of Human Development Has a Genetic Basis

Within nearly every cell in the body is the genome for making the entire organism. The genome is the master blueprint that provides detailed instructions for everything from how to grow a gallbladder to where the nose gets placed on a face. Whether a cell becomes part of a gallbladder or a nose is determined by which genes are turned on or off within that cell, and these actions are in turn determined by cues from outside the cell. The genome provides the option, and the environment determines which option is taken (Marcus, 2004).

Within each cell are **chromosomes.** These structures are made of *deoxyribonucleic acid (DNA),* a substance that consists of two intertwined strands of molecules in a double helix shape. Segments of those strands are called **genes** (**Figure 3.29**).

**chromosomes** Structures within the cell body that are made up of DNA. DNA consists of genes.

**genes** The units of heredity that help determine the characteristics of an organism.

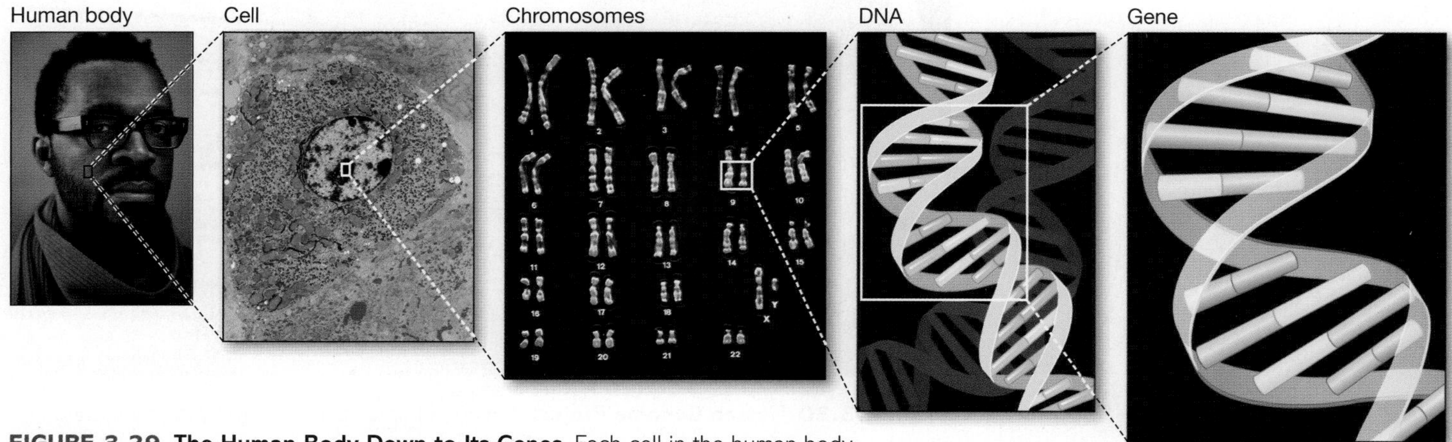


**FIGURE 3.29 The Human Body Down to Its Genes** Each cell in the human body includes pairs of chromosomes, which consist of DNA strands. DNA has a double helix shape and is composed of genes.

In a typical human, nearly every cell contains 23 pairs of chromosomes. One member of each pair comes from the person's mother, the other from the person's father. In other words, each parent contributes half of a person's DNA, half of a person's genes.

Each gene—a particular sequence of molecules along a DNA strand—specifies an exact instruction to manufacture a distinct polypeptide. One or more polypeptides make up a protein. Proteins are the basic chemicals that make up the structure of cells and direct their activities. There are thousands of different types of proteins, and each type carries out a specific task. The environment determines which proteins are produced and when they are produced. For example, a certain species of butterfly becomes colorful or drab, depending on the season in which it is born. The environment during its development probably causes a gene sensitive to temperature to be expressed. Similarly, although each cell in the human body contains the same DNA, cells become specialized, depending on which of their genes are expressed. Gene expression determines the body's basic physical makeup, but it also determines specific developments throughout life. It is involved in all psychological activity. Gene expression allows us to sense, to learn, to fall in love, and so on.

In February 2001, two groups of scientists published separate articles that detailed the results of the first phase of the *Human Genome Project,* an international research effort. This achievement represents the coordinated work of hundreds of scientists around the world to map the entire structure of human genetic material. The first step of the Human Genome Project was to map the entire structure of DNA. In other words, the researchers set out to identify the precise order of molecules that make up each of the thousands of genes on each of the 23 pairs of human chromosomes (**Figure 3.30**).

**FIGURE 3.30 Human Genome Project** A map of human genes is presented by J. Craig Venter, president of the research company Celera Genomics, at a news conference in Washington on February 12, 2001. This map is one part of the international effort by hundreds of scientists to map the entire structure of human genetic material.

One of the most striking findings from the Human Genome Project is that we have fewer than 30,000 genes. That number means we have only about twice as many genes as a fly (13,000) or a worm (18,000), not much more than the number in some plants (26,000), and fewer than the number estimated to be in an ear of corn (50,000). Indeed, more-recent estimates indicate that the human genome may consist of just over 20,000 genes (Pennisi, 2007). Why are we so complex if we have so few genes? The number of our genes might be less important than subtleties in how those genes are expressed and regulated (Baltimore, 2001).

## Heredity Involves Passing Along Genes through Reproduction

The first clues to the mechanisms responsible for heredity were discovered by the monk Gregor Mendel around 1866. At the monastery where Mendel lived, there was a long history of studying plants. For studying genetics, Mendel developed an experimental technique, *selective breeding,* that strictly controlled which plants bred with which other plants.

In one simple study, Mendel selected pea plants that had either only purple flowers or only white flowers. He then cross-pollinated the two types to see which color flowers the plants would produce. Mendel found that the first generation of pea offspring tended to be completely white or completely purple. If he had stopped there, he would never have discovered the basis of heredity. However, he then allowed each plant to self-pollinate into a second generation. This second generation revealed a different pattern: Of the hundreds of pea plants, about 75 percent had purple flowers and 25 percent had white flowers. This 3:1 ratio repeated itself in additional studies. It also held true for other characteristics, such as pod shape. From this pattern, Mendel deduced that the plants contained separate units, now referred to as genes, that existed in different versions (e.g., white and purple). In determining an offspring's features, some of these versions would be dominant and others would be recessive. We now know that a **dominant gene** from either parent is expressed (becomes apparent or physically visible) whenever it is present. A **recessive gene** is expressed only when it is matched with a similar gene from the other parent. In pea plants, white flowers are recessive, so white flowers occur only when the gene for purple flowers is not present. All "white genes" and no purple ones were one of the four possible combinations of white and purple genes in Mendel's experiments (**Figure 3.31**).

GENOTYPE AND PHENOTYPE The existence of dominant and recessive genes means that not all genes are expressed. The **genotype** is an organism's genetic makeup. That genetic constitution is determined at the moment of conception and never changes. The **phenotype** is that organism's observable physical characteristics and is always changing.

Genetics, or nature, is one of the two influences on phenotype. So, for instance, in Mendel's experiments, two plants with purple flowers had the same phenotype but might have differed in genotype. Either plant might have had two (dominant) genes for purple. Alternatively, either plant might have had one (dominant) purple gene and one (recessive) white gene. Environment, or nurture, is the second influence on phenotype. For instance, humans inherit their height and skin color; but good nutrition leads to increased size, and sunlight can change skin color. Another example of environmental influence on phenotype

**dominant gene** A gene that is expressed in the offspring whenever it is present.

**recessive gene** A gene that is expressed only when it is matched with a similar gene from the other parent.

**genotype** The genetic constitution of an organism, determined at the moment of conception.

**phenotype** Observable physical characteristics, which result from both genetic and environmental influences.

**FIGURE 3.31 Genotypes and Phenotypes** Mendel's experiments with cross-breeding pea plants resulted in purple flowers 75 percent of the time and white flowers 25 percent of the time.

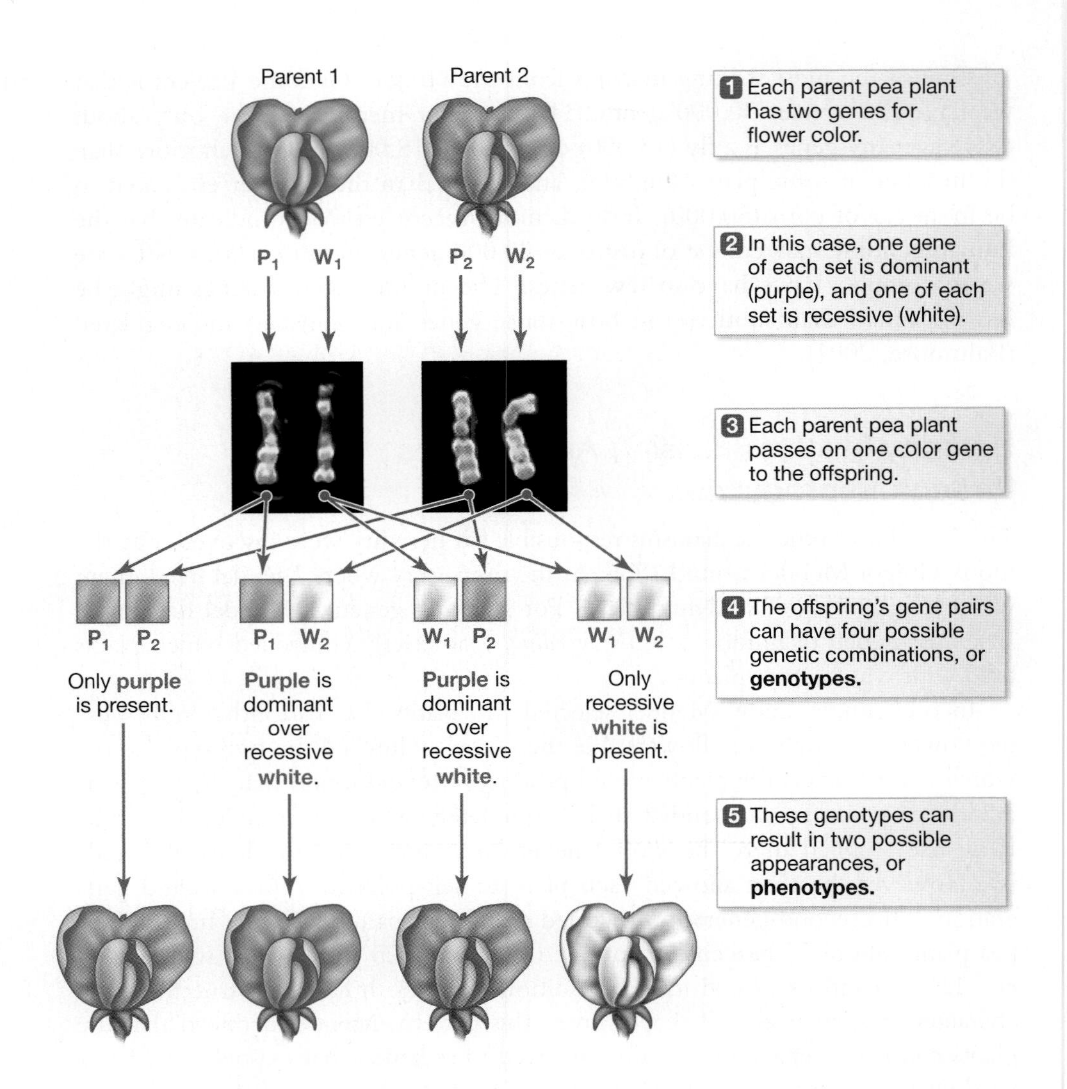


is *phenylketonuria (PKU)*. Infants who have this rare genetic disorder are unable to break down phenylalanine (an enzyme that appears in dairy and other products, including aspartame, a sweetener in diet soft drinks). The resulting excess of phenylalanine can lead to severe brain damage. Fortunately, providing such children with a low-phenylalanine diet until they pass the critical stages of neural development greatly helps reduce brain damage. The phenotype, then, is modified by diet.

**POLYGENIC EFFECTS** Mendel's flower experiments dealt with single-gene characteristics. Such traits appear to be determined by one gene each. But when a population displays a range of variability for a certain characteristic, such as height or intelligence, the characteristic is *polygenic*. In other words, the trait is influenced by many genes (as well as by environment).

Consider human skin color. There are not just three or four separate skin colors. There is a spectrum of colors. The U.S. Census of 2000 allowed respondents to select more than one race for the first time. The data from that census showed that approximately 2.4 percent of the population (over 6.8 million people) identify themselves as multiracial (CensusScope, 2000). The huge range of skin tones among Americans alone shows that human skin color is not inherited the same way as flower color was in Mendel's research. The rich variety of skin colors (phenotype) is not the end product of a single dominant/recessive gene pairing (genotype). Instead, the variety shows the effects of multiple genes.

## Genotypic Variation Is Created by Sexual Reproduction

Although they have the same parents, siblings may differ from each other in many ways, such as eye color, height, and personality. These differences occur because each person has a specific combination of genes, determined in part by random cell division before reproduction. Most cells in the human body contain 23 pairs of chromosomes. These pairs include the sex chromosomes, which are denoted X and Y due to their shapes. Females have two X chromosomes. Males have one X chromosome and one Y (**Figure 3.32**).

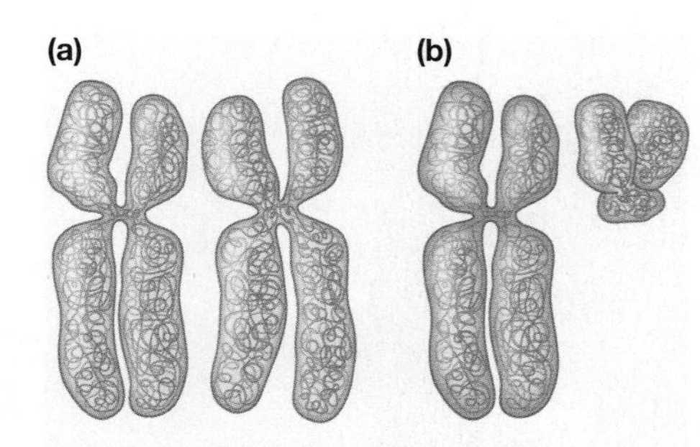


**FIGURE 3.32 Sex Chromosomes (a)** In females, the 23rd pair of chromosomes consists of two X chromosomes. **(b)** In males, the 23rd pair consists of one X and one Y chromosome. The Y chromosome is much smaller than the X chromosome.

In each parent, reproductive cells divide to produce *gametes,* the egg and sperm cells. Each gamete contains half of every chromosome pair. After one sperm and one egg combine during fertilization, the resulting fertilized cell, known as a *zygote,* contains 23 pairs of chromosomes. In other words, half of each pair of chromosomes comes from the mother, and the other half comes from the father. From any two parents, 8 million different combinations of the 23 chromosomes are possible. The net outcome is that a unique genotype is created at conception, and this accounts for the genetic variation of the human species (**Figure 3.33**).

The zygote grows through *cell division.* This process has two stages: First the chromosomes duplicate. Then the cell divides into two new cells with an identical chromosome structure. Cell division is the basis of the life cycle and

**FIGURE 3.33 Try for Yourself: Genetic Matching**

(a)

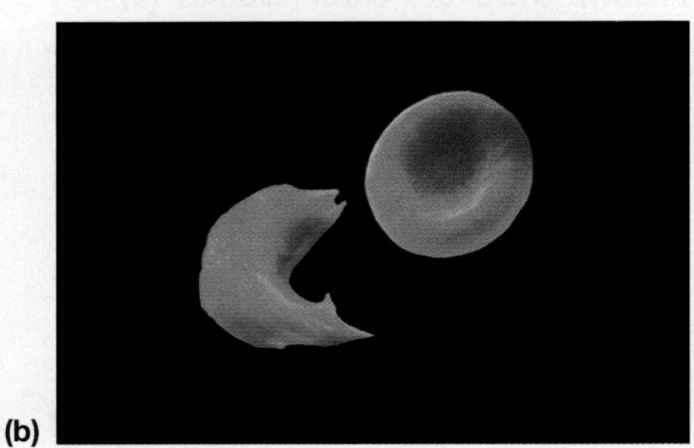

(b)

**FIGURE 3.34 Mutations (a)** These moths illustrate industrial melanism at work. As shown here, it is easier to spot light-colored insects against dark backgrounds. Because predators have an easier time catching insects they can spot, darker moths and darker butterflies are better able to survive in more-polluted areas. **(b)** Sickle-cell disease occurs when people receive recessive genes for the trait from both parents. It causes red blood cells to assume the distinctive "sickle" shape seen here in the left cell. Sickle-cell disease is most common among African Americans.

is responsible for growth and development. Errors sometimes occur during cell division and lead to *mutations,* most of which are benign and have little influence on the organism. Occasionally, a genetic mutation produces a selective advantage or disadvantage in terms of survival or reproduction. That is, mutations can be adaptive or maladaptive. The evolutionary significance of such a change in adaptiveness is complex. If a mutation produces an ability or behavior that proves advantageous to the organism, that mutation may spread through the gene pool. The mutation may spread because those who carry the gene are more likely to survive and reproduce.

Consider *industrial melanism.* This phenomenon accounts for the fact that in areas of the world with heavy soot or smog, moths and butterflies tend to be darker in color. What has created this dark coloration? Before industrialization, landscapes (trees, buildings, etc.) were lighter in color. Predators were more likely to spot darker insects against pale backgrounds, so any mutation that led to darker coloring in insects was eliminated quickly through natural selection. But with industrialization, pollution darkened the landscapes. Darker coloring in insects therefore became more adaptive because the darker insects were harder to see against the darker backgrounds (**Figure 3.34a**).

What about genetic mutations that are disadvantageous adaptively, such as by leading to disease? The dominance or recessiveness of a gene helps determine if it remains in the gene pool. For instance, *sickle-cell disease* is a genetic disorder that alters the bloodstream's processing of oxygen. It can lead to pain, organ and bone damage, and anemia. The disease occurs mainly in African Americans: Approximately 8 percent of African Americans are estimated to have the (recessive) gene for it (National Human Genome Research Institute, n.d.). Because the sickle-cell gene is recessive, only those African Americans who receive it from both parents will develop the disease. Those who receive a recessive gene from only one parent have what is called *sickle-cell trait.* They may exhibit symptoms under certain conditions (such as during exercise), but they will have a generally healthy phenotype in spite of a genotype that includes the trait (**Figure 3.34b**).

Recessive genes do not interfere with most people's health. For this reason, the recessive genes for diseases such as sickle-cell anemia can survive in the gene pool. This particular gene also has some benefit in that it increases resistance to malaria, a parasitic disease prevalent in certain parts of Africa. People with only one sickle-cell gene enjoy this resistance without suffering from sickle-cell disease. In contrast to recessive gene disorders like this one, most dominant gene disorders are lethal for most of their carriers and therefore do not last in the gene pool.

## Genes Affect Behavior

What determines the kind of person you are? What factors make you more or less bold, intelligent, or able to read a map? Your abilities and your psychological traits are influenced by the interaction of your genes and the environment in which you were raised or to which you are now exposed. The study of how genes and environment interact to influence psychological activity is known as *behavioral genetics.* Behavioral genetics has provided important information about the extent to which biology influences mind, brain, and behavior.

Any research suggesting that abilities to perform certain behaviors are biologically based is controversial. Most people do not want to be told that what they can achieve is limited by something beyond their control, such as their genes.

It is easy to accept that genes control physical characteristics such as sex, race, eye color, and predisposition to diseases such as cancer and alcoholism. But can genes determine whether people will get divorced, how smart they are, or what careers they choose? Increasingly, science indicates that genes lay the groundwork for many human traits. From this perspective, people are born essentially like undeveloped photographs: The image is already captured, but the way it eventually appears can vary based on the development process. Psychologists study the ways in which characteristics are influenced by nature, nurture, and their combination—in other words, by the ways genes are expressed in distinct environments.

**BEHAVIORAL GENETICS METHODS** Most of us, at one time or another, have marveled at how different siblings can be, even those raised around the same time and in the same household. The differences are to be expected, because most siblings share neither identical genes nor identical life experiences. Within the household and outside it, environments differ subtly and not so subtly. Siblings have different birth orders. Their mother may have consumed different foods and other substances during pregnancies. They may have different friends and teachers. Their parents may treat them differently. It is difficult to know what causes the similarities and differences between siblings, who always share some genes and often share much of their environments. Therefore, behavioral geneticists use two methods to assess the degree to which traits are inherited: twin studies and adoption studies.

*Twin studies* compare similarities between different types of twins to determine the genetic basis of specific traits. **Monozygotic twins,** or *identical twins,* result from one zygote (fertilized egg) dividing in two. Each new zygote, and therefore each twin, has the same chromosomes and the same genes on each chromosome. Interesting research indicates, however, that monozygotic twins' DNA might not be as identical as long thought, due to subtle differences in how the mother's and father's genes are combined (Bruder et al., 2008). **Dizygotic twins,** sometimes called *fraternal* or *nonidentical twins,* result when two separately fertilized eggs develop in the mother's womb simultaneously. The resulting twins are no more similar genetically than any other pair of siblings. To the extent that monozygotic twins are more similar than dizygotic twins, the increased similarity is considered most likely due to genetic influence. Even identical twins do not have the exact same environment (and in rare circumstances might even have some different genes due to random mutations), and therefore they have different phenotypes. Still, they are typically much more similar than dizygotic twins, who differ markedly in genotype.

*Adoption studies* compare the similarities between biological relatives and adoptive relatives. Nonbiological adopted siblings may share similar home environments but will have different genes. Therefore, the assumption is that similarities among nonbiological adopted siblings have more to do with environment than with genes. Growing up in the same home turns out to have relatively little influence on many traits, including personality traits. Indeed, after genetic similarity is controlled for, even biological siblings raised in the same home are no more similar than two strangers plucked at random off the street. (This point is examined in greater detail in Chapter 9, "Human Development," and Chapter 13, "Personality.")

One way to conduct a behavioral genetic study is to compare monozygotic twins who have been *raised together* with ones who were *raised apart.* Thomas Bouchard and his colleagues at the University of Minnesota identified more than

**monozygotic twins** Also called *identical twins;* twin siblings that result from one zygote splitting in two and therefore share the same genes.

**dizygotic twins** Also called *fraternal twins;* twin siblings that result from two separately fertilized eggs and therefore are no more similar genetically than nontwin siblings.

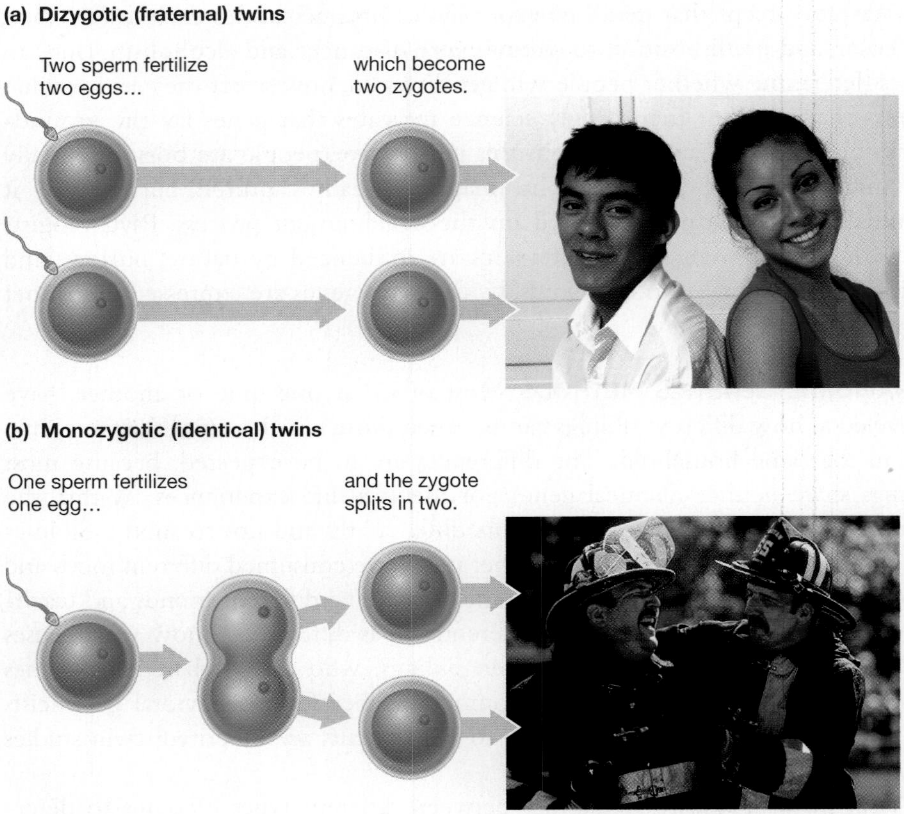

**FIGURE 3.35 Twins (a)** Fraternal twins, such as this pair pictured during their 13th birthday party, result when two separate eggs are fertilized at the same time. **(b)** Identical twins result when one fertilized egg splits in two. Identical twins Gerald Levey and Mark Newman, participants in Dr. Bouchard's study, were separated at birth. Reunited at age 31, they discovered they were both firefighters and had similar personality traits. **What other factors might account for the similarities between twins raised apart?**

**(a) Dizygotic (fraternal) twins**

Two sperm fertilize two eggs...

which become two zygotes.

**(b) Monozygotic (identical) twins**

One sperm fertilizes one egg...

and the zygote splits in two.

100 pairs of identical and nonidentical twins, some raised together and some raised apart (1990; **Figure 3.35**). The researchers examined a variety of these twins' characteristics, including intelligence, personality, well-being, achievement, alienation, and aggression. The general finding from the Minnesota Twin Project was that identical twins, raised together or not, were likely to be similar.

The "Jim twins" were among the most famous case studies to emerge from this project. These twin brothers were separated at birth and raised by different families. It is easy to guess about how each one was given the same name, but how is it possible that each James went on to marry a woman named Linda, divorce Linda and marry a woman named Betty, name a son James Alan (or James Allen), and name a dog Toy? In addition, both were part-time law enforcement officers who drove Chevrolets and vacationed in Florida. They were the same height and weight, chain-smoked the same brand of cigarettes, and drank the same brand of beer. Although no one would seriously suggest there are genes for naming dogs Toy or for marrying and divorcing women named Linda, the many similarities in the Jim twins' lives point to the strong genetic influences in shaping personality and behavior.

Some critics have argued that most of the adopted twins in the Minnesota study were raised in relatively similar environments. This similarity came about, in part, because adoption agencies try to match the child to the adoptive home. However, this argument does not explain the identical twins Oskar Stohr and Jack Yufe, who were born in Trinidad in 1933 (Bouchard, Lykken, McGue, Segal, & Tellegen, 1990). Oskar was raised a Catholic in Germany and eventually joined the Nazi Party. Jack was raised a Jew in Trinidad and lived for a while in Israel. Few twins have more-different backgrounds. Yet when they met, at an interview for the study, they were wearing similar clothes, exhibited similar mannerisms, and shared odd habits, such as flushing the toilet before using it, dipping toast in coffee, storing rubber bands on their wrists, and enjoying startling people by sneezing loudly in elevators. Some critics feel that nothing more than coincidence is at work in these case studies. They argue that if a researcher randomly selected any two people of the same age, many surprising similarities would exist in those people and their lives, just by coincidence, even if the people and their lives differed in most other ways. But twins and other relatives share similarities beyond coincidental attributes and behavior quirks. For instance, intelligence and personality traits such as shyness tend to run in families due to strong genetic components.

Moreover, some evidence suggests that twins raised apart may be more similar than twins raised together. This phenomenon might occur if parents encouraged individuality in twins raised together by emphasizing different strengths and interests as a way of helping each twin develop as an individual. In effect, the parents would actively create a different environment for each twin.

**UNDERSTANDING HERITABILITY** *Heredity* is the transmission of characteristics from parents to offspring by means of genes. A term that is often confused with *heredity* but means something different is **heritability.** This term refers to a statistical estimate of the genetic portion of the variation in some specific trait. The heritability for a trait depends on the *variation:* the measure of the overall difference among a group of people for that particular trait. That is, within a group of people (e.g., American women), how much do members vary in some trait (e.g., height)? Once we know the typical amount of variation within the population, we can see whether people who are related show less variation. For instance, do sisters tend to be more similar in height than unrelated women chosen at random?

Heritability refers to populations, not to individuals. If within a certain population a trait such as height has a heritability of .60, that means 60 percent of height variation among individuals within that population is genetic. It does not mean that anyone necessarily gets 60 percent of his or her height from genetics and 40 percent from environment. For instance, almost everyone has two legs. More people lose legs through accidents than are born without them. Thus the heritability value for having two legs is nearly zero, despite the obvious fact that the human genome includes instructions for growing two legs. The key lesson here is: Estimates of heritability are concerned only with the extent that people differ in terms of their genetic makeup within the group.

## Social and Environmental Contexts Influence Genetic Expression

In a longitudinal study of criminality, Avshalom Caspi and his colleagues (2002) followed a group of more than 1,000 New Zealanders from their births in 1972–73 until adulthood. Every few years, the researchers collected enormous amounts of information about the participants and their lives. When the participants were 26 years old, the investigators examined which factors predicted who became a violent criminal. Prior research had demonstrated that children who are mistreated by their parents are more likely to become violent offenders. But not all mistreated children become violent, and these researchers wanted to know why not. They hypothesized that the enzyme monoamine oxidase (MAO) is important in determining susceptibility to the effects of mistreatment, because low levels of MAO have been implicated in aggressive behaviors (this connection is discussed further in Chapter 14, "Psychological Disorders"). The gene that controls MAO comes in two forms, one of which leads to higher levels of MAO and one of which leads to lower levels. Caspi and colleagues found that boys with

**heritability** A statistical estimate of the extent to which variation in a trait within a population is due to genetic factors.

the low-MAO gene appeared to be especially susceptible to the effects of early-childhood mistreatment. Those boys were also much more likely to be convicted of a violent crime than those with the high-MAO gene. Only 1 in 8 boys was mistreated *and* had the low-MAO gene. That minority, however, was responsible for nearly half of the violent crimes committed by the group (**Figure 3.36**). The New Zealand study is a good example of how nature and nurture together affect behavior—in this case, unfortunately, violent behavior. Nature and nurture are inextricably entwined.

Many other studies have provided evidence that genes and social contexts interact to affect the phenotype. Sandra Scarr and her colleagues have proposed a theory of development that stresses the interactive nature of genes and

**FIGURE 3.36 Scientific Method: Caspi's Study of the Influence of Environment and Genes**

**Hypothesis:** The enzyme monoamine oxidase (MAO) may be important in determining susceptibility to the effects of maltreatment, because low levels of MAO have been implicated in aggressive behaviors.

**Research Method:**

1 A group of more than 1,000 New Zealanders were followed from birth to adulthood.

2 Researchers measured which children were mistreated by their parents (**nurture**).

3 Researchers measured the presence of the MAO gene, which comes in two forms. One form leads to higher levels of MAO, and the other form leads to lower levels (**nature**).

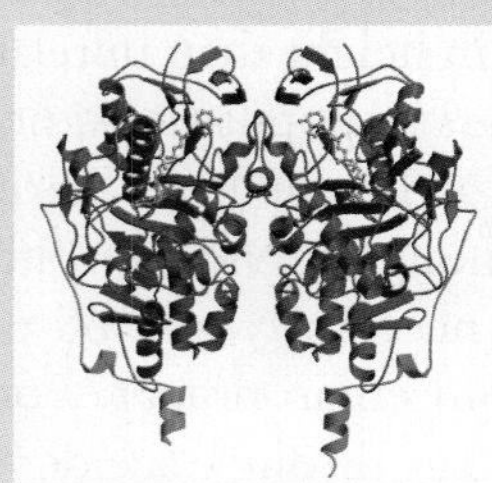

4 Researchers measured the tendency toward criminal behavior.

**Results:** Those who had the gene for low MAO activity were much more likely than others to have been convicted of violent crimes if they had been maltreated as children. The effects of maltreatment had less influence on those with the high-MAO gene.

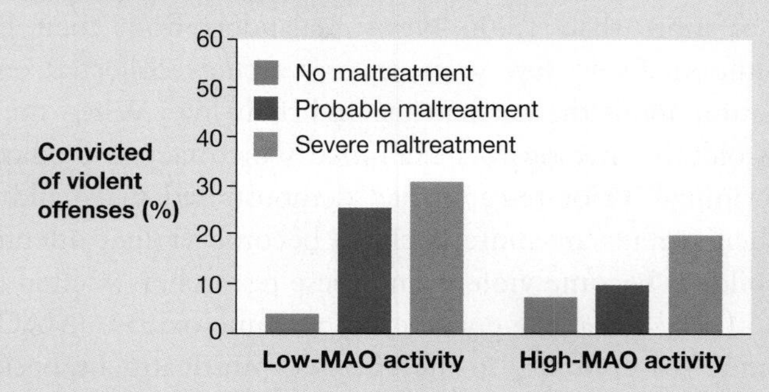


**Conclusion:** Nature and nurture can work together to affect human behavior.

**Source:** Caspi, A., McClay, J., Moffit, T. E., Mill, J., Martin, J., Craig, I. W., et al. (2002). Role of genotype in the cycle of violence in maltreated children. *Science, 29*, 851–854.

environment (Scarr & McCarthy, 1983). According to Scarr, early environments influence young children, but children's genes also influence the experiences they receive. For instance, children exposed to the same environment interpret and react to it in different ways. When teased, some children withdraw, others shrug it off without concern, and still others fight back. Because of differences in how they react to events, different children evoke different responses from others. A well-mannered, cuddly child prompts parents and caregivers to provide more nurturing than an irritable, fussy child does. Similarly, a child who seems to enjoy reading is likely to receive more books and be read to more often than a child who does not. And as children become older, they can choose their social situations. Some children prefer vigorous outdoor activities, others prefer quieter indoor activities, and so on. Thus genes predispose people to certain behaviors. Those behaviors prompt other people to respond in particular ways. Together, the behaviors, the responses, and subsequent actions shape people's phenotypes. Because genes and social contexts interact, separating their independent effects can be very difficult. Some argue that it is impossible.

**FIGURE 3.37 Genetic Modifications** The two white mice and three brown mice in this photo are genetically normal. The sixth mouse is hairless because it has been genetically modified. Specifically, this mouse has received two *nu* genes, which cause the "nude" mutation. These genes also cause the mouse to have no thymus and therefore no T cells (an important part of the immune system). The lack of T cells makes the mouse a good laboratory subject, as its body cannot reject tumors or transplants of cells from other animals.

## Genetic Expression Can Be Modified

Researchers can employ various gene manipulation techniques to enhance or reduce the expression of a particular gene or even to insert a gene from one animal species into the embryo of another. The researchers can then compare the genetically modified animal with an unmodified one to test theories about the affected gene's function (**Figure 3.37**). Such techniques have dramatically increased our understanding of how gene expression influences thought, feeling, and behavior. For instance, some of the transgenic mice discussed in Chapter 2 are called *knockouts.* Within these research mice, particular genes have been "knocked out," or rendered inactive by being removed from the genome or disrupted within the genome. If a gene is important for a specific function, knocking out that gene should interfere with the function. This experimental technique has revolutionized genetics, and in recognition the 2007 Nobel Prize in Physiology or Medicine was awarded to the three scientists who developed it: Mario Capecchi, Oliver Smithies, and Sir Martin Evans.

One remarkable finding from genetic manipulation is that changing even a single gene can dramatically change behavior. Through various gene manipulations, researchers have created anxious mice, hyperactive mice, mice that cannot learn or remember, mice that groom themselves to the point of baldness, mice that fail to take care of their offspring, and even mice that progressively increase alcohol intake when stressed (Marcus, 2004; Ridley, 2003). In one study, a gene from the highly social prairie vole was inserted into the developing embryos of normally antisocial mice. The resulting transgenic mice exhibited social behavior more typical of prairie voles than of mice (Insel & Young, 2001). Another study found that knocking out specific genes led mice to forget mice they had previously encountered. These knockouts also failed to investigate new mice placed in their cages, though normal mice would do so readily. In essence, knocking out one gene led to multiple impairments in social recognition (Choleris et al., 2003). This finding does not indicate that mice have a specific gene for being social. It indicates that changing one gene's expression leads to the expression of a series of other genes. This effect ultimately influences even complex behaviors. In other words, genes seldom work in isolation to influence mind and behavior. Rather, complex interaction among thousands of genes gives rise to the complexity of human experience.

CRITICAL THINKING SKILL

## Seeking Disconfirming Evidence

Most of us tend to focus on information that confirms what we already believe. Suppose you believe that genetics plays only a small role in the way people think, feel, and act. How would you test this belief? If you are like most people, you would look for studies that show a small genetic effect and criticize studies that show a large one. But a better way to gather and study information would be to draw a 2 × 2 chart and fill in every cell (**Figure 3.38**).

On the left, you would list each position: your thesis (A) and its opposite, or antithesis (B). In the middle, you would supply at least one or two reasons that support each position, provide evidence for each reason, and evaluate the relative strength of each piece of evidence. (For example, how reliable is your source for this information? If a study was conducted, did it use appropriate control groups?) On the right, you would supply at least one or two reasons that contradict each position; provide evidence for each of these reasons; and, as with the supporting evidence, evaluate the relative strength of each piece of evidence. The table would force you to consider information that supports your beliefs. It would also force you to consider information that fails to support those beliefs.

Suppose you believe that vitamin C reduces your likelihood of getting a cold. If you acted on the natural tendency to consider only confirming information, you would look for studies in which people who took vitamin C had fewer colds. If you employed this table, you would also need to consider other possibilities, such as studies in which people took vitamin C and did not have fewer colds, or did not take vitamin C and had fewer colds, or did not take vitamin C and had more colds. To consider the subject thoroughly, you would include all four kinds of studies in your thinking. This critical thinking skill (or strategy) will not only keep you from ignoring disconfirming evidence. It will also increase your ability to gather disconfirming evidence, evaluate it, and thereby strengthen your arguments—for and against.

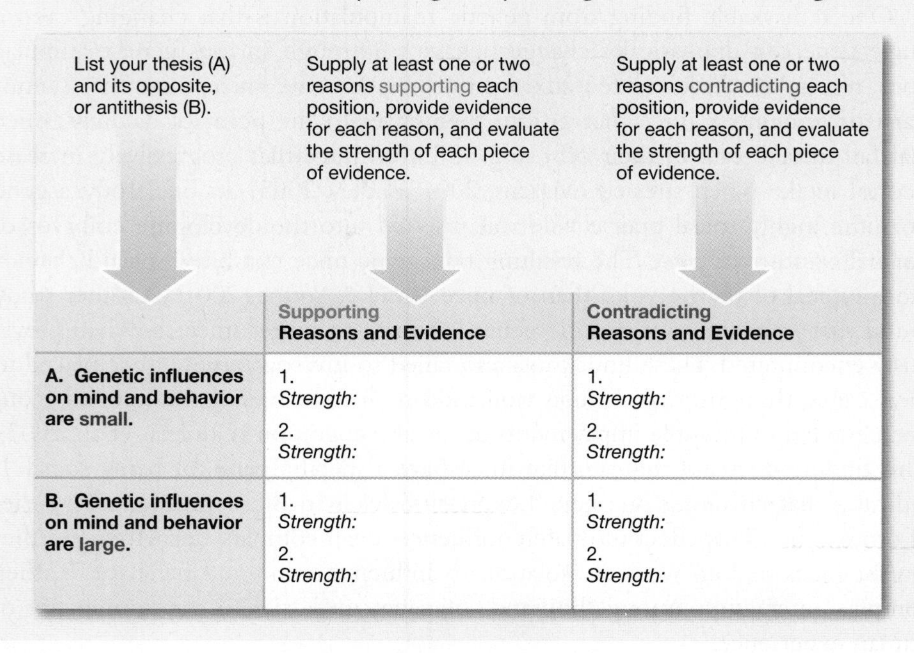


| | Supporting Reasons and Evidence | Contradicting Reasons and Evidence |
|---|---|---|
| **A. Genetic influences on mind and behavior are small.** | 1. *Strength:* 2. *Strength:* | 1. *Strength:* 2. *Strength:* |
| **B. Genetic influences on mind and behavior are large.** | 1. *Strength:* 2. *Strength:* | 1. *Strength:* 2. *Strength:* |

**FIGURE 3.38 Supporting and Contradictory Evidence**

## Summing Up

### What Is the Genetic Basis of Psychological Science?

Human behavior is influenced by genes. People inherit both physical attributes and personality traits from their parents. The Human Genome Project has mapped the basic sequence of DNA, providing information that will help scientists increase their understanding of individual differences in people's characteristics and develop treatments for genetically based disorders. In addition to studying the heritability of traits, researchers are interested in studying how and when genes are expressed. Genetic expression is affected by the environment and experience.

## Measuring Up

1. The difference between genotype and phenotype is that ________.
   a. genotype refers to an organism's genetic makeup; phenotype refers to observable characteristics that result from genetic and environmental influences
   b. genotype refers to monozygotic twins' (nearly) identical genetic makeup; phenotype refers to dizygotic twins' genetic makeup
   c. genotypes can be modified by experiences; phenotypes can be modified only if the underlying genes are knocked out
   d. genotypes direct the experiences organisms seek for themselves; phenotypes cannot affect environmental events
2. What is the principle behind knockout gene research?
   a. Aggressive behavior is inherited through so-called knockout genes.
   b. By rendering a single gene inactive, we can study that gene's effects on behavior.
   c. Knockout genes reveal the relative contributions of prenatal and postnatal experiences on offspring.
   d. Knockout genes reduce the need for using MRIs to study brain development.

**Answers:** 1. a. genotype refers to an organism's genetic makeup; phenotype refers to observable characteristics that result from genetic and environmental influences.
2. b. By rendering a single gene inactive, we can study that gene's effects on behavior.

## 3.5 How Does the Brain Change?

In a perfect illustration of how nurture can influence nature, the brain can reorganize itself based on which parts of it are used lightly and which are used heavily. In fact, despite the great precision and the specificity of its connections, the brain is extremely malleable. Over the course of development, throughout our constant stream of experience, and after injury, the brain continually changes. This property is known as **plasticity.**

Reptiles hatch from their leathery eggs ready to go; in contrast, human infants require lots of sleep and high-quality nutrition before they can function independently. As children's bodies grow and develop, their brains grow and develop, actively rewiring in major ways for many years. The brain's development follows set sequences. Different structures and abilities progress at different rates and mature at different points in life. In babies, for example, general vision develops before the ability to see depth. The prefrontal cortex is not anatomically fully mature until early adulthood. Each development is programmed in the genes. But even with these meticulously specified genetic instructions, environment plays a major role.

### Learning Objectives

- Explain how environmental factors and experience influence brain organization.
- Describe sex differences in brain structure and function.

**plasticity** A property of the brain that allows it to change as a result of experience, drugs, or injury.

## The Interplay of Genes and Environment Wires the Brain

Every life experience alters an individual brain's connections. In fact, gene expression is profoundly affected by environment. Which cells express which genes, and to what extent, depends to a large extent on environment. Through the constant interplay between nature and nurture, environment affects our DNA's activity and the products of that activity. Thus brain plasticity reflects the interactive nature of our biological and environmental influences.

**CELL IDENTITY BECOMES FIXED OVER TIME** In the developing embryo, each new cell receives signals, from its surroundings, that determine what type of cell it will become. If cells from one part of an embryo are surgically transplanted to another part, the transplant's success depends on how developed the cells' identity is. Tissue transplanted early enough completely transforms into whatever type is appropriate for its new location. As an embryo develops, each cell becomes more and more committed to its identity, so transplanting cells too late may disfigure the organism. Many people are therefore excited about the possibility of transplanting fetal cells. Because fetal cells are undeveloped enough to become any type of tissue, they might be used to cure diseases and even restore mobility to people who have lost some motor abilities. This work is in its infancy, so to speak, but it promises breakthroughs in how mental illness and other psychological conditions are treated. Neural cells transplanted early enough take on the identity appropriate to their new location, and the organism develops normally.

**EXPERIENCE FINE-TUNES NEURAL CONNECTIONS** Connections form between brain structures when growing axons are directed by certain chemicals that tell them where to go and where not to go. The major connections are established by chemical messengers, but the detailed connections are governed by experience. If a cat's eyes are sewn shut at birth, depriving the animal of visual input, the visual cortex fails to develop properly. If the sutures are removed weeks later, the cat is permanently blind, even though its eyes function normally. Adult cats that are similarly deprived do not lose their sight (Wiesel & Hubel, 1963). Evidently, ongoing activity is necessary in the visual pathways to refine the visual cortex enough for it to be useful. In general, such plasticity has *critical periods.* During these times, particular experiences must occur for development to proceed normally.

To study the effects of experience on development, researchers reared rats in two different laboratory environments. One group was raised in a normal environment for laboratory rats: featureless boxes with bedding at the bottom, plus dishes for food and water. The other group was raised in an enriched environment, with many interesting things to look at, puzzles to solve, obstacles to run, toys to play with, running wheels to exercise on, and even balance beams to hone athletic skills on. In the first environment, the rats suffered mental deprivation. The unused portions of their brains atrophied (failed to develop normally). In the second environment, the "luxury" items might simply have approximated rat life in the wild, allowing normal rat development. As a result, the second group developed bigger, heavier brains than the first group (Rosenzweig, Bennett, & Diamond, 1972). Thus experience is important for normal development and maybe even more so for superior development.

## Culture Affects the Brain

Our cultural experiences help shape how we view the world and how we think. As a result, cultural differences contribute to different patterns of brain activity.

For instance, cultures differ slightly in how they express emotions. As discussed further in Chapter 10, evidence indicates that people are better at identifying emotional expressions from members of their own cultures than from members of other cultures. This effect occurs in part, it seems, because people have more experience in interpreting emotional expressions among those with whom they interact regularly. If so, this greater recognition should mean that people's brain responses are enhanced when they are interpreting emotional expressions within their own cultural groups than from other cultural groups. A recent brain imaging study involved one group of participants in Japan and another group in the United States (Chiao et al., 2008). The researchers showed pictures of both neutral and fearful facial expressions portrayed by Japanese and American faces. As noted earlier in this chapter, the amygdala shows increased activity when people view fearful expressions. In this study, activity in the amygdala was greatest when participants viewed fearful expressions within their own cultural group. Thus cultural experience appears to fine-tune the brain's responses to such important environmental cues (**Figure 3.39**).

**FIGURE 3.39 Scientific Method: Chiao's Study of How Culture Affects the Brain**

**Hypothesis:** People are better at identifying emotional expressions from members of their own cultures than from members of other cultures.

**Research Method:**

1. Participants in Japan and the United States were shown pictures of both neutral expressions and fearful expressions portrayed by Japanese and American faces.

2. Participants' amygdala activity was measured using fMRI scans.

Left amygdala

% signal change (0–2.4); ■ Own culture ■ Other culture; Anger, Fear, Happy, Neutral

Right amygdala

% signal change (0–2.4); ■ Own culture ■ Other culture; Anger, Fear, Happy, Neutral

**Results:** Participants showed greatest amygdala activity in response to fear expressed by members of their own cultural group.

**Conclusion:** Cultural experience appears to fine-tune the brain's response to important environmental clues.

**Source:** Chiao, J. Y., Iidaka, T., Gordon, H. L., Nogawa, J., Bar, M., Aminoff, E., et al. (2008). Cultural specificity in amygdala response to fear faces. *Journal of Cognitive Neuroscience, 20(12)*, 2167–2174.

## The Brain Rewires Itself throughout Life

Brain plasticity decreases with age. Even into very old age, however, the brain can grow new connections among neurons and even grow new neurons. The rewiring and growth within the brain represents the biological basis of learning.

**CHANGE IN THE STRENGTH OF CONNECTIONS UNDERLIES LEARNING** In every moment of life, we gain memories: experiences and knowledge that are acquired instantaneously and may be recalled later, as well as habits that form gradually. All these memories are reflected in the brain's physical changes.

Psychologists widely accept that changes in the brain are most likely not in its larger wiring or general arrangement. The changes are mainly in the strength of existing connections. One possibility is that when two neurons fire simultaneously, the synaptic connection between them strengthens. The strengthened synaptic connection makes these neurons more likely to fire together in the future. Conversely, *not* firing simultaneously tends to weaken the connection between two neurons. This theory can be summarized by the catchphrase *Fire together, wire together.* First proposed in the 1940s, by the renowned psychologist Donald Hebb, it is consistent with a great deal of experimental evidence and many theoretical models. It accounts for both the "burning in" of an experience (a pattern of neural firing becomes more likely to recur, and its recurrence leads the mind to recall an event) and the ingraining of habits (repeating a behavior makes the repeater tend to perform that behavior automatically). Sometimes, entirely new connections grow between neurons. This new growth is a major factor in recovery from brain injury.

Until recently, scientists believed that adult brains produced no new brain cells. There is now evidence, however, that new neurons are produced in some brain regions (Eriksson et al., 1998). The production of new neurons is called *neurogenesis*. A fair amount of neurogenesis apparently occurs in the hippocampus. Recall from earlier in this chapter that memories are retained within (or at least require) the hippocampus initially. They eventually are transferred to the cortex, so the hippocampus is continuously overwritten. Perhaps, without disrupting memory, neurons in the hippocampus can be lost and replaced.

Elizabeth Gould and her colleagues have demonstrated that environmental conditions can play an important role in neurogenesis. For example, they have found that for rats, shrews, and marmosets, stressful experiences—such as being confronted by strange males in their home cages—interfere with neurogenesis during development and adulthood (Gould & Tanapat, 1999). When animals are housed together, they typically form dominance hierarchies that reflect social status. Dominant animals—those who possess the highest social status—show greater increases in new neurons than do subordinate animals (Kozorovitskiy & Gould, 2004). Thus social environment can strongly affect brain plasticity, a dynamic process we are only beginning to understand. Neurogenesis may underlie neural plasticity. If so, further research might enable us, through neurogenesis, to reverse the brain's natural loss of neurons and slow down age-based mental decline.

**synesthesia** Cross-sensory experience (e.g., a visual image has a taste).

**CHANGES IN THE BRAIN** The functions of portions of the cerebral cortex shift in response to their activity. Recall the somatosensory homunculus (see Figure 3.21a). As that representation makes clear, more cortical tissue is devoted to body parts that receive more sensation or are used more. Again, wiring in the brain is affected by amount of use. Another example of changes in cortical maps, discussed earlier, is the enlargement of hippocampi in experienced London taxi drivers.

Cortical reorganization can also have bizarre results. For example, an amputee can be afflicted with a *phantom limb,* the intense sensation that the amputated body part still exists. Some phantom limbs are experienced as moving normally, such as being used to gesture in conversation, whereas some are frozen in position. Moreover, a phantom limb often is accompanied by pain sensations, which may result from the misgrowth of the severed pain nerves at the stump. The cortex misinterprets the pain as coming from the place where those nerves originally came from. This phenomenon suggests that the brain has not reorganized in response to the injury and that the missing limb's cortical representation remains intact. The neurologist V. S. Ramachandran has discovered, however, that an amputee who has lost a hand may, when his or her eyes are closed, perceive a touch on the cheek as if it were on the missing hand (Ramachandran & Hirstein, 1998). Apparently, on the somatosensory homunculus the hand is represented next to the face. The unused part of the amputee's cortex (the part that would have responded to the now-missing limb) assumes to some degree the function of the closest group, representing the face. Somehow, the rest of the brain has not kept pace with the somatosensory area enough to figure out these neurons' new job, so the neurons are activated by a touch on the amputee's face (**Figure 3.40**).

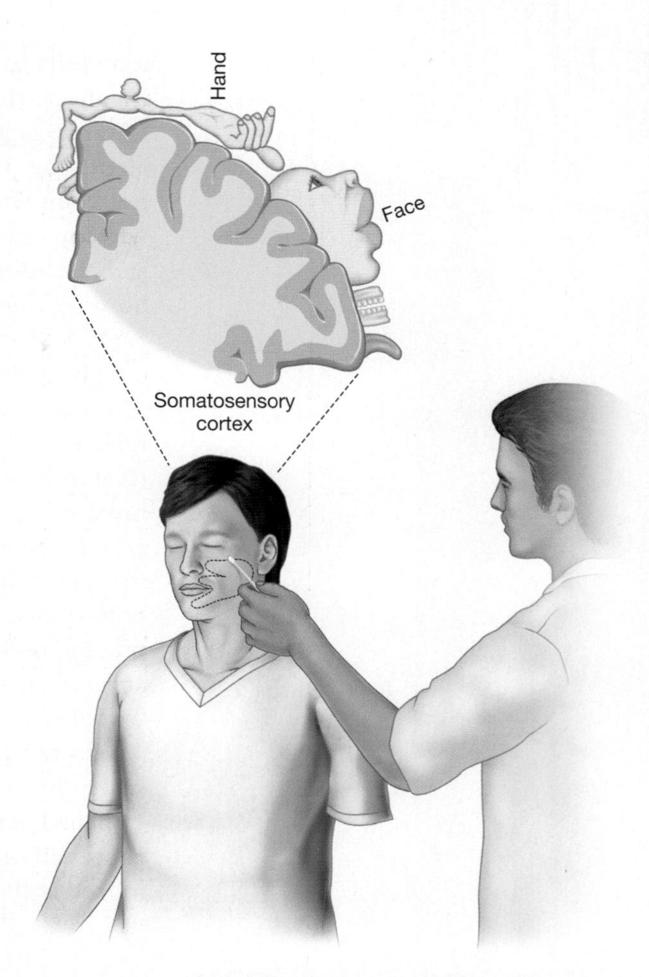


**FIGURE 3.40 Cortical Remapping Following Amputation** The participant felt a cotton swab touching his cheek as touching his missing hand. **What is the apparent reason for this effect?**

**THE PUZZLE OF SYNESTHESIA** People called *synesthetes* experience **synesthesia.** This kind of cross-sensory experience can take many forms. One man hates driving because the sight of road signs tastes to him like a mixture of pistachio ice cream and ear wax (McNeil, 2006). For another man, any personal name has a specific taste—for example, the name *John* tastes like cornbread (Simner et al., 2006). For yet another synesthete, each day of the week is colored (Monday is red, Tuesday is indigo), as is each month of the year (December is yellow, January is red; Ramachandran, 2003). For others, colors evoke smells, sights evoke sounds, and numbers come in colors (e.g., 5 is always red, 2 is always green; **Figure 3.41**). Such experiences are idiosyncratic. For one person, bread is always smooth in texture and silver in color, but for another person it sounds like a foghorn. For each person, the associations do not vary. If road signs have a taste, for example, they always taste the same.

Reports of people with synesthesia date as far back as ancient Greece (Ferry, 2002). Estimates of the percentage of the population that report these cross-sensory experiences range from 1 in 2,000 to 1 in 200. Since we cannot simply write these people off as "crazy," we need to understand their bizarre sensations.

Recent research into heredity and brain organization provides fascinating clues for understanding synesthesia. Because synesthesia tends to run in families,

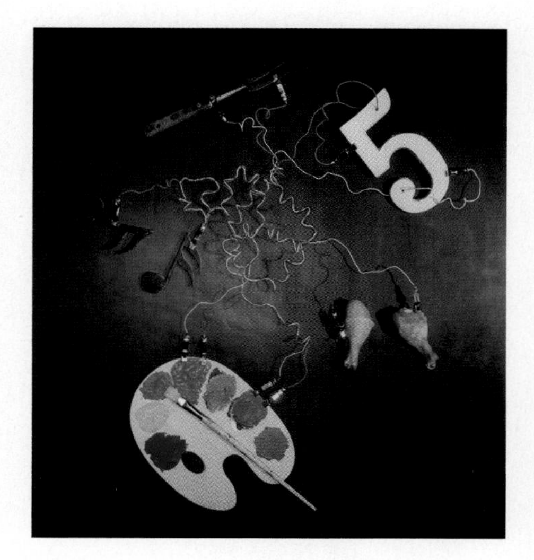


**FIGURE 3.41 Synesthesia** For synesthetes, sensory experiences are crossed. For example, colors may evoke smells, sights may evoke sounds, and numbers may come in colors.

it appears to have a genetic basis. Thus it may help us understand how heredity affects the way we experience the world. Even more provocatively, brain research suggests that cross-sensory experiences could be related to creativity. Could the mixture of colors, words, and images by artists be the result of "special brain wiring" that they inherited (Blakeslee, 2001)? Can synesthesia explain why we call some smells "sharp" and some colors "loud"? Questions like these, and the scientific research being used to answer them, are radically changing how we think about all human experience and behavior.

V. S. Ramachandran, the neurologist who conducted many of the studies on phantom limbs (discussed in the previous section), has also conducted a series of experiments to better understand what is happening when someone reports, for example, that a sound is lime green or that chicken tastes pointy (Ramachandran & Hubbard, 2001). Ramachandran inferred that the genes involved in synesthesia were related to brain formation. Because the brain area involved in seeing colors is physically close to the brain area involved in understanding numbers, he theorized that in people with color/number synesthesia, these two brain areas have some connections or cross-wiring. The process of linking these areas would have resembled the process of linking areas of an amputee's brain (again, discussed earlier): One portion of the brain would have adopted another portion's role.

To test his hypothesis, Ramachandran examined MRIs taken of synesthetes when they looked at black numbers on a white background. He found evidence of neural activity in the brain area responsible for color vision. Control participants without synesthesia did not experience activity in this brain area when they looked at the same numbers (**Figure 3.42**).

**FIGURE 3.42 Try for Yourself: Synesthesia Test**

Two stimuli used by Ramachandran and Hubbard (2003) to study synesthesia:

Look first at the square on the left, and as quickly as possible count the number of 2s.

Now do the same task with the square on the right.

**Explanation:** Unless you have synesthesia and it causes you to see particular numbers in particular colors, you were much faster at counting the 2s on the right. They "popped out" at you because they are a different color from the 5s. Some synesthetes are equally fast at both tasks because they see the numbers in different colors. This test is one of many used to determine if someone has color-related synesthesia.

CRITICAL THINKING SKILL

## Recognizing Unstated Assumptions

All human interactions are based partly on unstated assumptions. For example, the participants in a conversation assume the parties have some knowledge in common but that they do not all have the same knowledge. When you enter a classroom, you assume the instructor will act differently than the students. In writing this textbook, the authors explained information they assumed would be new for most readers, but they did not define words they assumed most readers would know.

When you are trying to understand a complex topic, begin by recognizing your assumptions about that topic. Also consider other people's assumptions. Once you make those assumptions explicit, you can apply reason to them.

Consider, for example, common assumptions about genetic influences and the brain. Many people assume that if a trait or tendency is passed along genetically, then those who inherit that trait or tendency cannot change it in themselves. By this thinking, those who inherit shyness, intelligence, or boldness cannot change how shy, intelligent, or bold they are.

When people learn about sex differences in the brain, they often assume that the brain does not change and that it "causes" sex differences in behaviors. In reality, the brain reflects genetic inheritance and experience, and together these variables determine the size, function, and structure of the brain.

In fact, because nature is inextricably intertwined with nurture, no biological effects can occur independent of environment. Just as all learning is influenced by assumptions, all choices are influenced by past learning and its influence on both thoughts and feelings.

There is one major difference between a phantom limb and synesthesia, however. The phantom limb is caused primarily by environment (the loss of the limb), whereas synesthesia appears to be caused primarily by genetics. Why has this sensory anomaly remained in the gene pool? Ramachandran suggests that it confers an adaptive advantage: Synesthetes' brains are wired to connect seemingly disparate topics, and the ability to make remote associations is an important part of creativity. As an example, Ramachandran and his collaborator E. M. Hubbard ask us to consider Shakespeare's line "It is the East and Juliet is the sun." The likening of Juliet to the sun is a metaphor, but where did it come from? Its association of a woman and a bright light resembles a synesthetic experience. In fact, these authors conclude that creative people experience a higher incidence of synesthesia than do noncreative people (2003).

### Females' and Males' Brains Are Similar and Different

The interplay of biological and environmental effects on the brain is reflected in the similarities and differences between females' and males' brains. Everything a person experiences alters his or her brain, of course, and females and males differ

in their life experiences and hormonal makeups. Hormonal differences might affect brain development, and thus they might influence the way males and females differ on some cognition tasks, such as on the ease with which they mentally rotate objects or recall parts of a story (Kimura, 1999).

Sex differences in anatomy are referred to as *sexual dimorphism*. The study of the brain's sexual dimorphism has a long history. Many comparisons of males' and females' brains, especially the earliest comparisons, were questionable scientifically and mostly used to show that female brains were inferior (for a review, see Halpern, 2000). The unstated assumption was always that if two groups (in this case, females and males) were different, one had to be inferior. But people do not have to be the same to be equal. In fact, there is evidence that men and women may perform a task, such as remembering a recent occurrence, equally well but by using different parts of the brain. For example, Richard Haier and colleagues (2005) have found that females and males may solve some complex problems, such as items on IQ tests, differently. Females show greater use of language-related brain regions, and males show greater use of spatial-related brain regions, even when participants are matched for intelligence.

Males generally have larger brains than females, but larger is not necessarily better. In fact, one developmental process in the brain involves disconnecting neurons so that only the most useful connections remain. Jay Giedd and his colleagues (1997) at the U.S. National Institutes of Health concluded that among both sexes, the sizes of brain structures are highly variable. They reported that boys' brains are approximately 9 percent larger than girls' brains, with some differences in the rate of maturation for different parts of the brain for girls and boys.

As discussed in Chapter 5, to some extent the brain's two hemispheres are lateralized: Each hemisphere is dominant for different cognitive functions. A considerable body of evidence says that females' brains are more bilaterally organized for language. In other words, the brain areas important in processing language are more likely to be found in both halves of females' brains. The equivalent language areas are more likely to be in only one hemisphere, usually the left, in males' brains (**Figure 3.43**). One source of data that supports

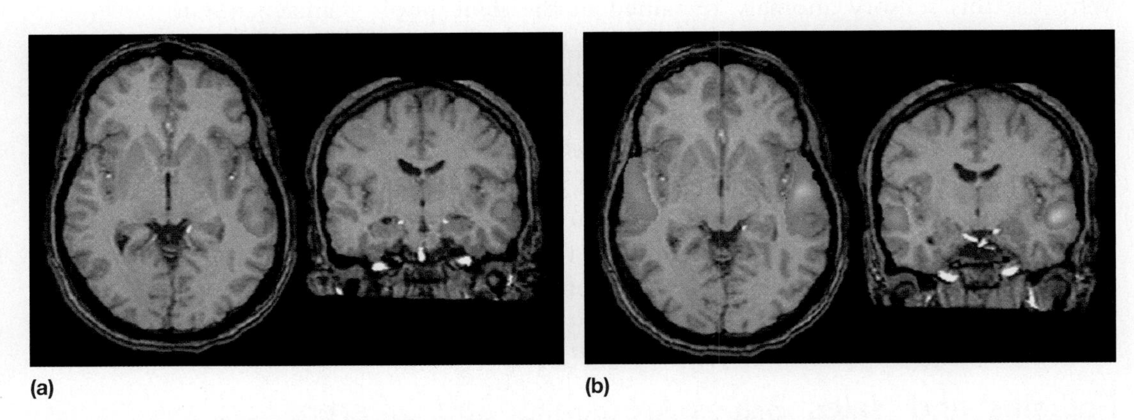


**FIGURE 3.43 Male versus Female Brains** A considerable body of evidence indicates that female brains are more bilaterally organized for language. For example, researchers studied men and women listening to someone reading aloud. As these fMRI images show, **(a)** the men listened with one side of their brains, whereas **(b)** the women tended to listen with both sides.

this distinction is people's experiences following strokes. Even when patients are matched on the location and severity of the brain damage caused by a stroke, women are less impaired in language use than men are (Jiang, Sheikh, & Bullock, 2006). A possible reason for women's better outcomes is that, because language is represented in both halves of women's brains, damage to half of a woman's brain will have less effect on that woman's ability to process language than it would if most of the language areas were in the damaged half of the brain. A related hypothesis, in accord with the idea that women's brains are more bilaterally organized, is that the halves of women's brains are connected by more neural fibers than men's are. Remember that a thick band of neurons, the corpus callosum, connects the brain's two halves (see Figure 3.20). Some researchers have found that a portion of this connective tissue is larger in women (Gur & Gur, 2004).

Before we can be confident about recent findings of sex differences in the brain, much more research is needed. We need to better understand normal, healthy brain development. We also need to better understand brain and behavior relationships before we can reason about human sex differences from our knowledge of brain structures (Halpern et al., 2007). Finally, although we tend to focus on the ways in which males and females are different, we need to keep in mind that their brains are similar in many (perhaps most) ways.

## The Brain Can Recover from Injury

Just as the brain reorganizes in response to amount of use, it also reorganizes in response to brain damage. Following an injury in the cortex, the surrounding gray matter assumes the function of the damaged area, like a local business scrambling to pick up the customers of a newly closed competitor. This remapping seems to begin immediately, and it continues for years. Such plasticity involves all levels of the central nervous system, from the cortex down to the spinal cord.

Reorganization is much more prevalent in children than in adults, in accord with the sensitive periods of normal development. Young children afflicted with severe and uncontrollable epilepsy that has paralyzed one or more limbs sometimes undergo *radical hemispherectomy,* the surgical removal of an entire cerebral hemisphere. The remaining hemisphere eventually takes on most of the lost hemisphere's functions, and the children regain almost complete use of their limbs. This procedure is not possible in adults. If it were performed on adults, the lack of neural reorganization in their brains would lead to permanent paralysis and loss of function.

As discussed earlier in this chapter, one of the most exciting areas of current neurological research is the transplantation of human fetal tissue into the brain to repair damage. The transplanted tissue consists specifically of *stem cells.* These "master" cells can regenerate themselves. They also can develop into any type of tissue, such as muscle or nerve cells. This relatively new procedure is being explored as a possible treatment for strokes and degenerative diseases such as Parkinson's and Huntington's. The significant challenge is to get the newly introduced cells to make the proper connections so that the damaged circuits regrow. Many people oppose the use of fetal tissue for any type of research, however, on religious or other philosophical grounds. Fortunately, many new methods are emerging that allow researchers to create stem cells by reprogramming adult cells (Kim et al., 2008).

## Summing Up

### How Does the Brain Change?

Experience affects the circuitry of the brain. During development and across the life span, the circuitry of the brain is constantly reworked in response to experience. Culture, as context for experience, affects brain activity. An understanding of the brain's organization and plasticity has allowed researchers to better understand conditions such as phantom limb syndrome and synesthesia. Although there are many similarities between the brains of females and males, research suggests that females' and males' brains differ in some ways. Males' brains are larger. Females' brains are organized more bilaterally. The brain can reorganize after a brain injury; however, children demonstrate greater reorganization following brain injury than adults.

## Measuring Up

1. A person's brain changes in response to environment, including all of that person's experiences. Place an X next to the statements below that support this idea.
   _____ a. The sizes of London taxi drivers' hippocampi were correlated with how long the participants had been London taxi drivers.
   _____ b. Some amputees can feel sensations in their amputated limbs when their eyes are closed and their faces are touched.
   _____ c. Many drugs can mimic neurotransmitters' actions.
   _____ d. Laboratory rats raised in enriched environments developed heavier brains than laboratory rats raised in standard environments.
   _____ e. Phineas Gage's personality changed profoundly after his frontal cortex was damaged.
   _____ f. Some brain responses to selected stimuli vary due to cultural influence.
2. Indicate whether the following statements, about the ways in which females' and males' brains differ, are true or false.
   _____ a. Males' brains generally are larger than females' brains.
   _____ b. Males' and females' brains have no differences.
   _____ c. Researchers have found that sex differences in the brain explain why males tend to hold executive positions more than females do.
   _____ d. Sex differences in the brain indicate that males and females have essentially different abilities.
   _____ e. A larger brain is a better brain—more advanced, plus more complex in its organization.

**Answers:** 1. Choices a, b, c, d, and f are all examples of environments's effect on the brain. Choice e is an extreme effect caused by a brain injury.
2. a. true; b. false; c. false; d. false; e. false.

Psychology: Knowledge You Can Use

# Will My Learning Disability Prevent Me from Succeeding in College?

Have you been diagnosed with a learning disability? Do you suspect you might have one?

According to the National Center for Learning Disabilities (2009), a learning disability is a "neurological disorder that affects the brain's ability to receive, process, store, and respond to information." According to the U.S. government (1990), a learning disability "substantially limits one or more major life activities." One of the most common learning disabilities is dyslexia, which involves difficulties in acquiring and processing language (**Figure 3.44**). Typically, a person with dyslexia has trouble reading, spelling, or writing. Someone who has difficulty spelling or writing might, alternatively, have the learning disability dysgraphia, a disorder of written expression.

Learning disabilities often become apparent in childhood, but some people first realize they have one in adulthood. These individuals might excel academically all the way through high school. They are able to mask or make up for their learning disabilities through intelligence and effort. What happens, though, when people with learning disabilities enter college? The new academic and organizational challenges of college might help reveal a person's learning disability. But that person is not therefore doomed to fail in college!

**FIGURE 3.44 An Inspiring Example** The celebrity chef Jamie Oliver suffers from dyslexia. His disability has hardly kept him from achieving his career goals. Here, in June 2010, Oliver is announcing Home Cooking Skills, a new and inspirational program he has cocreated to teach basic cooking skills to young people in England.

If you have a learning disability or suspect you have one, the first thing to do is get in touch with your campus's disability support services staff. Your campus may not have an entire office dedicated to disabilities. In that case, talk with a member of the Student Affairs staff (e.g., the dean of students, a director of residence life, or a mental health counselor on your campus). Someone at Student Affairs will be able to point you in the right direction. The earlier you contact the disability support office or Student Affairs, the sooner you will have access to the resources available on your campus. That way, you will be able to employ these resources if and when you need them (probably when the semester becomes most intense).

If your learning disability is verified, disability support office staff will work with you to determine the types of accommodations necessary to level the playing field for you. What does "level the playing field" mean? United States law requires colleges and universities to provide equal opportunity to the fruits of education for individuals with learning disabilities. Without accommodations of particular kinds, students with learning disabilities start off at a disadvantage.

Imagine if one football team had to play blindfolded while the opposing team was able to see perfectly. The "playing field" would be uneven, and thus the game would be unfair for the blindfolded team. While it is certainly *possible* to navigate college with a learning disability and with no formal support, it certainly is not fair. Students who go this route may not realize they have a learning disability or may feel that seeking the accommodations they are legally entitled to would be stigmatized by their peers, professors, and family. Thankfully, football players need not play blindfolded, and people with learning disabilities need not go through college wearing their own versions of blindfolds.

Given your particular strengths and weaknesses in processing information, some types of accommodations will be helpful, others will not. For example, a student with dyslexia might benefit from hearing exam questions read aloud. A student with dysgraphia might benefit from receiving notes from a classmate.

Disability support office staff will let your professors know you are entitled to a specific type of accommodation. Importantly, they will not tell your professors about the nature of your learning disability. They will simply note that you have a learning disability. For example, a disability support office staff member might send a note to your professors that reads "[Your name will go here], a student in your introductory psychology course, has provided evidence of a condition that requires academic accommodation. As a result, please provide [him or her] with time and a half on exams and on in-class writing assignments."

If you wish, you can also speak directly with individual professors about your learning disability and the kinds of resources likely to help you. Linda Tessler, a psychologist who works with persons with learning disabilities, writes:

> It must be clear that you are not asking for standards to be lowered. You are using tools to help you perform. To pass, you must perform the task that your classmates perform. You may, however, need to get there in a different way. Dyslexic students have to read the textbook just as nondyslexic students do. They may just do it differently through the use of books on tape. (Tessler, 1997)

Will a learning disability prevent you from succeeding in college? Not if you can help it, and you can help it by advocating for yourself. Line up the resources you need to ensure that you are able to reap the rewards of college.

# StudySpace: Your Place for a Better Grade

**Visit StudySpace to access free review materials, such as:**

- complete study outlines
- vocabulary flashcards of all key terms
- additional chapter review quizzes

## Chapter Summary

### 3.1 How Does the Nervous System Operate?

- **Neurons Are Specialized for Communication:** Neurons are the basic building blocks of the nervous system. They receive and send chemical messages. All neurons have the same basic structure, but neurons vary by function and by location in the nervous system.
- **Action Potentials Cause Neural Communication:** Changes in a neuron's electrical charge are the basis of an action potential, or neural firing. Firing is the means of communication within networks of neurons.
- **Neurotransmitters Bind to Receptors across the Synapse:** Neurons do not touch; they release chemicals (neurotransmitters) into the synaptic cleft, a small gap between the neurons. Neurotransmitters bind with the receptors of postsynaptic neurons, thus changing the charge in those neurons. Neurotransmitters' effects are halted by reuptake of the neurotransmitters into the presynaptic neurons, by enzyme deactivation, or by autoreception.
- **Neurotransmitters Influence Mental Activity and Behavior:** Neurotransmitters have been identified that influence aspects of the mind and behavior in humans. For example, neurotransmitters influence emotions, motor skills, sleep, dreaming, learning and memory, arousal, pain control, and pain perception. Drugs and toxins can enhance or inhibit the activity of neurotransmitters by affecting their synthesis, their release, and the termination of their action in the synaptic cleft.

### 3.2 What Are the Basic Brain Structures and Their Functions?

- **The Brain Stem Houses the Basic Programs of Survival:** The top of the spinal cord forms the brain stem, which is involved in basic functions such as breathing and swallowing. The brain stem contains the reticular formation, a network of neurons that influences general alertness and sleep.
- **The Cerebellum Is Essential for Movement:** The cerebellum ("little brain"), the bulging structure connected to the back of the brain stem, is essential for movement and controls balance.
- **Subcortical Structures Control Emotions and Appetitive Behaviors:** The subcortical structures play a key part in psychological functions because they control vital functions (the hypothalamus), sensory relay (the thalamus), memories (the hippocampus), emotions (the amygdala), and the planning and producing of movement (the basal ganglia).
- **The Cerebral Cortex Underlies Complex Mental Activity:** The lobes of the cortex play specific roles in vision (occipital), touch (parietal), hearing and speech comprehension (temporal), and movement, rational activity, social behavior, and personality (frontal).

### 3.3 How Does the Brain Communicate with the Body?

- **The Peripheral Nervous System Includes the Somatic and Autonomic Systems:** The somatic system transmits sensory signals and motor signals between the central nervous system and the skin, muscles, and joints. The autonomic system regulates the body's internal environment through the sympathetic division, which responds to alarm, and the parasympathetic division, which returns the body to its resting state.
- **The Endocrine System Communicates through Hormones:** Endocrine glands produce and release chemical substances. These substances travel to body tissues through the bloodstream and influence a variety of processes, including sexual behavior.
- **Actions of the Nervous System and Endocrine System Are Coordinated:** The endocrine system is largely controlled through the actions of the hypothalamus and the pituitary gland. The hypothalamus controls the release of hormones from the pituitary gland. The pituitary gland controls the release of hormones from other endocrine glands in the body.

### 3.4 What Is the Genetic Basis of Psychological Science?

- **All of Human Development Has a Genetic Basis:** Human behavior is influenced by genes. Through genes, people inherit both physical attributes and personality traits from their parents. Chromosomes are made of genes, and the Human Genome Project has mapped the genes that make up humans' 23 chromosomal pairs.
- **Heredity Involves Passing Along Genes through Reproduction:** Genes may be dominant or recessive. An organism's genetic constitution is referred to as its genotype. The organism's observable characteristics are referred to as its phenotype. Many characteristics are polygenic.
- **Genotypic Variation Is Created by Sexual Reproduction:** An offspring receives half of its chromosomes from its mother and half of its chromosomes from its father. Because so many combinations of the 23 pairs of chromosomes are possible, there is tremendous genetic variation in the human species. Mutations resulting from errors in cell division also give rise to genetic variation.
- **Genes Affect Behavior:** Behavioral geneticists examine how genes and environment interact to influence psychological activity and behavior. Twin studies and research on adoptees provide insight into heritability.
- **Social and Environmental Contexts Influence Genetic Expression:** Genes and social contexts interact in ways that influence our observable characteristics.

- **Genetic Expression Can Be Modified:** Genetic manipulation has been achieved in mammals such as mice. Animal studies using the technique of "knocking out" genes to determine their effects on behavior and on disease are a valuable tool for understanding genetic influences.

### 3.5 How Does the Brain Change?

- **The Interplay of Genes and Environment Wires the Brain:** Chemical signals influence cell growth and cell function. Environmental experiences, particularly during critical periods, influence cell development and neural connections.
- **Culture Affects the Brain:** The influence of experience on brain development is reflected in the different patterns of brain activity of people from different cultures.
- **The Brain Rewires Itself throughout Life:** Although plasticity decreases with age, the brain retains the ability to rewire itself throughout life. This ability is the biological basis of learning. Anomalies in sensation and in perception, such as synesthesia, are attributed to the cross-wiring of connections in the brain.
- **Females' and Males' Brains Are Similar and Different:** Females' and males' brains are more similar than different. They are different, however: Males' brains are larger than females' (on average), and females' verbal abilities are organized more bilaterally (more equally in both hemispheres).
- **The Brain Can Recover from Injury:** The brain can reorganize its functions in response to brain damage, although this capacity decreases with age.

## Key Terms

acetylcholine (ACh), p. 84
action potential, p. 79
agonists, p. 82
all-or-none principle, p. 80
amygdala, p. 92
antagonists, p. 82
autonomic nervous system (ANS), p. 98
axon, p. 77
basal ganglia, p. 92
brain stem, p. 90
Broca's area, p. 89
cell body, p. 77
central nervous system (CNS), p. 75
cerebellum, p. 90
cerebral cortex, p. 93
chromosomes, p. 105
dendrites, p. 77
dizygotic twins, p. 111
dominant gene, p. 107
dopamine, p. 84
endocrine system, p. 100
endorphins, p. 86
epinephrine, p. 84
frontal lobes, p. 94
GABA, p. 85
genes, p. 105
genotype, p. 107
glutamate, p. 86
gonads, p. 101
heritability, p. 113
hippocampus, p. 91
hormones, p. 101
hypothalamus, p. 91
interneurons, p. 76
monozygotic twins, p. 111
motor neurons, p. 76
myelin sheath, p. 77
neurons, p. 75
neurotransmitters, p. 80
nodes of Ranvier, p. 77
norepinephrine, p. 84
occipital lobes, p. 93
parasympathetic division, p. 99
parietal lobes, p. 94
peripheral nervous system (PNS), p. 75
phenotype, p. 107
pituitary gland, p. 102
plasticity, p. 117
prefrontal cortex, p. 94
receptors, p. 81
recessive gene, p. 107
resting membrane potential, p. 77
reuptake, p. 82
sensory neurons, p. 76
serotonin, p. 84
somatic nervous system, p. 98
substance P, p. 86
sympathetic division, p. 99
synapse, p. 77
synaptic cleft, p. 77
synesthesia, p. 121
temporal lobes, p. 94
terminal buttons, p. 77
thalamus, p. 91

## Practice Test

1. Complete the following analogy: Genes are to chromosomes as ______ are to ______.
   a. recipes, ingredients
   b. seeds, vegetables
   c. bricks, walls
   d. feet, shoes
2. Which of the following statements are true regarding the relationship between genetic makeup and environment?
   a. Environmental factors can influence gene expression.
   b. The presence of certain genes can influence an organism's susceptibility to environmental stressors.
   c. Genes and environment can interact to affect phenotype.
3. Which *two* labels accurately describe neurons that detect information from the physical world and pass that information along to the brain?
   a. motor neuron
   b. sensory neuron
   c. interneuron
   d. efferent neuron
   e. afferent neuron
4. Who do you predict would have a larger hippocampus?
   a. someone who plays computer games requiring the exploration of complex virtual worlds
   b. someone who plays computer games requiring extraordinarily quick reflexes and body awareness

The answer key for the Practice Tests can be found at the back of the book. It also includes answers to the green caption questions.

# 4

# Sensation and Perception

WHEN HELEN KELLER WAS 19 MONTHS OLD, she completely lost the senses of sight and hearing. Her life became dark and silent, and for her the world existed only through touch, smell, and taste. She recognized her parents, and determined her location, through touch and through smell. But otherwise she was completely isolated in a mental prison. Realizing that others could communicate but she could not, she became so enraged and frustrated that she threw daily tantrums. She later wrote, "Sometimes, I stood between two persons who were conversing and touched their lips. I could not understand, and was vexed. I moved my lips and gesticulated frantically without result. This made me so angry at times that I kicked and screamed until I was exhausted" (quoted by Diane Schuur in *Time* magazine, June 14, 1999).

When Keller was 6 years old, her parents sought assistance from Alexander Graham Bell. Bell was the inventor of devices such as the telephone, and he also taught a system called "Visible Speech" to

**FIGURE 4.1 Keller and Sullivan** Eight-year-old Helen Keller **(left)** sits with her teacher, Anne Sullivan, in Cape Cod in 1888.

to deaf children. He put the Kellers in touch with the Perkins School for the Blind, in Watertown, Massachusetts. Through the school, the Kellers hired a teacher, Anne Sullivan, to teach Helen to communicate through signs (**Figure 4.1**). At first, Helen simply mimicked Sullivan's strange hand motions, making no sense. One day, Sullivan ran water over one of Helen's hands while spelling *w-a-t-e-r* in the other, and Helen made the connection. She grabbed some dirt and asked Sullivan to spell its name. By evening, Helen had memorized her first 30 words in sign language. She had begun a life of both passionate learning and social activism.

What would your life be like if you could not see or hear? What would it be like if you were not only blind and deaf but also unable to smell, taste, and feel pain or temperature? You would still feel hunger and other bodily sensations, such as being tired, but you would have no way of knowing about other people or an environment outside your body. No one could communicate with you, and you could communicate with no one. What would you do without sensation, your windows to the world? How would you do anything if you lacked perception, your ability to make sense of your sensory experiences? ■

**Learning Objectives**

- Distinguish between sensation and perception.
- Describe the process of transduction.
- Distinguish between an absolute threshold and a difference threshold.
- Discuss sensory detection theory.
- Define sensory adaptation.

## 4.1 How Do We Sense Our Worlds?

Psychologists often divide the way we experience the world into two distinct phases: *sensation* and *perception*. **Sensation** is our sense organs' detection of external stimulus energy, such as light, air vibrations, and odors. It is also our sense organs' responses to the external stimulus energy and the transmission of those responses to the brain. Sensation is an elementary experience, such as color or motion, without the more complex perceptual experience of what is being seen or what is moving. **Perception** is the brain's further processing of these detected signals. It results in internal representations of the stimuli, representations that form a conscious experience of the world. Whereas the essence of sensation is detection, the essence of perception is construction of useful and meaningful information about a particular environment.

Say that you drive up to a traffic signal as the light turns green. The light emits its particular photons. Those photons are detected by specialized neurons in your eyes, and those neurons transmit signals to your brain. As a result of these steps, you have sensed the energy (photons). When the brain processes the resulting neural signals, you experience the green light and register the meaning of that signal. As a result of these additional steps, you have perceived the light and the signal. (The basic movement from sensation to perception is depicted in **Figure 4.2.**)

This chapter will discuss how the sense organs detect various types of stimulus energy, how the brain constructs useful information about the world on the basis of what has been detected, and how we use this constructed information to guide ourselves through the world around us. An important lesson in this chapter is that our sensation and perception of the world do not work like a camera or digital recorder, faithfully and passively capturing the physical properties of stimuli we encounter. Rather, what we *sense* (what we see, hear, taste, touch, or smell) is the result of how we *perceive*. Brain processes actively construct perceptual experiences from sensory experiences.

**sensation** The sense organs' detection of external stimuli, their responses to the stimuli, and the transmission of these responses to the brain.

**perception** The processing, organization, and interpretation of sensory signals; it results in an internal representation of the stimulus.

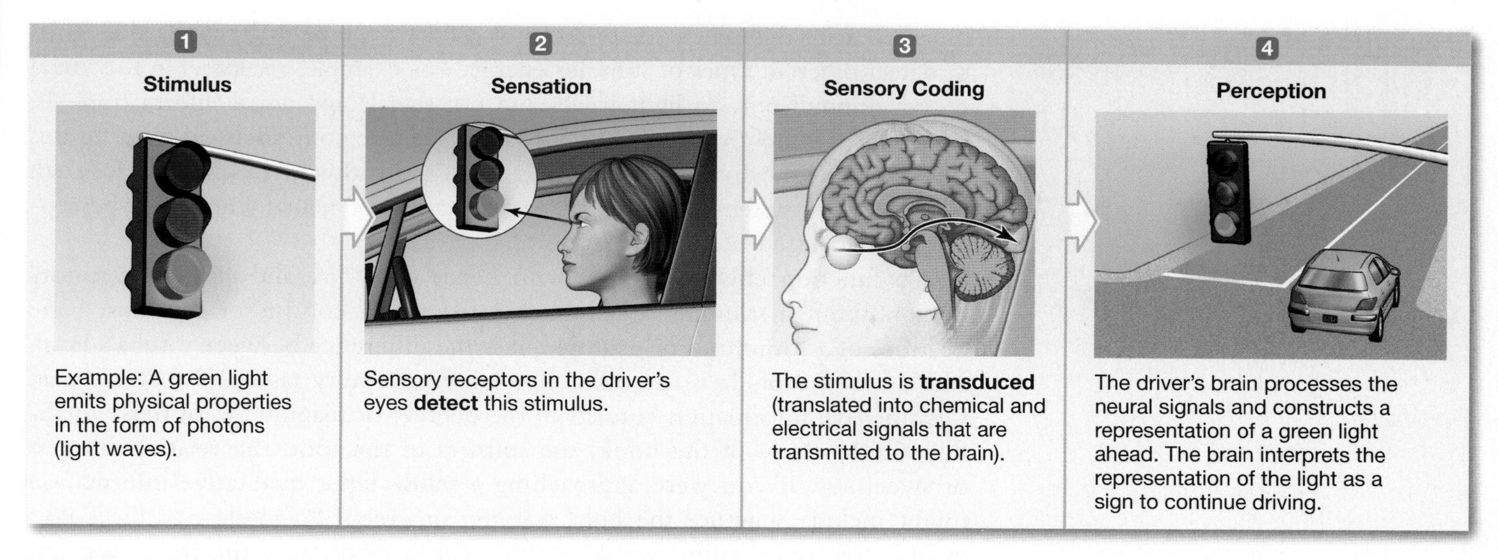


**FIGURE 4.2 From Sensation to Perception**

This constant conversion of sensation to perception allows us to adapt to the details of our environments. But sometimes our sensory systems can get the details wrong. For example, they sometimes fill in information that an environment has not provided. Even when sensory systems do something like fill in information, they do so in an intelligent and efficient way that produces a meaningful understanding of what is and what happens. Perception is often based on our prior experiences, which shape our expectations about new sensory experiences. For example, you are unlikely to see a blue, apple-shaped object as a real apple because you know from past experience that apples are not blue. Because of the different adaptive challenges that humans and the various nonhuman animals have faced, humans are sensitive to different types of physical energy than nonhuman animals are. This chapter focuses on sensation and perception as they operate in humans.

## Stimuli Must Be Coded to Be Understood by the Brain

Our sensory organs translate the physical properties of stimuli into patterns of neural impulses. This process is called *sensory coding*. The different features of the physical environment are coded by patterns of impulses in different neurons. Thus a green stoplight will be coded by a particular neural response pattern in the eye's retina before being read by other areas of the brain. (Technically, the retina is part of the brain. This point is discussed further in the section "In Vision, the Eye Detects Light Waves," later in this chapter.)

When a hand touches a hot skillet, neurons in the hand and in the brain will signal pain. The brain cannot process the physical stimuli directly, so the stimuli must be translated into chemical and electrical signals the brain can interpret. The translation of stimuli is called **transduction.** Through this process, specialized cells in the sense organs, called *sensory receptors,* receive physical or chemical stimulation and pass the resulting impulses to connecting neurons. Connecting neurons then transmit information to the brain in the form of neural impulses. Most sensory information first goes to the thalamus, a structure in the middle of the brain. Neurons in the thalamus then send information to the cortex, where incoming neural impulses are interpreted as sight, smell, sound, touch, or taste. Each sense

**transduction** A process by which sensory receptors produce neural impulses when they receive physical or chemical stimulation.

organ contains different types of receptor cells. Each type of receptor is designed to detect different types of stimulus energy. For example, receptors in the visual system respond only to light waves and can signal only visual information. (In Chapter 3, Figures 3.18 and 3.19 depict the brain regions discussed here. In this chapter, **Table 4.1** lists the stimuli, receptors, and pathways to the brain for each major sensory system. The brain's interpretation of neural impulses—perception—is discussed later in this chapter.)

To function effectively, the brain needs *qualitative* and *quantitative* information about a stimulus. Qualitative information consists of the most basic qualities of a stimulus. For example, it is the difference between a tuba's honk and a flute's toot. It is the difference between a salty taste and a sweet one. Quantitative information consists of the degree, or magnitude, of those qualities: the loudness of the honk, the softness of the toot, the relative saltiness or sweetness. If you were approaching a traffic light, qualitative information might include whether the light was red or green. Regardless of the color, quantitative information would include the brightness of the light. We can identify qualitative differences because different sensory receptors respond to qualitatively different stimuli. In contrast, quantitative differences in stimuli are coded by the rate of a particular neuron's firing. A more rapidly firing neuron is responding at a higher frequency to a more intense stimulus, such as a brighter light, a louder sound, or a heavier weight (**Figure 4.3**).

Sensory receptors—except, possibly, those involved in smell—provide *coarse coding*. The coding is called coarse because sensory qualities are coded by only a few different types of receptors. Each type of receptor responds to a broad range of stimuli. The combined responses by different receptors firing at different rates enable us to tell the difference between stimuli—between, for example, lime green and forest green or between a pinch on the arm and a shove. Sensation and perception result from a symphony of sensory receptors and the neurons those receptors communicate with. The receptors and neurons fire in different combinations and at different rates. As discussed in Chapter 5, the sum of this activity is consciousness, the huge range of perceptions that make up our experience of the world.

**TABLE 4.1 The Stimuli, Receptors, and Pathways for Each Sense**

| Sense | Stimuli | Receptors | Pathways to the Brain |
|---|---|---|---|
| Taste | Molecules dissolved in fluid on the tongue | Cells in taste buds on the tongue | Portions of facial, glossopharyngeal, and vagus nerves |
| Smell | Molecules dissolved in fluid on mucous membranes in the nose | Sensitive ends of olfactory neurons in the mucous membranes | Olfactory nerve |
| Touch | Pressure on the skin | Sensitive ends of touch neurons in skin | Cranial nerves for touch above the neck, spinal nerves for touch elsewhere |
| Hearing | Sound waves | Pressure-sensitive hair cells in cochlea of inner ear | Auditory nerve |
| Vision | Light waves | Light-sensitive rods and cones in retina of eye | Optic nerve |

**Qualitative Information**
Sensory receptors respond to qualitative differences by firing in different combinations.

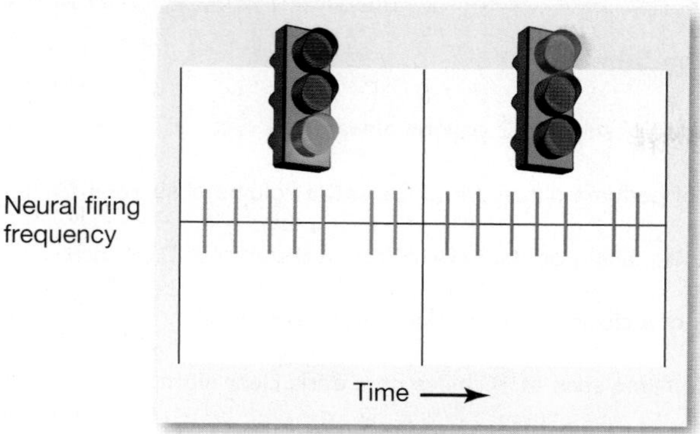


A green light is coded by different receptors than a red light.

**Quantitative Information**
Sensory receptors respond to quantitative differences by firing at different rates.

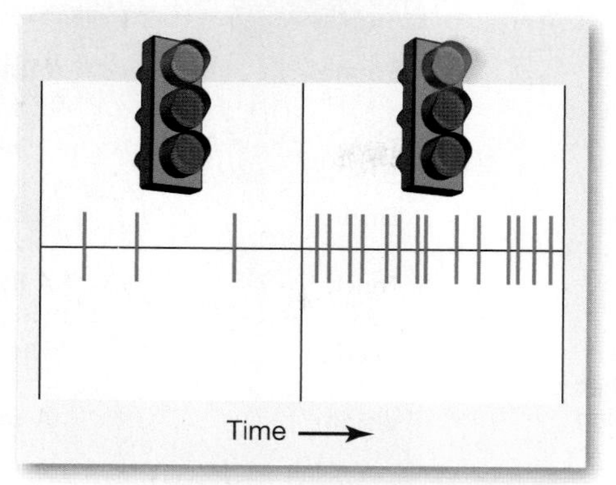


A bright light causes receptors to fire more rapidly (at a higher frequency) than a dim light.

**FIGURE 4.3 Qualitative versus Quantitative Sensory Information**

## Psychophysics Measures the Relationship between Stimuli and Perception

We have long understood that perceptual experience is constructed from information detected by the sense organs. For more than a century, psychologists have tried to understand the relationship between the world's physical properties and how we sense and perceive them. *Psychophysics,* a subfield developed during the nineteenth century by the researchers Ernst Weber and Gustav Fechner, examines our psychological experiences of physical stimuli. For example, how much physical energy is required for our sense organs to detect a stimulus? How much change is required before we notice that change? To test such things, researchers present very subtle changes in stimuli and observe how participants respond. They study the limits of humans' sensory systems.

SENSORY THRESHOLDS Your sensory organs constantly acquire information from your environment. You do not notice much of this information. The *absolute threshold* is the minimum intensity of stimulation that must occur before you experience a sensation. In other words, it is the stimulus intensity you would detect more often than by chance. The absolute threshold for hearing is the faintest sound a person can detect 50 percent of the time (**Figure 4.4**). For instance, how loudly must someone in the next room whisper for you to hear it? In this case, the absolute threshold for auditory stimuli would be the quietest whisper you could hear half the time. (**Table 4.2** lists some approximate minimum stimuli for each sense.)

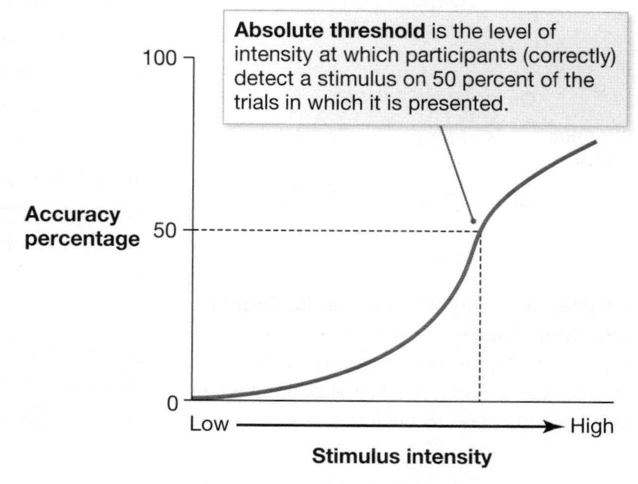


**FIGURE 4.4 Absolute Threshold**

A *difference threshold* is the just noticeable difference between two stimuli. In other words, it is the minimum amount of change required for a person to detect a difference. If your friend is watching a television show while you are reading and a commercial comes on that is louder than the show, you might look up, noticing that something has changed. The difference threshold is the minimum change in volume, the minimum quantitative change, required for you to detect a difference.

| TABLE 4.2 Approximate Absolute Sensory Threshold (Minimum Stimulus) for Each Sense | |
|---|---|
| **Sense** | **Minimum Stimulus** |
| Taste | 1 teaspoon of sugar in 2 gallons of water |
| Smell | 1 drop of perfume diffused into the entire volume of six rooms |
| Touch | A fly's wing falling on your cheek from a distance of 0.04 inch |
| Hearing | The tick of a clock at 20 feet under quiet conditions |
| Vision | A candle flame seen at 30 miles on a dark, clear night |

SOURCE: Galanter, 1962.

There are four possible outcomes when a participant is asked whether something occurred during a trial:

| Stimulus signal | Response given: Yes | Response given: No |
|---|---|---|
| On | Hit | Miss |
| Off | False alarm | Correct rejection |

Those who are biased toward reporting a signal tend to be "yea-sayers":

| Stimulus signal | Response given: Yes | Response given: No |
|---|---|---|
| On | 89% | 11% |
| Off | 41% | 59% |

Those who are biased toward denying that a signal occurred tend to be "nay-sayers":

| Stimulus signal | Response given: Yes | Response given: No |
|---|---|---|
| On | 45% | 55% |
| Off | 26% | 74% |

**FIGURE 4.5 Payoff Matrices for Signal Detection Theory** Note that the percentages in this figure were invented to show representative numbers. Actual percentages vary from question to question.

The difference threshold increases as the stimulus becomes more intense. Pick up a 1-ounce letter and a 2-ounce letter, and you will easily detect the difference. But pick up a 5-pound package and a package that weighs 1 ounce more, and the difference will be harder, maybe impossible, to discern. The principle at work here is called *Weber's law.* This law states that the just noticeable difference between two stimuli is based on a proportion of the original stimulus rather than on a fixed amount of difference. That is, the more intense the stimulus, the bigger the change needed for you to notice.

**SIGNAL DETECTION THEORY** Classical psychophysics was based on the idea of a sensory threshold. That is, either you saw something or you did not. Your detection depended on whether the intensity of the stimulus was above or below the sensory threshold. As research progressed, however, it became clear that early psychophysicists had ignored an important variable: human judgment.

Imagine you are a participant in a study of sensory thresholds. You are sitting in a dark room, and an experimenter asks if you detect a faint light, hear a faint sound, or feel a very light touch on your arm. You might fail to detect a weak stimulus that is presented. Even if you do not detect this stimulus, you might ask yourself if you do or if you should, since someone has asked about it. You might even convince yourself you had sensed a weak stimulus that had not been presented. After realizing that their methods of testing absolute thresholds were flawed, researchers formulated **signal detection theory (SDT).** This theory states that detecting a stimulus requires making a judgment about its presence or absence, based on a subjective interpretation of ambiguous information (Green & Swets, 1966).

For example, SDT applies to the work of radiologists, who scan medical images to detect early signs of disease. A radiologist might be looking for the kind of faint shadow that signals an early-stage cancer and have difficulty judging whether an abnormality in the image is likely cancerous. The radiologist's knowledge of the patient (e.g., age, sex, family medical history) will likely affect this judgment. So, of course, will factors such as the radiologist's training, experience, motivation, and attention. Moreover, the knowledge of the consequences can influence a radiologist's judgment. Being wrong could mean missing a fatal cancer or, conversely, causing unnecessary and potentially dangerous treatment.

Any research study on signal detection involves a series of trials in which a stimulus is presented in only some trials. In each trial, the participant must state whether he or she sensed the stimulus. A trial of this kind, in which a participant judges whether an event occurs, can have one of four outcomes. If the signal is presented and the participant detects it, the outcome is a *hit*. If the participant fails to detect the signal, the outcome is a *miss*. If the participant "detects" a signal that was not presented, the outcome is a *false alarm*. If the signal is not presented and the participant does not detect it, the outcome is a *correct rejection* (**Figure 4.5**). The participant's sensitivity to the signal is usually computed by comparing the hit rate with the false alarm rate. This comparison corrects for any bias the participant might bring to the testing situation.

*Response bias* refers to a participant's tendency to report detecting the signal in an ambiguous trial. The participant might be strongly biased against responding and need a great deal of evidence that the signal is present. Under other conditions, that same participant might need only a small amount of evidence.

The context of a judgment made outside the research lab will affect the person's judgment (see "Critical Thinking Skill: Recognizing the Effects of Context on Judgments," p. 138). A radiologist checking a CAT scan for signs of a brain tumor might be extra cautious about accepting any abnormality as a signal (i.e., a tumor), since a positive response could lead to drastic and dangerous neurosurgery. A doctor checking an X-ray for signs of a broken bone might be more willing to make a positive diagnosis, since treatment, although uncomfortable, will most likely not endanger the life of the patient. People's expectations often influence the extent to which they are biased. For instance, a soldier expecting an imminent attack will likely err on the side of responding, such as by mistaking a dim shape as an enemy when in fact no one is there. The important point is that personal beliefs and expectations, as well as the situation, influence how a person experiences sensations from the environment.

**signal detection theory (SDT)** A theory of perception based on the idea that the detection of a faint stimulus requires a judgment—it is not an all-or-none process.

**sensory adaptation** A decrease in sensitivity to a constant level of stimulation.

SENSORY ADAPTATION Our sensory systems are tuned to detect changes in our surroundings. It is important for us to be able to detect such changes because they might require responses. It is less critical to keep responding to unchanging stimuli. **Sensory adaptation** is a decrease in sensitivity to a constant level of stimulation (**Figure 4.6**).

Imagine you are studying and work begins at a nearby construction site. When the equipment starts up, the sound seems particularly loud and disturbing. After a few minutes, however, the noise seems to have faded into the background. Researchers have often noticed that if a stimulus is presented continuously, the responses of the sensory systems that detect it tend to diminish over time. Similarly, when a continuous stimulus stops, the sensory systems usually respond strongly as well. If the construction noise suddenly halted, you would likely notice the silence.

**FIGURE 4.6 Sensory Adaptation** Because of sensory adaptation, people who live near constant noise eventually become less aware of the noise. Pictured here are homes near Heathrow Airport, in London. **If jets were flying this close over your home, how long do you think it would take for you to adjust? What other kinds of constant stimulation must people adjust to?**

CRITICAL THINKING SKILL

## Recognizing the Effects of Context on Judgments

Are you smart? Are you beautiful? Are you good in math? If you make such a judgment, to what or to whom would you be comparing yourself? Any judgment you make about yourself will depend on the context. Likewise, any judgment you make *about anything* will be affected to a large extent by the specific situation in which you make that judgment.

Imagine sitting in a windowless room illuminated with one small candle. If you light a second candle, the room will appear much brighter. Now imagine sitting in a room lit brightly by several 200-watt lightbulbs. If you light a small candle here, the room's brightness might not differ perceptually, as would be predicted by Weber's law (described earlier). In an analogous way, the subtle effects of context within a situation can become obvious when that situation is viewed from afar or later or in the abstract (**Figure 4.7**).

**FIGURE 4.7 Context Matters** If you had seen just the detail, would you have guessed the bigger picture? The girl turns out to be crying because she is at a Justin Bieber performance.

The effects of context extend beyond immediate sensations and perceptions and across a wide range of events. For example, people generally define their own social and physical characteristics by comparing themselves with others (Alicke, LoSchiavo, Zerbst, & Zhang, 1997). We often make such comparisons automatically and usually without being conscious that we are relying on some comparator (i.e., some basis for comparison).

Often without realizing they are doing it, many people compare themselves with the highly attractive and ultrathin models in advertising. Since the viewers cannot match the perfect, often digitally manipulated images they encounter, they experience negative feelings (Bower, 2001). If the viewers are prone to making immediate comparisons, their moods become more negative, and they feel more dissatisfied with their own bodies (Tiggermann & McGill, 2004). One study found that when male and female college students viewed beautiful models, they rated photos of average-looking people as less attractive than did a similar group of college students who did not see the models' photos (Kenrick, Montello, Gutierres, & Trost, 1993).

Research has shown that we do not completely control comparisons we make unconsciously. Gilbert, Giesler, and Morris (1995) have found, however, that we can control comparisons by either avoiding some encounters or rejecting conclusions we have come to in the past. Thus people prone to feeling bad about themselves after seeing advertisements with seemingly perfect models could stop reading magazines that carry such advertisements, or they could continue to read the magazines but remind themselves that these models set unattainable standards that do not apply to real people. In other words, people can define themselves as students, writers, scientists, artists, athletes, parents, or whatever else they choose. They can choose to reject fashion models as their standards for comparison. And understanding the basis for any comparison is the key to making a sound judgment related to that comparison.

## Summing Up

### How Do We Sense Our Worlds?

The study of sensation focuses on the ways our sense organs detect and respond to external stimulus energy. When sensory receptors receive physical or chemical stimulation, the stimuli are converted to neural impulses through transduction. Transduction allows the brain to perceive sensory stimuli. Sensory coding for the qualitative aspects of a stimulus, such as color and bitterness, depends on the combination of receptors activated by the stimulus. Sensory coding for the quantitative aspects of a stimulus, such as intensity and loudness, depends on the number of neurons that fire and the frequency with which they fire. Psychophysics enables scientists to study psychological reactions to physical events. Psychophysical methods can be used to determine thresholds for detecting stimuli and noticing change. These thresholds can be influenced by human judgment and situational factors. Sensory systems are most responsive to changes in stimulation. When exposed to constant stimulation, the responses of sensory systems diminish over time.

## Measuring Up

1. Suppose you are designing an experiment to determine the absolute threshold for detecting a salty taste. You plan to give participants plain water that _______________.
   a. always has a small amount of salt in it
   b. sometimes has a small amount of salt in it and sometimes has no salt

   You plan to have them sip a small amount of water and tell you _______________.
   a. whether they taste salt or no salt
   b. how much salt is in each sip from different glasses of water

   You will use the participants' responses to calculate an absolute threshold for tasting salt by _______________.
   a. comparing hits and false alarms
   b. calculating the amount of salt used in each sip of water

2. What is Weber's law?
   a. When participants are unsure whether they can detect a stimulus, they will guess about it.
   b. Some people are biased toward saying they detected something, and others are biased toward saying they detected nothing.
   c. We are especially tuned to detect changes in stimulation.
   d. The amount of physical energy needed to detect a change in sensation depends on the proportional change from the original stimulus.

**Answers:** 1. b. sometimes has a small amount of salt in it and sometimes has no salt; a. whether they taste salt or no salt; a. comparing hits and false alarms.
2. d. The amount of physical energy needed to detect a change in sensation depends on the proportional change from the original stimulus.

## 4.2 What Are the Basic Sensory Processes?

How does information about the world get into the brain? Remember that neurons in the brain receive signals from other neurons. As discussed at the opening of this chapter, Helen Keller's perceptual experiences were restricted because her sensory systems were damaged. The neurons in her brain that

### Learning Objectives

- For each of the five major senses—taste, smell, touch, hearing, and vision—identify the type of receptor and trace the neural pathway to the brain.
- Distinguish between the neural processes associated with the experience of immediate pain and the experience of chronic pain.
- Understand how color is determined.

**FIGURE 4.8 How We Taste**

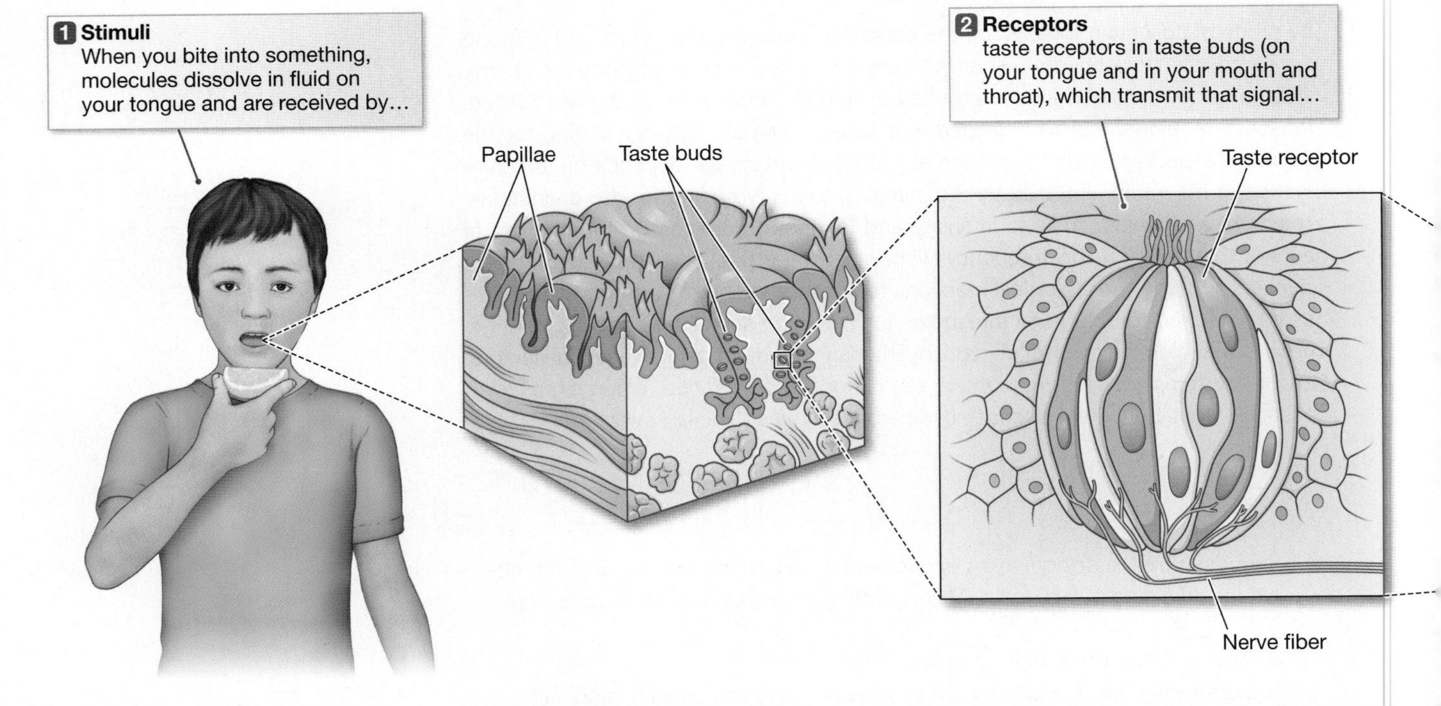

**1 Stimuli**
When you bite into something, molecules dissolve in fluid on your tongue and are received by...

**2 Receptors**
taste receptors in taste buds (on your tongue and in your mouth and throat), which transmit that signal...

constructed visual and auditory perceptions did not receive any sensory signals. This section discusses how each sense organ detects stimuli and how the resulting information is then sent to the brain for processing.

## In Taste, Taste Buds Detect Chemicals

The job of **gustation,** our sense of taste, is to keep poisons out of our digestive systems while allowing good food in. The stimuli for taste are chemical substances from food that dissolve in saliva, though how these stimuli work is still largely a mystery. The taste receptors are part of the **taste buds.** These sensory organs are mostly on the tongue (in the tiny, mushroom-shaped structures called *papillae*) but are also spread throughout the mouth and throat. Most individuals have approximately 8,000 to 10,000 taste buds. When food, fluid, or some other substance (e.g., dirt) stimulates the taste buds, they send signals to the brain, which then produces the experience of taste (**Figure 4.8**).

In all the senses, a near-infinite variety of perceptual experiences arises from the activation of unique combinations of receptors. Scientists once believed that different regions of the tongue are more sensitive to certain tastes, but they now know that the different taste buds are spread relatively uniformly throughout the tongue and mouth (Lindemann, 2001). Every taste experience is composed of a mixture of five basic qualities: sweet, sour, salty, bitter, and *umami* (Japanese for "savory" or "yummy").

Only within the last decade have scientists recognized umami as the fifth taste sensation (Krulwich, 2007). This delicious taste was perhaps first created intentionally in the late 1800s, when the French chef Auguste Escoffier invented a veal stock that did not taste primarily sweet, sour, salty, or bitter. Independently of Escoffier, in 1908, the Japanese cook and chemist Kikunae Ikeda identified the taste as arising from the detection of glutamate, a substance that occurs naturally in foods such as

**gustation** The sense of taste.

**taste buds** Sensory organs in the oral cavity that contain the receptors for taste.

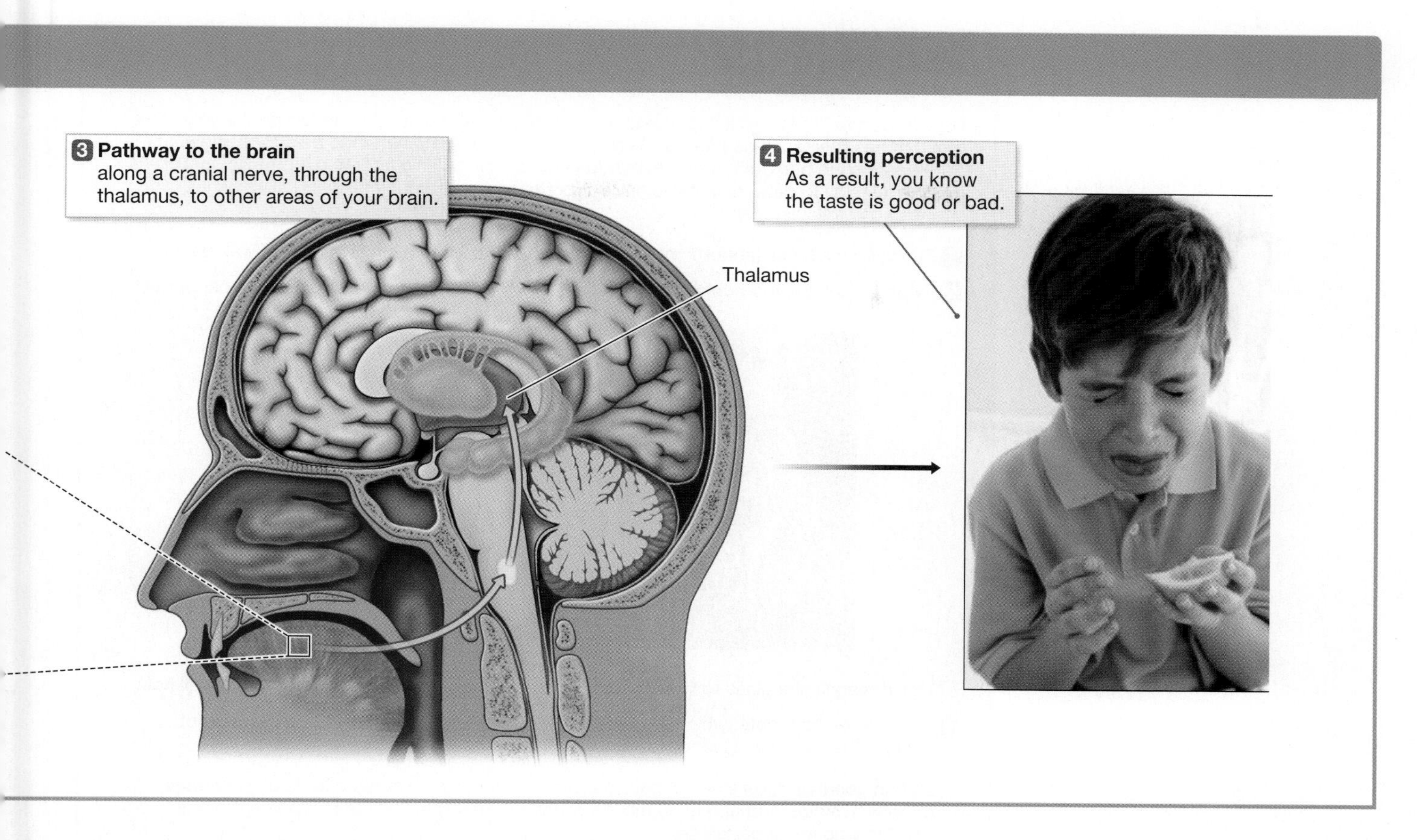


meat, some cheese, and mushrooms. Glutamate is the sodium salt in glutamic acid, and as *monosodium glutamate*—or *MSG,* which is commercially available under the brand name Accent—it can be added to various foods as a "flavor enhancer."

Taste alone does not affect how much you like a certain type of food. As you might know from having had colds, food seems tasteless if your nasal passages are blocked, since taste relies heavily on the sense of smell. A food's texture also matters: Whether a food is soft or crunchy, creamy or granular, tender or tough affects the sensory experience, as does the extent to which the food causes discomfort, as can happen with spicy chilies. The entire taste experience occurs not in your mouth but in your brain, which integrates these various sensory signals.

Some people experience especially intense taste sensations, a trait largely determined by genetics. These individuals, known as *supertasters,* are highly aware of flavors and textures and are more likely than others to feel pain when eating very spicy foods (Bartoshuk, 2000). First identified by their extreme dislike of bitter substances, supertasters have nearly six times as many taste buds as normal tasters. Although it might sound enjoyable to experience intense tastes, many supertasters are especially picky eaters because particular tastes can overwhelm them. When it comes to sensation, more is not necessarily better (**Figure 4.9**).

Each of us has individual taste preferences. For example, some people hate anchovies, while others love them. Some people love sour foods, while others prefer sweet ones. These preferences come partly from our different numbers of taste receptors. The same food can actually taste different, because the sensation associated with that food differs in different people's mouths. But cultural factors influence taste preferences as well.

Cultural influences on food preferences begin in the womb. In a study of infant food preferences, pregnant women were assigned to four groups: Some drank carrot juice every day during the last two months of pregnancy, then

## FIGURE 4.9 Try for Yourself: Are You a Supertaster?

Do you wonder if you are a supertaster? Supertasters tend to be thin and to dislike vegetables that can be bitter, such as broccoli. Women are more likely than men to be supertasters. Supertasters are born with more taste buds and are more likely to become professional chefs or wine tasters. To determine if you are a supertaster, the psychologist Linda Bartoshuk suggests the following test:

1. Punch a small hole (about 7 millimeters or .25 inches) into a small square of wax paper.
2. Swab some blue food coloring on the front of your tongue, then place the wax paper over it.

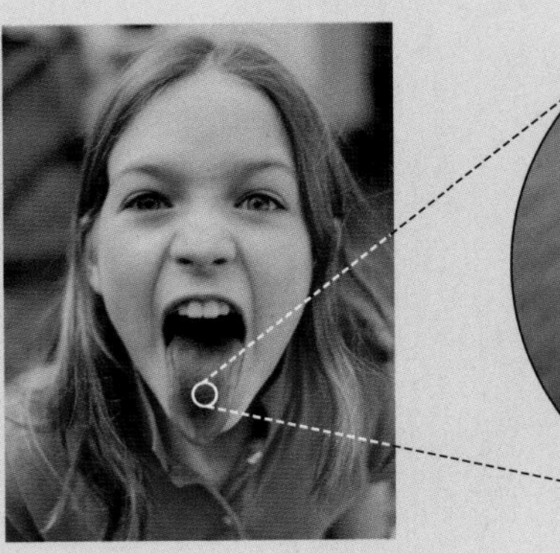
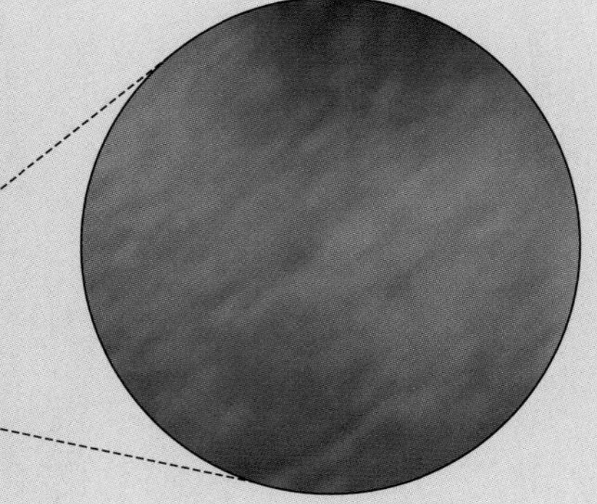

3. Use a magnifying glass to view the part of your tongue that shows through the small hole.
4. You will see pink dots, which are the papillae. They remain pink because they do not take up the blue dye. Count the number of pink dots you can see in the small hole.

**Result:** In general, fewer than 15 papillae means you have fewer taste buds than average, 15 to 35 is average, and above 35 means you are probably among the 25 percent of the population who are supertasters.

drank carrot juice again every day during the first two months *after* childbirth; some drank a comparable amount of water every day during both of those periods; some drank carrot juice during the first period, then drank water during the second period; and some drank water during the first period, then drank carrot juice during the second period (Mennella, Jagnow, & Beauchamp, 2001). All the mothers breast-fed their babies, so the taste of what each mother ate was in the breast milk that constituted each newborn's sole food source during the first few months of life. When the babies were several months old, they were all fed carrot juice (either alone or mixed with their cereal). The infants whose mothers drank carrot juice during the two months before childbirth, the first two months after childbirth, or both periods showed a preference for carrot juice compared with the infants whose mothers drank only water during those same months. Thus, through their own eating behaviors before and immediately following birth, mothers apparently pass their eating preferences on to their offspring. Once again, as noted throughout this book, nature and nurture are inextricably entwined (**Figure 4.10**).

## In Smell, the Nasal Cavity Gathers Odorants

Lacking vision and hearing, Helen Keller relied on her other senses. She called her sense of smell a "potent wizard" that guided her through life. In general, however, humans' sense of smell is vastly inferior to that of many animals. For example, dogs have 40 times more olfactory receptors than we do and are 100,000 to 1 million times more sensitive to odors. Our less developed sense of

**FIGURE 4.10 Scientific Method: Infant Taste Preferences Affected by Mother's Diet**

**Hypothesis:** Taste preferences in newborns are influenced by their mothers' food preferences during the months immediately before and after birth.

**Research Method:**

Pregnant women were assigned at random to one of four groups instructed to drink a certain beverage every day for two months before the baby's birth and two months after the baby's birth:

| | Before birth | After birth |
|---|---|---|
| Group 1: | carrot juice | water |
| Group 2: | carrot juice | carrot juice |
| Group 3: | water | carrot juice |
| Group 4: | water | water |

**Results:** Babies whose mothers were in Groups 1, 2, or 3 preferred the taste of carrot juice more than did babies whose mothers were in Group 4 and did not drink carrot juice.

**Conclusion:** Babies become familiar with the taste of foods their mothers consume around the time of their birth, and they prefer familiar tastes.

**Source:** Mennella, J. A., Jagnow, C. P., & Beauchamp, G. K. (2001). Prenatal and postnatal flavor learning by human infants. *Pediatrics, 107*, e88.

smell comes from our ancestors' reliance on vision. Yet smell's importance to us in our daily lives is made clear, at least in Western cultures, by the vast sums of money we spend on fragrances, deodorants, and mouthwash.

Of all the senses, smell, or **olfaction,** has the most direct route to the brain. It may, however, be the least understood sense. Like taste, it involves the sensing of chemicals that come from outside the body. We smell something when chemical particles, or *odorants,* pass into the nose and, when we sniff, into the nasal cavity's upper and back portions. In the nose and the nasal cavity, a warm, moist environment helps the odorant molecules come into contact with the **olfactory epithelium,** a thin layer of tissue embedded with smell receptors. These receptors transmit information to the **olfactory bulb,** the brain center for smell. From the olfactory bulb, which is just below the frontal lobes, smell information goes direct to other brain areas. Unlike other sensory information, smell signals bypass the thalamus, the early relay station. Information about whether a smell is pleasant or aversive is processed in the brain's prefrontal cortex. The smell's intensity is processed in brain areas also involved in emotion and memory (Anderson, Christoff, et al., 2003), so it is not surprising that olfactory stimuli can evoke feelings and memories (**Figure 4.11**). For example, many people find that the aromas of certain holiday foods cooking, the smell of bread baking, and/or the fragrances of particular perfumes generate fond childhood memories.

There are thousands of receptors in the olfactory epithelium, each responsive to different chemicals. It remains unclear exactly how these receptors

**olfaction** The sense of smell.

**olfactory epithelium** A thin layer of tissue, within the nasal cavity, that contains the receptors for smell.

**olfactory bulb** The brain center for smell, located below the frontal lobes.

**FIGURE 4.11 How We Smell**

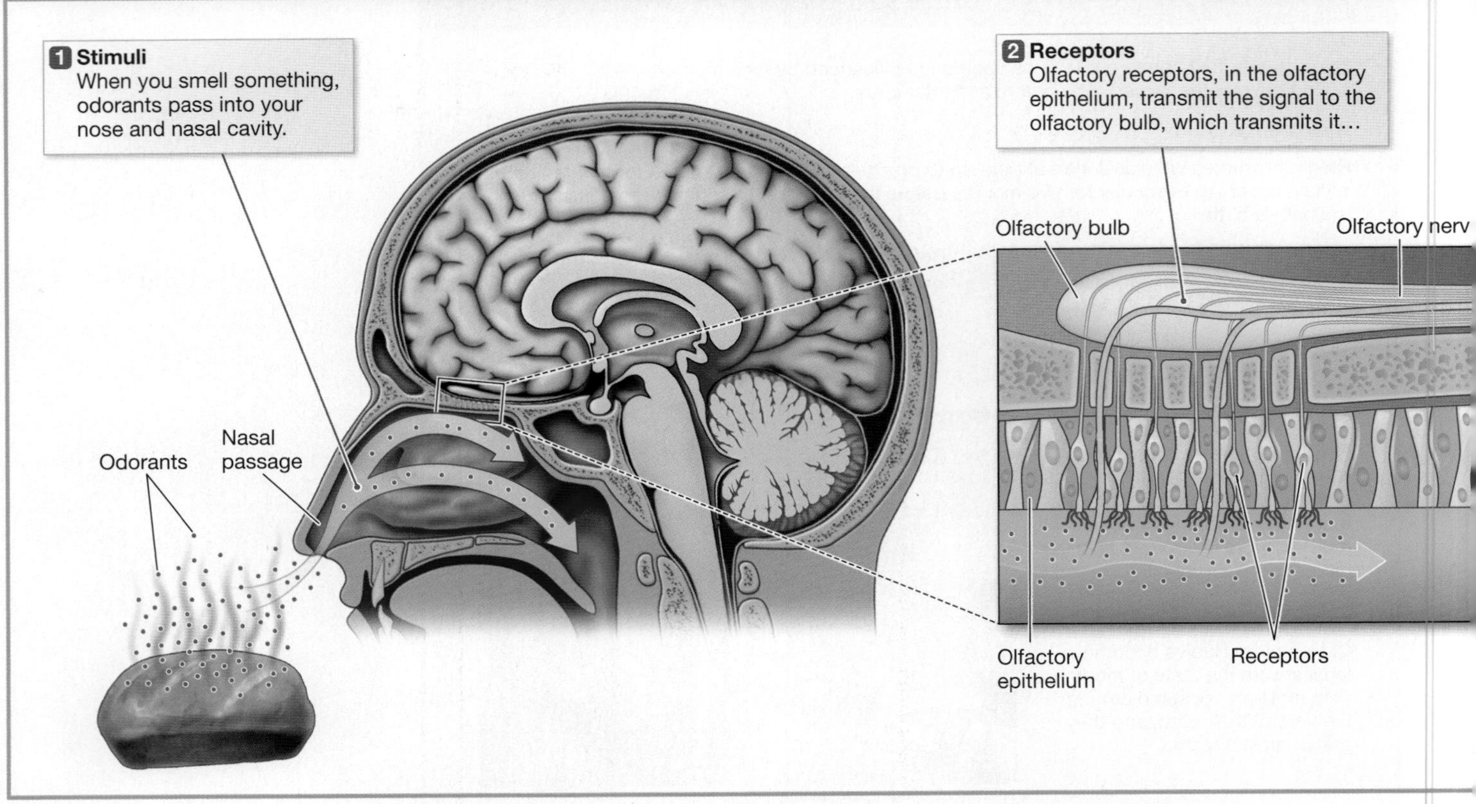

**1 Stimuli**
When you smell something, odorants pass into your nose and nasal cavity.

**2 Receptors**
Olfactory receptors, in the olfactory epithelium, transmit the signal to the olfactory bulb, which transmits it...

Olfactory bulb
Olfactory nerv
Nasal passage
Odorants
Olfactory epithelium
Receptors

encode distinct smells. One possibility is that each type of receptor is uniquely associated with a specific odor (for example, one type would encode only the scent of roses). This explanation is unlikely, however, given the huge number of scents we can detect. Another possibility, more likely to be correct, is that each odor stimulates several receptors and that the activation pattern across several types of receptors determines the olfactory perception (Lledo, Gheusi, & Vincent, 2005). In all sensory systems, sensation and perception result from the specificity of receptors and the pattern of receptor responses.

According to the researchers Yaara Yeshurun and Noam Sobel (2010), although humans can discriminate among thousands of different odors, most people are pretty bad at identifying odors by name. What humans can readily do is say whether an odor is pleasant or unpleasant. Many are often surprised to find out that people have difficulty naming odors, but you can test this claim by asking your friends or relatives to name familiar food items from the fridge. You will probably find that they are unable to name the smell of odorous household refrigerator items at least 50 percent of the time (de Wijk, Schab, & Cain, 1995). At the same time, the available evidence indicates that women are generally better than men at identifying odors (Bromley & Doty, 1995; Lehrner, 1993; Schab, 1991).

The sense of smell is also involved in an important mode of communication. *Pheromones* are chemicals released by animals, probably including humans, that trigger physiological or behavioral reactions in other animals. These chemicals do not elicit "smells" that we are conscious of, but they are processed in a manner similar to the processing of olfactory stimuli. Specialized receptors in the nasal cavity respond to the presence of pheromones. Pheromones play a major role in sexual signaling in many animal species, and they may affect humans in similar ways (as discussed in Chapter 10, "Emotion and Motivation"). For example,

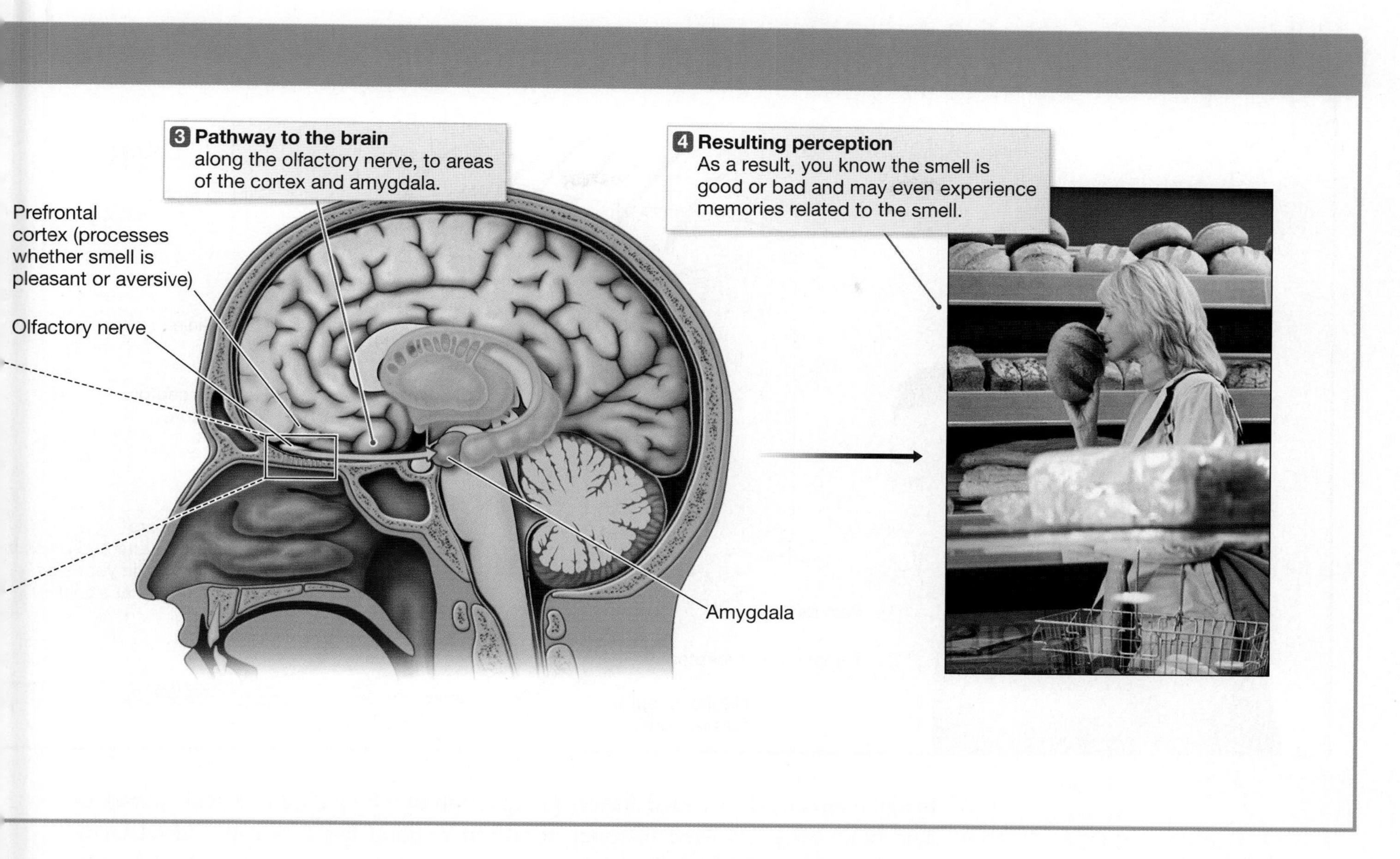


pheromones may explain why the menstrual cycles of women who live together tend to synchronize (McClintock, 1971).

## In Touch, Sensors in the Skin Detect Pressure, Temperature, and Pain

Touch, the **haptic sense,** conveys sensations of temperature, of pressure, and of pain. It also delivers a sense of where our limbs are in space. Anything that makes contact with our skin provides *tactile stimulation,* which gives rise to the experience of touch. In fact, skin is the largest organ for sensory reception.

The haptic receptors for both temperature and pressure are sensory neurons that reach to the skin's outer layer. Their long axons enter the central nervous system by way of spinal or cranial nerves. (Simply put, spinal nerves travel from the rest of the body into the spinal cord and then to the brain. By contrast, cranial nerves connect directly to the brain.) For sensing temperature, there appear to be receptors for warmth and receptors for cold. Intense stimuli can trigger both warmth and cold receptors, however. Such simultaneous activation can produce strange sensory experiences, such as a false feeling of wetness. Some receptors for pressure are nerve fibers at the bases of hair follicles. These receptors respond to movement of the hair. Four other types of pressure receptors are capsules in the skin. These receptors respond to continued vibration; to light, fast pressure; to light, slow pressure; or to stretching and steady pressure. Pain receptors, discussed in greater detail in the next section, are found throughout the body, not just in the skin. The integration of various signals and higher-level mental processes produces haptic experiences (**Figure 4.12**). For instance, stroking multiple pressure points can produce a tickling sensation, which can be pleasant or unpleasant, depending on the mental state of the person being tickled.

**haptic sense** The sense of touch.

FIGURE 4.12 How We Experience Touch: The Haptic Sense

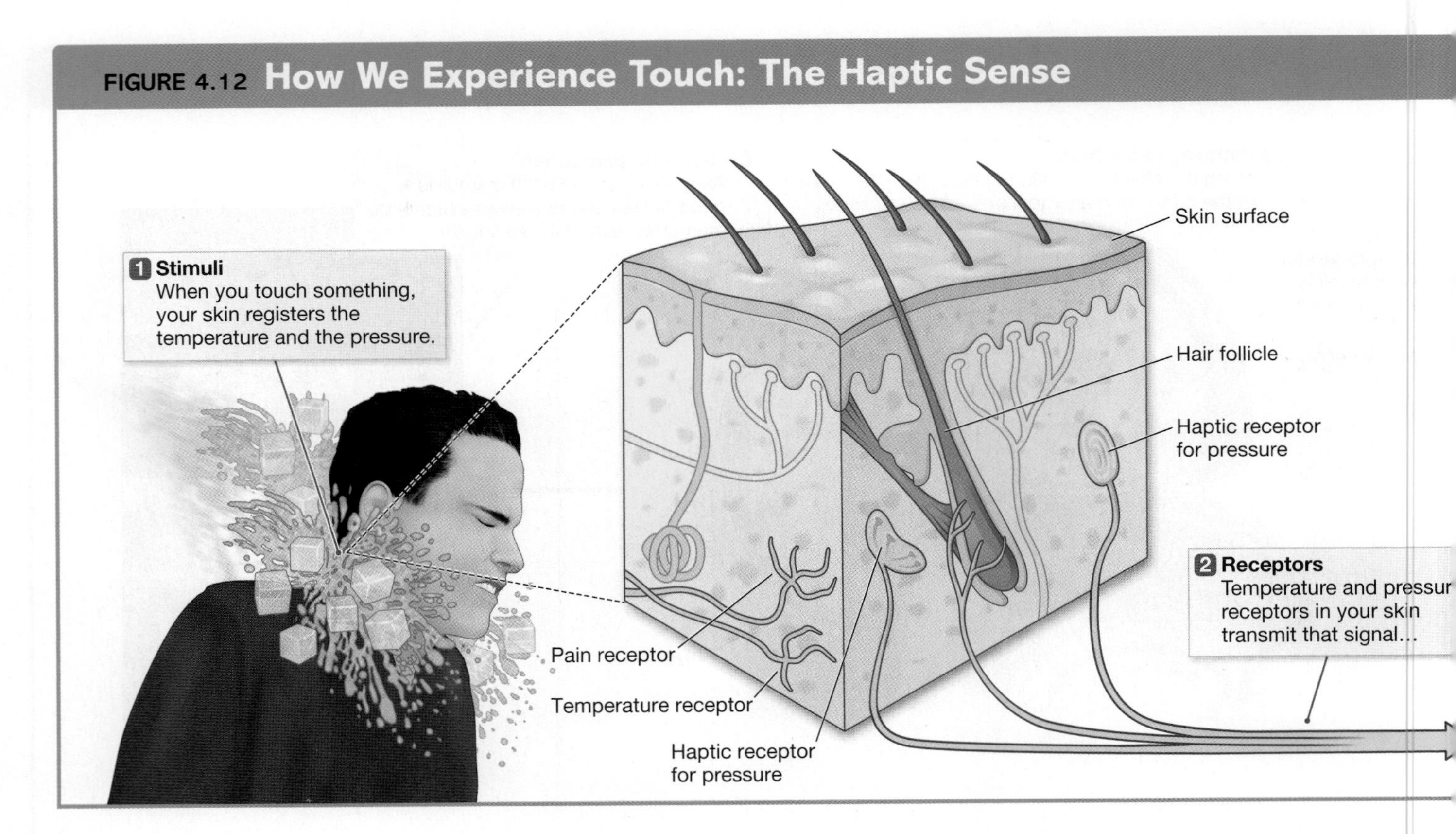


Imaging research has helped answer the question of why we cannot tickle ourselves: The brain areas involved in touch sensation respond less to self-produced tactile stimulation than to external tactile stimulation (Blakemore, Wolpert, & Frith, 1998).

**TWO TYPES OF PAIN** Pain is part of a warning system that stops you from continuing activities that may harm you. For example, the message may be to remove your hand from a jagged surface or to stop running when you have damaged a tendon. Children born with a rare genetic disorder that leaves them insensitive to pain usually die young, no matter how carefully they are supervised. They simply do not know how to avoid activities that harm them or to report when they are feeling ill (Melzack & Wall, 1982).

Like other sensory experiences, the actual experience of pain is created by the brain. For instance, a person whose limb has been amputated may sometimes feel phantom pain in the nonexistent limb (see Figure 3.40). The person really feels pain, but the pain occurs because of painful sensations *near* the site of the missing limb or even because of a nonpainful touch on the cheek. The brain simply misinterprets the resulting neural activity.

Most experiences of pain result when damage to the skin activates haptic receptors. The nerve fibers that convey pain information are thinner than those for temperature and for pressure and are found in all body tissues that sense pain: skin, muscles, membranes around both bones and joints, organs, and so on. Two kinds of nerve fibers have been identified for pain: *fast fibers* for sharp, immediate pain and *slow fibers* for chronic, dull, steady pain.

An important distinction between these fibers is the myelination or nonmyelination of their axons, which travel from the pain receptors to the spinal cord. As also discussed in Chapter 3, myelination speeds up neural communication. Myelinated axons, like heavily insulated wire, can send information quickly. Nonmyelinated axons send information more slowly. Think of a time when you

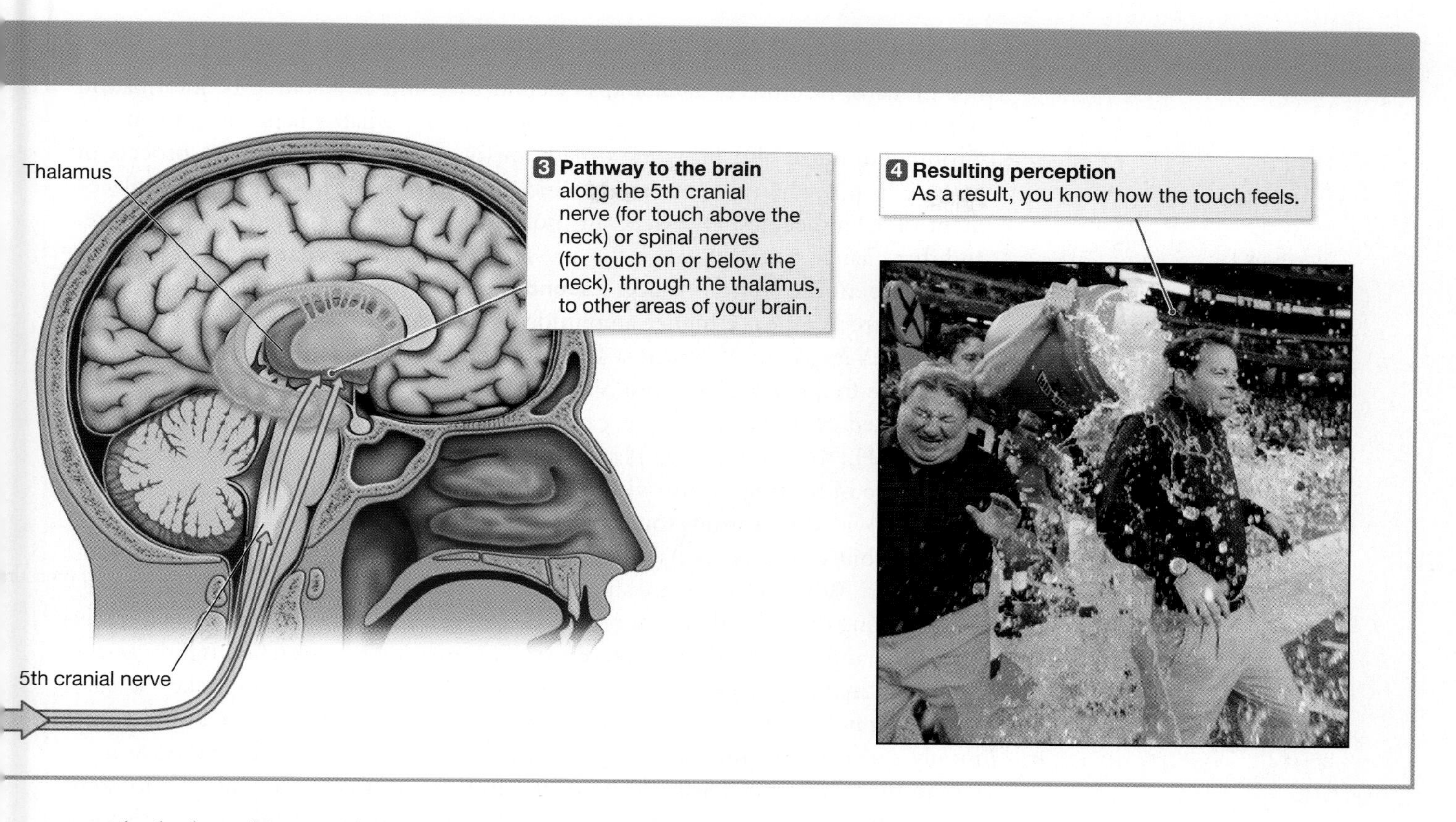


touched a hot object, such as a cooking pan. You probably can recall feeling two kinds of pain: a sharp, fast, localized pain at the moment your skin touched the pan, followed by a slow, dull, more diffuse burning pain. The fast-acting receptors are activated by strong physical pressure and temperature extremes, whereas the slow-acting receptors are activated by chemical changes in tissue when skin is damaged. In terms of adaptation, fast pain leads us to recoil from harmful objects and therefore is protective, whereas slow pain keeps us from using the affected body parts and therefore helps in recuperation (**Figure 4.13**).

**FIGURE 4.13 How We Experience Touch: The Sense of Pain**

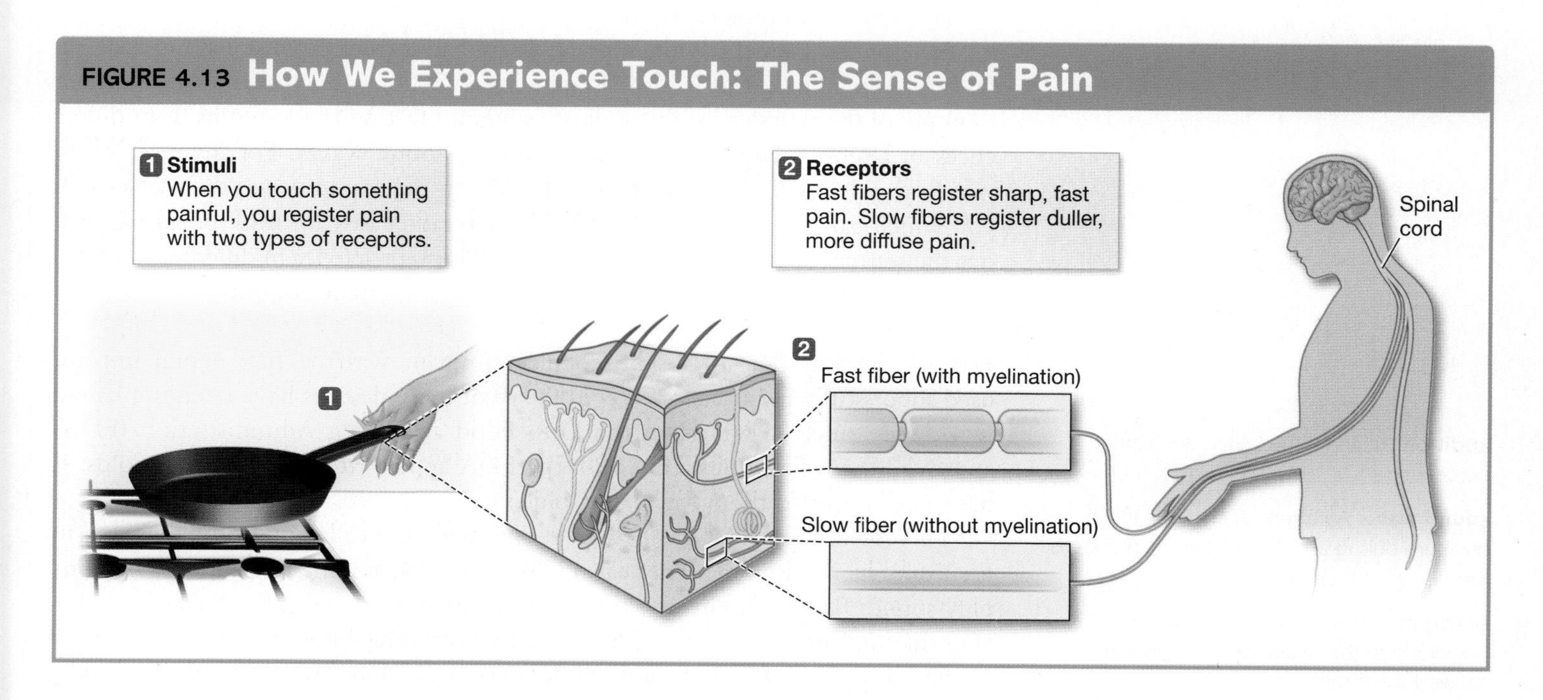

## In Hearing, the Ear Detects Sound Waves

For humans, hearing, or **audition,** is second to vision as a source of information about the world. It is a mechanism for determining what is happening in an environment, and it also provides a medium for spoken language. The process of hearing begins when the movements and vibrations of objects cause the displacement of air molecules. Displaced air molecules produce a change in air pressure, and that change travels through the air. The pattern of the changes in air pressure during a period of time is called a **sound wave.** The wave's *amplitude* determines its loudness: We hear a higher amplitude as a louder sound. The wave's *frequency* determines its pitch: We hear a higher frequency as a sound that is higher in pitch. The frequency of a sound is measured in vibrations per second, called *hertz* (abbreviated *Hz*). Most humans can detect sound waves with frequencies from about 20 Hz to about 20,000 Hz. Like all other sensory experiences, the sensory experience of hearing occurs within the brain, as the brain integrates the different signals provided by various sound waves.

Our ability to hear is based on the intricate interactions of various regions of the ear. When changes in air pressure produce sound waves within a person's hearing distance, those sound waves arrive at the person's *outer ear* and travel down the auditory canal to the **eardrum.** This membrane, stretched tightly across the canal, marks the beginning of the *middle ear.* The sound waves make the eardrum vibrate. These vibrations are transferred to *ossicles,* three tiny bones commonly called the hammer, anvil, and stirrup. The ossicles transfer the eardrum's vibrations to the *oval window.* The oval window is actually a membrane located within the *cochlea,* in the *inner ear.* The cochlea is a fluid-filled tube that curls into a snail-like shape, with a membrane at the end called the *round window.* Running through the center of the cochlea is the thin *basilar membrane.* The oval window's vibrations create pressure waves in the cochlear fluid; these waves prompt the basilar membrane to oscillate. Movement of the basilar membrane stimulates *hair cells* to bend and to send information to the *auditory nerve.* These hair cells are the primary auditory receptors. Thus sound waves, mechanical signals, hit the eardrum and are converted to neural signals that travel to the brain along the auditory nerve. This conversion of sound waves to brain activity produces the sensation of sound (**Figure 4.14**).

As noted by Daniel Levitin, a psychologist and former professional musician, in his best-selling book *This Is Your Brain on Music* (2006), music provides an excellent example of the wonders of the auditory system. Hearing music results from differences in brain activity, not from differentiated sound waves. For instance, when you hear guitars, drums, and singing, nothing in the sound waves themselves tells you which part of the music is which. Yet it is rather easy for most people to pick out the separate features in a piece of music. Through activity in different brain regions, the features all come together to create the experience of music.

**THE COCHLEAR IMPLANT** The cochlear implant was the first neural implant used successfully in humans. Over 100,000 of these devices have been implanted worldwide since 1984, when the U.S. Food and Drug Administration (FDA) approved them for adults. (In 1990, the FDA approved them for 2-year-olds. It has since approved them for 1-year-olds.)

The cochlear implant has helped people with severe hearing problems due to the loss of hair cells in the inner ear. Unlike a hearing aid, the implant does not amplify sound. Rather, it directly stimulates the auditory nerve. The downside is that after the implant is put in place, the person who received it loses all residual normal hearing in that ear, because sound no longer travels along the ear canal and middle

**audition** Hearing; the sense of sound perception.

**sound wave** A pattern of changes in air pressure during a period of time; it produces the percept of a sound.

**eardrum** A thin membrane that marks the beginning of the middle ear; sound waves cause it to vibrate.

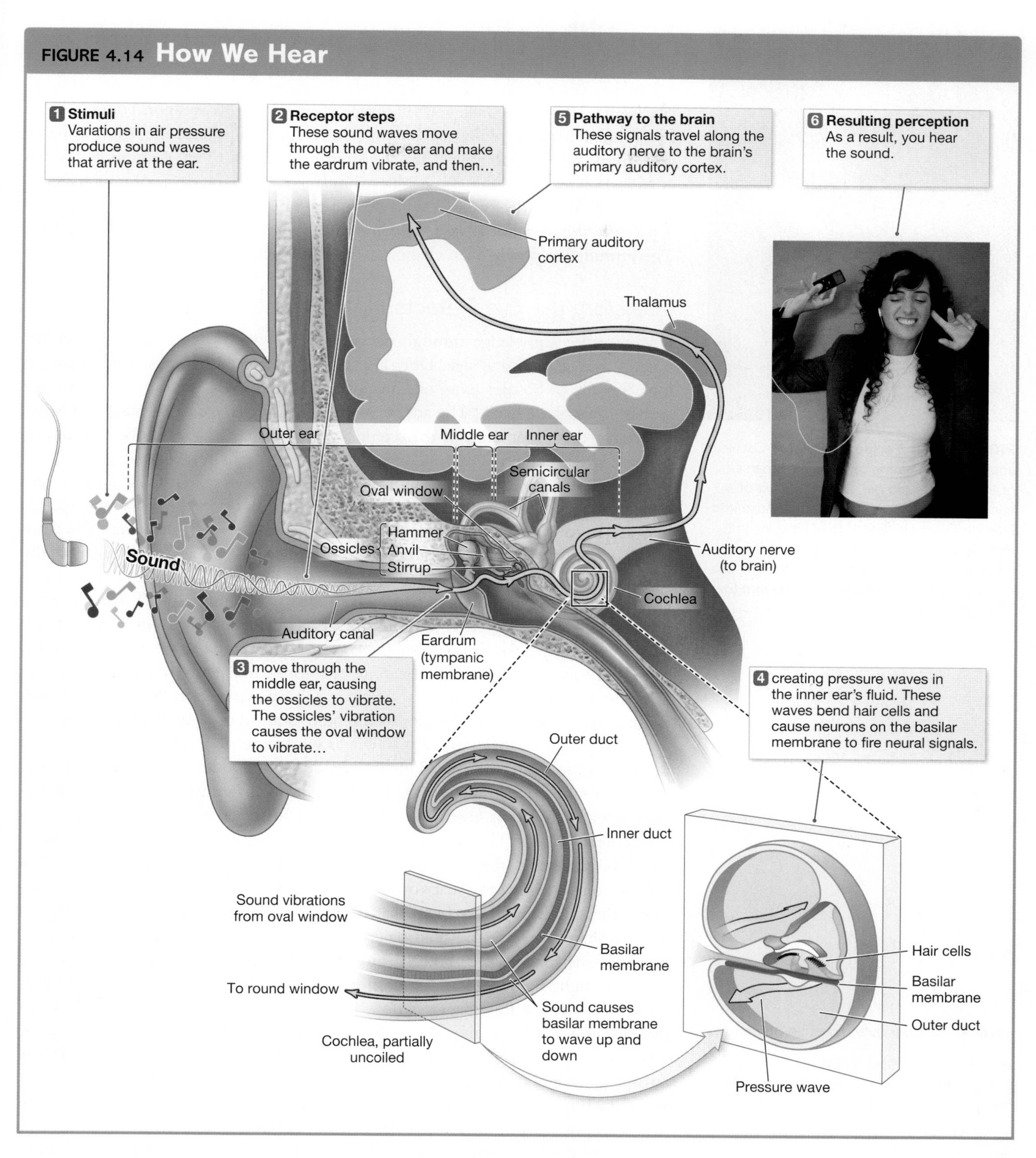


ear. Instead, sound is picked up by a tiny microphone behind the ear, sent through a computer processor, and then transmitted to the implant's electrodes inside the cochlea. If the devices are implanted at a young enough age in a child born deaf (younger than 2 years being optimal), the child's hearing will be quite functional. He or she will learn to speak reasonably normally (**Figure 4.15**).

**FIGURE 4.15 Cochlear Implants** Cochlear implants, such as the one fitted on the side of this 10-year-old girl's head, consist of a microphone around the ear and a transmitter fitted to the scalp, linked to electrodes that directly stimulate the auditory nerve. When implanted at a young age, these devices can enable people with hearing loss to learn to hear and speak.

The benefits of cochlear implants might seem indisputable to many people with normal hearing. In the 1990s, however, deaf people who do not consider deafness a disability voiced concerns that the implants might adversely affect deaf culture. In fact, some deaf people believe that cochlear implants are a weapon being wielded by the medical community to wipe out deaf culture. They see this effort as being an extreme result of prejudice and discrimination against them, commonly known as *audism*. They argue that the cochlear implants disrupt the deaf community's cohesiveness. While deaf people with cochlear implants can still use sign language, apparently they are not always welcome in the signing community (Chase, 2006). This attitude has slowly been changing, but is still held by many deaf signers.

## In Vision, the Eye Detects Light Waves

If we acquire knowledge through our senses, then vision is by far our most important source of knowledge. Does a place look safe or dangerous? Does a person look friendly or hostile? Even our metaphors for knowledge and for understanding are often visual: "I see," "The answer is clear," "I'm fuzzy on that point." It is not surprising, then, that most of the scientific study of sensation and of perception is concerned with vision.

Sight seems so effortless, so automatic, that most of us take it for granted. Every time a person opens his or her eyes, though, nearly half of that person's brain springs into action to make sense of the energy arriving in the eyes. Of course, the brain can do so only based on sensory signals from the eyes. If the eyes are damaged, the sensory system fails to process new information. This section focuses on how energy is transduced in the visual system, but what we commonly call *seeing* is much more than transducing energy. As the psychologist James Enns notes in his book *The Thinking Eye, the Seeing Brain* (2005), very little of what we call seeing takes place in the eyes. Rather, what we see results from constructive processes that occur throughout much of the brain to produce our visual experiences. Seeing is therefore a remarkable process that produces useful information about our environments.

Some people describe the human eye as working like a crude camera, in that it focuses light to form an image. This analogy does not do justice to the intricate processes that take place in the eye, however. Light first passes through the **cornea,** the eye's thick, transparent outer layer. The cornea focuses the incoming light, which then enters the *lens*. There, the light is bent farther inward and focused to form an image on the **retina,** the thin inner surface of the back of the eyeball. If you shine a light in someone's eyes so that you can see the person's retina, you are in fact looking at the only part of the brain that is visible from outside the skull. In fact, the retina is the one part of the central nervous system that is located where we can see it. The retina contains the photoreceptors that transduce light into neural signals.

More light is focused at the cornea than at the lens. The lens is adjustable, however, whereas the cornea is not. The **pupil,** the dark circle at the center of the eye, is a small opening in the front of the lens. By contracting (closing) or dilating (opening), the pupil determines how much light enters the eye. The **iris,** an opaque, circular muscle, determines the eye's color and controls the pupil's size. The pupil dilates in dim light but also when we see something we like, such as a beautiful painting or a cute baby (Tombs & Silverman, 2004).

Behind the iris, muscles change the shape of the lens. They flatten it to focus on distant objects and thicken it to focus on closer objects. This process is called *accommodation*. The lens and cornea work together to collect and focus light rays reflected from an object, to form on the retina an upside-down image of the

**cornea** The clear outer covering of the eye.

**retina** The thin inner surface of the back of the eyeball; it contains the photoreceptors that transduce light into neural signals.

**pupil** The small opening in the eye; it lets in light waves.

**iris** The colored muscular circle on the surface of the eye; it changes shape to let in more or less light.

object. The world looks right-side up to us even though the image of the world projected on the retina is upside down (**Figure 4.16**).

**RODS AND CONES** The retina has two types of receptor cells: **rods** and **cones.** The name of each type comes from its distinctive shape. Rods respond at extremely low levels of illumination and are responsible primarily for night vision. They do not support color vision, and they resolve fine detail poorly. This is why, on a moonless night, objects appear in shades of gray. In contrast to rods, cones are less sensitive to low levels of light. They are responsible primarily for vision under high illumination and for seeing both color and detail. Within the rods and cones, light-sensitive chemicals called *photopigments* initiate the transduction of light waves into electrical neural impulses.

Each retina holds approximately 120 million rods and 6 million cones. Near the retina's center, cones are densely packed in a small region called the **fovea.** Although cones are spread throughout the remainder of the retina (except in the blind spot, as you will see shortly), they become increasingly scarce near the outside edge. Conversely, rods are concentrated at the retina's edges. None are in the fovea. If you look directly at a very dim star on a moonless night, the star will appear to vanish because its light will fall on the fovea, where there are no rods. If you look just to the side of the star, however, the star will be visible, because its light will fall just outside the fovea, where there are rods.

**TRANSMISSION FROM THE EYE TO THE BRAIN** The visual process begins with the generation of electrical signals by the photoreceptors in the retina. Immediately after light is transduced into neural impulses by the rods and cones, other cells in the retina perform on those impulses a series of sophisticated computations that help the visual system process the incoming information. The outputs from these *bipolar, amacrine,* and *horizontal cells* converge on about a million retinal *ganglion cells* (see Figure 4.16). Ganglion cells are the first neurons in the visual pathway with axons. During the process of seeing, they are the first neurons to generate action potentials.

The ganglion cells send their signals along their axons from inside the eye to the thalamus. These axons are gathered into a bundle, the *optic nerve,* which exits the eye at the back of the retina. The point at which the optic nerve exits the retina has no rods or cones, and this lack produces a blind spot in each eye. If you stretch out one of your arms, make a fist, and look at your fist, the size that your fist appears to you is about the size of your blind spot. The brain normally fills in this gap automatically, so you assume the world continues and are not aware that a blind spot exists in the middle of your field of vision. However, you can isolate your blind spot (**Figure 4.17**).

At the optic chiasm, half of the axons in the optic nerves cross. (The axons that cross are the ones that project from the portion of the retina nearest the nose.) This arrangement causes all information from the left side of visual space (i.e., everything visible to the left of the point of gaze) to be projected to the right hemisphere of the brain and vice versa. In each case, the information reaches the visual areas of the thalamus and then travels to the *primary visual cortex,* cortical areas in the occipital lobes, at the back of the head. The pathway from the retina to this region carries all the information that we consciously experience as seeing.

**THE COLOR OF LIGHT IS DETERMINED BY ITS WAVELENGTH** We can distinguish among millions of shades of color. An object appears to be a particular color because of the wavelengths it reflects. The color is not a property of the

**rods** Retinal cells that respond to low levels of illumination and result in black-and-white perception.

**cones** Retinal cells that respond to higher levels of illumination and result in color perception.

**fovea** The center of the retina, where cones are densely packed.

## FIGURE 4.16 How We See

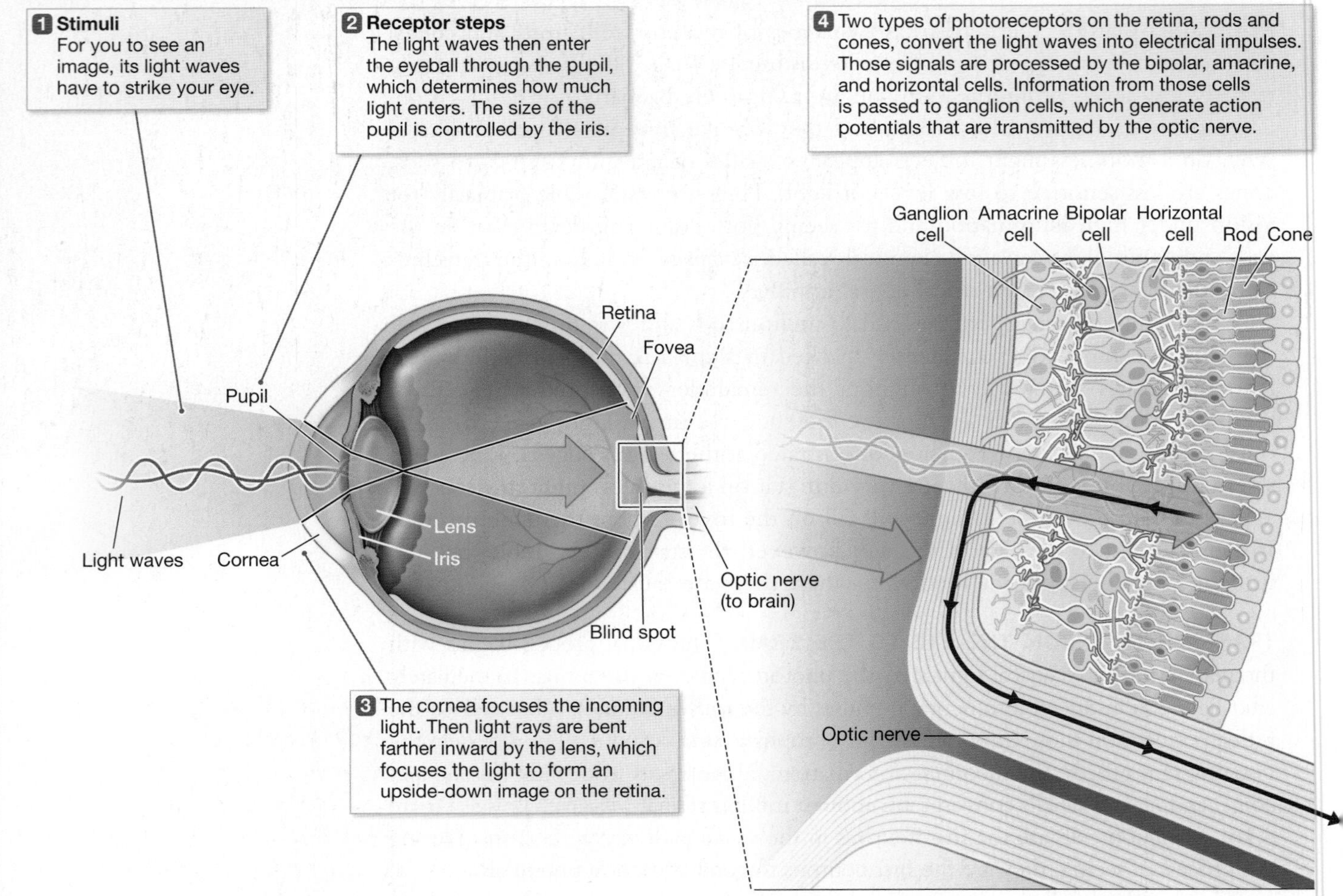

**1 Stimuli**
For you to see an image, its light waves have to strike your eye.

**2 Receptor steps**
The light waves then enter the eyeball through the pupil, which determines how much light enters. The size of the pupil is controlled by the iris.

3 The cornea focuses the incoming light. Then light rays are bent farther inward by the lens, which focuses the light to form an upside-down image on the retina.

4 Two types of photoreceptors on the retina, rods and cones, convert the light waves into electrical impulses. Those signals are processed by the bipolar, amacrine, and horizontal cells. Information from those cells is passed to ganglion cells, which generate action potentials that are transmitted by the optic nerve.

Light waves
Cornea
Pupil
Lens
Iris
Retina
Fovea
Blind spot
Optic nerve (to brain)
Ganglion cell
Amacrine cell
Bipolar cell
Horizontal cell
Rod
Cone
Optic nerve

## FIGURE 4.17 Try for Yourself: Find Your Blind Spot

To find your blind spot using your right eye, hold this book in front of you and look at the dot, closing your left eye. Move the book toward and away from your face until the rabbit disappears.

You can repeat this exercise for your left eye by turning the book upside down.

**Result:** The optic nerve creates the blind spot, a small point at the back of the retina. There are no receptors at this spot because it is where the nerves leave the eye.

object. In fact, color is always a product of our visual system; there is no color in the physical world.

Visible light consists of electromagnetic waves ranging in length from about 400 to 700 nanometers (abbreviated *nm;* this length is about one billionth of a meter). In simplest terms, the color of light is determined by the wavelengths of the electromagnetic waves that reach the eye. In the center of the retina, the cone cells transduce light into neural impulses. According to the *trichromatic theory,* color vision results from activity in three different types of cones that are sensitive to different wavelengths. One type of cone is most sensitive to short wavelengths (blue–violet light), another type is most sensitive to medium wavelengths (yellow–green light), and the third type is most sensitive to long wavelengths (red–orange light; **Figure 4.18**). The three types of cones in the retina are therefore called "S," "M," and "L" cones because they respond maximally to short, medium, and long wavelengths,

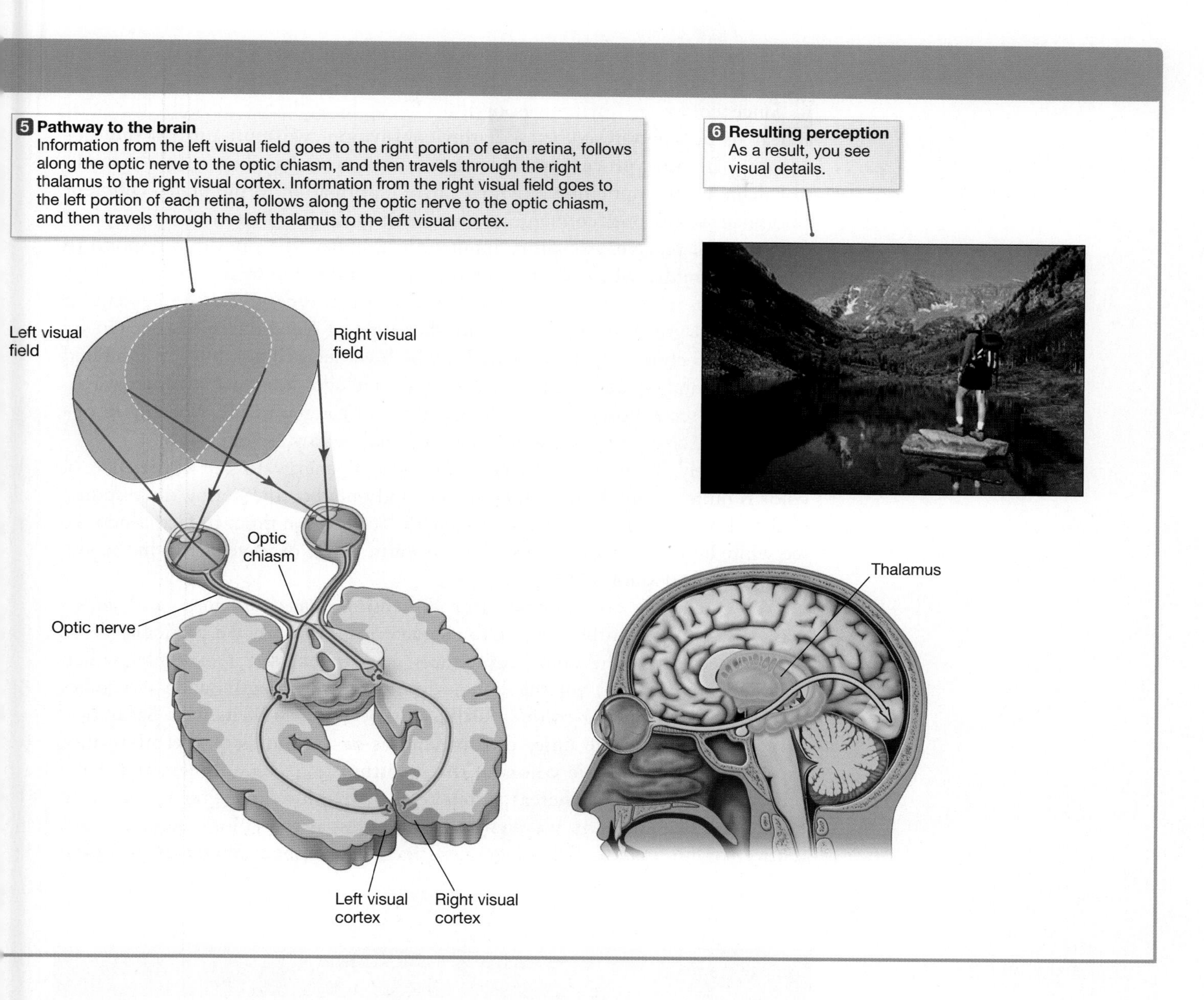


respectively. For example, yellow light looks yellow because it stimulates the L and M cones about equally and hardly stimulates the S cones at all. In fact, we can create yellow light by combining red light and green light because each type of light stimulates the corresponding cone population. As far as the brain can tell, there is no difference between yellow light and a combination of red light and green light!

Our perception of different colors is determined by the ratio of activity among the three types of cone receptors. Some aspects of color vision, however, cannot be explained by the responses of three types of cones in the retina. For example, we have trouble visualizing certain color mixtures. It is easier to imagine reddish yellow or bluish green, say, than reddish green or bluish yellow. In addition, some colors seem to be "opposites." This perceptual effect is the basis of *opponent-process theory* (Hering, 1878/1964). When we stare at a red image for some time, we see a green afterimage when we look away; when we stare at a green image, we see a red afterimage. Likewise, when we stare at a blue

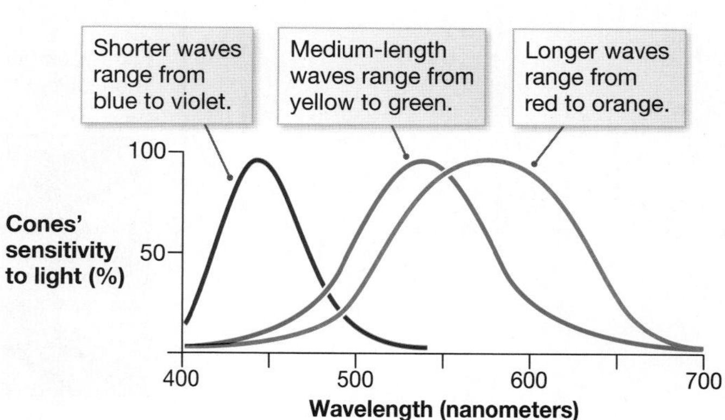


**FIGURE 4.18 The Experience of Color** The color of light is determined by the wavelength of the electromagnetic wave that reaches the eye. This graph shows the percentage of light at different wavelengths that is absorbed by each kind of cone.

image for some time, we see a yellow afterimage when we look away; when we stare at a yellow image, we see a blue afterimage (**Figure 4.19**).

Since colors are themselves optical effects, how do we account for what appear to be opposite colors? For this explanation, we must turn to the second stage in visual processing. This stage occurs in the ganglion cells—the cells that make up the optic nerve, which carries information to the brain. Different combinations of cones converge on the ganglion cells in the retina. One type of ganglion cell receives excitatory input from L cones (the ones that respond to long wavelengths, which we see as red), but it is inhibited by M cones (medium wavelengths, which we see as green). Cells of this type create the perception that red and green are opposites. Another type of ganglion cell is excited by input from S cones (short wavelengths, which we see as blue), but it is inhibited by both L- and M-cone activity (when light includes long and medium wavelengths, we see yellow). These different types of ganglion cells, working in opposing pairs, create the perception that blue and yellow are opposites.

Ultimately, how the brain converts physical energy to the experience of color is quite complex and can be understood only by considering the response of the visual system to different wavelengths at the same time. In fact, when we see white light, our eyes are receiving the entire range of wavelengths in the visible spectrum (**Figure 4.20**).

We categorize color along three dimensions: *hue, saturation,* and *brightness.* Hue consists of the distinctive characteristics that place a particular color in the spectrum—the color's greenness or orangeness, for example, which will depend primarily on the light's dominant wavelength when it reaches the eye. Saturation is a color's purity, or the vividness of its hue. Saturation varies according to the unity of wavelengths in a stimulus or the mixture of those wavelengths. Basic colors of the spectrum (e.g., blue, green, red) have only one wavelength, whereas pastels (e.g., baby blue, lime green, and pink) have a mixture of many wavelengths. Brightness is the color's perceived intensity, or luminance. This characteristic is determined chiefly by the total

**FIGURE 4.19 Try for Yourself: Afterimage**

For at least 30 seconds, stare at this version of the Union Jack, flag of the United Kingdom. Then look at the blank space to the right.

**Result:** Because your receptors have adapted to the green and orange in the first image, the afterimage appears in the complementary colors red and blue. You can tell that afterimages are caused by events in the retina, because the afterimage moves with you as you move your eyes, as though it is "painted" on the retina.

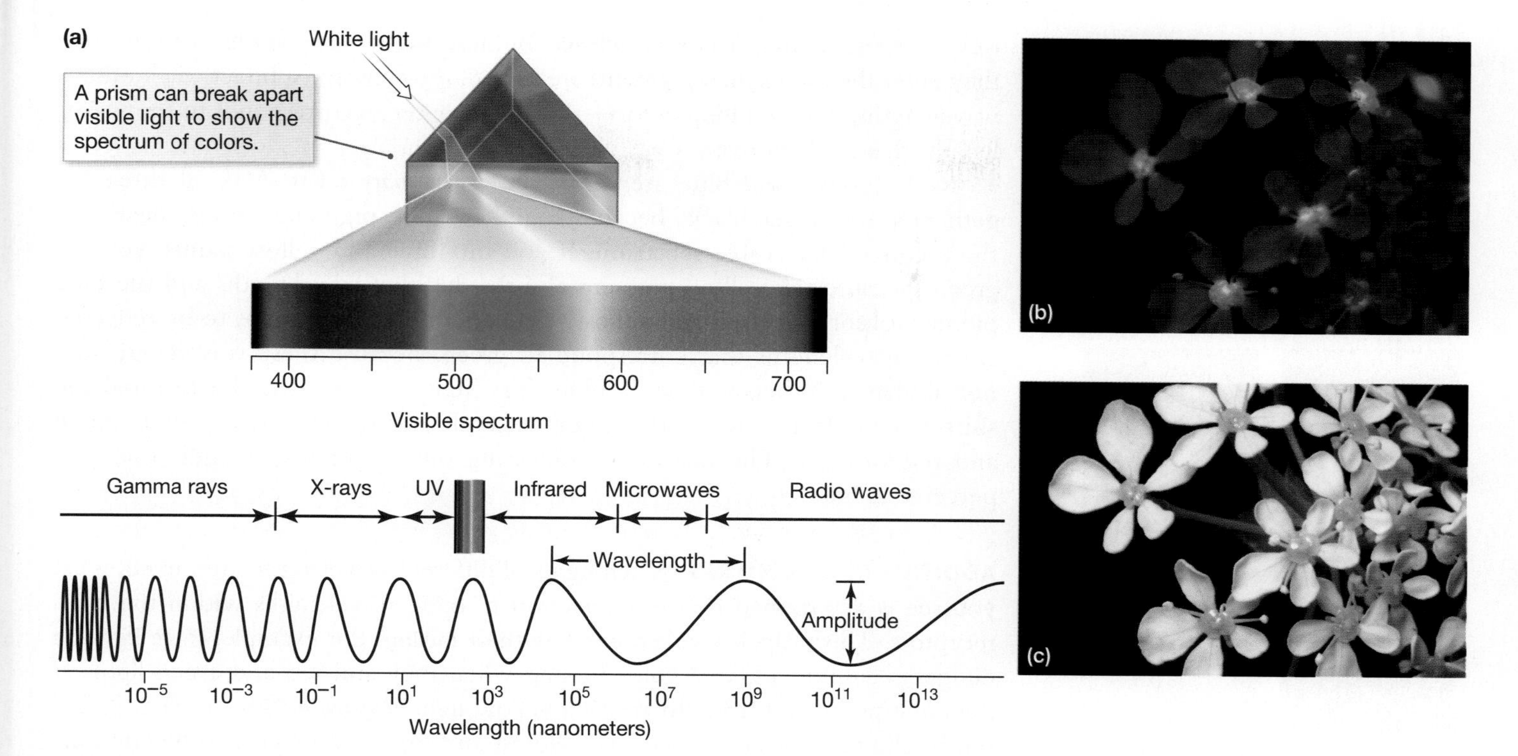


**FIGURE 4.20 The Color Spectrum (a)** When white light shines through a prism, the spectrum of color that is visible to humans is revealed. As shown here, the visible color spectrum is only a small part of the electromagnetic spectrum: It consists of electromagnetic wavelengths from just under 400 nm (the color violet) to just over 700 nm (the color red). By using night-vision goggles, humans are able to see infrared waves (i.e., waves below red in terms of frequency). **(b)** Some insects can see ultraviolet light (i.e., light greater than violet in terms of frequency). This ability helps them find nectar glands, which can appear fluorescent in UV illumination. **(c)** When humans view the same flowers under visible light, they do not see the same nectar patterns that the insects see.

amount of light reaching the eye—think of the difference between, say, a bright blue and a pale blue of the same shade (**Figure 4.21a**). However, do not confuse brightness with *lightness*. The lightness of a visual stimulus is determined by the brightness of the stimulus relative to its surroundings. Thus two examples of the same color—two grays with the same brightness, say—can differ in lightness. The lightness of each example will depend on the level of brightness that surrounds it. Because lightness is related to the context in which a color appears, it is more useful than brightness for describing appearance (**Figure 4.21b**).

**SUBTRACTIVE COLOR MIXING** A color is determined by the mixture of wavelengths from a stimulus. Depending on the particular stimulus, any given color can be produced through either the *subtractive* or the *additive* mixture of wavelengths. Mixing paints is one form of **subtractive color mixing,** because the mixture occurs within the stimulus and is a physical process (**Figure 4.22a**).

Paint colors are determined by pigments, which are chemicals on the surfaces of objects. Pigments absorb different wavelengths of light and prevent them from being reflected to the eye. Therefore, the color of a pigment is determined by

**subtractive color mixing** A process of color mixing that occurs within the stimulus itself; a physical, not psychological, process.

**FIGURE 4.21 Brightness versus Lightness** (a) Which blue is brighter? Why? (b) For each pair, which central square is lighter? In fact, the central squares in each pair are identical. Most people see the gray square that is surrounded with red, for example, as lighter than the gray square surrounded with green. Why do they look different?

the wavelengths that *it does not absorb*. Because these wavelengths are reflected, they enter the eye. When pigments are mixed, they absorb (subtract) each other's wavelengths. The resulting color—the color we see—corresponds to the wavelengths that are "left over."

Red, yellow, and blue are the *subtractive primary colors*. Mix all three together and you get black, because together these pigments absorb nearly all the colors of the visible spectrum. If you mix blue and yellow paints, you get green, because the yellow pigment absorbs the blue wavelengths and the blue pigment absorbs the red and yellow wavelengths. What remains to be reflected are the wavelengths that correspond to green, because these wavelengths are not absorbed. When you see a blue shirt, it is blue because the material the shirt is made from has absorbed medium and long wavelengths (yellow–green and red–orange). The material is reflecting only short wavelengths that you perceive as blue.

**ADDITIVE COLOR MIXING** When lights of different wavelengths are mixed, what you see is determined by the interaction of these wavelengths within the eye's receptors. This process is called **additive color mixing.** For example, stage lighting designers employ additive color mixing when they aim red and green lights at the same point on a stage to create a yellow light (**Figure 4.22b**). In fact, as laid out by the *three primaries law of color,* almost any color can be created by combining just three wavelengths, so long as one is from the long-wave end of the spectrum (red–orange), one is from the middle (yellow–green), and one is from the short end of the spectrum (blue–violet).

Psychologists consider the *additive primary colors* to be red, green, and blue. Whereas mixing red, yellow, and blue paint yields black paint, mixing red, green, and blue light yields white light. Because different wavelengths of light bend (refract) at different angles when they pass through a prism, white light entering a prism leaves it with all the colors of a rainbow (see Figure 4.20). Indeed, rainbows form in the sky because tiny water droplets in the air function as prisms, refracting sunlight in different directions.

## We Have Other Sensory Systems

In his book *Sensory Exotica* (1999), the psychologist Howard Hughes points out that humans, like other animals, have several internal sensory systems in addition to the five primary senses. One such system is the **kinesthetic sense,** which some researchers group with the touch senses. Kinesthetic sensations come from receptors in muscles, in tendons, and in joints. This information enables us to pinpoint the positions in space and the movements of both our bodies and our limbs. Thus it helps us coordinate voluntary movement and is invaluable in avoiding injury.

The **vestibular sense** uses information from receptors in the semicircular canals of the inner ear. These canals contain a liquid that moves when the head moves, bending hair cells at the ends of the canal. The bending generates nerve impulses that inform us of the head's rotation. In this way, it is responsible for a sense of balance. It explains why inner-ear infections or standing up quickly can make us dizzy. The experience of being seasick or carsick results in part from conflicting signals arriving from the visual system and the vestibular system.

**additive color mixing** A process of color mixing that occurs when different wavelengths of light interact within the eye's receptors; a psychological process.

**kinesthetic sense** Perception of the positions in space and movements of our bodies and our limbs.

**vestibular sense** Perception of balance.

CRITICAL THINKING SKILL

## Questioning the "Evidence" for Extrasensory Perception (ESP)

Do you believe in the so-called *sixth sense,* the "unexplainable" feeling that something is about to happen? Our many sensory systems provide information about the world, but they are sensitive to only a small range of the energy available in any environment. For instance, dogs can hear much higher frequencies than we can, and many insects can sense energy forms that we cannot detect. Is it possible that other frequencies or energy forms exist and scientists simply have not discovered them? If so, might these undiscovered energy forces allow people to read other people's minds, predict the future by examining the stars, or communicate with ghosts? In other words, could people be able to perceive information beyond ordinary sensory information through *extrasensory perception,* or *ESP*?

Many reports of ESP are anecdotal. Scientists reject claims supported only by anecdotes, no matter how scientific the stories sound. Anecdotes are not valid evidence, because they are difficult to test in the laboratory and in the world outside the lab. In addition, many claims made about people's ability to predict events can be explained away through logic. For instance, if you see a couple fighting all the time, you might predict accurately that they will break up, but that does not make you a psychic. Much of our social perception requires us to be sensitive to the subtle cues that guide behavior in a situation. But the information we glean from social situations does not arrive from some "extra" sensory system.

Some evidence for ESP was obtained by the social psychologist Daryl Bem and his collaborator Charles Honorton (1994). In their studies, a "sender" in a soundproof booth focused on a randomly generated image. A "receiver" in another room tried to sense the sender's imagery. The receiver was then asked to choose among four alternatives, one of which was correct. By chance, the receivers should have been correct 25 percent of the time. Across 11 studies, however, Bem and Honorton found that receivers were right about 33 percent of the time. Is this evidence of ESP? Many psychologists say that other factors in the experiments might have affected the results. A statistical review of many such studies found little support for ESP (Milton & Wiseman, 2001). Moreover, numerous scientific organizations and government agencies have reviewed decades of research and have concluded that no such phenomenon exists.

In 2011, Bem published a paper that presented data from a series of studies that were purported to show evidence of ESP. In some of the studies, participants reportedly responded to stimuli that they had not yet encountered. For instance, participants were asked to predict where erotic pictures would appear on a computer screen. On each trial, the participant would identify a location before a computer program would independently present the picture. At a rate better than chance, participants were able to predict where the computer would present the erotic

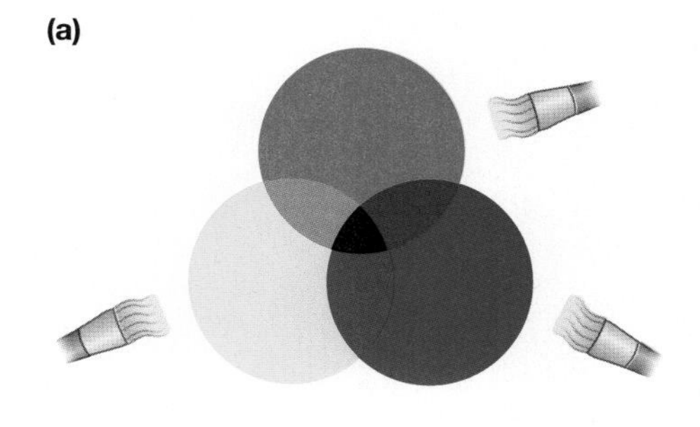


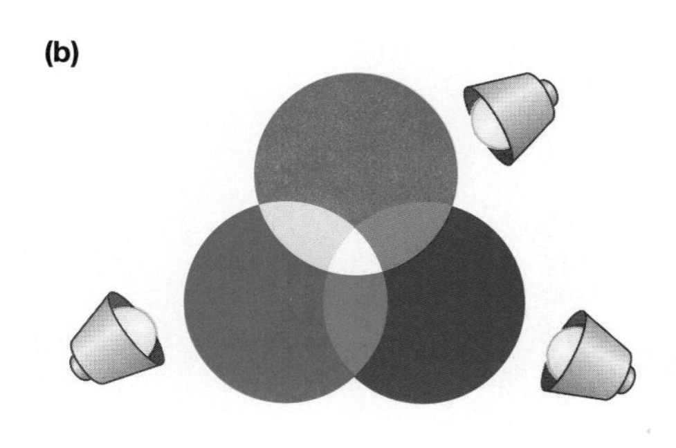


**FIGURE 4.22 Subtractive and Additive Color Mixing (a)** Subtractive color mixing is the physical process of color mixing that happens within the stimulus. The subtractive primary colors are red, yellow, and blue. **(b)** By contrast, additive color mixing happens when lights of different wavelengths are perceived by the eye. The additive primary colors are red, green, and blue.

images. The findings remain highly controversial, however. Many in the psychological community believe that extraordinary claims require extraordinary evidence, so they are concerned about the paper's lack of explanation for the findings. In addition, most of the positive results were quite small, and they may have been produced through an inappropriate use of statistical procedures. The only reasonable conclusion is that the evidence for ESP is currently weak and that healthy skepticism demands better evidence.

## Summing Up

### What Are the Basic Sensory Processes?

All the senses share similar processes. Each has receptors that respond to different physical or chemical stimuli by transducing them into some pattern of brain activity. Typically, different receptors respond to different types of stimuli, and most sensory systems integrate signals from these different receptors into an overall sensation. This system allows a relatively small number of receptors to code a wide variety of stimuli. For example, the entire range of colors is interpreted by three types of visual cones. These various sensory receptors help the perceptual system receive important information that assists in solving adaptive problems. Sensory information, although obtained from the outside world, is processed entirely in the brain to produce sensory experience through perception.

## Measuring Up

1. The sensory systems ______________.
   a. use all the available energy in their environment to create a true representation of both objects and events
   b. use only a small portion of the available energy in their environment
2. A general principle regarding sensation is that ______________.
   a. the combined firing of many different receptors and the neurons they connect with creates our sensations
   b. each sensation (for example, seeing a blue color or hearing a high-pitch tone) is coded by one type of receptor, which is sensitive to only one type of stimulus
3. An intense stimulus, such as a loud sound or a heavy touch, is coded by ______________.
   a. different sensory receptors that project to different areas of the brain
   b. an increase in the number of neurons that respond to the stimulation

**Answers:** 1. b. use only a small portion of the available energy in their environment.
2. a. the combined firing of many different receptors and the neurons they connect with creates our sensations.
3. b. an increase in the number of neurons that respond to the stimulation.

# 4.3 How Does Perception Emerge from Sensation?

**Learning Objectives**

- Identify the primary sensory areas for touch, hearing, and vision.
- Discuss the gate control theory of pain.
- Explain how the brain localizes sound.
- Distinguish between the "what" and "where" pathways of the visual system.
- Describe blindsight.

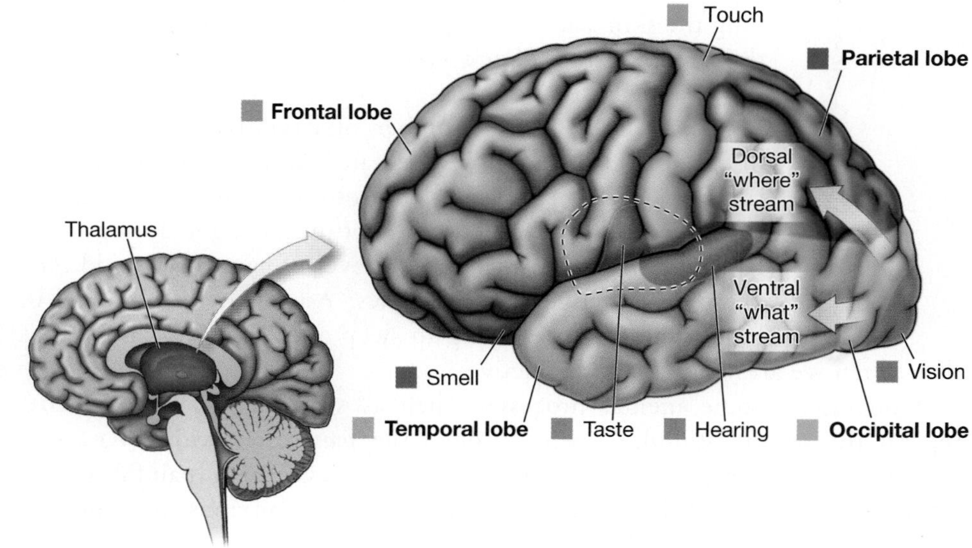

The perceptual system is stunningly intelligent in its ability to guide each of us around. For example, right this minute your brain is making millions of calculations to produce a coherent experience of your environment. Despite the illusion that the objects and events you are experiencing exist in the space around you, your experience is a construction of your brain and resides inside your skull. Neurons inside your brain do not directly experience the outside world. Instead, they communicate with other neurons inside and outside your brain. Neurons talk to neurons in total darkness. Yet your conscious experience of the world emerges from this communication. This process happens in milliseconds.

If you lay this book flat and look at the pages as a whole, you will see one image. You will not see the thousands of images that dance across your retina to create a constant, perhaps static view. What you perceive, then, is vastly different from the pattern of stimulation your retina is taking in. If you were aware of what your brain was doing every moment, you would be paralyzed by information overload. Most of the computations the brain performs never reach your consciousness. Only important new outcomes do. How does the brain extract a stable representation of the world from the information the senses provide?

So far, you have seen how sensation happens: Sensory receptors transduce stimuli into electrical impulses, and nerves then transmit those impulses to the brain. Working with just the electrical impulses it receives from nerves, the brain creates a rich variety of perceptual experiences. With the exception of olfaction, all sensory information is relayed to cortical and other areas of the brain from the thalamus. Information from each sense is projected separately from the thalamus to a specific region of the cerebral cortex. In these *primary sensory areas,* the perceptual process begins in earnest (**Figure 4.23**). Because the brain regions involved in taste and smell are not well understood, these senses are not discussed in the following sections.

**FIGURE 4.23 Primary Sensory Areas** These are the primary brain regions where information about taste, touch, hearing, smell, and vision are projected. Visual information travels in separate "streams"—what you see and where it is—from the occipital lobe (visual cortex) to different parts of the brain for further processing.

## In Touch, the Brain Integrates Sensory Information from Different Regions of the Body

Touch information from the thalamus is projected to the *primary somatosensory cortex,* in the parietal lobe. In the 1940s, in a classic series of studies of patients undergoing brain surgery, the neurosurgeon Wilder Penfield discovered that electrical stimulation of the primary somatosensory cortex could evoke the sensation of touch in different regions of the body (Penfield & Jasper, 1954). Penfield found that neighboring body parts tended to be represented next to one another, so that the body is effectively mapped out there according to physical proximity. As shown in Chapter 3's drawing of the homunculus (see Figure 3.21a), sensitive body parts have large amounts of cortical tissue dedicated to them. The most sensitive regions of the body, such as lips and fingers, have a great deal of cortex devoted to them. Other areas, such as the back and the calves, have very little.

**GATE CONTROL THEORY** The brain regulates the experience of pain, sometimes producing it, sometimes suppressing it. Pain is a complex experience that depends on biological, psychological, and cultural factors. The psychologist Ronald Melzack did pioneering research in this area. For example, he demonstrated that psychological factors, such as past experiences, are extremely important in determining how much pain a person feels.

With his collaborator Patrick Wall, Melzack formulated the *gate control theory of pain,* which states that for us to experience pain, pain receptors must be activated and a neural "gate" in the spinal cord must allow the signals through to the brain (Melzack & Wall, 1965). This theory was radical in that it conceptualized pain as a perceptual experience within the brain rather than simply a response to nerve stimulation. According to this theory, pain signals are transmitted by small-diameter nerve fibers, which can be blocked at the level of the spinal cord (prevented from reaching the brain) by the firing of larger sensory nerve fibers. Thus sensory nerve fibers can "close a gate" and prevent or reduce the perception of pain. This is why scratching an itch is so satisfying, why rubbing an aching muscle helps reduce the ache, and why vigorously rubbing the skin where an injection is about to be given reduces the needle's sting (**Figure 4.24**).

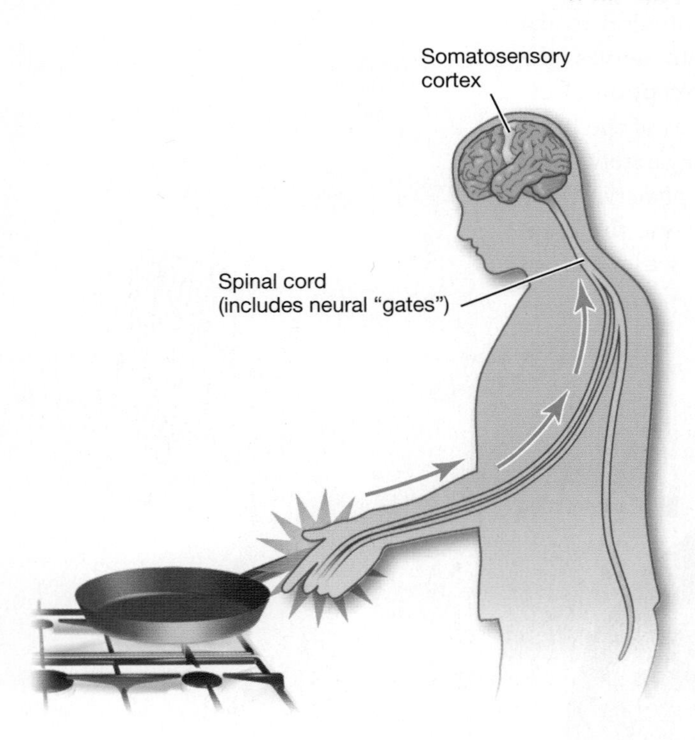


**FIGURE 4.24 Gate Control Theory**
According to the gate control theory of pain, neural "gates" in the spinal cord allow signals through. Those gates can be closed when information about touch is being transmitted (e.g., by rubbing a sore arm) or by distraction.

**CONTROLLING PAIN** A number of cognitive states, such as distraction, can also close the gate. Athletes sometimes play through pain because of their intense focus on the game. Wounded soldiers sometimes continue to fight during combat, often failing to recognize a level of pain that would render them inactive at other times. An insect bite bothers us more when we are trying to sleep and have few distractions than when we are wide awake and active.

Conversely, some mental processes, such as worrying about or focusing on the painful stimulus, seem to open the pain gates wider. Research participants who are well rested rate the same level of a painful stimulus as less painful than do participants who are fearful, anxious, or depressed

(Loggia, Mogil, & Bushnell, 2008; Sullivan et al., 2001). Likewise, positive moods help people cope with pain. In a systematic review of the literature, Swedish researchers found that listening to music was an extremely effective means of reducing postoperative pain, perhaps because it helps patients relax (Engwall & Duppils, 2009).

DeCharms and colleagues (2005) have pioneered techniques that offer hope for people who suffer from painful conditions. The researchers sought to teach people in pain—many of these people in chronic pain—to visualize their pain more positively. For example, participants were taught to think about a burning sensation as soothing, like the feeling of being in a sauna. As they tried to learn such techniques, they viewed fMRI images that showed which regions of their brains were active as they performed the tasks. Many participants learned techniques that altered their brain activity and reduced their pain.

Of course, there are more-traditional ways to control pain. Most of us have taken legal drugs, usually ibuprofen or acetaminophen, to reduce pain perception. If you have ever suffered from a severe toothache or needed surgery, you have probably experienced the benefits of pain medication. When a dentist administers Novocain to sensory neurons in the mouth, pain messages are not transmitted to the brain, so the mouth feels numb. General anesthesia slows down the firing of neurons throughout the nervous system, and the patient becomes unresponsive to stimulation (Perkins, 2007).

You can use your knowledge of pain perception anytime you need to reduce your own pain or to help others in pain. Distraction is usually the easiest way to reduce pain. If you are preparing for a painful procedure or suffering after one, watching an entertaining movie can help, especially if it is funny enough to elevate your mood. Music may help you relax, making it easier to deal with pain. Rapid rubbing can benefit a stubbed toe, for example, or a finger that was caught in a closing drawer. You will also feel less pain if you are rested, not fearful, and not anxious. Finally, try to visualize your pain as something more pleasant. Of course, severe pain is a warning that something in the body is seriously wrong. If you experience severe pain, you should be treated by a medical professional.

## In Hearing, the Brain Integrates Sensory Information from the Ears

Auditory neurons in the thalamus extend their axons to the *primary auditory cortex,* which is located in the temporal lobe. Neurons in the primary auditory cortex code the frequency (or pitch) of auditory stimuli. The neurons toward the front respond best to higher frequencies, such as that of a train whistle. Those toward the rear respond best to lower frequencies, such as that of a foghorn.

Locating the origin of a sound is an important part of auditory perception. In audition, the sensory receptors cannot code where events occur. Instead, the

*"Great! O.K., this time I want you to sound taller, and let me hear a little more hair."*

brain integrates the different sensory information coming from each of our two ears. Much of our understanding of auditory localization has come from research with barn owls. These nocturnal birds have finely tuned hearing, which helps them locate their prey. In fact, in a dark laboratory, a barn owl can locate a mouse through hearing alone. A barn owl uses two cues to locate a sound: the time the sound arrives in each ear and the sound's intensity in each ear. Unless the sound comes from exactly in front or in back of the owl, the sound will reach one ear first. Whichever side it comes from, it will sound softer on the other side because the owl's head acts as a barrier. These differences in timing and magnitude are minute, but they are not too small for the owl's brain to detect and act on. Although a human's ears are not as finely tuned to the locations of sounds as an owl's ears are, the human brain uses information from the two ears similarly (**Figure 4.25**).

## In Vision, the Brain Processes Sensory Information from the Eyes

The study of perception has focused to a large extent on the visual cortex and the multiple areas in which the retinal image is processed. The complexity of visual perception is underscored by the amount of cortical real estate dedicated to processing visual information. Some estimates suggest that up to half of the cerebral cortex may participate in visual perception in some way. As noted earlier, the *primary visual cortex* is in the occipital lobe.

**WHAT VERSUS WHERE** One important theory proposes that visual areas beyond the primary visual cortex form two parallel processing streams, or pathways. The lower, *ventral stream* appears to be specialized for the perception and recognition of objects, such as determining their colors and shapes. The upper, *dorsal stream* seems to be specialized for spatial perception—determining where an object is

**FIGURE 4.25 Auditory Localization (a)** Like barn owls, **(b)** humans draw on the intensity and timing of sounds to locate where the sounds are coming from.

and relating it to other objects in a scene. (Both streams are shown in Figure 4.23.) These two processing streams are therefore known as the *"what" stream* and the *"where" stream* (Ungerleider & Mishkin, 1982).

Damage to certain regions of the visual cortex provides evidence for distinguishing between these two streams of information. Consider the case of D.F. (Goodale & Milner, 1992). At age 34, this woman suffered carbon monoxide poisoning that damaged her visual system. Regions involved in the "what" pathway were particularly damaged. D.F. was no longer able to recognize the faces of her friends and family members, common objects, or even drawings of squares or of circles. She could recognize people by their voices, however, and objects if they were placed in her hands. Her condition—*object agnosia,* the inability to recognize objects—was striking in what she could and could not do. When presented with a drawing of, say, an apple, she could not identify or reproduce it. But if asked to draw an apple, she could do so from memory. Despite major deficits in her perception of objects, she could use visual information about the size, shape, and orientation of objects to control visually guided movements. In other words, her "where" pathway appeared to be intact. For instance, she could walk across a room and step around things adeptly. She could reach out and shake a person's hand. Most confounding, in laboratory tests, she could reach out and grasp a block. In performing this action, D.F. would put exactly the right distance between her fingers, even though she could not tell you what she was going to pick up or how large it was. Thus her conscious visual perception of objects—her "what" pathway—was impaired. She was not aware of taking in any visual information about objects she saw. Still, other aspects of her visual processing were unaffected. The intact regions of her visual cortex allowed her to use information about the size and location of objects despite her lack of awareness about those objects. As illustrated by D.F.'s case, different neurological systems operate independently to help us understand the world around us.

BLINDSIGHT Some research on visual awareness has examined **blindsight.** A person with this condition experiences some blindness because of damage to the visual system, but is unaware of having retained some sight. Typically, a blindsighted patient loses vision in only a portion of the visual field. For example, when looking forward, the person might not be able to see anything on his or her left. Researchers have discovered that when a stimulus is presented in this blind field, the patient can respond unconsciously to that stimulus. Say that a moving dot is presented in the blind field and the patient is asked to indicate the direction in which the dot is moving. Typically, the patient reports seeing nothing. When pressed to guess the direction of motion, however, more often than by chance the patient will guess correctly.

A 52-year-old physician became blind after two consecutive strokes destroyed his primary visual cortex (Pegna, Khateb, Lazeyras, & Seghier, 2005). Nothing was wrong with his eyes, but the visual regions of his brain could not process any information they received from them. Although alert and aware of his surroundings, the patient reported being unable to see anything, not even the presence of intense light. When the patient was shown a series of faces and was asked to guess their emotional expressions, he had no sense of having seen anything. Remarkably, however, he was able to identify the expressions at a level much better than by chance. He did not respond to other stimuli (such as shapes, animal faces, or scary stimuli).

**blindsight** A condition in which people who are blind have some spared visual capacities in the absence of any visual awareness.

## Summing Up

### How Does Perception Emerge from Sensation?

Sensory information is relayed from our receptors to our brain by nerves. Gate control theory maintains that pain perception may be blocked by "closing gates" at the level of the spinal cord. With the exception of smell, sensory information is relayed to the thalamus, which subsequently projects the information to distinct cortical regions. The primary sensory areas for touch, hearing, and vision are in the parietal, temporal, and occipital lobes, respectively. The cortical regions of the visual system are characterized by "what" and "where" streams. Damage to cortical regions can result in unusual perceptual conditions, such as blindsight.

## Measuring Up

1. The primary sensory area for touch is in the ____________ lobe; the primary sensory area for vision is in the ____________ lobe.
   a. frontal; parietal
   b. occipital; temporal
   c. temporal; parietal
   d. temporal; frontal
   e. parietal; occipital
2. After a stroke, patient X is unable to reach out to grasp an object that she can see and recognize. This deficit suggests that patient X has ____________.
   a. sustained damage to the ventral stream
   b. sustained damage to the dorsal stream
   c. blindsight

**Answers:** 1. e. parietal; occipital.
2. b. sustained damage to the dorsal stream.

**Learning Objectives**

- Describe the Gestalt principles of perceptual organization.
- Identify the brain regions associated with facial perception.
- Identify cues for depth perception.
- Explain how the visual system perceives motion.
- Discuss how perceptual constancy is achieved.

# 4.4 What Factors Influence Visual Perception?

## Object Perception Requires Construction

Within the brain, what exactly happens to the information the senses take in about an object's features? How does that information get organized?

Optical illusions are among the tools psychologists have for understanding how the brain uses such information. Many perceptual psychologists believe that illusions reveal the mechanisms that help our visual systems determine the sizes and distances of objects in the visual environment. In doing so, illusions illustrate how we form accurate representations of the three-dimensional world. Researchers rely on these tricks to reveal automatic perceptual systems that, in most circumstances, result in accurate perception (**Figure 4.26**).

**GESTALT PRINCIPLES OF PERCEPTUAL ORGANIZATION** As discussed in Chapter 1, Gestalt psychologists theorized that perception is more than the result of

## FIGURE 4.26 Try for Yourself: Optical Illusions

### (a) The Ouchi Illusion

Named for the Japanese artist Hajime Ouchi, who invented it, this illusion shows how we separate a figure from its background.

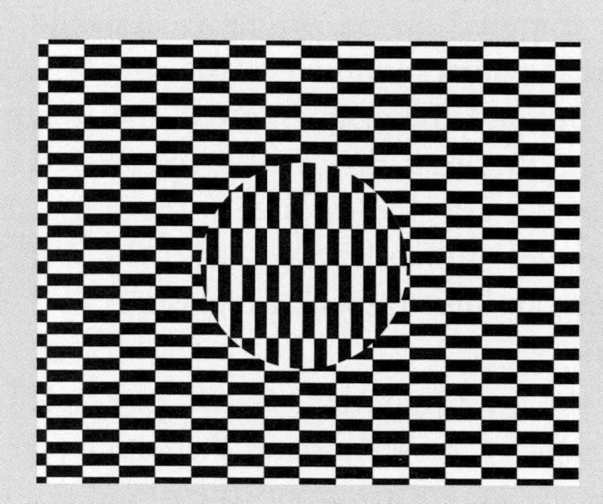

**Result:** The circle is made of lines offset from the rest of the display. Scrolling the image horizontally or vertically gives a much stronger effect. Some people report seeing colors and movement in this illusion.

### (b) The McCollough Effect

This illusion was named for the vision researcher Celeste McCollough, who first described it. Alternate your gaze from the green stimulus with vertical lines to the magenta stimulus with horizontal lines, changing from one to the other approximately every second for 40 seconds.

Then look at the black-and-white stimulus, composed of vertical and horizontal lines.

What do you see?

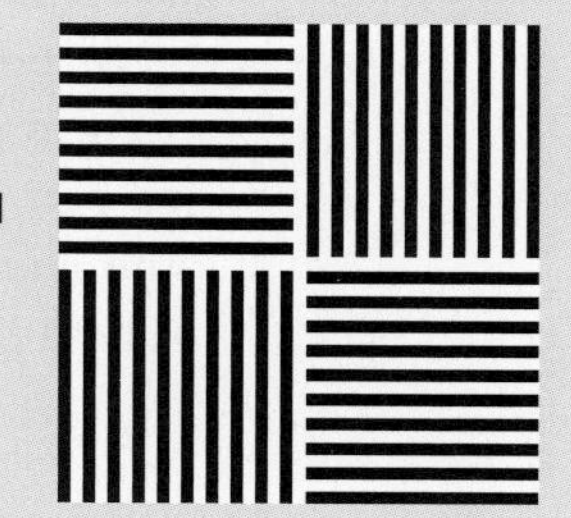

**Result:** You should see magenta vertical lines and green horizontal lines. Because the McCollough effect can last for hours or even a day, it cannot be explained by simple neural fatigue (where neurons reduce firing after repeated use). For this reason, the effect more likely occurs in higher brain regions, not in the eye. As noted in the text, the visual system is especially primed to process information about edges, and color-related edge perception may be involved.

accumulating sensory data. The German word *Gestalt* means "shape" or "form." As used in psychology, *Gestalt* means "organized whole." The founders of Gestalt psychology postulated a series of laws to explain how our brains group the perceived features of a visual scene into organized wholes. Gestalt psychology holds that our brains use innate principles to organize sensory information. These principles explain why we perceive, say, "a car" as opposed to "metal, tires, glass, door handles, hubcaps, fenders," and so on. For us, an object exists as a unit, not as a collection of features.

**FIGURE AND GROUND** One of the visual perception system's most basic organizing principles is distinguishing between figure and ground. A classic illustration of this is the *reversible figure illusion*. Look back at Figure 1.12, where you can see either a full face or two faces looking at each other—but not both at the same time. In identifying either figure—indeed, *any* figure—the brain assigns the rest of the scene to the background. In this illusion, the "correct" assignment of figure and ground is ambiguous. The figures periodically reverse (switch back and forth) as the visual system strives to make sense of the stimulation. In ways like this, visual perception is dynamic and ongoing.

As discussed in Chapter 1, Richard Nisbett and colleagues (2001) have demonstrated cultural differences between Eastern people's perceptions and Western people's perceptions. Easterners focus on a scene holistically, whereas Westerners focus on single elements in the forefront. Thus Easterners are more likely to be influenced by the (back)ground of a figure, and Westerners are more likely to extract the figure from its (back)ground.

Now look back at Figure 1.11. In this illusion, it is hard to see the Dalmatian standing among the many black spots scattered on the white background. This effect occurs because the part of the image corresponding to the dog lacks contours that define the dog's edges and because the dog's spotted coat resembles that of the background. Many observers find that they first recognize one part of the dog—say, the head—and from that are able to discern the dog's shape. Once you perceive the dog, it becomes very difficult to *not* see it the next time you look at the figure. Thus experience can inform shape processing.

**PROXIMITY AND SIMILARITY** Two of the most important Gestalt principles concern proximity and similarity. The *principle of proximity* states that the closer two figures are to each other, the more likely we are to group them and see them as part of the same object (**Figure 4.27a**). You might already be familiar with the *principle of similarity* as illustrated by the *Sesame Street* song and game "One of These Things Is Not Like the Others." We tend to group figures according to

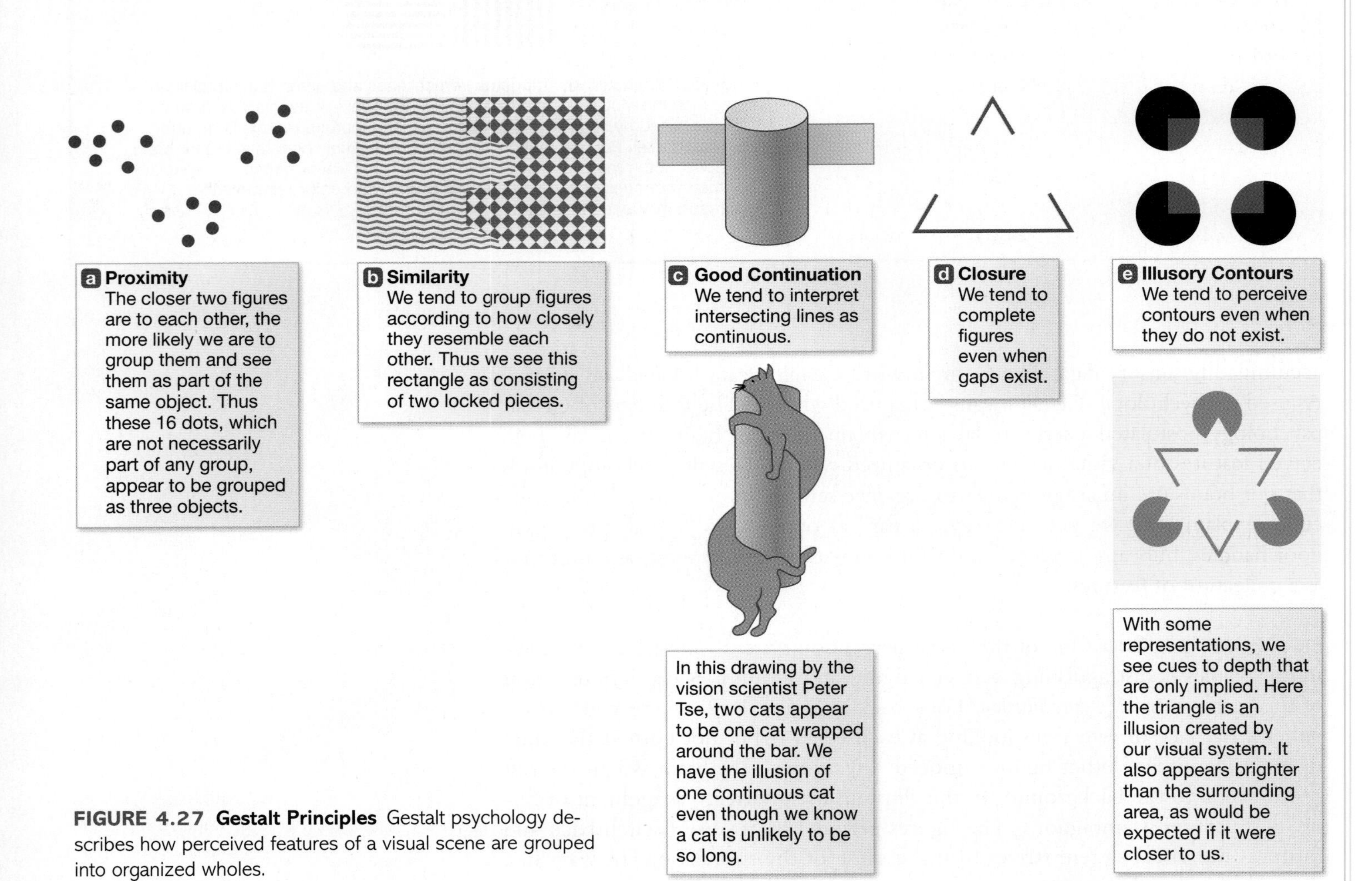


**FIGURE 4.27 Gestalt Principles** Gestalt psychology describes how perceived features of a visual scene are grouped into organized wholes.

how closely they resemble each other, whether in shape, color, or orientation (**Figure 4.27b**). In accordance with both of these principles, we tend to cluster elements of the visual scene. Clustering enables us to consider a scene as a whole rather than as individual parts. For example, we often perceive a flock of birds as a single entity because all the elements, the birds, are similar and in close proximity.

**THE "BEST" FORMS** Other Gestalt principles describe how we perceive a form's features. *Good continuation* is the tendency to interpret intersecting lines as continuous rather than as changing direction radically. Good contour (boundary line) continuation appears to play a role in completing an object behind an *occluder,* which can be anything that hides from view a portion of an object or an entire object. For example, in **Figure 4.27c** the bar in the top illustration appears to be completely behind the occluder. Good continuation may operate over features that are more complex than contours, however. In the bottom illustration, two cats appear to be one extremely long cat wrapped around the pole, yet no continuous contours permit this completion. *Closure* refers to the tendency to complete figures that have gaps, as in **Figure 4.27d.** *Illusory contours* refers to the fact that we sometimes perceive contours and cues to depth even though they do not exist (**Figure 4.27e**).

**BOTTOM-UP AND TOP-DOWN INFORMATION PROCESSING** How do we assemble the information about parts into a perception of a whole object? According to most models of the process, pattern recognition is hierarchical. Specifically, pattern recognition occurs through **bottom-up processing.** This term means that data are relayed in the brain from lower to higher levels of processing. But perception is actually a combination of bottom-up and **top-down processing.** In top-down processing, information at higher levels of mental processing can influence lower, "earlier" levels in the processing hierarchy. For this reason, context affects perception: What we expect to see (higher level) influences what we perceive (lower level). Consider the Dalmatian illustration discussed earlier. Also consider the incomplete letters in **Figure 4.28.** The same shape appears in the center of each word, but you perceive the shape first as "H" and then as "A" (lower level). Your perception depends on which interpretation makes sense in the context of the particular word (higher level).

Knowing how information is processed can help us understand and avoid mistakes. For example, faulty expectations can lead to faulty perceptions. On November 28, 1979, Air New Zealand Flight 901 crashed into the slopes of Mount Erebus, on Ross Island in Antarctica, causing the deaths of the 237 passengers and 20 crew members. Because the aircraft's flight computer had been programmed incorrectly, the plane was far off course. In addition, the pilots had descended below the minimum altitude allowed for the flight. However, these factors do not explain why, until moments before impact, the flight crew failed to notice the 12,000-foot volcano looming in front of them (**Figure 4.29**).

Psychologists testifying at the commission of inquiry offered a possible, if startling, explanation: The pilots saw what they expected to see. One unique hazard of Antarctic aviation is "whiteout," in which the sky and the snow-covered terrain appear to merge and pilots are unable visually to distinguish the ground or the horizon. The pilots believed they were flying over the Ross Ice Shelf, hundreds of miles from their actual location. They did not expect to encounter mountains anywhere near their flight path. The psychologists argued that the few visual cues available to the pilots were sufficiently consistent with what they

**bottom-up processing** A hierarchical model of pattern recognition in which data are relayed from one level of mental processing to the next, always moving to a higher level of processing.

**top-down processing** A hierarchical model of pattern recognition in which information at higher levels of mental processing can also influence lower, "earlier" levels in the processing hierarchy.

THE CAT

**FIGURE 4.28 Context** Context plays an important role in object recognition. **How does context aid your interpretation of the shapes shown here?**

**FIGURE 4.29 Mount Erebus** Because the pilots on Air New Zealand Flight 901 did not expect to see this Antarctic volcano ahead of them, they failed to see it.

Participants were shown an array of faces and objects.

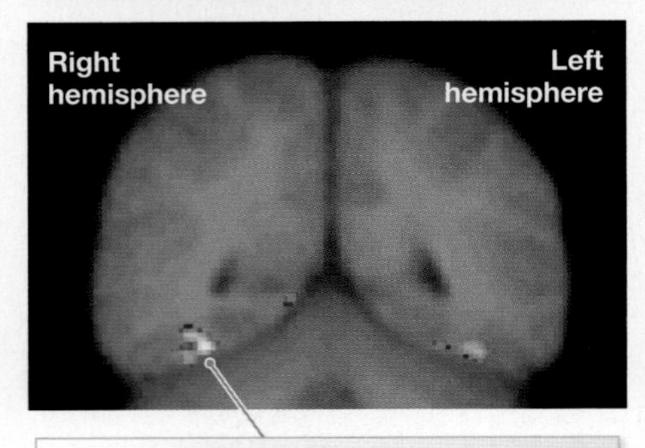


The visual perception of faces activated an area of the brain known as the fusiform gyrus. The right hemisphere responded more strongly than the left, especially when faces were presented among objects.

**FIGURE 4.30 Perceiving Faces** Brain imaging shows increased activity in the right hemisphere when faces are viewed.

expected to see that in their minds their expectations were confirmed. Since there appeared to be no danger, the pilots decided, fatally, to reduce altitude to give the passengers a better view of the spectacular Antarctic landscape. The combination of an unusually sparse visual environment and the pilots' beliefs conspired to fool their visual systems into seeing terrain that was not there—and failing to see the mountain that was.

**FACE PERCEPTION** One special class of object that the visual system is sensitive to is faces. As highly social animals, humans are well able to perceive and interpret facial expressions. Several studies support the idea that human faces reveal "special" information that is not available in any other way. For example, we can more readily discern information about a person's mood, attentiveness, sex, race, age, and so on by looking at that person's face than by listening to the person talk, watching the person walk, or studying his or her clothing (Bruce & Young, 1986).

People are better at recognizing members of their own race or ethnic group, however, than at recognizing members of other races or ethnic groups. There is some truth to the saying *they all look alike,* but the saying applies to all groups. This effect may occur because people have more exposure to people of their own race or ethnicity (Gosselin & Larocque, 2000). In the United States, where whites greatly outnumber blacks, whites are much better at recognizing white faces than at recognizing black faces (Brigham & Malpass, 1985).

Some people have particular deficits in the ability to recognize faces—a condition known as *prosopagnosia*—but not in the ability to recognize other objects (Farah, 1996). As discussed earlier in this chapter, patient D.F. has trouble with object recognition. Because D.F. also has prosopagnosia, she cannot tell one face from another. Still, she is able to judge whether something is a face or not and whether that face is upside down or not. This ability implies that facial recognition differs from nonfacial object recognition (Steeves et al., 2006).

Faces are so important that certain brain regions appear to be dedicated solely to perceiving them. As part of the "what" stream discussed earlier, certain cortical regions, and even specific neurons, seem to be specialized to perceive faces. A number of separate brain imaging studies have found that a region of the *fusiform gyrus,* in the right hemisphere, may be specialized for perceiving faces (Grill-Spector, Knouf, & Kanwisher, 2004; McCarthy, Puce, Gore, & Allison, 1997; **Figure 4.30**). Indeed, this brain area responds most strongly to upright faces, as we would perceive them in the normal environment (Kanwisher, Tong, & Nakayama, 1998).

People have a surprisingly hard time recognizing faces, especially unknown faces, that are upside down. We are much worse at this task than we are at recognizing other inverted objects. The inversion interferes with the way people perceive the relationship between facial features (Hancock, Bruce, & Burton, 2000). For instance, if the eyebrows are bushier than usual, this facial characteristic is obvious if the face is upright but not detectable when the face is inverted. One interesting example of the perceptual difficulties associated with inverted faces is evident in the Thatcher illusion, so called because the effect was first studied using photos of the former British prime minister Margaret Thatcher (Thompson, 1980; **Figure 4.31**).

Other brain areas are sensitive to facial expression and gaze direction. For example, a face's emotional significance appears to activate the amygdala, which is involved in calculating potential danger (Adams, Gordon, Baird, Ambady, & Kleck, 2003; Adolphs, 2003). As discussed in Chapter 10, one theory suggests that the amygdala processes visual information very crudely and quickly, to help identify potential threats. For example, the amygdala becomes activated when people observe subliminal presentations of faces expressing fear (Whalen et al., 2001). When the blind physician discussed earlier was shown a series of faces and was asked to guess their emotional expression, he had no sense of having seen anything, but he was able to identify the expression at a level much better than by chance. He did not respond to other stimuli (such as shapes, animal faces, or scary stimuli). A brain scanner showed that his amygdala became activated when he was presented with emotional faces but not with faces showing neutral expressions. Thus his amygdala might have processed the faces' emotional content despite his lack of awareness. This possibility raises the intriguing question of whether the physician was "seeing" the faces. It also may help illuminate how visual information reaches the amygdala when primary visual areas are damaged.

**FIGURE 4.31 Try for Yourself: The Thatcher Illusion**

These two inverted pictures of Margaret Thatcher look normal. Turn your book upside down to reveal a different perspective.

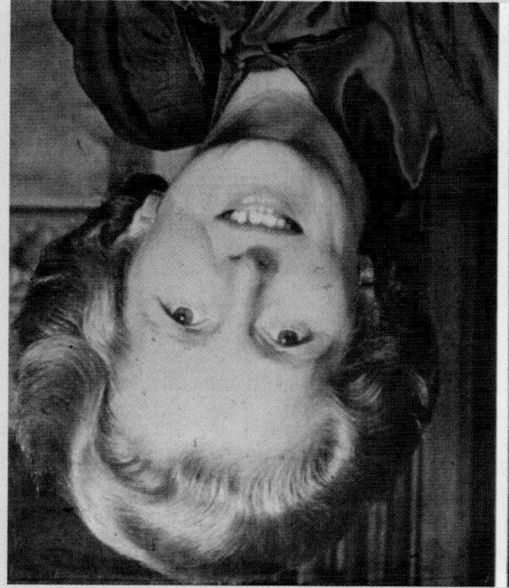

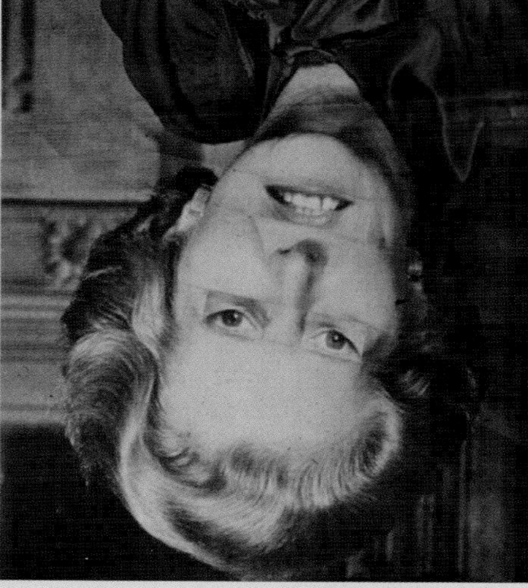

**Result:** Inversion of the whole face interferes with the perception of the individual components. This effect implies that we pay most attention to the eyes and mouth. As long as those features are oriented correctly, the rest of the face appears normal even if it is not.

In a series of studies, researchers found that people more quickly and accurately recognize angry facial expressions than happy ones (Becker, Kenrick, Neuberg, Blackwell, & Smith, 2007). In addition, the researchers found that most people recognize anger more quickly on a man's face than on a woman's, and they found the reverse for happiness. The researchers think these results are due partly to people's beliefs that men express anger more often than women do and that women express happiness more often than men do (i.e., the beliefs would be contributing to top-down processing—we are more likely to "see" what we expect to see). They also think that female and male facial features drive the effect. For example, bushy eyebrows low on the face are more likely to be perceived as an expression of anger, and men typically have bushier and lower eyebrows than women. According to evolutionary psychology, there is an adaptive advantage to the detection of angry faces. Given that men in every society commit most violent crimes, it is adaptive to be especially fast and accurate at recognizing angry male faces. Thus facial recognition supports an idea emphasized throughout this book: The brain is adaptive.

## Depth Perception Is Important for Locating Objects

One of the visual system's most important tasks is to locate objects in space. Without this capacity, we would find it difficult to navigate in the world and interact with things and people. One of the most enduring questions in psychological research is how we are able to construct a three-dimensional mental representation of the visual world from two-dimensional retinal input. Our ability to see depth in a photograph illustrates this point: A three-dimensional array of objects creates exactly the same image on the retina that a photograph of the same array of objects does. Despite this inherent ambiguity, we do not confuse pictures with the scenes they depict.

We are able to perceive depth in the two-dimensional patterns of photographs, movies, videos, and television images because the brain applies the same rules or mechanisms that it uses to work out the spatial relations between objects in the three-dimensional world. To do this, the brain rapidly and automatically exploits certain prior assumptions it has about the relationship between two-dimensional image cues and the three-dimensional world. Among these assumptions are cues that help the visual system perceive depth. These depth cues can be divided into two types: **Binocular depth cues** are available from both eyes together and contribute to bottom-up processing. **Monocular depth cues** are available from each eye alone and provide organizational information for top-down processing.

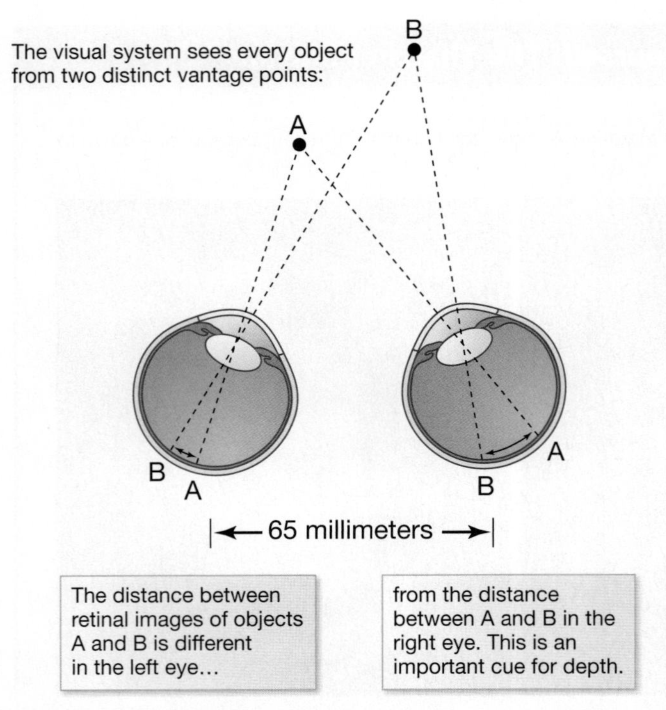


**FIGURE 4.32 Binocular Disparity** To demonstrate your own binocular disparity, hold one of your index fingers out in front of your face and close first one eye and then the other. Your finger appears to move because each eye, due to its position relative to the finger, has a unique retinal image.

**BINOCULAR DEPTH PERCEPTION** One of the most important cues to depth perception is **binocular disparity** (or *retinal disparity*). This cue is caused by the distance between humans' two eyes. Because each eye has a slightly different view of the world, the brain has access to two different but overlapping retinal images. The brain uses the disparity between these two retinal images to compute distances to nearby objects (**Figure 4.32**). The ability to determine an object's depth based on that object's projections to each eye is called *stereoscopic vision*.

A related binocular depth cue is **convergence.** This term refers to the way that our eye muscles turn our eyes inward when we view nearby objects. The brain knows how much the eyes are converging, and it uses this information to perceive distance (**Figure 4.33**).

**MONOCULAR DEPTH PERCEPTION** Although binocular disparity is an important cue for depth perception, it is useful only for objects relatively close to us. Furthermore, we can perceive depth even with one eye closed, because of monocular depth cues. Artists routinely use these cues to create a sense of depth, so monocular depth cues are also called *pictorial depth cues*. The Renaissance painter,

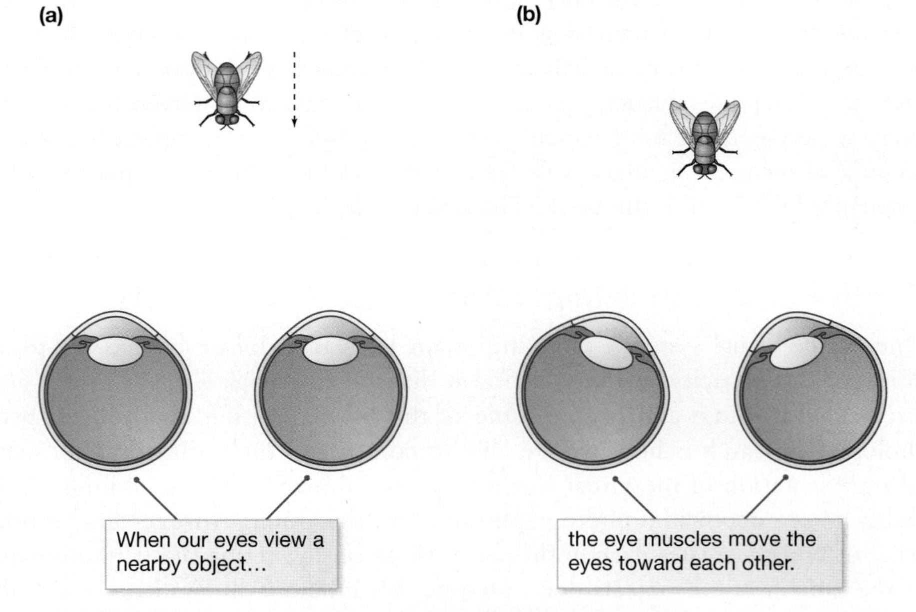


**FIGURE 4.33 Convergence** Hold one of your index fingers out in front of your face, about a foot away. Slowly bring your finger toward your eyes. Are you able to perceive your eyes converging?

**binocular depth cues** Cues of depth perception that arise from the fact that people have two eyes.

**monocular depth cues** Cues of depth perception that are available to each eye alone.

**binocular disparity** A depth cue; because of the distance between a person's eyes, each eye receives a slightly different retinal image.

**convergence** A cue of binocular depth perception; when a person views a nearby object, the eye muscles turn the eyes inward.

**FIGURE 4.34 Pictorial Depth Cues** Using the bulleted list below as a reference, try to identify the six depth cues in Edvard Munch's painting *Evening on Karl Johan Street* (circa 1892).

sculptor, architect, and engineer Leonardo da Vinci first identified many of these cues, which include:

- *Occlusion:* A near object occludes (blocks) an object that is farther away.
- *Relative size:* Far-off objects project a smaller retinal image than close objects do, if the far-off and close objects are the same physical size.
- *Familiar size:* We know how large familiar objects are, so we can tell how far away they are by the size of their retinal images.
- *Linear perspective:* Seemingly parallel lines appear to converge in the distance.
- *Texture gradient:* As a uniformly textured surface recedes, its texture continuously becomes denser.
- *Position relative to horizon:* All else being equal, objects below the horizon that appear higher in the visual field are perceived as being farther away. Objects above the horizon that appear lower in the visual field are perceived as being farther away (**Figure 4.34**).

MOTION CUES FOR DEPTH PERCEPTION Motion is another cue for depth. *Motion parallax* is the relative movements of objects that are at various distances from the observer. For example, when you watch the scenery from a moving car, near objects such as mailboxes seem to pass quickly, far objects more slowly (**Figure 4.35**). If you fixate on an object farther away, such as a mountain, it appears to match your speed. If you fixate on an object at an intermediate distance, such as a house set back from the road, anything closer (e.g., the mailbox) moves opposite your direction relative to that object (e.g., house). Anything farther (e.g., mountain) moves in your direction relative to the object (e.g., house). Motion cues such as these help the brain calculate which objects are closer and which are farther away.

**FIGURE 4.35 Motion Parallax** Near objects seem to pass us more quickly in the opposite direction of our movement. Objects farther away seem to move more slowly.

## Size Perception Depends on Distance Perception

The size of an object's retinal image depends on that object's distance from the observer. The farther away the object is, the smaller its retinal image. To determine an object's size, then, the visual system needs to know how far away it is. Most of the time, enough depth information is available for the visual system to work out an object's distance and thus infer how large the object is. Size perception sometimes fails, however, and an object may look bigger or smaller than it really is (**Figure 4.36**). This optical illusion arises when normal perceptual processes incorrectly represent the distance between the viewer and the stimuli. In other words, depth cues can fool us into seeing depth when it is not there. Alternatively, a lack of depth cues can fool us into *not* seeing depth when it *is* there. This section considers two phenomena related to both depth perception and distance perception: *Ames boxes* (also called *Ames rooms*) and the *Ponzo illusion*.

**FIGURE 4.36 Distance Perception** This picture, by Rebecca Robinson, captures what appears to be a tiny Sarah Heatherton standing on James Heatherton's head. This illusion occurs because the photo fails to present depth information: It does not convey the hill on which Sarah is standing.

**AMES BOXES** Ames boxes were crafted in the 1940s by Adelbert Ames, a painter turned scientist. These constructions present powerful depth illusions. Inside the Ames boxes, rooms play with linear perspective and other distance cues. One such room makes a far corner appear the same distance away as a near corner (**Figure 4.37**). In a normal room and in this Ames box, the nearby child projects a larger retinal image than the child farther away. Normally, however, the nearby child would not appear to be a giant, because the perceptual system would take depth into account when assessing size. Here, the depth cues are wrong, so the nearby child appears farther away than he is, and the disproportionate size of his image on your retina makes him look huge.

**THE PONZO ILLUSION** The Ponzo illusion, first described by the psychologist Mario Ponzo in 1913, is another classic example of a size/distance illusion (**Figure 4.38**). The common explanation for this effect is that monocular depth cues make the two-dimensional figure seem three-dimensional (Rock, 1984). As noted earlier, seemingly parallel lines appear to converge in the distance. Here, the two lines drawn to look like railroad tracks receding in the distance trick your brain into thinking they are parallel. Therefore, you perceive the two

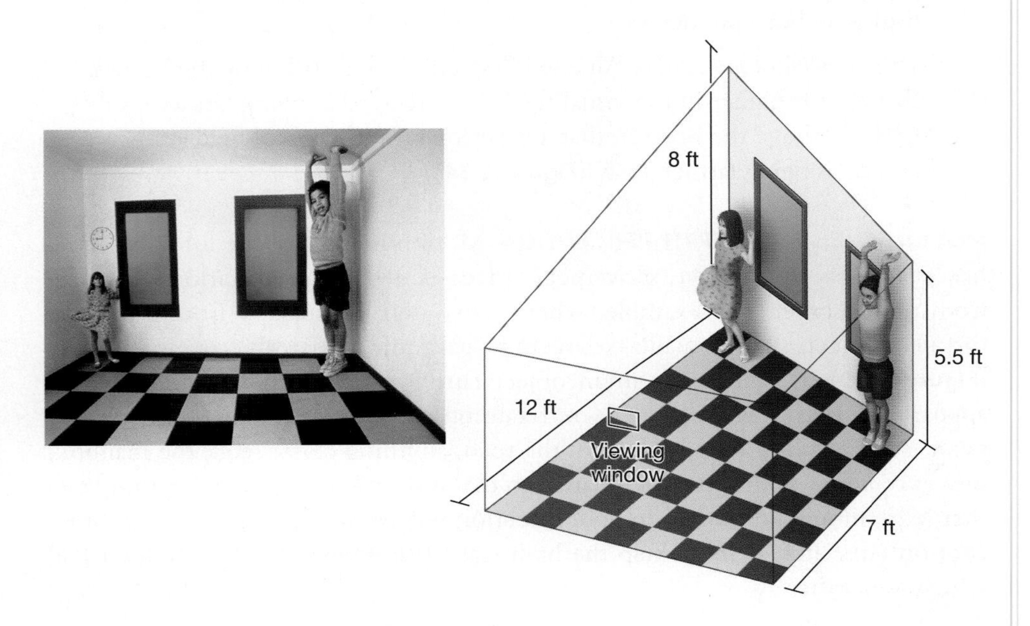


**FIGURE 4.37 The Ames Box** Ames played with depth cues to create size illusions. For example, as illustrated here, he made a diagonally cut room appear rectangular by using crooked windows and floor tiles. When one child stands in a near corner and another (of similar height) stands in a far corner, the room creates the illusion that they are equidistant from the viewer. Therefore, the closer child looks like a giant compared with the child farther away.

parallel lines in the center as if they are at different distances and thus different in size when they actually are the same size. This illusion shows how much we rely on depth perception to gauge size. The brain defaults to using depth cues even when depth is absent. Once again, the brain responds as efficiently as possible.

**FIGURE 4.38 The Ponzo Illusion** The two horizontal lines appear to be different sizes but are actually the same length.

## Motion Perception Has Internal and External Cues

We know how motion can cue depth perception, but how does the brain perceive motion? One answer is that we have neurons specialized for detecting movement. In other words, these neurons fire when movement occurs. But how does the brain know what is moving? If you look out a window and see a car driving past a house, how does your brain know the car is moving and not the house?

Consider the dramatic case of M.P., a German woman. After receiving damage to secondary visual areas of her brain—areas critical for motion perception—M.P. saw the world as a series of snapshots rather than as a moving image (Zihl, von Cramon, & Mai, 1983). Pouring tea, she would see the liquid frozen in air and be surprised when her cup overflowed. Before crossing a street, she might spot a car far away. When she tried to cross, however, that car would be right in front of her. M.P. had a unique deficit: She could perceive objects and colors but not continuous movement.

This section considers three phenomena that offer insights into how the visual system perceives motion: *motion aftereffects, compensation for head and eye motion,* and *stroboscopic motion perception.*

**MOTION AFTEREFFECTS** Motion aftereffects may occur when you gaze at a moving image for a long time and then look at a stationary scene. You experience a momentary impression that the new scene is moving in the opposite direction from the moving image. This illusion is also called the *waterfall effect,* because if you stare at a waterfall and then turn away, the scenery you are now looking at will seem to move upward for a moment.

Motion aftereffects are strong evidence that motion-sensitive neurons exist in the brain. According to the theory that explains this illusion, the visual cortex has neurons that respond to movement in a given direction. When you stare at a moving stimulus long enough, these direction-specific neurons begin to adapt to the motion. That is, they become fatigued and therefore less sensitive. If the stimulus is suddenly removed, the motion detectors that respond to all the other directions are more active than the fatigued motion detectors. Thus you see the new scene moving in the other direction.

**COMPENSATION FOR HEAD AND EYE MOVEMENT** The existence of motion-sensitive neurons does not completely explain motion perception. For instance, when you see what appears to be a moving object, how do you know whether the object is moving, you are moving, or your eyes are moving? Images move across your retina all the time, and you do not always perceive them as moving. Each slight blink or eye movement creates a new image on the retina. Why is it that every time you move your eye or your head, the images you see do not jump around? One explanation is that the brain calculates an object's perceived movements by monitoring the movement of the eyes, and perhaps also of the head, as they track a moving object. In addition, motion detectors track an image's motion across the retina, as the receptors in the retina fire one after the other (**Figure 4.39**).

**perceptual constancy** Correctly perceiving objects as constant in their shape, size, color, and lightness, despite raw sensory data that could mislead perception.

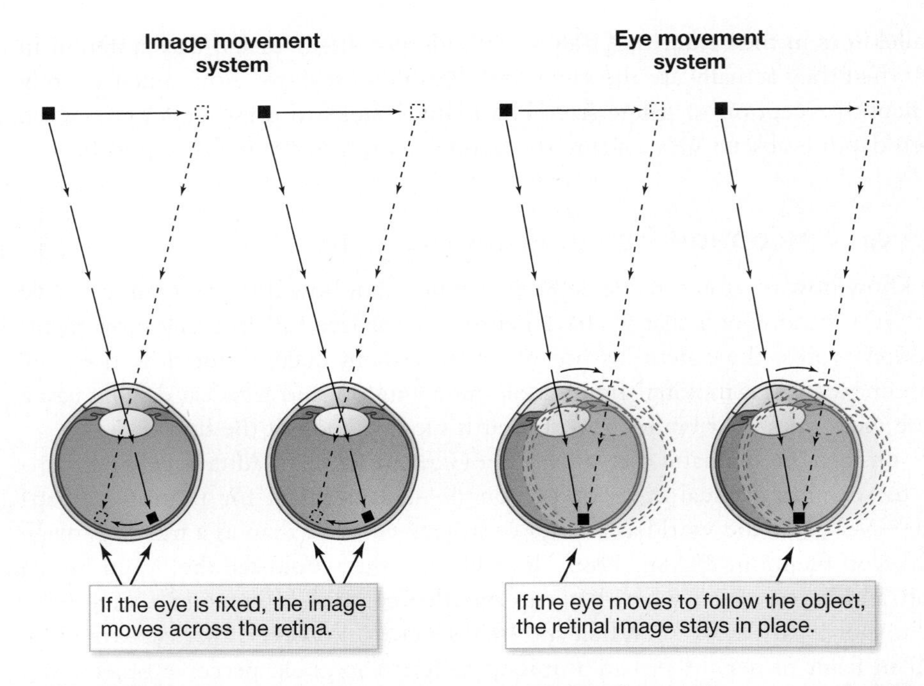


**FIGURE 4.39 Perceiving Movement** These diagrams illustrate the two ways that the visual system detects movement.

**STROBOSCOPIC MOTION PERCEPTION** Movies are made up of still-frame images, presented one after the other to create the illusion of motion pictures. This phenomenon is based on stroboscopic movement, a perceptual illusion that occurs when two or more slightly different images are presented in rapid succession (**Figure 4.40**). The Gestalt psychologist Max Wertheimer conducted experiments in 1912 by flashing, at different intervals, two vertical lines placed close together. He discovered that when the interval was less than 30 milliseconds, subjects thought the two lines were flashed simultaneously. When the interval was greater than 200 milliseconds, they saw two lines being flashed at different times. Between those times, movement illusions occurred: When the interval was about 60 milliseconds, the line appeared to jump from one place to another. At slightly longer intervals, the line appeared to move continuously—a phenomenon called *phi movement*.

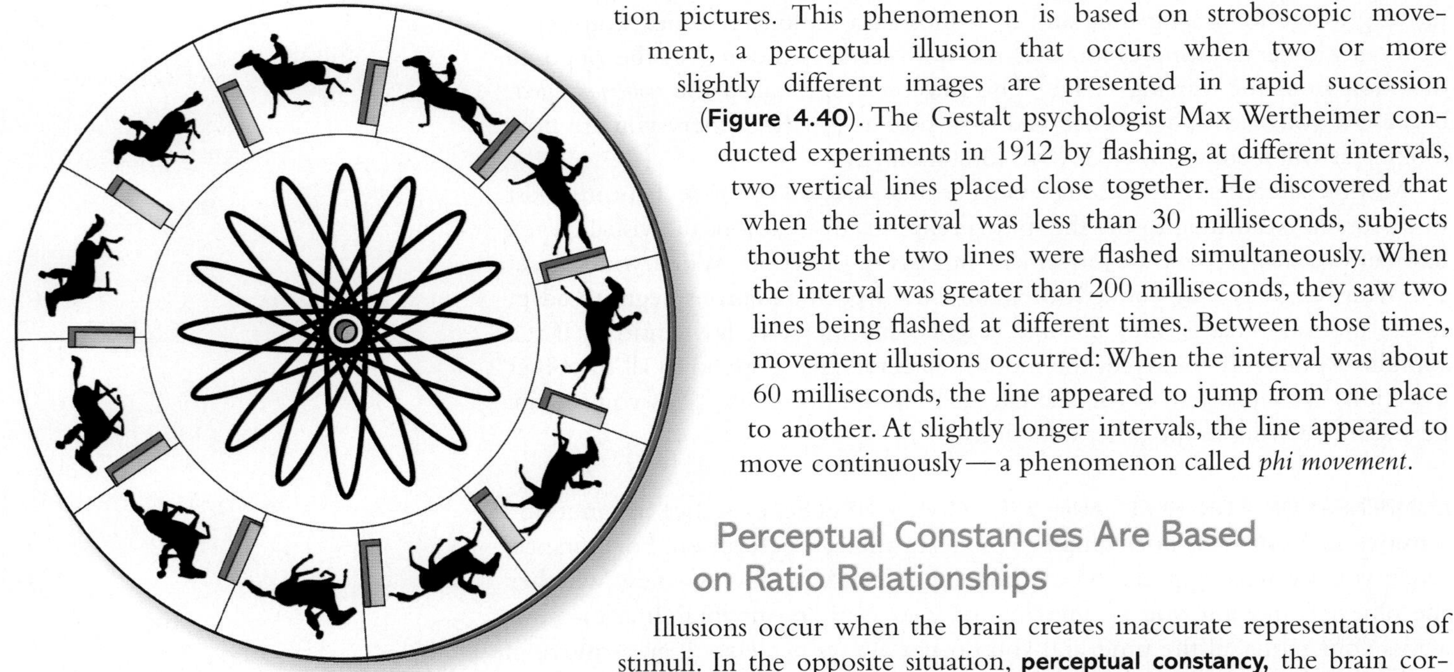

**FIGURE 4.40 How Moving Pictures Work** This static series would appear transformed if you spun the wheel. When the slightly different images were presented in rapid succession, the stroboscopic movement would tell your brain that you were watching a moving horse.

## Perceptual Constancies Are Based on Ratio Relationships

Illusions occur when the brain creates inaccurate representations of stimuli. In the opposite situation, **perceptual constancy,** the brain correctly perceives objects as constant despite sensory data that could lead it to think otherwise. Consider your image in the mirror. What you see in the mirror might look like it is your actual size, but the image is much smaller than the parts of you being reflected. (If you doubt this claim, try tracing around the image of your face in a steamy bathroom mirror.) Similarly, how does the brain know that a person is 6 feet tall when the retinal image of that person changes size according to how near or far the person is (**Figure 4.41**)? How does the brain know that snow is white and a tire is black, even when snow at night or a tire in bright light might send the same luminance cues to the retina?

For the most part, changing an object's angle, distance, or illumination does not change our perception of that object's size, shape, color, or lightness. But to perceive any of these four constancies, we need to understand the relationship between the object and at least one other factor. For *size constancy,* we need to know how far away the object is from us. For *shape constancy,* we need to know from what angle we are seeing the object. For *color constancy,* we need to compare the wavelengths of light reflected from the object with those reflected from its background. Likewise, for *lightness constancy,* we need to know how much light is being reflected from the object and from its background. In each case, the brain computes a ratio based on the relative magnitude rather than relying on each sensation's absolute magnitude. The perceptual system's ability to make relative judgments allows it to maintain constancy across various perceptual contexts. Although their precise mechanisms are unknown, these constancies illustrate that perceptual systems are tuned to detect changes from baseline conditions, not just to respond to sensory inputs.

By studying how illusions work, many perceptual psychologists have come to believe that the brain has built-in assumptions that influence perceptions. The vast majority of visual illusions appear to be beyond our conscious control—we cannot make ourselves not see illusions, even when we know they are not true representations of objects or events (**Figure 4.42**). Thus the visual system is a complex interplay of constancies, which allow us to see both a stable world and perceptual illusions that we cannot control.

(a)

(b)

**FIGURE 4.41 Perceptual Constancy** When you look at each of these photos, your retinal image of the bearded man is the same. Why, then, does he appear larger in (a) than in (b)?

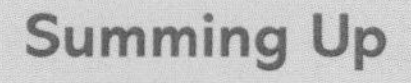

## Summing Up

### What Factors Influence Visual Perception?

Information first arrives in primary sensory regions. Multiple brain regions then contribute to our unified perceptual experience. The perceptual system uses cues from the perceiver's environment to help interpret sensory information. For example, the brain uses depth cues to determine the location of objects, and it uses ratio relationships to determine the perceptual constancy of objects. Contemporary theorists emphasize that perceptions are not faithful reproductions of the physical world. Instead, perceptions are constructed by the brain through multiple processes.

## Measuring Up

1. Match each of the following monocular depth cues with its description: familiar size, linear perspective, occlusion, position relative to horizon, relative size, texture gradient.
   a. Seemingly parallel lines appear to converge in the distance.
   b. Near objects block those that are farther away.
   c. We use our knowledge of an object's size to judge the object's distance.
   d. Smaller objects are judged to be farther away.
   e. Uniform surfaces appear denser in the distance.
   f. Objects below the horizon that appear higher in the visual field are judged to be farther away.

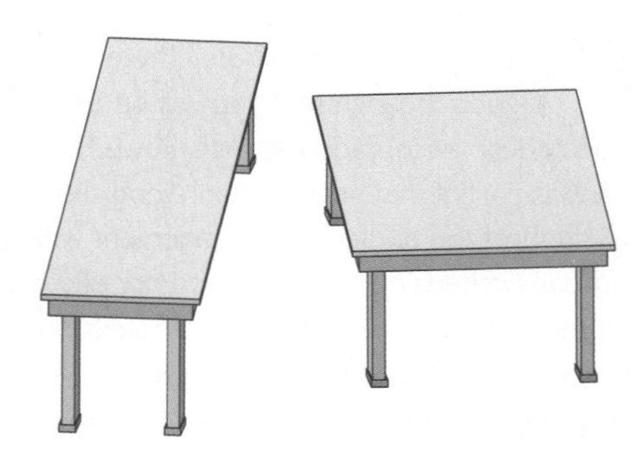

**FIGURE 4.42 The Tabletop Illusion** Created by the psychologist Roger Shepard, this illusion demonstrates the brain's automatic perceptual processes. Even when we know the two tabletops are the same size and shape—even if we have traced one image and placed it on top of the other—perspective cues make us see them as different.

2. What is binocular disparity?
   a. a disorder in which a person loses depth perception
   b. a cue to depth caused by the formation of a slightly different retinal image in each eye
   c. the distance between our eyes
   d. the ability to see depth in a two-dimensional stimulus by defocusing our vision
3. Perceptual constancy ________.
   a. allows us to see objects as stable even when there are large fluctuations in the sensory information we receive
   b. allows us to understand how physical energy is transduced into neural activity
   c. is a misnomer because our perceptions are not constant
   d. was based on the idea that different parts of the brain underlie different perceptual experiences

**Answers:** 1. a. linear perspective; b. occlusion; c. familiar size; d. relative size; e. texture gradient; f. position relative to the horizon.
2. b. a cue to depth caused by the formation of a slightly different retinal image in each eye.
3. a. allows us to see objects as stable even when there are large fluctuations in the sensory information we receive.

**Psychology: Knowledge You Can Use**

# How Can I Use Psychology to Improve My Next PowerPoint Presentation?

At some point in your college career, you will probably be asked to give a formal presentation. There is a good chance that you will be either expected or encouraged to use PowerPoint slides as part of that presentation. Good slides will support the audience's engagement with and comprehension of your talk. Poor slides will muddle your message, confuse your audience, and reflect negatively on you. If you are going to use slides in a presentation, you want those slides to sparkle. Psychology has a lot to say about how to make this happen.

The cognitive psychologist Stephen Kosslyn is an expert in how people process information. While attending many academic presentations, he noticed a trend, which he describes in his book *Clear and to the Point: 8 Principles for Compelling PowerPoint Presentations* (2007): "I realized that virtually all of [the problems in PowerPoint presentations] occur because the presentations failed to respect the fundamental characteristics of how we humans perceive, remember, and comprehend information" (p. 2). Kosslyn has translated his observations into three principles that you can use to direct and hold the attention of your audience. These principles are *salience, discriminability, and perceptual organization.*

**Salience** Our brains pay attention to things that are prominent, or salient. For example, when you look at a line of people, you are likely to notice an especially tall or short person. When you walk through a parking lot, you might notice an especially old, dirty, or damaged car or an especially bright and shiny one. You notice, and you pay attention.

Of course, members of your audience have the same tendency. If you want the audience to pay attention to a particular point in your presentation, make that point salient. For example, use a larger font for the titles of slides than for the body of the slides. Use colored text to call attention to key words in a quote or diagram.

Be mindful of some pitfalls, however. First, if items are not centrally important, avoid making them salient. Avoid using a flashy animation to introduce a small piece of supporting evidence. Resist splashing a rainbow of colors across each slide. Be selective. Second, avoid many of the nifty backgrounds available in PowerPoint. Because they are loaded with bright colors and bold

**Now, on this slide, may I direct your attention to the flashy animation and cool transition effects... because I worked really, really hard on them.**

patterns, your audience may focus attention on the package of your presentation. You want them, instead, to focus on the content.

**Discriminability** As you learned earlier in this chapter, we are able to detect differences between two stimuli only if those differences exceed some threshold (see the discussions of difference threshold and Weber's law). As Kosslyn explains, "We need contrast to distinguish shapes, colors, or positions from each other and from the background" (2007, p. 123).

Suppose you want to create a bar graph that shows differences in religiosity between urban and rural participants. It would be unwise for you to represent urban participants using a teal bar and rural participants using a turquoise bar. The two colors are insufficiently different. In fact, audience members may not detect any difference between them and thus might not understand the slide. To vary the colors, you might make one bar teal and the second bar orange. These two colors will be easy for most audience members to discriminate.

By the way, a relatively common deficit in color vision makes it difficult for people to perceive distinctions between reds and greens. When preparing slides, you should avoid contrasting reds and greens.

**Perceptual Organization** Our brains like to group things. For example, we see *** *** as two groups of three and ** ** ** as three groups of two. Likewise, we see ♥■●♦♣♠ as two groups and ♥■●♦♣♠ as three groups. Why does this tendency matter? When creating PowerPoint slides, make all elements associated with a particular point one color. Make all elements associated with a different point another color. For example, in illustrating differences in religiosity between urban and rural participants, you might make the bar representing urban participants and the label that says "Urban Participants" the exact same color. You would then make the bar representing rural participants and the label that says "Rural Participants" a second color.

A cautionary note is warranted here, too. If you have used PowerPoint, you might know that you can use the animations tool to make pieces of text "fly in" at different times. For example, one bullet point might move quickly from the left margin to the center of the screen. A second bullet point might scoot up from the bottom of the screen. If you would like audience members to perceive two elements as part of the same group, be sure to bring those pieces onto the slide at the same time. For example, in creating the bar graph about religiosity, you might make the bar representing the religiosity of urban participants appear at the same time as a bullet point describing the mean and standard deviation of that variable. Shared motion, like shared color, signals group membership.

These are just a few of the many great ideas Kosslyn shares in his book. If you really want to make your next presentation shine, read his book and employ the many practices it recommends. And when you are up in front of the group, please remember not to chew gum.

# StudySpace: Your Place for a Better Grade

**Visit StudySpace to access free review materials, such as:**

- complete study outlines
- vocabulary flashcards of all key terms
- additional chapter review quizzes

## Chapter Summary

### 4.1 How Do We Sense Our Worlds?

- **Stimuli Must Be Coded to Be Understood by the Brain:** Stimuli reaching the receptors are converted to neural impulses through the process of transduction.
- **Psychophysics Measures the Relationship between Stimuli and Perception:** By studying how people respond to different sensory levels, scientists can determine thresholds and perceived change (based on signal detection theory). Our sensory systems are tuned to both adapt to constant levels of stimulation and detect changes in our environment.

### 4.2 What Are the Basic Sensory Processes?

- **In Taste, Taste Buds Detect Chemicals:** The gustatory sense uses taste buds to respond to the chemical substances that produce at least five basic sensations: sweet, sour, salty, bitter, and umami (savory). The number and distribution of taste buds vary among individuals. Cultural taste preferences begin in the womb.
- **In Smell, the Nasal Cavity Gathers Odorants:** Receptors in the olfactory epithelium respond to chemicals and send signals to the olfactory bulb in the brain. Humans can discriminate among thousands of odors. Females are more accurate than males at detecting and identifying odors.
- **In Touch, Sensors in the Skin Detect Pressure, Temperature, and Pain:** The haptic sense relies on tactile stimulation to activate receptors for pressure, for temperature, and for distinct types of pain (immediate, sharp pain and chronic, dull pain).
- **In Hearing, the Ear Detects Sound Waves:** Sound waves activate hair cells in the inner ear. The receptors' responses depend on the sound waves' amplitude and frequency.
- **In Vision, the Eye Detects Light Waves:** Receptors (rods and cones) in the retina detect different forms of light waves. The lens helps the eye focus the stimulation on the retina for near versus far objects. Color is determined by wavelengths of light, which activate certain types of cones; by the absorption of wavelengths by objects; or by the mixing of wavelengths of light.
- **We Have Other Sensory Systems:** In addition to the five "basic" senses, humans and other animals have a kinesthetic sense (ability to judge where one's body and limbs are in space) and a vestibular sense (ability to judge the direction and intensity of head movements, associated with a sense of balance).

### 4.3 How Does Perception Emerge from Sensation?

- **In Touch, the Brain Integrates Sensory Information from Different Regions of the Body:** The primary sensory area for touch information is the primary somatosensory cortex in the parietal lobe. Neural "gates" in the spinal cord control pain. We can reduce pain perception by distracting ourselves, visualizing pain as more pleasant, being rested and relaxed, learning how to change the brain activity that underlies pain perception, and taking drugs that interfere with the neural transmission of pain.
- **In Hearing, the Brain Integrates Sensory Information from the Ears:** The primary sensory area for auditory information is the primary auditory cortex in the temporal lobe. The neurons at the front of the auditory cortex respond best to higher frequencies. The neurons at the rear of the auditory cortex respond best to lower frequencies. The brain localizes sound by comparing the times that a sound arrives at the individual ears and by comparing the magnitudes of the resulting sound waves at the ears.
- **In Vision, the Brain Processes Sensory Information from the Eyes:** The primary sensory area for visual information is the primary visual cortex in the occipital lobe. The visual system is characterized by a ventral stream that is specialized for object perception and recognition (what) and a dorsal stream that is specialized for spatial perception (where). Blindsight occurs when individuals who are blind retain some visual capacities of which they are unaware.

### 4.4 What Factors Influence Visual Perception?

- **Object Perception Requires Construction:** The Gestalt principles of organization account for some of the brain's perceptions of the world. The principles include distinguishing figure and ground, the grouping of objects on the basis of proximity and similarity, and the perception of "best" forms. Perception involves two processes: bottom-up processes (sensory information) and top-down processes (expectations about what we will perceive). Researchers have identified brain regions that are specialized for the perception of faces.
- **Depth Perception Is Important for Locating Objects:** The brain uses binocular cues, monocular cues, and motion cues to perceive depth. Binocular disparity and convergence are binocular depth cues. Pictorial depth cues such as occlusion, relative size, and linear perspective are monocular depth cues. Motion parallax is a motion depth cue.
- **Size Perception Depends on Distance Perception:** Illusions of size can be created when the retinal size conflicts with the known size of objects in the visual field, as in the Ames box illusion and the Ponzo illusion.
- **Motion Perception Has Internal and External Cues:** Motion detectors in the cortex respond to stimulation. The perceptual system establishes a stable frame of reference and relates object movement to it. Intervals of stimulation of repeated objects give the impression of continuous movement. Motion aftereffects, which are opposite in motion from things that have been observed, tell us about the fatigue of neural receptors that fire in response to motion in certain directions.
- **Perceptual Constancies Are Based on Ratio Relationships:** We create expectations about the world that allow us to use information about the shape, size, color, and lightness of objects in their surroundings to achieve constancy.

## Key Terms

additive color mixing, p. 156
audition, p. 148
binocular depth cues, p. 170
binocular disparity, p. 170
blindsight, p. 163
bottom-up processing, p. 167
cones, p. 151
convergence, p. 170
cornea, p. 150
eardrum, p. 148
fovea, p. 151
gustation, p. 140
haptic sense, p. 145
iris, p. 150
kinesthetic sense, p. 156
monocular depth cues, p. 170
olfaction, p. 143
olfactory bulb, p. 143
olfactory epithelium, p. 143
perception, p. 132
perceptual constancy, p. 174
pupil, p. 150
retina, p. 150
rods, p. 151
sensation, p. 132
sensory adaptation, p. 137
signal detection theory (SDT), p. 136
sound wave, p. 148
subtractive color mixing, p. 155
taste buds, p. 140
top-down processing, p. 167
transduction, p. 133
vestibular sense, p. 156

## Practice Test

1. Which answer accurately lists the order in which these structures participate in sensation and perception (except for smell)?
   a. specialized receptors, thalamus, cortex
   b. specialized receptors, cortex, thalamus
   c. cortex, specialized receptors, thalamus
   d. thalamus, specialized receptors, cortex

2. While listening to a string quartet, you find you can easily decipher the notes played by the violins, by the viola, and by the cello. When you focus on the viola, you find some of the notes especially loud and others barely discernable. Which of the following statements best describes your sensations of the quartet?
   a. You can decipher qualitative differences among the instruments because of the rate of firing of your sensory neurons, whereas you can make quantitative distinctions—recognizing variations in the notes' intensity—due to the involvement of specific sensory receptors.
   b. You can decipher quantitative differences among the instruments because of the rate of firing of your sensory neurons, whereas you can make qualitative distinctions—recognizing variations in the notes' intensity—due to the involvement of specific sensory receptors.
   c. You can decipher qualitative differences among the instruments because of the involvement of specific sensory receptors, whereas you can make quantitative distinctions—recognizing variations in the notes' intensity—due to the rate of firing of your sensory neurons.
   d. You can decipher quantitative differences among the instruments because of the involvement of specific sensory receptors, whereas you can make qualitative distinctions—recognizing variations in the notes' intensity—due to the rate of firing of your sensory neurons.

3. When the violist plays a solo, you cannot hear it. Which of the following statements is the most likely explanation?
   a. The differences in intensity between the notes of the solo are too small to be noticeable.
   b. The intensity of the auditory stimulation does not exceed the minimum threshold needed for you to detect a sensation.
   c. The quartet's playing has left your hearing receptors overstimulated and thus unable to process less intense stimuli.

4. Imagine you have a steady, radiating pain across your lower back. No matter how you position yourself, you cannot make the pain go away. Select the answer choices most relevant to this type of pain. More than one choice may be correct.
   a. activated by chemical changes in tissue
   b. activated by strong physical pressure of temperature extremes
   c. fast fibers
   d. myelinated axons
   e. nonmyelinated axons
   f. slow fibers

5. A 1-year-old girl skins her knees on a rough sidewalk. The girl cries in pain. Which of the following interventions will most likely calm her?
   a. Promising to give her a piece of candy if she stops crying.
   b. Quickly cleaning and bandaging the skinned knees.
   c. Looking intently into her eyes and saying, "Let's take some deep breaths together. Ready. . . . Breathe in. . . . Now breathe out."
   d. Directing the girl's hand on a quick touching tour of the nearby environment and saying things such as "Feel this tree's rough bark. Touch the grass; it tickles. Feel how smooth this rock is!"

The answer key for the Practice Tests can be found at the back of the book. It also includes answers to the green caption questions.

# 5

# Consciousness

IN 2000, WHEN HE WAS 16 YEARS OLD, ERIK RAMSEY was involved in a car crash. His brain stem was damaged in the accident. Since then, as a result of that injury, Ramsey has suffered from *locked-in syndrome*. In this rare condition, all or nearly all of a person's voluntary muscles are paralyzed. Even when Ramsey is awake and alert, he cannot communicate with those around him except by moving his eyes up and down (**Figure 5.1**). As a psychological state, locked-in syndrome has been compared to being buried alive. Imagine that you see all the sights around you and hear every noise, but you cannot respond physically to these sights and noises. Imagine that you can feel every itch, but you cannot scratch yourself or move to gain relief.

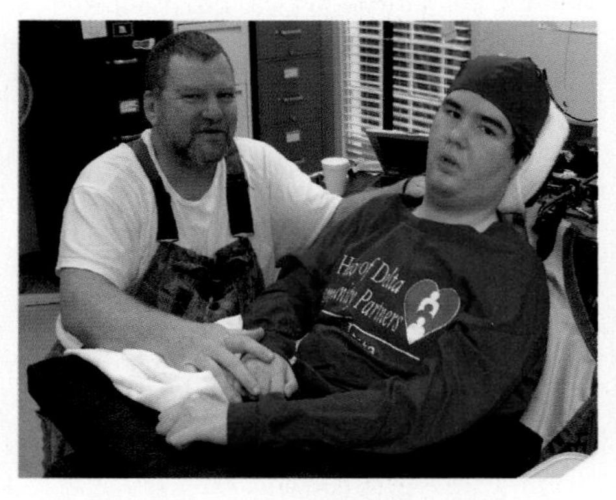

**FIGURE 5.1 Conscious but Locked In** Erik Ramsey (**right,** with his father, Eddie) suffers from locked-in syndrome. He has total awareness, but his condition leaves him almost completely unable to communicate.

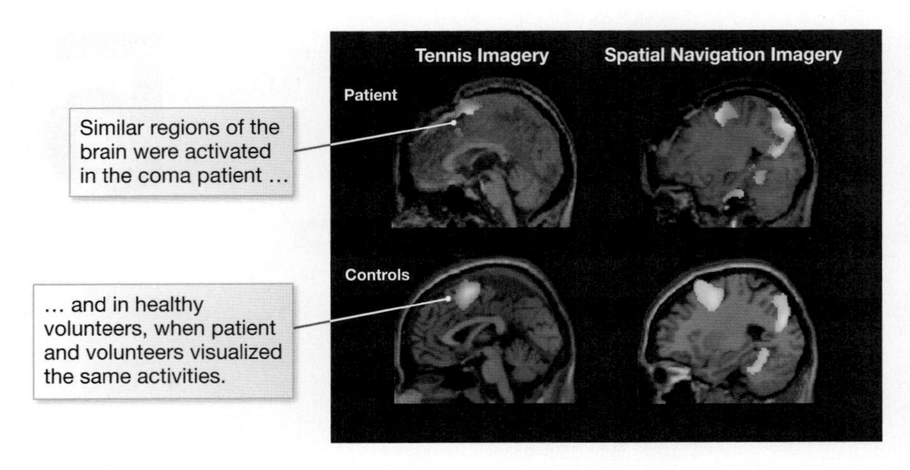


**FIGURE 5.2 In a Coma but Aware** The brain images on the top are from the patient, a young woman in a coma who showed no outward signs of awareness. The images on the bottom are a composite from the control group, which consisted of healthy volunteers. Both the patient and the control group were told to visualize playing tennis and walking around. Right after the directions were given, the neural activity in the patient's brain appeared similar to the neural activity in the control group's brains.

Recent scientific advances have raised the possibility that Ramsey and patients like him will be able to communicate. That is, we might be able to "read" their thoughts by imaging brain activity in real time. Communication of this kind is the goal of researchers who, in 2004, planted electrodes in the speech region of Ramsey's left hemisphere. For the past several years, Ramsey has been listening to recordings of vowel sounds and mentally simulating those sounds. His simulation of each vowel sound should produce its own pattern of brain activity. Ultimately, the researchers hope to use this brain activity to create a voice synthesizer that will translate Ramsey's neural patterns into understandable speech (Bartels et al., 2008). So far, researchers working with Ramsey have demonstrated that he can produce numerous specific vowel sounds (Guenther et al., 2009).

Other researchers have obtained similarly promising results. A 23-year-old woman in an apparent coma was asked to imagine playing tennis or walking through her house (Owen et al., 2006). This woman's pattern of brain activity became quite similar to the patterns of control subjects who also imagined playing tennis or walking through a house (**Figure 5.2**). The woman could not give outward signs of awareness, but researchers believe she was able to understand language and respond to the experimenters' requests. The implications of this finding are extraordinary. Could the researchers' method be used to reach other people who are in comas, aware of their surroundings, but unable to communicate? Indeed, this research team has now evaluated 54 coma patients and found 5 who could willfully control brain activity to communicate (Monti et al., 2010). One 29-year-old man was able to answer five of six yes/no questions correctly by thinking of one type of image to answer yes and another type to answer no. The ability to communicate from a coma might allow some patients to express thoughts, ask for more medication, and increase the quality of their lives. These advances add up to one astonishing fact: Some people in comas are conscious! ■

**Learning Objectives**

- Define consciousness.
- Identify varied states of consciousness.
- Explain how brain activity gives rise to consciousness.
- Summarize research findings on consciousness and "the interpreter" among individuals with split brain.
- Discuss how unconscious processes influence thought and behavior.

## 5.1 What Is Consciousness?

This chapter looks at consciousness and its variations. The cases discussed in the chapter opener highlight the chapter's two main points. First, people can be conscious of their surroundings even when they do not appear to be. Second, conscious experiences are associated with brain activity. To understand the relationship between the brain and consciousness, we need to consider how conscious experiences differ. As explored later in this chapter, there are natural variations in consciousness (e.g., sleep). Moreover, people manipulate consciousness through natural methods (e.g., meditation) as well as artificial methods (e.g., drugs). In addition, because of the very nature of consciousness, conscious experiences differ from person to person.

## Consciousness Is a Subjective Experience

**Consciousness** refers to moment-by-moment subjective experiences. Paying attention to your immediate surroundings is one such experience. Reflecting on your current thoughts is another. You know you are conscious because you are experiencing the outside world through your senses and because you are aware that you are thinking. But what gives rise to your consciousness? Are you conscious simply because many neurons are firing in your brain? If so, how are the actions of these brain circuits related to your subjective experiences of the world?

**consciousness** One's subjective experience of the world, resulting from brain activity.

An iPad's electrical circuits produce images and sound when they are energized, but gadgets such as iPads are neither conscious nor unconscious in the same way humans are. The difference is not simply that the circuitry in gadgets works one way and the circuitry in human brains works another way. Nor is the difference simply that humans are biological and gadgets are not. Your body includes many highly active biological systems, such as your immune system, that do not produce the sort of consciousness you are experiencing right now. At every minute, your brain is regulating your body temperature, controlling your breathing, calling up memories as necessary, and so on. You are not conscious of the brain operations that do these things. Why are you conscious only of certain experiences?

Philosophers have long debated questions about the nature of consciousness. As discussed in Chapter 1, the seventeenth-century philosopher René Descartes stated that the mind is physically distinct from the brain, a view called *dualism*. Most psychologists reject dualism. Instead, they believe that the brain and the mind are inseparable. According to this view, the activity of neurons in the brain produces the contents of consciousness: the sight of a face, the smell of a rose. More specifically, for each type of content—each sight, each smell—there is an associated pattern of brain activity. The activation of this particular group of neurons in the brain somehow gives rise to conscious experience.

But because each of us experiences consciousness personally—that is, subjectively—we cannot know if any two people experience the world in exactly the same way. What does the color red look like to you (**Figure 5.3**)? How does an apple taste? As discussed in Chapter 1, early pioneers in psychology attempted to understand consciousness through introspection, but psychologists largely abandoned this method because of its subjective nature. Conscious experiences exist, but their subjective nature makes them difficult to study empirically. When children play the game "I spy, with my little eye," the players might be looking at the same thing—say, "something that is red"—but they might be experiencing that thing differently. In other words, there is no way to know whether each player's experience of the thing (its shape, size, color, and so on) is the same or whether each player is using the same words to describe a different experience. The labels applied to experience do not necessarily do justice to the experience. When you experience heartbreak and a friend consoles you by saying, "I know how you feel," does your friend definitely know?

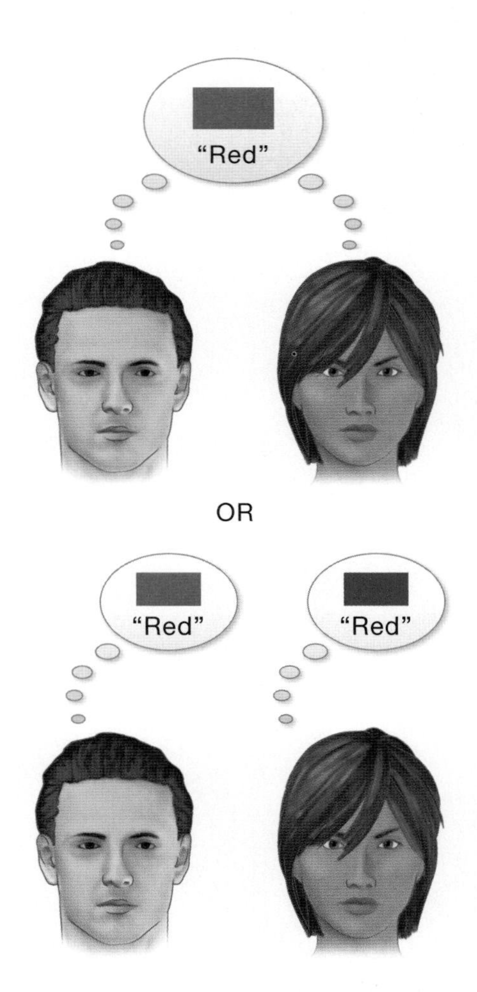


**FIGURE 5.3 Seeing Red** One difficult question related to consciousness is whether people's subjective experiences of the world are similar. For instance, does red look the same to everyone who has normal color vision?

## There Are Variations in Conscious Experience

Conscious experience can be seen as unified and coherent. In this view, the mind is a continuous stream and thoughts float on that stream. There is a limit, however, to how many things the mind can be conscious of at the same time.

For example, as you read this chapter, what are you conscious of, and how conscious are you? Are you focused intently on the material? Is your mind wandering, occasionally or often? You cannot pay attention to reading while doing

several other things, such as watching television or instant messaging. As you focus on developments in the show or in the messages, you might realize that you have no idea what you just read or what your friend just replied. Likewise, you can think about what you will do tomorrow, what kind of car you would like to own, and where you most recently went on vacation—but you cannot think about them all at the same time. While driving to a familiar destination, have you ever begun to think about something other than your driving? Before you knew it, you had arrived. But how did you get there? You knew you had driven, but you could not remember details of the drive, such as whether you stopped at traffic lights or passed other vehicles.

As you go through any day, you experience variations in consciousness. As discussed later, your level of consciousness varies naturally through the day in your sleep/wake cycle. It is also affected by your actions (such as eating or meditating) and by consciousness-altering substances you consume (such as caffeine or alcohol).

In general, all of us can execute routine or *automatic* tasks (such as driving, walking, or catching a baseball) that are so well learned that we do them without much conscious effort. Indeed, paying too much attention can interfere with these automatic behaviors. By contrast, difficult or unfamiliar tasks require greater conscious effort. Such *controlled* processing is slower than automatic processing, but it helps us perform in complex or novel situations. For example, if a rainstorm starts while you are driving, you will need to pay more attention to your driving and be very conscious of the road conditions.

Through such variations, consciousness serves at least three vital functions (Baumeister & Masicampo, 2010; Baumeister, Masicampo, & Vohs, 2011). First, consciousness lets us perform complex actions that may require input from several different brain regions. Second, consciousness helps us connect with one another by sharing our thoughts and feelings and even imagining ourselves in another person's situation. Third, consciousness is required for complicated thinking, such as understanding the development of a plot in a story, using logical reasoning, and performing mathematical calculations. Most of us are fortunate enough to take these functions for granted. But to understand the importance of these functions, consider cases in which the basic operations of consciousness are impossible or compromised.

**EXTREME STATES** As noted by the cognitive neuroscientist Steven Laureys (2007), medical advances are enabling a greater number of people to survive traumatic brain injuries. For example, doctors now save the lives of many people who previously would have died from injuries sustained in car accidents or on battlefields. A good example is the remarkable survival of Congresswoman Gabrielle Giffords, who was shot in the head by an assailant in 2011. Surviving is just the first step toward recovery, however, and many of those who sustain serious brain injuries fall into comas or, like Giffords, are induced into coma as part of medical treatment. The coma allows the brain to rest. Most people who regain consciousness after such injuries do so within a few days, but some people do not regain consciousness for weeks. In this state, they have sleep/wake cycles—they open their eyes and appear to be awake, close their eyes and appear to be asleep—but they do not seem to respond to their surroundings. When this condition lasts longer than a month, it is known as a *persistent vegetative state*. Evidence indicates that the brain sometimes can process information in this state (Gawryluk, D'Arcy, Connolly, & Weaver, 2010). But the persistent vegetative state is not associated with consciousness. Normal brain activity does not occur when a person is in this state, in part because much of the person's brain may be dead. The longer the persistent vegetative state lasts, the less likely it is that the person will ever recover consciousness or show normal brain activity. Terri Schiavo, a woman living in Florida, spent more than 15 years in a persistent vegetative state. Eventually, her husband wanted to terminate her life support, but her parents wanted to continue it. Both sides waged a legal battle. A court ruled in the husband's favor, and life support was terminated. After Schiavo's death, an autopsy revealed substantial and irreversible damage throughout her brain and especially in cortical regions known to be important for consciousness (**Figure 5.4a**).

Between the vegetative state and full consciousness is the *minimally conscious state*. In this state, people make some deliberate movements, such as following an object with their eyes. They may try to communicate. The prognosis for those in a minimally conscious state is much better than for those in a persistent vegetative state. Consider the case of the Polish railroad worker Jan Grzebski, who in June 2007, at age 67, woke up from a 19-year coma. He lived for another 18 months. Grzebski remembered events that were going on around him during his coma, including his children's marriages. There is some indication that he tried to speak on occasion but was not understood (Scislowska, 2007; **Figure 5.4b**). Differentiating between states of consciousness by behavior alone is difficult, but brain imaging may prove useful for identifying the extent of a patient's brain injury and likelihood of recovery.

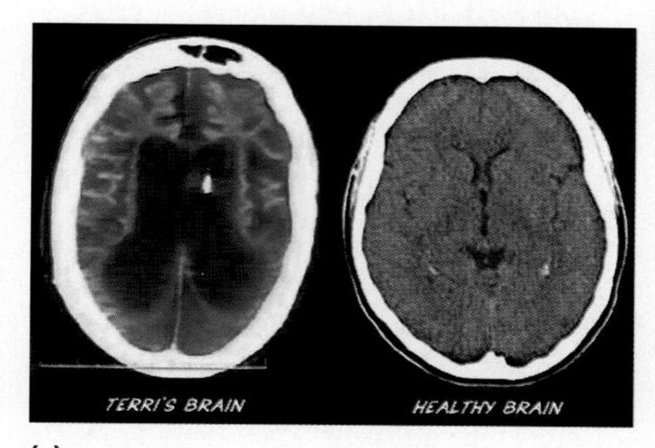


(a)

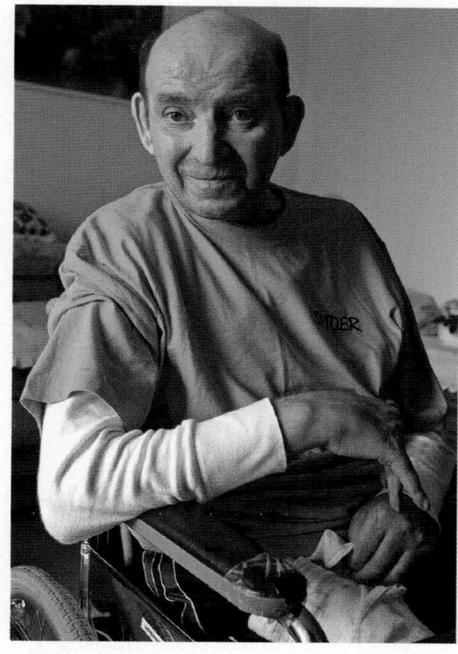

(b)

**FIGURE 5.4 Persistent Vegetative State versus Minimally Conscious State (a)** Terri Schiavo spent more than 15 years in a persistent vegetative state before she was taken off life support. Her parents and their supporters believed she showed some awareness. As the dark areas of the brain scan on the left indicate, however, there was no activity in Schiavo's brain because her cortex had deteriorated beyond recovery. By using imaging to examine the brain of a person in an apparent coma, doctors can determine whether the patient is a good candidate for treatment. **(b)** Jan Grzebski was in a minimally conscious state for 19 years before he awoke and reported that he had in fact been aware of events around him. **Suppose you were trapped in a minimally conscious state for even half that time. How might you respond to the world after regaining full consciousness?**

## Brain Activity Gives Rise to Consciousness

As psychological science is beginning to reveal, common brain activity may give rise to people's subjective experiences. Scientists cannot (yet) read your mind by looking at your brain activity, but they can identify objects you are seeing by looking at your brain activity (Kay, Naselaris, Prenger, & Gallant, 2008). For instance, researchers can use fMRI (see Chapter 2, "Research Methodology") to determine, based on your pattern of brain activity at that moment, whether the picture you are seeing is of a house, a shoe, a bottle, or a face (O'Toole, Jiang, Abdi, & Haxby, 2005). Similarly, brain imaging can reveal whether a person is looking at a striped pattern that is moving horizontally or vertically, whether a person is looking at a picture or a sentence, which of three categories a person is thinking about during a memory task, and so on (Norman, Polyn, Detre, & Haxby, 2006).

Philosophers have long debated what it means to be conscious of something. Psychologists now examine, even measure, consciousness and other mental states that were previously viewed as too subjective to be studied. For example, Frank Tong and colleagues (1998) studied the relationship between consciousness and neural responses in the brain. Participants were shown images in which houses were superimposed on faces. When participants reported seeing a face, neural activity increased within temporal lobe regions associated with face recognition. When participants reported seeing a house, neural activity increased within temporal lobe regions associated with object recognition. This finding suggests that different types of sensory information are processed by different brain areas: The particular type of neural activity determines the particular type of awareness (**Figure 5.5**).

**THE GLOBAL WORKSPACE MODEL** The *global workspace model* posits that consciousness arises as a function of which brain circuits are active (Baars, 1988; Dehaene, Changeux, Naccache, Sachur, & Sergent, 2006). That is, you experience your brain regions' output as conscious awareness. Studying people with brain injuries, who are sometimes unaware of their deficits (that is, the consciousness-related problems that arise from their injuries), supports this idea. For instance, a

**FIGURE 5.5 Scientific Method: The Relationship between Consciousness and Neural Responses in the Brain**

**Hypothesis:** Specific patterns of brain activity can predict what a person is seeing.

**Research Method:**

1. Participants were shown images with houses superimposed on faces.

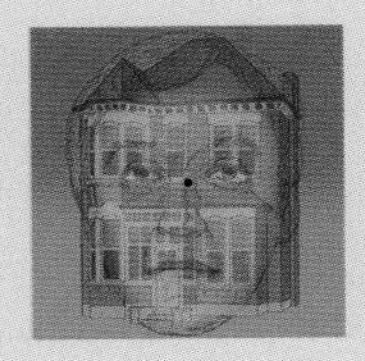

2. Participants were asked to report whether they saw a house or a face.

3. Researchers used fMRI to measure neural responses in participants' brains.

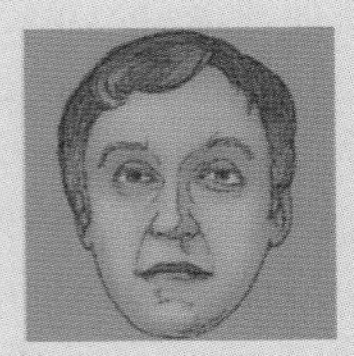

**Results:** Activity increased in the fusiform face area when participants reported seeing a face, but activity increased in temporal cortex regions associated with object recognition when participants reported seeing a house.

**Conclusion:** Type of awareness is related to which brain region processes the particular sensory information.

**Source:** Tong, F., Nakayama, K., Vaughan, J. T., & Kanwisher, N. (1998). Binocular rivalry and visual awareness in human extrastriate cortex. *Neuron, 21*, 753–759.

person who has vision problems caused by an eye injury will know about those problems because the brain's visual areas will notice something is wrong. But if that same person then suffers damage to the brain's visual areas so that they stop delivering output, the person may have no visual information to consider and thus will not be aware of vision problems. Of course, if the person suddenly becomes blind, that person will know he or she cannot see. But a person who loses part of the visual field because of a brain injury tends not to notice the gap in visual experience. This tendency appears with hemineglect, for example (see Figure 3.22). A hemineglect patient is not aware of missing part of the visual world. In one patient's words, "I knew the word 'neglect' was a sort of medical term for whatever was wrong but the word bothered me because you only neglect something that is actually there, don't you? If it's not there, how can you neglect it?" (Halligan & Marshall, 1998, p. 360). The hemineglect patients' unawareness of their visual deficits supports the idea that consciousness arises through the brain processes active at any point in time.

Most importantly, the global workspace model presents no single area of the brain as responsible for general "awareness." Rather, different areas of the brain deal with different types of information. Each of these systems in turn is responsible for conscious awareness of its type of information (**Figure 5.6**). From this perspective, consciousness is the mechanism that makes us actively aware of information and that prioritizes what information we need or want to deal with at any moment.

**THE SPLIT BRAIN** Studying people who have undergone brain surgery has given researchers a better understanding of the conscious mind. On rare occasions, for example, epilepsy does not respond to modern medications. Surgeons may then remove the part of the brain in which the epileptic seizures begin. Another strategy, pioneered in the 1940s and still practiced on occasion when other interventions have failed, is to cut connections within the brain to try to isolate the site where the seizures begin. After the procedure, a seizure that begins at that site is less likely to spread throughout the cortex.

The major connection between the hemispheres that may readily be cut without damaging the gray matter is the massive fiber bundle called the corpus callosum (see Figure 3.20). When the corpus callosum is severed, the brain's halves are almost completely isolated from each other. The resulting condition is called **split brain.** This surgical procedure has provided many important insights into the basic organization and specialized functions of each brain hemisphere (**Figure 5.7**).

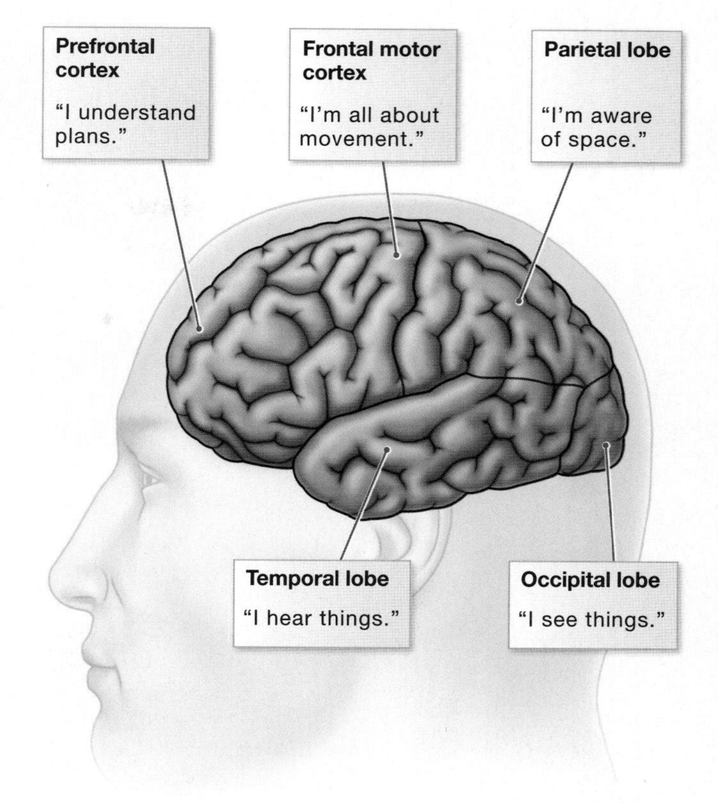


**FIGURE 5.6 Areas of Awareness** A central theme emerging from cognitive neuroscience is that awareness of different aspects of the world is associated with functioning in different parts of the brain. This simplified diagram indicates major areas of awareness.

What is it like to have your brain split in half? Perhaps the most obvious thing about split-brain patients after their operations is how normal they are. Unlike patients after other types of brain surgery, split-brain patients have no immediately apparent problems. In fact, some early investigations suggested the surgery had not affected the patients in any discernible way. They could walk normally, talk normally, think clearly, and interact socially. In the 1960s, this book's coauthor Michael Gazzaniga, working with the Nobel laureate Roger Sperry, conducted a series of tests on the first split-brain patients. The results were stunning: Just as the brain had been split in two, so had the mind!

As discussed in Chapter 4, images from the visual field's left side (left half of what you are looking at) go to the right hemisphere. Images from the visual field's right side go to the left hemisphere. The left hemisphere also controls the right hand, and the right hemisphere controls the left hand. With a split-brain patient, these divisions enable researchers to provide information to, and receive information from, a single hemisphere at a time (**Figure 5.8**).

Psychologists have long known that in most people the left hemisphere is dominant for language. If a split-brain patient sees two pictures flashed on a

**split brain** A condition in which the corpus callosum is surgically cut and the two hemispheres of the brain do not receive information directly from each other.

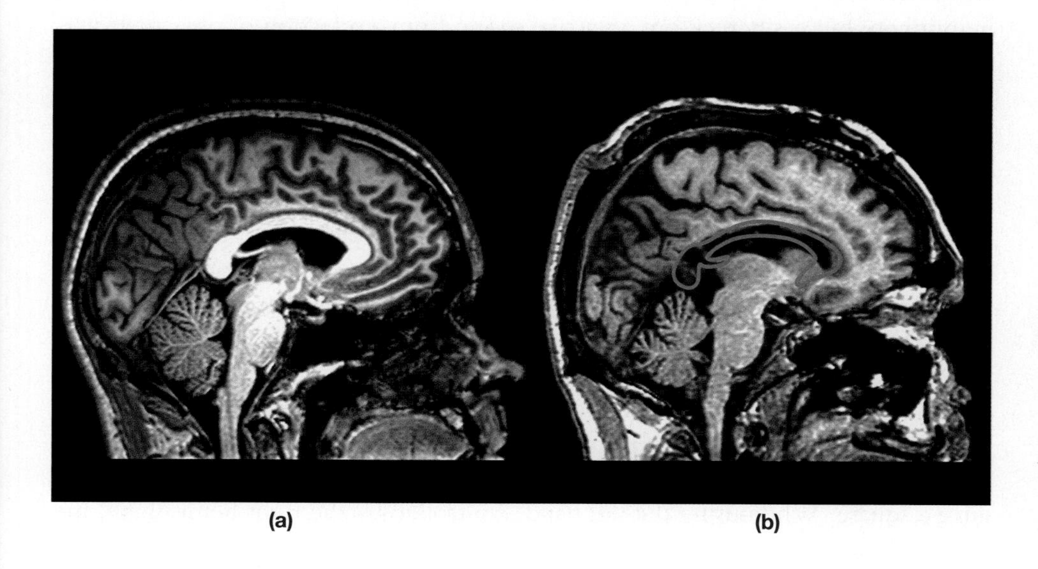


**FIGURE 5.7 Split Brain (a)** This image shows the brain of a normal person whose corpus callosum is intact. **(b)** This image shows the brain of a patient whose corpus callosum has been removed (as indicated by the red outline). With the corpus callosum removed, the two hemispheres of the brain are almost completely separated.

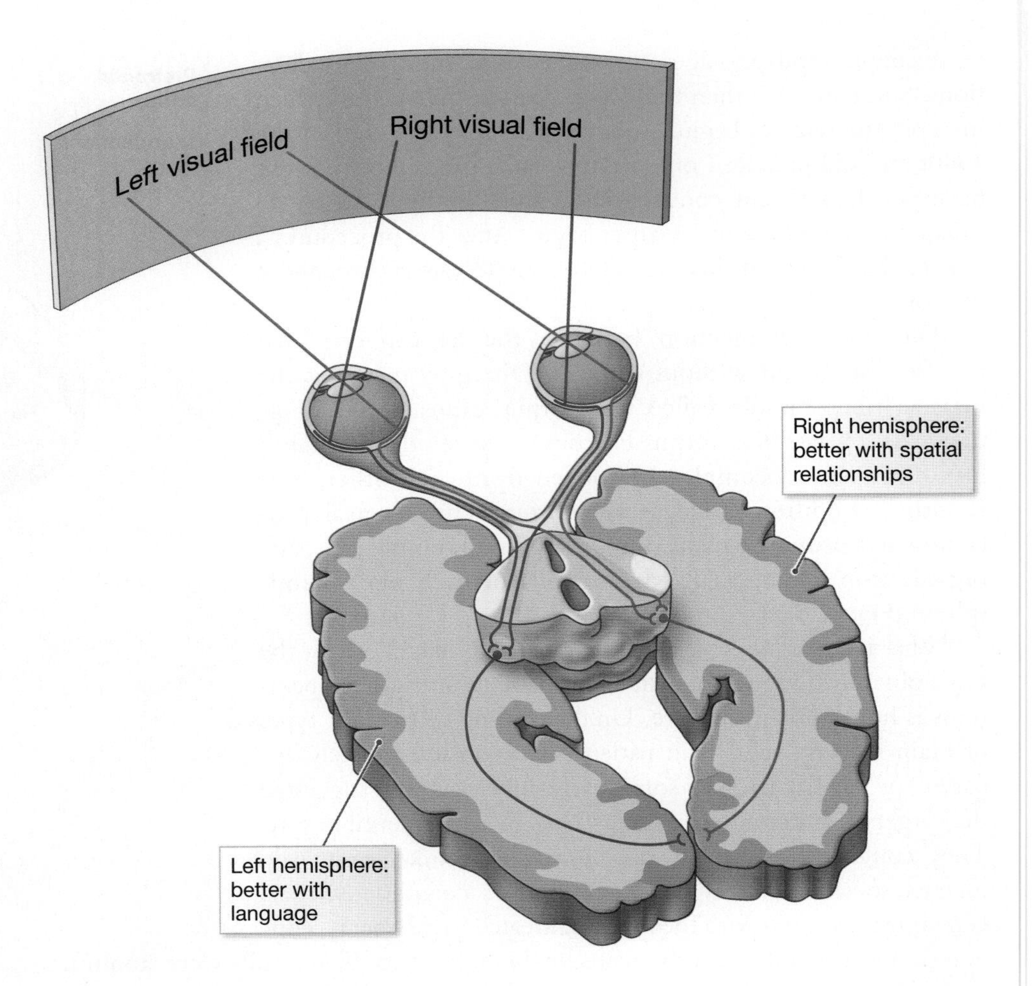


**FIGURE 5.8 Visual Input** Images from the left side go to the brain's right hemisphere. Images from the right side go to the left hemisphere.

screen briefly and simultaneously—one to the visual field's right side and one to the left side—the patient will report that only the picture on the right was shown. Why is this? The left hemisphere (or "left brain"), with its control over speech, sees only the picture on the right side. It is the only picture a person with a split brain can talk about. In many patients, the right hemisphere has no discernable language capacity. The mute right hemisphere (or "right brain"), having seen the picture on the left, is unable to articulate a response. The right brain can act on its perception, however: If the picture on the left was of a spoon, the right hemisphere can easily pick out an actual spoon from a selection of objects. It uses the left hand, which is controlled by the right hemisphere. Still, the left hemisphere does not know what the right one saw. Splitting the brain, then, produces two half brains. Each half has its own perceptions, thoughts, and consciousness (**Figure 5.9**).

In some patients, the right hemisphere displays rudimentary language comprehension, such as the ability to read simple words. Such right hemisphere language capabilities tend to improve in the years following the split-brain operation. Presumably, the right hemisphere attains communication skills that were not needed when that hemisphere was connected to the fluent left brain.

Normally, the competencies of each hemisphere complement those of the other. The left brain is generally hopeless at spatial relationships. In one experiment, a split-brain participant is given a pile of blocks and a drawing of a simple arrangement in which to put them. For example, the participant needs to produce a square. When using the left hand, controlled by the right hemisphere, the

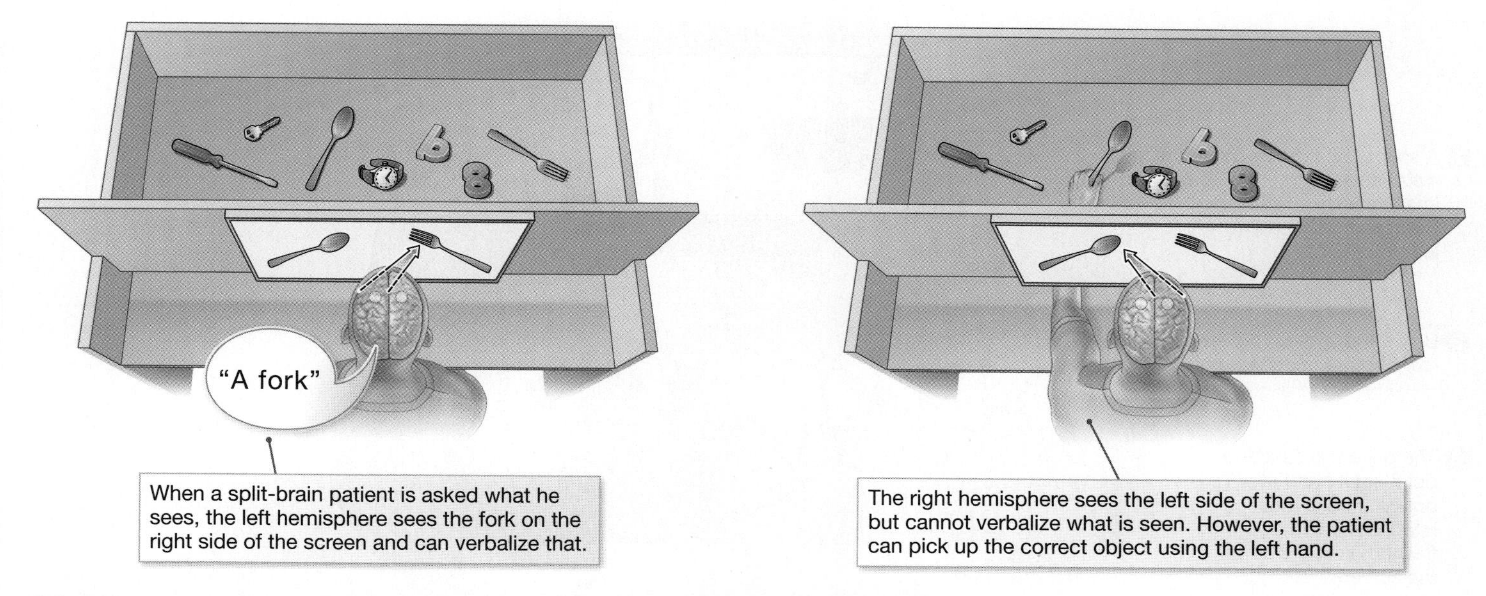


**FIGURE 5.9 Split-Brain Experiment: The Left Hemisphere versus the Right Hemisphere**

participant arranges the blocks effortlessly. When using the right hand, controlled by the left brain, the participant produces only an incompetent, meandering attempt. During this dismal performance, the right brain presumably grows frustrated, because it makes the left hand try to slip in and help!

**THE INTERPRETER** Another interesting dimension to the relationship between the brain's hemispheres is how they work together to reconstruct our experiences. This collaboration can be demonstrated by asking a disconnected left hemisphere what it thinks about previous behavior that has been produced by the right hemisphere. In one such experiment, the split-brain patient sees different images flash simultaneously on the left and right sides of a screen. Below those images is a row of other images. The patient is asked to point with each hand to a bottom image that is most related to the image flashed on that side of the screen above. In one such study, a picture of a chicken claw was flashed to the left hemisphere. A picture of a snow scene was flashed to the right hemisphere. In response, the left hemisphere pointed the right hand at a picture of a chicken head. The right hemisphere pointed the left hand at a picture of a snow shovel. The (speaking) left hemisphere could have no idea what the right hemisphere had seen. When the participant was asked why he pointed to those pictures, he (or, rather, his left hemisphere) calmly replied, "Oh, that's simple. The chicken claw goes with the chicken, and you need a shovel to clean out the chicken shed." The left hemisphere evidently had interpreted the left hand's response in a manner consistent with the left brain's knowledge (**Figure 5.10**).

The left hemisphere's propensity to construct a world that makes sense is called the **interpreter.** This term means that the left hemisphere is interpreting what the right hemisphere has done (Gazzaniga, 2000). In this last example, the left hemisphere interpreter created a ready way to explain the left hand's action. The left hand was controlled by the disconnected right hemisphere. The left hemisphere's explanation, however, was unrelated to the right hemisphere's real reason for commanding that action. Yet to the patient, the movement seemed perfectly plausible once the action had been interpreted. Usually, the interpreter's

**interpreter** A term specific to the left hemisphere; refers to the left hemisphere's attempts to make sense of actions and ongoing events.

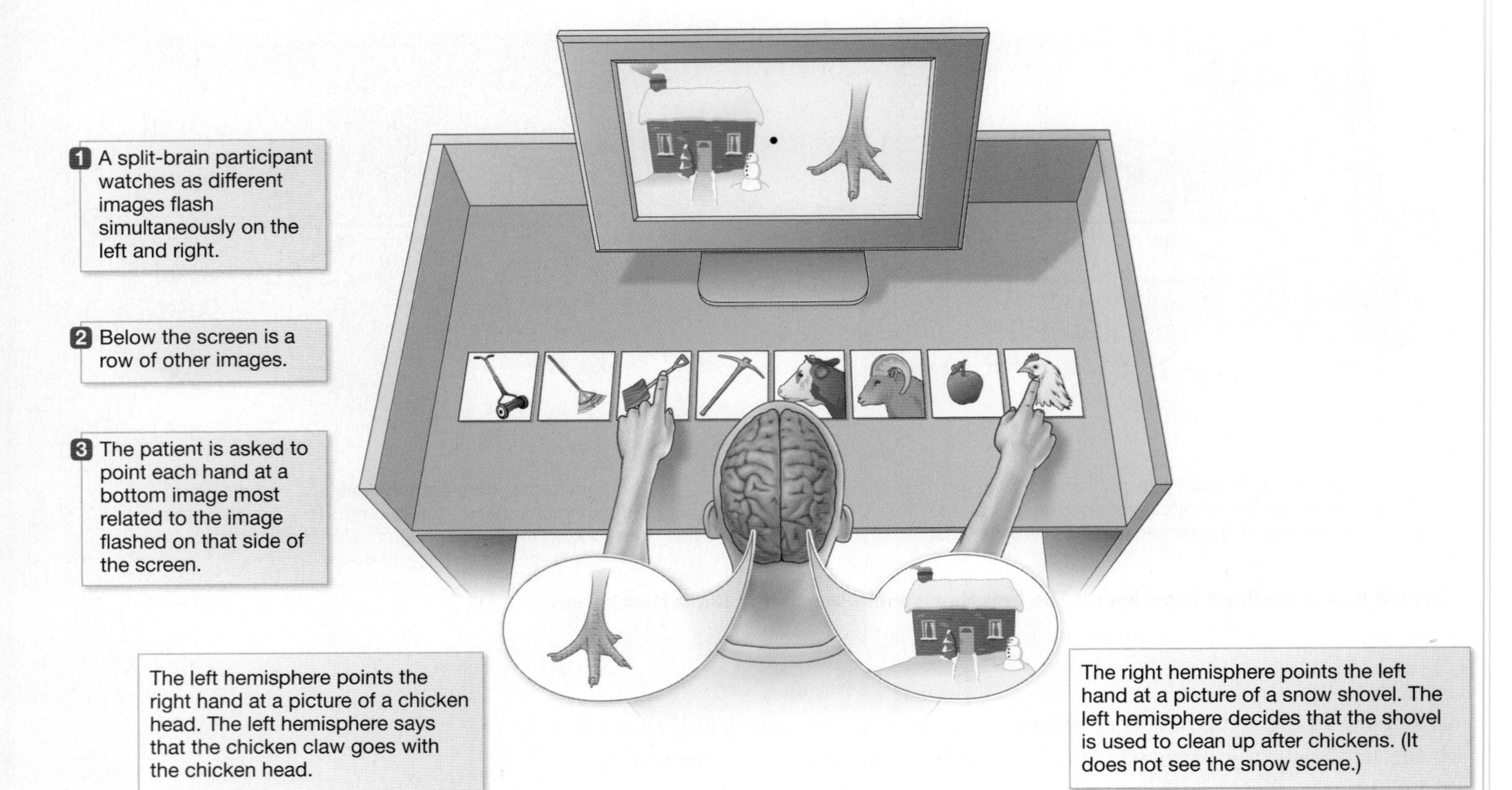


**FIGURE 5.10 The Left Hemisphere Interpreter** On the basis of limited information, the left hemisphere attempts to explain behavior governed by the right hemisphere.

explanations come readily. In fact, Jeffrey Cooney and Michael Gazzaniga (2003) explain hemineglect by arguing that the left hemisphere interpreter can make sense only of available information. Even though normally sighted people might find the hemineglect patients' attitude bizarre, the hemineglect patients see their particular limited visual states as perfectly normal. To give another example: If the command *Stand up* is flashed to a split-brain patient's right hemisphere, the patient will stand up. But when asked why he or she has stood up, the patient will not reply, "You just told me to," because the command is not available to the (speaking) left hemisphere. Instead, unaware of the command, the patient will say something like, "I just felt like getting a soda." The left hemisphere is compelled to concoct a story that explains, or interprets, the patient's action after it has occurred.

Such interpretation does not always happen instantly. Sometimes it takes the patient's left hemisphere as long to figure out why the left hand is acting as it would take an outside observer. In one session, Gazzaniga and his colleagues presented the word *phone* to the right hemisphere of patient J.W. and asked him to verbalize what he saw. J.W. replied that he did not see anything. Of course, J.W. was speaking from his left hemisphere, which did not see the word *phone,* and his right hemisphere was mute. When a pen was placed in his left hand, however, and he was asked to draw what he saw, J.W. immediately started drawing a phone. Outside observers who had not seen the word *phone* took some time to make out what J.W. was drawing. J.W.'s left hemisphere had the same difficulty in interpreting the drawing. Fortunately, J.W. tended to articulate what he was thinking. He was initially confused by what he was drawing and started guessing about what it was. Not until the picture was almost complete did the outside observers, including J.W.'s left hemisphere, understand what his left hand was drawing. At that point, J.W. exclaimed, "Duh, it's a phone!" The communication between the hemispheres occurred on the paper and not within his head. J.W.'s right hemisphere drew what it saw. After viewing the drawing, his left hemisphere identified it as a phone. In the meantime, his interpreter struggled to guess what his hand was drawing.

**THE INTERPRETER SPECULATES** The interpreter strongly influences the way we view and remember the world. Say that normal participants are shown a series of pictures that form a story. Later, these same participants are shown another group of pictures and are asked to identify which pictures they had seen previously. They will have a strong tendency to falsely "recognize" pictures consistent with the theme of the original series and to reject those inconsistent with the theme. The left brain, then, tends to "compress" its experiences into a comprehensible story and to reconstruct remembered details based on the gist of that story. The right brain seems simply to experience the world and remember things in a manner less distorted by narrative interpretation.

Sometimes the left brain interpreter makes life more difficult than it needs to be. In one experiment, human or (nonhuman) animal participants must predict, on each trial, whether a red light or a green light will flash. A correct prediction produces some small reward. Both lights flash in a random sequence, but overall the red light flashes 70 percent of the time. Nonhuman participants, such as rats, pretty quickly notice that the red light comes on more often. So to receive the most reward, what strategy do they follow? After doing this task a number of times, most animals simply choose the red light—the most probable response—100 percent of the time. By doing so, they receive rewards on 70 percent of the trials. This strategy makes great sense in terms of adaptiveness, because it guarantees that the animals receive the maximum rewards. Humans do something much different, however. They try to figure out patterns in the way the lights flash, and they choose the red light about 70 percent of the time. That is, overall their choices match the frequency of how often red flashes. Because the lights flash randomly, humans may choose incorrectly on any given trial. Indeed, when humans choose the red light 70 percent of the time, they generally receive rewards on only 58 percent of the trials.

Why do humans not follow the optimal strategy, which even rats can figure out? According to George Wolford and colleagues (2000), the left hemisphere interpreter leads people to search for patterns that might not even exist. To test this idea, the researchers had two split-brain patients perform a version of the task described in the previous paragraph. The patients' right hemispheres tended to respond in the optimal way that animals did, choosing the same thing 100 percent of the time. The patients' left hemispheres chose red only 70 percent of the time. The left hemisphere interpreter's tendency to seek relationships between things may be adaptive in some contexts, but it can produce less-than-optimal outcomes when such relationships (e.g., patterns) do not exist.

The split brain is a rare condition, of course, and nearly all people have two hemispheres that communicate and cooperate on the tasks of daily living. The popular media have sometimes exaggerated the findings of this research. They have suggested that certain people are "left brain" logical types and others are "right brain" artistic types. It is true that the hemispheres are specialized for certain functions, such as language or spatial navigation. Still, most cognitive processes involve the coordinated efforts of both hemispheres.

## Unconscious Processing Influences Behavior

Before reading further, think of your phone number. If you are familiar enough with the number, you probably remembered it quickly. Yet you have no idea how your brain worked this magic. That is, you do not have direct access to the neural or cognitive processes that lead to your thoughts and behavior. You thought about your phone number, and (if the magic worked) the number popped into your consciousness.

This brief exercise illustrates a central property of consciousness: We are aware of some mental processes and not aware of others. Over the last several decades, many researchers have explored different ways in which unconscious cues, or **subliminal perception,** can influence cognition. Subliminal perception refers to stimuli that get processed by sensory systems but, because of their short durations or subtle forms, do not reach consciousness.

**subliminal perception** The processing of information by sensory systems without conscious awareness.

Advertisers have long been accused of using subliminal cues to persuade people to purchase products (**Figure 5.11**). The evidence suggests that subliminal messages have quite small effects on purchasing behavior (Greenwald, 1992). Material presented subliminally can influence how people think, however, even if it has little or no effect on complex actions. (Buying something you did not intend to buy would count as a complex action.) That is, considerable evidence indicates that people are affected by events—stimuli—they are not aware of (Gladwell, 2005). In one study, participants exerted greater physical effort when large images of money were flashed at them, even though the flashes were so brief the participants did not report seeing the money (Pessiglione et al., 2007). The subliminal images of money also produced brain activity in areas of the limbic system, which is involved in emotion and motivation. Subliminal cues may be most powerful when they work on people's motivational states. For example, flashing the word *thirst* may prove more effective than flashing the explicit directive *Buy Coke.* Indeed, researchers found that subliminal presentation of the word *thirst* led participants to drink more Kool-Aid, especially when they were actually thirsty (Strahan, Spencer, & Zanna, 2002).

**FIGURE 5.11 Try for Yourself: Subliminal Perception**

Try to pick out the subliminal message in the advertisement below.

**Answer:** The ice cubes spell out S-E-X.

Other events can influence our thoughts without our awareness. In a classic experiment by the social psychologists Richard Nisbett and Timothy Wilson (1977), the participants were asked to examine word pairs, such as *ocean-moon,* that had obvious semantic associations between the words. They were then asked to free-associate on other, single words, such as *detergent.* Nisbett and Wilson wanted to find out the degree, if any, to which the word pairs would influence the free associations. And if the influence occurred, would the participants be conscious of it? When given the word *detergent* after the word pair *ocean-moon,* participants typically free-associated the word *tide.* However, when asked why they said "tide," they usually gave reasons citing the detergent's brand name, such as "My mom used Tide when I was a kid." They were not aware that the word pair had influenced their thoughts. Here again, the left hemisphere interpreter was at work, making sense of a situation and providing a plausible explanation for cognitive events when complete information was not available. We are, of course, frequently unaware of the many different influences on our thoughts, feelings, and behaviors. Similar effects underlie the classic mistake called a *Freudian slip,* in which an unconscious thought is suddenly expressed at an inappropriate time or in an inappropriate social context.

To study the power of unconscious influences, John Bargh and colleagues (1996) supplied participants with different groups of words. Some of the participants received words associated with the elderly, such as *old, Florida,* and *wrinkles.* The participants were asked to make sentences out of the supplied words. After they had made up a number of sentences, they were told the experiment was over. But the researchers continued observing the participants. They wanted to know whether the unconscious activation of beliefs about the elderly would influence the participants' behavior. Indeed, participants primed with stereotypes about old people walked much more slowly than did those who had been given words unrelated to the elderly. When questioned later, the slow-walking participants were not aware that the concept of "elderly" had been activated or that it had changed their behavior.

Other researchers have obtained similar findings. For instance, Ap Dijksterhuis and Ad van Knippenberg (1998) found that people at Nijmegen University, in the Netherlands, were better at answering trivia questions when they were subtly presented with information about "professors" than when they were subtly presented with information about "soccer hooligans." The participants were unaware that their behavior was influenced by the information. Such findings indicate that much of our behavior occurs without our awareness or intention (Bargh & Morsella, 2008; Dijksterhuis & Aarts, 2010).

**THE SMART UNCONSCIOUS** Common sense tells us that consciously thinking about a problem or deliberating about the options is the best strategy for making a decision. Consider the possibility that *not* consciously thinking can produce an outcome superior to that of consciously thinking. In a study by Ap Dijksterhuis (2004), participants evaluated complex information regarding real-world choices. One situation involved selecting an apartment. In each case, the participants chose between alternatives that had negative features (e.g., high rent, bad location) and positive features (e.g., nice landlord, good view). Objectively, one apartment was the best choice. Some participants were required to make an immediate choice (no thought). Some had to think for 3 minutes and then choose (conscious thought). Others had to work for 3 minutes on a difficult, distracting task and then choose (unconscious thought). Across three separate trials, those in the unconscious thought condition made the best decisions. According to Dijksterhuis and Nordgren (2006), unconscious processing is especially valuable for complex decisions in which it is difficult to weigh the pros and cons consciously. Perhaps this is why, for very important decisions, people often choose to "sleep on it." (Chapter 8, "Thinking and Intelligence," will return to this idea in discussing problem solving strategies.)

Consider also the possibility that consciously thinking can undermine good decision making. The social psychologist Tim Wilson and the cognitive psychologist Jonathan Schooler (1991) asked research participants to rate jams. When the participants simply tasted the jams, their ratings were very similar to experts' ratings. However, when the participants had to explain their ratings jam by jam, their ratings differed substantially from the experts'. Unless the experts were wrong, the participants had made poorer judgments: Having to reflect consciously about their reasons apparently altered their perceptions of the jams.

## Summing Up

### What Is Consciousness?

Consciousness is a person's subjective experience of the world. The relationship between the physical brain and consciousness has been debated for centuries. Psychologists have developed tools to assess the experience of consciousness and have suggested that consciousness serves several important functions. Brain activity gives rise to conscious experience. The global workspace model posits that different brain regions produce different types of conscious experience; no one region is associated with consciousness. Substantial insight into consciousness has been gained from the study of patients with split brain. From the assessment of split-brain patients, the role of the left hemisphere as an interpreter of experience has become evident. Information can be processed subliminally—that is, without conscious awareness. The unconscious processing of information can influence thought and behavior, and such processing may produce better decisions than conscious thought.

## Measuring Up

1. Which of the following statements are correct according to our understanding of consciousness? Choose as many as apply.
   a. The presence of consciousness is one of the main ways we can distinguish between humans' thoughts and nonhuman animals' thoughts.
   b. Brain research shows that some people in comas have higher brain activity levels than others.
   c. The contents of consciousness cannot be labeled.
   d. Any biological process can be made conscious through effortful processing.
   e. Our behaviors and thoughts are affected by some events about which we have no conscious knowledge.
   f. Consciousness is subjective.
   g. Without brain activity, there is no consciousness.
   h. People in comas may differ in levels of consciousness.
   i. People are either conscious or unconscious; there is no middle ground.
2. In a split-brain patient, the left hemisphere interpreter ______________.
   a. explains what to do when the patient does not understand instructions
   b. translates from one language to another until the patient understands what is being said
   c. makes sense of actions
   d. uses language to direct the right hemisphere's activities

**Answers:** 1. Choices b, e, f, g, and h are correct.
2. c. makes sense of actions.

## 5.2 What Is Sleep?

**Learning Objectives**

- Describe the stages of sleep.
- Identify common sleep disorders.
- Discuss the functions of sleeping and dreaming.

**circadian rhythms** The regulation of biological cycles into regular patterns.

At regular intervals, the brain does a strange thing: It goes to sleep. A common misconception is that the brain shuts itself down during sleep. Nothing could be further from the truth. Many brain regions are more active during sleep than during wakefulness. It is even possible that some complex thinking, such as working on difficult problems, occurs in the sleeping brain (Walker & Stickgold, 2006).

Sleep is part of the normal rhythm of life. Brain activity and other physiological processes are regulated into patterns known as **circadian rhythms.** (*Circadian* roughly translates to "about a day.") For example, body temperature, hormone levels, and sleep/wake cycles operate according to circadian rhythms. Regulated by a biological clock, circadian rhythms are influenced by the cycles of light and dark. Humans and nonhuman animals continue to show these rhythms, however, when removed from light cues.

Multiple brain regions are involved in producing and maintaining circadian rhythms and sleep. For instance, information about light detected by the eyes is sent to a small region of the hypothalamus called the *suprachiasmatic nucleus*. This region then sends signals to a tiny structure called the *pineal gland* (**Figure 5.12**). The pineal gland may then secrete *melatonin,* a hormone that travels through the bloodstream and affects various receptors in the body, including the brain. Bright light suppresses the production of melatonin, whereas darkness triggers its release. Researchers recently have noted that taking melatonin can help people cope with jet lag and shift work, both of which interfere with circadian rhythms. Taking melatonin also appears to help people fall asleep, although it is unclear why this happens.

The average person sleeps around 8 hours per night, but individuals differ tremendously in the number of hours they sleep. Infants sleep much of the day. People tend to sleep less as they age. Some adults report needing 9 or 10 hours of sleep a night to feel rested, whereas others report needing only an hour or two a night. It might be that your genes influence the amount of sleep you need, as researchers have identified a gene that influences sleep (Koh et al., 2008). Called *SLEEPLESS,* this gene regulates a protein that, like many anesthetics, reduces action potentials in the brain. Loss of this protein leads to an 80 percent reduction in sleep. But people's sleep habits can be quite extreme. When a 70-year-old retired nurse, Miss M., reported sleeping only an hour a night, researchers were skeptical. On her first two nights in a research laboratory, Miss M. was unable to sleep, apparently because of the excitement. But on her third night, she slept for only 99 minutes, then awoke refreshed, cheerful, and full of energy (Meddis, 1977). You might like the idea of sleeping so little and having all those extra hours of spare time, but most of us do not function well on so little sleep. And as discussed in later chapters, sufficient sleep is important for memory and good health and is often affected by psychological disorders, such as depression.

## Sleep Is an Altered State of Consciousness

The difference between being awake and being asleep has as much to do with conscious experience as with biological processes. When you sleep, you are not fully conscious. Your conscious experience of the outside world is largely turned off. To some extent, however, you remain aware of your surroundings and your brain still processes information. Your mind is analyzing potential dangers, controlling body movements, and shifting body parts to maximize comfort. For this reason, people who sleep next to children or to pets tend not to roll over onto them. Nor do most people fall out of bed while sleeping—in this case, the brain is aware of at least the edges of the bed. (Because the ability to not fall out of bed when asleep is learned or perhaps develops with age, infant cribs have side rails and young children may need bed rails when they transition from crib to bed.)

Before the development of objective methods to assess brain activity, most people believed the brain went to sleep along with the rest of the body. In the 1920s, researchers invented the electroencephalograph, or EEG. As discussed in Chapter 2, this machine measures the brain's electrical activity. When people are awake, they

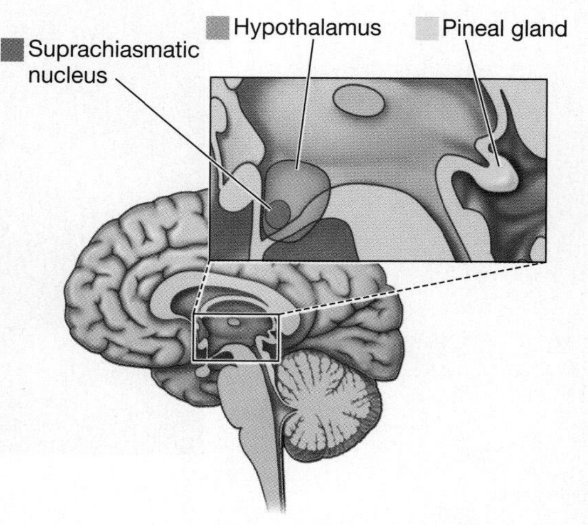


**FIGURE 5.12 The Pineal Gland and the Sleep/Wake Cycle** Changes in light register in the suprachiasmatic nucleus of the hypothalamus. In response, this region signals the pineal gland when the time for sleep or the time for wakefulness has come.

have many different sources of sensory activity. As a result, the neurons in their brains are extremely active. The EEG shows this activity as short, frequent, irregular brain signals known as *beta waves* (shown in **Figure 5.13**). When people really focus their attention on something or when they close their eyes and relax, brain activity slows and becomes more regular. This pattern produces *alpha waves*.

**STAGES OF SLEEP** As evidenced by changes in EEG readings, sleep occurs in stages (see Figure 5.13). When you drift off to sleep, you enter stage 1. Here, the EEG shows *theta waves*. You can easily be aroused from stage 1, and if awakened, you will probably deny that you were sleeping. In this light sleep, you might see fantastical images or geometric shapes. You might have the sensation of falling or that your limbs are jerking. As you progress to stage 2, your breathing becomes more regular, and you become less sensitive to external stimulation. You are now really asleep. Although the EEG continues to show theta waves, it also shows occasional bursts of activity called *sleep spindles* and large waves called *K-complexes*. Some researchers believe that these bursts are signals from brain mechanisms involved with shutting out the external world and keeping people asleep (Steriade, 1992). Two findings indicate that the brain must work to maintain sleep. First, abrupt noise can trigger K-complexes. Second, as people age and sleep more lightly, their EEGs show fewer sleep spindles.

The progression to deep sleep occurs through stages 3 and 4, which nowadays are typically seen as one stage because their brain activity is nearly identical (Silber et al., 2007). This period is marked by large, regular brain patterns called *delta waves*, and it is often referred to as *slow-wave sleep*. People in slow-wave sleep are very hard to wake and often very disoriented when they do wake up. People still process some information in slow-wave sleep, however, because the mind continues to evaluate the environment for potential danger. For example, parents in slow-wave sleep can be aroused by their children's cries. Yet they can blissfully

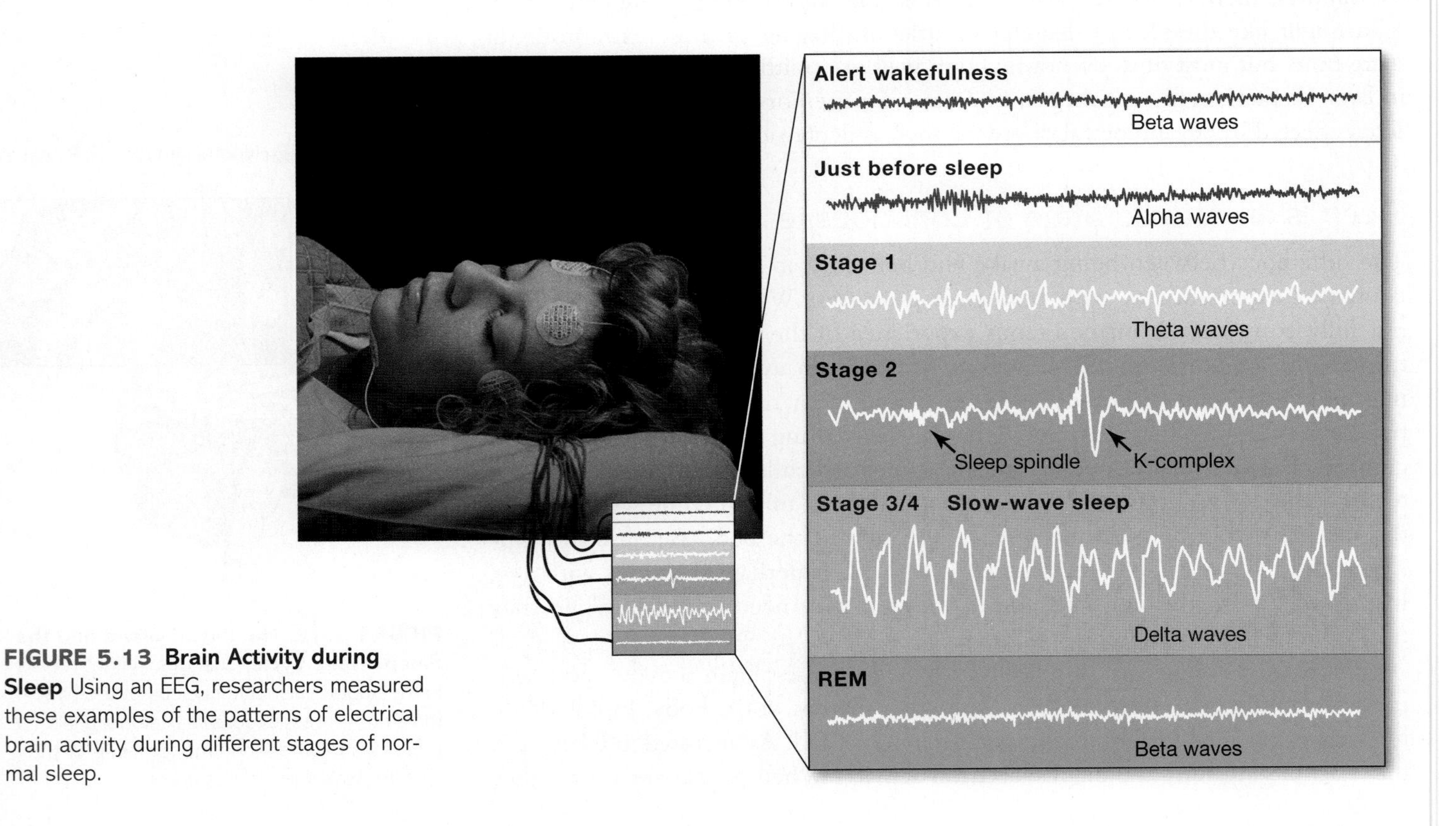


**FIGURE 5.13 Brain Activity during Sleep** Using an EEG, researchers measured these examples of the patterns of electrical brain activity during different stages of normal sleep.

ignore sounds, such as sirens or traffic noise, that are louder than the crying children but are not necessarily relevant.

**REM sleep** The stage of sleep marked by rapid eye movements, dreaming, and paralysis of motor systems.

**insomnia** A disorder characterized by an inability to sleep.

**REM SLEEP** After about 90 minutes of sleep, the sleep cycle reverses, returning to stage 1. At this point, the EEG suddenly shows a flurry of beta wave activity that usually represents an awake, alert mind. The eyes dart back and forth rapidly beneath closed eyelids. Because of these *rapid eye movements,* this stage is called **REM sleep.** It is sometimes called *paradoxical sleep* because of the paradox of a sleeping body with an active brain. Indeed, some neurons in the brain, especially in the occipital cortex and brain stem regions, are more active during REM sleep than during waking hours. But while the brain is active during REM episodes, most of the body's muscles are paralyzed. At the same time, the body shows signs of genital arousal: Most males of all ages develop erections, and most females of all ages experience clitoral engorgement.

REM sleep is psychologically significant because of its relation to dreaming. About 80 percent of the time when people are awakened during REM sleep, they report dreaming, compared with less than half of the time during non-REM sleep (Solms, 2000). As discussed later, the dreams differ between these two types of sleep.

Over the course of a typical night's sleep, the cycle repeats about five times. The sleeper progresses from slow-wave sleep through to REM sleep, then back to slow-wave sleep and through to REM sleep (**Figure 5.14**). As morning approaches, the sleep cycle becomes shorter, and the sleeper spends relatively more time in REM sleep. People briefly awaken many times during the night, but they do not remember these awakenings in the morning. As people age, they sometimes have more difficulty going back to sleep after awakening.

**SLEEP DISORDERS** Sleep problems are relatively common throughout life. Nearly everyone occasionally has trouble falling asleep, but for some people the inability to sleep causes significant problems in their daily lives. **Insomnia** is a sleep disorder in which people's mental health and ability to function are compromised by their inability to sleep. Indeed, chronic insomnia is associated with diminished psychological well-being, including feelings of depression (Bootzin & Epstein, 2011; Hamilton et al., 2007). An estimated 12 percent to 20 percent of adults have persistent insomnia; it is more common in women than in men and in older adults than in younger adults (Espie, 2002; Ram, Seirawan, Kumar, & Clark, 2010). One factor that complicates the estimation of how many people have insomnia is that many people who believe

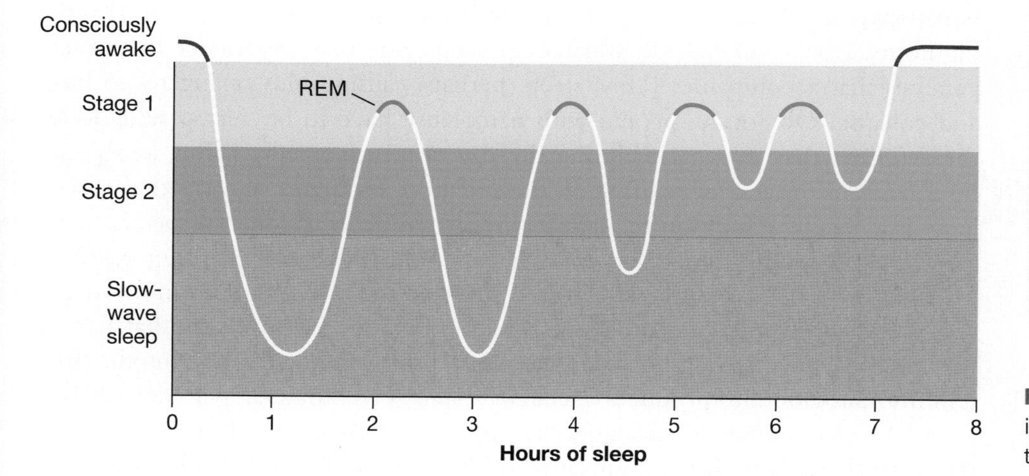


**FIGURE 5.14 Stages of Sleep** This chart illustrates the normal stages of sleep over the course of the night.

**obstructive sleep apnea** A disorder in which a person, while asleep, stops breathing because his or her throat closes; the condition results in frequent awakenings during the night.

**narcolepsy** A sleep disorder in which people experience excessive sleepiness during normal waking hours, sometimes going limp and collapsing.

they are poor sleepers overestimate how long it takes them to fall asleep and often underestimate how much sleep they get on a typical night. For instance, some people experience *pseudoinsomnia,* in which they basically dream they are not sleeping. Their EEGs would indicate sleep. But if you roused them, they would claim to have been awake.

In an odd twist, a major cause of insomnia is worrying about sleep. When people experience this kind of insomnia, they may be tired enough to sleep. As they try to fall asleep, however, they worry about whether they will get to sleep and may even panic about how a lack of sleep will affect them. This anxiety leads to heightened arousal, which interferes with normal sleep patterns. To overcome these effects, many people take sleeping pills, which may work in the short run but can cause significant problems down the road. People may come to depend on the pills to help them sleep. Then if they try to stop taking the pills, they may lie awake wondering whether they can get to sleep on their own. According to research, the most successful treatment for insomnia combines drug therapy with *cognitive-behavioral therapy* (CBT, discussed in Chapter 15, "Treatment of Psychological Disorders"). CBT helps people overcome their worries about sleep and relieves the need for the drugs, which should be discontinued before the end of therapy (Morin et al., 2009). Other factors that contribute to insomnia include poor sleeping habits. Ways to improve sleeping habits are given in this chapter's "Psychology: Knowledge You Can Use" feature, "Can Sleep Deprivation Hurt Me?" (p. 201).

Another fairly common sleeping problem is **obstructive sleep apnea.** While asleep, a person with this disorder stops breathing for short periods. Basically, the sleeper's throat closes during these periods. In struggling to breathe, the person briefly awakens and gasps for air. Obstructive sleep apnea is most common among middle-aged men and is often associated with obesity, although it is unclear if obesity is the cause or consequence of apnea (Pack & Pien, 2011; Spurr, Graven, & Gilbert, 2008). People with apnea are often unaware of their condition, since the main symptom is loud snoring and they do not remember their frequent awakenings during the night. Yet chronic apnea causes people to have poor sleep, which is associated with daytime fatigue and even problems such as an inability to concentrate while driving. Moreover, apnea is associated with cardiovascular problems and stroke. For serious cases, physicians often prescribe a continuous positive airway pressure (CPAP) device. During sleep, this device blows air into the person's nose or nose and mouth (**Figure 5.15**).

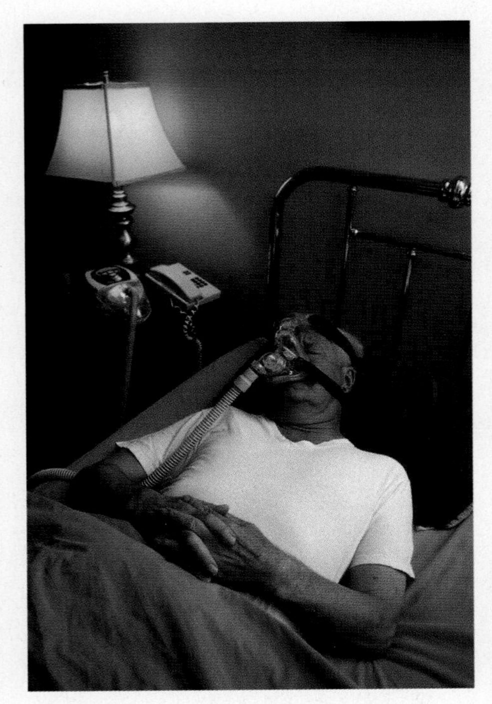

**FIGURE 5.15 Obstructive Sleep Apnea** This man suffers from obstructive sleep apnea. Throughout the night, a continuous positive airway pressure device blows air into his nose or mouth to keep his throat open.

A student who falls asleep during a lecture is likely sleep deprived, but a professor who falls asleep while lecturing is probably experiencing an episode of **narcolepsy.** In this rare disorder, excessive sleepiness occurs during normal waking hours. During an episode of narcolepsy, a person may experience the muscle paralysis that accompanies REM sleep, perhaps causing him or her to go limp and collapse. Obviously, people with narcolepsy have to be very careful about the activities they engage in during the day, as unexpectedly falling asleep can be dangerous or fatal, depending on the situation. Evidence suggests that narcolepsy is a genetic condition that affects the neural transmission of a specific neurotransmitter in the hypothalamus (Chabas, Taheri, Renier, & Mignot, 2003; Nishino, 2007). The most widely used treatments for this condition are drugs that act as stimulants. Researchers have found evidence, however, that narcolepsy may be an autoimmune disorder and that treating it as such (using the protein immunoglobulin) produces excellent results (Cvetkovic-Lopes et al., 2010).

*REM behavior disorder* is roughly the opposite of narcolepsy. In this condition, the normal paralysis that accompanies REM sleep is disabled. Sufferers act out their dreams while sleeping, often striking their sleeping partners. No treatment exists for this rare sleep disorder. The condition is caused by a neurological deficit and is most often seen in elderly males.

By contrast, sleepwalking is most common among young children. Technically called *somnambulism,* this relatively common behavior occurs during slow-wave sleep, typically within the first hour or two after falling asleep. During an episode, the person is glassy-eyed and seems disconnected from other people and/or the surroundings. No harm is done if the sleepwalker wakes up during the episode. Being gently walked back to bed is safer for the sleepwalker than being left to wander around and potentially get hurt.

## Sleep Is an Adaptive Behavior

In terms of adaptiveness, sleep might seem illogical. Tuning out the external world during sleep can be dangerous and thus a threat to survival. Beyond that, humans might have advanced themselves in countless ways if they had used all their time productively rather than wasting it by sleeping. But people cannot override indefinitely the desire to sleep. Eventually, our bodies shut down and we sleep whether we want to or not.

Why do we sleep? Some animals, such as some frogs, never exhibit a state that can be considered sleep (Siegel, 2008). Most animals sleep, however, even if they have peculiar sleeping styles. (For example, some dolphin species have *unihemispherical sleep,* in which the cerebral hemispheres take turns sleeping.) Sleep must serve an important biological purpose. Researchers have proposed three general explanations for sleep's adaptiveness: *restoration, circadian rhythms,* and *facilitation of learning.*

**RESTORATION AND SLEEP DEPRIVATION** According to the *restorative theory,* sleep allows the body, including the brain, to rest and repair itself. Various kinds of evidence support this theory: After people engage in vigorous physical activity, such as running a marathon, they generally sleep longer than usual. Growth hormone, released only during deep sleep, facilitates the repair of damaged tissue. Sleep apparently enables the brain to replenish energy stores and also strengthens the immune system (Hobson, 1999).

Numerous laboratory studies have examined sleep deprivation's effects on physical and cognitive performance. Surprisingly, most studies find that two or three days of sleep deprivation have little effect on strength, athletic ability, or the performance of complex tasks. When deprived of sleep, however, people find it difficult to perform quiet tasks, such as reading. They find it nearly impossible to perform boring or mundane tasks.

A long period of sleep deprivation causes mood problems and decreases cognitive performance. People who suffer from chronic sleep deprivation may experience attention lapses and reduced short-term memory. Studies using rats have found that extended sleep deprivation compromises the immune system and leads to death. Sleep deprivation is also dangerous and potentially disastrous because it makes people prone to *microsleeps,* in which they fall asleep during the day for periods ranging from a few seconds to a minute (Coren, 1996).

Sleep deprivation might serve one very useful purpose: When people are suffering from depression, depriving them of sleep sometimes alleviates their depression. This effect appears to occur because sleep deprivation leads to increased activation of serotonin receptors, as do drugs used to treat depression

**FIGURE 5.16 Sleeping Predator** After a fresh kill, a lion may sleep for days.

(Benedetti et al., 1999; the treatment of depression is discussed in Chapter 15, "Treatment of Psychological Disorders"). For people who are not suffering from depression, however, sleep deprivation is more likely to produce negative moods than positive ones.

**CIRCADIAN RHYTHMS** The *circadian rhythm theory* proposes that sleep has evolved to keep animals quiet and inactive during times of the day when there is greatest danger, usually when it is dark. According to this theory, animals need only a limited amount of time each day to accomplish the necessities of survival, and it is adaptive for them to spend the remainder of the time inactive, preferably hidden. Thus an animal's typical amount of sleep depends on how much time that animal needs to obtain food, how easily it can hide, and how vulnerable it is to attack. Small animals tend to sleep a lot. Large animals vulnerable to attack, such as cows and deer, sleep little. Large predatory animals that are not vulnerable sleep a lot (**Figure 5.16**). We humans depend greatly on vision for survival. We are adapted to sleeping at night because our early ancestors were more at risk in the dark.

**FACILITATION OF LEARNING** Scientists have also proposed that sleep is important because it is involved in the strengthening of neural connections that serve as the basis of learning. The general idea is that circuits wired together during the waking period are consolidated, or strengthened, during sleep (Wilson & McNaughton, 1994). When research participants sleep after learning, their recall is better than in control conditions where participants remain awake (Drosopoulos, Schulze, Fischer, & Born, 2007). Robert Stickgold and colleagues (2000) conducted a study in which participants had to learn a complex task. After finding that participants improved at the task only if they had slept for at least 6 hours following training, the researchers argued that learning the task required neural changes that normally occur only during sleep. Both slow-wave sleep and REM sleep appear to be important for learning to take place, but people may be especially likely to perform better if they dream about the task while sleeping. In one study, participants learned how to run a complex maze. Those who then slept for 90 minutes went on to perform better on the maze. Those who dreamed about the maze, however, performed much better (Wamsley, Tucker, Payne, Benavides, & Stickgold, 2010).

Indeed, there is some evidence that students experience more REM sleep during exam periods, when a greater mental consolidation of information might be expected to take place (Smith & Lapp, 1991). The argument that sleep, especially REM sleep, promotes the development of brain circuits for learning is also supported by the changes in sleep patterns that occur over the life course. Infants and the very young, who learn an incredible amount in a few years, sleep the most and also spend the most time in REM sleep.

Findings linking sleep to learning should give caution to students whose main style of studying is the all-nighter. In one recent study, students who were sleep deprived for one night showed reduced activity the next day in the hippocampus, a brain area essential for memory (Yoo, Hu, Gujar, Jolesz, & Walker, 2007). These sleep-deprived students also showed poorer memory at subsequent testing. According to the investigators, there is substantial evidence that sleep does more than consolidate memories. Sleep also seems to prepare the brain for its memory needs for the next day.

**Psychology: Knowledge You Can Use**

# Can Sleep Deprivation Hurt Me?

College students are incredibly busy. They juggle their academic work with extracurricular activities, jobs, volunteer positions, social calendars, and family commitments. Obligations seemingly expand beyond the available hours in a day. Not surprisingly, many students steal hours from their sleep in hope of making room for all the to-dos (**Figure 5.17**). Is cutting back on sleep a healthy strategy for fitting it all in? Psychological research says, emphatically, no.

Sleep deprivation poses risks to mind, body, and spirit. It undermines your ability to think and solve problems, interferes with memory, and makes it more difficult to concentrate. Sleep deprivation also interferes with your body's hunger signals, contributing to overeating and weight gain (late-night pizza run, anyone?). It impairs your motor abilities, contributing to accidents and injuries. Moreover, sleep deprivation increases anxiety, depression, and distress. In addition—to add insult to injury—others perceive us as less attractive when we are sleep deprived, compared with when we are well rested (Axelsson et al., 2010).

In short, if you restrict your amount of sleep so that you can study more, you are setting yourself up for poor mental health, poor physical health, and an academic struggle. Yet you have to do the work and accomplish all your other tasks. What are your options?

If you voluntarily skip sleep, think about the facts just presented. Perhaps just knowing the potential impact of your decision will help you modify your behavior. Then again, you might find these specific strategies helpful:

1. **Plan.** Create a weekly calendar. Use it to schedule your classes, study time, social time, exercise, down time, and so on. Honestly estimate the amount of time it will take you to complete tasks. Schedule sufficient time for each task in your calendar.
2. **Know your priorities.** There will be times when your schedule simply cannot accommodate all the to-dos. When you are so pressed for time, you will need to make decisions about what to cut. Knowing your priorities can help you make those decisions. If doing well on your biology exam is a top priority, consider skipping the party that weekend. Yes, your decision will have consequences (you might miss your friend's crazy antics), but knowing your priorities will make it easier to accept those consequences.
3. **Stick to the plan.** Procrastination can wreak havoc on your sleep. If you find yourself procrastinating on important tasks, consider working with a mental health practitioner to figure out why you procrastinate and how you might overcome this tendency.
4. **Practice saying no.** College is a great time to explore the activities available on your campus or in your community, but exploring all those options simultaneously is a recipe for disaster. Be selective.

**FIGURE 5.17 Sleep Deprivation** Students may try to avoid sleep. Sleep will catch up with them!

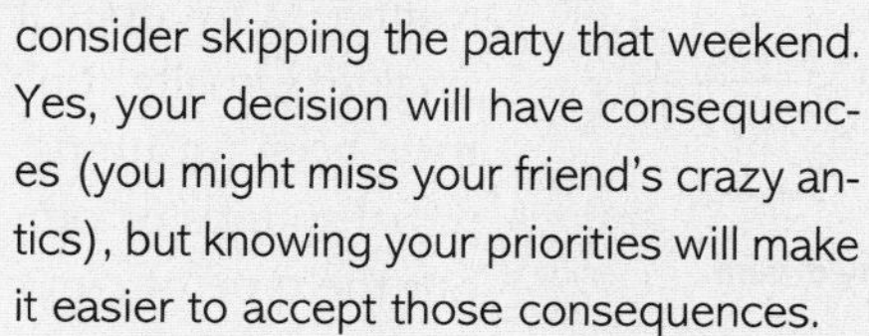

Of course, sometimes sleep may elude you. Even when you long for sleep as you lie in bed, you may find yourself dog-tired but unable to doze off. In such cases, the strategies described below might help you develop better sleep:

1. **Establish a routine to help set your biological clock.** Every day (including weekends), go to bed at the same time and wake up at the same time. Changing the time you go to bed or wake up each day alters your regular nightly sleep cycle and can disrupt other physiological systems.
2. **Avoid alcohol and caffeine just before going to bed.** Alcohol might help you get to sleep more quickly, but it will interfere with your sleep cycle and most likely cause you to wake up early the next day. Caffeine is a stimulant: It interferes with a chemical (adenosine) that helps you sleep, so it will prevent you from falling asleep.
3. **Exercise regularly.** Regular exercise will help maintain your sleep cycle. Exercising creates arousal that interferes with sleep, however, so do not exercise right before going to bed. But a little stretching before bedtime can help your mind and body relax.
4. **Remember, your bed is for sleeping.** Most of us do not sleep in our kitchens, nor should we eat in our beds. Or watch TV. Or study. Your mind needs to associate your bed with sleeping. The best way to make that association is to use your bed exclusively for sleeping. And maybe a little cuddling.

*(continued)*

5. **Relax.** Do not worry about the future (easier said than done, right?). Have a warm bath or listen to soothing music. Download a couple of meditation and relaxation podcasts. Use the techniques presented in them to help you deal with chronic stress and guide you to restfulness.
6. **Get up.** When you cannot fall asleep, get up and do something else. Do not lie there trying to force sleep (we all know how well that works, or rather does not work). If you start feeling sleepy a bit later, crawl back into bed and give sleep another try.
7. **Let bygones be bygones.** When you have trouble falling asleep on a particular night, do not try to make up for the lost sleep by sleeping late the next morning or napping during the day. Those zzzz's are gone. You want to be sleepy when you go to bed the next night. Sleeping late, napping, or both will make the next night's sleep more difficult.

The sleep attitudes and habits you establish during college will be with you for the rest of your life. Be good to yourself. Set yourself up for academic success, as well as physical and mental health, by prioritizing good sleep and taking charge of your sleep.

For additional resources, visit the National Sleep Foundation's Web site: www.sleepfoundation.org/

**"Look, don't try to weasel out of this. It was my dream, but you had the affair in it."**

## People Dream while Sleeping

Because **dreams** are the products of an altered state of consciousness, dreaming is one of life's great mysteries. Indeed, no one knows if dreaming serves any biological function. Why does the sleeper's mind conjure up images, fantasies, stories that make little sense, and scenes that ignore physical laws and rules of both time and space? Why does the mind then confuse these conjurings with reality? Why does it sometimes allow them to scare the dreamer awake? Usually, only when people wake up do they realize they have been dreaming. Of course, dreams sometimes incorporate external sounds or other sensory experiences, but this happens without the type of consciousness experienced during wakefulness.

Although some people report that they do not remember their dreams, everyone dreams unless a particular kind of brain injury or a particular kind of medication interferes. In fact, the average person spends six years of his or her life dreaming. If you want to remember your dreams better, you can teach yourself to do so: Keep a pen and paper or a voice recorder next to your bed so you can record your dreams as soon as you wake up. If you wait, you are likely to forget most of them.

**REM DREAMS AND NON-REM DREAMS** Dreams occur in REM and non-REM sleep, but the dreams' contents differ in the two types of sleep. REM dreams are more likely to be bizarre. They may involve intense emotions, visual and auditory hallucinations (but rarely taste, smell, or pain), and an uncritical acceptance of illogical events. Non-REM dreams are often very dull. They may concern mundane activities such as deciding what clothes to wear or taking notes in class.

The activation and deactivation of different brain regions during REM and non-REM sleep may be responsible for the different types of dreams. During non-REM sleep, there is general deactivation of many brain regions; during REM sleep, some areas of the brain show increased activity, whereas others show decreased activity (Hobson, 2009). The contents of REM dreams result from the activation of brain structures associated with motivation, emotion, and reward (i.e., the amygdala); the activation of visual association areas; and the deactivation of the prefrontal cortex (Schwartz & Maquet, 2002; **Figure 5.18**). As discussed in Chapter 3, the prefrontal cortex is indispensable for self-awareness, reflective thought, and conscious input from the external world. Because this brain region is deactivated during REM dreams, the brain's emotion centers and visual

**dreams** Products of an altered state of consciousness in which images and fantasies are confused with reality.

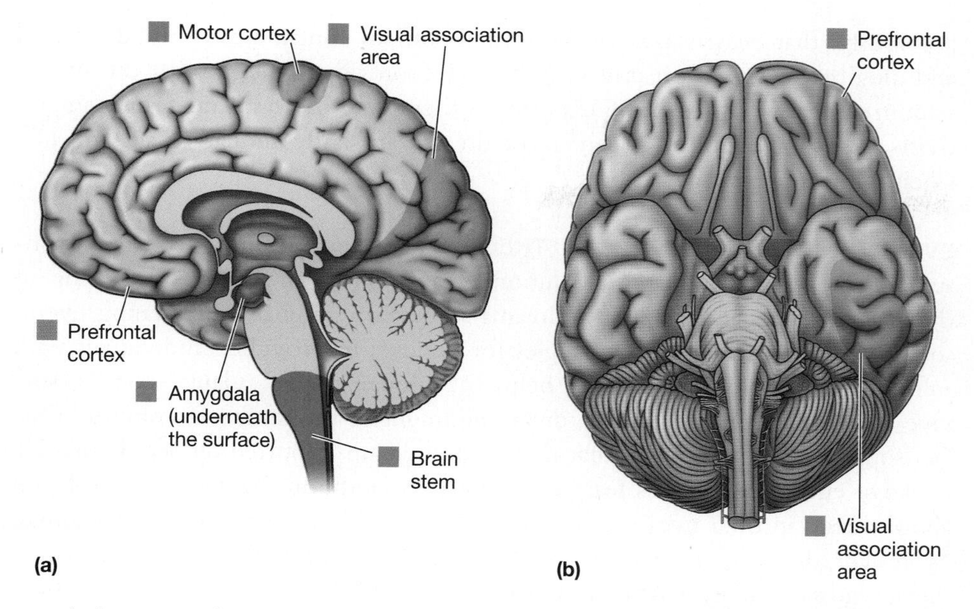


**FIGURE 5.18 Brain Regions and REM Dreams** These two views of the brain show the regions that are activated and deactivated during REM sleep. **(a)** As seen here from the side, the motor cortex, the brain stem, and visual association areas are activated, as are brain regions involved in motivation, emotion, and reward (e.g., the amygdala). The prefrontal cortex is deactivated. **(b)** As shown here from below, other visual association areas are activated as well. (This view also reveals the full size of the prefrontal cortex.)

association areas interact without rational thought. Note, however, that REM and dreaming appear to be controlled by different neural signals (Solms, 2000). In other words, REM does not produce the dream state. REM is simply linked with the contents of dreams.

WHAT DO DREAMS MEAN? Sigmund Freud presented one of the first major theories of dreams. According to Freud, dreams contain hidden content that represents unconscious conflicts within the mind of the dreamer. The **manifest content** is the dream the way the dreamer remembers it. The **latent content** is what the dream symbolizes; it is the material disguised to protect the dreamer from confronting a conflict directly. Virtually no support exists for Freud's ideas that dreams represent hidden conflicts and that objects in dreams have special symbolic meanings. Daily life experiences do, however, influence the contents of dreams. For example, you may be especially likely to have dreams with anxious content while studying for exams.

Some dreams have thematic structures. They unfold as events or stories rather than as jumbles of disconnected images. Still, such structures apparently hold no secret meanings. Although most people think their dreams are uniquely their own, many common themes occur in dreams. Have you ever dreamed about showing up for an exam and being unprepared or finding that you are taking the wrong test? Many people in college have dreams like these. Even after you graduate and no longer take exams routinely, you probably will have similar dreams about being unprepared. Retired professors sometimes dream about being unprepared to teach classes!

ACTIVATION-SYNTHESIS THEORY The sleep researchers John Alan Hobson and Robert McCarley proposed a model that has dominated scientific thinking about dreaming. According to Hobson and McCarley's **activation-synthesis theory,** random brain activity occurs during sleep. This neural firing can activate mechanisms that normally interpret sensory input. The sleeping mind tries to make sense of the resulting sensory activity by synthesizing it with stored memories. From this perspective, dreams are the side effects of mental processes produced by random neural firing.

In 2000, Hobson and his colleagues revised the activation-synthesis theory to take into account recent findings in cognitive neuroscience. For instance, they included activation of the limbic regions, associated with emotion and motivation, as the source of dreams' emotional content. They also proposed (as mentioned

**manifest content** According to Sigmund Freud, the plot of a dream; the way a dream is remembered.

**latent content** According to Sigmund Freud, what a dream symbolizes; the material that is disguised in a dream to protect the dreamer from confronting a conflict directly.

**activation-synthesis theory** A theory of dreaming; this theory proposes that the brain tries to make sense of random brain activity that occurs during sleep by synthesizing the activity with stored memories.

previously) that deactivation of the frontal cortices contributes to the delusional and illogical aspects of dreams. Critics of Hobson's theory argue that dreams are seldom as chaotic as might be expected if they were based on random brain activity (Domhoff, 2003). Indeed, most dreams are fairly similar to waking life, albeit with some strange features.

**EVOLVED THREAT-REHEARSAL THEORY** The neuroscientist Antti Revonsuo (2000) has proposed an evolutionary account of dreaming. According to the *evolved threat-rehearsal theory,* dreams sometimes simulate threatening events so that people can rehearse strategies for coping. In providing individuals with solutions to problems, dreaming helps the human species adapt—that is, survive and reproduce. In this way, dreaming might be the result of evolution. One fact supporting this theory is that most of the dreams reported by people involve negative emotions, such as fear and anxiety. In addition, people tend to dream about threats in their lives and to have nightmares about even long-past traumas. Moreover, dreaming is associated with the activation of limbic structures, such as the amygdala, that are activated by real dangers.

## Summing Up

### What Is Sleep?

Most animals experience sleep. In this altered state of consciousness, the sleeper loses substantial contact with the external world. Sleep is characterized by stages. Each stage is associated with a unique pattern of electrical activity in the brain, as reflected in EEG readings. Insomnia, sleep apnea, and narcolepsy are among the sleep disorders that have been identified. Dreams occur in both REM sleep and non-REM sleep, but the content of dreams differs between these two types of sleep. This variation may be due to the activation and deactivation of different brain structures during REM sleep and non-REM sleep. A number of theories have been proposed to explain why we sleep and dream. The biological functions of sleeping and dreaming remain unknown.

## Measuring Up

1. When people sleep, ________________.
   a. the brain shuts down so it can rest
   b. brain activity goes through several cycles of different stages, and each stage has its own characteristic pattern of brain waves
   c. the brain goes into a random pattern of firing that causes dreaming; dreaming is the left hemisphere interpreter making sense of brain activity
   d. REM sleep occurs continuously throughout the sleep period as different types of brain waves determine how deeply we sleep

2. Select the hypothesized reasons why we dream. Select as many as apply.
   a. Dreams get rid of excessive energy that accumulates throughout the day.
   b. Dreams are a way of making sense of neural firing patterns.
   c. Dreams allow us to rehearse coping strategies for anxiety-producing events.
   d. Dreams help us forget information we no longer need to remember.
   e. Dreams restore natural brain waves to their original state.

**Answers:** 1. b. brain activity goes through several cycles of different stages, and each stage has its own characteristic pattern of brain waves.
2. b. Dreams are a way of making sense of neural firing patterns; c. Dreams allow us to rehearse coping strategies for anxiety-producing events.

# 5.3 What Is Altered Consciousness?

A person's consciousness varies naturally over the course of the day. Often this variation is due to the person's actions. Watching television might encourage the mind to zone out, whereas learning to play a piece on the piano might focus attention. The following sections discuss three ways of potentially reaching altered states of consciousness: *hypnosis, meditation, and immersion in an action.*

**Learning Objectives**

- Discuss the effects of hypnosis and meditation on consciousness.
- Define the concept of "flow."
- Discuss the consequences of escaping the self.

## Hypnosis Is Induced through Suggestion

As part of an act, a stage performer or magician might hypnotize audience members and instruct them to perform silly behaviors, such as making animal noises. Has this hypnotist presented a real change in mental state or just good theater? What exactly is hypnosis?

**Hypnosis** involves a social interaction during which a person, responding to suggestions, experiences changes in memory, perception, and/or voluntary action (Kihlstrom, 1985; Kihlstrom & Eich, 1994). Psychologists generally agree that hypnosis affects some people, but they do not agree on whether it produces a genuinely altered state of consciousness (Jamieson, 2007).

**hypnosis** A social interaction during which a person, responding to suggestions, experiences changes in memory, perception, and/or voluntary action.

During a hypnotic induction, the hypnotist makes a series of suggestions to at least one person (**Figure 5.19**). "You are becoming sleepy," the hypnotist might say. "Your eyelids are drooping. . . . Your arms and legs feel very heavy." As the listener falls more deeply into the hypnotic state, the hypnotist makes more suggestions. "You cannot move your right arm," "You feel warm," "You want to bark like a dog," and so on. If everything goes according to plan, the listener follows all the suggestions as though they are true. For example, the person really barks like a dog.

Sometimes the hypnotist suggests that, after the hypnosis session, the listener will experience a change in memory, perception, or voluntary action. Such a *posthypnotic suggestion* is usually accompanied by the instruction to not remember the suggestion. For example, a stage performer or magician serving as a hypnotist might suggest, much to the delight of the audience, "When I say the word *dog,* you will stand up and bark like a dog. You will not remember this suggestion." Therapists sometimes hypnotize patients and give them posthypnotic suggestions to help them diet or quit smoking, but evidence suggests that hypnosis has quite modest effects on these behaviors. Evidence clearly indicates, however, that posthypnotic suggestions can at least subtly influence behaviors.

Consider a study of moral judgment conducted by Thalia Wheatley and Jonathan Haidt (2005). Participants in this study received a posthypnotic suggestion to feel a pang of disgust whenever they read a certain word. The word itself was neutral (e.g., the word *often*). Subsequently, participants made more-severe moral judgments when reading stories that included the word, even when the stories were innocuous. Like split-brain patients, the participants were surprised by their reactions and sometimes made up justifications for their harsh ratings, such as saying that the lead character seemed "up to something." This result suggests that the left hemisphere interpreter might be involved in people's understanding their own behavior when that behavior results from posthypnotic suggestion or other unconscious influence.

**FIGURE 5.19 Hypnotized?** **Are hypnotized people merely playing a part suggested to them by the hypnotist? What theory informs your conclusion?**

To the extent that hypnosis works, it relies mostly on the person being hypnotized rather than the hypnotist: Most of us could learn to hypnotize other people, but most of us cannot be hypnotized. Why not? Standardized tests exist for hypnotic suggestibility, and hypnosis works primarily for people who are highly suggestible (Kallio & Revonsuo, 2003). What does it mean to be among the approximately 1 in 5 people who are highly suggestible? Researchers have a hard time identifying the personality characteristics of people who can or cannot be hypnotized. Suggestibility seems related less to obvious traits such as intelligence and gullibility than to the tendencies to get absorbed in activities easily, to not be distracted easily, and to have a rich imagination (Balthazard & Woody, 1992; Crawford, Corby, & Kopell, 1996; Silva & Kirsch, 1992). Furthermore, a person who dislikes the idea of being hypnotized or finds it frightening would likely not be hypnotized easily. To be hypnotized, a person must go along with the hypnotist's suggestions willingly. No reliable evidence indicates that people will do things under hypnosis that they find immoral or otherwise objectionable.

**THEORIES OF HYPNOSIS** Some psychologists believe that a person under hypnosis essentially plays the role of a hypnotized person. That person is not faking hypnosis. Rather, he or she acts the part as if in a play, willing to perform actions called for by the "director," the hypnotist. According to this *sociocognitive theory of hypnosis,* hypnotized people behave as they expect hypnotized people to behave, even if those expectations are faulty (Kirsch & Lynn, 1995; Spanos & Coe, 1992). Alternatively, the *dissociation theory of hypnosis* acknowledges the importance of social context to hypnosis, but it views the hypnotic state as an altered state. According to this theory, hypnosis is a trancelike state in which conscious awareness is separated, or dissociated, from other aspects of consciousness (Gruzelier, 2000).

It seems unlikely that a person could alter his or her brain activity to please a hypnotist, even if that hypnotist is a psychological researcher, and numerous brain imaging studies have supported the dissociation theory of hypnosis (Rainville, Hofbauer, Bushnell, Duncan, & Price, 2002). In one of the earliest such studies, Stephen Kosslyn and colleagues (2000) demonstrated that when hypnotized participants were asked to imagine black-and-white objects as having color, they showed activity in visual cortex regions involved in color perception. Hypnotized participants asked to drain color from colored images showed diminished activity in those same brain regions. This activity pattern did not occur when participants were not hypnotized. These results suggest that the brain follows hypnotic suggestions.

Another study used the Stroop test. As you may recall from Figure 2.17, this test involves naming the color in which a color's name is printed. For example, it takes longer to name the color of the word *red* when that word is printed in blue ink than when it is printed in red ink. Participants took the test having received the posthypnotic suggestion that they would be looking at meaningless symbols instead of words. The participants apparently followed that suggestion and therefore did not show the standard Stroop interference effect, which is believed to result from automatic cognitive processes that cannot be controlled (Raz, Shapiro, Fan, & Posner, 2002). In a subsequent imaging study, the same researchers found that their suggestion to view the words as meaningless was associated with less activity in brain regions typically activated when people read or perform the Stroop test. Thus these participants seem to have perceived the stimuli as nonwords. This alteration of brain activity would be hard for people to accomplish just to please a hypnotist—or a researcher (Raz, Fan, & Posner, 2005).

**HYPNOSIS FOR PAIN** One of the most powerful uses of hypnosis is *hypnotic analgesia,* a form of pain reduction. Laboratory research has demonstrated that this technique works reliably (Hilgard & Hilgard, 1975; Nash & Barnier, 2008). For instance, a person who plunges one of his or her arms into extremely cold water will feel great pain, and the pain will intensify over time. On average, a person can leave the arm in the water for only about 30 seconds, but a person given hypnotic analgesia can hold out longer. As you might expect, people high in suggestibility who are given hypnotic analgesia can tolerate the cold water the longest (Montgomery, DuHamel, & Redd, 2000).

There is overwhelming evidence that in clinical settings, hypnosis is effective in dealing with immediate pain (e.g., during surgery, dental work, burns) and chronic pain (e.g., from arthritis, cancer, diabetes; Patterson & Jensen, 2003). A patient can also be taught self-hypnosis to improve recovery from surgery (**Figure 5.20**). Hypnosis may work more by changing the patient's interpretation of pain than by diminishing pain. That is, the patient feels the sensations associated with pain, but feels detached from those sensations (Price, Harkins, & Baker, 1987). An imaging study confirmed this pattern by showing that while hypnosis does not affect the sensory processing of pain, it reduces brain activity in regions that process the emotional aspects of pain (Rainville, Duncan, Price, Carrier, & Bushnell, 1997). Findings such as these provide considerable support for the dissociation theory of hypnosis. It seems implausible that either expectations about hypnosis or social pressure not to feel pain could explain how people given hypnotic analgesia are able to undergo painful surgery and not feel it. Nor does it seem likely that either expectations about hypnosis or social pressure not to feel pain could result in the changes in brain activity seen during hypnotic analgesia.

**FIGURE 5.20 Self-Hypnosis** This advertisement promotes one way that patients can learn self-hypnosis.

**meditation** A mental procedure that focuses attention on an external object or on a sense of awareness.

## Meditation Produces Relaxation

With a growing awareness of different cultural and religious practices and alternative approaches to medicine, people in the West have become more interested in examining Eastern techniques, including acupuncture and meditation. Different forms of meditation are popular in many Eastern religions, including Hinduism, Buddhism, and Sikhism. **Meditation** is a mental procedure that focuses attention on an external object or on a sense of awareness. Through intense contemplation, the meditator develops a deep sense of tranquility.

Mark Leary (2004) notes that one goal of meditation is to quiet the internal voices we experience as we go through the day or as we try to sleep. Do you ever find that while you are trying to concentrate on a lecture or carry on a conversation, an inner voice keeps interrupting you, perhaps reminding you of things you need to do or wondering what the other person thinks of you? Or perhaps, as you lie in bed at night, the inner voice chatters on about worries and concerns that you would prefer to forget so that you can get some sleep. During meditation, people learn to calm this inner voice, sometimes by simply letting it continue without paying attention to it.

There are two general forms of meditation. In *concentrative meditation,* you focus attention on one thing, such as your breathing pattern, a mental image, or a specific phrase (sometimes called a *mantra*). In *mindfulness meditation,* you let your thoughts flow freely, paying attention to them but trying not to react to them. You hear the contents of your inner voice, but you allow them to flow from one topic to the next without examining their meaning or reacting to them in any way. Why not take a break from reading and try one of these methods (**Figure 5.21**)?

**FIGURE 5.21 Try for Yourself: Meditation**

For at least 20 minutes, try meditating. To practice concentrative meditation, focus your attention on your breathing pattern, in and out. To practice mindfulness meditation, let your thoughts flow freely without reacting to them.

**Result:** The goal of meditation is to help people achieve a deep state of relaxation. How close did you come to that goal? What does this experience suggest to you about consciousness and its variations?

Religious forms of meditation are meant to bring spiritual enlightenment. Most forms of meditation popular in the West are meant to expand the mind, bring about feelings of inner peace, and help people deal with the tensions and stresses in their lives. These methods include *Zen, yoga,* and *transcendental meditation*, or *TM.*

Perhaps the best-known meditation procedure, TM involves meditating with great concentration for 20 minutes twice a day. Many early studies found a number of benefits from TM, including lower blood pressure, fewer reports of stress, and changes in the hormonal responses underlying stress. These studies have been criticized, however, because they had small samples and lacked appropriate control groups. In a more rigorous recent study, a large number of heart patients were randomly assigned to TM or an educational program. After 16 weeks, the patients performing TM improved more than the control group on a number of health measures, such as blood pressure, blood lipids, and insulin resistance (Paul-Labrador et al., 2006). Unfortunately, this study does not show which aspects of TM produced the health benefits. Was it simply relaxing, or was it the altered state of consciousness? (As discussed in Chapter 11, reducing stress, no matter how it is done, yields substantial health benefits.)

Psychologists also study how meditation affects cognitive processing and brain function (Cahn & Polich, 2006). In one study, participants were assigned randomly to five days of either intensive meditation training or relaxation training. Those who underwent the meditation training showed greater stress reduction and more significant improvement in attention than did the group that underwent relaxation training (Tang et al., 2007). When participants in another study were made to feel sad, those who had received meditation training felt less sad than those in a control group who did not receive meditation training (Farb et al., 2010; **Figure 5.22**). Some researchers argue that long-term meditation brings about structural changes in the brain that help maintain brain function over the life span. For instance, the volume of gray matter typically diminishes with age. One study found that this volume did not diminish in older adults who practiced Zen meditation (Pagnoni & Cekic, 2007). This finding suggests that Zen

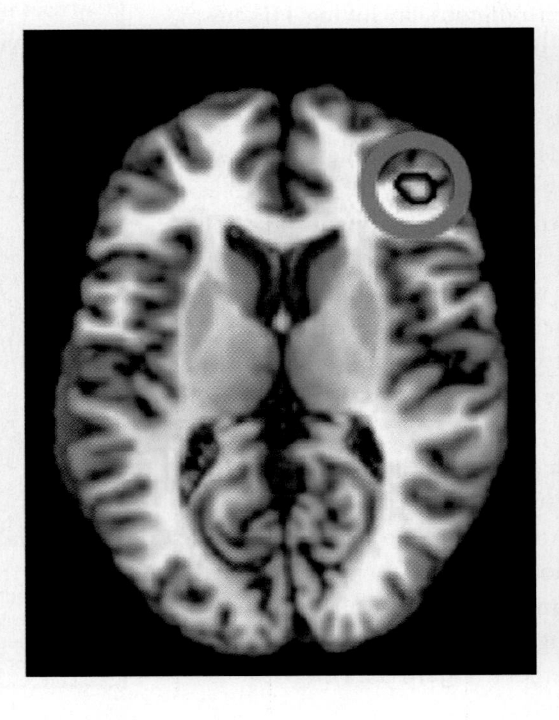

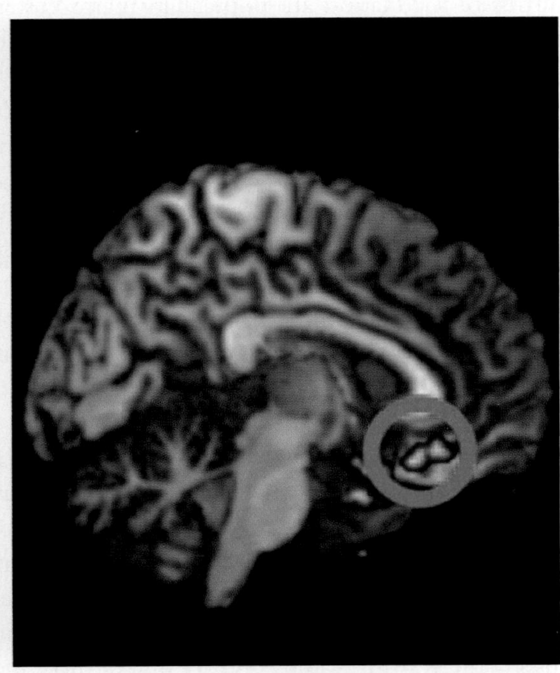

**FIGURE 5.22 The Brain on Meditation** In these fMRI scans, the circles indicate brain areas that typically show less activity when people are sad. After control subjects watched sad clips from movies, these areas of their brains were less active, as expected. In the brains of participants who had received eight weeks of meditation training, these areas remained active, indicating that these participants felt less sadness.

meditation might help preserve cognitive functioning as people age. But people who meditate may differ substantially from people who do not, especially in terms of lifestyle choices such as diet and a willingness to take care of their health. As Chapter 2 notes, such correlational data do not prove causation. Careful empirical research using the methods of psychological science should contribute significantly to our understanding of meditation's effects.

## People Can Lose Themselves in Activities

Hypnosis and meditation involve doing something to alter consciousness. As noted throughout this chapter, however, a person's level of conscious awareness changes as a result of the time of day as well as the person's activities. For instance, when a person performs an automatic task, such as driving, that person's conscious thoughts might not include the experience of driving. Instead, the driver's brain shifts to "autopilot" and automatically goes through the process. During most of our daily activities, of course, we are consciously aware of only a small portion of both our thoughts and our behaviors.

**EXERCISE, RELIGIOUS PRAYER, AND FLOW** Why do many people listen to music while exercising? In offering a distraction from physical exertion, music can bring about an energizing shift in consciousness. Many people have had a similar but more extreme experience during exercise. One minute they are in pain and feeling fatigued, and the next minute they are euphoric and feeling a glorious release of energy. Commonly known as *runner's high,* this state is partially mediated by physiological processes (especially endorphin release; see Chapter 3, "Biology and Behavior"). It also occurs because of a shift in consciousness.

Shifts in consciousness that are similar to runner's high occur at other moments in our lives. Religious ceremonies often decrease awareness of the external world and create feelings of euphoria. Indeed, such rituals often involve chanting, dancing, and/or other behaviors as a way for people to lose themselves in *religious ecstasy*. Like meditation, religious ecstasy directs attention away from the self. In this way, it allows a person to focus on his or her spiritual awareness (**Figure 5.23**).

One psychological theory about such peak experiences is based on the concept of *flow,* "a particular kind of experience that is so engrossing and enjoyable [that it is] worth doing for its own sake even though it may have no consequence outside itself" (Csikszentmihalyi, 1999, p. 824). That is, a person might perform a particular task out of fascination with it rather than out of a desire for a reward. Flow is an optimal experience in that the activity is completely absorbing and completely satisfying. The person experiencing flow loses track of time, forgets about his or her problems, and fails to notice other things going on (Csikszentmihalyi, 1990). The person's skills are well matched with the task's demands; the situation is less like driving, where much of the work happens automatically, than like rock climbing, where every thought is on the next step and is concrete, not deep and abstract (Leary, 2004). Flow experiences have been reported during many activities, including playing music (O'Neil, 1999) or a moderately challenging version of the computer game *Tetris* (Keller & Bless, 2008), participating in sports (Jackson, Thomas, Marsh, & Smethurst, 2001), and simply doing satisfying jobs (Demerouti, 2006). In the view of the psychologist Mihaly Csikszentmihalyi (1999), flow experiences bring personal fulfillment and make life worth living.

**FIGURE 5.23 Religious Ecstasy** During a service at a Baptist church in Beulah, Mississippi, a woman is overcome with religious ecstasy. According to the photographer, the woman was speaking in tongues.

**FIGURE 5.24 Escapist Entertainment** Simple entertainment can veer toward obsession. **What would you say are the possible benefits of devoting time to video games? What are the potential negative effects?**

**ESCAPING THE SELF** Our conscious thoughts can be dominated by worries, frustrations, and feelings of personal failure. Sometimes people get tired of dealing with life's problems and try to make themselves feel better through escapist pursuits. Potential flow activities such as sports or work may help people escape thinking about their problems, but people engage in such activities mainly to feel personally fulfilled. The difference is between escaping and engaging. Sometimes people choose to escape the self rather than engage with life: To forget their troubles, they drink alcohol, take drugs, play video games, watch television, surf the Web, text, and so on. The selective appeal of escapist entertainment is that it distracts people from reflecting on their problems or their failures, thereby helping them avoid feeling bad about themselves.

Some escapist activities—such as running or reading—tend to have positive effects; some tend to be relatively harmless distractions; and some tend to come at great personal expense. For example, people obsessively playing online games such as *World of Warcraft* have lost their jobs and even their marriages (**Figure 5.24**). They have even taken the lives of their offspring: In South Korea in 2010, Kim Jae-beom and his common-law wife, Kim Yun-jeong, neglected their 3-month-old daughter to the point that she died of starvation. The couple reportedly spent every night raising a virtual daughter as part of a role-playing game they engaged in at an Internet café. Some ways of escaping the self can also be associated with self-destructive behaviors, such as binge eating, unsafe sex, and, at the extreme, suicide. According to the social psychologist Roy Baumeister (1991), people engage in such behaviors because, to escape their problems, they seek to reduce self-awareness. The state of being in lowered self-awareness may reduce long-term planning, reduce meaningful thinking, and help bring about uninhibited actions. Chapter 12 further discusses the connections between behavior and self-awareness. The next section of this chapter looks at a common way people try to escape their problems—namely, using drugs or alcohol to alter consciousness.

**Summing Up**

## What Is Altered Consciousness?

Altered states of consciousness may be achieved through hypnosis. Some people are more susceptible to hypnosis than others. Posthypnotic suggestions can alter how people react, even though they are not aware that a suggestion was given to them. Hypnosis can also be used to control pain. Patterns of brain activity suggest that individuals who are hypnotized are not simply faking their responses or engaging in theatrical tricks. Altered states of consciousness may also be achieved through concentrative or mindfulness meditation. The results of some studies suggest that meditation may contribute to improved health. Altered states of consciousness—in particular, flow states—may also occur as a consequence of extreme physical exertion, profound religious experiences, or engaging in tasks that are deeply absorbing. Those who attempt to decrease self-awareness by escaping the self often face devastating consequences.

### Measuring Up

**Mark each statement below with a T if it is true and an F if it is false.**

a. Participants under hypnosis who were told that they would not see real words did not show the Stroop effect. (To review the Stroop effect, see Figure 2.17.)

b. Brain imaging showed that hypnotized subjects really were asleep.

c. Brain imaging showed that hypnosis changes brain activity in ways inconsistent with the idea that people are simply role-playing.

d. People who are hypnotized will do anything the hypnotist tells them to.

e. Hypnosis is not useful in reducing pain.

f. Hypnotized people are aware of the hypnotist's suggestions and simply go along with what they are asked to do.

**Answers:** a. T; b. F; c. T; d. F; e. F; f. F

## 5.4 How Do Drugs Affect Consciousness?

#### Learning Objectives

- Describe the neurochemical, psychological, and behavioral effects of marijuana, stimulants, MDMA, opiates, and alcohol.
- Identify physiological and psychological factors associated with addiction.

Throughout history, people have discovered that ingesting certain substances can alter their mental states in various ways. Some of those altered states, however momentary, can be pleasant. Some, especially over the long term, can have negative consequences, including injury or death. According to the United Nations Office on Drugs and Crime (2009), upward of 250 million people around the globe use illicit drugs each year. Societal problems stemming from drug abuse are well known. Most people probably know and care about someone addicted to a commonly abused drug, such as alcohol, an illegal substance, or a prescription medication. If we include nicotine and caffeine on that list, most people probably are drug addicts. To investigate the biological, individual, and societal effects of drug use, psychologists ask questions such as *Why do people use drugs? Why do some people become addicted to drugs? Why do drug addicts continue to abuse drugs when doing so causes turmoil and suffering?*

### People Use—and Abuse—Many Psychoactive Drugs

Drugs are a mixed blessing. If they are the right ones, taken under the right circumstances, they can provide soothing relief from severe pain or a moderate headache. They can help people suffering from depression lead more satisfying lives. They can help children who have attention deficits or hyperactivity disorders settle down and learn better. But many of these same drugs can be used for "recreational" purposes: to alter physical sensations, levels of consciousness, thoughts, moods, and behaviors in ways that users believe are desirable. This recreational use sometimes can have negative consequences.

*Psychoactive drugs* are mind-altering substances. These drugs change the brain's neurochemistry by activating neurotransmitter systems. The effects of a particular drug depend on which neurotransmitter systems it activates. *Stimulants,* for example, are drugs that increase behavioral and mental activity. They include caffeine and nicotine as well as cocaine and amphetamines. These substances generally work by interfering with the normal reuptake of dopamine by the releasing neuron, allowing dopamine to remain in the synapse and thus prolonging its effects, although sometimes stimulants also increase the release of dopamine (Fibiger, 1993). Activation of dopamine receptors seems to be involved in drug use in two ways. First, the increased dopamine is associated with greater reward, or increased liking (Volkow, Wang, & Baler, 2011). Second, the increased dopamine leads to a greater desire to take a drug, even if that drug does not produce pleasure. Thus sometimes an addict *wants* a drug even if the addict does not *like* the drug when he or she uses it (Kringelbach & Berridge, 2009). The available evidence suggests that dopamine is particularly important for the wanting aspect of addiction. Stimulants activate the sympathetic nervous system, increasing heart rate and blood pressure. They improve mood, but they also cause people to become restless, and they disrupt sleep.

This section considers a few common psychoactive drugs. Some of them have legitimate medical uses, but all of these drugs are commonly abused outside of treatment.

**MARIJUANA** The most widely used illicit drug in the world is marijuana, the dried leaves and flower buds of the cannabis plant. Many drugs can easily be categorized as a stimulant, a depressant, or a hallucinogen, but marijuana can have the effects of all three types. The psychoactive ingredient in marijuana is THC, or tetrahydrocannabinol. This chemical produces a relaxed mental state, an uplifted or contented mood, and some perceptual and cognitive distortions. Marijuana users report that THC also makes perceptions more vivid, and some say it especially affects taste. Most first-time users do not experience the "high" obtained by more experienced users. Novice smokers might use inefficient techniques, they might have trouble inhaling, or both, but users apparently must learn how to appreciate the drug's effects (Kuhn, Swartzwelder, & Wilson, 2003). In this way, marijuana differs from most other drugs. Generally, the first time someone uses a drug other than marijuana, the effects are very strong, and subsequent uses lead to tolerance, in which a person has to use more of the drug to get the same effect.

Although the brain mechanisms that marijuana affects remain somewhat mysterious, researchers have discovered a class of receptors that are activated by naturally occurring THC-like substances. Activation of these *cannabinoid* receptors appears to adjust and enhance mental activity and perhaps alter pain perception. The large concentration of these receptors in the hippocampus may partly explain why marijuana impairs memory (Ilan, Smith, & Gevins, 2004). Marijuana is also used for its medicinal properties, and this use is legal in many countries and American states. For instance, cancer patients undergoing chemotherapy report that marijuana is effective for overcoming nausea. Nearly 1 in 4 AIDS patients reports using marijuana to relieve nausea and pain (Prentiss, Power, Balmas, Tzuang, & Israelski et al., 2004). The medical use of marijuana is controversial because of the possibility that chronic use can cause health problems or lead to abuse of the drug.

**COCAINE** Cocaine is derived from the leaves of the coca bush, which grows primarily in South America. After inhaling (snorting) cocaine as a powder or smoking it in the form of crack cocaine, users experience a wave of confidence. They feel good, alert, energetic, sociable, and wide awake. Cocaine produces its stimulating effects by increasing the concentration of dopamine in the neural synapse. These short-term effects are especially intense for crack cocaine users. In contrast, habitual use of cocaine in large quantities can lead to paranoia, psychotic behavior, and violence (Ottieger, Tressell, Inciardi, & Rosales, 1992).

Cocaine has a long history of use in America. John Pemberton, a pharmacist from Georgia, was so impressed with cocaine's effects that in 1886 he added the drug to soda water for easy ingestion, thus creating Coca-Cola. In 1906, the U.S. government outlawed cocaine, so it was removed from the drink. To this day, however, coca leaves from which the cocaine has been removed are used in the making of Coke (**Figure 5.25**).

COCA-COLA

SYRUP AND EXTRACT.

For Soda Water and other Carbonated Beverages.

This "INTELLECTUAL BEVERAGE" and TEMPERANCE DRINK contains the valuable TONIC and NERVE STIMULANT properties of the Coca plant and Cola (or Kola) nuts, and makes not only a delicious, exhilarating, refreshing and invigorating Beverage, (dispensed from the soda water fountain or in other carbonated beverages), but a valuable Brain Tonic, and a cure for all nervous affections — SICK HEAD-ACHE, NEURALGIA, HYSTERIA, MELANCHOLY, &c.

The peculiar flavor of COCA-COLA delights every palate; it is dispensed from the soda fountain in same manner as any of the fruit syrups.

J. S. Pemberton;

Chemist,

Sole Proprietor, Atlanta, Ga.

**FIGURE 5.25 Early Coke Ad** This advertisement's claim that Coca-Cola is "a valuable Brain Tonic" may have been inspired by the incorporation of cocaine into the drink before 1906.

**AMPHETAMINES** Amphetamines are synthesized using simple lab methods. They go by street names such as *speed, meth* (for *methamphetamine*), *ice,* and *crystal.* Amphetamines have a long history of use for weight loss and staying awake. However, their numerous negative side effects include insomnia, anxiety, and heart, skin, and dental problems. In addition, people quickly become addicted to them. They are seldom used for legitimate medical purposes.

Methamphetamine is the world's second most commonly used illicit drug, after marijuana (Barr et al., 2006). It was first developed in the early twentieth century as a nasal decongestant, but its recreational use became popular in the 1980s. The National Institute of Drug Abuse (2006) estimates that around 4 percent of the U.S. population have tried methamphetamine at some point in their lives. The use of methamphetamine may have declined in recent years, however (Gonzales, Mooney, & Rawson, 2010). One factor that encourages the use of this drug and may explain its popularity over the past decade is that methamphetamine is easy to make from common over-the-counter drugs.

By blocking the reuptake of dopamine and increasing its release, methamphetamine yields much higher levels of dopamine in the synapse. In addition, methamphetamine stays in the body and brain much longer than, say, cocaine, so its effects are prolonged. Over time, methamphetamine damages various brain structures, including the frontal lobes (**Figure 5.26**). Ultimately, it depletes dopamine levels. The drug's effects on the temporal lobes and the limbic system may explain the harm done to memory and emotion in long-term users (Kim et al., 2006; Thompson et al., 2004). Methamphetamine also causes considerable physical damage (**Figure 5.27**).

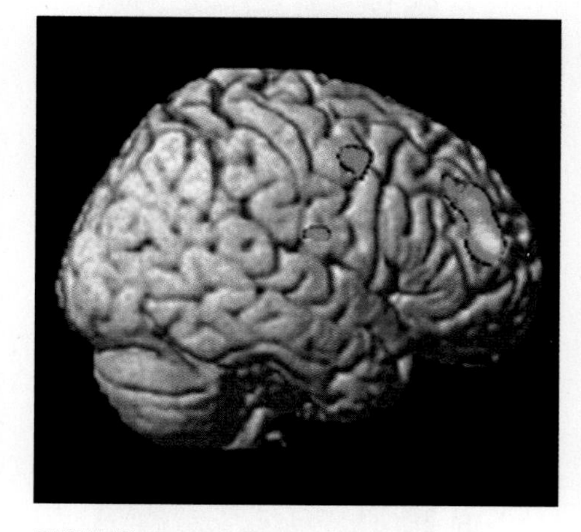

**FIGURE 5.26 Methamphetamine's Effects on the Brain** This image is a composite of brain scans from 29 methamphetamine addicts. The red and yellow areas represent the brain damage that typically occurs in the frontal cortex as a result of methamphetamine abuse (Kim et al., 2006). Such damage may explain the cognitive problems associated with methamphetamine use.

**MDMA** MDMA, or ecstasy, has become popular since the 1990s. It produces an energizing effect similar to that of stimulants, but it also causes slight hallucinations. According to the National Institute of Drug Abuse (2010), MDMA use by high school students increased from 3.7 percent to 4.7 percent between 2009 and 2010. The drug first became popular among young adults in nightclubs and at all-night parties known as raves. Compared with amphetamines, MDMA is associated with less dopamine release and more serotonin release. The serotonin release may explain ecstasy's hallucinogenic properties. Although many users believe it to be relatively safe, researchers have documented a number of impairments from long-term ecstasy use, especially memory problems and a diminished ability to perform complex tasks (Kalechstein, De La Garza II, Mahoney III, Fantegrossi, & Newton, 2007). Because ecstasy also depletes serotonin, users

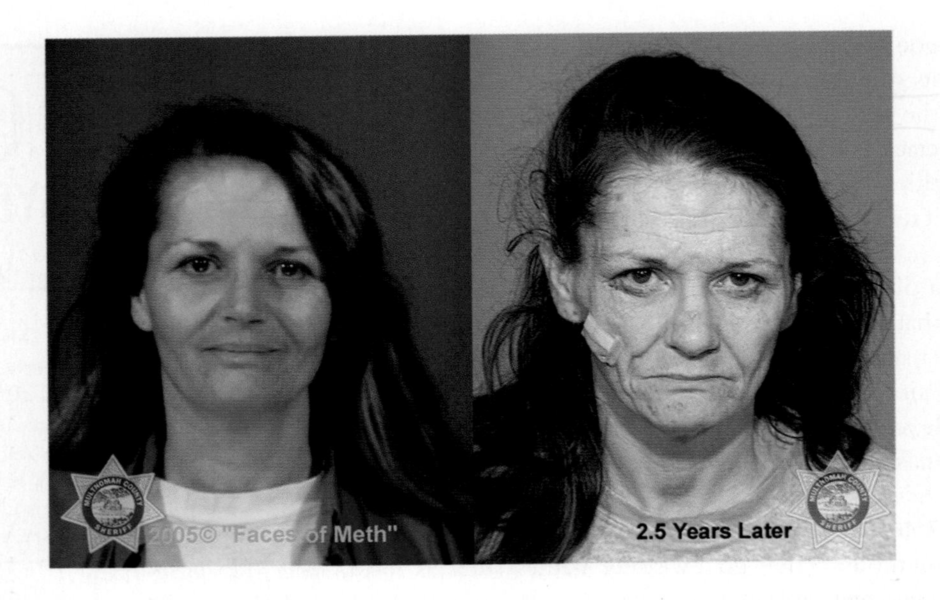


**FIGURE 5.27 Methamphetamine's Effects on the Person** These before-and-after photos dramatically illustrate how the physical damage from methamphetamine can affect appearance. When the photo on the left was taken, Theresa Baxter was 42 and not a methamphetamine addict. The photo on the right was taken 2½ years later, after Baxter was arrested for crimes she committed to support her addiction.

often feel depressed when the drug's rewarding properties wear off (Fischer, Hatzidimitriou, Wlos, Katz, & Ricaurte, 1995; **Figure 5.28**).

**OPIATES** Opiates are a type of depressant. They include heroin, morphine, and codeine. These drugs provide enormous reward value, producing feelings of relaxation, analgesia, and euphoria. Heroin provides a rush of intense pleasure that most addicts describe as similar to orgasm. This rush evolves into a pleasant, relaxed stupor. Heroin and morphine may be so highly addictive because they have dual physical effects: They increase pleasure by binding with opiate receptors and increase wanting of the drug by activating dopamine receptors (Kuhn et al., 2003).

Opiates have been used to relieve pain and suffering for hundreds of years. Indeed, before the twentieth century, heroin was widely available without prescription and was marketed by Bayer, the aspirin company (**Figure 5.29**). The benefits of short-term opiate use to relieve severe pain seem clear, but long-term opiate use to relieve chronic pain will much more likely lead to abuse or addiction than will short-term use (Ballantyne & LaForge, 2007). Moreover, long-term use of opiates is associated with a number of neurological and cognitive deficits, such as attention and memory problems (Gruber, Silveri, & Yurgelun-Todd, 2007). Therefore, clinicians need to be cautious in prescribing opiates, such as Vicodin, especially when the drugs will be used over extended periods.

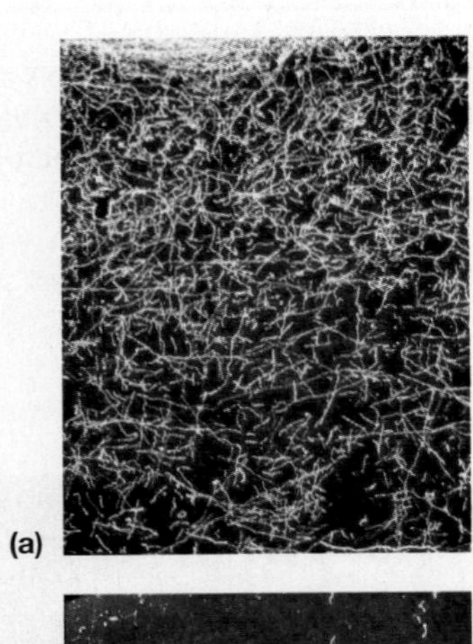


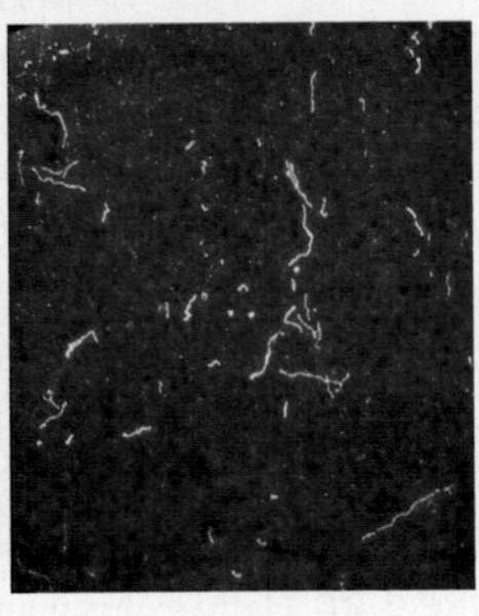


**FIGURE 5.28 MDMA's Effects on the Brain (a)** This image shows serotonin nerve fibers in the cortex of a normal monkey. **(b)** This image shows the same brain area of a monkey that received multiple doses of MDMA (ecstasy). Eighteen months after the monkey received the MDMA, the monkey's serotonin nerve fibers remain drastically reduced.

## Alcohol Is the Most Widely Abused Drug

Like other addictive drugs, alcohol may offer its rewards by activating dopamine receptors. But alcohol also interferes with the neurochemical processes involved in memory, and memory loss can follow excessive alcohol intake. Heavy long-term alcohol intake can cause extensive brain damage. *Korsakoff's syndrome,* a disorder sometimes caused by alcoholism, is characterized by both severe memory loss and intellectual deterioration.

Many societies have a love/hate relationship with alcohol. On the one hand, moderate drinking is an accepted aspect of social interaction and may even be good for one's health. On the other hand, alcohol is a major contributor to many societal problems, such as spousal abuse and other forms of violence. Although the percentage of traffic fatalities due to alcohol is dropping, alcohol is a factor in more than one-third of fatal accidents (Mayhew, Brown, & Simpson, 2002). One study found that approximately one-third of college students reported having had sex during a drinking binge, and the heaviest drinkers were likely to have had sex with a new or casual partner (Leigh & Schafer, 1993), thus increasing their risk for exposure to AIDS and other sexually transmitted diseases. The overall cost of problem drinking in the United States—from lost productivity due to employee absence, from health care expenses, and so on—is estimated to be more than $100 billion annually.

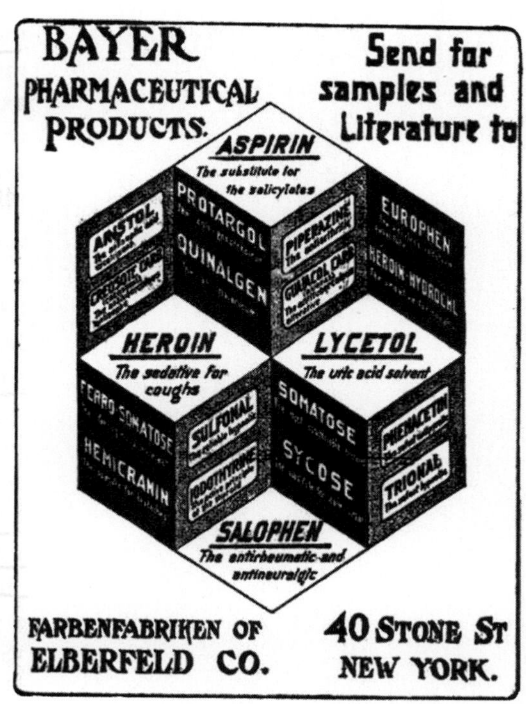


**FIGURE 5.29 Early Heroin Ad!** Before 1904, Bayer advertised heroin as "the sedative for coughs."

### GENDER DIFFERENCES IN ALCOHOL CONSUMPTION ACROSS CULTURES

The World Health Organization conducts a massive international study of gender-related and culture-related differences in alcohol consumption (Obot & Room, 2005). The study's main premise is that to understand alcohol consumption worldwide, we need to study the various ways alcohol is used, by men and by women, across cultural and social contexts. The authors call the gap between men and women in alcohol consumption "one of the few universal gender differences in human social behavior" (Wilsnack, Wilsnack, & Obot, 2005, p. 1). Can you guess whether men or women consume more alcohol? In every region of the world, across a wide variety of measures (e.g., drinking versus abstinence, heavy drinking versus occasional drinking, alcohol-related disorders), men drink a lot more. Men are twice as likely to report binge drinking (drinking five or more servings in one evening), chronic drinking, and recent alcohol intoxication. Gender gaps in binge drinking may be smaller among university students, however.

What accounts for the large and universal difference between men's drinking and women's drinking? One possible explanation is that because women do not

CRITICAL THINKING SKILL

## Recognizing Slippery Slope Thinking

What happens when you slip while walking down a slope? Might you fall to the bottom? A person making a *slippery slope argument* reasons that some first slippery step must lead down to a larger, more slippery step or even a large fall. For example, a slippery slope argument against all "recreational" drug use proposes that if you start using a drug that is not likely to have lasting effects (say, marijuana), this behavior will lead you to take "harder" drugs (say, cocaine), and soon you will be robbing to support your heroin habit. The "starter," less powerful drug is referred to as a *gateway drug* because it supposedly opens the gate to more-regular and more-dangerous drug use.

The data are mixed on whether using drugs such as marijuana is associated with later use of drugs such as heroin. Even if the relationship were strong, what might be wrong with these data? The conclusion that taking marijuana *causes* people to take harder drugs cannot be inferred from these data. There are many other possible explanations for this relationship. For example, people with a tendency to get addicted could start with any drug and generally do start with the cheapest and most available one, marijuana. It might or might not be true that a minor action will lead to a more serious one. There is no reason to assume, however, that this progression is always true or is even usually true.

metabolize alcohol as quickly as men do and generally have smaller body volumes, they consume less alcohol than men to achieve the same effects. Another possible explanation is that women's drinking may be more hidden because it is less socially accepted than men's drinking. According to this view, women's alcohol consumption may be underreported, especially in cultures where it is frowned upon or forbidden. In some cultures, "real men" are expected to drink a lot and prove they can "hold" their liquor, whereas women who do the same are seen as abnormal.

**EXPECTATIONS** Alan Marlatt (1999), a leading researcher on substance abuse, has noted that people view alcohol as the "magic elixir," capable of increasing social skills, sexual pleasure, confidence, and power. They anticipate that alcohol will have positive effects on their emotions and behavior. For example, people tend to think that alcohol reduces anxiety, so both light and heavy drinkers turn to alcohol after a difficult day. Alcohol *can* interfere with the cognitive processing of threat cues, so that anxiety-provoking events are less troubling when people are intoxicated. This effect occurs, however, only if people drink *before* the anxiety-provoking events. In fact, according to the research, drinking after a hard day can increase people's focus on and obsession with their problems (Sayette, 1993). In addition, while moderate doses of alcohol are associated with more-positive moods, larger doses are associated with more-negative moods.

Expectations about alcohol's effects are learned very early in life, through observation. Children may see that people who drink have a lot of fun and that drinking is an important aspect of many celebrations. Teenagers may view drinkers as sociable and grown up, two things they desperately want to be. Studies have shown that children who have very positive expectations about alcohol are more likely to start drinking and become heavy drinkers than children who do not share those expectations (Leigh & Stacy, 2004).

According to the social psychologists Jay Hull and Charles Bond (1986), expectations about alcohol profoundly affect behavior. These researchers gave study participants tonic water with or without alcohol. Regardless of the drinks' actual

CRITICAL THINKING SKILL

## Recognizing Circular Reasoning

Have you ever seen a cat chase its tail? It can be a pretty funny sight, as the cat never gets closer to its "prey." Similarly, a person who engages in circular reasoning moves around without truly reaching a conclusion. The argument ends up where it started, because the reason for believing the conclusion is just a restatement of the conclusion. Here is an example: "We need to raise the legal drinking age from 21 to 25 because 21-year-olds are too young to drink." Can you see what is wrong with this argument? Saying that 21-year-olds are too young to drink is just another way of saying "We need to raise the legal drinking age from 21." The argument does not explain *why* 21 is too young. If the speaker had said, "We need to raise the legal drinking age from 21 to 25 because research shows that 25-year-olds have half the number of traffic accidents that 21-year-olds do" or ". . . because the frontal areas of the brain mature between ages 21 and 25" or ". . . because 25-year-olds are more responsible," she or he would have provided a reason to support the conclusion.

contents, they told some participants they were drinking just tonic water and some they were drinking tonic water with alcohol. This balanced-placebo design allowed for a comparison of those who thought they were drinking tonic water but were actually drinking alcohol with those who thought they were drinking alcohol but were actually drinking tonic water. The researchers demonstrated that alcohol impairs motor processes, information processing, and mood, independent of whether the person thinks he or she has consumed it. In addition, the researchers demonstrated that the belief that one has consumed alcohol leads to disinhibition regarding various social behaviors, such as sexual arousal and aggression, whether or not the person has consumed alcohol. Thus some behaviors generally associated with drunkenness are accounted for by learned beliefs about intoxication rather than by alcohol's pharmacological properties. Sometimes the learned expectations and the pharmacology work in opposite ways. For instance, alcohol tends to increase sexual arousal, but it interferes with sexual performance.

(a)

(b)

**FIGURE 5.30 Physical Dependence versus Psychological Dependence** Both types of dependence can force people to go to extremes. **(a) What does this scene, outside a restaurant in Germany, suggest about patrons such as this woman? (b) How do casinos, such as this one in Las Vegas, encourage patrons' "addiction" to gambling?**

## Addiction Has Physical and Psychological Aspects

Addiction is drug use that remains compulsive despite its negative consequences. The condition consists of physical and psychological factors. Physical dependence on a drug is a physiological state associated with *tolerance*, whereby a person needs to consume more of a particular substance to achieve the same subjective effect. Failing to ingest the substance leads to symptoms of *withdrawal*, a physiological and psychological state characterized by feelings of anxiety, tension, and cravings for the addictive substance. The physical symptoms of withdrawal vary widely from drug to drug and from individual to individual, but they include nausea, chills, body aches, and tremors. A person can be psychologically dependent, however, without showing tolerance or withdrawal. This section focuses on addiction to substances that alter consciousness, but people can also become psychologically dependent on behaviors, such as shopping or gambling (**Figure 5.30**).

**ADDICTION'S CAUSES** How do people become addicted? One central factor appears to be dopamine activity in the limbic system, because this activity underlies the rewarding properties of taking drugs (Baler & Volkow, 2006; Chapter 6, "Learning," further discusses dopamine's role in the experience of reward). A brain region called the *insula* seems to be important for craving and addiction (Goldstein et al., 2009), since this region becomes active when addicts view images of drug use (**Figure 5.31**). Patients with insula damage report that immediately after being injured, they quit smoking easily. In fact, they no longer experience conscious urges to smoke. One patient who had a stroke to his left insula commented that he quit smoking because his "body forgot the urge to smoke" (Naqvi, Rudrauf, Damasio, & Bechara, 2007, p. 534).

Only about 5 percent to 10 percent of those who use drugs become addicted. Indeed, more than 90 million Americans have experimented with illicit drugs, yet most of them use drugs only occasionally or try them for a while and then give them up. In a longitudinal study, Jonathan Shedler and Jack Block (1990) found that those who had experimented with drugs as adolescents were better adjusted in adulthood than those who had never tried them. Complete abstainers and heavy drug users had adjustment problems compared with those who had experimented. This finding does not suggest, however, that everyone should try drugs or that parents should encourage drug experimentation. After all, no one can predict just who will become addicted or know who is prepared to handle a drug's effects on behavior.

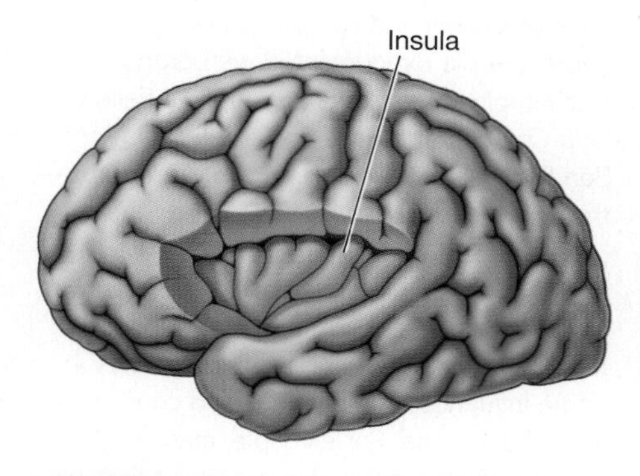


**FIGURE 5.31 Insula** This brain region appears to play a role in craving and addiction.

Some adolescents are especially likely to experiment with illegal drugs and to abuse alcohol. Children high in sensation seeking (a personality trait that involves attraction to novelty and risk taking) are more likely to associate with deviant peer groups and to use alcohol, tobacco, and drugs (Wills, DuHamel, & Vaccaro, 1995). These children and their parents tend to have poor relationships, which in turn promote the children's association with deviant peer groups. Does the family environment determine alcohol and drug use? Some theorists suggest that an inherited predisposition to sensation seeking may predict behaviors, such as affiliating with drug users, that increase the possibility of substance abuse.

Some evidence points to genetic components of addiction, especially for alcoholism, but little direct evidence points to a *single* "alcoholism" or "addiction" gene. Rather, what people inherit is a cluster of characteristics. These inherited risk factors might include personality traits such as risk taking and impulsivity, a reduced concern about personal harm, a nervous system chronically low in arousal, or a predisposition to finding chemical substances pleasurable. In turn, such factors may make some people more likely to explore drugs and enjoy them.

Social learning theorists have sought to account for the initiation of drug or alcohol use among either children or adolescents. They emphasize the roles of parents, the mass media, and peers, including self-identification with high-risk groups (e.g., "stoners" or "druggies"). Teenagers want to fit in somewhere, even with groups that society perceives as deviant. And as discussed further in Chapter 6, children imitate the behavior of role models, especially those they admire or with whom they identify. For children whose parents smoke, the modeling of the behavior may be continuous through early childhood and elementary school. When parents smoke, their children tend to have positive attitudes about smoking and to begin smoking early (Rowe, Chassin, Presson, & Sherman, 1996).

(a)

(b)

**FIGURE 5.32 The Sixties, Drugs, and Vietnam (a)** By the late 1960s, youth culture had taken many new forms in the United States and elsewhere. In exploring the boundaries of society and consciousness, many young people experimented with drugs. Here, two people share drugs at the Shiva Fellowship Church Earth Faire at Golden Gate Park, San Francisco, in April 1969. **(b)** Through those years and beyond, the United States played a leading role in the Vietnam War, a military conflict that took place in the "faraway lands" of Vietnam, Laos, and Cambodia. Perhaps inevitably, the changes and conflicts at home influenced the changes and conflicts away from home. For example, many U.S. soldiers abused drugs. Here, two soldiers exchange vials of heroin in Quang Tri Province, South Vietnam, July 1971.

**ADDICTION'S CONTEXT** Some evidence suggests that context is important for understanding addiction. For example, in the late 1960s, drug abuse among U.S. soldiers, including the use of narcotics such as heroin and opium, appeared to be epidemic. The widespread drug use was not surprising. It was a time of youthful drug experimentation, soldiers in Vietnam had easy access to various drugs, and drugs helped the soldiers cope temporarily with fear, depression, homesickness, boredom, and the repressiveness of army regulations (**Figure 5.32**). The military commanders mostly ignored drug use among soldiers, viewing it as "blowing off steam."

Beginning in 1971, the military began mandatory drug testing of soldiers to identify and detoxify drug users before they returned to the United States. Amid speculation that a flood of addicted soldiers returning from Vietnam would swamp treatment facilities back home, the White House asked a team of behavioral scientists to study a group of returning soldiers and assess the extent of the addiction problem. Led by the behavioral epidemiologist Lee Robins, the research team examined a random sample of 898 soldiers who were leaving Vietnam in September 1971. Robins and her colleagues found extremely high levels of drug use among them (Robins, Helzer, & Davis, 1975). Over 90 percent reported drinking alcohol, nearly three-quarters smoked marijuana, and nearly half used narcotics such as heroin, morphine, and opium. About half the soldiers who used narcotics either had symptoms of addiction or reported believing they would be unable to give up their drug habits. The team's findings suggested that approximately 1 soldier in 5 returning from Vietnam was a drug addict. Given the prevailing view that addiction was a biological disorder with a low rate of recovery, these results indicated that tens of thousands of heroin addicts would soon be inundating the United States. But this did not happen.

Robins and her colleagues examined drug use among the soldiers after they returned to the United States. Of those who were apparently addicted to narcotics in Vietnam, only half sought out drugs when they returned to the States, and fewer still maintained their narcotic addictions. Approximately 95 percent of the addicts no longer used drugs within months of their return—an astonishing quit rate considering that the success rate of the best treatments is typically only 20 percent to 30 percent. A long-term follow-up study conducted in the early 1990s confirmed that only a handful of those who were addicts in Vietnam remained addicts.

Why did coming home help the addicts recover? In the United States, they likely did not have the same motivations for taking the drugs as they did in Vietnam. No longer needing the drugs to escape combat's horrors, they focused on other needs and goals, such as careers and family obligations. An important lesson from this case study is that we cannot ignore environment when we try to understand addiction. Knowing drugs' physical actions in the brain may give us insights into addiction's biology, but that information fails to account for how these biological impulses can be overcome by other motivations.

## Summing Up

### How Do Drugs Affect Consciousness?

People have long ingested drugs that alter the way they think, feel, and act. Commonly used psychoactive drugs include marijuana, cocaine, amphetamines, MDMA, opiates, and alcohol. These drugs produce their psychological and behavioral effects by affecting neurotransmitter systems. The abuse of these drugs is costly to society, contributing to illness, violence, crime, and death. Excessive drug use can lead to addiction, a condition characterized by physical and psychological dependence. A brain region called the insula has been implicated in the experience of addiction. Addiction is influenced by personality factors, such as sensation seeking. Addiction is also influenced by the environment or context in which drug use occurs.

## Measuring Up

1. All drugs work by ________________.
   a. increasing neural firing in the cerebellum
   b. decreasing the amount of neurotransmitter affected by reuptake
   c. creating dizziness, which the interpreter translates as a drug state
   d. activating neurotransmitter systems

2. Match each of the following drugs or drug categories to the appropriate statement below: stimulants, MDMA, opiates, marijuana, alcohol.
   a. It is involved in more than one-third of fatal car accidents.
   b. It is the only drug that does not have its strongest effect on first-time users.
   c. They include heroin, morphine, and codeine.
   d. Its psychoactive ingredient is THC, or tetrahydrocannabinol.
   e. They include cocaine, nicotine, caffeine, and amphetamines.
   f. It is known as ecstasy.
   g. According to their reports, one-third of college students had sex while under its influence.
   h. One of them was used in Coca-Cola's original recipe.
   i. It is associated with Korsakoff's syndrome, a disorder characterized by severe memory loss and intellectual impairment.

**Answers:** 1. d. activating neurotransmitter systems.
2. a. alcohol; b. marijuana; c. opiates; d. marijuana; e. stimulants; f. MDMA; g. alcohol; h. stimulants; i. alcohol.

# StudySpace: Your Place for a Better Grade

**Visit StudySpace to access free review materials, such as:**

- complete study outlines
- vocabulary flashcards of all key terms
- additional chapter review quizzes

## Chapter Summary

### 5.1 What Is Consciousness?

- **Consciousness Is a Subjective Experience:** Consciousness is difficult to study because of the subjective nature of our experience of the world. Brain imaging research has shown that particular brain regions are activated by particular types of sensory information.
- **There Are Variations in Conscious Experience:** Consciousness is each person's unified and coherent experience of the world around him or her. At any one time, each person can be conscious of a limited number of things. A person's level of consciousness varies throughout the day and depends on the task at hand. Whereas people in a persistent vegetative state show no brain activity, people in minimally conscious states show brain activity. That activity indicates some awareness of external stimuli.
- **Brain Activity Gives Rise to Consciousness**: The global workspace model maintains that consciousness arises from activity in different cortical areas. The corpus callosum connects the brain's two sides; cutting it in half results in two independently functioning hemispheres. The left hemisphere is responsible primarily for language, and the right hemisphere is responsible primarily for images and spatial relations. The left hemisphere strives to make sense of experiences, and its interpretations influence the way a person views and remembers the world.
- **Unconscious Processing Influences Behavior:** Research findings indicate that much of a person's behavior occurs automatically, without that person's conscious awareness. Thought and behavior can be influenced by stimuli that are not experienced at a conscious level.

### 5.2 What Is Sleep?

- **Sleep Is an Altered State of Consciousness:** Sleep is characterized by stages that vary in brain activity. REM sleep is marked by rapid eye movements, dreaming, and body paralysis. Sleep disorders include insomnia, sleep apnea, and narcolepsy.
- **Sleep Is an Adaptive Behavior:** Sleep allows the body, including the brain, to rest and restore itself. Sleep also protects animals from harm at times of the day when they are most susceptible to danger, and it facilitates learning through the strengthening of neural connections.
- **People Dream while Sleeping:** REM dreams and non-REM dreams activate and deactivate distinct brain regions. Sigmund Freud believed that dreams reveal unconscious conflicts. Evidence does not support this view. Activation-synthesis theory posits that dreams are the product of the mind's efforts to make sense of random brain activity during sleep. Evolved threat-rehearsal theory maintains that dreaming evolved as a result of its adaptive value. That is, dreaming may have enabled early humans to rehearse strategies for coping with threatening events.

### 5.3 What Is Altered Consciousness?

- **Hypnosis Is Induced through Suggestion:** Scientists have debated whether hypnotized people merely play the role they are expected to play or whether they experience an altered state of consciousness. Consistent with the latter view, brain imaging research has demonstrated changes in brain activity among hypnotized subjects.
- **Meditation Produces Relaxation:** The goal of meditation, particularly as it is practiced in the West, is to bring about a state of deep relaxation. Studies suggest that meditation can have multiple benefits for people's physical and mental health.
- **People Can Lose Themselves in Activities:** Exercise, religious practices, and other engaging activities can produce a state of altered consciousness called flow. In this state, people become completely absorbed in what they are doing. Flow is experienced as a positive state. In contrast to activities that generate flow, activities used to escape the self or reduce self-awareness can have harmful consequences.

### 5.4 How Do Drugs Affect Consciousness?

- **People Use—and Abuse—Many Psychoactive Drugs:** Stimulants, including cocaine and amphetamines, increase behavioral and mental activity. THC (the active ingredient in marijuana) produces a relaxed state, an uplifted mood, and perceptual and cognitive distortions. MDMA, or ecstasy, produces energizing and hallucinogenic effects. Opiates produce a relaxed state, analgesia, and euphoria.
- **Alcohol Is the Most Widely Abused Drug:** Alcohol impairs motor processes, informational processing, mood, and memory. Research has demonstrated that, across the globe, males consume more alcohol than females. A drinker's expectations can significantly affect his or her behavior while under the influence of alcohol.
- **Addiction Has Physical and Psychological Aspects:** Physical dependence occurs when the body develops tolerance for a drug. Psychological dependence occurs when someone habitually and compulsively uses a drug or engages in a behavior, despite its negative consequences.

## Key Terms

activation-synthesis theory, p. 203
circadian rhythms, p. 194
consciousness, p. 183
dreams, p. 202
hypnosis, p. 205
insomnia, p. 197
interpreter, p. 189
latent content, p. 203
manifest content, p. 203
meditation, p. 207
narcolepsy, p. 198
obstructive sleep apnea, p. 198
REM sleep, p. 197
split brain, p. 187
subliminal perception, p. 192

## Practice Test

1. What is a key distinction between a person in a persistent vegetative state and a person in a minimally conscious state?
   a. The person in the minimally conscious state is less responsive to her or his surroundings.
   b. The person in the persistent vegetative state is more likely to regain full consciousness at some point in the future.
   c. The person in the minimally conscious state shows some degree of brain activity, whereas the person in the persistent vegetative state shows no brain activity.
   d. The person in the minimally conscious state is dreaming, whereas the person in the persistent vegetative state is in a coma.

2. A researcher asks study participants to play a word game in which they unscramble letters to form words. In Condition A, the unscrambled words are *outgoing, talkative,* and *smile.* In Condition B, the unscrambled words are *standoffish, silent,* and *frown.* After participants complete the word game, they meet and interact with a stranger. What do you predict participants' behavior during that interaction will reveal?
   a. Participants in Conditions A and B will behave nearly identically.
   b. Participants in Condition A will be more friendly toward the stranger than will participants in Condition B.
   c. Participants in Condition B will be more friendly toward the stranger than will participants in Condition A.

3. A study participant who has a severed corpus callosum is asked to focus on a dot in the middle of a computer screen. After a few seconds, a car appears on the left half of the screen while an automobile tire appears on the right half of the screen. How will the participant most likely respond if asked to describe the objects in the pictures?
   a. The participant will say he saw a tire and will draw a car.
   b. The participant will say he saw a car and will draw a tire.
   c. The participant will say he saw a car and a tire, but he will not be able to draw either object.
   d. The participant will draw a car and a tire, but he will not be able to name either object.

4. For each description below, name the sleep disorder: insomnia, apnea, narcolepsy, or somnambulism.
   a. _____ Despite feeling well rested, Marcus falls asleep suddenly while practicing piano.
   b. _____ Emma walks through the living room in the middle of the night, seemingly oblivious to those around her.
   c. _____ Sophia spends most of the night trying to fall asleep.
   d. _____ Ivan's roommate regularly complains that Ivan's snoring wakes him multiple times throughout the night.

5. Which of the following pieces of evidence suggest sleep is an adaptive behavior? Check all that apply.
   a. A few days of sleep deprivation do not impair physical strength.
   b. All animals sleep.
   c. It is impossible to resist indefinitely the urge to sleep.
   d. Sleep deprivation helps people feel less depressed.
   e. Animals die when deprived of sleep for extended periods.

6. Four students discuss a hypnotist's performance on campus. Which student's claim about hypnotism is most consistent with current evidence?
   a. "We just witnessed a bunch of people acting goofy solely because they thought they were supposed to act goofy."
   b. "I can't believe the hypnotist was able to make those people do things they would usually be so opposed to!"
   c. "What worries me is that someone could hypnotize me without my even knowing about it."
   d. "It's pretty cool that a hypnotist could help those people enter an altered state of consciousness."

7. Which of the following instruction sets would a yoga teacher trained in concentrative meditation be most likely to give?
   a. "Close your eyes while sitting in a comfortable position. Let your thoughts move freely through your mind, like clouds passing through the sky. Acknowledge them, but do not react to them."
   b. "Lying on your back, rest your hands gently on your abdomen. As you breathe in and out, focus attention on your breath. Notice the rhythmic rise and fall of your abdomen and the slow, deep movement of your chest."

The answer key for the Practice Tests can be found at the back of the book. It also includes answers to the green caption questions.

# 6

# Learning

IN THE MID-1940s, BURRHUS FREDERIC SKINNER and his wife, Yvonne, were living in Minnesota. When their daughter Deborah was born, Skinner kept the infant in a box. After the magazine *Ladies' Home Journal* published an article about Skinner with a photo of the "Baby in a Box," Skinner's treatment of Deborah became notorious. Readers of the piece, and even people who only heard about it, were outraged. What kind of monster would deprive a child of human contact?

In fact, this incident was a perfect example of how the media can misrepresent facts. Skinner developed the sleeping chamber for Deborah so that she could remain comfortable during the cold winters in Minnesota without being constrained by clothing and blankets (**Figure 6.1**). He called the box a "baby tender," and it maintained an optimal temperature and provided a continuous supply of fresh linens. There was also a smaller, portable version. Each of these cribs had

**FIGURE 6.1 "Baby in a Box"** B. F. Skinner developed this crib for his daughter in 1945. **If you were offered a contemporary version of Skinner's invention, would you accept it or reject it as a crib for one of your own children? Why?**

a safety-glass front that adults could open. Contrary to rumors, Skinner did not lock Deborah in the box. She did not grow up to be depressed, sue her father, or commit suicide. In fact, Deborah—a successful artist living in London, England—has denounced such rumors. She and her sister, Julie—an author and educator—had excellent relationships with their father until his death, in 1990.

Even at the time of the "Baby in a Box" incident, B. F. Skinner was a famous behavioral scientist. He is now seen as the person who arguably had the greatest influence on contemporary psychological science. He and Yvonne raised Deborah and Julie according to the ideas established through his research. Especially important to Skinner was emphasizing reward over punishment. He was not a cold, mad scientist or a child abuser.

As a young man, Skinner had wanted to be a novelist so that he could explore large questions about the human condition. Then he read two works of nonfiction that changed his life. The first was the 1924 book *Behaviorism,* by the psychologist John B. Watson. The second was a 1927 article in the *New York Times Magazine,* in which the novelist H. G. Wells expressed admiration for the work of the physiologist Ivan Pavlov. Increasingly, the behaviorists' perspective made sense to Skinner. He became convinced that psychology was his calling.

Skinner received his Ph.D. from Harvard University in 1931, but he differed with his professors about what psychologists should study. Many faculty members were concerned about his disregard for their efforts to analyze the mind through introspection, an approach then common at Harvard. As discussed in Chapter 1, introspection is the process of using verbal reports to assess mental states. After thinking about your own thoughts and feelings, you talk about them as a way of making them public and available for others to study. The main objection to using introspection as a research method is that it is not very reliable. Behaviorists such as Skinner believed that, to be scientists, psychologists had to instead study observable actions. In other words, psychologists needed to focus on the behaviors that people and nonhuman animals display.

Inspired by the work of Watson and of Pavlov, Skinner believed that he could dramatically change an animal's behavior by providing incentives to the animal for performing particular acts. For the next half century, he conducted systematic studies of animals, often pigeons or rats, to discover the basic rules of learning. His groundbreaking work led Skinner to form radical ideas about behaviorism. In the process, he outlined many of the most important principles that shape the behavior of animals, including humans. These principles remain as relevant today as they were more than 50 years ago. And as you will learn in this chapter, a device known as the Skinner box—a different Skinner box—played a major part in this scientist's work. ■

**Learning Objectives**

- Define classical conditioning.
- Differentiate between US, UR, CS, and CR.
- Describe the role of learning in the development and treatment of phobias and drug addiction.
- Discuss the evolutionary significance of classical conditioning.
- Describe the Rescorla-Wagner model of classical conditioning.

## 6.1 What Ideas Guide the Study of Learning?

B. F. Skinner's ideas have been enormously influential throughout society, from classrooms to clinics and beyond. Dismissing the importance of mental states and questioning philosophical concepts such as free will, Skinner believed that the application of basic learning principles could create a better, more humane world. In fact, he felt that his ideas could free the world of poverty and violence. In *Walden Two* (1948), a best-selling novel, he depicts a utopia in which children are raised only with praise and incentives, never with punishment. *Walden Two* has inspired many people. Entire communities, such as northern Mexico's Los Horcones and rural Virginia's Twin Oaks, were founded on the principles in it.

This chapter focuses on what Skinner and a number of other learning theorists have discovered about how learning takes place. This material represents some of psychology's central contributions to our understanding of behavior. Learning theories have been used to improve quality of life and to train humans and nonhuman animals to learn new tasks. They have also contributed to the other major areas of psychology. To understand what humans and nonhuman animals are, we need to know what learning is.

## Learning Results from Experience

**Learning** is a relatively enduring change in behavior. That change results from experience. Learning occurs when an animal benefits from experience so that its behavior is better adapted to the environment. The ability to learn is crucial for all animals. To survive, animals need to learn things such as which types of foods are dangerous, when it is safe to sleep, and which sounds indicate potential dangers. Learning is central to almost all aspects of human existence. It makes possible our basic abilities (such as walking and speaking) and our complex ones (such as flying airplanes, performing surgery, or maintaining intimate relationships). Learning also shapes many aspects of daily life: clothing choices, musical tastes, social rules about how close we stand to each other, cultural values about either exploiting or preserving the environment, and so on.

The essence of learning is understanding how events are related. For example, you might associate going to the dentist with being in pain. You might associate working with getting paid. Associations develop through *conditioning,* a process in which environmental stimuli and behavioral responses become connected. Psychologists study two types of conditioning. The first, *classical conditioning, or Pavlovian conditioning,* occurs when you learn that two types of events go together. For example, you learn that certain music plays during scary scenes in a movie. Now you feel anxious when you hear that music. The second type, *operant conditioning, or instrumental conditioning,* occurs when you learn that a behavior leads to a particular outcome. For example, you grasp that studying leads to better grades. This latter type of learning was of greatest interest to B. F. Skinner. Other types include learning by observing others. For example, you might learn about new fashions by paying attention to what celebrities are wearing.

Learning theory arose in the early twentieth century. Its development was due partly to the dissatisfaction among some psychologists with the widespread use of introspection. At the time, Freudian ideas were at the heart of psychological theorizing. For their research, Freud and his followers used verbal report techniques, such as dream analysis and free association. They aimed to assess the unconscious mental processes that they believed were the primary determinants of behavior. John B. Watson, however, argued that Freudian theory was unscientific and ultimately meaningless. He rejected any psychological enterprise that focused on things that could not be observed directly, such as people's mental experiences. Although he acknowledged that thoughts and beliefs existed, he believed they could not be studied using scientific methods. According to Watson, observable behavior was the only valid indicator of psychological activity.

**learning** A relatively enduring change in behavior, resulting from experience.

As discussed in Chapter 1, Watson founded behaviorism on such principles. This school of thought was based on the belief that humans and nonhuman animals are born with the potential to learn just about anything. In formulating his ideas, Watson was influenced by the seventeenth-century philosopher John Locke. An infant, Locke argued, is a *tabula rasa* (Latin for "blank slate"). Born knowing nothing, the infant acquires all of its knowledge through sensory experiences. In this way, a person develops. Building on this foundation, Watson stated that environment and its associated effects on animals were the sole determinants of learning. Watson felt so strongly about the preeminence of environment that he issued the following bold challenge: "Give me a dozen healthy infants, well formed, and my own specified world to bring them up in and I'll guarantee to take any one at random and train him to become any type of specialist I might select—doctor, lawyer, artist, merchant-chief, and yes, even beggar-man and thief, regardless of his talents, penchants, tendencies, abilities, vocations and race of his ancestors" (Watson, 1924, p. 82). In North America, Watson enormously influenced the study of psychology. Behaviorism was the dominant psychological paradigm there well into the 1960s. It affected the methods and theories of every area of psychology.

## Behavioral Responses Are Conditioned

Watson developed his ideas about behaviorism after reading the work of Ivan Pavlov, who had won a Nobel Prize in 1904 for his research on the digestive system. Pavlov was interested in the *salivary reflex*. This automatic, unlearned response occurs when a food stimulus is presented to a hungry animal, including a human. For his work on the digestive system, Pavlov created an apparatus that collected saliva from dogs. With this device, he measured the different amounts of saliva that resulted when he placed various types of food into a dog's mouth (**Figure 6.2**).

Like so many major scientific advances, Pavlov's contribution to psychology started with a simple observation. One day he realized that the laboratory dogs were salivating before they tasted their food. Indeed, the dogs started salivating the moment a lab technician walked into the room or whenever they saw the bowls that usually contained food. Pavlov's genius was in recognizing that this

(a)

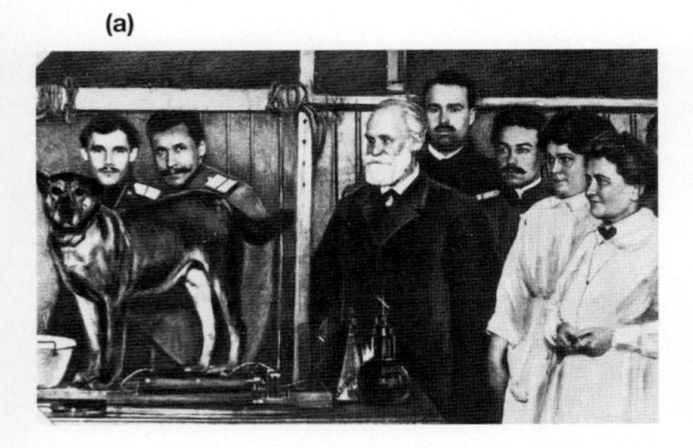

(b)

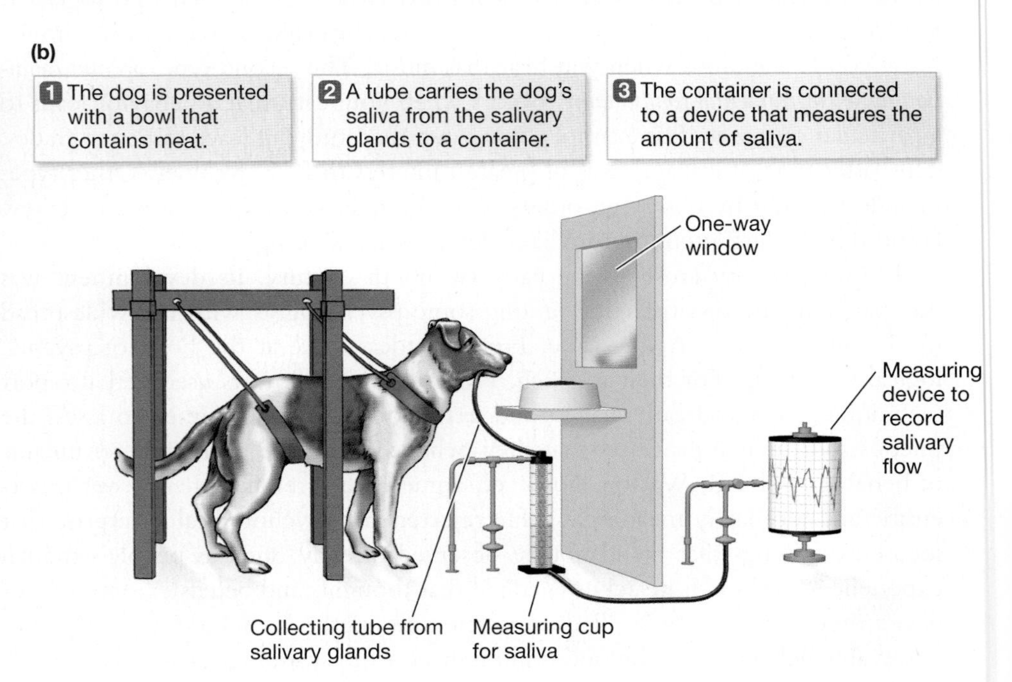


**FIGURE 6.2 Pavlov's Apparatus and Classical Conditioning (a)** Ivan Pavlov, pictured here with his colleagues and one of his canine subjects, conducted groundbreaking work on classical conditioning. **(b)** Pavlov's apparatus collected and measured a dog's saliva.

behavioral response was a window to the working mind. Unlike inborn reflexes, salivation at the sight of a bowl or of a person is not automatic. Therefore, that response must have been acquired through experience. This insight led Pavlov to devote the rest of his life to studying the basic principles of learning.

A researcher at the University of Pennsylvania, Edwin Twitmyer, independently made the same discovery of classical conditioning. Twitmyer studied the patellar (knee-jerk) reflex in humans. He informed his study participants that a bell would be rung when the knee tap was delivered. In one presentation, the bell accidentally rang without the tap occurring, and the knee-jerk response followed. The participants not only acquired the conditioned response. They also found it difficult or impossible to suppress the response. Twitmyer published this serendipitous discovery in his doctoral dissertation and presented it at the annual APA meeting a year before Pavlov's discovery, but he received little attention (Fernberger, 1943).

**PAVLOV'S EXPERIMENTS** Consider a typical Pavlovian experiment. A *neutral stimulus* unrelated to the salivary reflex, such as the clicking of a metronome, is presented along with a stimulus that reliably produces the reflex, such as food. The neutral stimulus can be anything that the animal can see or hear as long as it is not something that is usually associated with being fed. This pairing is called a *conditioning trial*. It is repeated a number of times. Then come the *critical trials*. Here, the metronome sound is presented alone and the salivary reflex is measured. Pavlov found that under these conditions, the sound of the metronome on its own produced salivation. This type of learning is now referred to as **classical conditioning,** or **Pavlovian conditioning.** In this type of conditioning, a neutral stimulus elicits a response because it has become associated with a stimulus that already produces that response.

Pavlov called the salivation elicited by food the **unconditioned response (UR).** The response is "unconditioned" because it occurs without prior training. It is an unlearned, automatic behavior, such as any simple reflex. Similarly, the food is the **unconditioned stimulus (US).** In the normal reflex response, the food (US) leads to salivation (UR). Because the clicking of the metronome produces salivation only after training, it is the **conditioned stimulus (CS).** That is, the clicking stimulates salivation only after learning takes place. The increased salivation that occurs when only the conditioned stimulus is presented is the **conditioned response (CR).** Both the unconditioned and the conditioned responses are salivation, but they are not identical: The conditioned response usually is weaker than the unconditioned response. Thus the metronome sound produces less saliva than the food does. (The process of conditioning is outlined in **Figure 6.3.**)

Suppose you are watching a movie in which a character is attacked. As you watch the attack scene, you feel tense, anxious, and perhaps disgusted. In this scenario, the frightening scene and your feelings occur naturally. That is, the stimulus and your response to it are unconditioned. Now imagine a piece of music that does not initially have much effect on you but that you hear in the movie just before each frightening scene. (A good example is the musical theme from the classic 1970s movie *Jaws*.) Eventually, you will begin to feel tense and anxious as soon as you hear the music. You have learned that the music, the conditioned stimulus, predicts scary scenes. Because of this learning, you feel the tension and anxiety, the conditioned response. As in Pavlov's studies, the CS (music) produces a somewhat different emotional response than the US (the scary scene). The response may be

**classical conditioning (Pavlovian conditioning)** A type of learned response; a neutral object comes to elicit a response when it is associated with a stimulus that already produces that response.

**unconditioned response (UR)** A response that does not have to be learned, such as a reflex.

**unconditioned stimulus (US)** A stimulus that elicits a response, such as a reflex, without any prior learning.

**conditioned stimulus (CS)** A stimulus that elicits a response only after learning has taken place.

**conditioned response (CR)** A response to a conditioned stimulus; a response that has been learned.

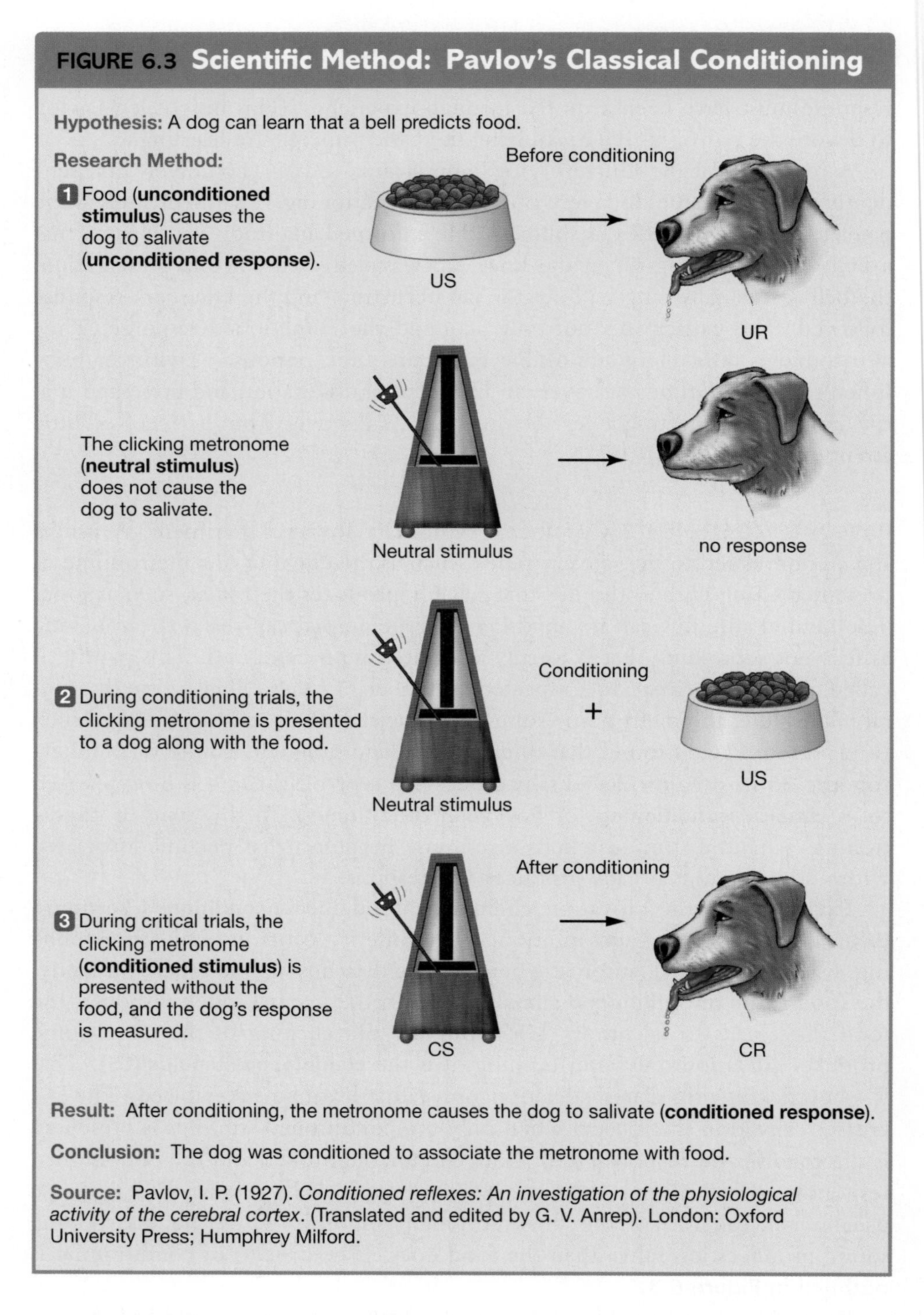


**FIGURE 6.3 Scientific Method: Pavlov's Classical Conditioning**

weaker. It may be more a feeling of apprehension than one of fear or disgust. If you later hear this music in a different context, however, such as on the radio, you will again feel tense and anxious even though you are not watching the movie. You have been classically conditioned to be anxious when you hear the music. Because this association is learned, however, your anxious feeling from the music will always be weaker than your response to the scary scene was.

**ACQUISITION, EXTINCTION, AND SPONTANEOUS RECOVERY** Like many other scientists (of his time and subsequently), Pavlov was greatly influenced by Darwin's *On the Origin of Species*. Pavlov believed that conditioning is the basis for how animals learn to adapt to their environments. By learning to predict what objects

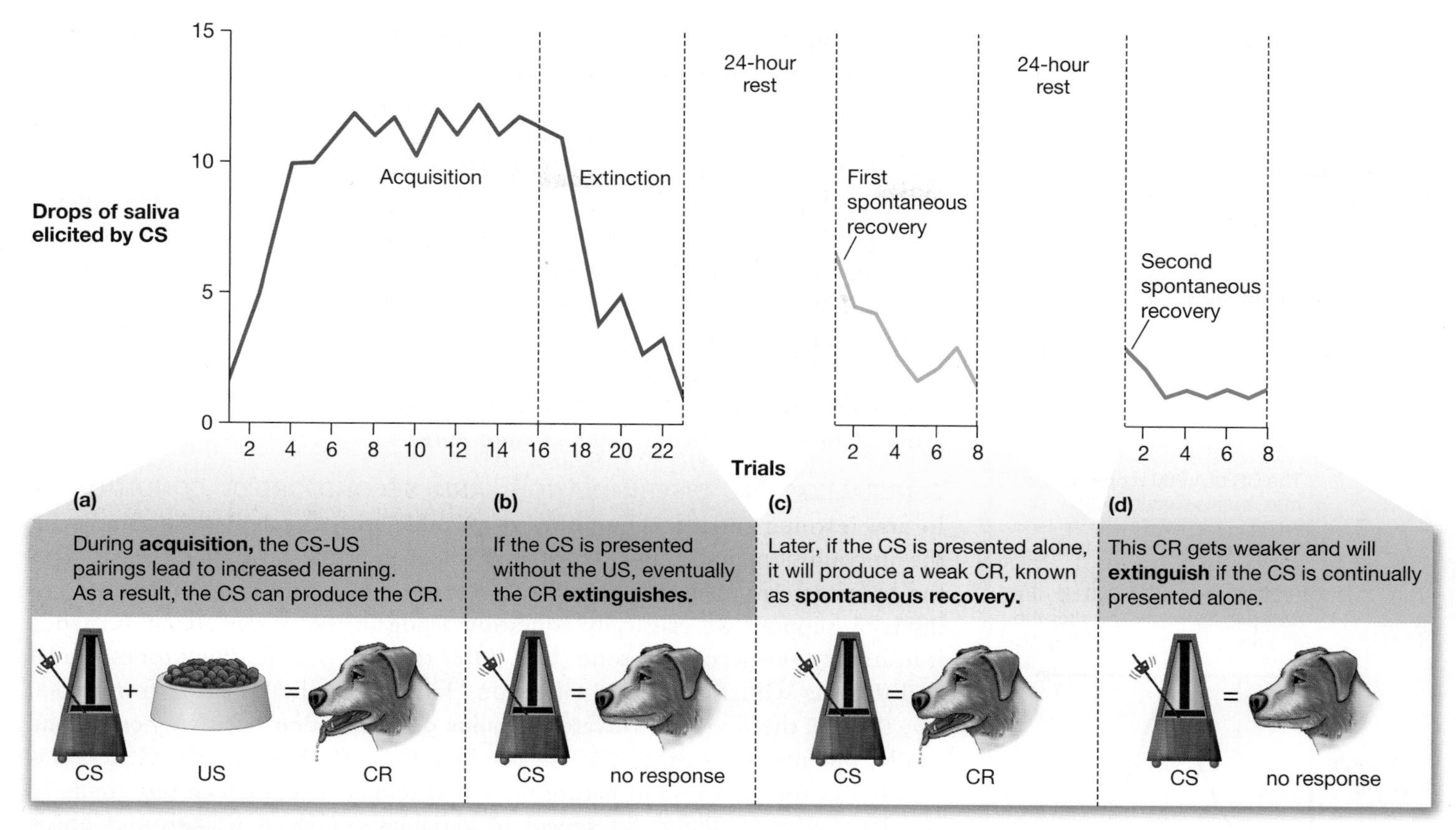


**FIGURE 6.4 Acquisition, Extinction, and Spontaneous Recovery**

bring pleasure or pain, animals acquire new adaptive behaviors. For instance, when an animal learns that a metronome beat predicts the appearance of food, this process of association is called **acquisition.** Acquisition is the gradual formation of an association between a conditioned stimulus (here, a metronome) and an unconditioned stimulus (here, food; **Figure 6.4a**).

From his research, Pavlov concluded that the critical element in the acquisition of a learned association is that the stimuli occur together in time. This bond is referred to as *contiguity*. Subsequent research has shown that the strongest conditioning occurs when there is a very brief delay between the conditioned stimulus and the unconditioned stimulus. Thus you will develop a stronger conditioned response to a piece of music if it comes just before a scary scene than if it occurs during or after the scary scene: The music's role in predicting the frightening scene is an important part of the classical conditioning. The next time you watch a horror movie, pay attention to the way the music gets louder just before a scary part begins.

Once a behavior is acquired, how long does it persist? For instance, what if the animal expects to receive food every time it hears the beat of the metronome, but after a long time no food appears? Animals sometimes have to learn when associations are no longer adaptive. Normally, after standard Pavlovian conditioning, the metronome (CS) leads to salivation (CR) because the animal learns to associate the metronome with the food (US). If the metronome is presented many times and food does not arrive, the animal learns that the metronome is no longer a good predictor of food. Because of this new learning, the animal's salivary response gradually disappears. This process is known as **extinction.** The conditioned response is *extinguished* when the conditioned stimulus no longer predicts the unconditioned stimulus (**Figure 6.4b**).

**acquisition** The gradual formation of an association between the conditioned and unconditioned stimuli.

**extinction** A process in which the conditioned response is weakened when the conditioned stimulus is repeated without the unconditioned stimulus.

**spontaneous recovery** A process in which a previously extinguished response reemerges after the presentation of the conditioned stimulus.

**stimulus generalization** Learning that occurs when stimuli that are similar but not identical to the conditioned stimulus produce the conditioned response.

**stimulus discrimination** A differentiation between two similar stimuli when only one of them is consistently associated with the unconditioned stimulus.

Now suppose, a long time after extinction, the metronome is set in motion now and then. The adaptive response is to check back once in a while to see if the metronome is beating. Starting the metronome will once again produce the conditioned response of salivation. Through such **spontaneous recovery,** the extinguished CS again produces a CR (**Figure 6.4c**). This recover is temporary, however. It will fade quickly unless the CS is again paired with the US. Even a single pairing of the CS with the US will reestablish the CR, which will then again diminish if CS-US pairings do not continue. Thus extinction inhibits (reduces the strength of) the associative bond, but it does not eliminate that bond. Extinction is a form of learning that overwrites the previous association: The animal learns that the original association no longer holds true (e.g., the metronome no longer signals that it will be followed by meat; Bouton, 1994; Bouton, Westbrook, Corcoran, & Maren, 2006; **Figure 6.4d**).

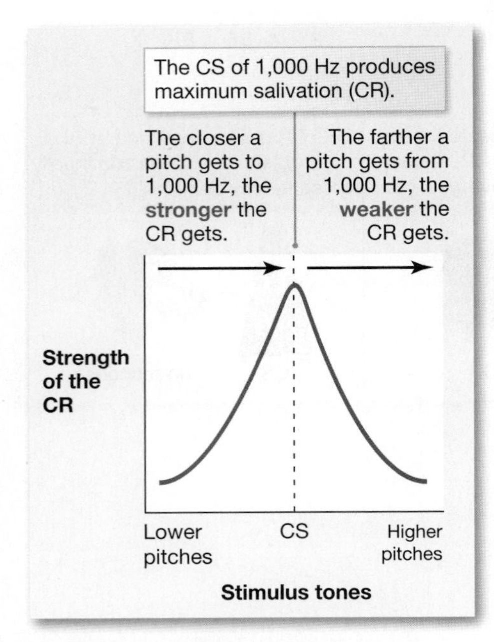


**FIGURE 6.5 Stimulus Generalization**

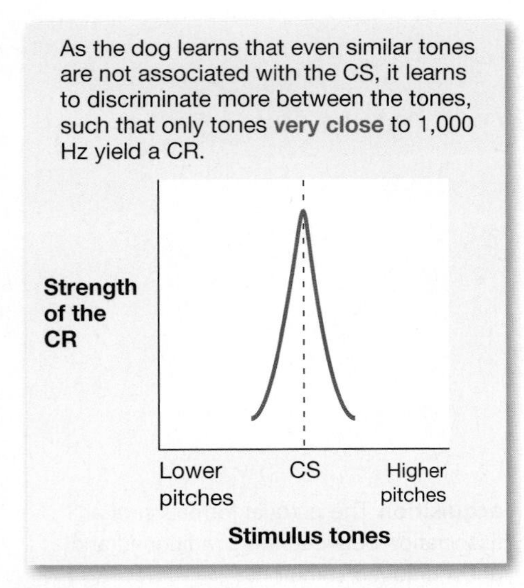


**FIGURE 6.6 Stimulus Discrimination**

### GENERALIZATION, DISCRIMINATION, AND SECOND-ORDER CONDITIONING

In any learning situation, hundreds of possible stimuli can be associated with the unconditioned stimulus to produce the conditioned response. How does the brain determine which stimulus is—or which stimuli are—relevant? For instance, suppose we classically condition a dog so that it salivates (CR) when it hears a 1,000-hertz (Hz) tone (CS). After the CR is established, tones similar to 1,000 Hz will also produce salivation. The farther the tones are from 1,000 Hz, the less the dog will salivate. **Stimulus generalization** occurs when stimuli similar but not identical to the CS produce the CR (**Figure 6.5**). Generalization is adaptive, because in nature the CS is seldom experienced repeatedly in an identical way. Slight differences in variables—such as background noise, temperature, and lighting—lead to slightly different perceptions of the CS. As a result of these different perceptions, animals learn to respond to variations in the CS.

Of course, generalization has limits. Sometimes it is important for animals to distinguish among similar stimuli. For instance, two plant species might look similar, but one might be poisonous. In **stimulus discrimination,** animals learn to differentiate between two similar stimuli if one is consistently associated with the unconditioned stimulus and the other is not. Pavlov and his students demonstrated that dogs can learn to make very fine distinctions between similar stimuli. For example, dogs can learn to detect subtle differences in shades of gray or in tones (**Figure 6.6**).

Sometimes a conditioned stimulus does not become directly associated with an unconditioned stimulus. Instead, the conditioned stimulus becomes associated with other stimuli associated with the US. This phenomenon is known as *second-order conditioning*. In one of Pavlov's early studies, a CS-US bond was formed between a tone (CS) and food (US) so that the tone (CS) led to salivation (CR). In a second training session, a black square was repeatedly presented at the same time as the tone. There was no US (no presentation of the meat) during this phase of the study. After a few trials, the black square was presented alone. It too produced salivation.

Second-order conditioning helps account for the complexity of learned associations, especially in people. For instance, suppose a child has been conditioned to associate money with desirable objects, such as candy and toys. Now suppose that whenever the child's uncle visits, the uncle gives the child some money. Through second-order conditioning, the child will learn to associate the uncle with money. If the child feels affection for the uncle, some of that affection will come from the association with money (Domjan, 2003).

## Phobias and Addictions Have Learned Components

Classical conditioning helps explain many behavioral phenomena. Among the examples are phobias and addictions.

**PHOBIAS AND THEIR TREATMENT** A **phobia** is an acquired fear out of proportion to the real threat of an object or of a situation. Common phobias include the fears of heights, of dogs, of insects, of snakes, and of the dark. According to classical-conditioning theory, phobias develop through the generalization of a fear experience, as when a person stung by a wasp develops a fear of all flying insects. (Phobias are discussed further in Chapter 14, "Psychological Disorders.")

Animals can be classically conditioned to fear neutral objects. This process is known as *fear conditioning*. In a typical study of fear conditioning, a rat is classically conditioned to produce a fear response to an auditory tone: Electric shock follows the tone, and eventually the tone produces fear responses on its own. These responses include specific physiological and behavioral reactions. One interesting response is *freezing,* or keeping still. Humans are among the many species that respond to fear by freezing. For example, as captured in video footage, right after a bomb exploded at the Atlanta Summer Olympics in 1996, most people froze for a few seconds. Immediately keeping still might be a hardwired response that helps animals deal with predators, which often are attracted by movement (LeDoux, 2002).

In 1919, John B. Watson became one of the first researchers to demonstrate the role of classical conditioning in the development of phobias. In this case study, Watson taught an infant named Albert B. to fear neutral objects. It is important to note Watson's motives for conditioning "Little Albert." At the time, the prominent theory of phobias was based on Freudian ideas about unconscious repressed sexual desires. Believing that Freudian ideas were unscientific and unnecessarily complex, Watson proposed that phobias could be explained by simple learning principles, such as classical conditioning. To test his hypothesis, Watson devised a learning study. He asked a woman he knew to let him use her son, Albert B., in the study. Because this child was emotionally stable, Watson believed the experiment would cause him little harm. When Albert was 9 months old, Watson and his lab assistant, Rosalie Rayner, presented him with various neutral objects, including a white rat, a rabbit, a dog, a monkey, costume masks, and a ball of white wool. Albert showed a natural curiosity about these items, but he displayed no overt emotional responses.

When Albert was 11 months old, Watson and Rayner began the conditioning trials. This time, as they presented the white rat and Albert reached for it, Watson smashed a hammer into an iron bar, producing a loud clanging sound. The sound scared the child, who immediately withdrew and hid his face. Watson did this a few more times at intervals of five days until Albert would whimper and cringe when the rat was presented alone. Thus the US (smashing sound) led to a UR (fear). Eventually, the pairing of the CS (rat) and US (smashing sound) led to the rat's producing fear (CR) on its own. The fear response generalized to other stimuli that Watson had presented along with the rat at the initial meeting. Over time, Albert became frightened of them all, including the rabbit and the ball of wool. Even a Santa Claus with a white beard produced a fear response. Thus classical conditioning was shown to be an effective method of inducing phobia (**Figure 6.7**).

Watson had planned to conduct extinction trials to remove the learned phobias. Albert's mother removed the child from the study, however, before Watson

**phobia** An acquired fear that is out of proportion to the real threat of an object or of a situation.

**FIGURE 6.7 Scientific Method: Watson's "Little Albert" Experiment**

**Hypothesis:** Phobias can be explained by classical conditioning.

**Research Method:**

1. Little Albert was presented with neutral objects that provoked a neutral response. These objects included a white rat and costume masks.

2. During conditioning trials, when Albert reached for the white rat (CS) a loud clanging sound (US) scared him (UR).

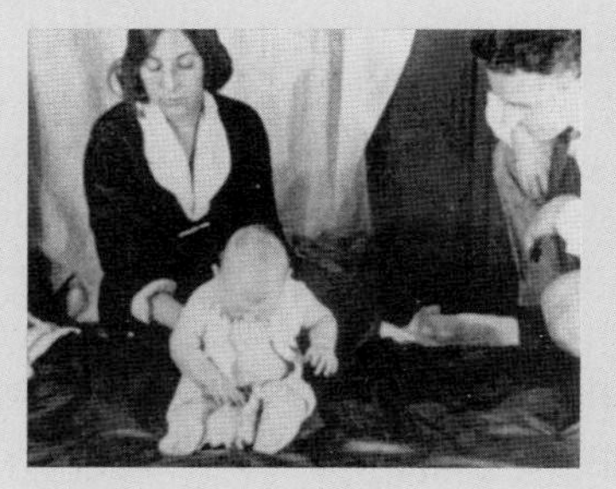

**Results:** Eventually, the pairing of the rat (CS) and the clanging sound (US) led to the rat's producing fear (CR) on its own. The fear response generalized to other stimuli presented with the rat initially, such as the costume masks.

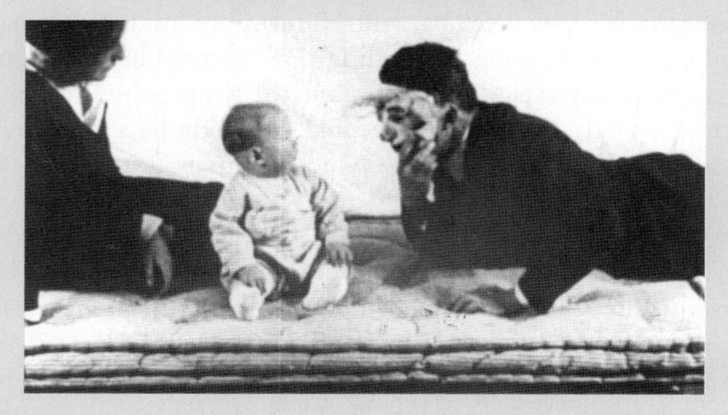

**Conclusion:** Classical conditioning can cause people to fear neutral objects.

**Source:** Watson, J. B., & Rayner, R. (1920). Conditioned emotional reactions. *Journal of Experimental Psychology, 3*, 1–14.

could conduct those trials. For many years, no one seemed to know what had become of Little Albert. His fate was one of psychology's great mysteries. Finally, an investigative team led by the psychologist Hall Beck uncovered evidence that Little Albert was actually Douglas Merritte. Merritte died at age 6, likely of meningitis (a brain infection; Beck, Levinson, & Irons, 2009). Watson's conditioning of Albert has long been criticized as unethical. An ethics committee probably would not approve such a study today.

In his detailed plans for the reconditioning, Watson described a method of continually presenting the feared items to Albert paired with more pleasant things, such as candy. A colleague of Watson's used this method on a child who was afraid of rabbits and other furry objects. The behavioral pioneer Mary Cover Jones eliminated the fear of rabbits in a 3-year-old named Peter by bringing the rabbit closer as she provided Peter with a favorite food (Jones, 1924). Such classical-conditioning techniques have since proved valuable for developing very effective behavioral therapies to treat phobias. For instance, when a person is suffering from a phobia, a clinician might expose the patient to small doses of the feared stimulus while having the client engage in an enjoyable task. This technique, called *counterconditioning,* may help the client overcome the phobia.

The behavioral therapist Joseph Wolpe has developed a formal treatment based on counterconditioning (Wolpe, 1997). Wolpe's treatment is called *systematic desensitization*. First the client is taught how to relax his or her muscles. Then the client is asked to imagine the feared object or situation while continuing to use the relaxation exercises. Eventually, the client is exposed to the feared stimulus while relaxing. The general idea is that the CS → $CR_1$ (fear) connection can be broken by developing a CS → $CR_2$ (relaxation) connection. As discussed in Chapter 15, psychologists now believe that in breaking the fear connection, repeated exposure to the feared stimulus is more important than relaxation.

**DRUG ADDICTION** Classical conditioning also plays an important role in drug addiction. (Addiction is discussed fully in Chapter 5, "Consciousness.") Conditioned drug effects are common and demonstrate conditioning's power. For example, the smell of coffee can become a conditioned stimulus. The smell alone can lead coffee drinkers to feel activated and aroused—as though they have actually consumed caffeine. Likewise, for heroin addicts, the sight of the needle and the feeling when it is inserted into the skin become a CS. For this reason, addicts sometimes inject themselves with water to reduce their cravings when heroin is unavailable. Sometimes, the sight of a straight-edge razor blade, which is often used to "cut" heroin, can briefly increase a drug addict's cravings (Siegel, 2005). When former heroin addicts are exposed to environmental cues associated with their drug use, they often experience cravings. If such cravings are not satisfied, the addict may experience *withdrawal,* the unpleasant state of tension and anxiety that occurs when addicts stop using drugs. Addicts who quit using drugs in treatment centers often relapse when they return to their old environments because they experience conditioned craving.

In laboratory settings, researchers have presented heroin addicts or cocaine addicts with cues associated with drug ingestion. These cues have led the addicts to experience cravings and various physiological responses associated with withdrawal, such as changes in heart rate and blood pressure. Brain imaging studies have found that such cues lead to activation of the prefrontal cortex and various regions of the limbic system, areas of the brain involved in the experience of reward (Volkow et al., 2008). Seeing a tantalizing food item when you are hungry activates these same brain regions as you anticipate enjoying your tasty meal. In the same way, the sight of drug cues produces an expectation that the drug high will follow (**Figure 6.8**). According to the psychologist Shepard Siegel (2005), it is therefore important that treatment for addiction include exposing addicts to drug cues. Such exposure helps extinguish responses, in the brain and the rest of the body, to those cues. In this way, the cues are prevented from triggering cravings in the future.

Siegel and his colleagues have also conducted research into the relationship between drug tolerance and situation. As discussed in Chapter 5, tolerance is a process by which addicts need more and more of a drug to experience the same effects. Siegel's research has shown that tolerance is greatest when the drug is taken in the

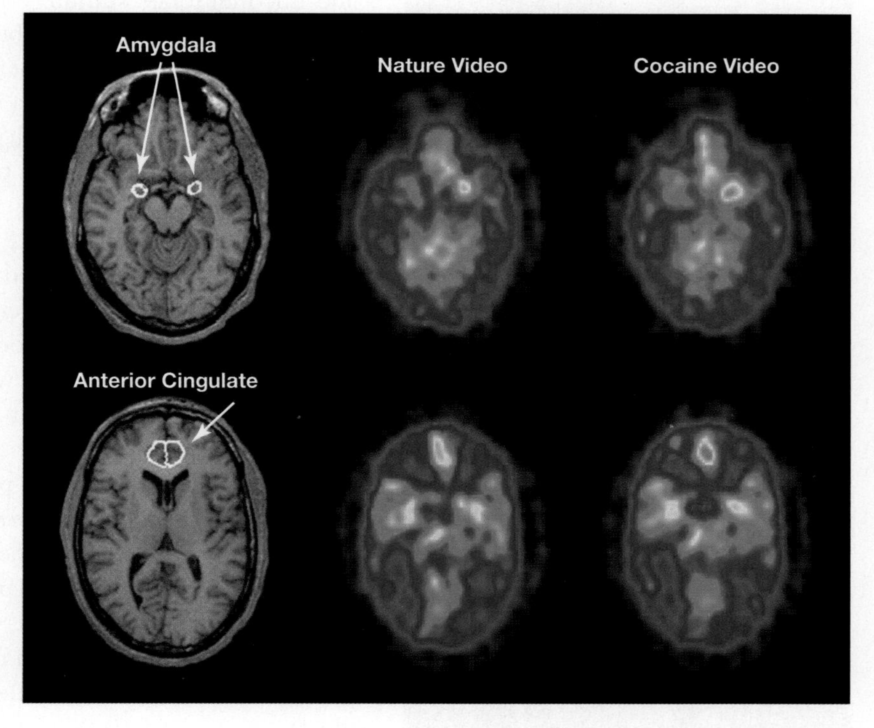


**FIGURE 6.8 PET Scans Showing Activation of Limbic System Structures** Cocaine addicts were shown videos of nature scenes and videos of cocaine cues. The cocaine-related videos sparked activation in brain regions associated with reward and emotion, such as the anterior cingulate and the amygdala. Watching nature videos did not lead to increased activity in these areas. (Areas with greatest activation are shown in orange and red.)

same location as previous drug use occurred in. Presumably, the body has learned to expect the drug in that location and then to compensate for the drug, such as by altering neurochemistry or physiology to metabolize it. For example, college students show greater tolerance to alcohol when it is provided with familiar cues (e.g., a drink that looks and tastes like beer) than when the same amount of alcohol is provided in a novel form (e.g., a blue, peppermint-flavored drink; Siegel, Baptista, Kim, McDonald, & Weise-Kelly, 2000). Tolerance can be so great that addicts regularly use drug doses that would be fatal for the inexperienced user. Conversely, Siegel's findings imply that if addicts take their usual large doses in novel settings, they are more likely to overdose. That is, because the addicts are taking drugs under different conditions, their bodies will not respond sufficiently to compensate for the drugs (Siegel, 1984; Siegel, Hinson, Krank, & McCully,1982).

## Classical Conditioning Involves More Than Events Occurring at the Same Time

Pavlov's original explanation for classical conditioning was that any two events presented in contiguity would produce a learned association. Any object or phenomenon could be converted to a conditioned stimulus when associated with any unconditioned stimulus. Pavlov and his followers believed that the association's strength was determined by factors such as the intensity of the conditioned and unconditioned stimuli. For example, the more intense the stimuli were, the greater the learning would be. (A louder metronome or larger piece of meat would produce stronger associations than a quieter metronome or smaller piece of meat.) In the mid-1960s, a number of challenges to Pavlov's theory suggested that some conditioned stimuli were more likely than others to produce learning. Contiguity was not sufficient to create CS-US associations.

(a)

(b)

**FIGURE 6.9 Conditioned Food Aversion in Animals (a)** After eating a monarch butterfly, **(b)** this blue jay vomited and thus learned to avoid eating anything that looks like the butterfly. **What evolutionary value do you see in this learned behavior?**

**EVOLUTIONARY SIGNIFICANCE** Research conducted by the psychologist John Garcia and colleagues showed that certain pairings of stimuli are more likely to become associated than others. For instance, when animals receive nonlethal amounts of poison in their food that make them ill, they quickly learn to avoid the tastes or smells associated with the food (Garcia & Koelling, 1966).

Likewise, most people can recall a time when they ate a particular food and then became ill with nausea, stomach upset, and vomiting. Whether or not the food caused the illness, most people respond to this sequence of events by demonstrating a *conditioned food aversion*. This response occurs even if the illness clearly was caused by a virus or some other condition. It is especially likely to occur if the food was not part of the person's usual diet. The association between eating a novel food and getting sick, even when the illness occurs hours after eating, is so strong that a food aversion can be formed in one trial (**Figure 6.9**). Some people cannot stand even the smell of a food they associate with a stomach-related illness.

Conditioned food aversions are easy to produce with smell or taste, but they are very difficult to produce with light or sound. This difference makes sense, since smell and taste are the main cues that guide an animal's eating behavior. From an evolutionary viewpoint, animals that quickly associate a certain flavor with illness, and therefore avoid that flavor, will be more successful. That is, they will be more likely to survive and pass along their genes.

Contemporary researchers are interested in how classical conditioning helps animals learn adaptive responses (Hollis, 1997; Shettleworth, 2001). The adaptive value of a particular response varies according to the animal's evolutionary history. For example, taste aversions are easy to condition in rats but difficult to condition in birds. This difference occurs because in selecting food, rats rely more on taste and birds rely more on vision. Accordingly, birds quickly learn to avoid a visual cue they associate with illness. Different types of stimuli cause different reactions even within a species. Rats freeze and startle if a CS is auditory, but they rise on their hind legs if the CS is visual (Holland, 1977).

Such differences in learned adaptive responses may reflect the survival value that different auditory and visual stimuli have for particular animals in particular environments. Those meanings are of course related to the potential dangers associated with the stimuli. For example, monkeys can more easily be conditioned to fear snakes than to fear objects such as flowers or rabbits (Cook & Mineka, 1989). The psychologist Martin Seligman (1970) has argued that animals are genetically programmed to fear specific objects. He refers to this programming as *biological preparedness*. Preparedness helps explain why animals tend to fear potentially dangerous things (e.g., snakes, fire, heights) rather than objects that pose little threat (e.g., flowers, shoes, babies).

The threats may also come from within an animal's own species. For example, when people participate in conditioning experiments in which aversive stimuli are paired with members of their own racial group or members of a different racial group, they more easily associate the negative stimuli with outgroup members (Olsson, Ebert, Banaji, & Phelps, 2005). This finding indicates that people are predisposed to wariness of outgroup members. Presumably, this tendency has come about because outgroup members have been more dangerous over the course of human evolution. The tendency has sometimes been exploited to create or enhance prejudice toward outgroups during wars and other intergroup conflicts. For example, as the Nazis prepared for and conducted their extermination of Jews during World War II, they created films in which Jews' faces morphed into those of rats crawling in filth. By showing these images to the German population, the Nazis aimed to condition a national response of repulsion to facial features associated with being Jewish. (Videos of these films are cataloged at the Museum of Tolerance, in Los Angeles, California.)

## Learning Involves Cognition

Until the 1970s, most learning theorists were concerned only with observable stimuli and observable responses. Since then, learning theorists have placed a greater emphasis on trying to understand the mental processes that underlie conditioning. An important principle has emerged from this work: Classical conditioning is a way that animals come to *predict* the occurrence of events. Psychologists' increasing consideration of mental processes such as prediction and expectancy is called the *cognitive perspective* on learning (Hollis, 1997).

The psychologist Robert Rescorla (1966) conducted one of the first studies that highlighted the role of cognition in learning. He argued that for learning to take place, the conditioned stimulus must accurately predict the unconditioned stimulus. For instance, a stimulus that occurs *before* the US is more easily conditioned than one that comes *after* it. Even though the two are both contiguous presentations with the US (close to it in time), the first stimulus is more easily learned because it predicts the US. Across all learning conditions, as mentioned earlier, some delay between the CS and the US is optimal for learning. The length of delay varies, depending on the natures of the conditioned and unconditioned stimuli. For instance, eyeblink conditioning occurs when a sound (CS) is associated with a puff of air blown into the eye (US), which leads to a blink. Optimal

CRITICAL THINKING SKILL

## Avoiding the Association of Events with Other Events That Occur at the Same Time

**FIGURE 6.10 Questioning Superstitions** According to superstition, bad luck will come your way if a black cat crosses your path or if you walk under a ladder. **What misfortunes could actually occur in the situations shown here?**

Do you have a lucky charm? Do you wear your "good luck" socks every time you take an exam? Do you try to blow out the candles on your birthday cake in just one breath so that your silent wish will come true? The list of people's superstitions is virtually endless. In North America and Europe, people avoid the number 13. In China, Japan, Korea, and Hawaii, they avoid the number 4. The basketball player Michael Jordan, a graduate of the University of North Carolina, always wore shorts with the North Carolina logo under his uniform for good luck. The baseball player Wade Boggs ate only chicken on the day of a game (Morrison, n. d.). Even pigeons *might* be superstitious. In conditioning pigeons' pecking behavior, Skinner found that, during each trial, a particular pigeon would swing its head in the same way before responding, while another would do a half turn before responding.

The tendency to associate events that occur together in time is incredibly strong. When a chance event happens to occur close in time to a second event, humans and nonhuman animals sometimes associate the chance event with the second event. People, and apparently other animals, have a strong need to understand what causes or predicts events. Their resulting associations can lead people, at least, to cling to superstitions.

Most superstitions are harmless, but some can interfere with daily living, as when people stay in bed on the 4th or 13th of every month or refuse to get off on the 4th or 13th floor of a building. As a critical thinker, be aware of the tendency to associate events with other events that occur, perhaps simply by chance, at the same time (**Figure 6.10**).

learning for eyeblink conditioning is measured in milliseconds. By contrast, conditioned food aversions often take many hours, since the ill effects of consuming poisons or food that has gone bad may not be felt for hours after eating.

The cognitive model of classical learning, published by Rescorla and his colleague Allan Wagner, profoundly changed our understanding of learning (Rescorla & Wagner, 1972). The **Rescorla-Wagner model** states that an animal learns an expectation that some predictors (potential CSs) are better than others. According to this model, the strength of the CS-US association is determined by the extent to which the US is unexpected or surprising. The greater the surprise of the US, the more effort an organism puts into trying to understand its occurrence so that it can predict future occurrences. The result is greater classical conditioning of the event (CS) that predicted the US.

**Rescorla-Wagner model** A cognitive model of classical conditioning; it states that the strength of the CS-US association is determined by the extent to which the unconditioned stimulus is unexpected or surprising.

Say you always use an electric can opener to open a can of dog food. Your dog associates the sound of the can opener (CS) with the appearance of food (US). The dog wags its tail and runs around in circles when it hears that sound. Now say the electric can opener breaks and you replace it with a manual one. Without hearing the sound of the electric can opener, your dog receives food. According to Rescorla and Wagner, when an animal encounters a novel stimulus, it pays attention to it. This behavior is known as an *orienting response*. In other words, the unexpected appearance of the food (US) will cause your dog to pay attention to events in the environment that might have produced the food. Through this *orienting response,* your dog soon will learn to associate being fed with your use of the new can opener (**Figure 6.11**).

Other aspects of classical conditioning are consistent with the Rescorla-Wagner model. First, an animal will more easily associate an unconditioned stimulus with a novel stimulus than with a familiar stimulus. For example, a dog can be conditioned more easily with a smell new to it (such as that of almonds) than with a smell it knows (that of dog biscuits, perhaps). Second, once a conditioned stimulus is learned, it can prevent the acquisition of a new conditioned stimulus. This phenomenon is known as the *blocking effect*. For example, if a dog has learned that the smell of almonds (CS) is a good predictor of food (US), that dog will not look for other predictors, even if they now also predict the availability of food. Third, a stimulus associated with a CS can act as an *occasion setter,* or trigger, for the CS (Schmajuk, Lamoureux, & Holland, 1998). For example, a dog might

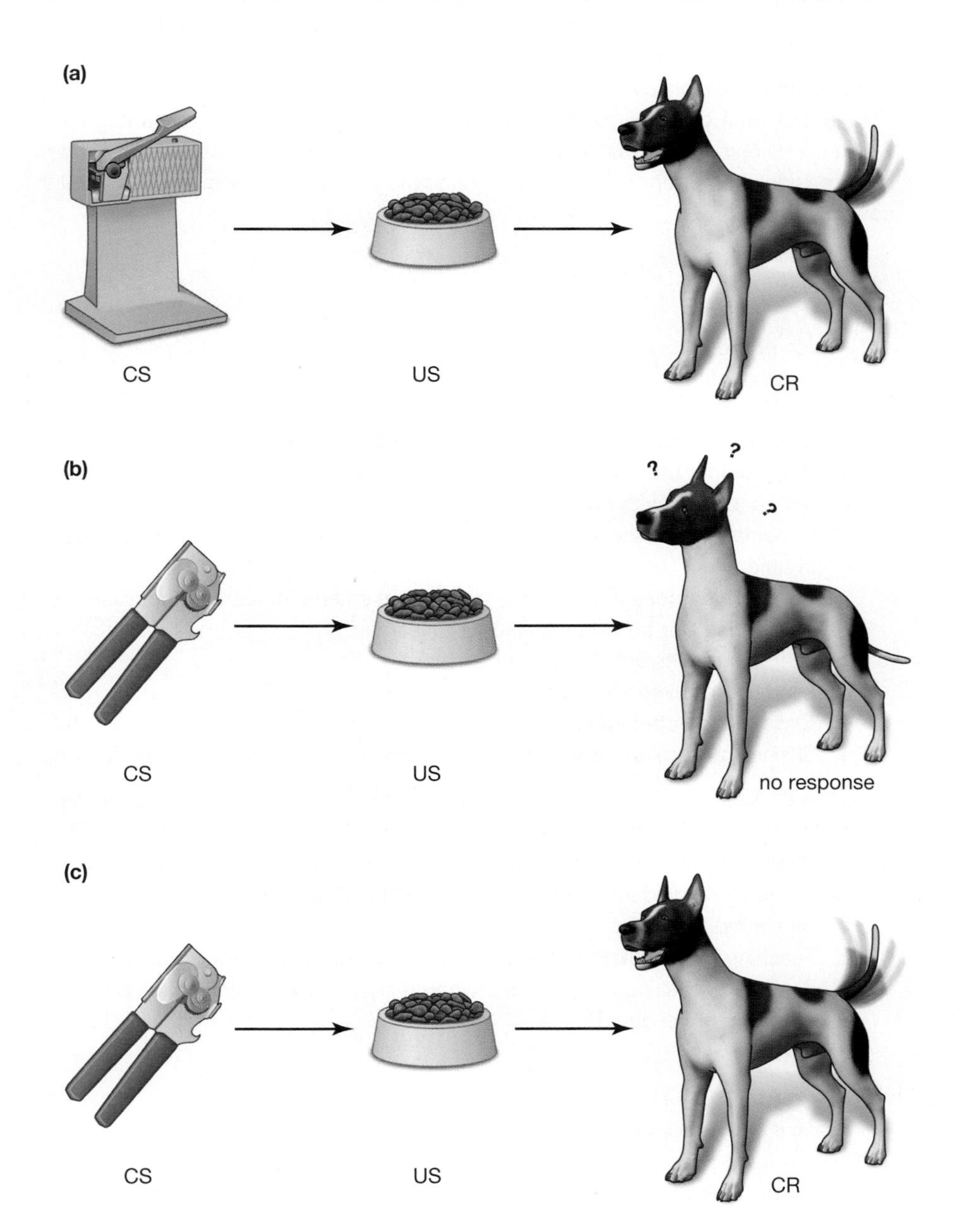


**FIGURE 6.11 Rescorla-Wagner Model** The Rescorla-Wagner model of learning emphasizes the substitution of one stimulus for another. **(a)** Here a dog associates the sound of an electric can opener with the arrival of food. **(b)** With the substitution of a manual can opener for the electric one, the dog is initially surprised. What happened to the reliable predictor of the dog's food? **(c)** The orienting response causes the dog to check the environment for a new stimulus. When the dog comes to associate the manual can opener with the arrival of food, the new stimulus has become the better predictor of the expected event: time to eat!

learn that the smell of almonds predicts food only when the smell is preceded by a sound or by a flash of light. The sound or light lets the dog know whether the association between the smell of almonds and food is active.

## Summing Up

### What Ideas Guide the Study of Learning?

Behaviorism, founded by John B. Watson, focuses on observable aspects of learning. Ivan Pavlov developed classical-conditioning theory to account for the learned association between neutral stimuli and reflexive behaviors. Conditioning occurs when a conditioned stimulus becomes associated with an unconditioned stimulus. For learning to occur, the conditioned stimulus needs to reliably predict the unconditioned stimulus, not simply be contiguous with it. Classical conditioning explains the development of phobias and contributes to drug addiction. Accordingly, techniques based on classical conditioning may be used to treat phobias and drug addiction. Many psychologists believe that classical conditioning evolved because it helps animals learn adaptive responses—that is, responses that facilitate survival. The Rescorla-Wagner model, a cognitive model of classical conditioning, states that the degree to which conditioning occurs is determined by the extent to which the US is unexpected or surprising, with stronger effects occurring when a novel or unusual CS is used in conditioning.

## Measuring Up

1. Which of the following are true statements about conditioning? Check as many as apply.
   - **a.** Conditioning is one kind of learning.
   - **b.** Only nonhuman animals can be conditioned.
   - **c.** B. F. Skinner used rats and pigeons in most of his research because he was not concerned with human learning.
   - **d.** Conditioning usually involves the association of two events that occur close in time.
   - **e.** Conditioning does not meet the definitional criteria for learning because the association can be extinguished, or unlearned.
   - **f.** Learning results only from experiences.
   - **g.** Learning involves short-term changes in behavior.
   - **h.** Classical and operant conditioning are the same.
   - **i.** Skinner came to appreciate the introspection methods used by his professors.
2. John B. Watson had planned to extinguish Little Albert's conditioned response to the rat. Which of the following techniques would have achieved that goal?
   - **a.** Repeatedly showing Little Albert the rat without making a loud sound.
   - **b.** Making a loud sound every time a different and unrelated object was presented.
   - **c.** Teaching Little Albert to strike the bar so he could make the loud sound.
   - **d.** Repeatedly making a loud sound when related objects, such as the ball of wool, were presented.

**Answers:** 1. Choices a, d, and f are true.
2. a. Repeatedly showing Little Albert the rat without making a loud sound.

# 6.2 How Does Operant Conditioning Differ from Classical Conditioning?

Learning Objectives

- Define operant conditioning.
- Distinguish between positive reinforcement, negative reinforcement, positive punishment, and negative punishment.
- Distinguish between schedules of reinforcement.
- Identify biological and cognitive factors that influence operant conditioning.

Classical conditioning is a relatively passive process. In it, an animal learns predictive connections between stimuli, regardless of what the animal does beyond that. This form of conditioning does not account for the many times that one of the events occurs because the animal has taken some action.

Our behaviors often represent means to particular ends. They are *instrumental*—done for a purpose. We buy food to eat it, we study to get good grades, we work to receive money, and so on. We learn that behaving in certain ways leads to rewards, and we learn that not behaving in other ways keeps us from punishment. This type of learning is called **operant conditioning,** or **instrumental conditioning.** B. F. Skinner, the psychologist most closely associated with this process, chose the term *operant* to express the idea that animals *operate* on their environments to produce effects. Operant conditioning is the learning process in which an action's consequences determine the likelihood that the action will be performed in the future.

The study of operant conditioning began in the late nineteenth century, in Cambridge, Massachusetts, at the home of the Harvard psychologist William James. A young graduate student working with James, Edward Thorndike, took inspiration from Charles Darwin's painstakingly precise observations of animal behavior. In James's basement, Thorndike performed the first reported carefully controlled experiments in comparative animal psychology. Specifically, he studied whether nonhuman animals showed signs of intelligence. As part of his research, Thorndike built a *puzzle box,* a small cage with a trapdoor (**Figure 6.12a**). The trapdoor would open if the animal inside performed a specific action, such as pulling a string. Thorndike placed food-deprived animals, initially chickens, inside the puzzle box to see if they could figure out how to escape.

**operant conditioning (instrumental conditioning)** A learning process in which the consequences of an action determine the likelihood that it will be performed in the future.

(a)

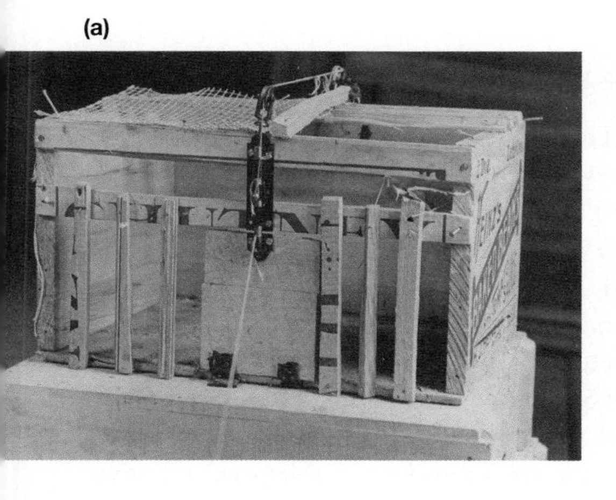

(b)

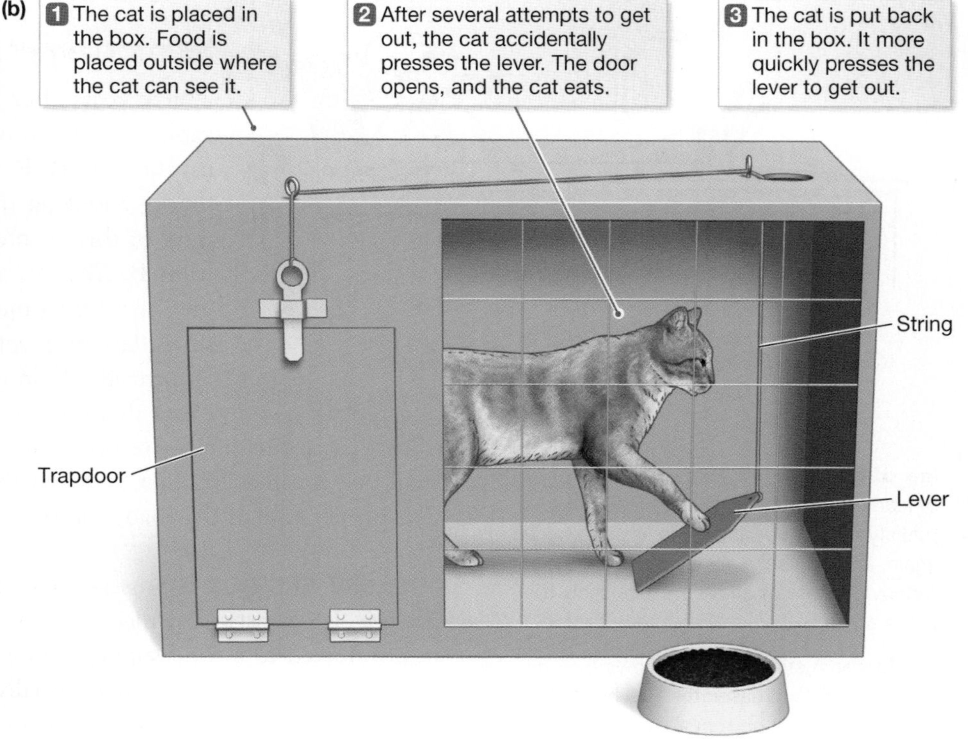


**FIGURE 6.12 Thorndike's Puzzle Box**
**(a)** Thorndike used puzzle boxes, such as the one depicted here, **(b)** to assess learning in animals.

**FIGURE 6.13 Law of Effect** By studying cats' attempts to escape from a puzzle box, Thorndike was able to formulate his general theory of learning.

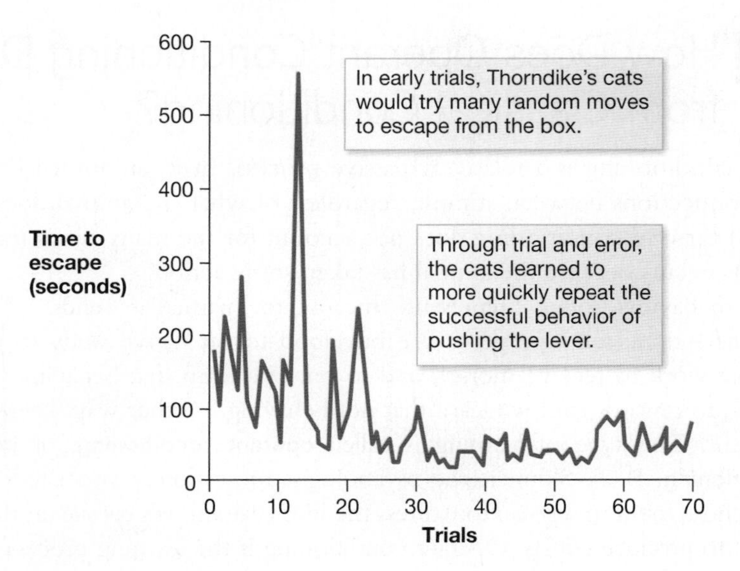


When Thorndike moved to Columbia University to complete his Ph.D., he switched from using chickens to using cats in his studies. To motivate the cats, he would place food just outside the box. When a cat was first placed in the box, it usually attempted to escape through numerous nonproductive behaviors. After 5 to 10 minutes of struggling, the cat would *accidentally* pull the string, and the door would open. Thorndike would then return the cat to the box and repeat the trial. The cat would pull the string more quickly on each subsequent trial. Soon, it would learn to escape from the puzzle box within seconds (**Figure 6.10b**). From this line of research, Thorndike developed a general theory of learning. According to this **law of effect,** any behavior that leads to a "satisfying state of affairs" is likely to occur again. Any behavior that leads to an "annoying state of affairs" is less likely to occur again (**Figure 6.13**).

*"Oh, not bad. The light comes on, I press the bar, they write me a check. How about you?"*

## Reinforcement Increases Behavior

Thirty years after Thorndike experimented with animals escaping puzzle boxes, another Harvard graduate student in psychology, B. F. Skinner, developed a more formal learning theory based on the law of effect. As discussed at the beginning of this chapter, Skinner had been greatly influenced by John B. Watson and shared his philosophy of behaviorism. He therefore objected to the subjective aspects of Thorndike's law of effect: States of "satisfaction" are not observable empirically. Skinner coined the term *reinforcer* to describe an event that produces a learned response. A **reinforcer** is a stimulus that occurs after a response and increases the likelihood that the response will be repeated. Skinner believed that behavior—studying, eating, driving on the proper side of the road, and so on—occurs because it has been reinforced.

**law of effect** Thorndike's general theory of learning: Any behavior that leads to a "satisfying state of affairs" is likely to occur again, and any behavior that leads to an "annoying state of affairs" is less likely to occur again.

**reinforcer** A stimulus that follows a response and increases the likelihood that the response will be repeated.

**THE SKINNER BOX** To assess operant conditioning, Skinner developed a simple device. It consists of a small chamber or cage. Inside, one lever or response key is connected to a food supply, and a second lever or response key is connected to a water supply. An animal, usually a rat or pigeon, is placed in the chamber or cage. The animal learns to press one lever or key to receive food, the other

(a)

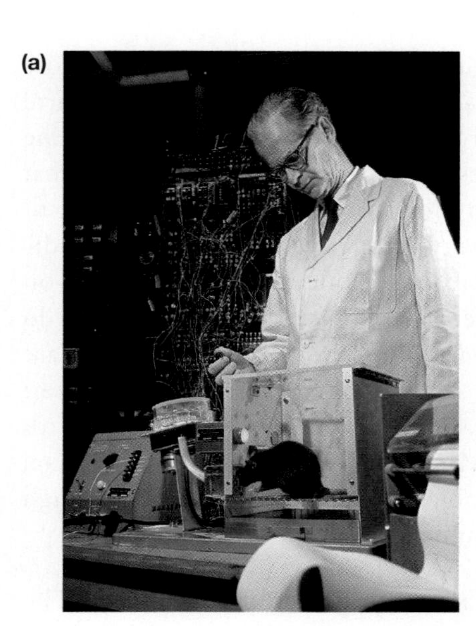

(b)

**FIGURE 6.14 Skinner Box (a)** B. F. Skinner and one of his subjects demonstrate **(b)** the operant chamber, now known as the Skinner box.

lever or key to receive water. In his earlier research, Skinner had used a maze. There, a rat had to make a specific turn to get access to the reinforcer, usually a small piece of food in the goal box. After the rat completed a trial, Skinner had to return the rat to the beginning of the maze. He developed the *operant chamber,* as he called it, basically because he grew tired of fetching rats. With the device—which came to be known as the *Skinner box,* although he never used that term—he could expose rats or pigeons to repeated conditioning trials without having to do anything but observe (**Figure 6.14**). Skinner later built mechanical recording devices that allowed the experimenter to conduct trials without being present.

SHAPING When performing operant conditioning, you cannot provide the reinforcer until the animal displays the appropriate response. An animal inside the Skinner box has so little to do that it typically presses the lever or key sooner rather than later. One major problem with operant conditioning outside the Skinner box is that the same animal might take a while to perform the action you are looking for. Rather than wait for the animal to spontaneously perform the action, you can use an operant-conditioning technique to teach the animal to do so. This powerful process is called **shaping.** It consists of reinforcing behaviors that are increasingly similar to the desired behavior.

Suppose you are trying to teach your dog to roll over. You initially reward the dog for any behavior that even slightly resembles rolling over, such as lying down. Once this behavior is established, you reinforce behaviors more selectively. Reinforcing *successive approximations* eventually produces the desired behavior. In other words, the animal learns to discriminate which behavior is being reinforced.

Shaping has been used to condition animals to perform amazing feats: pigeons playing table tennis, dogs playing the piano, pigs doing housework such as picking up clothes and vacuuming, and so on (**Figure 6.15**). Shaping has also been used to teach appropriate social skills to mentally ill people; to teach language to children with autism; and to teach basic skills, such as dressing themselves, to mentally retarded individuals. More generally, parents and educators often use shaping to encourage appropriate behavior in children. For example, they praise children for their initial—often illegible—attempts at handwriting.

**FIGURE 6.15 Shaping** Shaping, an operant conditioning technique, consists of reinforcing behaviors that are increasingly similar to the desired behavior. This technique can be used to train animals to perform extraordinary behaviors. Here a trained dog water-skis for a boat show. **Suppose you wanted to teach yourself to do something. Which behavior would you choose, and how would you go about shaping it?**

**REINFORCERS CAN BE CONDITIONED** The most obvious reinforcers are those necessary for survival, such as food or water. Because they satisfy biological needs, they are called *primary reinforcers*. From an evolutionary standpoint, the learning value of primary reinforcers makes a great deal of sense: Animals that repeatedly perform behaviors reinforced by food or water are more likely to survive and pass along their genes. But many apparent reinforcers do not directly satisfy biological needs. For example, a compliment, money, or an A on a paper can be reinforcing. Events or objects that serve as reinforcers but do not satisfy biological needs are called *secondary reinforcers*. These reinforcers are established through classical conditioning, as described earlier in this chapter: We learn to associate a neutral stimulus, such as money (CS), with rewards such as food, security, and power (US). Money is really only pieces of metal or of paper, but these and other neutral objects become meaningful through their associations with unconditioned stimuli.

**REINFORCER POTENCY** Some reinforcers are more powerful than others. The psychologist David Premack (1959; Holstein & Premack, 1965) theorized about how a reinforcer's value could be determined. The key is the amount of time an organism, when free to do anything, engages in a specific behavior associated with the reinforcer. For instance, most children would choose to spend more time eating ice cream than eating spinach. Ice cream is therefore more reinforcing for children than spinach is. One great advantage of Premack's theory is that it can account for differences in individuals' values. For people who prefer spinach to ice cream, spinach serves as a more potent reinforcer.

A logical application of Premack's theory, now called the *Premack principle,* is that a more valued activity can be used to reinforce the performance of a less valued activity. Parents use the Premack principle all the time. They tell their children, "Eat your spinach and then you'll get dessert," "Finish your homework and then you can go out," and so on.

## Both Reinforcement and Punishment Can Be Positive or Negative

Reinforcement and punishment have the opposite effects on behavior. Whereas reinforcement increases a behavior's probability, punishment decreases its probability. For example, feeding a rat after it presses a lever will increase the probability that the rat will press the lever. Giving a rat an electric shock after it presses a lever will decrease that action's probability. Both reinforcement and punishment can be positive or negative. The designation depends on whether something is given or removed, not on whether any part of the process is good or bad.

**POSITIVE AND NEGATIVE REINFORCEMENT** Through the administration of a stimulus, **positive reinforcement** increases the probability that a behavior will be repeated. Positive reinforcement is often called *reward*. Rewarded behaviors increase in frequency, as when people work harder in response to praise or increased pay. In contrast, **negative reinforcement** increases behavior through the *removal* of an unpleasant stimulus. For instance, when a rat is required to press a lever to turn off an electric shock, the pressing of the lever has been negatively reinforced. Negative reinforcement differs from punishment. If the rat were being punished, it would receive a shock *for* pressing the lever. The key point is that reinforcement—positive or negative—*increases* the likelihood of a behavior, whereas punishment *decreases* the likelihood of a behavior.

**positive reinforcement** The administration of a stimulus to increase the probability of a behavior's being repeated.

**negative reinforcement** The removal of a stimulus to increase the probability of a behavior's being repeated.

Negative reinforcement is quite common in everyday life. You take a pill to get rid of a headache. You close the door to your room to shut out noise. You change the channel to avoid watching an awful program. You pick up a crying baby. In each case, you are trying to avoid or escape an unwanted stimulus. If the action you take successfully reduces the unwanted stimulus, then the next time you have a headache, hear noise in your room, see an awful program, or are with a crying baby, the more likely you are to repeat the behavior that reduced the stimulus. The behavior has been negatively reinforced.

**positive punishment** The administration of a stimulus to decrease the probability of a behavior's recurring.

**negative punishment** The removal of a stimulus to decrease the probability of a behavior's recurring.

POSITIVE AND NEGATIVE PUNISHMENT Punishment reduces the probability that a behavior will recur. It can do so through positive or negative means. Again, "positive" or "negative" here means whether something is added or removed, not whether it is good or bad. **Positive punishment** decreases the behavior's probability through the administration of a stimulus. Usually the stimulus in positive punishment is unpleasant. When a rat receives a shock for pressing a lever, the rat has received positive punishment. **Negative punishment** decreases the behavior's probability through the removal of a usually pleasant stimulus. When a teenager loses driving privileges for speeding, the teenager has received negative punishment. If that same teen has received a speeding ticket, the ticket serves as a positive punishment. Here, the negative and positive forms of punishment may produce the same result: The teen will be less likely to speed the next time he or she gets behind the wheel.

In thinking about these terms, which can be confusing, consider whether the behavior is more likely to occur (reinforcement) or less likely to occur (punishment). A reinforcement or punishment is positive if something is applied or given and negative if something is removed or terminated. Likewise, you have to think in terms of which behavior is being reinforced or punished. Suppose a teacher gives students a special treat for being quiet in class. Subsequently, the students talk less. In this case, the treat is a positive punishment for talking because it reduces the probability that talking will occur again. At the same time, the treat is a reinforcement for being quiet. Giving the treat led to a decrease in talking and an increase in being quiet. (For an overview of positive and negative kinds of both reinforcement and punishment, see **Figure 6.16**.)

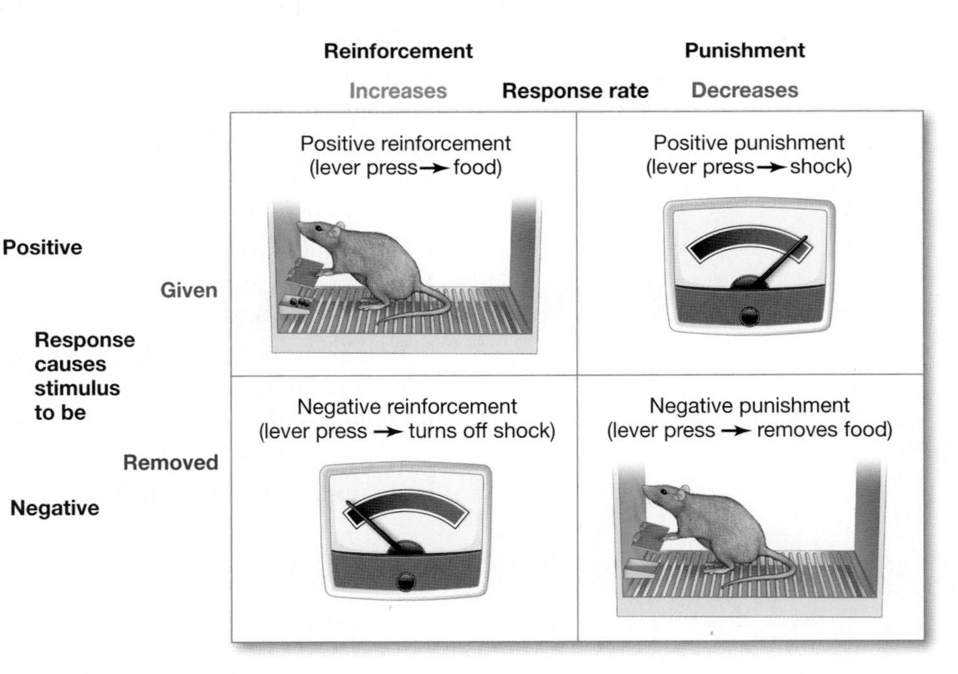


**FIGURE 6.16 Negative and Positive Reinforcement, Negative and Positive Punishment** Use this chart to help solidify your understanding of the terms in this section.

EFFECTIVENESS OF PARENTAL PUNISHMENT To make their children behave, parents sometimes use punishment as a means of discipline. Many contemporary psychologists believe that punishment is often applied ineffectively, however, and that it may have unintended and unwanted consequences. Research has shown that for punishment to be effective, it must be reasonable, unpleasant, and applied immediately so that the relationship between the unwanted behavior and the punishment is clear (Goodall, 1984; O'Leary, 1995). But considerable potential exists for confusion. For example, sometimes punishment is applied after a desired action. If a student is punished after admitting to cheating on an exam, the student may then associate the punishment with being honest rather than with the original offense. As a result, the student learns not to tell the truth. As Skinner once pointed out, one thing people learn from punishment is how to avoid it. Rather than learning how to behave appropriately, they may learn not to get caught.

Punishment can also lead to negative emotions, such as fear and anxiety. Through classical conditioning, these emotions may become associated with the person who administers the punishment. If a child thus learns to fear a parent or teacher, the long-term relationship between child and adult may be damaged (Gershoff, 2002). In addition, punishment often fails to offset the reinforcing aspects of the undesired behavior. In real life, any behavior can be reinforced in multiple ways. For instance, thumb sucking may be reinforced because it makes a child feel good, because it provides relief from negative emotions, and because it alleviates hunger. Punishment may not be sufficient to offset such rewards, but it may reinforce the child's secrecy about thumb sucking. For these and other reasons, most psychologists agree with Skinner's recommendation that reinforcement be used rather than punishment. A child complimented for being a good student is likely to perform better academically than one punished for doing poorly. After all, reinforcing good behavior tells the child what to do. Punishing the child for bad behavior does not tell the child how to improve.

One form of punishment that most psychologists believe is especially ineffective is physical punishment, such as spanking. Spanking is very common, however. Nearly three-quarters of American parents spank their children and thus apparently believe it is effective (Gallup, 1995). As noted by Alan Kazdin and Corina Benjet (2003), beliefs about the appropriateness of spanking involve religious beliefs and cultural views, as well as legal issues. Many countries (e.g., Austria, Denmark, Israel, Sweden, and Italy) have banned corporal punishment in homes or schools. Even the United Nations has passed resolutions discouraging it.

Some researchers have provided evidence of numerous negative outcomes associated with spanking, especially severe spanking (Bender et al., 2007). These problems include poor parent/child relations, weaker moral values, mental health problems, increased delinquency, and future child abuse. One concern is that physical punishment teaches the child that violence is an appropriate behavior for adults. (*Imitation learning* is discussed later in this chapter.) Although the extent to which mild forms of spanking cause problems is open to debate (Baumrind, Larzelere, & Cowan, 2002), the evidence indicates that other forms of punishment are more effective for decreasing unwanted behaviors (Kazdin & Benjet, 2003). Time-outs, small fines, and grounding can effectively modify behavior. Yet many psychologists believe that any method of punishment is less effective than providing positive reinforcement for "better" behaviors. By rewarding the behaviors they wish to see, parents are able to increase those behaviors while building more positive bonds with their children.

## Operant Conditioning Is Influenced by Schedules of Reinforcement

How often should a reinforcer be given? For fast learning, behavior might be reinforced each time it occurs. This process is known as **continuous reinforcement.** In the real world, behavior is seldom reinforced continuously. Animals do not find food each time they look for it, and people do not receive praise each

**continuous reinforcement** A type of learning in which behavior is reinforced each time it occurs.

time they behave acceptably. The intermittent reinforcement of behavior is more common. This process is known as **partial reinforcement.** Partial reinforcement's effect on conditioning depends on the reinforcement schedule.

**partial reinforcement** A type of learning in which behavior is reinforced intermittently.

**ratio schedule** A schedule in which reinforcement is based on the number of times the behavior occurs.

**interval schedule** A schedule in which reinforcement is provided after a specific unit of time.

**fixed schedule** A schedule in which reinforcement is provided after a specific number of occurrences or after a specific amount of time.

**variable schedule** A schedule in which reinforcement is provided at different rates or at different times.

**RATIO AND INTERVAL SCHEDULES** Partial reinforcement can be administered according to either the number of behavioral responses or the passage of time. For instance, factory workers can be paid by the piece (behavioral responses) or by the hour (passage of time). A **ratio schedule** is based on the number of times the behavior occurs, as when a behavior is reinforced on every third or tenth occurrence. An **interval schedule** is based on a specific unit of time, as when a behavior is reinforced when it is performed every minute or hour. Ratio reinforcement generally leads to greater responding than does interval reinforcement. For example, factory workers paid by the piece are usually more productive than those paid by the hour, especially if the workers receive incentives for higher productivity.

**FIXED AND VARIABLE SCHEDULES** Partial reinforcement also can be given on a *fixed schedule* or a *variable schedule*. In a **fixed schedule,** the reinforcer is given consistently after a specific number of occurrences or after a specific amount of time. For example, whether factory workers are paid by the piece or by the hour, they usually are paid according to a fixed rate. They earn the same amount for each piece or for each hour, so the rate of reinforcement is entirely predictable. In a **variable schedule,** the reinforcer is given at different rates or at different times. The responder does not know how many behaviors need to be performed or how much time needs to pass before reinforcement will occur. One example of variable reinforcement is when a salesperson receives a commission only when a customer agrees to purchase a product. (The patterns of behavior typically observed under different schedules of reinforcement are illustrated in **Figure 6.17.**)

**BEHAVIORAL PERSISTENCE** The schedule of reinforcement also affects the persistence of behavior. Continuous reinforcement is highly effective for teaching a behavior. If the reinforcement is stopped, however, the behavior extinguishes quickly. For instance, normally when you put money in a vending machine, it gives you a product in return. If it fails to do so, you quickly stop putting your money into it. By contrast, at a casino you might drop a lot

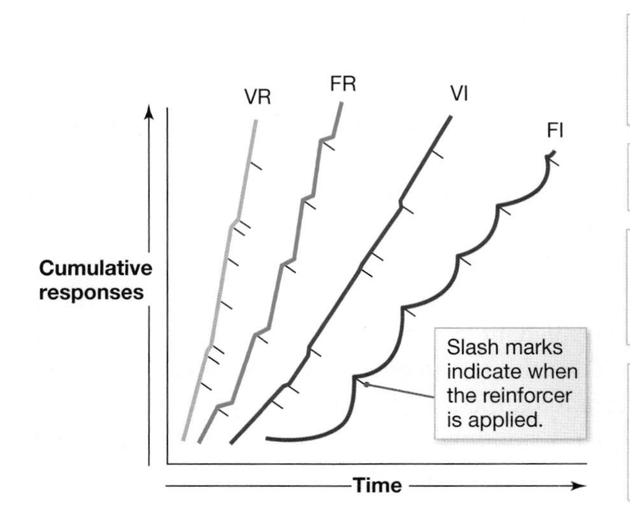


Variable ratio: A slot machine pays off on average every few pulls, but you never know which pull will pay.

Fixed ratio: You are paid each time you complete a chore.

**Variable interval**: You listen to the radio to hear your favorite song. You do not know when you will hear it.

**Fixed interval**: When quizzes are scheduled at fixed intervals, students study only when the quiz is to be administered (the grade is the reinforcer).

**FIGURE 6.17 Behavior and Reinforcement** The curves on this graph show cumulative responses under different schedules of reinforcement over time. The steeper the line, the higher the response rate. Ratio reinforcement leads to the highest rates of response.

Psychology: Knowledge You Can Use

## Can Behavior Modification Help Me Stick with an Exercise Program?

The U.S. surgeon general recommends that each adult engage in at least 30 minutes of moderate physical activity daily, but most of us fail to achieve this goal (Centers for Disease Control and Prevention, 1999). Maybe you intend to exercise daily, then struggle to find the time to get to the gym. Or maybe you make working out a priority for a few weeks, then fall off the wagon. How can psychology help you stick with your exercise program (**Figure 6.18**)?

As you learned earlier in this chapter, experts regularly use the principles of operant conditioning to change the behaviors of animals, including humans. You do not have to be an expert, however, to condition yourself to perform healthful behaviors. Consider these steps:

1. **Identify a behavior you wish to change.** Before you begin a behavior modification program, you need to know which behavior you wish to modify. If your lack of physical activity is a concern, the behavior you need to target is being sedentary.
2. **Set goals.** Set goals that are realistic, specific, and measurable. If your current exercise program consists of a daily race to beat the closing elevator door, setting a goal to run 10 miles per day every day this month is not realistic. Likewise, a goal of "exercise more" will not do the trick, because it is too vague. Instead, you might set one of the following goals: Jog 1 mile on the treadmill at least four days this week, attend three yoga sessions this week, or walk at least 10,000 steps each day this week. Note that you can measure each of these goals objectively. You can use the treadmill's odometer to know whether you hit the 1-mile mark, or a calendar to indicate your performance of yoga, or the readout on a pedometer to track your daily steps.

   Note, too, that these goals sit on a relatively short time horizon. Setting goals you can meet in short order allows for more opportunities for reinforcement. If your ultimate goal is to run a marathon 12 months from now, you need to set small, incremental subgoals that you can reinforce along the way.
3. **Monitor your behavior.** Monitor your behavior for a week or more before you begin your activity. Simply noting the behavior will likely move you toward your goal, since you will be more conscious of it. Keeping careful track will also enable you to get a sense of your baseline. By using this baseline as a point of comparison later, you will be able to assess your progress. Record your observations. If you have a smart phone, you might download an app for recording physical activity. Register at an exercise-tracking Web site. Or just use a paper notebook.
4. **Select a reinforcer and decide on a reinforcement schedule.** When you choose a reinforcer, pick something attainable that you genuinely find enjoyable. For example, you could buy one song from iTunes after every other yoga class. Alternatively, you could treat yourself to a movie each week that you meet your goal. Or you could give yourself one penny for every hundred

of money into a slot machine that rarely rewards you with a "win." Such behavior is not simply the result of an "addiction" to gambling. Rather, people put money in slot machines because the machines *sometimes* provide monetary rewards. Psychologists explain this persistent behavior as the effect of a *variable-ratio schedule* of reinforcement.

The **partial-reinforcement extinction effect** refers to the greater persistence of behavior under partial reinforcement than under continuous reinforcement. During continuous reinforcement, the learner easily can detect when reinforcement has stopped. But when the behavior is reinforced only some of the time, the learner needs to repeat the behavior comparatively more times to detect the absence of reinforcement. Thus the less frequent the reinforcement during training, the greater the resistance to extinction. To condition a behavior so that it persists, you need to reinforce it continuously during early acquisition and then slowly change to partial reinforcement. Parents naturally follow this strategy in teaching behaviors to their children, as in toilet training.

**partial-reinforcement extinction effect**
The greater persistence of behavior under partial reinforcement than under continuous reinforcement.

**FIGURE 6.18 Behavior Modification in Action** To see behavior modification in action, select a target behavior of your own that you wish to change. Maybe you feel that you should be studying more, exercising more, or watching less television. Any behavior will do, as long as it is specific and you have a realistic goal for changing it. Over time, as you successfully change the behavior, phase out the reinforcer and simply perform the behavior out of habit. For example, once you are used to exercising regularly, you will exercise regularly. The reinforced behavior may even become reinforcing on its own.

steps you take each day. Eventually, you could use the money to buy something you do not normally spend money on.

5. **Reinforce the desired behavior.** To cause the behavior change you want to see, you need to reinforce the desired behavior whenever it occurs. Be consistent. Suppose that if you work out at the gym three times this week, you treat yourself by watching the new episode of *Glee*. This is important: If you do not work out at the gym three times this week, do not watch *Glee*. If you're a *Gleek*, it might be hard to resist streaming the newest episode (perhaps as you lounge on the couch instead of heading to the gym). But if you want the behavior modification to work, you have to resist. If you do not behave appropriately, you do not receive the reinforcer! Allow yourself no exceptions.

6. **Modify your goals, reinforcements, or reinforcement schedules, as needed.** Once you begin consistently hitting your stated goals, make the goals more challenging. Add more days per week, more miles per run, or more laps per workout. If you find yourself getting bored with a reinforcer, mix it up a bit. Just be sure to select reinforcers that are genuinely appealing. And change the reinforcement schedule so you have to work harder to get the reward. For example, rather than reinforcing your good behavior after each workout, use reinforcement after you complete two workouts or after you work out consistently for a week.

Of course, you can use these principles to address other behaviors, such as procrastinating on your studies, neglecting to call your family, spending too much time on Facebook, and so on. For now, just pick one behavior you want to modify and try implementing the steps above. Once you get the hang of it, see if you can translate these steps to other areas of your life. Give it a try! You might amaze yourself with the power of behavior modification.

BEHAVIOR MODIFICATION **Behavior modification** is the use of operant-conditioning techniques to eliminate unwanted behaviors and replace them with desirable ones. The general rationale behind behavior modification is that most unwanted behaviors are learned and therefore can be unlearned. Parents, teachers, and animal trainers use conditioning strategies widely. People can be taught, for example, to be more productive at work, to save energy, and to drive more safely. Children with profound learning disabilities can be trained to communicate and to interact. As discussed in Chapter 15, operant techniques are also effective for treating many psychological conditions, such as depression and anxiety disorders.

Another widespread behavior modification method draws on the principle of secondary reinforcement. Chimpanzees can be trained to perform tasks in exchange for tokens, which they can later trade for food. The tokens thus reinforce behavior, and the chimps work as hard to obtain the tokens as they work to obtain food. Prisons, mental hospitals, schools, and classrooms often use *token economies*, in which people earn tokens for completing tasks and lose tokens for behaving

**behavior modification** The use of operant-conditioning techniques to eliminate unwanted behaviors and replace them with desirable ones.

badly. The people can later trade their tokens for objects or privileges. Here, the rewards not only reinforce good behavior but also give participants a sense of control over their environment. So, for instance, teachers can provide tokens to students for obeying class rules, turning in homework on time, and helping others. At some future point, the tokens can be exchanged for rewards, such as fun activities or extra recess time. In mental hospitals, token economies can encourage good grooming and appropriate social behavior and can discourage bizarre behavior.

**FIGURE 6.19 Biological Constraints** Animals have a hard time learning behaviors that run counter to their evolutionary adaptation. For example, raccoons are hardwired to rub food between their paws, as this raccoon is doing. They have trouble learning *not* to rub objects.

## Biology and Cognition Influence Operant Conditioning

Behaviorists such as B. F. Skinner believed that all behavior could be explained by straightforward conditioning principles. Recall from the beginning of this chapter that Skinner's *Walden Two* describes a utopia in which all of society's problems are solved through operant conditioning. In reality, however, reinforcement schedules explain only a certain amount of human behavior. Biology constrains learning, and reinforcement does not always have to be present for learning to take place.

**BIOLOGICAL CONSTRAINTS** Behaviorists believed that any behavior could be shaped through reinforcement. We now know that animals have a hard time learning behaviors that run counter to their evolutionary adaptation. A good example of biological constraints was obtained by Marian and Keller Breland, a husband-and-wife team of psychologists who used operant-conditioning techniques to train animals for commercials (Breland & Breland, 1961). Many of their animals refused to perform certain tasks they had been taught. For instance, a raccoon learned to place coins in a piggy bank, but eventually it refused to perform this task. Instead, the raccoon stood over the bank and briskly rubbed the coins in its paws. This rubbing behavior was not reinforced. In fact, it delayed reinforcement. One explanation for the raccoon's behavior is that the task was incompatible with innate adaptive behaviors. The raccoon associated the coin with food and treated it the same way: Rubbing food between the paws is hardwired for raccoons (**Figure 6.19**).

Similarly, pigeons can be trained to peck at keys to obtain food or secondary reinforcers, but it is difficult to train them to peck at keys to avoid electric shock. They can learn to avoid shock by flapping their wings, however, because wing flapping is their natural means of escape. The psychologist Robert Bolles has argued that animals have built-in defense reactions to threatening stimuli (Bolles, 1970). Conditioning is most effective when the association between the response and the reinforcement is similar to the animal's built-in predispositions.

**ACQUISITION/PERFORMANCE DISTINCTION** There is another challenge to the idea that reinforcement is responsible for all behavior. Namely, learning can take place without reinforcement. Edward Tolman, an early cognitive theorist, argued that reinforcement has more impact on performance than on learning. At the time, Tolman was conducting experiments in which rats had to learn to run through complex mazes to obtain food. Tolman believed that each rat developed a **cognitive map.** That is, during an experiment, each rat held in its brain a visual/spatial representation of the particular maze. The rat used this knowledge of the environment to help it find the food quickly.

**cognitive map** A visual/spatial mental representation of an environment.

To test his theory, Tolman and his students studied three groups of rats. The first group traveled through the maze but received no reinforcement: The rats reached the "goal box," found no food in the box, and simply wandered through the maze on each subsequent trial. The second group received reinforcement on every trial: Because the rats found food in the goal box, they learned to find the box quickly. The third group, critically, started receiving re-

**FIGURE 6.20 Scientific Method: Tolman's Study of Latent Learning**

**Hypothesis:** Reinforcement has more impact on performance than on learning.

**Research Method:**

**1 One group of rats** is put through trials running in a maze with a goal box that never has any food reward as reinforcement.

**2 A second group of rats** is put through trials in a maze with a goal box that always has food reinforcement.

**3 A third group of rats** is put through trials in a maze that has food reinforcement only after the first 10 trials.

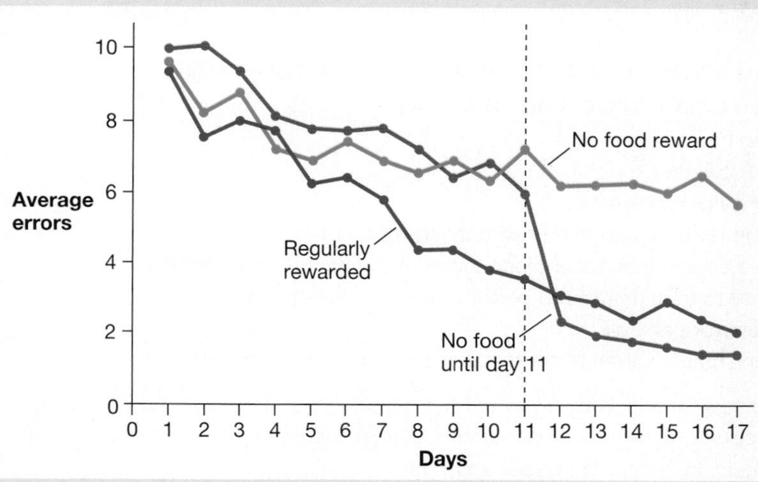


**Results:** Rats that were regularly reinforced for correctly running through a maze (**blue**) showed improved performance over time compared with rats that did not receive reinforcement (**green**). Rats that were not reinforced for the first 10 trials but were reinforced thereafter showed an immediate change in performance (**red**). Note that between days 11 and 12 the red group's average number of errors decreased dramatically.

**Conclusion:** Rats may learn a path through a maze but not reveal their learning. They do not reveal the learning because the maze running behavior has not been reinforced. Learning of this kind is called latent learning. It may be revealed once the behavior is reinforced. In other words, there is a distinction between acquisition of a behavior and performance of that behavior.

**Source:** Tolman, E. C., & Honzik, C. H. (1930). Introduction and removal of reward, and maze performance in rats. *University of California Publications in Psychology, 4*, 257–275.

inforcement only after the first 10 trials: At that point, the rats showed an amazingly fast learning curve and immediately caught up to the group that had been continuously reinforced (Tolman & Honzik, 1930). This result implies that the rats had learned a cognitive map of the maze and used it when the reinforcement began. Tolman's term **latent learning** refers to learning that takes place without reinforcement (**Figure 6.20**). For example, latent learning occurs when a person learns something simply by observing it. When most people drive for the first time, they do not need to be told that rotating the steering wheel turns the car. They already know that they need to rotate the steering wheel, even though they have never been reinforced for doing so.

Another form of learning that takes place without reinforcement is *insight learning*. In this form of problem solving, a solution suddenly emerges after either a period of inaction or contemplation of the problem. (Problem solving is discussed further in Chapter 8, "Thinking and Intelligence.") You probably have had this sort of experience, in which you mull over a problem for a while and then suddenly know the answer. The presence of reinforcement does not adequately explain insight learning, but it helps determine whether the behavior is subsequently repeated.

**latent learning** Learning that takes place in the absence of reinforcement.

## Summing Up

### How Does Operant Conditioning Differ from Classical Conditioning?

Whereas classical conditioning involves the learned association between two events, operant conditioning involves the learned association between a behavior and its consequences. B. F. Skinner developed the concept of operant conditioning to explain why some behaviors are repeated and others are not. Reinforcement increases a behavior's likelihood of being repeated. Punishment reduces that likelihood. Positive reinforcement and positive punishment involve the administration of a stimulus. Negative reinforcement and negative punishment involve the removal of a stimulus. Four schedules of reinforcement have been identified: variable ratio, fixed ratio, variable interval, and fixed interval. Each schedule has a distinct effect on behavior. Although Skinner maintained that operant conditioning could explain all behavior, contemporary theorists recognize that biological predispositions and cognitive processes influence organisms' ability to learn.

## Measuring Up

1. Indicate whether each of the following people and phenomena is related to operant conditioning or classical conditioning.
   a. Ivan Pavlov
   b. B. F. Skinner
   c. behavior modification
   d. A behavior is associated with its consequences.
   e. Two events that occur close together in time are associated.
   f. used to train animals to perform tricks and useful tasks
   g. Premack principle
   h. Punishment's effects are explained by this type of conditioning.

2. Suppose a mother is trying to get her 8-year-old to stop cursing. Each time the child curses, the mother waits until the child's father is present before spanking the child. Select the better answers:
   a. The time interval between the cursing and the punishment is
      _____ too long for optimal learning.
      _____ fine as long as the punishment is administered on the same day as the cursing.
   b. One likely outcome to the continued use of this punishment is
      _____ the child will curse at times he or she is unlikely to be caught.
      _____ the child will gradually extinguish the cursing response.
   c. Generalization is likely to occur such that
      _____ the child curses only when the father is at work.
      _____ the child comes to fear the father and mother.
   d. What is the child likely to learn?
      _____ Do not get caught cursing.
      _____ Cursing is a nasty behavior that must be stopped.
   e. A more effective approach would be to
      _____ spank the child as soon as the cursing occurs.
      _____ provide rewards for not cursing.

**Answers:** 1. a. classical; b. operant; c. operant; d. operant; e. classical; f. operant; g. operant; h. operant.
2. a. _X_ too long for optimal learning; b. _X_ the child will curse at times he or she is unlikely to be caught; c. _X_ the child comes to fear the father and mother; d. _X_ Do not get caught cursing; e. _X_ provide rewards for not cursing.

# 6.3 How Does Watching Others Affect Learning?

**Learning Objectives**

- Describe the concept of the meme.
- Define observational learning.
- Generate examples of observational learning, modeling, and vicarious learning.
- Discuss contemporary evidence regarding the role of mirror neurons in learning.

Suppose you were teaching someone to fly an airplane. How might you apply the learning principles discussed in this chapter to accomplish your goal? Obviously, reinforcing arbitrary correct behaviors would be a disastrous way to train an aspiring pilot. Similarly, teaching someone to play football, eat with chopsticks, or perform complex dance steps requires more than simple reinforcement. We learn many behaviors not by doing them but by watching others do them. For example, we learn social etiquette through observation. We sometimes learn to be anxious in particular situations by seeing that other people are anxious. We often acquire attitudes about politics, religion, and the habits of celebrities from parents, peers, teachers, and the media.

## Learning Can Be Passed On through Cultural Transmission

All humans belong to the same species and share the vast majority of genes. Around the world, however, there is enormous cultural diversity in what people think and how they behave. Would you be the same person if you had been raised in a small village in China, or in the jungles of South America, or in the mountains of Afghanistan? Probably not, since your religious beliefs, your values, and even your musical tastes are shaped by the culture in which you are raised. Each unit of cultural knowledge that is transmitted is a **meme.** Evolutionary psychologists view memes as analogous to genes. Like genes, memes are selectively passed on from one generation to the next. But unlike natural selection, which typically occurs slowly over thousands of years, memes can spread quickly, as in the worldwide adoption of the Internet. Although memes can be conditioned through association or reinforcement, many memes are learned by watching the behavior of other people. Some memes, however—such as fads—die out quickly.

One good example of the cultural transmission of knowledge is the case of Imo the monkey. In the 1950s, researchers who were studying monkeys in Japan threw some sweet potatoes onto a sandy beach for the monkeys there to eat. Imo developed the habit of washing her sweet potatoes in the ocean to remove the sand. Within a short time, other monkeys copied Imo, and soon many monkeys were washing their potatoes before eating them. Through social learning, this behavior has continued to be passed along from one generation to the next, and monkeys there still wash their potatoes (Dugatkin, 2004; **Figure 6.21**).

**FIGURE 6.21 Memes** In the 1950s, a Japanese macaque named Imo developed and unwittingly passed along to her fellow monkeys the meme of washing sweet potatoes in the ocean. The descendants of these sweet potato–washing macaques continue the behavior, as shown here. **Think of an example of meme transmission in humans. How is it similar to the behavior of these monkeys? How is it different?**

## Learning Can Occur through Observation and Imitation

**Observational learning** is the acquisition or modification of a behavior after exposure to at least one performance of that behavior. This kind of learning is a powerful adaptive tool for humans and other animals. For example, offspring can learn basic skills by watching adults perform those skills. They can learn which things are safe to eat by watching what adults eat. They can learn to fear dangerous objects and dangerous situations by watching adults avoid those objects and situations. Children even acquire beliefs through observation. Young children are sponges, absorbing everything that goes on around them. They learn by watching as much as by doing.

**meme** A unit of knowledge transmitted within a culture.

**observational learning** The acquisition or modification of a behavior after exposure to at least one performance of that behavior.

**BANDURA'S OBSERVATIONAL STUDIES** The most thorough work on observational learning was conducted in the 1960s by the psychologist Albert Bandura. In a now-classic series of studies, Bandura divided preschool children into two groups. One group watched a film of an adult playing quietly with a large inflatable doll called Bobo. The other group watched a film of the adult attacking Bobo furiously: whacking the doll with a mallet, punching it in the nose, and kicking it around the room. When the children were later allowed to play with a number of toys, including the Bobo doll, those who had seen the more aggressive display were more than twice as likely to act aggressively toward the doll (Bandura, Ross, & Ross, 1961). These results suggest that exposing children to violence may encourage them to act aggressively (**Figure 6.22**).

**MEDIA AND VIOLENCE** On average, a television in the United States is on for 5 or 6 hours per day, and young children often spend more time watching television than doing any other activity, including schoolwork (Roberts, 2000). Worldwide, children consume an average of 3 hours per day of screen media (television, movies, and video games; Groebel, 1998). The most popular media, including Sat-

**FIGURE 6.22 Scientific Method: Bandura's Bobo Doll Studies**

**Hypothesis:** Children can acquire behaviors through observation.

**Research Method:**

1. Two groups of preschool children were shown a film of an adult playing with a large inflatable doll called Bobo.
2. One group saw the adult play quietly with the doll (activity not shown below).
3. The other group saw the adult attack the doll (activity shown in top row below).

**Result:** When children were allowed to play with the doll later, those who had seen the aggressive display were more than twice as likely to act aggressively toward the doll.

**Conclusion:** Exposing children to violence may encourage them to act aggressively.

**Source:** Bandura, A., Ross, D., & Ross, S. (1961). Transmission of aggression through imitation of aggressive models. *Journal of Abnormal and Social Psychology, 66*, 3–11.

urday morning cartoons, contain considerable amounts of violence (Carnagey, Anderson, & Bartholow, 2007).

**FIGURE 6.23 Media and Violent Behavior** Studies have shown that playing violent video games desensitizes children to violence.

Media violence has been found to increase the likelihood of short-term and long-term aggressive and violent behavior (Anderson et al., 2003). In one study, after children played a violent video game for only 20 minutes, they were less physiologically aroused by scenes of real violence. In other words, they had become desensitized to violence, showing fewer helping behaviors and increased aggression (Carnagey, Anderson, & Bushman, 2007; **Figure 6.23**). In another study, Leonard Eron and colleagues found that TV viewing habits at age 8 predicted, for age 30, amounts of both violent behavior and criminal activity (Eron, 1987). A 2002 meta-analysis of studies involving the effects of media violence—taking into account laboratory experiments, field experiments, cross-sectional correlational studies, and longitudinal studies—showed that exposure to violent media increases the likelihood of aggression (Gentile, Saleem, & Anderson, 2007).

A number of problems exist, however, with the studies on this topic. The social psychologist Jonathan Freedman (1984) has noted that many of the so-called aggressive behaviors displayed by children could be interpreted as playful rather than aggressive. A more serious concern is whether the studies generalize to the real world. Viewing a violent film clip in a lab is not like watching TV in one's living room. The film clips used in studies are often brief and extremely violent, and the child watches them alone. In the real world, violent episodes are interspersed with nonviolent material, and children often watch them with others, who may buffer the effect.

Even the longitudinal studies that assess childhood TV watching and later violent behavior fail to empirically support satisfactorily that TV caused the behavior. Extraneous variables, such as personality, poverty, or parental negligence, could have affected both TV viewing habits and violent tendencies. After all, not all of those who view violence on TV become aggressive later in life. Perhaps those who watch excessive amounts of TV, and therefore have fewer opportunities to develop social skills, act aggressively. Correlation does not prove causation (as discussed in Chapter 2, "Research Methodology"; see, for example, "Critical Thinking Skill: Identifying the Need for Control Groups," p. 42). Only through careful laboratory studies in which participants are randomly assigned to experimental conditions can we determine causality. Obviously, it is not practical to assign children randomly to experience different types of media, and it is ethically questionable to expose any children to violence if it might make them more aggressive.

Despite the problems with specific studies, most scientists see a relation between exposure to violence and aggressive behavior. How might media violence promote aggression in children? One possibility is that exposure to massive amounts of violence in movies, which misrepresent the prevalence of violence in real life, leads children to believe that violence is common and inevitable. Because in movies few people are punished for acting violently, children may come to believe that such behaviors are justified (Bushman & Huesmann, 2001). That is, the portrayal of violence in movies teaches children questionable social scripts for solving personal problems. By mentally rehearsing a violent scenario or observing the same violent scenario enacted many times and perhaps in different movies, a child might come to believe that engaging in brutality is an effective way to both solve problems and dispense with annoying people (Huesmann, 1998).

**FIGURE 6.24 Scientific Method: Fear Response in Rhesus Monkeys**

**Hypothesis:** Monkeys can develop phobias about snakes by observing other monkeys reacting fearfully to snakes.

**Research Method:**

1. Two sets of monkeys, one reared in the laboratory and one reared in the wild, had to reach past a clear box to get food.

2. When the clear box contained a snake, the laboratory-reared monkeys reached across the box, but the wild-reared monkeys refused to reach across the box.

**Results:** After watching wild-reared monkeys react, laboratory-reared monkeys no longer reached across the box.

**Conclusion:** Fears can be learned through observation.

**Source:** Mineka, S., Davidson, M., Cook, M., & Keir, R. (1984). Observational conditioning of snake fear in rhesus monkeys. *Journal of Abnormal Psychology, 93*, 355–372.

SOCIAL LEARNING OF FEAR The psychologist Susan Mineka noticed that monkeys raised in laboratories do not fear snakes, whereas monkeys raised in the wild fear snakes intensely. She set out to explore whether monkeys, by observing other monkeys reacting fearfully to snakes, could develop a phobia of snakes. Mineka and colleagues set up an experiment with two groups of rhesus monkeys. One group was reared in the laboratory, and one group was reared in the wild. To obtain food, the monkeys had to reach beyond a clear box that contained either a snake or a neutral object. When a snake was in the box, the wild-reared monkeys did not touch the food. They also showed signs of distress, such as clinging to their cages and making threatening faces. The laboratory-raised monkeys reached past the box even if it contained a snake, and they showed no overt signs of fear. The researchers then showed the laboratory-raised monkeys the wild monkeys' fearful response, to see if it would affect the laboratory monkeys' reactions to the snake. The laboratory monkeys quickly developed a fear of the snakes, and this fear was maintained over a three-month period (Mineka, Davidson, Cook, & Keir, 1984; **Figure 6.24**).

Humans too can learn to fear particular stimuli by observing others. For example, a person might become afraid of a specific neighborhood after watching news video of a person being assaulted there. In fact, people can learn to fear particular things simply by hearing that the things are dangerous. Thus social forces play an important role in the learning of fear (Olsson & Phelps, 2007).

DEMONSTRATION AND IMITATION Because humans can learn through observation, they can be taught many complex skills through demonstration. For instance, parents use slow and exaggerated motions to show their children how to tie their shoes. Some nonhuman animals also appear to teach their offspring certain skills through demonstration, although this idea remains controversial among scientists (Caro & Hauser, 1992). For instance, cheetah mothers seem to facilitate the stages in which their young learn to hunt. At first, the mothers kill their prey. Later, they simply knock down the prey and let their cubs kill it, or they injure the prey to make it easier for the cubs to knock down and kill.

Humans readily imitate the actions of others. Within a few days (or even hours) of birth, human newborns will imitate facial expressions, and they will continue to imitate gestures and other actions as they mature (**Figure 6.25**). These forms of copying resemble the behavior of the monkeys, discussed earlier, who copied Imo the monkey's potato washing. Indeed, one study found that infant macaque monkeys also imitate facial expressions when they are 3 days old (Ferrari et al., 2006). But the issue of whether nonhuman animals engage in imitation in the same way that humans do is controversial. For example, pigeons will more quickly learn to step on bars to receive food pellets when they observe other pigeons receiving food this way (Zentall, Sutton, & Sherburne, 1996). It is possible, however, that in such situations, the animals are learning about features of their environment rather than imitating the particular actions. According to the most recent research, imitation is much less common in nonhuman animals than in humans.

**modeling** The imitation of behavior through observational learning.

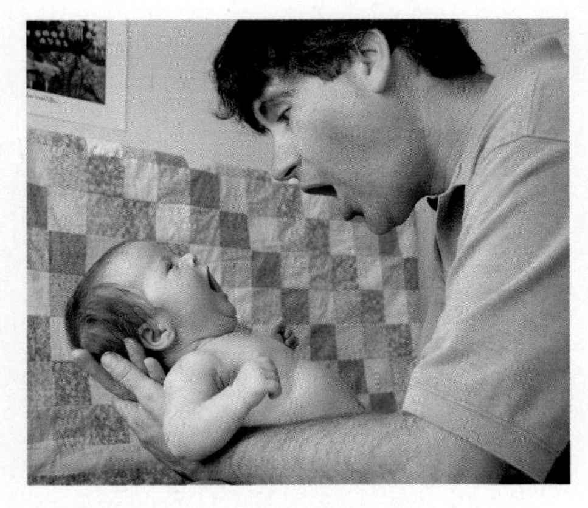

**FIGURE 6.25 Early Modeling** Babies frequently imitate expressions and behaviors.

The imitation of observed behavior is commonly called **modeling.** The term indicates that people are reproducing the behaviors of *models*—those being observed. Modeling in humans is influenced by numerous factors. Generally, we are more likely to imitate the actions of models who are attractive, have high status, and are somewhat similar to ourselves. In addition, modeling is effective only if the observer is physically capable of imitating the behavior. Simply watching Tiger Woods blast 300-yard drives does not mean we could do so if handed a golf club.

The influence that models have on behavior often occurs implicitly, without our being aware that our behaviors are being altered. People might not want to admit that they have changed their ways of speaking or dressing to resemble those of celebrities. Overwhelming evidence says, however, that we imitate what we see in others. We especially imitate the behaviors of people we admire. Adolescents whose favorite actors smoke in movies are much more likely to smoke (Tickle, Sargent, Dalton, Beach, & Heatherton, 2001). The more smoking that adolescents observe in movies, the more positive their attitudes about smoking become and the more likely they are to begin smoking (Sargent et al., 2005). Surprisingly, these effects are strongest among children whose parents do not smoke. Why would this be so? Perhaps what such children learn about smoking comes completely through the media, which tend to glamorize the habit. For example, movies often present smokers as attractive, healthy, and wealthy, not like the typical smoker. Adolescents do not generally decide to smoke after watching one movie's glamorous depiction of smoking. Rather, images of smokers as mature, cool, sexy—things adolescents want to be—shape adolescents' attitudes about smoking and subsequently lead to imitation (**Figure 6.26**). As adolescent viewers learn to associate smoking with people they admire, they incorporate the general message that smoking is desirable.

**FIGURE 6.26 Imitation and Smoking**
This shot appears in the movie *The Killer Inside Me* (2010). The movie's title might be appropriate, because eye-catching images such as this one contribute to viewers' sense that smoking is a mature, cool, sexy behavior worth imitating. Notice how the character's pose is wrapped by the tight framing, the colors, and the swirls. These effects give the impression that the life of Lou Ford (played by Casey Affleck) depends on some mysterious power in his cigarette.

VICARIOUS REINFORCEMENT Another factor that determines whether observers imitate a model is whether the model is reinforced for performing the behavior. In one study, Bandura and colleagues showed children a film of an adult aggressively playing with a Bobo doll, but this time the film ended in one of three different ways (Bandura, Ross, & Ross, 1963). In the first version, a control condition, the adult experienced no consequences for the aggressive behavior. In the second version, the adult was rewarded for the behavior with candy and praise. In the third version, the adult was punished for the behavior by being both spanked and verbally reprimanded. When subsequently allowed to play with the Bobo doll, the children who observed the model being rewarded were much more likely to be aggressive toward the doll than were the children in the control group. In contrast, those who saw the model being punished were less likely to be aggressive than were those in the control group. Through **vicarious learning,** people learn about an action's consequences by watching others being rewarded or punished for performing the action.

These findings do not mean that the children who did not show aggression did not learn the behavior. Later, all the children were offered small gifts to perform the model's actions, and all performed the actions reliably. As noted earlier, a key distinction in learning is between the *acquisition* of a behavior and its *performance.* Here, all the children acquired the behavior. But only those who saw the model being rewarded performed the behavior—at least until the children themselves were rewarded. Direct rewards prompted the children in the control group to reveal the behavior they had acquired.

**vicarious learning** Learning the consequences of an action by watching others being rewarded or punished for performing the action.

MIRROR NEURONS What happens in the brain during imitation learning? When a monkey observes another monkey reaching for an object, **mirror neurons** in the observing monkey's brain become activated (Rizzolatti, Fadiga, Gallese, & Fogassi, 1996). These same (mirror) neurons would be activated if the observing monkey

**mirror neurons** Neurons that are activated when one observes another individual engage in an action and when one performs the action that was observed.

performed the behavior. Mirror neurons are especially likely to become activated when a monkey observes the target monkey engaging in movement that has some goal. For example, the target monkey might be reaching to grasp an object. Neither the sight of the object alone nor the sight of the target monkey at rest leads to activation of these mirror neurons.

Brain imaging techniques have identified similar mirror neurons in humans (Rizzolatti & Craighero, 2004). Thus every time you observe another person engaging in an action, similar neural circuits are firing in your brain and in the other person's brain. Scientists are debating the function of mirror neurons. This system may serve as the basis of imitation learning, but the firing of mirror neurons in the observer's brain does not always lead to imitative behavior in the observer. Therefore, some theorists speculate, mirror neurons may help us explain and predict others' behavior. In other words, mirror neurons may allow us to step into the shoes of people we observe so we can better understand those people's actions. One speculation is that mirror neurons are the neural basis for empathy, the emotional response of feeling what other people are experiencing.

Humans also have mirror neurons for mouth movements, and these neurons are stimulated when observers see a mouth move in a way typical of chewing or speaking (Ferrari, Gallese, Rizzolatti, & Fogassi, 2003). This phenomenon has led to speculation that mirror neurons are not just important for imitation learning. They may also play a role in humans' ability to communicate through language. Mirror neurons may be a brain system that creates a link between the sender of a message and the receiver of that message. Rizzolatti and Arbib (1998) have proposed that the mirror neuron system evolved to make language possible. Their theory relies on the idea that speech evolved mainly from gestures. Indeed, people readily understand many nonverbal behaviors, such as waving or thrusting a fist in the air. Evidence indicates that listening to sentences that describe actions activates the same brain regions active when those actions are observed (Tettamanti et al., 2005). Even reading words that represent actions leads to brain activity in relevant motor regions, as when the word *lick* activates brain regions that control tongue movements (Hauk, Johnsrude, & Pulvermüller, 2004).

The idea of mirror neurons has been expanded to include even our understanding of other people's mental states. There are a number of questions, however, about the meaning of brain activity observed during mirror neuron studies, such as whether brain activity reflects prior learning rather than imitation (Hickok, 2009). As the evidence accumulates, support grows for at least this idea: Mirror neurons in brain regions responsible for movement track the behaviors of targets as those behaviors unfold over time (Press, Cook, Blakemore, & Kilner, 2011).

**Summing Up**

## How Does Watching Others Affect Learning?

Humans learn behavior by observing the behavior of others. We acquire basic and complex skills, beliefs, attitudes, habits, and emotional responses by observing others—for example, parents, peers, teachers, and individuals in popular media. We tend to imitate models who are attractive, who have high status, who are similar to ourselves, and whom we admire. Through vicarious learning, we learn about an action's consequences. We are more likely to perform a behavior when a model has been rewarded for the behavior than when a model has been punished for the behavior. Mirror neurons, which fire when a behavior is observed and performed, may be the neural basis of imitation learning.

## Measuring Up

1. The critical finding from Bandura's Bobo doll research was that ________.
   a. children who viewed a model being rewarded for acting aggressively toward the doll exhibited more aggressive behaviors toward the doll than did children in the control condition
   b. using a control group is vital
   c. children who learned to exhibit aggression toward the Bobo doll later generalized this behavior to their own dolls
   d. it allowed researchers to prove that watching violence on television causes children to become more violent

2. Mirror neurons ______________.
   a. fire when we are watching behavior in other people
   b. connect to sensory neurons, except in olfaction because little or no motion occurs when people smell an odor
   c. are probably more important in learning a second language than in learning a first language
   d. are among the smallest neurons in the human body

**Answers:** 1. a. children who viewed a model being rewarded for acting aggressively toward the doll exhibited more aggressive behaviors toward the doll than did children in the control condition.
2. a. fire when we are watching behavior in other people.

# 6.4 What Is the Biological Basis of Learning?

### Learning Objectives

- Discuss the role of dopamine and the nucleus accumbens in the experience of reinforcement.
- Define habituation, sensitization, and long-term potentiation.
- Describe the neural basis of habituation, sensitization, long-term potentiation, and fear conditioning.

Scientists have long understood the basics of learning: The brain undergoes relatively permanent changes as a result of exposure to environmental events. That is, your experience of the world changes your brain, and these changes reflect learning.

Over the past few decades, psychologists have made numerous discoveries about the biological basis of learning. For instance, researchers have explored the brain processes that underlie reinforcement. They have demonstrated that similar brain activity occurs for most rewarding experiences. Likewise, researchers have provided considerable information about how learning occurs at the neuronal level. This section discusses the findings regarding learning's biological basis that have emerged through the methods of psychological science.

## Dopamine Activity Underlies Reinforcement

As noted earlier, people often use the term *reward* as a synonym for positive reinforcement. By contrast, Skinner and other traditional behaviorists defined reinforcement strictly in terms of whether it increased behavior. They were relatively uninterested in *why* it increased behavior. For instance, they carefully avoided any speculation about whether subjective experiences had anything to do with behavior. After all, they believed that mental states were impossible to study empirically.

Studies of learning have made clear, however, that positive reinforcement works in two ways: It provides the subjective experience of pleasure, and it increases wanting for the object or event that produced the reward. More generally, behaviors that have favorable outcomes create responses in the brain that support the recurrence of those behaviors. One important component of the neural basis of reinforcement is the neurotransmitter dopamine. As discussed in Chapter 5, dopamine is involved in addictive behavior, especially in terms of increased wanting for the addictive substance. Research over the past 50 years has shown that dopamine plays an important role in reinforcement (Schultz, 2010; Wise & Rompre, 1989).

**PLEASURE CENTERS** One of the earliest discoveries that pointed to the role of neural mechanisms in reinforcement came about because of a small surgical error. In the early 1950s, the brain researchers Peter Milner and James Olds were testing whether electrical stimulation to a specific brain region would facilitate learning. To see whether the learning they observed was caused by brain activity or by the aversive qualities of the electrical stimulus, Olds and Milner administered electrical stimulation to rats' brains only while the rats were in one specific location in the cage. The logic was that if the application of electricity was aversive, the rats would selectively avoid that location. Fortunately for science, Milner and Olds administered each shock to the wrong part of the brain. Instead of avoiding the area of the cage associated with electrical stimulation, the rats quickly came back. Apparently, they were looking for more stimulation!

Olds and Milner then set up an experiment to see whether rats would press a lever to self-administer shock to specific sites in their brains. This procedure was subsequently referred to as *intracranial self-stimulation* (*ICSS;* **Figure 6.27**). The rats self-administered electricity to their brains with gusto, pressing the lever hundreds of times per hour (Olds & Milner, 1954). Olds and Milner referred to brain regions that support ICSS as *pleasure centers.* Although behaviorists objected to the term *pleasure,* ICSS was a powerful reinforcer. In one experiment, rats that had been on a near-starvation diet for 10 days were given a choice between food and the opportunity to administer ICSS. They chose the electrical stimulation more than 80 percent of the time. Deprived rats also chose electrical stimulation over water or receptive sexual partners. They even crossed a painful electrified grid to receive ICSS. Rats will continue intracranial self-stimulation until they collapse from exhaustion. Monkeys tested in similar studies have been found to press a bar for electrical stimulation up to 8,000 times per hour (Olds, 1962)!

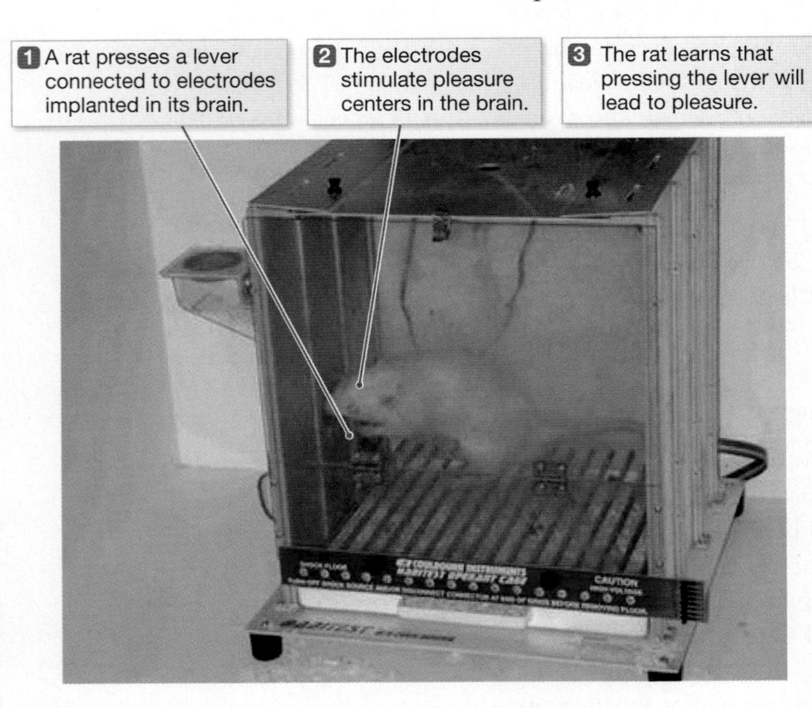


**FIGURE 6.27 Intracranial Self-Stimulation (ICSS)** Here a rat presses a lever to administer ICSS.

Most psychologists believe that ICSS acts on the same brain regions as those activated by natural reinforcers, such as food, water, and sex. When electrical stimulation is applied to the pleasure center in a rat and then turned off, the rat will engage in a naturally motivated behavior. For example, the rat might eat, drink, or copulate with an available partner. Also, depriving an animal of food or of water leads to increased ICSS. This finding is taken to indicate that the animal is trying to obtain the same reward experience it would obtain from drinking water or eating. Finally, the neural mechanisms underlying both ICSS and natural reward appear to use the same neurotransmitter, namely, dopamine. This evidence suggests that dopamine serves as the neurochemical basis of positive reinforcement in operant conditioning. For instance, ICSS activates dopamine receptors. Interfering with dopamine eliminates self-stimulation as well as naturally motivated behaviors, such as eating, drinking, and copulating.

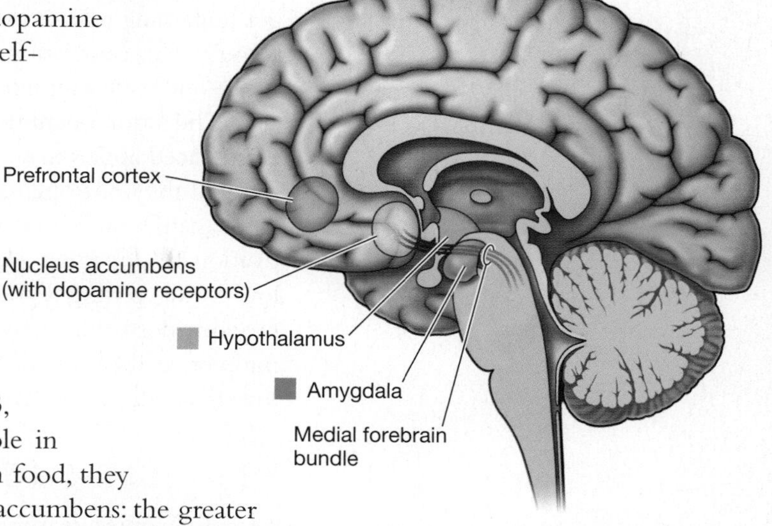


**FIGURE 6.28 Pleasure Centers of the Brain**

**DOPAMINE AND REWARD** The nucleus accumbens is a subcortical brain region that is part of the limbic system. Reward results from activation of dopamine neurons in the nucleus accumbens (**Figure 6.28**). Other brain regions, such as the amygdala and the prefrontal cortex, are involved, as are other neurotransmitters, such as endorphins (discussed in Chapter 3, "Biology and Behavior"). Still, dopamine plays a key role in reward (Volkow et al., 2011). When hungry rats are given food, they experience an increased dopamine release in the nucleus accumbens: the greater the hunger, the greater the dopamine release (Rolls, Burton, & Mora, 1980). Food tastes better when you are hungry, and water is more rewarding when you are thirsty, because more dopamine is released under deprived conditions than under nondeprived conditions. Even looking at funny cartoons activates the nucleus accumbens (Mobbs, Greicius, Abdel-Azim, Menon, & Reiss, 2003). Have you ever experienced the chills while listening to a favorite piece of music—a tingling sense that feels like a shiver down the spine and that might give you goose bumps? Using PET imaging and fMRI, researchers have shown that when people experience optimal pleasure while listening to music, there is dopamine activity in the nucleus accumbens (Salimpoor, Benovoy, Larcher, Dagher, & Zatorre, 2011).

In operant conditioning, dopamine release sets the value of a reinforcer. Drugs that block dopamine's effects disrupt operant conditioning. In one study, rats were taught to run a maze to receive electrical stimulation; but after being injected with a dopamine blocker, the rats would not run the maze until the electrical current was turned up (Stellar, Kelley, & Corbett, 1983). The blocker decreased the value of the reinforcement. Dopamine blockers are often given to individuals with Tourette's syndrome, a motor control disorder, to help them regulate their involuntary body movements. These individuals often have trouble staying on their drug regimens, however, because they feel the drugs prevent them from enjoying life. Conversely, as you might expect, drugs that enhance dopamine activation, such as cocaine and amphetamines, increase the reward value of stimuli.

Until recently, psychologists believed that rewards increased behavior primarily because of the pleasure those rewards produce. Robinson and Berridge (1993) introduced an important distinction between the *wanting* and *liking* aspects of reward. With drugs, for instance, wanting refers to the desire or craving a user has to take the substance. Liking refers to the subjective sense of pleasure the user receives from consuming the substance. Although wanting and liking often go together, there are circumstances under which wanting occurs without liking (Berridge et al., 2010; Kringelbach & Berridge, 2009). For example, a smoker may desire a cigarette but then not particularly enjoy smoking it. As mentioned in Chapter 5, dopamine appears to be especially important for the wanting aspect of reward.

**SECONDARY REINFORCERS ALSO RELY ON DOPAMINE** Natural reinforcers appear to signal reward directly. Primarily, they work through the activation of dopamine receptors in the nucleus accumbens. But what about secondary reinforcers, such as money or good grades? Neutral stimuli that at first fail to trigger dopamine release may do so readily after they are paired with unconditioned stimuli. This association comes about through a classical-conditioning process.

In one study, monkeys were presented with a trapdoor that opened occasionally. The door opening did not activate dopamine activity. The experimenters then placed apples in the doorway. As a result of this placement, the monkeys associated the door opening with the unconditioned stimulus of eating a tasty food. After many conditioning trials, the door opening led on its own to increased activation of dopamine (Ljungberg, Apicella, & Schultz, 1992). Similarly, seeing a loved one, getting a good grade, or receiving a paycheck may be conditioned to produce dopamine activation. Money is an excellent example of a secondary reinforcer, as mentioned earlier, and anticipated monetary rewards have been found to activate dopamine systems (Knutson, Fong, Adams, Varner, & Hommer, 2001).

## Habituation and Sensitization Are Simple Models of Learning

As noted earlier, learning involves relatively permanent changes in the brain, and these changes result from exposure to environmental events. The roots of this idea can be traced back to numerous scientists, including the researcher Richard Semon. In 1904, Semon proposed that memories are stored through changes in the nervous system. He called the storage of learned material an *engram,* a term later popularized by the psychologist Karl Lashley.

**FIGURE 6.29 Simple Model of Learning** The aplysia, a marine invertebrate, is used to study the neurochemical basis of learning.

In 1948, the psychologist Donald Hebb proposed that learning results from alterations in synaptic connections. According to Hebb, when one neuron excites another, some change takes place that strengthens the connection between the two neurons. Subsequently, the firing of one neuron becomes increasingly likely to cause the firing of the other neuron. In other words, basically, "cells that fire together wire together" (a concept discussed in Chapter 3, "Biology and Behavior"). Hebb did not have the technology to examine whether his hypothesis was valid, but his basic theory has been confirmed.

What activity at the synapse leads to learning? One answer is found in research using simple invertebrates such as the aplysia, a small marine snail that eats seaweed (**Figure 6.29**). The aplysia is an excellent species to use in the study of learning because it has relatively few neurons, and some of its neurons are large enough to be seen without a microscope (Kandel, Schwartz, & Jessell, 1995). The neurobiologist Eric Kandel and colleagues have used the aplysia to study the neural basis of two types of simple learning: *habituation* and *sensitization*. As a result of this research, Kandel received a Nobel Prize in Physiology or Medicine in 2000.

**Habituation** is a decrease in behavioral response after repeated exposure to nonthreatening stimuli. As discussed earlier, an animal will orient, or pay attention, to a novel stimulus. Through the process of habituation, if the stimulus is neither harmful nor rewarding, the animal learns to ignore it.

**habituation** A decrease in behavioral response after repeated exposure to a nonthreatening stimulus.

We constantly habituate to meaningless events around us. For instance, sit back and listen to the background sounds wherever you are. Perhaps you can hear a clock, or a computer fan, or your roommates playing music in the next room. Had you really noticed this noise before being directed to or had you habituated to it? Habituation can be demonstrated quite easily by repeatedly touching an aplysia. The first few touches cause it to withdraw its gills. After about 10 touches, it stops responding, and this lack of response lasts about 2 to 3 hours. Repeated habituation trials can lead to a state of habituation that lasts several weeks.

**Sensitization** is an increase in behavioral response after exposure to a threatening stimulus. For instance, imagine that while studying you smell something burning. You probably will not habituate to this smell. You might focus even greater attention on your sense of smell to assess the possible threat of fire, and you will be highly vigilant for any indication of smoke or of flames. In general, sensitization leads to heightened responsiveness to other stimuli. Giving a strong electric shock to an aplysia's tail leads to sensitization. Following the shock, a mild touch anywhere on the body will cause the aplysia to withdraw its gills.

Kandel's research on the aplysia has shown that alterations in the functioning of the synapse lead to habituation and sensitization. For both types of simple learning, presynaptic neurons alter their neurotransmitter release. A reduction in neurotransmitter release leads to habituation. An increase in neurotransmitter release leads to sensitization. Knowing the neural basis of simple learning gives us the building blocks to understand more-complex learning processes in both human and nonhuman animals.

## Long-Term Potentiation Is a Candidate for the Neural Basis of Learning

To understand how learning occurs in the brain, researchers have investigated *long-term potentiation*. This phenomenon was first observed in a laboratory in Oslo, Norway, in the late 1960s. The word *potentiate* means to strengthen, to make something more potent. **Long-term potentiation (LTP)** is the strengthening of a synaptic connection, resulting in postsynaptic neurons that are more easily activated.

To demonstrate long-term potentiation, researchers first establish the extent to which electrically stimulating one neuron leads to neural firing in a second neuron. (Recall from Chapter 3 that neurons fire when they receive sufficient stimulation.) The researchers then provide intense electrical stimulation to the first neuron. For example, they might give it 100 pulses of electricity in 5 seconds. Finally, they readminister a single electrical pulse to measure the extent of the second neuron's firing. LTP occurs when the intense electrical stimulation increases the likelihood that stimulating one neuron leads to increased firing in the second neuron (**Figure 6.30**). In the aplysia, habituation and sensitization are each due to changes in the release of a neurotransmitter from the presynaptic neuron. LTP results from changes in the postsynaptic neuron that make it more easily activated.

Numerous lines of evidence support the idea that long-term potentiation is involved in learning and memory (Beggs et al., 1999; Cooke & Bliss, 2006). For instance, LTP effects are most easily observed in brain sites known to be involved in learning and memory, such as the hippocampus. Moreover, the same drugs that improve memory also lead to increased LTP, and those that block memory also block LTP. Finally, behavioral conditioning produces neurochemical effects nearly identical to LTP.

The process of long-term potentiation also supports Hebb's contention that learning results from a strengthening of synaptic connections between neurons that fire together. Hebb's rule—"cells that fire together wire together"—can be used to explain a variety of learning phenomena. Consider classical conditioning. Neurons that signal the unconditioned stimulus are active at the same time as those that

**sensitization** An increase in behavioral response after exposure to a threatening stimulus.

**long-term potentiation (LTP)** The strengthening of a synaptic connection, making the postsynaptic neurons more easily activated.

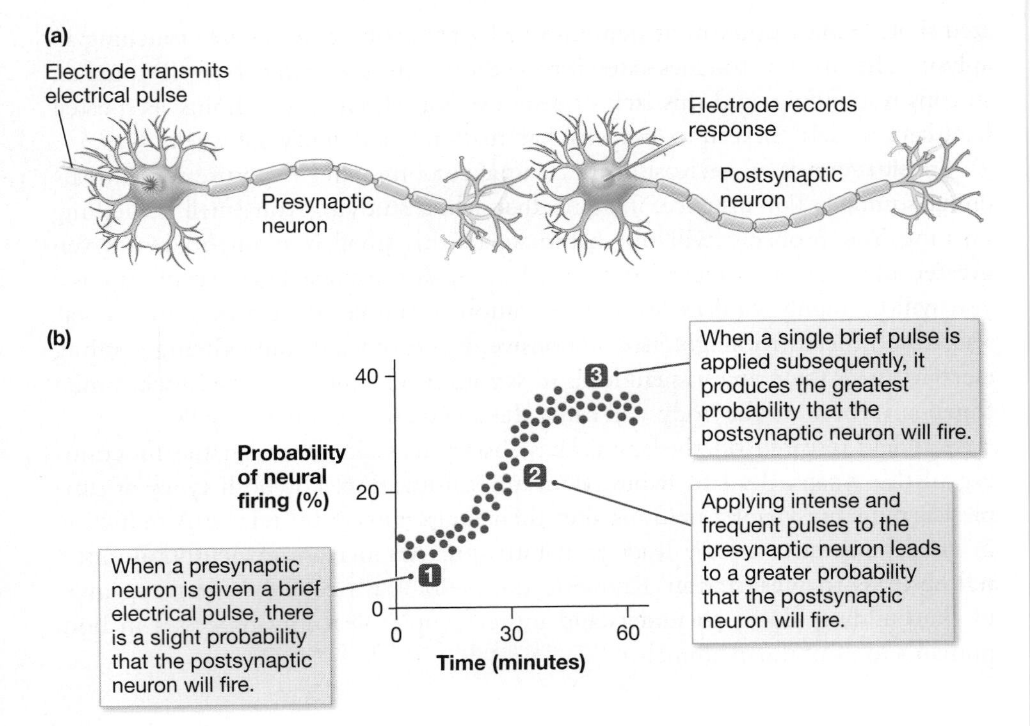


**FIGURE 6.30 Long-Term Potentiation (LTP)** **(a)** This diagram depicts the basic process used in testing for LTP between two neurons. **(b)** This graph shows the steps involved in LTP.

signal the conditioned stimulus. Over repeated trials, the synapses that connect these two events become strengthened. As a result of this strengthened synaptic connection, when one neuron fires, the other fires automatically. In other words, the conditioned response results from the increased connection between the two neurons.

**LTP AND THE NMDA RECEPTOR** Over the last decade, researchers have made considerable progress in understanding how long-term potentiation works. The *NMDA receptor* (a type of glutamate receptor) is required for it and has a special property: It opens only if a nearby neuron fires at the same time. This phenomenon supports Hebb's rule.

The finding that the NMDA receptor is involved in LTP led researchers to examine genetic processes that might influence learning. For instance, the neuroscientist Joseph Tsien modified genes in mice to make the genes' NMDA receptors more efficient. When tested in standard learning tasks, these transgenic mice performed amazingly well, learning novel tasks more quickly and showing increased fear conditioning (Tsien, 2000). The mice were such great learners that Tsien named them "Doogie mice," after the prime-time television character Doogie Howser, a boy doctor (**Figure 6.31**).

**FIGURE 6.31 Doogie Mice** Doogie mice (such as the one pictured here) and regular mice were given a test of learning and memory. In the first part, both kinds of mice had the chance to familiarize themselves with two objects. In the second part, the researchers replaced one of the objects with a novel object. The Doogie mice quickly recognized the change, but the normal mice did not recognize it.

Might we be able to modify human genes so that people learn more quickly? This fascinating question raises many ethical issues, but some pharmaceutical companies are exploring drugs that might enhance the learning process by manipulating gene expression or activating NMDA receptors. If successful, such treatments might prove valuable for treating patients with diseases such as Alzheimer's. This especially active area of research is increasing our understanding of how genes, neurotransmitters, and the environment interact to produce learning.

**FEAR CONDITIONING** Long-term potentiation was first observed in the hippocampus, but recent evidence indicates that fear conditioning may induce LTP in the amygdala (Kim & Jung, 2006). In fact, there is substantial evidence that the amygdala is crucial for fear conditioning. If a particular part of the amygdala is removed, an animal is unable to learn that one particular event (such as an electric shock) will follow another one (such as a tone; Davis, 1997). The neuroscientist Joseph LeDoux and his students have demonstrated that fear conditioning and the induction of LTP lead to similar changes in amygdala neurons. This finding suggests that fear conditioning might produce long-lasting learning through the induction of LTP (Rogan, Stäubli, & LeDoux, 1997; Sigurdsson, Doyère, Cain, & LeDoux, 2007).

As discussed earlier, fear learning can occur through observation. For example, monkeys can learn to fear objects by seeing other monkeys fear those objects. This social learning of fear likely relies on the amygdala. In one imaging study, research participants watched another person experience and display distress when receiving an electric shock paired with a conditioned stimulus. The observing participants subsequently were presented with the CS. To ensure that all their learning was vicarious, however, they did not receive a shock. During the observation period and during the trials when the observers were presented with the CS, the investigators found heightened activity in the amygdala (Olsson, Nearing, & Phelps, 2007). This finding suggests that similar mechanisms are involved in conditioned and observational fear learning.

## Summing Up

### What Is the Biological Basis of Learning?

Researchers are rapidly identifying the neurophysiological basis of learning. Research has demonstrated that activation of dopamine receptors in the nucleus accumbens is associated with the experience of reinforcement. Research has also supported Hebb's theory that neurons that fire together wire together. Kandel's work on the aplysia has shown that habituation and sensitization, two simple forms of learning, occur through alteration in neurotransmitter release. Through long-term potentiation, intense stimulation of neurons strengthens synapses, increasing the likelihood that one neuron's activation will increase the firing of other neurons. LTP occurs when NMDA receptors are stimulated by nearby neurons. LTP in the amygdala appears to play a role in fear conditioning.

## Measuring Up

1. What can we learn from the superlearner Doogie mice?
   a. NMDA receptors are important in producing learning.
   b. A breed of extremely smart mice provides a good model for understanding how some people are able to become doctors at a young age.
   c. Neurons that fire together wire together.
   d. Animal models of human learning cannot account for mirror neurons' action.
2. What is the evidence that dopamine is a critical neurotransmitter for the effects of reinforcers on behavior?
   a. The increased administration of self-stimulation suppresses dopamine release.
   b. Rats will work continuously to deliver electrical stimulation to a portion of the brain that uses dopamine in its neural processes.
   c. When rats press a lever to self-administer dopamine directly into the brain, they stop eating and drinking.
   d. When rats receive dopamine, they increase the rate at which they deliver intracranial self-stimulation.

**Answers:** 1. a. NMDA receptors are important in producing learning.
2. b. Rats will work continuously to deliver electrical stimulation to a portion of the brain that uses dopamine in its neural processes.

**Visit StudySpace to access free review materials, such as:**

- complete study outlines
- vocabulary flashcards of all key terms
- additional chapter review quizzes

## Chapter Summary

### 6.1 What Ideas Guide the Study of Learning?

- **Learning Results from Experience:** Learning is a relatively enduring change in behavior that results from experience. Learning enables animals to better adapt to the environment, and thus it facilitates survival. Learning involves understanding the associations between events. These associations are acquired through classical conditioning and operant conditioning.
- **Behavioral Responses Are Conditioned:** Pavlov established the principles of classical conditioning. Through classical conditioning, associations are made between two stimuli, such as the clicking of a metronome and a piece of meat. What is learned is that one stimulus predicts another. Acquisition, extinction, spontaneous recovery, generalization, discrimination, and second-order conditioning are processes associated with classical conditioning.
- **Phobias and Addictions Have Learned Components:** Phobias are learned fear associations. Similarly, addiction involves a conditioned response, which can result in withdrawal symptoms at the mere sight of drug paraphernalia. Addiction also involves tolerance: the need for more of a drug, particularly when that drug is administered in a familiar context, to get a high comparable to the one obtained earlier.
- **Classical Conditioning Involves More Than Events Occurring at the Same Time:** Not all stimuli are equally potent in producing conditioning. Animals are biologically prepared to make connections between stimuli that are potentially dangerous. This biological preparedness to fear specific objects helps animals avoid potential dangers, and thus it facilitates survival.
- **Learning Involves Cognition:** Animals are predisposed to form predictions that enhance survival, such as judging the likelihood that food will continue to be available at one location. The Rescorla-Wagner model maintains that the strength of a CS-US association is determined by the extent to which the US is unexpected or surprising.

### 6.2 How Does Operant Conditioning Differ from Classical Conditioning?

- **Reinforcement Increases Behavior:** A behavior's positive consequences will make it more likely to occur. Shaping is a procedure in which successive approximations of a behavior are reinforced, leading to the desired behavior. Reinforcers may be primary (those that satisfy biological needs) or secondary (those that do not directly satisfy biological needs).
- **Both Reinforcement and Punishment Can Be Positive or Negative:** For positive reinforcement and positive punishment, a stimulus is delivered after the animal responds. For negative reinforcement and negative punishment, a stimulus is removed after the animal responds. Positive and negative reinforcement increase the likelihood that a behavior will recur. Positive and negative punishment decrease the likelihood that a behavior will recur.
- **Operant Conditioning Is Influenced by Schedules of Reinforcement:** Learning occurs in response to continuous reinforcement and partial reinforcement. Partial reinforcement may be delivered on a ratio schedule or an interval schedule. Moreover, partial reinforcement may be fixed or variable. Partial reinforcement administered on a variable-ratio schedule is particularly resistant to extinction. Behavior modification involves the use of operant conditioning to eliminate unwanted behaviors and replace them with desirable behaviors.
- **Biology and Cognition Influence Operant Conditioning:** An organism's biological makeup restricts the types of behaviors the organism can learn. Latent learning takes place without reinforcement. Latent learning may not influence behavior until a reinforcer is introduced.

### 6.3 How Does Watching Others Affect Learning?

- **Learning Can Be Passed On through Cultural Transmission:** Memes (units of knowledge transmitted within a culture) are analogous to genes in that memes are selectively passed on from generation to generation.
- **Learning Can Occur through Observation and Imitation:** Observational learning is a powerful adaptive tool. Humans and other animals learn by watching the behavior of others. The imitation of observed behavior is referred to as modeling. Vicarious learning occurs when people learn about an action's consequences by observing others being reinforced or punished for their behavior. Mirror neurons are activated when a behavior is observed and performed and may be the neural basis of imitation learning.

### 6.4 What Is the Biological Basis of Learning?

- **Dopamine Activity Underlies Reinforcement:** The brain has specialized centers that produce pleasure when stimulated. Behaviors that activate these centers are reinforced. The nucleus accumbens (a part of the limbic system) has dopamine receptors, which are activated by pleasurable behaviors. Through conditioning, secondary reinforcers can also activate dopamine receptors.
- **Habituation and Sensitization Are Simple Models of Learning:** Habituation is a decrease in behavioral response after repeated exposure to a nonthreatening stimulus. In contrast, sensitization is an increase in behavioral response after exposure to a new and threatening stimulus.

- **Long-Term Potentiation Is a Candidate for the Neural Basis of Learning:** Long-term potentiation refers to the strengthening of synaptic connections. Long-term potentiation has been observed in the hippocampus (learning and memory) and amygdala (fear conditioning). The receptor NMDA is involved in long-term potentiation.

## Key Terms

acquisition, p. 229
behavior modification, p. 247
classical conditioning (Pavlovian conditioning), p. 227
cognitive map, p. 248
conditioned response (CR), p. 227
conditioned stimulus (CS), p. 227
continuous reinforcement, p. 244
extinction, p. 229
fixed schedule, p. 245
habituation, p. 260
interval schedule, p. 245
latent learning, p. 249
law of effect, p. 240
learning, p. 225
long-term potentiation (LTP), p. 261
meme, p. 251
mirror neurons, p. 255
modeling, p. 254
negative punishment, p. 243
negative reinforcement, p. 242
observational learning, p. 251
operant conditioning (instrumental conditioning), p. 239
partial reinforcement, p. 245
partial-reinforcement extinction effect, p. 246
phobia, p. 231
positive punishment, p. 243
positive reinforcement, p. 242
ratio schedule, p. 245
reinforcer, p. 240
Rescorla-Wagner model, p. 236
sensitization, p. 261
shaping, p. 241
spontaneous recovery, p. 230
stimulus discrimination, p. 230
stimulus generalization, p. 230
unconditioned response (UR), p. 227
unconditioned stimulus (US), p. 227
variable schedule, p. 245
vicarious learning, p. 255

## Practice Test

1. Every night for a few weeks, you feed your pet rat while watching the evening news. Eventually, the rat learns to sit by its food dish when the news program's opening theme song plays. In this example of classical conditioning, what are the US, UR, CS, and CR?

2. At a psychology lecture, each student receives 10 lemon wedges. The professor instructs the students to bite into a lemon wedge anytime a large blue dot appears within her slide presentation. Nearly every time the students bite into lemons, their mouths pucker. The 11th time a blue dot appears on the screen, many students' mouths pucker visibly. In this case, what are the US, UR, CS, and CR?

3. A few minutes later in that same psychology lecture, the professor projects the image of a turquoise dot. How will the students likely respond to this image?
   a. The students will not experience puckering responses, because the conditioned association has been extinguished.
   b. The students will not experience puckering responses, because they are able to discriminate between the two dot colors.
   c. The students will experience puckering responses, because of stimulus generalization.

4. Which pairing of stimuli will most quickly create a learned association?
   a. Eating a box of raisins and experiencing extreme nausea at the same time.
   b. Eating a box of raisins and experiencing extreme nausea a few hours later.
   c. Seeing clouds in the sky and experiencing a severe rain shower a few minutes later.
   d. Seeing clouds in the sky and experiencing a severe rain shower a few hours later.

5. Identify each statement as an example of negative punishment, positive punishment, negative reinforcement, or positive reinforcement.
   a. Whenever a puppy barks, it gets its belly rubbed, so it barks more.
   b. A professor directs all questions to the student who arrives late to class.
   c. A person with a clean driving record receives a reduced insurance premium.
   d. Your date arrives an hour late, and you refuse to speak for the rest of the evening.

The answer key for the Practice Tests can be found at the back of the book. It also includes answers to the green caption questions.

# 7

# Attention and Memory

HENRY MOLAISON, ONE OF THE MOST FAMOUS PEOPLE IN MEMORY RESEARCH, was born in 1926 and died in 2008. In vital ways, though, his world stopped in 1953, when he was 27.

As a young man, Molaison suffered from severe epilepsy. Every day, he had several grand mal seizures, an affliction that made it impossible for him to lead a normal life. Seizures are

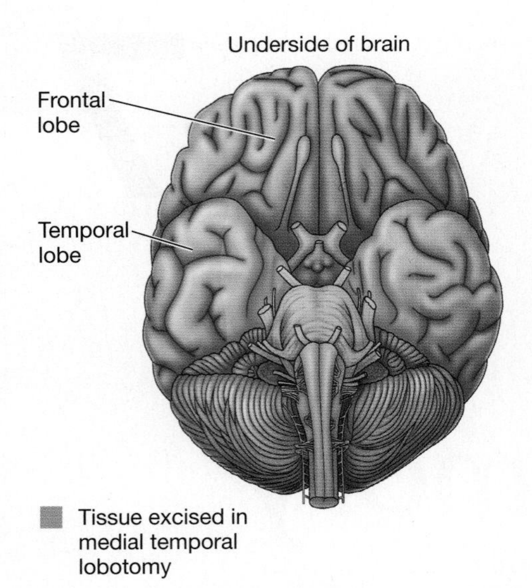


**FIGURE 7.1 A Drawing of H.M.'s Brain** The portions of the medial temporal lobe that were removed from H.M.'s brain are indicated by the shaded regions.

**FIGURE 7.2 Henry Molaison (H.M.)** Known to the world only by his initials, Molaison became one of the most famous people in memory research by participating in countless experiments. He died at a nursing home on December 2, 2008.

uncontrolled random firing of groups of neurons, and they can spread across the brain. Molaison's seizures originated in the temporal lobes of his brain and would spread from there. Because the anticonvulsive drugs available at that time could not control his seizures, surgery was the only choice for treatment. The reasoning behind this surgery was that if the seizure-causing portion of his brain was removed, he would stop having seizures. In September 1953, Molaison's doctors removed parts of his medial temporal lobes, including the hippocampus (**Figure 7.1**). The surgery quieted his seizures, but it had an unexpected and very unfortunate side effect: Molaison lost the ability to remember things over long periods of time.

Until his death, the larger world did not know Molaison's real name or what he looked like (**Figure 7.2**), because his privacy was guarded by the researchers who studied his memory. H.M., as he was known, never remembered the day of the week, what year it was, or his own age. Still, he could talk about his childhood, explain the rules of baseball, and describe members of his family, things he knew at the time of the surgery. According to the psychologists who tested him, his IQ was slightly above average. His thinking abilities remained intact. He could hold a normal conversation as long as he was not distracted, but he forgot the conversation in a minute or less. H.M.'s ability to hold a conversation showed that he was still able to remember things for short periods. After all, to grasp the meaning of spoken language, a person needs to remember the words recently spoken, such as the beginning and end of a sentence. But H.M. did not appear to remember any new information over time. People who worked with H.M. — such as the psychologist Brenda Milner, who followed his case for over 40 years — had to introduce themselves to him every time they met. As H.M. put it, "Every day is alone in itself." Because of his profound memory loss, he remembered nothing from minute to minute. But he knew that he remembered nothing. How could this have been the case? What did it mean for H.M. to have memory at all? ■

**Learning Objectives**

- Describe the three phases of memory.
- Identify brain regions involved in learning and memory.
- Describe the processes of consolidation and reconsolidation.

# 7.1 What Is Memory?

## Memory Is the Nervous System's Capacity to Acquire and Retain Usable Skills and Knowledge

H.M. learned some new things, although he did not know he had learned them. Most impressively, he learned new motor tasks. In one series of tests, he was required to trace the outline of a star while watching his hand in a mirror. Most people do poorly the first few times they try this difficult task. On each of three consecutive days, H.M. was asked to trace the star 10 times. His performance improved over the three days, and this result indicated that he had retained some information about the task. On each day, however, H.M. could not recall ever performing the task previously. His ability to learn new motor skills enabled him to get a job at a factory, where he mounted cigarette lighters on cardboard cases. But his condition left him unable to describe the job or the workplace. Studies of H.M.'s strange condition have contributed many clues to how memories are stored — normally and abnormally — in the brain.

Normally, each of us remembers millions of pieces of information, from the trivial to the vital. Each person's entire sense of self, or identity, is made up of what that person knows from memories, from his or her recollections of personal experiences and of things learned from others. Thus **memory** is the nervous system's capacity to acquire and retain skills and knowledge. This capacity enables organisms to take information from experiences and store it for retrieval later.

Yet memory does not work like a digital video camera that faithfully captures and just as faithfully retrieves the events its operator experiences. Instead, memories are often incomplete, biased, and distorted. Two people's memories for the same event can differ vastly, because each person stores and retrieves memories of the event distinctively. We tend to remember personally relevant information and filter our memories through our various perceptions and our knowledge of related events. In other words, memories are stories that can be altered subtly by the process of recollection.

In addition, all experiences are not equally likely to be remembered. Some life events pass swiftly, leaving no lasting memory. Others are remembered but later forgotten. Still others remain for a lifetime. We have multiple memory systems, and each memory system has its own "rules." For example, some brain processes underlie memory for information we will need to retrieve in 10 seconds. Those processes operate differently from the processes that underlie memory for information we will need to retrieve in 10 years. The following section looks at psychologists' basic model of how the mind remembers: the *information processing model.*

**memory** The nervous system's capacity to acquire and retain skills and knowledge.

**encoding** The processing of information so that it can be stored.

**storage** The retention of encoded representations over time.

## Memory Is the Processing of Information

Since the late 1960s, most psychologists have viewed memory as a form of information processing. In this model, the ways that memory works are analogous to the ways computers process information. A computer receives information through the keyboard or modem, and software determines how the information is processed; the information may then be stored in some altered format on the hard drive; and the information may be retrieved when it is needed. Likewise, the multiple processes of memory can be thought of as operating over time in three phases (**Figure 7.3**). The **encoding** phase occurs at the time of learning, as information is acquired by being encoded. That is, the brain changes information into a neural code that it can use. Consider the process of reading this book. In the encoding phase, your brain converts the sensory stimuli on the page to meaningful neural codes. The **storage** phase is the retention of

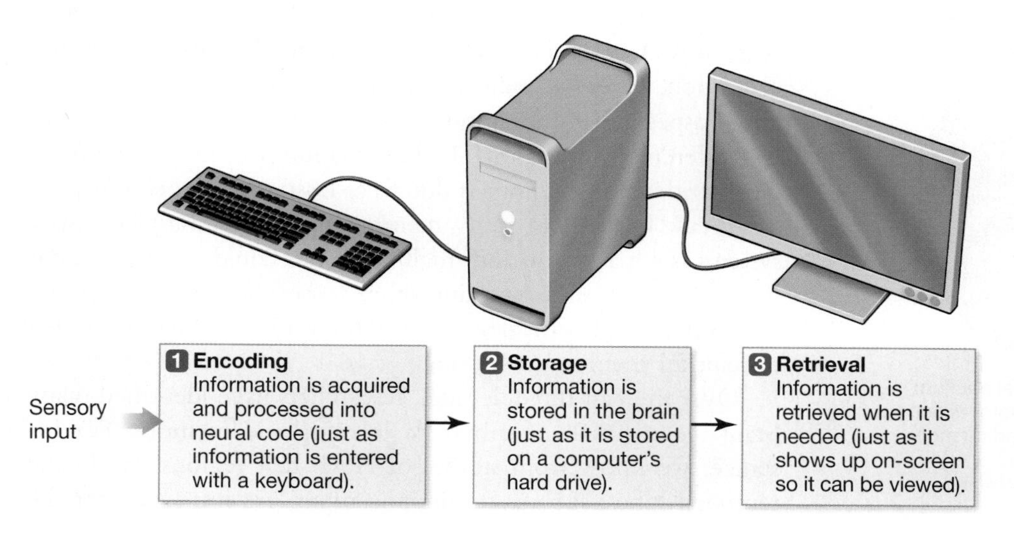


**FIGURE 7.3 Information Processing** The information processing model compares the working of memory to the actions of a computer. **How does human memory differ from a computer's memory?**

**retrieval** The act of recalling or remembering stored information when it is needed.

the coded representation. It corresponds to some change in the nervous system, a change that registers what you read as a memorable event. Storage can last a fraction of a second or as long as a lifetime. Think of this phase as being when you keep material you read in mind until test time or longer. There are at least three storage systems, which differ in how long they store information. These systems will be discussed in detail later in this chapter. **Retrieval,** the third phase of memory, consists of reaching into memory storage to find and bring to mind a previously encoded and stored memory when it is needed. Think of this phase as being when you draw on the material in your brain for use on the midterm, on the final, or sometime long after graduation when someone asks you a question about psychology.

## Memory Is the Result of Brain Activity

What role does biology play in the processing of information? Memory researchers have made tremendous progress over the past two decades in understanding what happens in the brain when we acquire, store, and retrieve memories.

MEMORY'S PHYSICAL LOCATIONS As discussed in Chapter 3, Karl Lashley spent much of his career trying to figure out where in the brain memories are stored. Lashley's term *engram* refers to the physical site of memory storage—that is, the place where memory "lives." As part of his research, Lashley trained rats to run a maze, then removed different areas of their cortices. (For more information on the cortex and on other brain regions discussed here, such as the cerebellum and the amygdala, see **Figure 7.4.**) In testing how much of the maze learning the rats retained after the surgery, Lashley found that the size of the area removed was the most important factor in predicting retention. The location of the area was far less important. From these findings, he concluded that memory is distributed throughout the brain rather than confined to any specific location. This idea is known as *equipotentiality*. Lashley was right that memories are not stored in any one brain location. In many other ways, though, Lashley was wrong about how memories are stored.

The psychologist Donald Hebb built on Lashley's research. In Hebb's interpretation, memories are stored in multiple regions of the brain, and they are linked through memory circuits. As discussed in Chapter 6, Hebb proposed that when neurons "fire together," they "wire together." Through this firing and wiring, all learning leaves biological trails in the brain.

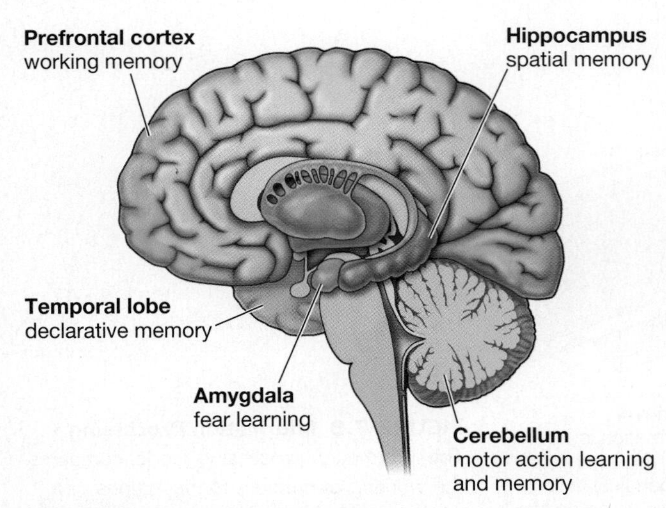


**FIGURE 7.4 Brain Regions Associated with Memory**

Not all brain areas are equally involved in memory, however. A great deal of neural specialization occurs. Because of this specialization, different brain regions are responsible for storing different aspects of information. Indeed, different memory systems use different brain regions. Lashley's failure to find the brain regions critical for memory is due to at least two factors. First, the maze task he used to study memory involved multiple sensory systems (such as vision and smell). The rats could compensate for the loss of one sense by using other senses. Second, Lashley did not examine subcortical areas, which are now known to be important for memory retention.

Over the past three decades, researchers have identified many brain regions that contribute to learning and memory. For instance, we know from studies of H.M. that regions within the temporal lobes, such as the hippocampus, are important for the ability to store new memories. The temporal lobes are important for being able to say what you remember, but they are less important for motor learning and classical conditioning (discussed in Chapter 6, "Learning"). As noted in Chapter 3, the cerebellum plays a role in how motor actions are learned and remembered. The amygdala, in contrast, is especially important for one type of classical conditioning, fear learning. As noted in Chapter 6, an animal without an amygdala cannot learn to fear objects that signal danger. The take-home message here is that memory is distributed among different brain regions. Memory does not "live" in one part of the brain. If you lose a particular brain cell, you will not therefore lose a memory.

**consolidation** A process by which immediate memories become lasting (or long-term) memories.

**CONSOLIDATION OF MEMORIES** Reading this chapter should be making some of your neural connections stronger. At the same time, new neural connections should be developing, especially in your hippocampus. Your brain is different than it was before you began reading the chapter. Neural connections that support memory have become stronger, and new synapses have been constructed (Miller, 2005). This process is known as **consolidation.** Through it, your immediate memories—memories acquired through encoding—become your lasting memories.

Most likely, the middle section of the temporal lobes (called the *medial temporal lobes*) are responsible for coordinating and strengthening the connections among neurons when something is learned. The medial temporal lobes are particularly important for the formation of new memories. The actual storage, however, occurs in the particular brain regions engaged during the perception, processing, and analysis of the material being learned. For instance, visual information is stored in the cortical areas involved in visual perception. Sound is stored in the areas involved in auditory perception. Thus memory for sensory experiences, such as remembering something seen or heard, involves reactivating the cortical circuits involved in the initial seeing or hearing (**Figure 7.5**). The medial temporal lobes form links, or pointers, between the different storage sites, and they direct the gradual strengthening of the connections between these links (Squire, Stark, & Clark, 2004). Once the connections are strengthened sufficiently, the medial temporal lobes become less important for memory. As discussed earlier, H.M.'s surgery removed parts of his medial temporal lobes. Without those parts, he could not make new memories (at least ones he could talk about), but he still was able to retrieve old memories.

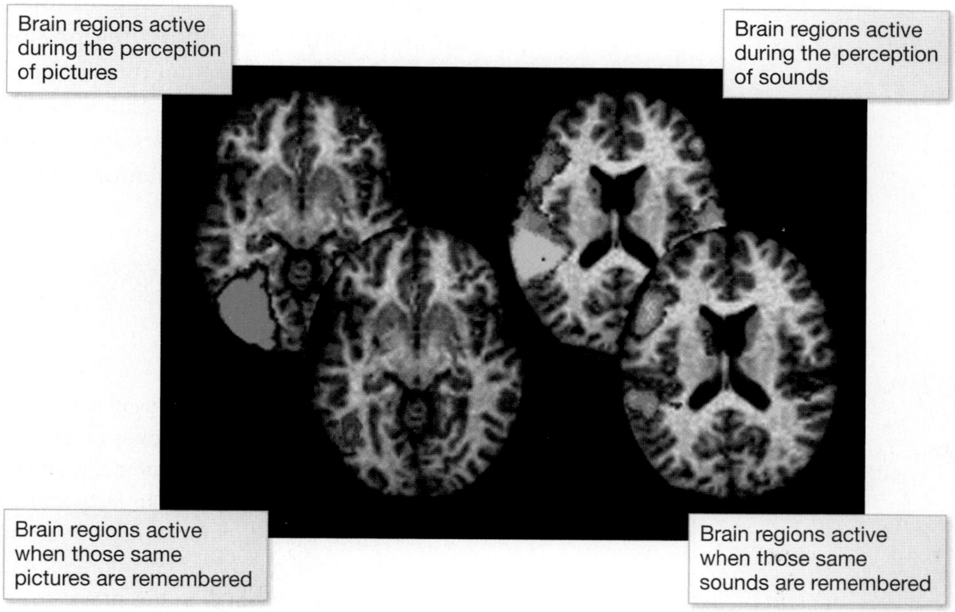

**FIGURE 7.5 Brain Activation during Perception and Remembering** These four horizontally sliced brain images were acquired using magnetic resonance imaging. In each pair, the top image shows the brain areas that are activated during a particular sensory-specific perception. The bottom image shows the regions of the sensory cortex that are activated when that sensory-specific information is remembered. Notice that the perceptions and the memories involve similar cortical areas.

To understand the basic consolidation process, consider that while reading this chapter you have come to understand that *medial* means middle. Now that you have acquired this information, you need to think about it over time so that it will be consolidated in your memory.

A good night's sleep might also contribute to this process. There is compelling evidence that sleep helps with the consolidation of memories and that disturbing

**FIGURE 7.6 Altering Memories** In the 2004 movie *Eternal Sunshine of the Spotless Mind,* Joel Barish (played by Jim Carrey) undergoes a procedure that eliminates memories of his former girlfriend. **If this procedure were real, would you choose to undergo it? Why would you want to eliminate parts of your past from your memory? What drawbacks might there be from losing even bad memories?**

sleep interferes with learning. Chronic sleep deprivation certainly will interfere with learning. (For more information on sleep, see Chapter 5, "Consciousness." Advice on improving your sleeping habits appears in that chapter's "Psychology: Knowledge You Can Use" feature, "Can Sleep Deprivation Hurt Me?")

**RECONSOLIDATION OF MEMORIES** An exciting theory developed by Karim Nader and Joseph LeDoux proposes that once memories are activated, they need to be consolidated again to be stored back in memory (LeDoux, 2002; Nader & Einarsson, 2010). These processes are known as **reconsolidation.** To understand how reconsolidation works, think of this image: A librarian returns a book to a shelf for storage so that it can be taken out again later.

When memories for past events are retrieved, those memories can be affected by new circumstances, and so the newly reconsolidated memories may differ from their original versions (Nader, Schafe, & LeDoux, 2000). In other words, our memories begin as versions of what we have experienced. Then they actually might change when we use them. In the library book analogy, this change would be like tearing pages out of the book or adding new pages or notes before returning it. The book placed on the shelf differs from the one taken out. The information in the torn-out pages is no longer available for retrieval, and the new pages or notes that were inserted alter the memory the next time it is retrieved.

The reconsolidation process repeats itself each time a memory is activated and placed back in storage, and it may explain why our memories for events can change over time. As you might imagine, this theory has received considerable attention. It not only has implications for what it means to remember something. It also opens up the intriguing possibility that bad memories could be erased by activating them and then interfering with reconsolidation. Recently, researchers have shown that using extinction (discussed in Chapter 6, "Learning") during the period when memories are susceptible to reconsolidation can be an effective method of altering bad memories (Schiller et al., 2010; **Figure 7.6**).

**reconsolidation** Neural processes involved when memories are recalled and then stored again for later retrieval.

## Summing Up

### What Is Memory?

Memory is the nervous system's capacity to acquire and retain skills and knowledge. Memory operates over time in three phases: encoding, storage, and retrieval. Multiple brain regions have been implicated in memory, including the hippocampus, temporal lobes, cerebellum, amygdala, and the brain structures involved in perception. The medial temporal regions of the brain are particularly important for the consolidation of memories into storage. As memories are consolidated, neurons link into distributed networks in the brain, and these networks become linked. Reconsolidation refers to the processes that occur when memories are retrieved, altered, and placed back into storage. Reconsolidation may explain why memories for events change over time.

## Measuring Up

1. Which of the following statements are true? Choose as many as apply.
   a. The hippocampus is particularly important in fear conditioning.
   b. Donald Hebb proposed the notion of equipotentiality.
   c. Encoding occurs before storage.

d. Reconsolidation is the first phase of memory.
e. The cerebellum is involved in the learning of motor actions.
f. Memory storage is limited to the parietal lobes.

2. What changes occur at the synapses when people learn and remember? Choose as many as apply.
   a. Neural connections are strengthened.
   b. Reuptake is enhanced.
   c. Neurons make more synaptic connections.
   d. Brain regions associated with learning and remembering become more sensitive to glucose.
   e. The cerebellum grows larger.

**Answers:** 1. c. Encoding occurs before storage.; e. The cerebellum is involved in the learning of motor actions.
2. a. Neuronal connections are strengthened.; c. Neurons make more synaptic connections.

## 7.2 How Does Attention Determine What We Remember?

**Learning Objectives**

- Distinguish between parallel processing and serial processing.
- Describe filter theory.
- Define change blindness.

Many students say they have memory problems. Specifically, they have trouble remembering the material covered in class and in their textbooks. Their problems often have nothing to do with the way their brains work, however. Instead, they simply do not pay attention when they are supposed to be learning. For example, students who overload their systems by studying while checking e-mail, instant messaging, and watching television will do worse at all these tasks than they would if they focused on one task at a time (Manhart, 2004).

Your elementary school teachers probably had a basic understanding of the way memory works. For this reason, they demanded that you and your fellow students "pay attention." Good teachers know that to get information into memory, a person needs to *attend*. That is, the person needs to focus on the subject and be alert. Think about the difference between the words *see* and *look, hear* and *listen. Look* and *listen* are commands that tell you where to direct your attention. Each of us has the ability to direct something in ourselves, called *attention,* to some information. We do so at the cost of paying less attention to other information. In fact, the word *pay* indicates that costs are associated with attending to some forms of information and not to others. Attention is limited. When it is divided among too many tasks or the tasks are difficult, performance suffers.

Attention is an important part of your ability to function in your daily life. Imagine how awful it would be if you could not block out the irrelevant information that comes at you all the time. Throughout any day, you try to focus attention on the tasks at hand and ignore other things that might distract you. A task as simple as having a conversation requires paying focused attention. If the other speaker has unusual facial features or has food on his or her chin, the unusual features or food might capture your attention and make it difficult to comprehend what the person is saying. If the other speaker is boring, your mind might wander. You might find your own thoughts, or even a nearby conversation, more interesting to attend to than your long-winded companion. In short, your attention can be distracted by external sensory cues or by internal thoughts

**parallel processing** Processing multiple types of information at the same time.

and memories (Chun, Golomb, & Turk-Browne, 2011). The following section presents the basic principles of how human attention works.

## Our Visual Attention Works Selectively and Serially

The psychologist Anne Treisman has made great advances in the study of attention. According to her theory about attention and recognition, we automatically identify "primitive" features within an environment. Such features include color, shape, size, orientation, and movement. Treisman has proposed that separate systems analyze the different visual features of objects. Through **parallel processing,** these systems all process information at the same time. We can attend selectively to one feature by effectively blocking the further processing of the others (Treisman & Gelade, 1980).

In studies that employ Treisman's *visual search tasks* (also called *feature search tasks*), participants look at a display of different objects on a computer screen. They search for *targets,* objects that differ from the others in only one feature. The other objects in the display are called *distractors.* A typical display might consist of a few red As (the targets) among many black ones (the distractors; **Figure 7.7**). In these conditions, the targets seem to pop out immediately, regardless of the number of distractors. Some features that seem to pop out when the targets differ from the distractors are color, shape, motion, orientation, and size (Wolfe & Horowitz, 2004). Suppose you are trying to find a friend of yours in a large crowd of people. This task will be fairly easy if your friend is wearing red and everyone else is wearing black, or if your friend is the only one waving, the only one standing up, or a much different size than everyone else.

As discussed in Chapter 3, a similar research paradigm was used to identify synesthetes, some of whom see particular numbers as printed in particular colors even when all the numbers are black. If you are not a synesthete, it might take you a while to find, for example, all the 2s in an array of 2s and 5s if all the numbers are black. A synesthete who sees 2s in one color and 5s in another color will be able to find the 2s very quickly.

Searching for a single feature, such as a red stimulus, is fast and automatic. Searching for two features is *serial* (you need to look at the stimuli one at a time) and *effortful* (takes longer and requires more attention). Imagine, for example, trying to find all the red Xs in a display of differently colored Xs and Ys. This effort would be called a *conjunction task* because the stimulus you are looking for is made up of two simple features conjoined (**Figure 7.8**).

(a)

(b)

**FIGURE 7.7 Parallel Processing**
**(a)** Parallel processing allows us to process information from different visual features at the same time by focusing on targets instead of distractors. Here the targets are the red objects. **(b) In this photo, which details serve as targets?**

## Our Auditory Attention Allows Us to Listen Selectively

Because attention is limited, it is hard to perform two tasks at the same time. It is especially hard if the two tasks rely on the same sensory mechanisms or the same mental mechanisms. We easily can listen to music and drive at the same time, but it is hard to listen to two conversations at once. Think about driving along an open road, singing along with a song on the radio and perhaps even talking with a passenger. What happens when you see the brake lights of cars ahead of you? You need to stop singing or talking and direct your attention to the task of driving. Suddenly, the task becomes more difficult and requires additional attention. Driving and listening to the radio at the same time can even be hazardous, depending on what you are listening to. For example, a sports broadcast might engage your visual system if it inspires you to imagine a game in progress. The game in your imagination would divert your attention from the visual cues on the road ahead.

As you might imagine, behaviors such as reading, eating, talking on a cell phone, or texting are dangerous while driving because they distract the driver's attention. It is estimated that in the United States from 2005 to 2008, deaths from distracted driving increased by 28 percent (National Highway Traffic Safety Administration, 2009; Wilson & Stimpson, 2010). Simulated-driving experiments have shown that talking on a cell phone is especially dangerous. In fact, talking on a cell phone can impair driving skills nearly as much as alcohol. For instance, drivers' braking reactions are reduced, possibly because talking impairs visual processing (Strayer, Drews, & Johnston, 2003). Talking on a cell phone while driving is likely more hazardous than talking with a passenger in the car while driving. A cell phone conversation will not vary naturally with the driving conditions, because the person talking with the driver will not know what is happening. Suppose that traffic has become heavy or the car ahead has suddenly braked. A driver talking with a passenger can signal in many ways that the conversation needs to pause as situations demand (Drews, Pasupathi, & Strayer, 2008). Hands-free cell phones do not solve the attention problem. Because drivers using hands-free phones still have to divide their attentional resources among multiple tasks, hands-free cell phone use may be just as dangerous as talking while holding the phone (Ishigami & Klein, 2009).

**FIGURE 7.8 Try for Yourself: Conjunction Tasks**

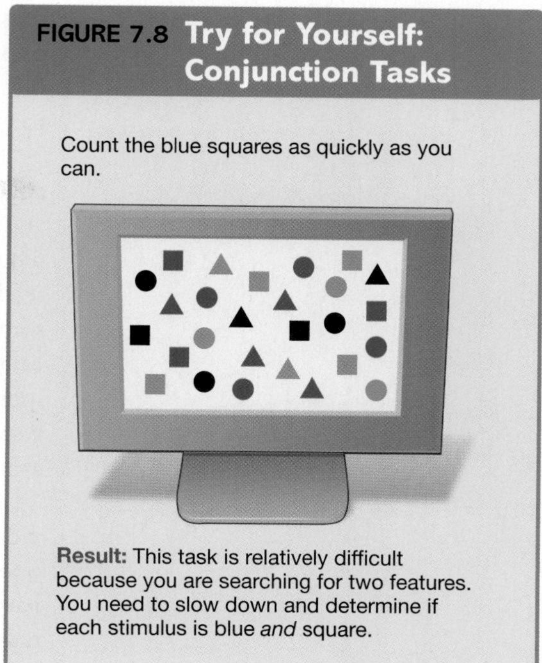


In thinking about the power of distraction, consider the *cocktail party phenomenon*. In 1953, the psychologist E. C. Cherry described the process this way: You can focus on a single conversation in the midst of a chaotic cocktail party. A particularly pertinent stimulus, however—such as hearing your name mentioned in another conversation or hearing a juicy piece of gossip—can capture your attention. If you really want to hear the other conversation or piece of gossip, you can focus your attention on it. Of course, when you redirect your attention in this way, you probably will not be able to follow what the closer (and therefore probably louder) partygoer is saying. You will lose the thread of your original conversation.

Cherry developed selective-listening studies to examine what the mind does with unattended information when a person pays attention to one task. He used a technique called *shadowing*. In this procedure, a participant wears headphones that deliver one message to one ear and a different message to the other. The person is asked to attend to one of the two messages and "shadow" it by repeating it aloud. As a result, the person usually notices the unattended sound (the message given to the other ear), but will have no knowledge about the content of the unattended sound (**Figure 7.9**).

Imagine you are participating in an experiment about what happens to unattended messages. You are repeating whatever is spoken into one ear (shadowing) and ignoring the message spoken into the other ear. What would happen if your own name were spoken into the unattended ear? You would probably hear your own name but know nothing about the rest of the message. Some important information gets through the filter of attention. It has to be personally relevant information, such as your name or the name of someone close to you, or it has to be particularly loud or different in some obvious physical way.

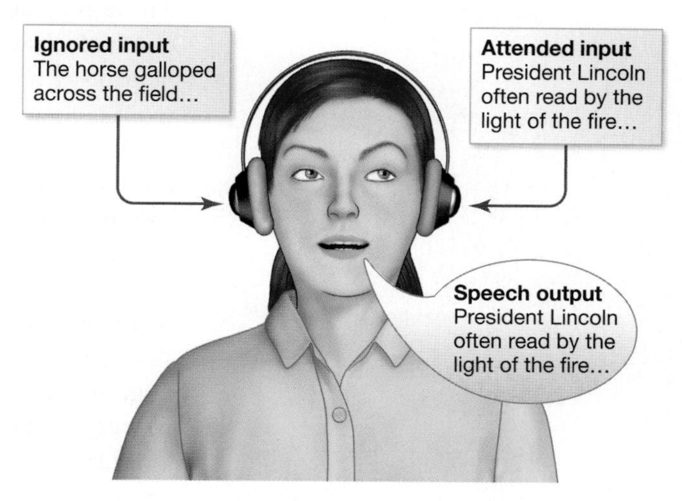


**FIGURE 7.9 Shadowing** In this procedure, the participant receives a different auditory message in each ear. The participant is required to repeat, or "shadow," only one of the messages.

## Through Selective Attention, We Filter Incoming Information

In 1958, the psychologist Donald Broadbent developed *filter theory* to explain the selective nature of attention. He assumed that people have a limited capacity for sensory information. They screen incoming information to let in only the most important material. In this model, attention is like a gate that opens for important information and closes for irrelevant information. But can we really close the gate to ignore some information? When and how do we close the gate?

Some stimuli demand attention and virtually shut off the ability to attend to anything else. Imagine you are focusing all your attention on reading this book, and suddenly you develop a muscle cramp. What will happen to your attention? The sharp jab of the cramp will demand your attention, and whatever you are reading will leave your consciousness until you attend to the muscle. Similarly, some stimuli, such as those that evoke emotions, may readily capture attention because they provide important information about potential threats in an environment (Phelps, Ling, & Carrasco, 2006). An object produces a stronger attentional response when it is viewed as socially relevant (e.g., an eye) than when it is viewed as nonsocial (e.g., an arrowhead; Tipper, Handy, Giesbrecht, & Kingstone, 2008).

Faces are a good example of stimuli that capture attention because they provide important social information. For example, a face indicates whether someone is a potential mate (i.e., has an attractive face) or may intend to cause physical harm (i.e., has an angry face). A series of studies found that the attentional system prioritizes faces, especially when they appear threatening, over less meaningful stimuli (West, Anderson, & Pratt, 2009). Indeed, threatening information receives priority over other stimuli within $\frac{1}{20}$ of a second after it is presented (West, Anderson, Ferber, & Pratt, 2011).

Studies such as the one just described indicate that decisions about what to attend to are made early in the perceptual process. At the same time, however, unattended information is processed at least to some extent. As discussed in Chapter 5, people are often influenced by information delivered subliminally or incidentally. Several selective-listening studies have found that even when participants cannot repeat an unattended message, they still have processed its contents. In one experiment, participants were told to attend to the message coming in one ear: *They threw stones at the bank yesterday*. At the same time, the unattended ear was presented with one of two words: *river* or *money*. Afterward, participants could not report the unattended words. However, those presented with the word *river* interpreted the sentence to mean someone had thrown stones at a riverbank. Those presented with the word *money* interpreted the sentence to mean someone had thrown stones at a financial institution (MacKay, 1973). Thus the participants extracted meaning from the word even though they did not process the word consciously.

To understand just how inattentive we can be, consider the phenomenon known as **change blindness.** Because we cannot attend to everything in the vast array of visual information available, often we are "blind" to large changes in our environments. For example, would you notice if the person you were talking to suddenly changed into another person? In two studies, participants were on a college campus when they were approached by a stranger. The stranger asked for directions. Then the stranger was momentarily blocked by a large object and replaced with another person of the same sex and race. Fifty percent of the people giving directions never noticed that they were talking to a different person. When giving directions to a stranger, we normally do not attend to the distinctive features of the stranger's face or clothing. If we are unable to recall those features later, it is not because we forgot them. More likely, it is because we never processed those features very much in the first place. After all, how often do we need to recall such information? (Simons & Levin, 1998; **Figure 7.10**).

**change blindness** A failure to notice large changes in one's environment.

**FIGURE 7.10 Scientific Method: Change Blindness Studies by Simons and Levin**

**Hypothesis:** People can be "blind" to large changes around them.

**Research Method:**

1. A participant is approached by a stranger asking for directions.

2. The stranger is momentarily blocked by a larger object.

3. While being blocked, the original stranger is replaced by another person.

**Results:** Half the participants giving directions never noticed they were talking to a different person (as long as the replacement was of the same race and sex as the original stranger).

**Conclusion:** Change blindness results from inattention to certain visual information.

**Source:** Photos from Simons, D. J., & Levin, D. T. (1998). Failure to detect changes to people during a real-world interaction. *Psychonomic Bulletin and Review, 5*, 644–649. © 1998 Psychonomic Society, Inc. Figure courtesy Daniel J. Simons.

In the first study, older people were especially likely not to notice a change in the person asking them for directions. Younger people were pretty good at noticing the change. Are older people especially inattentive? Or do they tend to process a situation's broad outlines rather than its details? Perhaps the older people encoded the stranger as simply "a college student" and did not look for more-individual characteristics. To test this idea, Simons and Levin (1998) conducted an additional study. This time, the stranger was an easily recognizable type of person from a different social group. That is, the same experimenters dressed as construction workers and asked college students for directions. Sure enough, the college students failed to notice the replacement of one construction worker with another. This finding supports the idea that the students encoded the strangers as belonging to a broad category of "construction workers" without looking more closely at them. For these students, construction workers seemed pretty much all alike and interchangeable. Subsequent research has shown that people with a greater ability to maintain attention in the face of distracting information are less likely to experience a similar type of change blindness (Seegmiller, Watson, & Strayer, 2011).

As change blindness illustrates, we can attend to a limited amount of information. Large discrepancies exist between what most of us believe we see and what we actually see. Thus our perceptions of the world are often inaccurate, and we have little awareness of our perceptual failures. We simply do not know how much information we miss in the world around us. Every time we miss a piece of information, we run the risk of not storing it as a memory. Every time we fail to pay attention, in other words, we are likely to forget what just happened.

CRITICAL THINKING SKILL

## Recognizing When "Change Blindness Blindness" May Be Occuring

The main message from studies of change blindness is that we can miss obvious changes in what we see and hear. Despite this possibility, most of us believe that we will always notice large changes—that important events automatically draw our attention. This erroneous belief persists because we often do not find out about the things we fail to perceive (Simons & Ambinder, 2005). In addition, the phenomenon of change blindness is so counterintuitive that few of us believe how much we do not see. *Change blindness blindness* is our unawareness that we often do not notice apparently obvious changes in our environments.

Imagine you are driving up a hill. At the top of the hill, there is an intersection. When you reach the top, you see another car heading straight into your lane, and in a flash you swerve to avoid a collision. The other car hits yours, but your last-minute swerve convinces eyewitnesses that you caused the accident by driving erratically. Change blindness blindness could be a factor in their reports: Perhaps out of a desire to help, the eyewitnesses believe they saw the whole accident. They may have missed the critical moments, however, because they were attending to their own activities. Attention, of course, influences memory.

Being aware of change blindness blindness is a critical thinking skill. Thinking that we always notice large changes may lead us to perceive things incorrectly, such as in erroneously believing something did or did not happen. Recognizing the limitations of attention may help prevent us from misleading ourselves about our perceptions. Knowledge about change blindness should make us more humble about what we really see and what we remember.


### Summing Up

### How Does Attention Determine What We Remember?

Attention is the ability to focus on certain stimuli. This ability is adaptive in that it facilitates functioning by enabling us to block out irrelevant information. Using visual search tasks, researchers have found that we process basic features of stimuli (e.g., color, motion, orientation, shape, and size) through parallel processing. Parallel processing is fast and automatic. Using conjunction tasks, researchers have found that we process multiple features of stimuli (e.g., trying to find red Xs) serially and effortfully. Filter theory maintains that attention is selective. Consistent with this theory, we can choose the stimuli to which we attend. For example, we can ignore a nearby conversation in favor of a more interesting one farther away. To some extent, however, we process information contained in sensory stimuli to which we are not consciously attending. We commonly exhibit change blindness, failing to notice major changes in the environment. Change blindness illustrates that our perceptions can be inaccurate.

## Measuring Up

1. Which statement correctly describes the processes associated with visual attention?
   a. Attention can be captured by stimuli that vary along multiple dimensions (e.g., red, tilted squares) and stimuli that are important for survival (e.g., high-pitched screams).
   b. Attention has a rapid process that searches for one feature and a slower, serial process that searches for multiple features one at a time.
   c. Attention first segregates stimuli and then uses a binding process to build perceptions.
   d. Attention is first narrow in focus and then broadens to include all items in the visual field.

2. What happens to information when we are not paying attention?
   a. Some of the unattended information is passed on for further processing, but it is weaker than attended information.
   b. It is always lost because attention filters out unattended information.
   c. Unattended information is always available in some form; we just need to design experiments to demonstrate that it is available.

**Answers:** 1. b. Attention has a rapid process that searches for one feature and a slower, serial process that searches for multiple features one at a time.
2. a. Some of the unattended information is passed on for further processing, but it is weaker than attended information.

# 7.3 How Are Memories Maintained over Time?

### Learning Objectives

- Distinguish between sensory memory, short-term memory, and long-term memory.
- Describe working memory and chunking.
- Review evidence that supports the distinction between working memory and long-term memory.
- Explain how information is transferred from working memory to long-term memory.

Have you been paying attention to your reading? How well do you remember this chapter's opening discussions of memory? Recall from the start of the chapter that the information processing model is based on the model of the computer (**Figure 7.11a**). Information is encoded in the brain during learning, stored in memory, and then retrieved for later use. In 1968, the psychologists Richard Atkinson and Richard Shiffrin proposed a different model. Atkinson and Shiffrin's three-part model consists of *sensory memory, short-term memory,* and *long-term memory* (**Figure 7.11b**). Each of these terms refers to the length of time that information is retained in memory. In addition, the three parts of this model differ in their capacity for storage, with sensory memory having the least capacity and long-term memory having the most. The following sections will look at these parts in more detail.

## Sensory Memory Is Brief

**Sensory memory** is a temporary memory system closely tied to the sensory systems. It is not what we usually think of when we think about memory, because it lasts only a fraction of a second. In fact, normally we are not aware that it is operating.

As discussed in Chapter 4, we obtain all our information about the world through our senses. Our sensory systems transduce, or change, that information into neural impulses. Everything we remember, therefore, is the result of neurons firing in the brain. For example, a memory of a sight or of a sound is created by intricate patterns of neural activity in the brain. A sensory memory occurs when a light, a sound, an odor, a taste, or a tactile impression leaves a vanishing trace

**sensory memory** A memory system that very briefly stores sensory information in close to its original sensory form.

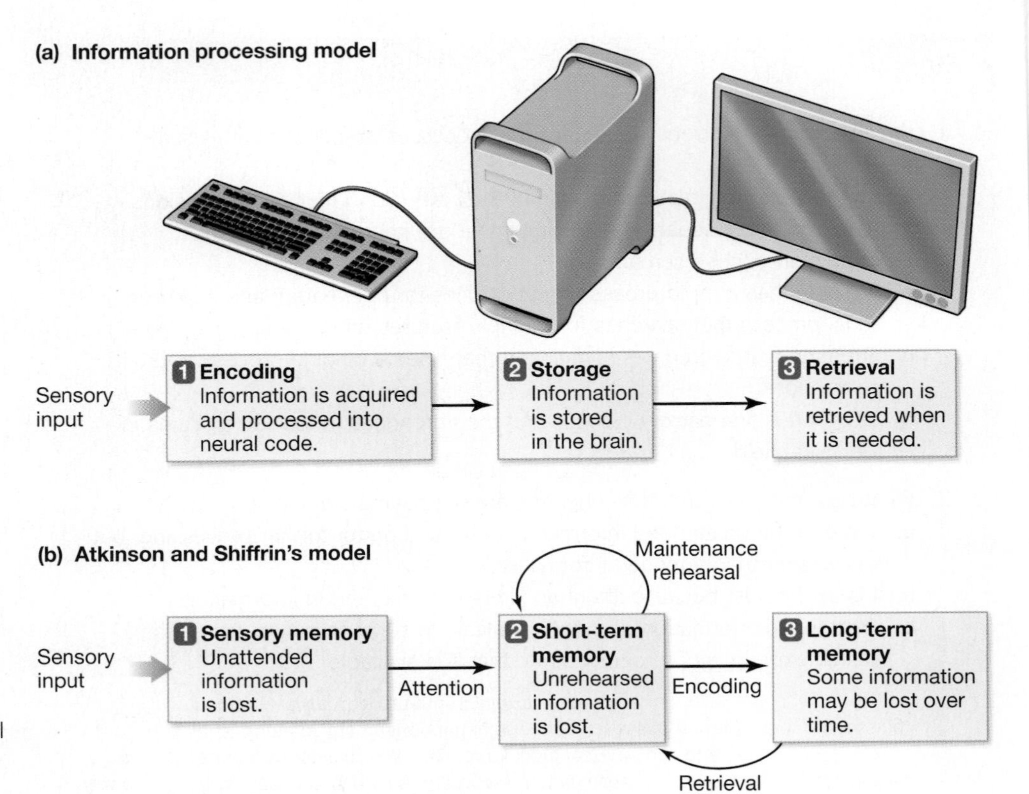


**FIGURE 7.11 Three-Part Memory Systems (a)** Recall that the information processing model compares the working of memory to the actions of a computer. **(b)** By contrast, Atkinson and Shiffrin's model emphasizes that memory storage varies in duration and capacity.

on the nervous system for a fraction of a second. When you look at something and quickly glance away, you can briefly picture the image and recall some of its details. When someone protests, "You're not paying attention to me," you often can repeat back the last few words the person spoke, even if you were thinking about something else.

In 1960, the cognitive psychologist George Sperling provided the initial empirical support for sensory memory. In this classic experiment, three rows of letters were flashed on a screen for 1/20 of a second. Participants were asked to recall all the letters. Most people believed they had seen all the letters, but they could recall only three or four. That is, in the time it took them to name the first three or four, they forgot the other letters. These reports suggested the participants had very quickly lost their memories of exactly what they had seen. Sperling tested this hypothesis by showing all the letters exactly as he had done before, but signaling with a high-, medium-, or low-pitched sound as soon as the letters disappeared. A high pitch meant the participants should recall the letters in the top row, a medium pitch meant they should recall the letters in the middle row, and a low pitch meant they should recall the letters in the bottom row. When the sound occurred very shortly after the letters disappeared, the participants correctly remembered almost all the letters in the signaled row. But the longer the delay between the letters' disappearance and the sound, the worse the participants performed. Sperling concluded that the visual memory persisted for about 1/3 of a second. After that very brief period, the trace of the sensory memory faded progressively until it was no longer accessible (**Figure 7.12**).

Our sensory memories enable us to experience the world as a continuous stream rather than in discrete sensations. Thanks to visual memory, when you turn your head the scene passes smoothly in front of you rather than in jerky bits. Your memory retains information just long enough for you to connect one image with the next in a smooth way that corresponds to the way objects move in the

**FIGURE 7.12** **Scientific Method: Sperling's Sensory Memory Experiment**

**Hypothesis:** Information in sensory memories is lost very quickly if it is not transferred for further processing.

**Research Method:**

1. Participants looked at a screen on which three rows of letters flashed for 1/20 of a second.

2. When a high-pitched tone followed the letters, it meant the participants should recall the letters in the top row. When a medium-pitched tone followed the letters, it meant the participants should recall the middle row. And when a low-pitched tone followed the letters, it meant the participants should recall the bottom row.

3. The tones sounded at various intervals: .15, .30, .50, or 1 second after the display of the letters.

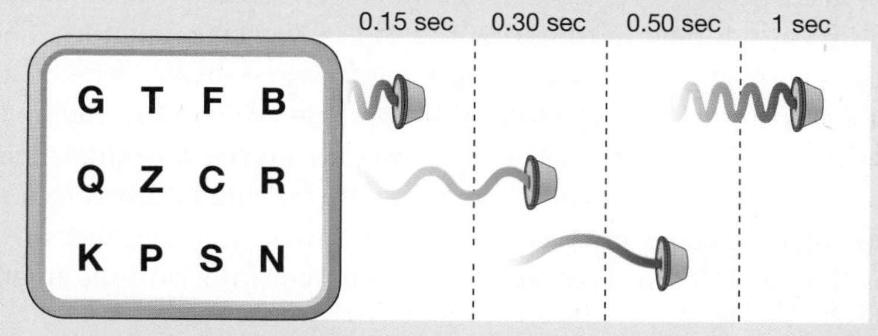


**Results:** When the tone sounded very shortly after the letters disappeared, participants remembered almost all the letters in the signaled row. The longer the delay between the disappearance of the letters and the tone, the worse the participants performed.

**Conclusion:** Sensory memory persists for about 1/3 of a second and then progressively fades.

**Source:** Sperling, G. (1960). The information available in brief visual presentations. *Psychological Monographs, 74*, 1–29.

real world. In much the same way, a movie projector plays a series of still pictures that follow each other closely enough in time to look like continuous action.

## Working Memory Is Active

Information attended to is passed from sensory stores to **short-term memory.** This memory system has a limited capacity, but it has more capacity than sensory memory. Researchers initially saw short-term memory as simply a buffer, or holding place, in which verbal information was rehearsed until it was stored or forgotten. Subsequently, however, researchers learned that short-term memory is not a single storage system. Instead, it is an active processing unit that deals with multiple types of information. A more contemporary model of the short-term retention of information is **working memory.** This storage system works on the information we have in memory, partly by combining information from different sources (Baddeley & Hitch, 1974; Baddeley, 2002). For example, working memory includes sounds, images, and ideas.

Information remains in working memory for about 20 to 30 seconds. It then disappears unless you actively prevent that from happening by thinking about or rehearsing the information. As an example, try to remember some new information: the meaningless three-letter string of consonants X C J. As long as you keep repeating the string over and over, you will keep it in working memory. But if

**short-term memory** A memory storage system that briefly holds a limited amount of information in awareness.

**working memory** An active processing system that keeps different types of information available for current use.

you stop rehearsing, you probably will soon forget the letters. After all, you are bombarded with other events that compete for your attention, and you may not be able to stay focused. Try again to remember X C J, but this time count backward in threes from the number 309. Most people find it difficult to remember the meaningless consonants after a few seconds of backward counting. The longer they spend counting, the less able they are to remember the consonant string. After only 18 seconds of counting, most people recall the consonants extremely poorly. This result indicates that working memory lasts less than half a minute without continuous rehearsing as a way to remember.

Researchers have recently demonstrated how working memory is updated to take into account new information (Ecker, Lewandowsky, Oberauer, & Chee, 2010). For instance, suppose a restaurant manager is told to expect 20 people for dinner. If subsequently told that 5 more people are coming, the manager needs to retrieve the original number, transform it by adding 5, and then substitute the new number for the old in working memory. These three processes—*retrieval, transformation,* and *substitution*—make distinct and independent contributions to updating the contents of working memory. Sometimes only one of the processes is necessary to update working memory. For instance, if the manager is expecting 20 people for dinner but is told there will be 25, the manager does not have to retrieve the original number or transform it. He or she just has to substitute the new number into working memory.

**MEMORY SPAN AND CHUNKING** Why do new items in working memory interfere with the recall of older items? Working memory can hold a limited amount of information. The cognitive psychologist George Miller has noted that the limit is generally seven items (plus or minus two). This figure is referred to as *memory span*. More-recent research suggests that Miller's estimate may be too high and that working memory may be limited to as few as four items (Conway et al., 2005). Memory span also varies among individuals. Indeed, some intelligence tests use memory span as part of the measure of IQ. Perhaps luckily for those of us whose memory spans may be tested, there is growing evidence that we can increase the capacity of working memory through exercises, such as working to maintain material in working memory in the face of interference or while performing other cognitive tasks (Morrison & Chein, 2011). The capacity of working memory increases as children develop (Garon, Bryson, & Smith, 2008) and decreases with advanced aging (McCabe et al., 2010).

Because working memory is limited, you might expect almost everyone to have great difficulty remembering a string of letters such as UTPHDNYUMAU CLABAMIT.

These 20 letters would tax even the largest memory span. But what if we organized the information into smaller, meaningful units? For instance, UT PHD NYU MA UCLA BA MIT.

Here the letters are separated to produce acronyms for universities and academic degrees. This organization makes them much easier to recall, for two reasons. First, memory span is limited to seven items, probably fewer, but the items can be letters or groups of letters, numbers or groups of numbers, words, or even concepts. Second, meaningful units are easier to remember than nonsense units. This process of organizing information into meaningful units is known as **chunking.** The term means that information is broken down into chunks. The more efficiently you chunk information, the more you can remember. Master chess players who glance at a scenario on a chessboard, even for a few seconds, later can reproduce the exact arrangement of pieces (Chase & Simon, 1973).

**chunking** Organizing information into meaningful units to make it easier to remember.

They can do so because they instantly chunk the board into a number of meaningful subunits based on their past experiences with the game. If the pieces are arranged on the board in ways that make no sense in terms of chess, however, experts are no better than novices at reproducing the board. In general, the greater your expertise with the material, the more efficiently you can chunk information and therefore the more you can remember (**Figure 7.13**).

**long-term memory** The relatively permanent storage of information.

**serial position effect** The ability to recall items from a list depends on order of presentation, with items presented early or late in the list remembered better than those in the middle.

## Long-Term Memory Is Relatively Permanent

When people talk about memory, they usually are referring to the relatively permanent storage of information: **long-term memory.** In the computer analogy presented earlier, long-term memory is like the storage of information on a hard drive. When you think about long-term memory's capacity, try to imagine counting everything you know and everything you are likely to know in your lifetime. It is hard to imagine what that number might be, because you can always learn more. Unlike computer storage, human long-term memory is nearly limitless. It enables you to remember nursery rhymes from childhood, the meanings and spellings of words you rarely use (such as *aardvark* and *cantankerous*), what you had for lunch yesterday, and so on, and so on.

**FIGURE 7.13 Memory Olympics** Contestants in the Memory Olympics memorize names, faces, and even decks of cards, as shown here at the meet in Kuala Lumpur, October 2003. Almost all participants in such memory contests use strategies involving chunking. **What strategies do you use for remembering? Why do they work?**

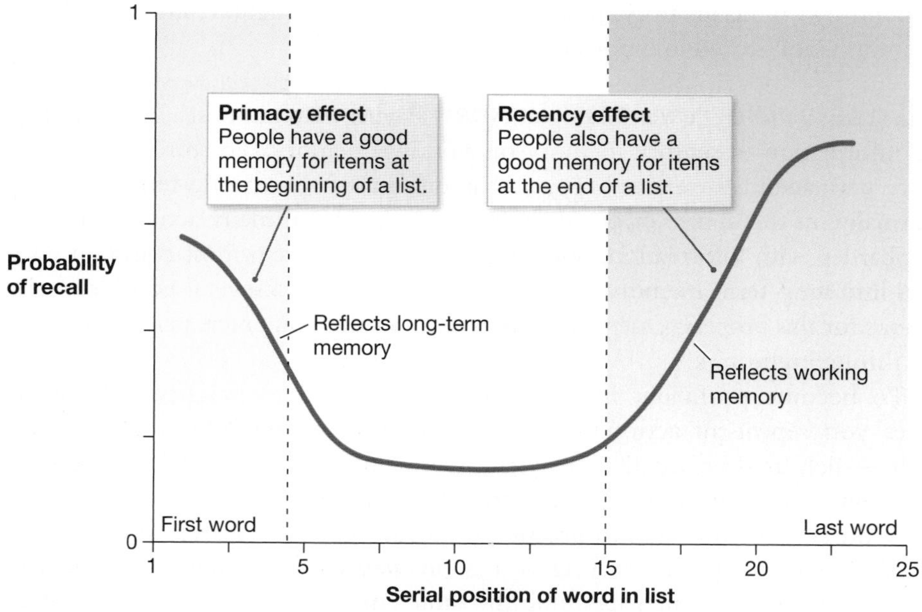

**DISTINGUISHING LONG-TERM MEMORY FROM WORKING MEMORY** Long-term memory is distinct from working memory in two important ways: It has a longer duration and a far greater capacity. A controversy exists, however, as to whether long-term memory represents a truly different type of memory storage from working memory. Initial evidence that long-term memory and working memory are separate systems came from research that required people to recall long lists of words. The ability to recall items from the list depended on the order of presentation. That is, items presented early or late in the list were remembered better than those in the middle. This phenomenon is known as the **serial position effect.** This effect actually consists of two separate effects: The *primacy effect* refers to the better memory people have for items presented at the beginning of the list. The *recency effect* refers to the better memory people have for the most recent items, the ones at the end of the list (**Figure 7.14**).

Primacy effect
People have a good memory for items at the beginning of a list.
Recency effect
People also have a good memory for items at the end of a list.
Reflects long-term memory
Reflects working memory
Probability of recall
1
0
First word
Last word
1 5 10 15 20 25
Serial position of word in list

**FIGURE 7.14 The Serial Position Effect** This graph helps illustrate the primacy effect and the recency effect, which together make up the serial position effect. The serial position effect, in turn, helps illustrate the difference between long-term memory and working memory.

One explanation for the serial position effect relies on a distinction between working memory and long-term memory. When research participants study a long list of words, they rehearse the earliest items the most. As a result, that information is transferred into long-term memory. By contrast, the last few items are still in working memory when the participants have to recall the words immediately after reading them. The idea that primacy effects are due to long-term memory, whereas recency effects are due to working memory, is supported by studies in which there is a delay between the presentation of the list and the recall task. Such delays interfere with the recency effect but not the primacy effect. You would expect this result if the recency effect involves working memory and the primacy effect involves long-term memory. The recency effect might not be entirely related to working memory, however. After all, you probably remember your most recent class better than the classes you had earlier, even though you are not holding that material in working memory. If you had to recall the past presidents or past prime ministers of your country, you would probably recall the early ones and most recent ones best and have poorer recall for those in between, but it is unlikely that you maintain the information about presidents or prime ministers in working memory.

Perhaps the best support for the distinction between working memory and long-term memory comes from case studies such as that of H.M., the patient described at the beginning of this chapter. His working memory system was perfectly normal, as shown by his ability to keep track of a conversation as long as he stayed actively involved in it. Much of his long-term memory system was intact, since he remembered events that occurred before his surgery. He was unable, however, to transfer new information from working memory into long-term memory. In another case, a 28-year-old accident victim with damage to the left temporal lobe had extremely poor working memory, with a span of only one or two items. However, he had perfectly normal long-term memory: a fine memory for day-to-day happenings and reasonable knowledge of events that occurred before his surgery (Shallice & Warrington, 1969). Somehow, despite the bottleneck in his working memory, he was relatively good at retrieving information from long-term memory. These case studies demonstrate that long-term memory can be separated from working memory. Still, the two memory systems are highly interdependent, at least for most of us. For instance, to chunk information in working memory, people need to form meaningful connections based on information stored in long-term memory.

**WHAT GETS INTO LONG-TERM MEMORY** Paying attention is a way of storing information in sensory memory or working memory. To store information more permanently, we need to get that information into long-term memory. Normally, in the course of our daily lives, we engage in many activities and are bombarded with information. Some type of filtering system must constrain what goes into long-term memory. Researchers have provided several possible explanations for this process. One possibility is that information enters permanent storage through rehearsal.

To become proficient in any activity, you need to practice. The more times you repeat an action, the easier it is to perform that action. Motor skills—such as those used to play the piano, play golf, and drive—become easier with practice. Memories are strengthened with retrieval, so one way to make durable memories is to practice retrieval. Recent research in classrooms has shown that repeated testing is a good way to strengthen memories. In fact, it is even better than spending the same amount of time reviewing information you have already read (Roediger & Karpicke, 2006). In a recent study, one group of students read a passage and then took a test on it, a second group studied the information in depth for a week, and a third group made concept maps to organize the information by linking together different ideas (Karpicke & Blunt, 2011). One week later, the students that took the test remembered the information better.

When you practice retrieving information, you basically are doing what you will need to do on a test. So, for example, after reading a section in this or any other book, look back at the main section heading and, if it is not already a question, rephrase it as a question. Then be sure you can answer the heading's question without looking at the text. You might also practice retrieval by working with other students, quizzing each other so you can spot gaps in your knowledge. (In addition, remember to answer the Measuring Up questions at the end of every section in this book; take the Practice Test at the end of each chapter; and visit the book's Web site to take additional tests. The Web site provides feedback and explanations of the correct answers for the additional tests.)

The deeper the level of processing, the more likely you are to remember the material later (Craik & Lockhart, 1972). This fact is another reason that critical thinking skills are important. Rather than just reading the material, think about its meaning and how it is related to other concepts. Try to organize the material in a way that makes sense to you, putting the concepts into your own words. Making the material relevant to you is an especially good way to process material deeply and therefore to remember it easily.

With the material right in front of you, you may be overly confident that you will remember it later. But recognition is easier than recall, and information in a book might not be as accessible when the book is closed and you have to answer questions about what you read. Rehearse material even after you think you have learned it. Test yourself by trying to recall the material a few hours after studying. Keep rehearsing until you can recall the material easily. Distributing your study over time rather than cramming will help you retain the information for longer periods of time (Cepeda, Pashler, Vul, Wixted, & Rohrer, 2006). Six sessions of 1 hour each are much better for learning than one 6-hour marathon. The study sessions should be long enough to get a meaningful amount of information into memory, but they should be spread out over several days or weeks.

Rehearsal is a way to get some information into long-term memory, but simply repeating something many times is not a good method for making information memorable. After all, sometimes we have extremely poor memory for objects that are highly familiar (**Figure 7.15**). Merely seeing something countless times does not enable us to recall its details. For example, try covering a person's watch and then asking that person to describe the watch face. A surprising number of people will not know details such as whether all the numbers are on the face, even if they look at the watch many times a day. This loss of information in memory really shows how well attention and memory function: We attend just enough for the task at hand and lose information that seems irrelevant.

Generally, information about an environment that helps us adapt to that environment is likely to be transformed into a long-term memory. Of the billions of

**FIGURE 7.15 Try for Yourself: The Penny Quiz**

Can you tell which drawing of the U.S. penny is correct?

**Answer:** Even if you live in the United States and see pennies all the time, you might have had trouble identifying "(a)" as the accurate version. In any county, most people do not pay much attention to the specific details of their currency.

both sensory experiences and thoughts we have each day, we want to store only useful information so as to benefit from experience. Remembering that a penny is money and being able to recognize one when you see it are much more useful than being able to recall its specific features—unless you receive counterfeit pennies and have to separate them from real ones.

Evolutionary theory helps explain how we decide in advance what information will be useful. Memory allows us to use information in ways that assist in reproduction and survival. For instance, animals that can use past experiences to increase their chances of survival have a selective advantage over animals that

**Summing Up**

## How Are Memories Maintained over Time?

Atkinson and Shiffrin's model maintains that memory has three components: sensory memory, short-term memory, and long-term memory. Sensory memory consists of brief traces on the nervous system that reflect perceptual processes. Material is passed from sensory memory to short-term memory, a limited system that briefly holds information in awareness. More recently, psychologists have come to think of short-term memory as working memory. Working memory may be limited to as few as four chunks of information. Long-term memory is a relatively permanent, virtually limitless store. The distinction between working memory and long-term memory has been demonstrated by studies that investigated the serial position effect and studies that investigated memory impairments. Information is most likely to be transferred from working memory to long-term memory if it is repeatedly retrieved, deeply processed, or helps us adapt to an environment.

## Measuring Up

1. Indicate how long each of the three stages of memory holds information, and indicate its capacity.

   *Stage:*
   a. sensory memory
   b. short-term (working) memory
   c. long-term memory

   *Duration:*
   i. one week
   ii. a fraction of a second
   iii. about one day
   iv. between 20 and 30 seconds
   v. potentially as long as a person lives
   vi. until middle age

   *Capacity:*
   i. 20 chunks, plus or minus 10
   ii. 4 to 9 chunks
   iii. much of the visual world
   iv. almost limitless
   v. about 100,000 pieces of information
   vi. equal to the number of neurons in the brain

2. Which memory system is responsible for your ability to remember the first word in this question?
   a. sensory memory
   b. working memory
   c. long-term memory

**Answers:** 1. a. Duration: ii, capacity: iii; b. Duration: iv, capacity: ii; c. Duration: v, capacity: iv.
2. b. working memory

fail to learn from past experiences. Recognizing a predator and remembering an escape route will help an animal avoid being eaten. Accordingly, remembering which objects are edible, which people are friends and which are enemies, and how to get home is typically not challenging for people with intact memory systems, but it is critical for survival.

# 7.4 How Is Information Organized in Long-Term Memory?

**Learning Objectives**

- Discuss the levels of processing model.
- Explain how schemas influence memory.
- Describe spreading activation models of memory.
- Identify retrieval cues.
- Identify common mnemonics.

Imagine if a library put each of its books wherever there was empty space on a shelf. To find a particular book, a librarian would have to look through the inventory book by book. Just as this random storage would not work well for books, it would not work well for memories. When an event or some information is important enough, you want to remember it permanently. Thus you need to store it in a way that allows you to retrieve it later. The following section discusses the organizational principles of long-term memory.

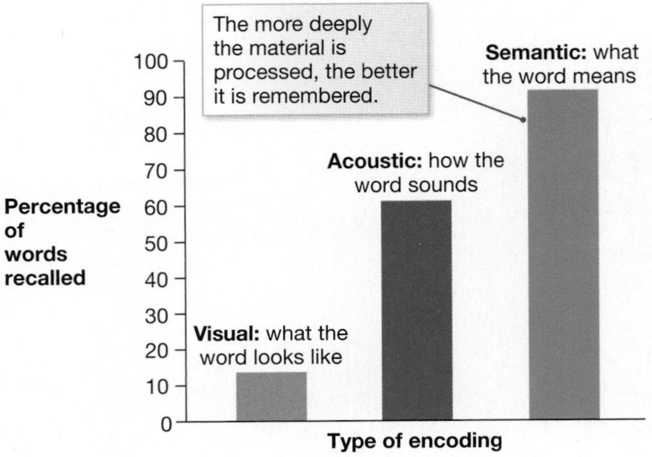


**FIGURE 7.16 Encoding** This graph shows the results of a hypothetical study of encoding. Participants are asked to consider a list of words according to how the words are printed, how they sound, or what they mean. Later they are asked to recall the words.

## Long-Term Storage Is Based On Meaning

As discussed in Chapter 4, within our brains our perceptual experiences are transformed into representations. These representations are then stored in networks of neurons. For instance, when your visual system senses a shaggy, four-legged animal and your auditory system senses barking, you perceive a dog. The concept of "dog" is a *mental representation* for a category of animals that share certain features, such as barking and fur. You do not have a tiny picture of a dog stored in your head. Rather, you have a mental representation. The mental representation for "dog" differs from that for "cat," even though the two are similar in many ways. You also have mental representations for complex and abstract ideas, including beliefs and feelings.

Mental representations are stored by meaning. In the early 1970s, the psychologists Fergus Craik and Robert Lockhart developed an influential theory of memory based on depth of elaboration. According to their *levels of processing model,* the more deeply an item is encoded, the more meaning it has and the better it is remembered. Craik and Lockhart proposed that different types of rehearsal lead to different types of encoding. *Maintenance rehearsal* is simply repeating the item over and over. *Elaborative rehearsal* encodes the information in more meaningful ways, such as thinking about the item conceptually or deciding whether it refers to oneself. In other words, in this type of rehearsal, we elaborate on basic information by linking it to knowledge from long-term memory.

How does the levels of processing model work? Suppose you show research participants a list of words and then ask them to do one of three things. You might ask them to make simple perceptual judgments, such as whether each word is printed in capital or lowercase letters. You might ask them to judge the sound of each word, as in whether the word rhymes with *boat.* Or you might ask them about each word's semantic meaning, as in "Does this word fit the sentence *They had to cross the _____ to reach the castle*?" Once participants have completed the task (that is, processed the information), you might ask them to recall as many words as possible. You will find that words processed at the deepest level, based on semantic meaning, are remembered the best (**Figure 7.16**). Brain imaging studies have shown that semantic encoding activates more brain regions than shallow encoding and this greater brain activity is associated with better memory (Kapur et al., 1994).

## Schemas Provide an Organizational Framework

If people store memories by meaning, how do they determine the meanings of particular memories? Chunking, discussed earlier, is a good way to encode groups of items for memorization. The more meaningful the chunks, the better they will be remembered. Decisions about how to chunk information depend on **schemas.** These structures in long-term memory help us perceive, organize, process, and use information. As we sort out incoming information, schemas guide our attention to an environment's relevant features. Thanks to schemas, we construct new memories by filling in holes within existing memories, overlooking inconsistent information, and interpreting meaning based on past experiences.

Although schemas help us make sense of the world, however, they can lead to biased encoding. This bias occurs in part because culture heavily influences schemas. In a classic demonstration conducted in the early 1930s, the psychologist Frederic Bartlett asked British participants to listen to a Native American folktale.

**schemas** Cognitive structures that help us perceive, organize, process, and use information.

The story involved supernatural experiences, and it was difficult to understand for non–Native Americans unfamiliar with such tales. Fifteen minutes later, Bartlett asked the participants to repeat the story exactly as they had heard it. The participants altered the story greatly. They also altered it consistently, so that it made sense from their own cultural standpoint. Sometimes they simply forgot the supernatural parts they could not understand.

To understand the influence of schemas on which information is stored in memory, consider a study in which students read a story about an unruly girl (Sulin & Dooling, 1974). Some participants were told that the subject of the story was the famous blind girl Helen Keller. Others were told it was Carol Harris, a made-up name. One week later, the participants who had been told the girl was Helen Keller were more likely to mistakenly report having read the sentence *She was deaf, mute, and blind* in the story than those who thought the story was about Carol Harris. The students' schema for Helen Keller included her disabilities. When they retrieved information about Keller from memory, they retrieved everything they knew about her along with the story they were trying to remember.

To see how schemas affect your ability to recall information, read the following paragraph carefully:

> The procedure is actually quite simple. First arrange things into different bundles depending on makeup. Don't do too much at once. In the short run this may not seem important, however, complications easily arise. A mistake can be costly. Next, find facilities. Some people must go elsewhere for them. Manipulation of appropriate mechanisms should be self-explanatory. Remember to include all other necessary supplies. Initially the routine will overwhelm you, but soon it will become just another facet of life. Finally, rearrange everything into their initial groups. Return these to their usual places. Eventually they will be used again. Then the whole cycle will have to be repeated. (Bransford & Johnson, 1972, p. 722)

How easy did you find this paragraph to understand? Could you now recall specific sentences from it? It might surprise you to know that in a research setting, college students who read this paragraph found it easy to understand and relatively straightforward to recall. How is that possible? It was easy when the participants knew that the paragraph described washing clothes. Go back and reread the paragraph. Notice how your schema for doing laundry helps you understand and remember how the words and sentences are connected to one another. You will learn more about schemas in the next chapter.

## Information Is Stored in Association Networks

One highly influential set of theories about memory organization is based on *networks of associations*. In a network model proposed by the psychologists Allan Collins and Elizabeth Loftus, an item's distinctive features are linked so as to identify the item. Each unit of information in the network is a *node*. Each node is connected to many other nodes. The resulting network is like the linked neurons in your brain, but nodes are simply bits of information. They are not physical realities. For example, when you look at a fire engine, all the nodes that represent a fire engine's features are activated. The resulting activation pattern gives rise to the knowledge that the object is a fire engine rather than, say, a car, a vacuum cleaner, or a cat.

An important feature of network models is that activating one node increases the likelihood that closely associated nodes will also be activated. As shown in

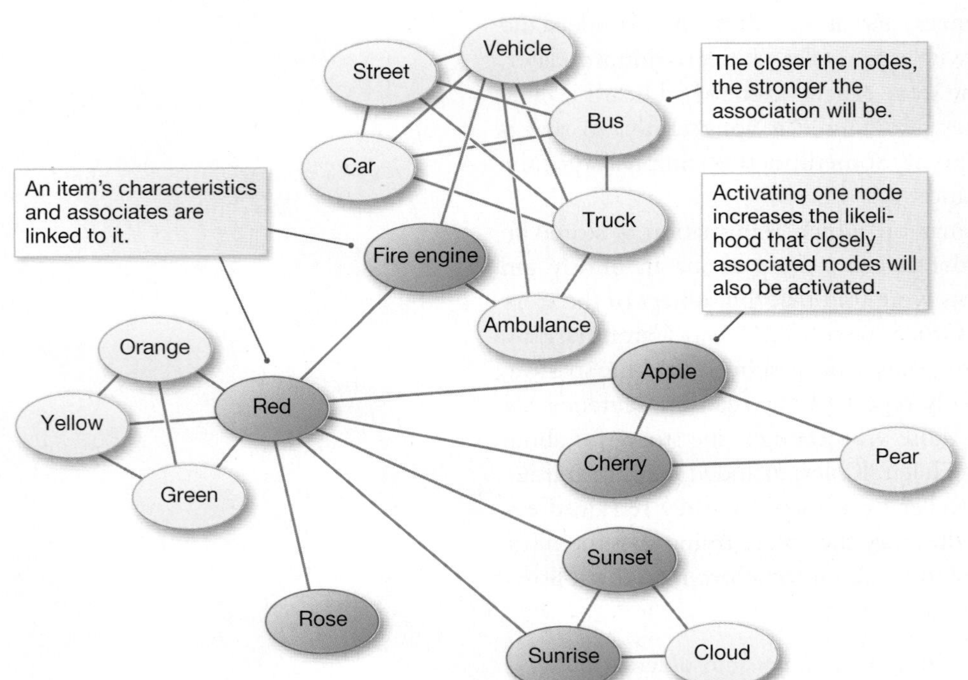


**FIGURE 7.17 A Network of Associations**
In this semantic network, similar concepts are connected through their associations.

**Figure 7.17,** the closer the nodes, the stronger the association between them and therefore the more likely it is that activating one node will activate the other. Seeing a fire engine activates nodes that indicate other vehicles. Once your fire engine nodes are activated, you will more quickly recognize other vehicles than, for instance, fruits or animals.

The main idea here—that activating one node increases the likelihood of associated nodes becoming active—is central to *spreading activation models* of memory. According to these models, stimuli in working memory activate specific nodes in long-term memory. This activation increases the ease of access to that material and thus makes retrieval easier. Indeed, a recent study showed that retrieval of some items led to enhanced memory for related items even when participants were told to forget those items (Bäuml & Samenieh, 2010).

An associative network is organized by category. The categories are structured in a hierarchy, and they provide a clear and explicit blueprint for where to find needed information quickly. Given the vast amount of material in memory, it is amazing how quickly we can search for and obtain needed memories from storage. Each time you hear a sentence, you not only have to remember what all the words mean. You also have to recall all relevant information that helps you understand the sentence's overall meaning. For this process to occur, the information needs to be organized logically. Imagine trying to find a specific file on a full 40-gigabyte hard disk by opening one file at a time. Such a method would be hopelessly slow. Instead, most computer disks are organized into folders, within each folder are more-specialized folders, and so on. Associative networks in the brain work similarly.

## Retrieval Cues Provide Access to Long-Term Storage

A **retrieval cue** can be anything that helps a person (or nonhuman animal) recall a memory. Encountering stimuli—such as the smell of turkey, a favorite song from years past, a familiar building, and so on—can trigger unintended memories. According to Endel Tulving's **encoding specificity principle,** any stimulus encoded along with an experience can later trigger a memory of the experience.

In one study of encoding, participants studied 80 words in either of two rooms. The rooms differed in ways such as location, size, and scent. The participants were then tested for recall in the room in which they studied or in the other room. When they studied and were tested in the same room, participants recalled an average of 49 words correctly. In contrast, when they were tested in the room in which they did not study, participants recalled an average of 35 words correctly (Smith, Glenberg, & Bjork, 1978). This kind of memory enhancement, when the recall situation is similar to the encoding situation, is known as

**retrieval cue** Anything that helps a person (or a nonhuman animal) recall information stored in long-term memory.

**encoding specificity principle** The idea that any stimulus that is encoded along with an experience can later trigger memory for the experience.

*context-dependent memory.* Context-dependent memory can be based on things such as physical location, odors, and background music, many of which produce a sense of familiarity (Hockley, 2008). In the most dramatic research demonstration of context-dependent memory, scuba divers learned information underwater, and they later recalled that information better underwater than on land (Godden & Baddeley, 1975; **Figure 7.18**).

Like physical context, internal cues such as mood can affect the recovery of information from long-term memory. When a person's internal states match during encoding and recall, memory can be enhanced. This effect is known as *state-dependent memory*. Research on this topic was inspired by the observation that alcoholics often misplace important objects, such as paychecks, because they store them in safe places while they are drinking but cannot remember where when they are sober. The next time they are drinking, however, they may remember where they hid the objects. Eric Eich and colleagues (1975) conducted a study of state-dependent memory and marijuana use. The participants best remembered items on a list when tested in the same state in which they had studied the list, either sober or high. Overall, however, they recalled the information best when they were sober during studying and testing. In a study involving alcohol, participants performed worst when they studied intoxicated and took the test sober (Goodwin, Powell, Bremer, Hoine, & Stern, 1969). They did worse than

**FIGURE 7.18 Scientific Method: Godden and Baddeley's Study of Context-Dependent Memory**

**Hypothesis:** When the recall situation is similar to the encoding situation, memory is enhanced.

**Research Method:**

1. One group of scuba divers learned a list of words on land.

2. Another group of scuba divers learned a list of words underwater.

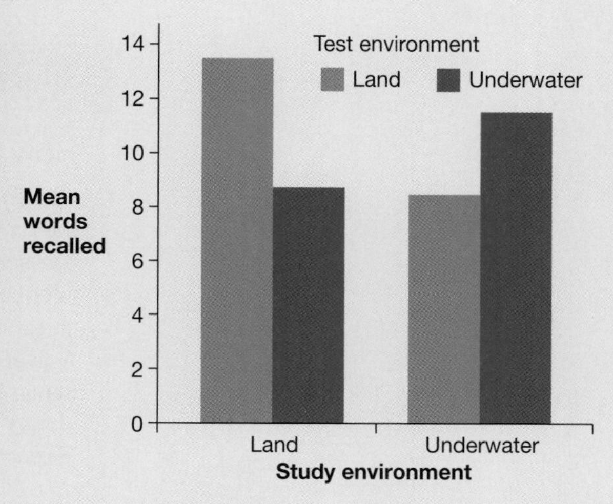


**Results:** The scuba divers who learned information underwater tested better underwater than on land. Those who studied on land tested better on land than underwater.

**Conclusion:** Information is best recalled in the same environment where it is learned.

**Source:** Godden, D. R., & Baddeley, A. D. (1975). Context-dependent memory in two natural environments: On land and underwater. *British Journal of Psychology, 66*, 325–331.

**mnemonics** Learning aids, strategies, and devices that improve recall through the use of retrieval cues.

participants who studied sober and took the test intoxicated. Participants who studied intoxicated and took the test intoxicated did much worse than those who were sober during study and test. It would be a mistake, then, to take an exam high or intoxicated. For the best results, study sober and take your tests sober.

MNEMONICS **Mnemonics** are learning aids or strategies that use retrieval cues to improve recall. People often find them helpful for remembering items in long lists, for example. One of the oldest methods dates back to the ancient Greeks, when the poet Simonides was able to recall who was killed by a ceiling collapse by visualizing where people were seated at the banquet table. Now referred to as the *method of loci* or the *memory palace,* this mnemonic consists of associating items you want to remember with physical locations. Suppose you want to remember the names of classmates you just met. First, you might visualize items from various places on your typical route across campus, or you might visualize parts of the physical layout of some familiar location, such as your bedroom. Then you would associate your classmates' names with the items or parts you have visualized. You might picture Sam climbing on your dresser, Latisha sitting on a chair, and Jerome hiding under the bed. When you later need to remember the names, you would visualize your room and retrieve the information associated with each piece of furniture.

The journalist Joshua Foer used this method when he competed in the U.S.A. Memory Championships in 2006 (Foer, 2011). During the contest, one of Foer's tasks was to memorize the order of two shuffled decks of playing cards. By imagining the cards in various locations in the house where he grew up, Foer was able to correctly remember the order of the cards in the two decks in just under 2 minutes. To keep from being distracted, he wore headphones and dark glasses. Strategies such as these enable people to excel at memory contests. The contest winners do not necessarily have better-functioning memories than most people. They are simply better able to use their memories.

## Summing Up

### How Is Information Organized in Long-Term Memory?

Human memory is stored according to meaning. The more an item is elaborated at the time of storage, the richer the later memory will be because more connections can serve as retrieval cues. Schemas help people perceive, organize, and process information. Thus schemas influence memory. Culture shapes our schemas. Hierarchical networks of associated nodes provide semantic links between related items. Activation of a node spreads throughout its network, enhancing memory of related items. Retrieval cues, including contextual cues and internal states, help us access stored information. Mnemonics, such as the method of loci and verbal mnemonics, involve the use of retrieval cues to improve recall.

## Measuring Up

1. Which is the best way to teach scuba divers how to surface safely?
   a. Teach them in a classroom so they can use their declarative knowledge on a written test.

b. Teach them underwater because the situation will provide retrieval cues for when they need to use the knowledge.
c. Teach them when they are on land and better able to pay attention.
d. Have them learn from experience so the method becomes part of a schema.

2. One strategy for improving memory is to relate something you are learning to information you already know. Why would that strategy be effective?
   a. Because the known information can act as a retrieval cue to help you remember the new information when you need it.
   b. Because the known information will create a feeling of familiarity, which will make the new information similar to what you already know.
   c. Because new information is easier to remember than known information and can help you remember older memories by making them more distinct and exciting.
   d. Because old and new information need to mingle in memory so you are not confused when you implicitly try to retrieve information.

**Answers:** 1. b. Teach them underwater because the situation will provide retrieval cues for when they need to use the knowledge.
2. a. Because the known information can act as a retrieval cue to help you remember the new information when you need it.

## 7.5 What Are the Different Long-Term Memory Systems?

**Learning Objectives**

- Distinguish between episodic, semantic, implicit, explicit, and prospective memories.
- Generate examples of each of these types of memory.

In the last few decades, most psychologists have come to view long-term memory as composed of several systems. The older view was that memories differed in terms of their strength (how likely something would be recalled) and their accessibility (the context in which something would be recalled). Generally, all memories were considered to be of the same type. In the late 1970s and early 1980s, cognitive psychologists began to challenge this view. They argued that memory is not just one entity. Rather, they saw it as a process that involves several interacting systems (Schacter & Tulving, 1994). The systems share a common function: to retain and use information. They encode and store different types of information in different ways, however. For instance, several obvious differences exist between your remembering how to ride a bicycle, your recalling what you ate for dinner last night, and your knowing that the capital of Canada is Ottawa. These are long-term memories, but they differ in how they were acquired (learned) and in how they are stored and retrieved. Remembering how to ride a bike requires a behavioral component. That is, it means integrating specific motor and perceptual skills that you acquired over time. You are not consciously aware of your efforts to maintain balance or to follow the basic rules of the road. By contrast, recalling a specific event you experienced or knowledge you learned from another source sometimes requires a conscious effort to retrieve the information from long-term memory.

Scientists do not agree on the number of human memory systems. For instance, some researchers have distinguished between memory systems based on how information is stored in memory, such as whether the storage occurs with or without deliberate effort. Other researchers have focused on the types of

**implicit memory** The system underlying unconscious memories.

**explicit memory** The system underlying conscious memories.

**declarative memory** The cognitive information retrieved from explicit memory; knowledge that can be declared.

**episodic memory** Memory for one's personal past experiences.

information stored: words and meaning, particular muscle movements, information about a city's spatial layout, and so on. The following sections explore how the different memory systems work.

## Explicit Memory Involves Conscious Effort

The most basic distinction between memory systems is a division of memories: On one hand are memories we are consciously aware of. On the other hand are memories we acquire without conscious effort or intention—memories we do not know we know. Remember that H.M., the memory loss sufferer described at the beginning of this chapter, improved at mirror tracing (tracing a pattern when only its mirror image is visible). He must have learned this motor task even without knowing he had. Peter Graf and Daniel Schacter (1985) referred to unconscious memory as **implicit memory.** They contrasted it with **explicit memory,** the processes we use to remember information we can say we know. The cognitive information retrieved from explicit memory is **declarative memory,** knowledge we can declare (consciously bring to mind).

For example, you use explicit memory when you recall what you had for dinner last night or what the word *aardvark* means. Declarative memories can involve words or concepts, visual images, or both. When you imagine the earth's orbit around the sun, you might also retrieve the images and names of the other planets. You could describe this knowledge in words, so it is declarative memory. Most of the examples presented in this chapter so far are of explicit memories. Every exam you ever took in school likely tested declarative memory.

In 1972, Endel Tulving found that explicit memory can be divided into *episodic memory* and *semantic memory*. **Episodic memory** refers to a person's past experiences and includes information about the time and place the experiences occurred (**Figure 7.19a**). If you can remember aspects of your 16th birthday, for example, such as where you were and what you did there, this information

(a)

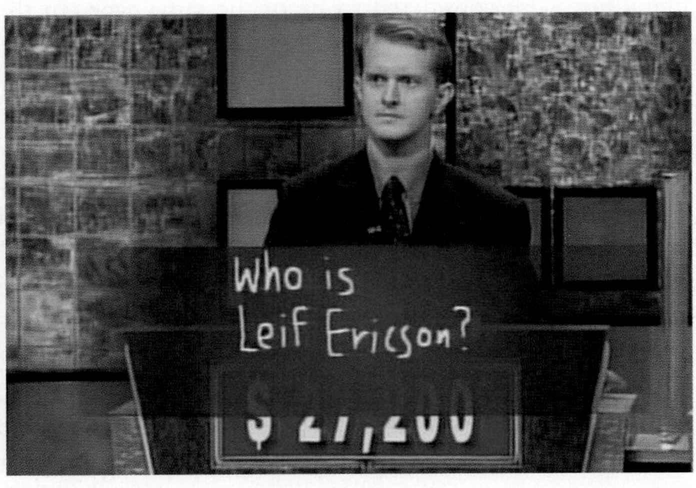


(b)

**FIGURE 7.19 Explicit Memory** Explicit memory involves information that individuals are aware of knowing. **(a)** When these World War II veterans assembled aboard the USS *Intrepid* to reminisce on Memorial Day, they were drawing on episodic memory, which is based on past experiences. **(b)** Game shows such as *Jeopardy!* test semantic memory: the memory of facts independent of personal experience. In 2004, Ken Jennings (pictured here) became the longest-defending champion on *Jeopardy!* when he won 75 games in a row.

is part of your episodic memory. **Semantic memory** represents the knowledge of facts independent of personal experience. We might not remember where or when we learned it, but we know it (**Figure 7.19b**). For instance, people know what Jell-O is, they know the capitals of countries they have never visited, and even those who have never played baseball know that three strikes mean the batter is out.

**semantic memory** Memory for knowledge about the world.

**procedural memory** A type of implicit memory that involves motor skills and behavioral habits.

Scientists have learned a great deal about normal memory by studying people such as H.M. and others who have impaired memory (Jacoby & Witherspoon, 1982). Evidence that episodic and semantic systems of explicit memory are separate can be found in cases of brain injury in which semantic memory is intact even though episodic memory is impaired. Researchers found this pattern of abnormal memory in three British people who had experienced brain damage (Vargha-Khadem et al., 1997). One child suffered the damage during a difficult delivery. The other two suffered it during early childhood (one had seizures at age 4; the other had an accidental drug overdose at age 9). Each of the three developed poor memory for episodic information. As children, they had trouble reporting what they had for lunch, what they were watching on television 5 minutes earlier, what they did during summer vacation. Their parents reported that the children had to be constantly monitored to make sure they remembered things such as going to school. Remarkably, these three children attended mainstream schools and did reasonably well. Moreover, when tested as young adults, their IQs fell within the normal range. They learned to speak and read, and they could remember many facts. For instance, when asked "Who is Martin Luther King Jr.?" one of the subjects, tested at age 19, responded, "An American; fought for Black rights, Black rights leader in the 1970s; got assassinated." These three, then, were able to encode and retrieve semantic information even though they could not remember their own personal experiences.

**FIGURE 7.20 Implicit Memory** The innate muscle memory for knowing how to ride a bicycle is procedural, or motor, memory. It is also an example of implicit memory—memory without the awareness of having the memory. Once you learn how to ride a bike, you can usually remember how to do it again, unconsciously, at any age.

## Implicit Memory Occurs without Deliberate Effort

Implicit memory consists of memories without awareness of them. In other words, you are not able to put these memories into words. Classical conditioning—discussed in Chapter 6, "Learning"—employs implicit memory. For example, if you always experience fear at the sight of a person in a white lab coat, you might have past associations (implicit memories) between a person in a white lab coat and pain.

Implicit memories do not require conscious attention. They happen automatically, without deliberate effort. Suppose that while driving you realize you have been daydreaming and have no episodic memory of the past few minutes. During that time, you employed implicit memories of how to drive and where you were going. Thus you did not crash the car or go in the wrong direction. This type of implicit memory is called **procedural memory,** or *motor memory*. It involves motor skills, habits, and other behaviors employed to achieve goals, such as coordinating muscle movements to ride a bicycle or following the rules of the road while driving (**Figure 7.20**). You remember to stop when you see a red light because you have learned to do so, and you might drive home on a specific route without even thinking about it. Procedural memories are generally so unconscious that most people find that consciously thinking about automatic behaviors interferes with the smooth production of those behaviors. For instance, the next time you are riding a bicycle, try to think about each step involved in the process. These memories are also very resistant to decay. Once you learn to ride a bike, it is likely that, unless you suffer some brain damage, you will always be able to do so.

Implicit memory influences our lives in subtle ways, as when our attitudes are influenced by implicit learning. For example, you might like someone because he or she reminds you of another person you like, even if you are unaware of the connection. Advertisers rely on implicit memory to influence our purchasing decisions. Constant exposure to brand names makes us more likely to think of them when we buy products. If you find yourself wanting a particular brand of something, you might be "remembering" advertisements for that brand, even if you cannot recall the specifics.

Our implicit formation of attitudes can affect our beliefs about people, such as whether particular people are famous. Ask yourself: Is Richard Shiffrin famous? Try to think for a second how you know him. If you thought he was famous, you might have recalled that Shiffrin was one of the psychologists who introduced the model of sensory, short-term, and long-term memory (an accomplishment that might make him famous in scientific circles). Alternatively, you might have remembered reading his name before even if you could not remember where.

In studying what he called the *false fame effect,* the psychologist Larry Jacoby had research participants read aloud a list of made-up names (Jacoby, Kelley, Brown, & Jasechko, 1989). The participants were told that the research project was about pronunciation. The next day, Jacoby had the same people participate in an apparently unrelated study. This time, they were asked to read a list of names and decide whether each person was famous or not. The participants misjudged some of the made-up names from the previous day as being those of famous people. Because the participants knew they had heard the names before but probably could not remember where, implicit memory led them to assume the familiar names were those of famous people.

## Prospective Memory Is Remembering to Do Something

"When you see Juan, tell him to call me, okay? And don't forget to bring the DVD tonight so we can watch the movie." Unlike the other types of remembering discussed so far in this chapter, **prospective memory** is future oriented. It means that a person remembers to do something at some future time (Graf & Uttl, 2001). As noted earlier in this chapter, paying attention has a "cost": The cognitive effort involved in attending to certain information makes us unable to attend closely to other information. Likewise, remembering to do something takes up valuable cognitive resources. It reduces either the number of items we can deal with in working memory or the number of things we can attend to (Einstein & McDaniel, 2005).

In a study of prospective memory, participants had to learn a list of words (Cook, Marsh, Clark-Foos, & Meeks, 2007). In one condition, they also had to remember to do something, such as press a key when they saw a certain word. The group that had to remember to do something took longer to learn the list than the control group that learned the same list of words but did not have to remember to do something.

**prospective memory** Remembering to do something at some future time.

Prospective memory involves both automatic and controlled processes. As discussed in Chapter 5, automatic processes happen without conscious awareness or intent (McDaniel & Einstein, 2000). Sometimes a retrieval cue occurs in a particular environment. For example, seeing Juan might automatically trigger your memory, so you effortlessly remember to give him the message. Sometimes particular environments do not have obvious retrieval cues for particular prospective memories. For example, you might not encounter a retrieval cue for remembering to fetch the DVD. Remembering to bring the disc might require some ongoing remembering as you head back to your room, even if you are not aware of that remembering. Prospective memory for events without retrieval cues is the reason sticky notes are so popular. In this case, you might stick a note that says "Bring DVD" on your notebook or on the steering wheel of your car. By jogging your memory, the note helps you avoid the effort of remembering. For an even more urgent reminder, you might set your cell phone alarm or electronic calendar (**Figure 7.21**).

**FIGURE 7.21 Prospective Memory** Prospective memory involves remembering to do something in the future. When you use a device, such as this personal digital assistant (PDA), to remember appointments and deadlines, you are assisting your prospective memory.

## Summing Up

### What Are the Different Long-Term Memory Systems?

Long-term memory is composed of multiple systems. Fundamental differences exist among episodic and semantic memory, explicit and implicit memory, and prospective memory. Explicit memory involves the conscious storage and retrieval of declarative memories—these memories may be episodic or semantic. Episodic memory deals with personally experienced events, such as where and when the events occurred. For example, you might remember that you had eggs for breakfast at home this morning. Semantic memory deals with facts independent of personal experiences and does not include memory for where and when the facts were learned. Implicit memory does not require conscious attention. Examples of implicit memory include procedural (or motor) memory and attitudes influenced by implicit learning. Prospective memory involves remembering to do something at a future time. If a cue to remember is available in the person's environment, prospective memory can operate automatically. Without a retrieval cue, remembering requires conscious effort.

## Measuring Up

**Indicate whether each of the following examples of memory is prospective, implicit, or explicit. If it is explicit, also indicate whether it is episodic or semantic.**

a. walking (for an adult)
b. the value of pi to six decimal places
c. writing a computer program
d. the fact that working memory is brief
e. the fact that you need to drive your sister home from school
f. the fact that the smell of eggs makes you sick and you do not know why

**Answers:** a. implicit; b. semantic and explicit; c. semantic and explicit; d. explicit and either semantic or episodic, depending on whether you remember when and where you learned it; e. prospective; f. implicit.

Learning Objectives

- List the seven sins of memory.
- Explain transience, blocking, and absentmindedness.
- Distinguish between retrograde and anterograde amnesia.
- Discuss methods to reduce persistence.

## 7.6 When Do People Forget?

In addition to remembering events and information, people fail to remember them. **Forgetting,** the inability to retrieve memory from long-term storage, is a perfectly normal, everyday experience. Ten minutes after you see a movie, you probably remember plenty of its details, but the next day you might remember mostly the plot and the main characters. Years later, you might remember the gist of the story, or you might not remember having seen the movie at all. We forget far more than we remember.

Most people bemoan forgetting. They wish they could better recall the material they study for exams, the names of childhood friends, the names of all seven dwarfs who lived with Snow White, what have you. But imagine what life would be like if you could not forget. Imagine, for example, walking up to your locker and recalling not just its combination but the 10 or 20 combinations for all the locks you have ever used. Consider the case of a Russian newspaper reporter who had nearly perfect memory. If someone read him a tremendously long list of items and he visualized the items for a few moments, he could recite the list, even many years later. But his memory was so cluttered with information that he had great difficulty functioning in normal society. Tortured by this condition, he eventually was institutionalized (Luria, 1968). Not being able to forget is as maladaptive as not being able to remember. It is therefore not surprising that we tend to best remember meaningful points. We remember the forest rather than the individual trees. Normal forgetting helps us remember and use important information.

The study of forgetting has a long history in psychological science. The late-nineteenth-century psychologist Hermann Ebbinghaus used the so-called *methods of savings* to examine how long it took people to relearn lists of nonsense syllables (e.g., vut, bik, kuh). Ebbinghaus provided compelling evidence that forgetting occurs rapidly over the first few days but then levels off. Most of us do not need to memorize nonsense syllables, but Ebbinghaus's general findings apply to meaningful material as well. You may remember very little of the Spanish or calculus you took in high school, but relearning these subjects would take you less time and effort than it took to learn them the first time. The difference between the original learning and relearning is "savings." In other words, you save time and effort because of what you remember.

Daniel Schacter (1999) has identified what he calls *the seven sins of memory* (**Table 7.1**). The first four sins—*transience, absentmindedness, blocking,* and *persistence*—are related to forgetting and remembering and are discussed here. The next three—*misattribution, suggestibility,* and *bias*—are discussed later in this chapter as distortions of memory. These so-called sins are very familiar to most people. Schacter sees them as by-products of otherwise desirable aspects of human memory. In fact, he argues that they are useful and perhaps even necessary characteristics for survival.

### Transience Is Caused by Interference

Memory **transience** is forgetting over time. Ebbinghaus observed this pattern in his studies of nonsense syllables. Many early theorists argued that such forgetting results from the memory trace's *decay* in a person's nervous system. Indeed, some evidence indicates that unused memories are forgotten. Research over the last few decades, however, has established that most forgetting occurs because of *interference* from other information. Additional information can lead to forgetting

**forgetting** The inability to retrieve memory from long-term storage.

**transience** Forgetting over time.

**TABLE 7.1 Seven Sins of Memory**

| Error | Type | Definition | Example |
|---|---|---|---|
| Transience | Forgetting | Reduced memory over time | Forgetting the plot of a movie |
| Blocking | Forgetting | Inability to remember needed information | Failing to recall the name of a person you meet on the street |
| Absentmindedness | Forgetting | Reduced memory due to failing to pay attention | Losing your keys or forgetting a lunch date |
| Persistence | Undesirable | The resurgence of unwanted or disturbing memories that we would like to forget | Remembering an embarrassing faux pas |
| Misattribution | Distortion | Assigning a memory to the wrong source | Falsely thinking that Richard Shiffrin is famous because his name is well known |
| Bias | Distortion | Influence of current knowledge on our memory for past events | Remembering past attitudes as similar to current attitudes even though they have changed |
| Suggestibility | Distortion | Altering a memory because of misleading information | Developing false memories for events that did not happen |

SOURCE: Based on Schacter (2001).

**proactive interference** When prior information inhibits the ability to remember new information.

**retroactive interference** When new information inhibits the ability to remember old information.

through *proactive interference* or *retroactive interference*. In both cases, competing information displaces the information we are trying to retrieve.

In **proactive interference,** old information inhibits the ability to remember new information. For instance, if you study for your psychology test, switch to studying for your anthropology test, and then take the anthropology test, your performance on the test might be impaired by your knowledge about psychology (**Figure 7.22a**). In **retroactive interference,** new information inhibits the ability to remember old information. So once you take the psychology test, your performance might suffer because you recall the freshly reinforced anthropology material instead (**Figure 7.22b**).

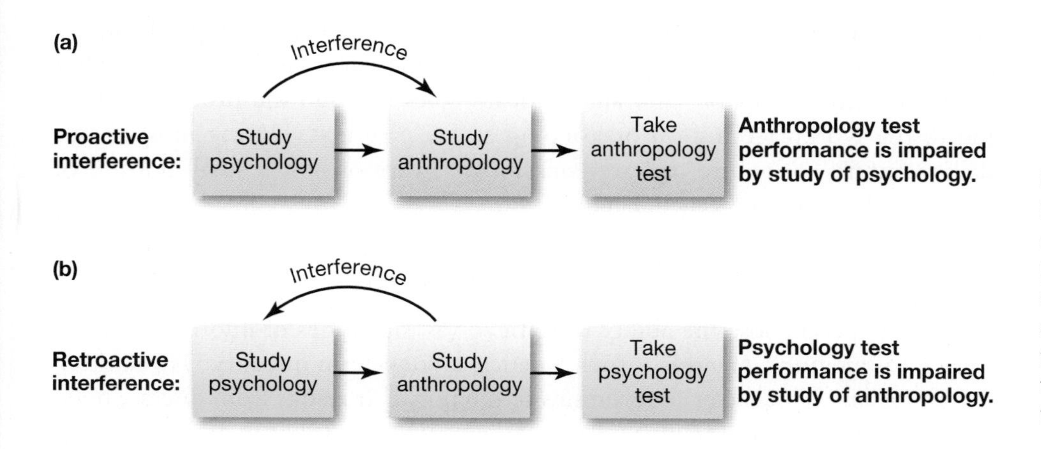


**FIGURE 7.22 Proactive and Retroactive Interference (a)** Proactive interference occurs when information already known (here, psychology material) interferes with the ability to remember new information (here, anthropology material). **(b)** Retroactive interference occurs when new information (anthropology material) interferes with memory for old information (psychology material).

**blocking** The temporary inability to remember something that is known.

**absentmindedness** The inattentive or shallow encoding of events.

**amnesia** A deficit in long-term memory, resulting from disease, brain injury, or psychological trauma, in which the individual loses the ability to retrieve vast quantities of information from long-term memory.

## Blocking Is Temporary

**Blocking** occurs when a person is temporarily unable to remember something: You cannot recall the name of a favorite song, you forget the name of someone you are introducing, you "blank" on some lines when acting in a play, and so on. Such temporary blockages are common and frustrating. Roger Brown and David MacNeill (1966) described another good example of blocking: the *tip-of-the-tongue phenomenon,* in which people experience great frustration as they try to recall specific, somewhat obscure words. For instance, when asked to provide a word that means "patronage bestowed on a relative, in business or politics" or "an astronomical instrument for finding position," people often struggle (Brown, 1991). Sometimes they know which letter the word begins with, how many syllables it has, and even what it sounds like, but even with these partial retrieval cues they cannot pull the precise word into working memory. (Did you know the words were *nepotism* and *sextant*?) Blocking often occurs because of interference from words that are similar in some way, such as in sound or meaning, and that recur. For example, you might repeatedly call an acquaintance Margaret although her name is Melanie. The tip-of-the-tongue phenomenon increases with age, perhaps because older people have greater memories that might interfere.

## Absentmindedness Results from Shallow Encoding

**Absentmindedness** is the inattentive or shallow encoding of events. The major cause of absentmindedness is failing to pay attention. For instance, you absentmindedly forget where you left your keys because when you put them down, you were also reaching to answer your phone. You forget the name of a person you are talking with because when you met, 5 minutes before, you were wondering where your keys went. You forget whether you took your vitamins this morning because you were deciding whether to study for your psychology test or your anthropology test (**Figure 7.23**).

Recall that when prospective memory fails, you fail to remember to do something. Often, this form of absentmindedness occurs because you are caught up in another activity. For instance, when you perform an automatic task, such as driving, your conscious thoughts might not include the driving experience. Your mind might wander to other ideas or memories.

There can be a negative side to this lack of attention: In the United States over the past decade, more than 300 children have died because they were left unattended in hot cars (49 in 2010 alone). In many cases, the parent forgot to drop the child off at day care on his or her way to work. It is easy to imagine forgetting your lunch in the car, but your child? Fortunately, such incidents are rare, but they seem to be especially likely when the parent's typical routine does not include day care drop-off duty. While the parent is driving, his or her brain shifts to "autopilot" and automatically goes through the process of driving to the workplace instead of stopping at day care first. During most of our daily activities, of course, we are consciously aware of only a small portion of both our thoughts and our behaviors.

**FIGURE 7.23 Absentmindedness** The major cause of absentmindedness is failing to pay sufficient attention when encoding memories. The celebrated musician Yo-Yo Ma is pictured here with his $2.5 million eighteenth-century cello, which was returned to him after he absentmindedly left it in a cab.

## Amnesia Is a Deficit in Long-Term Memory

Sometimes people lose the ability to retrieve vast quantities of information from long-term memory. **Amnesia** is such a deficit in long-term memory. This kind of loss is not one of Schacter's "seven sins of memory." It results from disease, brain injury, or psychological trauma.

The two basic types of amnesia are *retrograde amnesia* and *anterograde amnesia.* In **retrograde amnesia,** people lose past memories for events, facts, people, and even personal information. Most portrayals of amnesia in the media are of retrograde amnesia, as when a character in a soap opera awakens from a coma and does not know who he or she is (**Figure 7.24a**). By contrast, in **anterograde amnesia,** people lose the ability to form new memories (**Figure 7.24b**). As discussed at the beginning of this chapter, H.M. had a classic case of anterograde amnesia. He could remember old information about his past, but after his surgery he lost the ability to form new memories. However, H.M. may have acquired some new semantic knowledge about things that occurred after 1953. For instance, when given a list of people who became famous or infamous after 1953, H.M. was able to provide some information about them (O'Kane, Kensinger, & Corkin, 2004). This new learning may have occurred through his extensive repetition of materials over a long time. Given the name Lee Harvey Oswald, H.M. described him as the man who "assassinated the president." Oswald is believed to have shot U.S. president John F. Kennedy to death, in 1963.

(a)

(b)

**FIGURE 7.24 The Two Forms of Amnesia (a)** Jeff Ingram, pictured here, developed retrograde amnesia after leaving his home, in Washington state. When he arrived in Denver, Colorado, four days later, he had no memory of his previous life. He was recognized two months later, when he appeared on the news pleading for help from anyone who knew who he was. Though he did not remember his three-year relationship with his fiancée (here seated next to him), the two eventually married. **(b)** Most portrayals of amnesia in the media are of retrograde amnesia. In the 2000 film *Memento,* however, Leonard Shelby (played by Guy Pearce) suffers from anterograde amnesia. In other words, he cannot form new memories and therefore cannot remember recent events. In search of his wife's killer, he tattoos words onto his body to remind himself of information he has discovered.

## Persistence Is Unwanted Remembering

Sometimes you want to forget something but have difficulty doing so. **Persistence** occurs when unwanted memories recur in spite of the desire not to have them. Some unwanted memories are so traumatic that they destroy the life of the individual who suffers from them.

One prominent example of persistence occurs in posttraumatic stress disorder (PTSD; discussed further in Chapter 14, "Psychological Disorders"). PTSD is a serious mental health problem, with an estimated prevalence of 7.8 percent in the United States alone (Kessler, Sonnega, Bromet, Hughes, & Nelson, 1995). The most common triggers of PTSD include events that threaten people or those close to them. For example, the unexpected death of a loved one, a physical or sexual assault, a car accident, a natural disaster, or seeing someone badly injured or killed can be a source of PTSD. As mentioned earlier in this chapter, emotional events are associated with amygdala activity, which might underlie the persistence of certain memories.

Considerable research is under way to produce drugs that will erase unwanted memories. One drug, propranolol, blocks the postsynaptic norepinephrine receptors. If it is given before or right after a traumatic experience, the hormonally enhanced memories and fear response for that event are reduced, and the effect lasts for months (Cahill, Prins, Weber, & McGaugh, 1994; Pitman et al., 2002). Drugs such as propranolol might have side effects, however. Alternatively, as discussed earlier, extinction can be used during reconsolidation to yield the same or similar results, potentially without side effects (Schiller et al., 2010).

But erasing memories leads to many ethical questions. If we can erase traumatic memories, should we remove only the memories of traumas that were beyond the sufferer's control? Or should a person be treated for suffering a guilty conscience after an intentional malicious act? Will reducing memories to take the emotional sting out of life make us less human?

**retrograde amnesia** A condition in which people lose past memories, such as memories for events, facts, people, or even personal information.

**anterograde amnesia** A condition in which people lose the ability to form new memories.

**persistence** The continual recurrence of unwanted memories.

## Summing Up

### When Do People Forget?

Forgetting is the inability to retrieve memory from long-term storage. The ability to forget is as important as the ability to remember. Transience results from proactive or retroactive interference. That is, prior information inhibits the ability to remember new information, or new information inhibits the ability to remember old information. Blocking is a temporary inability to retrieve specific information, as exemplified by the tip-of-the-tongue phenomenon. Like transience, blocking results from interference during retrieval. Absentmindedness is caused by shallow encoding, which occurs when people fail to pay sufficient attention. Amnesia is a deficit in long-term memory. This condition results from disease, brain injury, or psychological trauma. Individuals with retrograde amnesia lose past memories. Individuals with anterograde amnesia lose the ability to form new memories. Persistence is the recurrence of unwanted memories. This problem is characteristic of posttraumatic stress disorder. Contemporary researchers are investigating methods to erase unwanted memories.

## Measuring Up

**Indicate whether each of the following is an example of retroactive interference or proactive interference or neither.**

**a.** You learned Russian as a teenager, but now you speak Hungarian. You have forgotten much of the Russian you used to know.

**b.** According to an old Yiddish saying, you should never marry someone with a name similar to that of your last spouse. Although the expression loses a lot in translation, the idea is that you will forget and call your new spouse by the old spouse's name.

**c.** For years you took a bus home from work, and then you got a new car. One night after work, you take the bus home, forgetting that you drove your new car to work.

**Answers:** a. retroactive; b. proactive; c. proactive.

**Learning Objectives**

- Define memory bias.
- Generate examples of source misattribution.
- Identify factors that contribute to errors in eyewitness testimony.
- Discuss susceptibility to false memories.
- Describe contemporary views on repressed memories.
- Discuss neuroscientific advancements in the identification of true and false memories.

# 7.7 How Are Memories Distorted?

Most people believe that human memory is permanent storage. Research has shown clearly, however, that human memory is biased, flawed, and distorted. In this section, you will learn how the human memory systems provide less-than-accurate portrayals of past events.

## People Reconstruct Events to Be Consistent

**Memory bias** is the changing of memories over time so that they become consistent with current beliefs or attitudes. As one of psychology's greatest thinkers, Leon Festinger (1987, p. 1), put it: "I prefer to rely on my memory. I have lived with that memory a long time, I am used to it, and if I have rearranged or distorted anything, surely that was done for my own benefit."

Consider students who take courses in study skills. Students often fail to heed the advice they receive in such courses, and there is only modest evidence that the courses are beneficial. Yet most students who take them describe them as extremely helpful. How can something that generally produces unimpressive outcomes be endorsed so positively? To understand this phenomenon, researchers randomly assigned students to either a genuine study skills course or a control group that received no special training. Students who took the real course showed few signs of improvement. In fact, their final-exam performances were slightly poorer than the control group's performances. Still, they considered the study skills program helpful. The experiment had one feature that helps explain why. At the beginning of the course, participants were asked to rate their studying skills. At the end of the course, they again rated themselves and were asked to recall how they had originally rated themselves. In describing their earlier ratings, students in the study skills course recalled themselves as having been significantly worse than they had rated themselves at the beginning. In this way, the students were "getting what they want[ed] by revising what they had" (Conway & Ross, 1984).

**memory bias** The changing of memories over time so that they become consistent with current beliefs or attitudes.

**flashbulb memories** Vivid episodic memories for the circumstances in which people first learned of a surprising, consequential, or emotionally arousing event.

People tend to recall their past beliefs and past attitudes as being consistent with their current ones. Often, they revise their memories when they change attitudes and beliefs. People also tend to remember events as casting them in prominent roles or favorable lights. As discussed further in Chapter 12, people also tend to exaggerate their contributions to group efforts, take credit for successes and blame failures on others, and remember their successes more than their failures. Societies, too, bias their recollections of past events. Groups' collective memories can seriously distort the past. Most societies' official histories tend to downplay their past behaviors that were unsavory, immoral, and even murderous. Perpetrators' memories are generally shorter than victims' memories.

## Flashbulb Memories Can Be Wrong

Some events cause people to experience what Roger Brown and James Kulik (1977) termed **flashbulb memories.** These vivid memories are of the circumstances in which people first learn of a surprising and consequential or emotionally arousing event. When in 1977 Brown and Kulik interviewed people about their memories of the assassination of U.S. president John F. Kennedy, they found that people described these 14-year-old memories in highly vivid terms. The details included who they were with, what they were doing or thinking, who told them or how they found out, and what their emotional reactions were to the event. In other words, flashbulb memories are an example of episodic memory. They do not reflect the problem of persistence, however, in that they are not recurring unwanted memories.

(a)

(b)

(c)

**FIGURE 7.25 Flashbulb Memories** Surprising and consequential or emotionally arousing events can produce flashbulb memories. For example, **(a)** the death of Michael Jackson, in 2009; **(b)** the explosion of the *Challenger*, in 1986; and **(c)** the resignation of Margaret Thatcher, in 1990, have left flashbulb memories of different kinds. The differences depend on how consequential the events were to the people remembering them.

**DO YOU REMEMBER WHERE YOU WERE WHEN . . . ?** Do you remember where you were when you found out that the pop star Michael Jackson had died (**Figure 7.25a**)? Or when you first heard that the jihadist leader Osama bin Laden had been killed? An obvious problem affects research into the accuracy of flashbulb memories. Namely, researchers have to wait for a "flash" to go off and then immediately conduct their study. The explosion of the U.S. space shuttle *Challenger,* on January 28, 1986, provided a unique opportunity for research on this topic. Ulric Neisser and Nicole Harsch (1993) had 44 psychology students fill out a questionnaire the day the shuttle exploded. When they tested the students' memories three years later, only three students had perfect recall, and the rest were incorrect about multiple aspects of the situation (**Figure 7.25b**).

Other researchers have documented better memory for flashbulb experiences. For example, Martin Conway and colleagues (1994) studied participants' responses to the news that the British prime minister Margaret Thatcher had resigned, in 1990. They found that participants who found the news surprising and felt the event was important had the strongest flashbulb memories. Thus students in the United Kingdom experienced stronger flashbulb memories for the Thatcher resignation than did students in the United States (**Figure 7.25c**).

For three years after the terrorist attacks on September 11, 2001, a study was conducted of more than 3,000 people across the United States (Hirst et al., 2009). Memories related to 9/11—such as where the person first heard about the attacks and the person's knowledge about the events—declined somewhat during the first year, but memory remained stable thereafter. As might be expected, people who were living in New York City on 9/11 had, over time, the most accurate memories of the World Trade Center attacks.

**EMPHASIS AND MEMORY** Although flashbulb memories are not perfectly accurate, they are at least as accurate as memory for ordinary events. Indeed, people are more confident about their flashbulb memories than they are about their ordinary memories (Talarico & Rubin, 2003). Any event that produces a strong emotional response is likely to produce a vivid, although not necessarily accurate, memory (Christianson, 1992). Or a distinctive event might simply be recalled more easily than a trivial event, however inaccurate the result. This latter pattern is known as the *von Restorff effect,* named after the researcher who first described it, in 1933. It is also possible that greater media attention to major events leads to greater exposure to the details of those events, thus encouraging better memory (Hirst et al., 2009).

## People Make Source Misattributions

**Source misattribution** occurs when people misremember the time, place, person, or circumstances involved with a memory. A good example of this phenomenon is the false fame effect, discussed earlier. This effect causes people to mistakenly believe that someone is famous simply because they have encountered the person's name before. Another example is the *sleeper effect.* Here, an argument initially is not very persuasive because it comes from a questionable source, but it becomes more persuasive over time. Suppose you see an online ad for a way to learn French while you sleep. You probably will not believe the claims in the ad. Yet over time you might remember the promise but fail to remember the source. Because the promise occurs to you without the obvious reason for rejecting it, you might come to believe that people can learn French while sleeping, or you might at least wonder if it is possible.

**SOURCE AMNESIA** **Source amnesia** is a form of misattribution that occurs when a person has a memory for an event but cannot remember where he or she encountered the information. Consider your earliest childhood memory. How vivid is it? Are you actually recalling the event or some retelling of the event? How do you know you are not remembering either something you saw in a photograph or a story related to you by family members? Most people cannot remember specific memories from before age 3. The absence of early memories, *childhood amnesia,* may be due to the early lack of linguistic capacity as well as to immature frontal lobes.

**source misattribution** Memory distortion that occurs when people misremember the time, place, person, or circumstances involved with a memory.

**source amnesia** A type of amnesia that occurs when a person shows memory for an event but cannot remember where he or she encountered the information.

**CRYPTOMNESIA** An intriguing example of source misattribution is **cryptomnesia.** Here, a person thinks he or she has come up with a new idea, but really has retrieved an old idea from memory and failed to attribute the idea to its proper source (Macrae, Bodenhausen, & Calvini, 1999). For example, students who take verbatim notes while conducting library research sometimes experience the illusion that they have composed the sentences themselves. This mistake can later lead to an accusation of plagiarism. (Be especially vigilant about indicating verbatim notes while you are taking them; see **Figure 7.26.**)

**cryptomnesia** A type of misattribution that occurs when a person thinks he or she has come up with a new idea, yet has only retrieved a stored idea and failed to attribute the idea to its proper source.

George Harrison, the late former Beatle, was sued because his 1970 song "My Sweet Lord" is strikingly similar to the song "He's So Fine," recorded in 1962 by the Chiffons. Harrison acknowledged having known "He's So Fine," but vigorously denied having plagiarized it. He argued that with a limited number of musical notes available to all musicians, and an even smaller number of chord sequences appropriate for rock and roll, some compositional overlap is inevitable. In a controversial verdict, the judge ruled against Harrison.

**FIGURE 7.26 Cryptomnesia** The 2006 novel *How Opal Mehta Got Kissed, Got Wild, and Got a Life* turned into a possible case of cryptomnesia. The author, a student at Harvard University named Kaavya Viswanathan, admitted that several passages in the work were taken from books that she read in high school. As a result, *How Opal Mehta Got Kissed* had to be recalled from bookstores. Perhaps Viswanathan, thinking she had come up with new material, had retrieved other people's writing from memory.

## People Are Bad Eyewitnesses

One of the most powerful forms of evidence is the eyewitness account. Research has demonstrated that very few jurors are willing to convict an accused individual on the basis of circumstantial evidence alone. But add one person who says, "That's the one!" and conviction becomes much more likely. This effect occurs even if it is shown that the witness had poor eyesight or some other condition that raises questions about the testimony's accuracy. Eyewitness testimony's power is troubling because witnesses are so often in error. When Gary Wells and colleagues (1998) studied 40 cases in which DNA evidence indicated that a person had been falsely convicted of a crime, they found that in 36 of these cases the person had been misidentified by at least one eyewitness (**Figure 7.27**). Why is eyewitness testimony so prone to error?

Recall the phenomenon of change blindness, discussed earlier. In studies of change blindness, people failed to notice that a person they were talking with had been replaced with a new person! Eyewitness testimony depends critically on a person's paying sufficient attention to an incident when it happens rather than after it happens. Therefore, the testimony is prone to error because often the eyewitness is not paying attention to the right details when the event happens.

**CROSS-ETHNIC IDENTIFICATION** One factor that contributes to poor eyewitness identification is that people are particularly bad at accurately identifying individuals of other ethnicities or races. This effect occurs among Caucasians, Asians, African Americans, and Hispanics. In brain imaging studies discussed in Chapter 4, African Americans and Caucasian Americans showed better memory for same-race faces. Apparently, people's superior memory for members of their own racial group is caused by greater activation in the fusiform face area (Golby, Gabrieli, Chiao, & Eberhardt, 2001). As discussed in Chapter 3, this area responds more strongly to faces than to other objects. Perhaps this area responds most strongly to same-race faces because people tend to have less frequent contact with members of other races and ethnicities. Or perhaps people encode race and ethnicity

**FIGURE 7.27 Eyewitness Accounts Can Be Unreliable** William Jackson **(left)** served five years in prison because he was wrongly convicted of a crime based on the testimony of two eyewitnesses. Note the similarities and differences between Jackson and the man on the right, the real perpetrator.

**suggestibility** The development of biased memories from misleading information.

according to rules of categorization, and they do not notice much about individuals beyond this group description.

**SUGGESTIBILITY AND MISINFORMATION** During the early 1970s, a series of important studies conducted by Elizabeth Loftus and colleagues demonstrated that people can develop biased memories when provided with misleading information. This error is the "sin" of **suggestibility.** The general methodology of this research involved showing research participants an event and then asking them specific questions about it. The different wordings of the questions altered the participants' memories for the event. In one experiment, a group of participants viewed a videotape of a car—a red Datsun—approaching a stop sign (Loftus, Miller, & Burns, 1978). A second group viewed a videotape of that same scene but with a yield sign instead of a stop sign. Each group was then asked, "Did another car pass the red Datsun while it was stopped at the stop sign?" Some participants in the second group claimed to have seen the red Datsun stop at the stop sign, even though they had seen it approaching a yield sign (**Figure 7.28**).

In another experiment, Loftus and John Palmer (1974) showed participants a videotape of a car accident. When participants heard the word *smashed* applied to the tape, they estimated the cars to be traveling faster than when they heard *contacted, hit, bumped,* or *collided.* In a related study, participants saw a videotape of a car accident and then were asked about seeing the cars either *smash into* or *hit* each other. One week later, they were asked if they had seen broken glass on the ground in the video. No glass broke in the video, but nearly one-third of those who heard *smashed* falsely recalled having seen broken glass. Very few of those who heard *hit* recalled broken glass.

**FIGURE 7.28 Scientific Method: Loftus's Studies on Suggestibility**

**Hypothesis:** People can develop biased memories when provided with misleading information.

**Research Method:**

1. One group of participants was shown a videotape of a red Datsun approaching a stop sign.

2. Another group of participants was shown a videotape of a red Datsun approaching a yield sign.

3. Immediately after viewing the tapes, the participants were asked, "Did another car pass the red Datsun while it was stopped at the stop sign?"

**Results:** Some participants who had seen the yield sign responded to the question by claiming they had seen the car at the stop sign.

**Conclusion:** People can "remember" seeing nonexistent objects.

**Source:** Loftus, E. F., Miller, D. G., & Burns, H. J. (1978). Semantic integration of verbal information into a visual memory. *Journal of Experimental Psychology: Human Learning and Memory, 4*, 19–31.

Are these sorts of laboratory analogues appropriate for studying eyewitness accuracy? After all, the sights and sounds of a traffic accident, for example, impress the event on the witness's awareness. Some evidence supports the idea that such memories are better in the real world than in the laboratory. One study examined the reports of witnesses to a fatal shooting (Yuille & Cutshall, 1986). All the witnesses had been interviewed by the police within two days of the incident. Months afterward, the researchers found the eyewitness reports, including the details, highly stable. Given that emotional state affects memories, it makes sense for accounts from eyewitnesses to be more vivid than accounts from laboratory research participants. It remains unclear, however, how accurate those stable memories were in the first place. And by retelling their stories over and over again—to the police, to friends and relatives, to researchers, and so on—eyewitnesses might inadvertently develop stronger memories for inaccurate details. This alteration may occur due to reconsolidation.

**FIGURE 7.29 Fallibility of Memory** For her photo essay *The Innocents,* Taryn Simon collaborated with members of the Innocence Project, an organization devoted to correcting errors in the criminal justice system. Here John Stickels **(right),** a member of the Innocence Project's board of directors, congratulates the exultant Patrick Waller on July 3, 2008, in a Dallas courthouse. Waller has just been told that he has been exonerated of a crime for which he had been wrongly convicted and sent to prison for 15 years. DNA evidence convinced the jury to reverse Waller's conviction.

**EYEWITNESS CONFIDENCE** How good are observers, such as jurors, at judging eyewitnesses' accuracy? The general finding from a number of studies is that people cannot differentiate accurate eyewitnesses from inaccurate ones (Clark & Wells, 2008; Wells, 2008). The problem is that eyewitnesses who are wrong are just as confident as (or *more* confident than) eyewitnesses who are right. Eyewitnesses who vividly report trivial details of a scene are probably less credible than those with poor memories for trivial details. After all, eyewitnesses to real crimes tend to be focused on the weapons or on the action. They fail to pay attention to minor details. Thus strong confidence for minor details may be a cue that the memory is likely to be inaccurate or even false. Some people are particularly confident, however, and jurors find them convincing. Taryn Simon, a photographer for the *New York Times,* created *The Innocents,* a photo essay of people who were wrongfully convicted of crimes they did not commit, most because of faulty eyewitness testimony (**Figure 7.29**). As Simon explained, "Police officers and prosecutors influence memory—both unintentionally and intentionally—through the ways in which they conduct the identification process. They can shape, and even generate, what comes to be known as eyewitness testimony" (Simon, 2003, para. 2). Simon described many compelling examples of memory's malleability. In one case, a victim, Jennifer Thompson, misidentified her attacker after being shown multiple images of possible assailants. According to Thompson, "All the images became enmeshed to one image that became Ron, and Ron became my attacker" (quoted in Simon, 2003, para. 3).

## People Have False Memories

How easily can people develop false memories (**Figure 7.30**)? Think back to when you were 5. Do you remember getting lost in a mall and being found by a kind old man who returned you to your family? No? Well, what if your family told you about this incident, including how panicked your parents were when they could not find you? According to research by Elizabeth Loftus, you might then remember the incident, even if it did not happen.

In an initial study, a 14-year-old named Chris was told by his older brother Jim, who was part of the study, about the "lost in the mall" incident. The context was a game called "Remember when. . . ." All the other incidents narrated by Jim were true. Two days later, when asked if he had ever been lost in a mall, Chris began reporting memories of how he felt during the mall episode. Within two weeks he reported the following:

**FIGURE 7.30 Try for Yourself: Creating False Recognition**

Read the following list out loud:

***sour candy sugar bitter good taste tooth nice honey soda chocolate heart cake tart pie***

Now put your book aside and write down as many of the words as you remember.

**Result:** Researchers have devised tests such as this for investigating whether people can be misled into recalling or recognizing events that did not happen (Roedigger & McDermott, 1995). For instance, without looking back, which of the following words did you recall? *Candy, honey, tooth, sweet, pie.*

If you recalled *sweet* (or think you did), you have experienced a false memory, because *sweet* was not on the original list. All the words on that list are related to sweetness, though. This basic paradigm produces false recollections reliably. Moreover, people are often extremely confident in saying they have seen or heard the words they recollect falsely.

> I was with you guys for a second and I think I went over to look at the toy store, the Kay-bee toy and uh, we got lost and I was looking around and I thought, "Uh-oh. I'm in trouble now." You know. And then I . . . I thought I was never going to see my family again. I was really scared you know. And then this old man, I think he was wearing a blue flannel shirt, came up to me. . . . [H]e was kind of old. He was kind of bald on top. . . . [H]e had like a ring of gray hair . . . and he had glasses. (Loftus, 1993, p. 532)

You might wonder if there was something special about Chris that made him susceptible to developing false memories. In a later study, however, Loftus and her colleagues used the same paradigm to assess whether they could implant false memories in 24 participants. Seven of the participants falsely remembered events that had been implanted by family members who were part of the study. How could this be so?

When a person imagines an event happening, he or she forms a mental image of the event. The person might later confuse that mental image with a real memory. Essentially, the person has a problem monitoring the source of the image. To Chris, the memory of being lost in the mall became as real as other events in childhood. Children are particularly susceptible, and false memories—such as of getting fingers caught in mousetraps or having to be hospitalized—can easily be induced in them. It is unlikely, however, that false memories can be created for certain types of unusual events, such as receiving an enema (Pezdek & Hodge, 1999).

CONFABULATION Some types of brain injury are associated with **confabulation,** the unintended false recollection of episodic memories. Morris Moscovitch, a memory research pioneer, has described confabulating as "honest lying," because the person does not intend to deceive and is unaware that his or her story is false. Moscovitch (1995) provides a striking example of confabulation in a patient he refers to as H.W. (not to be confused with H.M., the patient discussed at the opening of this chapter). The patient, a 61-year-old man, was the biological father of four children. All of his children were adults by the time H.W. experienced severe frontal lobe damage following a cerebral hemorrhage. Here is part of the clinical interview:

**confabulation** The unintended false recollection of episodic memories.

> Q. Are you married or single?

CRITICAL THINKING SKILL

## Recognizing How the Fallibility of Human Memory Can Lead to Faulty Conclusions

Brooke Patterson (2004) refers to the *tyranny of the eyewitness*. This phrase means that people generally believe eyewitnesses even though, as memory researchers have shown, eyewitnesses are frequently wrong. Of course, beliefs often remain strong despite data showing those beliefs are unjustified. And when a person confidently reports what he or she heard or saw, other people tend to assume the report reflects an accurate memory.

Most people do not like to have their memories questioned. For the most part, however, there is little or no relationship between a person's confidence about a memory and the probability of that memory's accuracy (Weber & Brewer, 2004). Unless an independent party can verify the information, it is difficult to distinguish between a valid memory and a faulty one. An unknown number of innocent people have been imprisoned or even put to death because of memory errors. No doubt, guilty people have gone free because of either faulty memories or failure to believe valid memories.

As a critical thinker with an understanding of psychological science, you must recognize the fallibility of memories. Even when you believe your own memories are accurate, you must consider the possibility that they are not. When a memory is important to some outcome, consider that memory's likely accuracy. Whenever possible, check the memory against related objective facts, such as video or audio recordings.

H.W. Married.

Q. How long have you been married?

H.W. About four months.

Q. How many children do you have?

H.W. Four. (He laughs.) Not bad for four months!

Q. How old are your children?

H.W. The eldest is 32, his name is Bob, and the youngest is 22, his name is Joe.

Q. How did you get those children in four months?

H.W. They're adopted.

Q. Does this all sound strange to you, what you are saying?

H.W. (He laughs.) I think it is a little strange.

Patients such as H.W. confabulate for no apparent purpose. They simply recall mistaken facts. When questioned, they try to make sense of their recollections by adding facts that make the story more coherent. (Chapter 5 discusses Michael Gazzaniga's theory of the interpreter and how split-brain patients confabulate to make sense of conflicting information fed to each cerebral hemisphere.)

A dramatic example of confabulation occurs in *Capgras syndrome*. People with Capgras believe that their family members have been replaced by impostors. Even when confronted with contradictory evidence, they invent facts to support their delusions. No amount of evidence can convince them that their siblings, parents, spouses, children, and other relatives are real. This bizarre syndrome is devastating

Psychology: Knowledge You Can Use

## How Can I Study More Effectively for Exams?

During your college years, you will likely take many exams. What sorts of tools does psychology offer to help you study more effectively for exams? As mentioned throughout this chapter, researchers have identified a number of methods that will help you remember information more easily. Here are some key methods. Because some of these methods are drawn from the material in this chapter, paying attention to this section will help reinforce in your mind some of the important concepts you have just read about.

1. **Distribute your learning.** Cramming does not work. Instead, distribute your study sessions. Six sessions of 1 hour each are much better for learning than one 6-hour marathon. By spreading your studying over multiple sessions, you will retain the information for longer periods of time.

2. **Elaborate the material.** Imagine you and two friends decide to engage in a little friendly competition. The challenge is to memorize a list of 20 words. Friend A simply reads the words. Friend B, after reading each word, copies the word's definition from a dictionary. You, after reading each word, think about how the word is relevant to you. For example, you see the word *rain* and think, "My car once broke down in the middle of a torrential rainstorm." Who is most likely to remember that list of words later? You are. The deeper your level of processing, the more likely you are to remember material, particularly if you make the material personally relevant.

   When you are learning something new, do not just read the material or copy down textbook descriptions. Think about the meaning of the material and how the concepts are related to other concepts. Organize the material in a way that makes sense to you, putting the concepts in your own words. Making the material relevant to you is an especially good way to process material deeply and therefore to remember it easily.

3. **Practice.** To make your memories more durable, you need to practice retrieving the information you are trying to learn. In fact, repeated testing is a more effective memory-building strategy than spending the same amount of time reviewing information you have already read. Most exams ask you to recall information. For example, you might be asked to provide a definition, apply a principle, or evaluate the relative strengths of two theories. To be successful at any of those tasks, you need to recall the relevant information. Thus, to prepare for the exam, you should practice recalling that information over and over again.

   After reading a section in this or any other book, look back to the main section heading. If that heading is not already a question, rephrase it as a question. Test yourself by trying to answer the heading's question without looking at the text. Make use of in-chapter or end-of-chapter test questions by answering these questions as you encounter them. Then answer them again a couple of days later.

   You can also develop your own practice materials. Write quiz questions. Make flash cards on either pieces of card stock or on the computer (quizlet.com is a great Web site for creating and using flash cards). For example, on one side of the flash card, write a key term. On the other side, write the definition of that term. Then drill using the flash cards in both directions. Can you recall the term when you see the definition? Can you provide the definition when you see the term? A good way to drill is to study with another member of your class and take turns quizzing each other.

to the family members accused of being imposters. People with Capgras often have damage to the frontal lobes and the limbic brain regions. The most likely cause is that the brain region involved in emotions is separated from the visual input, so the images of family members are no longer associated with warm feelings. The visual image is the same, but the feeling is not. Because of the change in feeling, the sufferer concludes that the people are not his or her real relatives. Once we understand the underlying brain mechanisms, bizarre behaviors such as this become more understandable.

### Repressed Memories Are Controversial

Over the past few decades, one of the most heated debates in psychological science has centered on repressed memories. On one side, some psychotherapists

4. **Overlearn.** With material in front of us, we are often overly confident that we "know" the information and believe we will remember it later. But recognition is easier than recall. Thus if you want to be able to recall information, you need to put in extra effort when encoding the material. Even after you *think* you have learned it, review it again. Test yourself by trying to recall the material a few hours (and a few days) after studying. Keep rehearsing until you can recall the material easily.
5. **Use verbal mnemonics.** Whatever their goals for remembering, people employ many types of mnemonics. For example, how many days are there in September? In the Western world, at least, most people can readily answer this question thanks to the old saying that begins *Thirty days hath September*. Children also learn *i before e except after c* and, along with that saying, *"weird" is weird*. By memorizing such phrases, we more easily remember things that are difficult to remember. Advertisers, of course, often create slogans or jingles that rely on *verbal mnemonics* so that consumers cannot help but remember them.

   Students have long used acronyms to remember information, such as HOMES to remember the great lakes (Huron, Ontario, Michigan, Erie, and Superior). In studying Chapter 13, the acronym OCEAN will help you remember the major personality traits: openness to experience, conscientiousness, extraversion, agreeableness, and neuroticism. Even complex ideas can be understood through simple mnemonics. For example, the phrase *cells that fire together wire together* is a way to remember long-term potentiation, the brain mechanism responsible for learning (discussed in Chapter 6).
6. **Use visual imagery.** Creating a mental image of material is an especially good way to remember. Visual imagery strategies you can use include doodling a sketch to help you link ideas to images, creating a flow chart to show how some process unfolds over time, or drawing a concept map that shows the relationships between ideas (**Figure 7.31**).

To use all of these strategies, you need to remember them. As a first step toward improving your study skills, create a mnemonic to remember these strategies!

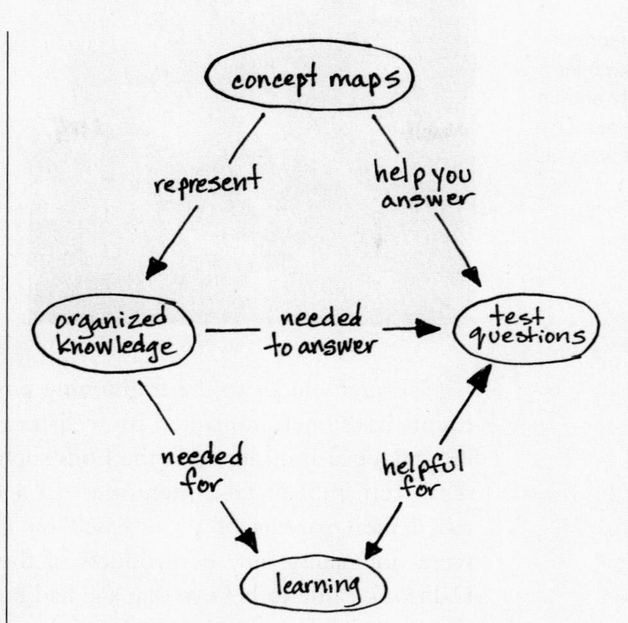


**FIGURE 7.31 Concept Map as Memory Aid** This concept map presents some ideas about—you guessed it—concept maps. When you need to visualize the relationships between different ideas about any subject, you can adapt this model. The ovals represent main ideas. The arrows indicate connections between ideas. A concept map can become far more complex. In fact, it can become as complex as you need it to be. For example, you might visually distinguish between main ideas and less important concepts by putting the main ideas in ovals and the less important concepts in triangles.

and patients claim that long-repressed memories for traumatic events can resurface during therapy. Recovered memories of sexual abuse are the most commonly reported repressed memories, and in the early 1990s there was a rash of reports about celebrities who had recovered memories of early childhood sexual abuse. On the other side, memory researchers such as Elizabeth Loftus point out that little credible evidence indicates that recovered memories are genuine or at least sufficiently accurate to be believable. Part of the problem is best summarized by a leading memory researcher, Daniel Schacter: "I am convinced that child abuse is a major problem in our society. I have no reason to question the memories of people who have always remembered their abuse, or who have spontaneously recalled previously forgotten abuse on their own. Yet I am deeply concerned by some of the suggestive techniques that have been recommended to recover repressed memories" (Schacter, 1996, p. 251).

(a)

(b)

**FIGURE 7.32 Fallibility of "Repressed Memory" (a)** Eileen Franklin **(center)** claimed to have recovered a previously repressed memory that her father had murdered a friend of hers two decades earlier. **(b)** George Franklin was found guilty and imprisoned based on his daughter's testimony. Evidence subsequently emerged proving his innocence, and he was released.

Schacter alludes to the frightening possibility that false memories for traumatic events have been implanted by well-meaning but misguided therapists. Convincing evidence indicates that methods such as hypnosis, age regression, and guided recall can implant false memories. In a few infamous examples, adults have accused their parents of abuse based on memories that the accusers later realized were not reality but the products of therapy (**Figure 7.32**). For instance, Diana Halbrook came to believe that she had been abused. She also believed that she had been involved in satanic ritualistic abuse, as part of which she had killed a baby. When she expressed doubts to her therapist and her "support" group about these events' veracity, they told her she was in denial and not listening to "the little girl" within. After all, the other members of the support group had recovered memories of being involved in satanic ritualistic abuse. After Halbrook left her therapy group, she came to believe she had not been abused and had not killed. Tellingly, "though thousands of patients have 'remembered' ritual acts, not a single such case has ever been documented in the United States despite extensive investigative efforts by state and federal law enforcement" (Schacter, 1996, p. 269).

Understandably, people on both sides of the debate about repressed memories hold strong and passionate beliefs. While research shows that some therapeutic techniques seem especially likely to foster false memories, it would be a mistake to dismiss all adult reports of early abuse. Some abuse certainly could have occurred and been forgotten until later, and we cannot ignore the memories of actual victims. In the latter half of the 1990s, the incidence of recovered memories fell dramatically, but we do not know whether this decline occurred because of less media attention to reports, because fewer people sought therapy to uncover their past memories, or because therapists stopped using these suggestive methods.

## Neuroscience May Make It Possible to Distinguish between "True" and "False" Memories

Given the many advances in the neuroscience of how we learn and remember, can any neuroscientific techniques help us distinguish between "true" memories and "false" ones? That is, can we determine when memories refer to events as they really happened? Alternatively, can we determine when memories refer to events that did not happen or that happened very differently than remembered?

Recall that when we remember something, the brain areas activated are the same ones that were active when we first learned it. For example, auditory memories activate auditory areas of the brain. Retrieving a memory seems to require the same neural activity that was involved in the initial encoding. If the memory is "true," the brain areas activated should be the same as those active when the event occurred, but if the memory is "false," unrelated brain areas would be activated (Garoff-Eaton, Slotnick, & Schacter, 2006). Some preliminary data suggest that we can make this distinction, but this emerging area of research needs a great deal of further testing. One problem with this method is that false memories tend to be similar in many ways to true memories. For example, you might correctly recall an event that occurred in high school gym class but have a false memory about the teacher involved. In a case like this one, the area of the brain involved in true memory for similar events in high school would probably also be involved in the retrieval of the false memory. A totally unrelated memory, such as a song you heard earlier today, would involve different brain regions.

## Summing Up

### How Are Memories Distorted?

Memory is far from a faithful, objective recorder of facts and events. Instead, memory often includes biases and distortions. The mind has a general bias toward maintaining consistency between our memories, beliefs, and attitudes. Nevertheless, people display unjustified confidence in their personal memories, such as flashbulb memories. People frequently display source misattribution—misremembering the time, place, person, or circumstances involved in a memory. Examples of source misattribution include source amnesia and cryptomnesia. People tend to make poor eyewitnesses: They often fail to pay attention to the incidents and people they observe, and they are suggestible to misleading information. Memories can be distorted, or even implanted, by false information. Confabulation, or "honest lying," has been documented among individuals with Capgras syndrome, characterized by damage to the frontal lobes and limbic system. The legitimacy of repressed memories continues to be debated by contemporary psychologists, many of whom argue that such memories may be implanted by suggestive techniques. Neuroscientists are attempting to develop techniques to distinguish between true and false memories on the basis of patterns of brain activation.

## Measuring Up

1. Flashbulb memories ______________.
   a. are almost always true memories because they involve emotional events
   b. are likely to be wrong because people misattribute the source of information
   c. are often distorted in the same way as other memories, but "feel" true to the people whose memories they are
   d. are less important for men than for women because, on average, men are less emotional and have less need to remember emotional events
2. Suppose a teacher accuses you of plagiarizing a term paper. To back up his accusation, he shows you a published passage similar to one you wrote in your paper. Of course, you did not commit plagiarism—you would never do that. Which of the following phenomena might be cited in your defense?
   a. cryptomnesia
   b. social comparison
   c. absentmindedness
   d. temporary blocking

**Answers:** 1. c. are often distorted in the same way as other memories, but "feel" true to the people whose memories they are.
2. a. cryptomnesia.

# StudySpace: Your Place for a Better Grade

**Visit StudySpace to access free review materials, such as:**

- complete study outlines
- vocabulary flashcards of all key terms
- additional chapter review quizzes

## Chapter Summary

### 7.1 What Is Memory?

- **Memory Is the Nervous System's Capacity to Acquire and Retain Usable Skills and Knowledge:** Memory enables organisms to take information from experiences and store it for retrieval at a later time.
- **Memory Is the Processing of Information:** Memory involves three phases. The first phase, encoding, is the processing of information so that it can be stored. The second phase, storage, is the retention of encoded information. The third phase, retrieval, is the recall of previously encoded and stored information.
- **Memory Is the Result of Brain Activity:** Multiple brain regions have been implicated in memory, including the hippocampus, temporal lobes, cerebellum, amygdala, prefrontal cortex, and the brain structures involved in perception. Through consolidation, immediate memories become lasting memories. Through reconsolidation, memories may be altered.

### 7.2 How Does Attention Determine What We Remember?

- **Our Visual Attention Works Selectively and Serially:** Simple searches for stimuli that differ in only one primary factor (e.g., shape, motion, size, color, orientation) occur automatically and rapidly through parallel processing. In contrast, searches for objects that are the conjunction of two or more properties (e.g., red and X shaped) occur slowly and serially.
- **Our Auditory Attention Allows Us to Listen Selectively:** We can attend to more than one message at a time, but we cannot do this well. There is evidence that we weakly process some unattended information.
- **Through Selective Attention, We Filter Incoming Information:** We often do not notice large changes in an environment because we fail to pay attention. This phenomenon is known as change blindness.

### 7.3 How Are Memories Maintained over Time?

- **Sensory Memory Is Brief:** Visual, auditory, olfactory, gustatory, and tactile memories are maintained long enough to ensure continuous sensory experiences.
- **Working Memory Is Active:** Working memory is an active processing system that keeps information available for current use. Chunking reduces information into units that are easier to remember. Research suggests that working memory may be limited to as few as four chunks of information.
- **Long-Term Memory Is Relatively Permanent:** Long-term memory is a relatively permanent, virtually limitless store. Information that is repeatedly retrieved, that is deeply processed, or that helps us adapt to an environment is most likely to enter long-term memory.

### 7.4 How Is Information Organized in Long-Term Memory?

- **Long-Term Memory Is Based on Meaning:** Maintenance rehearsal involves repetition. Elaborative rehearsal involves encoding information more meaningfully—for example, on the basis of semantic meaning. Elaborative rehearsal is more effective for long-term remembering than maintenance rehearsal.
- **Schemas Provide an Organizational Framework:** Schemas are cognitive structures that help people perceive, organize, and process information. Thus schemas influence memory. Culture shapes schemas. As a result, people from distinct cultures process information in different ways.
- **Information Is Stored in Association Networks:** Networks of associations are formed by nodes of information. The nodes are linked together and activated through spreading activation.
- **Retrieval Cues Provide Access to Long-Term Storage:** According to the encoding specificity principle, any stimulus encoded along with an experience can later trigger the memory of the experience. Mnemonics are learning aids or strategies that use retrieval cues to improve recall. Examples include the method of loci and verbal mnemonics.

### 7.5 What Are the Different Long-Term Memory Systems?

- **Explicit Memory Involves Conscious Effort:** Explicit, declarative memories that we consciously remember include personal events (episodic memory) and general, factual knowledge (semantic memory).
- **Implicit Memory Occurs without Deliberate Effort:** Procedural (motor) memories of how to do things automatically are implicit.
- **Prospective Memory Is Remembering to Do Something:** Prospective memory has "costs" in terms of reducing working memory capacity and reducing attention.

### 7.6 When Do People Forget?

- **Transience Is Caused by Interference:** Forgetting over time occurs because of interference from old information and new information.
- **Blocking Is Temporary:** The tip-of-the-tongue phenomenon is a person's temporary trouble retrieving the right word. This phenomenon is usually due to interference from a similar word.
- **Absentmindedness Results from Shallow Encoding:** Inattentive or shallow processing causes memory failure.

- **Amnesia Is a Deficit in Long-Term Memory:** Disease, injury, or psychological trauma can result in amnesia. Retrograde amnesia is the inability to recall past memories. Anterograde amnesia is the inability to form new memories.
- **Persistence Is Unwanted Remembering:** Persistence is the recurrence of unwanted memories. This problem is common among individuals with posttraumatic stress disorder. Researchers are investigating methods to erase unwanted memories.

### 7.7 How Are Memories Distorted?

- **People Reconstruct Events to Be Consistent:** People exhibit memory bias. That is, over time they make their memories consistent with their current beliefs or attitudes.
- **Flashbulb Memories Can Be Wrong:** The strong emotional response that attends a flashbulb memory may affect the memory's strength and accuracy.
- **People Make Source Misattributions:** People can misremember the time, place, person, or circumstances involved with a memory (source misattribution). In source amnesia, a person cannot remember where she or he encountered the information associated with a memory. In cryptomnesia, a person believes that he or she came up with a new idea, but only retrieved the idea from memory.
- **People Are Bad Eyewitnesses:** Poor eyewitness recall occurs because people often fail to pay attention to events and are suggestible to misleading information. People are particularly poor at identifying those whose ethnicities are different from their own.
- **People Have False Memories:** False memories can be implanted. Children are particularly susceptible to false memories. Confabulation, or "honest lying," is associated with some forms of brain damage.
- **Repressed Memories Are Controversial:** Psychologists continue to debate the validity of repressed memories. Some therapeutic techniques are highly suggestive and may contribute to the occurrence of false repressed memories.
- **Neuroscience May Make It Possible to Distinguish between "True" and "False" Memories:** By examining brain activity during encoding and retrieval, researchers hope to distinguish between true and false memories. Further research is needed in this emerging area of neuroscience.

## Key Terms

absentmindedness, p. 300
amnesia, p. 300
anterograde amnesia, p. 301
blocking, p. 300
change blindness, p. 276
chunking, p. 282
confabulation, p. 308
consolidation, p. 271
cryptomnesia, p. 305
declarative memory, p. 294
encoding, p. 269
encoding specificity principle, p. 290
episodic memory, p. 294
explicit memory, p. 294
flashbulb memories, p. 303
forgetting, p. 298
implicit memory, p. 294
long-term memory, p. 283
memory, p. 269
memory bias, p. 302
mnemonics, p. 292
parallel processing, p. 274
persistence, p. 301
proactive interference, p. 299
procedural memory, p. 295
prospective memory, p. 296
reconsolidation, p. 272
retrieval, p. 270
retrieval cue, p. 290
retroactive interference, p. 299
retrograde amnesia, p. 301
schemas, p. 288
semantic memory, p. 295
sensory memory, p. 279
serial position effect, p. 283
short-term memory, p. 281
source amnesia, p. 304
source misattribution, p. 304
storage, p. 269
suggestibility, p. 306
transience, p. 298
working memory, p. 281

## Practice Test

1. The card game Set requires players to attend to four features (shape, color, shading, and number) across 12 cards in an effort to identify a "Set." A player has identified a Set when "any feature in the 'Set' of three cards is either common to all three cards or is different on each card" (directions from Set Enterprises, Inc.). Playing this game requires participants to engage in a _____, which is _____.
   a. conjunction task; effortful
   b. conjunction task; fast and automatic
   c. primitive features task; effortful
   d. primitive features task; fast and automatic
2. Sarah and Anna are chatting at a coffee shop. Anna notices that Sarah does not seem to be paying attention to what she, Anna, is saying. Which strategy could Anna use to effectively pull Sarah's attention back to the conversation?
   a. Anna should buy Sarah a fresh cup of coffee; more caffeine will help her pay attention.
   b. Anna should covertly modify something about her own appearance (e.g., remove her earrings); even subtle changes in a person's visual field draw attention.
   c. Anna should lower her voice to a near-whisper.
   d. Anna should use Sarah's name in a sentence.

The answer key for the Practice Tests can be found at the back of the book. It also includes answers to the green caption questions.

# GLOSSARY

**absentmindedness** The inattentive or shallow encoding of events.

**accommodation** The process by which we create a new schema or drastically alter an existing schema to include new information that otherwise would not fit into the schema.

**accuracy** The extent to which an experimental measure is free from error.

**acetylcholine (ACh)** The neurotransmitter responsible for motor control at the junction between nerves and muscles; also involved in mental processes such as learning, memory, sleeping, and dreaming.

**acquisition** The gradual formation of an association between the conditioned and unconditioned stimuli.

**action potential** The neural impulse that passes along the axon and subsequently causes the release of chemicals from the terminal buttons.

**activation-synthesis theory** A theory of dreaming; this theory proposes that the brain tries to make sense of random brain activity that occurs during sleep by synthesizing the activity with stored memories.

**adaptations** In evolutionary theory, the physical characteristics, skills, or abilities that increase the chances of reproduction or survival and are therefore likely to be passed along to future generations.

**additive color mixing** A process of color mixing that occurs when different wavelengths of light interact within the eye's receptors; a psychological process.

**aggression** Any behavior that involves the intention to harm someone else.

**agonists** Drugs that enhance the actions of neurotransmitters.

**agoraphobia** An anxiety disorder marked by fear of being in situations in which escape may be difficult or impossible.

**all-or-none principle** The principle whereby a neuron fires with the same potency each time, although frequency can vary; a neuron either fires or not—it cannot partially fire.

**altruism** The providing of help when it is needed, without any apparent reward for doing so.

**amnesia** A deficit in long-term memory, resulting from disease, brain injury, or psychological trauma, in which the individual loses the ability to retrieve vast quantities of information from long-term memory.

**amygdala** A brain structure that serves a vital role in our learning to associate things with emotional responses and in processing emotional information.

**analogical representations** Mental representations that have some of the physical characteristics of objects; they are analogous to the objects.

**anorexia nervosa** An eating disorder characterized by an excessive fear of becoming fat and thus a refusal to eat.

**antagonists** Drugs that inhibit the actions of neurotransmitters.

**anterograde amnesia** A condition in which people lose the ability to form new memories.

**anti-anxiety drugs** A class of psychotropic medications used for the treatment of anxiety.

**antidepressants** A class of psychotropic medications used for the treatment of depression.

**antipsychotics** A class of psychotropic medications used for the treatment of schizophrenia and other disorders that involve psychosis.

**antisocial personality disorder (APD)** A personality disorder marked by a lack of empathy and remorse.

**applied behavioral analysis (ABA)** An intensive treatment for autism, based on operant conditioning.

**arousal** Physiological activation (such as increased brain activity) or increased autonomic responses (such as increased heart rate, sweating, or muscle tension).

**assessment** In psychology, examination of a person's mental state to diagnose possible psychological disorders.

**assimilation** The process by which we place new information into an existing schema.

**attachment** A strong emotional connection that persists over time and across circumstances.

**attention deficit hyperactivity disorder (ADHD)** A disorder characterized by restlessness, inattentiveness, and impulsivity.

**attitudes** People's evaluations of objects, of events, or of ideas.

**attributions** People's explanations for why events or actions occur.

**audition** Hearing; the sense of sound perception.

**autistic disorder** A developmental disorder characterized by deficits in social interaction, by impaired communication, and by restricted interests.

**autonomic nervous system (ANS)** A component of the peripheral nervous system; it transmits sensory signals and motor signals between the central nervous system and the body's glands and internal organs.

**availability heuristic** Making a decision based on the answer that most easily comes to mind.

**axon** A long narrow outgrowth of a neuron by which information is transmitted to other neurons.

**basal ganglia** A system of subcortical structures that are important for the production of planned movement.

**behavior modification** The use of operant-conditioning techniques to eliminate unwanted behaviors and replace them with desirable ones.

**behavioral approach system (BAS)** The brain system involved in the pursuit of incentives or rewards.

**behavioral inhibition system (BIS)** The brain system that is sensitive to punishment and therefore inhibits behavior that might lead to danger or pain.

**behaviorism** A psychological approach that emphasizes the role of environmental forces in producing behavior.

**behavior therapy** Treatment based on the premise that behavior is learned and therefore can be unlearned through the use of classical and operant conditioning.

**binocular depth cues** Cues of depth perception that arise from the fact that people have two eyes.

**binocular disparity** A depth cue; because of the distance between a person's eyes, each eye receives a slightly different retinal image.

**biological therapies** Treatment based on medical approaches to illness and to disease.

**biopsychosocial model** A model of health that integrates the effects of biological, behavioral, and social factors on health and illness.

**bipolar disorder** A mood disorder characterized by alternating periods of depression and mania.

**blindsight** A condition in which people who are blind have some spared visual capacities in the absence of any visual awareness.

**blocking** The temporary inability to remember something that is known.

**body mass index (BMI)** A ratio of body weight to height, used to measure obesity.

**borderline personality disorder** A personality disorder characterized by disturbances in identity, in affect, and in impulse control.

**bottom-up processing** A hierarchical model of pattern recognition in which data are relayed from one level of mental processing to the next, always moving to a higher level of processing.

**brain stem** An extension of the spinal cord; it houses structures that control functions associated with survival, such as breathing, swallowing, vomiting, urination, and orgasm.

**Broca's area** A small portion of the left frontal region of the brain, crucial for the production of language.

**buffering hypothesis** The idea that other people can provide direct emotional support in helping individuals cope with stressful events.

**bulimia nervosa** An eating disorder characterized by dieting, binge eating, and purging.

**bystander intervention effect** The failure to offer help by those who observe someone in need.

**case studies** A research method that involves the intensive examination of unusual people or organizations.

**cell body** Site, in the neuron, where information from thousands of other neurons is collected and integrated.

**central nervous system (CNS)** The brain and the spinal cord.

**central tendency** A measure that represents the typical response or the behavior of a group as a whole.

**cerebellum** A large, convoluted protuberance at the back of the brain stem; it is essential for coordinated movement and balance.

**cerebral cortex** The outer layer of brain tissue, which forms the convoluted surface of the brain.

**change blindness** A failure to notice large changes in one's environment.

**chromosomes** Structures within the cell body that are made up of DNA. DNA consists of genes.

**chunking** Organizing information into meaningful units to make it easier to remember.

**circadian rhythms** The regulation of biological cycles into regular patterns.

**classical conditioning (Pavlovian conditioning)** A type of learned response; a neutral object comes to elicit a response when it is associated with a stimulus that already produces that response.

**client-centered therapy** An empathic approach to therapy; it encourages people to fulfill their individual potentials for personal growth through greater self-understanding.

**cognition** Mental activity that includes thinking and the understandings that result from thinking.

**cognitive-behavioral approach** A diagnostic model that views psychopathology as the result of learned, maladaptive thoughts and beliefs.

**cognitive-behavioral therapy (CBT)** A therapy that incorporates techniques from cognitive therapy and behavior therapy to correct faulty thinking and change maladaptive behaviors.

**cognitive dissonance** An uncomfortable mental state due to a contradiction between two attitudes or between an attitude and a behavior.

**cognitive map** A visual/spatial mental representation of an environment.

**cognitive neuroscience** The study of the neural mechanisms (mechanisms involving the brain, nerves, and nervous tissue) that underlie thought, learning, and memory.

**cognitive psychology** The study of how people think, learn, and remember.

**cognitive restructuring** A therapy that strives to help patients recognize maladaptive thought patterns and replace them with ways of viewing the world that are more in tune with reality.

**cognitive therapy** Treatment based on the idea that distorted thoughts produce maladaptive behaviors and emotions; treatment strategies attempt to modify these thought patterns.

**compliance** The tendency to agree to do things requested by others.

**concept** A mental representation that groups or categorizes objects, events, or relations around common themes.

**concrete operational stage** The third stage in Piaget's theory of cognitive development; during this stage, children begin to think about and understand logical operations, and they are no longer fooled by appearances.

**conditioned response (CR)** A response to a conditioned stimulus; a response that has been learned.

**conditioned stimulus (CS)** A stimulus that elicits a response only after learning has taken place.

**cones** Retinal cells that respond to higher levels of illumination and result in color perception.

**confabulation** The unintended false recollection of episodic memories.

**conformity** The altering of one's behaviors and opinions to match those of other people or to match other people's expectations.

**confound** Anything that affects a dependent variable and may unintentionally vary between the experimental conditions of a study.

**consciousness** One's subjective experience of the world, resulting from brain activity.

**consolidation** A process by which immediate memories become lasting (or long-term) memories.

**continuous reinforcement** A type of learning in which the desired behavior is reinforced each time it occurs.

**control group** A comparison group; the participants in a study that receive no intervention or receive an intervention that is unrelated to the independent variable being investigated.

**conventional level** Middle stage of moral development; at this level, strict adherence to societal rules and the approval of others determine what is moral.

**convergence** A cue of binocular depth perception; when a person views a nearby object, the eye muscles turn the eyes inward.

**coping response** Any response an organism makes to avoid, escape from, or minimize an aversive stimulus.

**cornea** The clear outer covering of the eye.

**correlational studies** A research method that examines how variables are naturally related in the real world, without any attempt by the researcher to alter them or assign causation between them.

**critical thinking** Systematically evaluating information to reach reasonable conclusions.

**cross-sectional studies** A research method that compares participants in different groups (e.g., young and old) at the same time.

**cryptomnesia** A type of misattribution that occurs when a person thinks he or she has come up with a new idea, yet has only retrieved a stored idea and failed to attribute the idea to its proper source.

**crystallized intelligence** Intelligence that reflects both the knowledge one acquires through experience and the ability to use that knowledge.

**culturally sensitive research** Studies that take into account the role that culture plays in determining thoughts, feelings, and actions.

**culture** The beliefs, values, rules, and customs that exist within a group of people who share a common language and environment and that are transmitted through learning from one generation to the next.

**data** Objective observations or measurements.

**decision making** Attempting to select the best alternative among several options.

**declarative memory** The cognitive information retrieved from explicit memory; knowledge that can be declared.

**deductive reasoning** Using general rules to draw conclusions about specific instances.

**defense mechanisms** Unconscious mental strategies that the mind uses to protect itself from distress.

**defining attribute model** A way of thinking about concepts: A category is characterized by a list of features that determine if an object is a member of the category.

**deindividuation** A state of reduced individuality, reduced self-awareness, and reduced attention to personal standards; this phenomenon may occur when people are part of a group.

**delusions** False beliefs based on incorrect inferences about reality.

**dendrites** Branchlike extensions of the neuron that detect information from other neurons.

**dependent variable** In an experiment, the variable that is affected by the manipulation of the independent variable.

**descriptive statistics** Statistics that summarize the data collected in a study.

**descriptive studies** A research method that involves observing and noting the behavior of people or other animals to provide a systematic and objective analysis of the behavior.

**developmental psychology** The study of changes, over the life span, in physiology, cognition, emotion, and social behavior.

**dialectical behavior therapy (DBT)** A form of therapy used to treat borderline personality disorder.

**diathesis-stress model** A diagnostic model that proposes that a disorder may develop when an underlying vulnerability is coupled with a precipitating event.

**directionality problem** A problem encountered in correlational studies; the researchers find a relationship between two variables, but they cannot determine which variable may have caused changes in the other variable.

**discrimination** The inappropriate and unjustified treatment of people as a result of prejudice.

**disorganized behavior** Acting in strange or unusual ways, including strange movement of limbs, bizarre speech, and inappropriate self-care, such as failing to dress properly or bathe.

**display rules** Rules learned through socialization that dictate which emotions are suitable to given situations.

**dissociative disorders** Mental disorders that involve disruptions of identity, of memory, or of conscious awareness.

**dissociative identity disorder (DID)** The occurrence of two or more distinct identities in the same individual.

**dizygotic twins** Also called *fraternal twins;* twin siblings that result from two separately fertilized eggs and therefore are no more similar genetically than nontwin siblings.

**dominant gene** A gene that is expressed in the offspring whenever it is present.

**dopamine** A monoamine neurotransmitter involved in motivation, reward, and motor control over voluntary movement.

**dreams** Products of an altered state of consciousness in which images and fantasies are confused with reality.

**drive** A psychological state that, by creating arousal, motivates an organism to satisfy a need.

**dynamic systems theory** The view that development is a self-organizing process, where new forms of behavior emerge through consistent interactions between a biological being and his or her cultural and environmental contexts.

**dysthymia** A form of depression that is not severe enough to be diagnosed as major depression.

**eardrum** A thin membrane that marks the beginning of the middle ear; sound waves cause it to vibrate.

**ego** In psychodynamic theory, the component of personality that tries to satisfy the wishes of the id while being responsive to the dictates of the superego.

**elaboration likelihood model** A theory of how persuasive messages lead to attitude changes.

**electroconvulsive therapy (ECT)** A procedure that involves administering a strong electrical current to the patient's brain to produce a seizure; it is effective for some cases of severe depression.

**electroencephalograph (EEG)** A device that measures electrical activity in the brain.

**emotion** Feelings that involve subjective evaluation, physiological processes, and cognitive beliefs.

**emotional intelligence (EI)** A form of social intelligence that emphasizes the abilities to manage, recognize, and understand emotions and use emotions to guide appropriate thought and action.

**emotion-focused coping** A type of coping in which people try to prevent having an emotional response to a stressor.

**encoding** The processing of information so that it can be stored.

**encoding specificity principle** The idea that any stimulus that is encoded along with an experience can later trigger memory for the experience.

**endocrine system** A communication system that uses hormones to influence thoughts, behaviors, and actions.

**endorphins** Neurotransmitters involved in natural pain reduction and reward.

**epinephrine** A monoamine neurotransmitter responsible for bursts of energy after an event that is exciting or threatening.

**episodic memory** Memory for one's personal past experiences.

**etiology** Factors that contribute to the development of a disorder.

**evolutionary theory** A theory presented by the naturalist Charles Darwin; it views the history of a species in terms of the inherited, adaptive value of physical characteristics, of mental activity, and of behavior.

**exemplar model** A way of thinking about concepts: All members of a category are examples (exemplars); together they form the concept and determine category membership.

**experiment** A study that tests causal hypotheses by measuring and manipulating variables.

**experimental groups** Treatment groups; the participants in a study that receive the intervention.

**experimenter expectancy effect** Actual change in the behavior of the people or nonhuman animals being observed that is due to the expectations of the observer.

**explicit attitudes** Attitudes that a person can report.

**explicit memory** The system underlying conscious memories.

**exposure** A cognitive-behavioral therapy technique that involves repeated exposure to an anxiety-producing stimulus or situation.

**expressed emotion** A pattern of negative actions by a client's family members; the pattern includes critical comments, hostility directed toward the client by family members, and emotional overinvolvement.

**external validity** The degree to which the findings of an experiment can be generalized outside the laboratory.

**extinction** A process in which the conditioned response is weakened when the conditioned stimulus is repeated without the unconditioned stimulus.

**extrinsic motivation** Motivation to perform an activity because of the external goals toward which that activity is directed.

**family systems model** A diagnostic model that considers symptoms within an individual as indicating problems within the family.

**fight-or-flight response** The physiological preparedness of animals to deal with danger.

**five-factor theory** The idea that personality can be described using five factors: openness to experience, conscientiousness, extraversion, agreeableness, and neuroticism.

**fixed schedule** A schedule in which reinforcement is provided after a specific number of occurrences or a specific amount of time.

**flashbulb memories** Vivid episodic memories for the circumstances in which people first learned of a surprising, consequential, or emotionally arousing event.

**fluid intelligence** Intelligence that reflects the ability to process information, particularly in novel or complex circumstances.

**forgetting** The inability to retrieve memory from long-term storage.

**formal operational stage** The final stage in Piaget's theory of cognitive development; during this stage, teenagers can think abstractly, and they can formulate and test hypotheses through deductive logic.

**fovea** The center of the retina, where cones are densely packed.

**framing** The effect of presentation on how information is perceived.

**frontal lobes** Regions of the cerebral cortex—at the front of the brain—important for movement and higher-level psychological processes associated with the prefrontal cortex.

**frustration-aggression hypothesis** The extent to which people feel frustrated predicts the likelihood that they will act aggressively.

**functionalism** An approach to psychology concerned with the adaptive purpose, or function, of mind and behavior.

**functional magnetic resonance imaging (fMRI)** An imaging technique used to examine changes in the activity of the working human brain.

**fundamental attribution error** In explaining other people's behavior, the tendency to overemphasize personality traits and underestimate situational factors.

**GABA** Gamma-aminobutyric acid; the primary inhibitory transmitter in the nervous system.

**gender identity** Personal beliefs about whether one is male or female.

**gender roles** The characteristics associated with males and females because of cultural influence or learning.

**gender schemas** Cognitive structures that reflect the perceived appropriateness of male and female characteristics and behaviors.

**general adaptation syndrome** A consistent pattern of responses to stress that consists of three stages: alarm, resistance, and exhaustion.

**general intelligence (g)** The idea that one general factor underlies intelligence.

**generalized anxiety disorder (GAD)** A diffuse state of constant anxiety not associated with any specific object or event.

**genes** The units of heredity that help determine the characteristics of an organism.

**genotype** The genetic constitution of an organism, determined at the moment of conception.

**Gestalt theory** A theory based on the idea that the whole of personal experience is different from simply the sum of its constituent elements.

**glutamate** The primary excitatory transmitter in the nervous system.

**gonads** The main endocrine glands involved in sexual behavior: in males, the testes; in females, the ovaries.

**gustation** The sense of taste.

**habituation** A decrease in behavioral response after repeated exposure to a nonthreatening stimulus.

**hallucinations** False sensory perceptions that are experienced without an external source.

**haptic sense** The sense of touch.

**health psychology** A field that integrates research on health and on psychology; it involves the application of psychological principles to promote health and well-being.

**heritability** A statistical estimate of the extent to which variation in a trait within a population is due to genetic factors.

**heuristics** Shortcuts (rules of thumb or informal guidelines) used to reduce the amount of thinking that is needed to make decisions.

**hippocampus** A brain structure that is associated with the formation of memories.

**homeostasis** The tendency for bodily functions to maintain equilibrium.

**hormones** Chemical substances, released from endocrine glands, that travel through the bloodstream to targeted tissues; the tissues are subsequently influenced by the hormones.

**humanistic approaches** Approaches to studying personality that emphasize how people seek to fulfill their potential through greater self-understanding.

**hypnosis** A social interaction during which a person, responding to suggestions, experiences changes in memory, perception, and/or voluntary action.

**hypothalamic-pituitary-adrenal (HPA) axis** The biological system responsible for the stress response.

**hypothalamus** A brain structure that is involved in the regulation of bodily functions, including body temperature, blood pressure, and blood glucose levels; it also influences our basic motivated behaviors.

**hypothesis** A specific prediction of what should be observed if a theory is correct.

**id** In psychodynamic theory, the component of personality that is completely submerged in the unconscious and operates according to the pleasure principle.

**idiographic approaches** Person-centered approaches to studying personality; they focus on individual lives and how various characteristics are integrated into unique persons.

**immune system** The body's mechanism for dealing with invading microorganisms, such as allergens, bacteria, and viruses.

**implicit attitudes** Attitudes that influence a person's feelings and behavior at an unconscious level.

**implicit memory** The system underlying unconscious memories.

**incentives** External objects or external goals, rather than internal drives, that motivate behaviors.

**independent variable** In an experiment, the variable that is manipulated by the experimenter to examine its impact on the dependent variable.

**inductive reasoning** Using specific instances to draw conclusions about general rules.

**infantile amnesia** The inability to remember events from early childhood.

**inferential statistics** A set of procedures used to make judgments about whether differences actually exist between sets of numbers.

**ingroup favoritism** The tendency for people to evaluate favorably and privilege members of the ingroup more than members of the outgroup.

**insecure attachment** The attachment style for a minority of infants; the infant may exhibit insecure attachment through various behaviors, such as avoiding contact with the caregiver, or by alternating between approach and avoidance behaviors.

**insight** (1) The sudden realization of a solution to a problem. (2) The goal of psychoanalysis; a patient's awareness of his or her own unconscious psychological processes and how these processes affect daily functioning.

**insomnia** A disorder characterized by an inability to sleep.

**institutional review boards (IRBs)** Groups of people responsible for reviewing proposed research to ensure that it meets the accepted standards of science and provides for the physical and emotional well-being of research participants.

**intelligence** The ability to use knowledge to reason, make decisions, make sense of events, solve problems, understand complex ideas, learn quickly, and adapt to environmental challenges.

**intelligence quotient (IQ)** An index of intelligence computed by dividing a child's estimated mental age by the child's chronological age, then multiplying this number by 100.

**interactionists** Theorists who believe that behavior is determined jointly by situations and underlying dispositions.

**internal validity** The extent to which the data collected in a study address the research hypothesis in the way intended.

**interneurons** One of the three types of neurons; these neurons communicate only with other neurons.

**interpreter** A term specific to the left hemisphere; refers to the left hemisphere's attempts to make sense of actions and ongoing events.

**interval schedule** A schedule in which reinforcement is available after a specific unit of time.

**intrinsic motivation** Motivation to perform an activity because of the value or pleasure associated with that activity, rather than for an apparent external goal or purpose.

**introspection** A systematic examination of subjective mental experiences that requires people to inspect and report on the content of their thoughts.

**iris** The colored muscular circle on the surface of the eye; it changes shape to let in more or less light.

**kinesthetic sense** Perception of the positions in space and movements of our bodies and our limbs.

**latent content** According to Sigmund Freud, what a dream symbolizes; the material that is disguised in a dream to protect the dreamer from confronting a conflict directly.

**latent learning** Learning that takes place in the absence of reinforcement.

**law of effect** Thorndike's general theory of learning: Any behavior that leads to a "satisfying state of affairs" is likely to occur again, and any behavior that leads to an "annoying state of affairs" is less likely to occur again.

**learned helplessness** A cognitive model of depression in which people feel unable to control events in their lives.

**learning** A relatively enduring change in behavior, resulting from experience.

**longitudinal studies** A research method that studies the same participants multiple times over a period of time.

**long-term memory** The relatively permanent storage of information.

**long-term potentiation (LTP)** The strengthening of a synaptic connection, making the postsynaptic neurons more easily activated.

**loosening of associations** A speech pattern among some people with schizophrenia in which their thoughts are disorganized or meaningless.

**magnetic resonance imaging (MRI)** A method of brain imaging that produces high-quality images of the brain.

**major depression** A disorder characterized by severe negative moods or a lack of interest in normally pleasurable activities.

**manifest content** According to Sigmund Freud, the plot of a dream; the way a dream is remembered.

**mean** A measure of central tendency that is the arithmetic average of a set of numbers.

**median** A measure of central tendency that is the value in a set of numbers that falls exactly halfway between the lowest and highest values.

**meditation** A mental procedure that focuses attention on an external object or on a sense of awareness.

**meme** A unit of knowledge transmitted within a culture.

**memory** The nervous system's capacity to acquire and retain skills and knowledge.

**memory bias** The changing of memories over time so that they become consistent with current beliefs or attitudes.

**mental age** An assessment of a child's intellectual standing compared with that of same-age peers; determined by comparing the child's test score with the average score for children of each chronological age.

**mental sets** Problem solving strategies that have worked in the past.

**meta-analysis** A "study of studies" that combines the findings of multiple studies to arrive at a conclusion.

**mind/body problem** A fundamental psychological issue: Are mind and body separate and distinct, or is the mind simply the physical brain's subjective experience?

**mirror neurons** Neurons that are activated when one observes another individual engage in an action and when one performs the action that was observed.

**mnemonics** Learning aids, strategies, and devices that improve recall through the use of retrieval cues.

**mode** A measure of central tendency that is the most frequent score or value in a set of numbers.

**modeling** The imitation of behavior through observational learning.

**monocular depth cues** Cues of depth perception that are available to each eye alone.

**monozygotic twins** Also called *identical twins;* twin siblings that result from one zygote splitting in two and therefore share the same genes.

**motivation** Factors that energize, direct, or sustain behavior.

**motor neurons** One of the three types of neurons; these efferent neurons direct muscles to contract or relax, thereby producing movement.

**multiaxial system** The system used in the *DSM;* it calls for assessment along five axes that describe important mental health factors.

**multiple intelligences** The idea that there are different types of intelligence that are independent of one another.

**myelin sheath** A fatty material, made up of glial cells, that insulates the axon and allows for the rapid movement of electrical impulses along the axon.

**narcolepsy** A sleep disorder in which people experience excessive sleepiness during normal waking hours, sometimes going limp and collapsing.

**naturalistic observation** A type of descriptive study in which the researcher is a passive observer, making no attempt to change or alter ongoing behavior.

**natural selection** In evolutionary theory, the idea that those who inherit characteristics that help them adapt to their particular environments have a selective advantage over those who do not.

**nature/nurture debate** The arguments concerning whether psychological characteristics are biologically innate or acquired through education, experience, and culture.

**need** A state of biological or social deficiency.

**need hierarchy** Maslow's arrangement of needs, in which basic survival needs must be met before people can satisfy higher needs.

**need to belong theory** The theory that the need for interpersonal attachments is a fundamental motive that has evolved for adaptive purposes.

**negative punishment** The removal of a stimulus to decrease the probability of a behavior's recurring.

**negative reinforcement** The removal of a stimulus to increase the probability of a behavior's being repeated.

**negative symptoms** Symptoms of schizophrenia that are marked by deficits in functioning, such as apathy, lack of emotion, and slowed speech and movement.

**neurons** The basic units of the nervous system; cells that receive, integrate, and transmit information in the nervous system. They operate through electrical impulses, communicate with other neurons through chemical signals, and form neural networks.

**neurotransmitters** Chemical substances that carry signals from one neuron to another.

**nodes of Ranvier** Small gaps of exposed axon, between the segments of myelin sheath, where action potentials are transmitted.

**nomothetic approaches** Approaches to studying personality that focus on how common characteristics vary from person to person.

**nonverbal behavior** The facial expressions, gestures, mannerisms, and movements by which one communicates with others.

**norepinephrine** A monoamine neurotransmitter involved in states of arousal and awareness.

**objective measures** Relatively direct assessments of personality, usually based on information gathered through self-report questionnaires or observer ratings.

**object permanence** The understanding that an object continues to exist even when it cannot be seen.

**observational learning** The acquisition or modification of a behavior after exposure to at least one performance of that behavior.

**observational techniques** A research method of careful and systematic assessment and coding of overt behavior.

**observer bias** Systematic errors in observation that occur because of an observer's expectations.

**obsessive-compulsive disorder (OCD)** An anxiety disorder characterized by frequent intrusive thoughts and compulsive actions.

**obstructive sleep apnea** A disorder in which a person, while asleep, stops breathing because his or her throat closes; the condition results in frequent awakenings during the night.

**occipital lobes** Regions of the cerebral cortex, at the back of the brain, important for vision.

**olfaction** The sense of smell.

**olfactory bulb** The brain center for smell, located below the frontal lobes.

**olfactory epithelium** A thin layer of tissue, within the nasal cavity, that contains the receptors for smell.

**operant conditioning (instrumental conditioning)** A learning process in which the consequences of an action determine the likelihood that it will be performed in the future.

**oxytocin** A hormone that is important for mothers in bonding to newborns and may encourage affiliation during social stress.

**panic disorder** An anxiety disorder that consists of sudden, overwhelming attacks of terror.

**parallel processing** Processing multiple types of information at the same time.

**parasympathetic division** A division of the autonomic nervous system; it returns the body to its resting state.

**parietal lobes** Regions of the cerebral cortex, in front of the occipital lobes and behind the frontal lobes, important for the sense of touch and for conceptualizing the spatial layout of an environment.

**partial reinforcement** A type of learning in which behavior is reinforced intermittently.

**partial-reinforcement extinction effect** The greater persistence of behavior under partial reinforcement than under continuous reinforcement.

**participant observation** A type of descriptive study in which the researcher is actively involved in the situation.

**perception** The processing, organization, and interpretation of sensory signals; it results in an internal representation of the stimulus.

**perceptual constancy** Correctly perceiving objects as constant in their shape, size, color, and lightness, despite raw sensory data that could mislead perception.

**peripheral nervous system (PNS)** All nerve cells in the body that are not part of the central nervous system. The peripheral nervous system includes the somatic and autonomic nervous systems.

**persistence** The continual recurrence of unwanted memories.

**personal attributions** Explanations that refer to people's internal characteristics, such as abilities, traits, moods, or efforts.

**personality** The characteristic thoughts, emotional responses, and behaviors that are relatively stable in an individual over time and across circumstances.

**personality trait** A characteristic; a dispositional tendency to act in a certain way over time and across circumstances.

**personality types** Discrete categories of people based on personality characteristics.

**persuasion** The active and conscious effort to change an attitude through the transmission of a message.

**phenotype** Observable physical characteristics, which result from both genetic and environmental influences.

**phobia** An acquired fear that is out of proportion to the real threat of an object or of a situation.

**pituitary gland** A gland located at the base of the hypothalamus; it sends hormonal signals to other endocrine glands, controlling their release of hormones.

**placebo effect** An improvement in health following treatment with a placebo—that is, with a drug or treatment that has no apparent physiological effect on the health condition for which it was prescribed.

**plasticity** A property of the brain that allows it to change as a result of experience, drugs, or injury.

**population** Everyone in the group the experimenter is interested in.

**positive punishment** The administration of a stimulus to decrease the probability of a behavior's recurring.

**positive reinforcement** The administration of a stimulus to increase the probability of a behavior's being repeated.

**positive symptoms** Symptoms of schizophrenia that are marked by excesses in functioning, such as delusions, hallucinations, and disorganized speech or behavior.

**positron emission tomography (PET)** A method of brain imaging that assesses metabolic activity by using a radioactive substance injected into the bloodstream.

**postconventional level** Highest stage of moral development; at this level, decisions about morality depend on abstract principles and the value of all life.

**posttraumatic stress disorder (PTSD)** A mental disorder that involves frequent nightmares, intrusive thoughts, and flashbacks related to an earlier trauma.

**preconventional level** Earliest level of moral development; at this level, self-interest and event outcomes determine what is moral.

**prefrontal cortex** The frontmost portion of the frontal lobes, especially prominent in humans; important for attention, working memory, decision making, appropriate social behavior, and personality.

**prejudice** Negative feelings, opinions, and beliefs associated with a stereotype.

**preoperational stage** The second stage in Piaget's theory of cognitive development; during this stage, children think symbolically about objects, but they reason based on intuition and superficial appearance rather than logic.

**primary appraisals** Part of the coping process that involves making decisions about whether a stimulus is stressful, benign, or irrelevant.

**primary emotions** Emotions that are evolutionarily adaptive, shared across cultures, and associated with specific physical states; they include anger, fear, sadness, disgust, happiness, and possibly surprise and contempt.

**proactive interference** When prior information inhibits the ability to remember new information.

**problem-focused coping** A type of coping in which people take direct steps to confront or minimize a stressor.

**problem solving** Finding a way around an obstacle to reach a goal.

**procedural memory** A type of implicit memory that involves motor skills and behavioral habits.

**projective measures** Personality tests that examine unconscious processes by having people interpret ambiguous stimuli.

**prosocial** Tending to benefit others.

**prospective memory** Remembering to do something at some time in the future.

**prototype model** A way of thinking about concepts: Within each category, there is a best example—a prototype—for that category.

**psychological science** The study of mind, brain, and behavior.

**psychoanalysis** A method developed by Sigmund Freud that attempts to bring the contents of the unconscious into conscious awareness so that conflicts can be revealed.

**psychodynamic theory** Freudian theory that unconscious forces determine behavior.

**psychopathology** Sickness or disorder of the mind.

**psychosexual stages** According to Freud, developmental stages that correspond to distinct libidinal urges; progression through these stages profoundly affects personality.

**psychotherapy** The generic name given to formal psychological treatment.

**psychotropic medications** Drugs that affect mental processes.

**pupil** The small opening in the eye; it lets in light waves.

**random assignment** Placing research participants into the conditions of an experiment in such a way that each participant has an equal chance of being assigned to any level of the independent variable.

**ratio schedule** A schedule in which reinforcement is based on the number of times the behavior occurs.

**reactivity** When the knowledge that one is being observed alters the behavior being observed.

**reasoning** Using information to determine if a conclusion is valid or reasonable.

**receptors** In neurons, specialized protein molecules on the postsynaptic membrane; neurotransmitters bind to these molecules after passing across the synaptic cleft.

**recessive gene** A gene that is expressed only when it is matched with a similar gene from the other parent.

**reconsolidation** Neural processes involved when memories are recalled and then stored again for later retrieval.

**reinforcer** A stimulus that follows a response and increases the likelihood that the response will be repeated.

**reliability** The extent to which a measure is stable and consistent over time in similar conditions.

**REM sleep** The stage of sleep marked by rapid eye movements, dreaming, and paralysis of motor systems.

**replication** Repetition of an experiment to confirm the results.

**representativeness heuristic** Placing a person or object in a category if that person or object is similar to one's prototype for that category.

**Rescorla-Wagner model** A cognitive model of classical conditioning; it states that the strength of the CS-US association is determined by the extent to which the unconditioned stimulus is unexpected or surprising.

**research** A scientific process that involves the systematic and careful collection of data.

**response performance** A research method in which researchers quantify perceptual or cognitive processes in response to a specific stimulus.

**resting membrane potential** The electrical charge of a neuron when it is not active.

**restructuring** A new way of thinking about a problem that aids its solution.

**retina** The thin inner surface of the back of the eyeball; it contains the photoreceptors that transduce light into neural signals.

**retrieval** The act of recalling or remembering stored information when it is needed.

**retrieval cue** Anything that helps a person (or a nonhuman animal) recall information stored in long-memory.

**retroactive interference** When new information inhibits the ability to remember old information.

**retrograde amnesia** A condition in which people lose past memories, such as memories for events, facts, people, or even personal information.

**reuptake** The process whereby a neurotransmitter is taken back into the presynaptic terminal buttons, thereby stopping its activity.

**rods** Retinal cells that respond to low levels of illumination and result in black-and-white perception.

**sample** A subset of a population.

**scatterplot** A graphical depiction of the relationship between two variables.

**schemas** Cognitive structures that help us perceive, organize, process, and use information.

**schizophrenia** A psychological disorder characterized by a split between thought and emotion; it involves alterations in thoughts, in perceptions, or in consciousness.

**scientific method** A systematic procedure of observing and measuring phenomena (observable things) to answer questions about *what* happens, *when* it happens, *what* causes it, and *why*; involves a dynamic interaction between theories, hypotheses, and research.

**secondary appraisals** Part of the coping process during which people evaluate their response options and choose coping behaviors.

**secondary emotions** Blends of primary emotions; they include remorse, guilt, submission, and anticipation.

**secure attachment** The attachment style for a majority of infants; the infant is confident enough to play in an unfamiliar environment as long as the caregiver is present and is readily comforted by the caregiver during times of distress.

**selection bias** In an experiment, unintended differences between the participants in different groups.

**self-actualization** A state that is achieved when one's personal dreams and aspirations have been attained.

**self-fulfilling prophecy** People's tendency to behave in ways that confirm their own expectations or other people's expectations.

**self-report methods** Methods of data collection in which people are asked to provide information about themselves, such as in questionnaires or surveys.

**self-serving bias** The tendency for people to take personal credit for success but blame failure on external factors.

**semantic memory** Memory for knowledge about the world.

**sensation** The sense organs' detection of external stimuli, their responses to the stimuli, and the transmission of these responses to the brain.

**sensitive periods** Time periods when specific skills develop most easily.

**sensitization** An increase in behavioral response after exposure to a threatening stimulus.

**sensorimotor stage** The first stage in Piaget's theory of cognitive development; during this stage, infants acquire information about the world through their senses and motor skills. Reflexive responses develop into more deliberate actions through the development and refinement of schemas.

**sensory adaptation** A decrease in sensitivity to a constant level of stimulation.

**sensory memory** A memory system that very briefly stores sensory information in close to its original sensory form.

**sensory neurons** One of the three types of neurons; these afferent neurons detect information from the physical world and pass that information along to the brain.

**serial position effect** The ability to recall items from a list depends on order of presentation, with items presented early or late in the list remembered better than those in the middle.

**serotonin** A monoamine neurotransmitter important for a wide range of psychological activity, including emotional states, impulse control, and dreaming.

**sexual response cycle** A four-stage pattern of physiological and psychological responses during sexual activity.

**sexual strategies theory** A theory that maintains that women and men have evolved distinct mating strategies because they faced different adaptive problems over the course of human history. The strategies used by each sex maximize the probability of passing along their genes to future generations.

**shaping** A process of operant conditioning; it involves reinforcing behaviors that are increasingly similar to the desired behavior.

**short-term memory** A memory storage system that briefly holds a limited amount of information in awareness.

**signal detection theory (SDT)** A theory of perception based on the idea that the detection of a faint stimulus requires a judgment—it is not an all-or-none process.

**situational attributions** Explanations that refer to external events, such as the weather, luck, accidents, or other people's actions.

**situationism** The theory that behavior is determined more by situations than by personality traits.

**social facilitation** When the mere presence of others enhances performance.

**social loafing** The tendency for people to work less hard in a group than when working alone.

**social norms** Expected standards of conduct, which influence behavior.

**social psychology** The study of how people are influenced by their interactions with others.

**sociocultural model** A diagnostic model that views psychopathology as the result of the interaction between individuals and their cultures.

**sociometer** An internal monitor of social acceptance or rejection.

**somatic markers** Bodily reactions that arise from the emotional evaluation of an action's consequences.

**somatic nervous system** A component of the peripheral nervous system; it transmits sensory signals and motor signals between the central nervous system and the skin, muscles, and joints.

**sound wave** A pattern of changes in air pressure during a period of time; it produces the percept of a sound.

**source amnesia** A type of amnesia that occurs when a person shows memory for an event but cannot remember where he or she encountered the information.

**source misattribution** Memory distortion that occurs when people misremember the time, place, person, or circumstances involved with a memory.

**split brain** A condition in which the corpus callosum is surgically cut and the two hemispheres of the brain do not receive information directly from each other.

**spontaneous recovery** A process in which a previously extinguished response reemerges after the presentation of the conditioned stimulus.

**standard deviation** A statistical measure of how far away each value is, on average, from the mean.

**stereotypes** Cognitive schemas that allow for easy, fast processing of information about people based on their membership in certain groups.

**stereotype threat** Apprehension about confirming negative stereotypes related to one's own group.

**stimulus discrimination** A differentiation between two similar stimuli when only one of them is consistently associated with the unconditioned stimulus.

**stimulus generalization** Learning that occurs when stimuli that are similar but not identical to the conditioned stimulus produce the conditioned response.

**storage** The retention of encoded representations over time.

**stream of consciousness** A phrase coined by William James to describe each person's continuous series of ever-changing thoughts.

**stress** A pattern of behavioral, psychological, and physiological responses to events, when the events match or exceed the organism's ability to respond in a healthy way.

**stressor** An environmental event or stimulus that threatens an organism.

**structuralism** An approach to psychology based on the idea that conscious experience can be broken down into its basic underlying components.

**subliminal perception** The processing of information by sensory systems without conscious awareness.

**substance P** A neurotransmitter involved in pain perception.

**subtractive color mixing** A process of color mixing that occurs within the stimulus itself; a physical, not psychological, process.

**suggestibility** The development of biased memories from misleading information.

**superego** In psychodynamic theory, the internalization of societal and parental standards of conduct.

**symbolic representations** Abstract mental representations that do not correspond to the physical features of objects or ideas.

**sympathetic division** A division of the autonomic nervous system; it prepares the body for action.

**synapse** The site at which chemical communication occurs between neurons.

**synaptic cleft** The gap between the axon of a "sending" neuron and the dendrites of a "receiving" neuron; it contains extracellular fluid.

**synaptic pruning** A process whereby the synaptic connections in the brain that are frequently used are preserved, and those that are not used are lost.

**synesthesia** Cross-sensory experience (e.g., a visual image has a taste).

**taste buds** Sensory organs in the oral cavity that contain the receptors for taste.

**telegraphic speech** The tendency for toddlers to speak using rudimentary sentences that are missing words and grammatical markings but follow a logical syntax and convey a wealth of meaning.

**temperaments** Biologically based tendencies to feel or act in certain ways.

**temporal lobes** Regions of the cerebral cortex—below the parietal lobes and in front of the occipital lobes—important for processing auditory information, for memory, and for object and face perception.

**tend-and-befriend response** Females' tendency to protect and care for their offspring and form social alliances rather than flee or fight in response to threat.

**teratogens** Environmental agents that harm the embryo or fetus.

**terminal buttons** Small nodules, at the ends of axons, that release chemical signals from the neuron into the synapse.

**thalamus** The gateway to the brain; it receives almost all incoming sensory information before that information reaches the cortex.

**theory** A model of interconnected ideas or concepts that explains what is observed and makes predictions about future events.

**theory of mind** The term used to describe the ability to explain and predict another person's behavior as a result of recognizing her or his mental state.

**thinking** The mental manipulation of representations of information (i.e., of objects we encounter in our environments).

**third variable problem** A problem that occurs when the researcher cannot directly manipulate variables; as a result, the researcher cannot be confident that another, unmeasured variable is not the actual cause of differences in the variables of interest.

**top-down processing** A hierarchical model of pattern recognition in which information at higher levels of mental processing can also influence lower, "earlier" levels in the processing hierarchy.

**trait approach** An approach to studying personality that focuses on how individuals differ in personality dispositions.

**transcranial magnetic stimulation (TMS)** The use of strong magnets to briefly interrupt normal brain activity as a way to study brain regions.

**transduction** A process by which sensory receptors produce neural impulses when they receive physical or chemical stimulation.

**transience** Forgetting over time.

**Type A behavior pattern** A pattern of behavior characterized by competitiveness, achievement orientation, aggressiveness, hostility, restlessness, impatience with others, and inability to relax.

**Type B behavior pattern** A pattern of behavior characterized by noncompetitive, relaxed, easygoing, and accommodating behavior.

**unconditioned response (UR)** A response that does not have to be learned, such as a reflex.

**unconditioned stimulus (US)** A stimulus that elicits a response, such as a reflex, without any prior learning.

**unconscious** The mental processes that operate below the level of conscious awareness.

**variability** In a set of numbers, how widely dispersed the values are from each other and from the mean.

**variable** Something in the world that can vary and that a researcher can measure.

**variable schedule** A schedule in which reinforcement is applied at different rates or at different times.

**vestibular sense** Perception of balance.

**vicarious learning** Learning the consequences of an action by watching others being rewarded or punished for performing the action.

**well-being** A positive state that includes striving for optimal health and life satisfaction.

**working memory** An active processing system that keeps different types of information available for current use.

**Yerkes-Dodson law** The psychological principle that performance increases with arousal up to an optimal point, after which it decreases with increasing arousal.

# REFERENCES


Aarts, H., Custers, R., & Marien, H. (2008). Preparing and motivating behavior outside of awareness. *Science, 319*, 1639.

Abizaid, A. (2009). Ghrelin and dopamine: New insights on the peripheral regulation of appetite. *Journal of Neuroendocrinology, 21*, 787–793.

Abraido-Lanza, A. F., Chao, M. T., & Florez, K. R. (2005). Do healthy behaviors decline with greater acculturation? Implications for the Latino mortality paradox. *Social Science and Medicine, 61*, 1243–1255.

Abramson, L. Y., Metalsky, G., & Alloy, L. (1989). Hopelessness depression: A theory-based subtype of depression. *Psychological Review, 96*, 358–372.

Ackerman, P. L., Beier, M. E., & Boyle, M. O. (2005). Working memory and intelligence: The same or different constructs? *Psychological Bulletin, 131*, 30–60.

Adair, J., & Kagitcibasi, C. (1995). Development of psychology in developing countries: Factors facilitating and impeding its progress. *International Journal of Psychology, 30*, 633–641.

Adams, H. E., Wright, L. W., & Lohr, B. A. (1996). Is homophobia associated with homosexual arousal? *Journal of Abnormal Psychology, 105*, 440–445.

Adams, R. B., Jr., Gordon, H. L., Baird, A. A., Ambady, N., & Kleck, R. E. (2003, June 6). Effects of gaze on amygdala sensitivity to anger and fear faces. *Science, 300*, 1536–1537.

Adolphs, R. (2003). Cognitive neuroscience of human social behavior. *Nature Reviews Neuroscience, 1*, 165–178.

Adolphs, R., Gosselin, F., Buchanan, T. W., Tranel, D., Schyns, P., & Damasio, A. R. (2005). A mechanism for impaired fear recognition after amygdala damage. *Nature, 433*, 68–72.

Adolphs, R., Sears, L., & Piven, J. (2001). Abnormal processing of social information from faces in autism. *Journal of Cognitive Neuroscience, 13*, 232–240.

Adolphs, R., Tranel, D., & Damasio, A. R. (1998). The human amygdala in social judgment. *Nature, 393*, 470–474.

Agawu, K. (1995). *African rhythm: A northern ewe perspective*. Cambridge, UK: Cambridge University Press.

Ainsworth, M. D. S., Blehar, M. C., Waters, E., & Wall, S. (1978). *Patterns of attachment: A psychological study of the strange situation*. Hillsdale, NJ: Lawrence Erlbaum.

Albus, C. (2010). Psychological and social factors in coronary heart disease. *Annals of Medicine, 42*, 487–494.

Algoe, S. B., & Fredrickson, B. L. (2011). Emotional fitness and the movement of affective science from lab to field. *American Psychologist, 66*, 35–42.

Ali, S. R., Liu, W. M., & Humedian, M. (2004). Islam 101: Understanding the religion and therapy implications. *Professional Psychology Research and Review, 35*, 635–642.

Alicke, M. D., Klotz, M. L., Breitenbecher, D. L., Yurak, T. J., & Vredenburg, D. S. (1995). Personal contact, individuation, and the better-than-average effect. *Journal of Personality and Social Psychology, 68*, 804–825.

Alicke, M. D., LoSchiavo, F. M., Zerbst, J., & Zhang, S. (1997). The person who outperforms me is a genius: Maintaining perceived competence in upward social comparisons. *Journal of Personality and Social Psychology, 73*, 781–789.

Allen, J. B., Coan, J. A., & Nazarian, M. (2004). Issues and assumptions on the road from raw signals to metrics of frontal EEG asymmetry in emotion. *Biological Psychology, 67*, 183–218.

Allport, G. W. (1954). *The nature of prejudice* (8th ed.). Oxford, UK: Addison-Wesley.

Allport, G. W. (1961). *Pattern and growth in personality*. New York: Holt, Rinehart & Winston.

Amanzio, M., & Benedetti, F. (1999). Neuropharmacological dissection of placebo analgesia: Expectation-activated opioid systems versus conditioning-activated specific subsystems. *Journal of Neuroscience, 19*, 484–494.

Amaral, D. G., Schumann, C. M., & Nordahl, C. W. (2008). Neuroanatomy of autism. *Trends in Neurosciences, 3*, 137–45.

Amato, P. R., Johnson, D. R., Booth, A., & Rogers, S. J. (2003). Continuity and change in marital quality between 1980 and 2000. *Journal of Marriage and Family, 65*, 1–22.

Ambady, N., Hallahan, M., & Conner, B. (1999). Accuracy of judgments of sexual orientation from thin slices of behavior. *Journal of Personality and Social Psychology, 77*, 538–547.

Ambady, N., & Rosenthal, R. (1993). Half a minute: Predicting teacher evaluations from thin slices of nonverbal behavior and physical attractiveness. *Journal of Personality and Social Psychology, 64*, 431–441.

American Academy of Pediatrics, Committee on Drugs. (1998). Neonatal drug withdrawal. *Pediatrics, 10*, 1079–1088.

American Association of Suicidology. (2011). *Youth suicidal behavior* [Fact sheet]. Retrieved from http://www.suicidology.org/c/document_library/get_file?folderId=232&name=DLFE-335.pdf

American Psychiatric Association. (2000a). *Diagnostic and statistical manual of mental disorders* (4th ed., text revision). Washington, DC: Author.

American Psychiatric Association. (2000b). Practice guidelines for the treatment of patients with eating disorders (revised). *American Journal of Psychiatry, 157* (Suppl.), 1–39.

American Psychological Association. (2007, February). *Guidelines for psychological practice with girls and women*. Retrieved from http://www.apa.org/practice/guidelines/girls-and-women.pdf

American Psychological Association (2010, May 13). *Dr. Katherine C. Nordal on How to Find a Therapist*. Retrieved from http://apa.org/news/press/releases/2010/05/locate-a-therapist.aspx

American Psychological Association, Health Psychology Division 38. (n.d.). *What is health psychology?* Retrieved August 4, 2008, from http://www.health-psych.org

Amiraian, D. E., & Sobal, J. (2009). Dating and eating. Beliefs about dating foods among university students. *Appetite, 53*(2), 226–232. doi:10.1016/j.appet.2009.06.012

Amminger, G. P., Pape, S., Rock, D., Roberts, S. A., Ott, S. L., Squires-Wheeler, E., et al. (1999). Relationship between childhood behavioral disturbance and later schizophrenia in the New York high-risk project. *American Journal of Psychiatry, 156*, 525–530.

Anderson, A. K., Christoff, K., Stappen, I., Panitz, D., Ghahremani, D. G., Glover, G., et al. (2003). Dissociated neural representations of intensity and valence in human olfaction. *Nature Neuroscience, 6*, 196–202.

Anderson, A. K., & Phelps, E. A. (2000). Expression without recognition: Contributions of the human amygdala to emotional communication. *Psychological Science, 11*, 106–111.

Anderson, C. A., Berkowitz, L., Donnerstein, E., Huesmann, L. R., Johnson, J., Linz, D., et al. (2003). The influence of media violence on youth. *Psychological Science in the Public Interest, 4*, 81–110.

Anderson, I. M. (2000). Selective serotonin reuptake inhibitors versus tricyclic antidepressants: A meta-analysis of efficacy and tolerability. *Journal of Affective Disorders, 58*, 19–36.

Anderson, N. H. (1968). Likableness ratings of 555 personality-trait words. *Journal of Personality and Social Psychology, 9*, 272–279.

Anderson, R., Lewis, S. Z., Gichello, A. L., Aday, L. A., & Chiu, G. (1981). Access to medical care among the Hispanic population of the Southwestern United States. *Journal of Health and Social Behavior, 22*, 78–89.

Anderson, S. W., Bechara, A., Damasio, H., Tranel, D., & Damasio, A. R. (1999). Impairment of social and moral behavior related to early damage in human prefrontal cortex. *Nature Neuroscience, 2*, 1032–1037.

Andreasen, N. C. (1984). *The broken brain: The biological revolution in psychiatry*. New York: Harper & Row.

Angell, M. (2000, June 23). The epidemic of mental illness: Why? *The New York Review of Books*. Retrieved from http://www.nybooks.com

Antonuccio, D., & Burns, D. (2004). Adolescents with depression [Letter to the editor]. *Journal of the American Medical Association, 292*, 2577.

Aouizerate, B., Cuny, E., Bardinet, E., Yelnik, J., Martin-Guehl, C., Rotge, J. Y., et al. (2009). Distinct striatal targets in treating obsessive-compulsive disorder and major depression. *Journal of Neurosurgery, 111*, 775–779.

Aouizerate, B., Cuny, E., Martin-Guehl, C., Guehl, D., Amieva, H., Benazzouz, A., et al. (2004). Deep brain stimulation of the ventral caudate nucleus in the treatment of obsessive-compulsive disorder and major depression: Case report. *Journal of Neurosurgery, 101*, 574–575.

Araneta, M. R. G., Schlanger, K. M., Edmonds, L. D., Destiche, D. A., Merz, R. D., Hobbs, C. A., & Gray, G. G. (2003). Prevalence of birth defects among infants of Gulf War veterans in Arkansas, Arizona, California, Georgia, Hawaii, and Iowa, 1989–1993. *Birth Defects Research, 67*, 246–260.

Arias, E., MacDorman, M. F., Strobino, D. M., & Guyer, B. (2003). Annual summary of vital statistics: 2002. *Pediatrics, 112*, 1215–1230.

Aron, A., Norman, C. C., Aron, E. N., McKenna, C., & Heyman, R. E. (2000). Couples' shared participation in novel and arousing activities and experienced relationship quality. *Journal of Personality and Social Psychology, 78*(2), 273–284. doi:10.1037/0022-3514.78.2.273

Aronne, L. J., Wadden, T., Isoldi, K. K., & Woodworth, K. A. (2009). When prevention fails: Obesity treatment strategies. *American Journal of Medicine, 122(4 Suppl 1)*, S24–S32.

Aronson, E., & Mills, J. (1959). The effects of severity of initiation on liking for a group. *Journal of Abnormal and Social Psychology, 59*, 177–181.

Asberg, M., Shalling, D., Traskman-Bendz, L., & Wagner, A. (1987). Psychobiology of suicide, impulsivity, and related phenomena. In H. Y. Melzer (Ed.), *Psychopharmacology: The third generation of progress* (pp. 655–668). New York: Raven Press.

Asch, S. E. (1955). Opinions and social pressure. *Scientific American, 193*, 31–35.

Asch, S. E. (1956). Studies of independence and conformity: A minority of one against a unanimous majority. *Psychological Monographs, 70*, Whole No. 416.

Assad, L. K., Donnellan, M. B., & Conger, R. D. (2007). Optimism: An enduring resource for romantic relationships. *Journal of Personality and Social Psychology, 93*, 285–297.

Austin, E. J., Saklofske, D. H., & Mastoras, S. M. (2010). Emotional intelligence, coping and exam-related stress in Canadian undergraduate students. *Australian Journal of Psychology, 62*, 42–50.

Austin, M. P., Hadzi-Pavlovic, D., Leader, L., Saint, K., & Parker, G. (2005). Maternal trait anxiety, depression, and life event stress in pregnancy: Relationship with infant temperament. *Early Human Development, 81*, 183–190.

Averill, J. R. (1980). A constructivist view of emotion. In R. Plutchik & H. Kellerman (Eds.), *Theories of emotion* (pp. 305–339). New York: Academic Press.

Aviezer, H., Hassin, R. R., Ryan, J., Grady, C., Susskind, J., Anderson, A., et al. (2008). Angry, disgusted, or afraid? Studies on the malleability of emotion perception. *Psychological Science, 19*, 724–732.

Axelsson, J., Sundelin, T., Ingre, M., Van Someren, E. J. W., Olsson, A., & Lekander, M. (2010). Beauty sleep: Experimental study on the perceived health and attractiveness of sleep deprived people. *British Journal of Medicine, 341*. Retrieved December 10, 2010, from http://www.bmj.com/content/341/bmj.c6614.abstract

Aylward, E. H., Reiss, A. L., Reader, M. J., & Singer, H. S. (1996). Basal ganglia volumes in children with attention-deficit hyperactivity disorder. *Journal of Child Neurology, 11*, 112–115.

Baars, B. (1988). *A cognitive theory of consciousness*. Cambridge, UK: Cambridge University Press.

Babson, K. A., Trainor, C. D., Feldner, M. T., & Blumenthal, H. (2010). A test of the effects of acute sleep deprivation on general and specific self-reported anxiety and depressive symptoms: An experimental extension. *Journal of Behavior Therapy and Experimental Psychiatry, 41*, 297–303.

Back, M. D., Stopfer, J. M., Vazire, S., Gaddis, S., Schmukle, S. C., Egloff, B., & Gosling, S. D. (2010). Facebook profiles reflect actual personality not self-idealization. *Psychological Science, 21*, 372–374.

Baddeley, A.D., & Hitch, G. (1974). Working memory. In G. H. Bower (Ed.), *The psychology of learning and motivation: Advances in research and theory* (Vol. 8, pp. 47–89). New York: Academic Press.

Baddeley, A. D. (2002). Is working memory still working? *European Psychologist, 7*, 85–97.

Bailey, A., Le Couteur, A., Gottesman, I., Bolton, P., Simonoff, E., Yuzda, E., et al. (1995). Autism as a strongly genetic disorder: Evidence from a British twin study. *Psychological Medicine, 25*, 63–78.

Baillargeon, R. (1987). Object permanence in 3½ and 4½ month old infants. *Developmental Psychology, 23*, 655–664.

Baillargeon, R. (1995). Physical reasoning in infancy. In M. S. Gazzaniga (Ed.), *The cognitive neurosciences* (pp. 181–204). Cambridge, MA: MIT Press.

Baillargeon, R., Li, J., Ng, W., & Yuan, S. (2009). A new account of infants' physical reasoning. In A. Woodward & A. Needham (Eds.), *Learning and the infant mind* (pp. 66–116). New York: Oxford University Press.

Baker, T. B., Brandon, T. H., & Chassin, L. (2004). Motivational influences on cigarette smoking. *Annual Review of Psychology, 55*, 463–491.

Baldwin, D. A. (1991). Infants' contribution to the achievement of joint reference. *Child Development, 62*, 875–890.

Baldwin, D. A., & Baird, J. A. (2001). Discerning intentions in dynamic human action. *Trends in Cognitive Sciences, 5*, 171–178.

Baler, R. D., & Volkow, N. D. (2006). Drug addiction: The neurobiology of disrupted self-control. *Trends in Molecular Medicine, 12*(12), 559–566.

Ballantyne, J. C., & LaForge, K. S. (2007). Opioid dependence and addiction during opioid treatment of chronic pain. *Pain, 129*, 235–255.

Balthazard, C. G., & Woody, E. Z. (1992). The spectral analysis of hypnotic performance with respect to 'absorption.' *International Journal of Clinical and Experimental Hypnosis, 40*, 21–43.

Baltimore, D. (2001). Our genome unveiled. *Nature, 409*, 814–816.

Banaji, M. R., & Greenwald, A. G. (1995). Implicit gender stereotyping in judgments of fame. *Journal of Personality and Social Psychology, 68*, 181–198.

Bandura, A. (1977). *Social learning theory*. Englewood Cliffs, NJ: Prentice-Hall.

Bandura, A., Ross, D., & Ross, S. (1961). Transmission of aggression through imitation of aggressive models. *Journal of Abnormal and Social Psychology, 66*, 3–11.

Bandura, A., Ross, D., & Ross, S. (1963). Vicarious reinforcement and imitative learning. *Journal of Abnormal and Social Psychology, 67*, 601–607.

Bao, W. N., Whitbeck, L. B., Hoyt, D. R., & Conger, R. D. (1999). Perceived parental acceptance as a moderator of religious transmission among adolescent boys and girls. *Journal of Marriage and Family, 61*, 362–374.

Barbui, C., Cipriani, A., Patel, V., Ayuso-Mateos, J., & van Ommeren, M. (2011). Efficacy of antidepressants and benzodiazepines in minor depression: Systematic review and meta-analysis. *British Journal of Psychiatry, 198*, 11–16.

Barch, D. M., Sheline, Y. I., Csernansky, J. G., & Snyder, A. Z. (2003). Working memory and prefrontal cortex dysfunction: Specificity to schizophrenia compared with major depression. *Biological Psychiatry, 53*, 376–384.

Bargh, J. A. (2006). What have we been priming all these years? On the development, mechanisms, and ecology of nonconscious social behavior. *European Journal of Social Psychology, 36*(147), 168.

Bargh, J. A., & Chartrand, T. L. (1999). The unbearable automaticity of being. *American Psychologist, 54*, 462–479.

Bargh, J. A., Chen, M., & Burrows, L. (1996). Automaticity of social behavior: Direct effects of trait construct and stereotype activation on action. *Journal of Personality and Social Psychology, 71*, 230–244.

Bargh, J. A., & Ferguson, M. J. (2000). Beyond behaviorism: On the automaticity of higher mental processes. *Psychological Bulletin, 126*, 925–945.

Bargh, J. A., & Morsella, E. (2008). The unconscious mind. *Perspectives on Psychological Science, 3*, 73–79.

Barlow, D. H. (2002). *Anxiety and its disorders: The nature and treatment of anxiety and panic* (2nd ed.). New York: Guilford Press.

Barlow, D. H. (2004). Psychological treatments. *American Psychologist, 59*, 869–878.

Barlow, D. H., Gorman, J. M., Shear, M. K., & Woods, S. W. (2000). Cognitive-behavioral therapy, imipramine, or their combination for panic disorder: A randomized controlled trial. *Journal of the American Medical Association, 283*, 2529–2536.

Barnett, R. C., & Hyde, J. S. (2001). Women, men, work, and family: An expansionist theory. *American Psychologist, 56*, 781–796.

Baron, A. S., & Banaji, M. R. (2006). The development of implicit attitudes. *Psychological Science, 17*, 53–58.

Baron-Cohen, S., Wheelwright, S., & Jolliffe, T. (1997). Is there a "language of the eyes"? Evidence from normal adults and adults with autism or Asperger syndrome. *Visual Cognition, 4*, 311–332.

Barr, A. M., Panenka, W. J., MacEwan, G. W., Thornton, A. E., Lang, D. J., Honer, W. G., et al. (2006). The need for speed: An update on methamphetamine addiction. *Journal of Psychiatry & Neuroscience, 31*(5), 301–313.

Barrett, L. F., Mesquita, B., Ochsner, K. N., & Gross, J. J. (2007). The experience of emotion. *Annual Review of Psychology, 58*, 373–403.

Bartels, A., & Zeki, S. (2004). The neural correlates of maternal and romantic love. *Neuroimage, 21*, 1155–1166.

Bartels, J., Andreasen, D., Ehirim, P., Mao, H., Seibert, S., Wright, E. J., et al. (2008). Neurotrophic electrode: Method of assembly and implantation into human motor speech cortex. *Journal of Neuroscience Methods, 174*, 168–176.

Barton, D. A., Esler, M. D., Dawood, T., Lambert, E. A., Haikerwal, D., Brenchley, C., et al. (2008). Elevated brain serotonin turnover in patients with depression: Effect of genotype and therapy. *Archives of General Psychiatry, 65*, 38–46.

Bartoshuk, L. M. (2000). Comparing sensory experiences across individuals: Recent psychophysical advances illuminate genetic variation in taste perception. *Chemical Senses, 25*, 447–460.

Batson, C. D., Dyck, J. L., Brandt, J. R., Batson, J. G., Powell, A. L., McMaster, M. R., et al. (1988). Five studies testing two new egoistic alternatives to the empathy-altruism hypothesis. *Journal of Personality and Social Psychology, 55*, 52–77.

Batson, C. D., Turk, C. L., Shaw, L. L., & Klein, T. (1995). Information function of empathic emotion: Learning that we value the other's welfare. *Journal of Personality and Social Psychology, 68*, 300–313.

Baumeister, R. F. (1991). *Escaping the self: Alcoholism, spirituality, masochism, and other flights from the burden of selfhood*. New York: Basic Books.

Baumeister, R. F. (2000). Gender differences in erotic plasticity: The female sex drive as socially flexible and responsive. *Psychological Bulletin, 126*, 347–374.

Baumeister, R. F., Campbell, J. D., Krueger, J. I., & Vohs, K. D. (2003). Does high self-esteem cause better performance, interpersonal success, happiness, or healthier lifestyles? *Psychological Science in the Public Interest, 4*, 1–44.

Baumeister, R. F., Campbell, J. D., Krueger, J. I., & Vohs, K. D. (2005, January). Exploding the self-esteem myth. *Scientific American, 292*, 84–91.

Baumeister, R. F., Catanese, K. R., & Vohs, K. D. (2001). Is there a gender difference in strength of sex drive? Theoretical views, conceptual distinctions, and a review of the relevant literature. *Social Psychology Review, 5*, 242–273.

Baumeister, R. F., Dale, K., & Sommers, K. L. (1998). Freudian defense mechanisms and empirical findings in modern social psychology: Reaction formation, projection, displacement, undoing, isolation, sublimation, and denial. *Journal of Personality, 66*, 1081–1124.

Baumeister, R. F., Heatherton, T. F., & Tice, D. (1994). *Losing Control: How and Why People Fail at Self-Regulation.* San Diego: Academic Press.

Baumeister, R. F., & Leary, M. R. (1995). The need to belong: Desire for interpersonal attachments as a fundamental human motivation. *Psychological Bulletin, 117*(3), 497–529. doi:10.1037/0033-2909.117.3.497

Baumeister, R. F., & Masicampo, E. J. (2010). Conscious thought is for facilitating social and cultural interactions: How mental simulations serve the animal–culture interface. *Psychological Review, 117*, 945–971.

Baumeister, R. F., Masicampo, E. J., & Vohs, K. D. (2011). Do conscious thoughts cause behavior? *Annual Review of Psychology, 62*, 331–361.

Baumeister, R. F., Smart, L., & Boden, J. M. (1996). Relation of threatened egotism to violence and aggression: The dark side of high self-esteem. *Psychological Review, 103*, 5–33.

Baumeister, R. F., Stillwell, A. M., & Heatherton, T. F. (1994). Guilt: An interpersonal approach. *Psychological Bulletin, 115*, 243–267.

Baumgartner, T., Lutz, K., Schmidt, C. F., & Jäncke, L. (2006). The emotional power of music: How music enhances the feeling of affective pictures. *Brain Research 1075*(1), 151–164.

Bäuml, K. T., & Samenieh, A. (2010). The two faces of memory retrieval. *Psychological Science, 21*, 793–795.

Baumrind, D., Larzelere, R. E., & Cowan, P. A. (2002). Ordinary physical punishment: Is it harmful? Comment on Gershoff (2002). *Psychological Bulletin, 128*, 580–589.

Baxter, L. R. (2000). Functional imaging of brain systems mediating obsessive-compulsive disorder. In D. S. Charney, E. J. Nestler, & B. S. Bunney (Eds.), *Neurobiology of mental illness* (pp. 534–547). New York: Oxford University Press.

Baxter, L. R., Schwartz, J. M., Bergman, K. S., Szuba, M. P., Guze, B., Mazziota, J. C., et al. (1992). Caudate glucose metabolic rate changes with both drug and behavior therapy for obsessive-compulsive disorder. *Archives of General Psychiatry, 49*, 681–689.

Baydala, L., Rasmussen, C., Birch, J., Sherman, J., Wikman, E., Charchun, J., et al. (2009). Self-beliefs and behavioural development as related to academic achievement in Canadian Aboriginal children. *Canadian Journal of School Psychology, 24*, 19–33.

Beck, A. T. (1967). *Depression: Clinical, experimental and theoretical aspects.* New York: Harper & Row.

Beck, A. T. (1976). *Cognitive therapy and the emotional disorders.* New York: International Universities Press.

Beck, A. T., Brown, G., Seer, R. A., Eidelson, J. L., & Riskind, J. H. (1987). Differentiating anxiety and depression: A test of the cognitive content-specificity hypothesis. *Journal of Abnormal Psychology, 96*, 179–183.

Beck, A. T., Freeman, A., & Associates. (1990). *Cognitive therapy of personality disorders.* New York: Guilford Press.

Beck, A. T., & Rector, N. A. (2005). Cognitive approaches to schizophrenia: Theory and therapy. *Annual Review of Clinical Psychology, 1*, 577–606.

Beck, A. T., Rush, A. J., Shaw, B., & Emery, G. (1979). *Cognitive therapy of depression.* New York: Guilford Press.

Beck, A. T., Steer, R. A., & Brown, G. K. (1996). *Beck depression inventory manual.* San Antonio, TX: The Psychological Corporation.

Beck, A. T., Ward, C. H., Mendelson, M., Mock, J., & Erbaugh, J. (1961). An inventory for measuring depression. *Archives of General Psychiatry, 4*, 561–571.

Beck, H. P., Levinson, S., & Irons, G. (2009). Finding Little Albert: A journey to John B. Watson's infant laboratory. *American Psychologist, 64*, 605–614.

Becker, D. V., Kenrick, D. T., Neuberg, S. L., Blackwell, K. C., & Smith, D. M. (2007). The confounded nature of angry men and happy women. *Journal of Personality and Social Psychology, 92*, 179–190.

Beggan, J. K. (1992). On the social nature of nonsocial perception: The mere ownership effect. *Journal of Personality and Social Psychology, 62*, 229–237.

Beggs, J. M., Brown, T. H., Byrne, J. H., Crow, T., LeDoux, J. E., LeBar, K., et al. (1999). Learning and memory: Basic mechanisms. In M. J. Zigmond, F. E. Bloom, S. C. Landis, J. L. Roberts, & L. R. Squire (Eds.), *Fundamentals of neuroscience* (pp. 1411–1454). San Diego, CA: Academic Press.

Behne, T., Carpenter, M., Call, J., & Tomasello, M. (2005). Unwilling versus unable: Infants' understanding of intentional action. *Developmental Psychology, 41*, 328–337.

Bellak, L., & Black, R. B. (1992). Attention-deficit hyperactivity disorder in adults. *Clinical Therapeutics, 14*, 138–147.

Belmaker, R. H., & Agam, G. (2008). Major depressive disorder. *New England Journal of Medicine, 358*, 55–68.

Belsky, J. (1990). Children and marriage. In F. D. Fincham & T. N. Bradbury (Eds.), *The psychology of marriage: Basic issues and applications* (pp. 172–200). New York: Guilford Press.

Belsky, J., Houts, R. M., & Fearon, R. M. P. (2010). Infant attachment security and the timing of puberty: Testing an evolutionary hypothesis. *Psychological Science, 21*, 1195–1201.

Bem, D. J. (1967). Self-perception: An alternative explanation of cognitive dissonance phenomena. *Psychological Review, 74*, 183–200.

Bem, D. J. (1996). Exotic becomes erotic: A developmental theory of sexual orientation. *Psychological Review, 103*, 320–335.

Bem, D. J. (2011). Feeling the future: Experimental evidence for anomalous retroactive influences on cognition and affect. *Journal of Personality and Social Psychology, 100*(3), 407–425.

Bem, D. J., & Honorton, C. (1994). Does psi exist? Replicable evidence for an anomalous process of information transfer. *Psychological Bulletin, 115*, 4–18.

Bem, S. L. (1981). Gender schema theory: A cognitive account of sex typing.

Bender, H. L., Allen, J. P., McElhaney, K. B., Antonishak, J., Moore, C. M., Kelly, H. O., et al. (2007). Use of harsh physical discipline and developmental outcomes in adolescence. *Development and Psychopathology, 19*, 227–242.

Benedetti, F., Mayberg, H. S., Wagner, T. D., Stohler, C. S., & Zubieta, J. K. (2005). Neurobiological mechanisms of the placebo effect. *Journal of Neuroscience, 25*, 10390–10402.

Benedetti, F., Serretti, A., Colombo, C., Campori, E., Barbini, B., di Bella, D., et al. (1999). Influence of a functional polymorphism within the promoter of the serotonin transporter gene on the effects of total sleep deprivation in bipolar depression. *American Journal of Psychiatry, 156*, 1450–1452.

Benjamin, L. T. (2005). A history of clinical psychology as a profession in America (and a glimpse at its future). *Annual Review of Clinical Psychology, 1*, 1–30.

Bentler, P.M., & Newcomb, M. D. (1978). Longitudinal study of marital success and failure. *Journal of Consulting and Clinical Psychology, 46*, 1053–1070.

Berkman, L. F., & Syme, S. L. (1979). Social networks, host resistance, and mortality: A nine-year follow-up study of Alameda County residents. *American Journal of Epidemiology, 109*, 186–204.

Berkowitz, L. (1990). On the formation and regulation of anger and aggression: A cognitive-neoassociationistic analysis. *American Psychologist, 45*, 494–503.

Bernhardt, P. C., Dabbs, J. M., Fielden, J. A., & Lutter, C. D. (1998). Testosterone changes during vicarious experiences of winning and losing among fans at sporting events. *Physiology & Behavior, 65*, 59–62.

Berns, G. S., Chappelow, J., Zink, C. F., Pagnoni, G., Martin-Skurski, M. E., & Richards, J. (2005). Neurobiological correlates of social conformity and interdependence during mental rotation. *Biological Psychiatry, 58*, 245–253.

Bernstein, C.A. (2011). Meta-structure in DSM-5 process. *Psychiatric News, 46*, 7.

Berridge, K. C., Ho, C. Y., Richard, J. M., & DiFeliceantonio, A. G. (2010). The tempted brain eats: Pleasure and desire circuits in obesity and eating disorders. *Brain Research, 1350*, 43–64.

Berscheid, E., & Regan, P. (2005). *The psychology of interpersonal relationships.* New York: Prentice-Hall.

Betancourt, H., & Lopez, S. R. (1993). The study of culture, ethnicity, and race in American psychology. *American Psychologist, 48*, 629–637.

Bewernick, B. H., Hurlemann, R., Matusch, A., Kayser, S., Grubert, C., Hadrysiewicz, B., et al. (2010). Nucleus accumbens deep brain stimulation decreases ratings of depression and anxiety in treatment-resistant depression. *Biological Psychiatry, 67*, 110–116.

Bickerton, D. (1998). The creation and re-creation of language. In C. B. Crawford & D. L. Krebs (Eds.), *Handbook of evolutionary psychology: Ideas, issues, and applications* (pp. 613–634). Mahwah, NJ: Erlbaum.

Bidell, T. R., & Fischer, K. W. (1995). Between nature and nurture: The role of agency in the epigenesis of intelligence. In R. Sternberg & E. Grigorenko (Eds.), *Intelligence: Heredity and environment.* New York: Cambridge University Press.

Biederman, J., Hirshfeld-Becker, D. R., Rosenbaum, J. F., Herot, C., Friedman, D., Snidman, N., et al. (2001). Further evidence of association between behavioral inhibition and social anxiety in children. *American Journal of Psychiatry, 158*, 1673–1679.

Biederman, J., Monuteaux, M. C., Spencer, T., Wilens, T. E., Macpherson, H. A., & Faraone, S. V. (2008). Stimulant therapy and risk for subsequent substance use disorders in male adults with ADHD: A naturalistic controlled 10-year follow-up study. *American Journal of Psychiatry, 165*, 597–603.

Biesanz, J., West, S. G., & Millevoi, A. (2007). What do you learn about someone over time? The relationship between length of acquaintance and consensus and self-other agreement in judgments of personality. *Journal of Personality and Social Psychology, 92*, 119–135.

Bjorklund, D. F. (2007). *Why Youth is Not Wasted on the Young: Immaturity in Human Development.* Malden, MA: Blackwell.

Blagys, M. D., & Hilsenroth, M. J. (2000). Distinctive feature of short-term psychodynamic-interpersonal psychotherapy: A review of the comparative psychotherapy process literature. *Clinical Psychology: Science and Practice, 7*, 167–188.

Blair, I. V. (2002). The malleability of automatic stereotypes and prejudice. *Personality and Social Psychology Review, 6*, 242–261.

Blair, R. J. (2003). Neurobiological basis of psychopathy. *British Journal of Psychiatry, 182*, 5–7.

Blakemore, C. (1983). *Mechanics of the mind.* Cambridge, UK: Cambridge University Press.

Blakemore, S. J., & Choudhury, S. (2006). Development of the adolescent brain: Implications for executive function and social cognition. *Journal of Child Psychology and Psychiatry, 47*, 296–312. doi: 10.1111/j.1469-7610.2006.01611.x

Blakemore, S. J., Wolpert, D. M., & Frith, C. D. (1998). Central cancellation of self-produced tickle sensation. *Nature Neuroscience, 1*, 635–640.

Blakeslee, S. (2001, April 10). A reason we call our cheddar cheese "sharp" and shirts "loud." *The New York Times.* Retrieved from http://www.nytimes.com

Blanchard, R., & Ellis, L. (2001). Birth weight, sexual orientation, and the sex of preceding siblings. *Journal of Biosocial Science, 33*, 451–467.

Blass, T. (1991). Understanding behavior in the Milgram obedience experiment: The role of personality, situations, and their interactions. *Journal of Personality and Social Psychology, 60*, 398–413.

Block, J., & Kremen, A. M. (1996). IQ and ego-resiliency: Conceptual and empirical connections and separateness. *Journal of Personality and Social Psychology, 70*(2), 349–361.

BloodAlcoholContent.Org. (2007–2010). Measuring BAC. Retrieved October 29, 2010, from http://bloodalcoholcontent.org/measuringbac.html

Bloom, B., & Cohen, R. A. (2007). Summary health statistics for U. S. children: National health interview survey, 2006 (Vital and Health Statistics, Series 10, No. 234). Hyattsville, MD: Centers for Disease Control and Prevention.

Blue, I., & Harpham, T. (1996). Urbanization and mental health in developing countries. *Current Issues in Public Health, 2*, 181–185.

Bogaert, A. F. (2006). Biological versus nonbiological older brothers and men's sexual orientation. *Proceedings of the National Academy of Sciences, USA, 103*, 10771–10774.

Bohlin, G., Hagekull, B., & Rydell, A. M. (2000). Attachment and social functioning: A longitudinal study from infancy to middle childhood. *Social Development, 9*, 24–39. doi: 10.1111/1467-9507.00109

Bolles, R. C. (1970). Species-specific defense reactions and avoidance learning. *Psychological Review, 77*, 32–48.

Bonanno, G. A. (2004). Loss, trauma, and human resilience: Have we underestimated the human capacity to thrive after extremely aversive events? *American Psychologist, 59*(1), 20–28.

Bootzin, R. R., & Epstein, D. R. (2011). Understanding and treating insomnia. *Annual Review of Clinical Psychology, 7*, 435–458.

Bornstein, R. F. (1999). Criterion validity of objective and projective dependency tests: A meta-analytic assessment of behavioral prediction. *Psychological Assessment, 11*, 48–57.

Bosson, J. K., Lakey, C. E., Campbell, W. K., Zeigler-Hill, V., Jordan, C. H., & Kernis, M. H. (2008). Untangling the links between narcissism and self-esteem: A theoretical and empirical review. *Social and Personality Psychology Compass, 2*, 1415–1439.

Bouchard, C., & Pérusse, L. (1993). Genetics of obesity. *Annual Review of Nutrition, 13*, 337–354.

Bouchard, C., Tremblay, A., Despres, J. P., Nadeau, A., Lupien, J. P., Theriault, G., et al. (1990). The response to long-term overfeeding in identical twins. *New England Journal of Medicine, 322*, 1477–1482.

Bouchard, T. J., Jr., Lykken, D. T., McGue, M., Segal, N. L., & Tellegen, A. (1990, October 12). Sources of human psychological differences: The Minnesota study of twins reared apart. *Science, 250*, 223–228.

Bouton, M. E. (1994). Context, ambiguity, and classical conditioning. *Current Directions in Psychological Science, 3*, 49–53.

Bouton, M. E., Westbrook, R. F., Corcoran, K. A., & Maren, S. (2006). Contextual and temporal modulation of extinction: Behavioral and biological mechanisms. *Biological Psychiatry, 60*, 352–360.

Bower, A. (2001). Attractive models in advertising and the women who loathe them: The implications of negative affect for spokesperson effectiveness. *Highly Journal of Advertising, 30*, 51–63.

Bowlby, J. (1982). Attachment and loss: Retrospect and prospect. *American Journal of Orthopsychiatry, 52*, 664–678.

Brackett, M. A., Rivers, S. E., & Salovey, P. (2011). Emotional intelligence: Implications for personal, social, academic, and workplace settings. *Social and Personality Psychology Compass, 5*, 88–103.

Bradbury, T. N., & Fincham, F. D. (1990). Attributions in marriage: Review and critique. *Psychological Bulletin, 107*, 3–33.

Bransford, J. D., & Johnson, M. K. (1972). Contextual prerequisites for understanding: Some investigations of comprehension and recall. *Journal of Verbal Learning and Verbal Behavior, 11*, 717–726. (Reprinted and modified in *Human memory*, p. 305, by E. B. Zechmeister & S. E. Nyberg, Eds., 1982, Pacific Grove, CA: Brooks Cole.)

Braunschweig, D., Ashwood, P., Krakowiak, P., Hertz-Picciotto, I., Hansen, R., Croen, L. A., et al. (2008). Autism: Maternally derived antibodies specific for fetal brain proteins. *Neurotoxicology, 29*, 226–231.

Breedlove, S. M., Rosenzweig, M. R., & Watson, N. V. (2007). *Biological psychology* (5th ed.). Sunderland, MA: Sinauer Associates.

Breland, K., & Breland, M. (1961). The misbehavior of organisms. *American Psychologist, 16*, 681–684.

Brent, D. A. (2004). Antidepressants and pediatric depression: The risk of doing nothing. *New England Journal of Medicine, 351*, 1598–1601.

Brewer, M. B., & Caporael, L. R. (1990). Selfish genes vs. selfish people: Sociobiology as origin myth. *Motivation and Emotion, 14*, 237–243.

Brigham, J. C., & Malpass, R. S. (1985). The role of experience and contact in the recognition of faces of own- and other-races persons. *Journal of Social Issues, 41*, 139–155.

Brody, A. L., Saxena, S., Stoessel, P., Gillies, L. A., Fairbanks, L. A., Alborzian, S., et al. (2001). Regional brain metabolic changes in patients with major depression treated with either paroxetine or interpersonal therapy: Preliminary findings. *Archives of General Psychiatry, 58*, 631–640.

Brody, J. E. (1997, December 30). Personal health: Despite the despair of depression, few men seek treatment. *The New York Times*. Retrieved from http://www.nytimes.com

Brody, N. (1992). *Intelligence*. San Diego, CA: Academic Press.

Bromley, S. M., & Doty, R. L. (1995). Odor recognition memory is better under bilateral than unilateral test conditions. *Cortex, 31*, 25–40.

Brown, A. S. (1991). A review of the tip-of-the-tongue phenomenon. *Psychological Bulletin, 109*, 204–223.

Brown, B. B., Mounts, N., Lamborn, S. D., & Steinberg, L. (1993). Parenting practices and peer group affiliations in adolescence. *Child Development, 64*, 467–482.

Brown, G. W., & Harris, T. O. (1978). *Social origins of depression: A study of psychiatric disorders in women*. New York: Free Press.

Brown, J. D., & Kobayashi, C. (2002). Self-enhancement in Japan and America. *Asian Journal of Social Psychology, 5*, 145–168.

Brown, R. (1973). Development of the first language in the human species. *American Psychologist, 28*, 97–106. doi: 10.1037/h0034209

Brown, R., & Kulik, J. (1977). Flashbulb memories. *Cognition, 5*(1), 73–99.

Brown, R., & McNeill, D. (1966). The "tip-of-the-tongue" phenomenon. *Journal of Verbal Learning and Verbal Behavior, 5*, 325–337.

Brownell, C. A., & Brown, E. (1992). Peers and play in infants and toddlers. In V. Van Hasselt & M. Hersen (Eds.), *Handbook of social development: A lifespan perspective* (pp. 183–200). New York: Plenum Press.

Brownell, K. D., Greenwood, M. R. C., Stellar, E., & Shrager, E. E. (1986). The effects of repeated cycles of weight loss and regain in rats. *Physiology & Behavior, 38*, 459–464.

Bruce, V., & Young, A. (1986). Understanding face recognition. *British Journal of Psychology, 77*, 305–327.

Bruck, M. L., & Ceci, S. (1993). Amicus brief for the case of State of New Jersey v. Michaels. Presented by Committee of Concerned Social Scientists. Supreme Court of New Jersey Docket No. 36, 633. (Reprinted in *Psychology, Public Policy and Law, 1*, 1995, 272–322.)

Bruder, C. E., Piotrowski, A., Gijsbers, A. A., Andersson, R., Erickson, S., de Ståhl, T. D., et al. (2008). Phenotypically concordant and discordant monozygotic twins display different DNA copy-number-variation profiles. *American Journal of Human Genetics, 82*, 763–771.

Burger, J. M. (2009). Replicating Milgram: Would people still obey today? *American Psychologist, 64*, 1–11.

Burke, B. L., Arkowitz, H., & Menchola, M. (2003). The efficacy of motivational interviewing: A meta-analysis of controlled clinical trials. *Journal of Consulting and Clinical Psychology, 71*, 843–861.

Bush, E. C., & Allman, J. M. (2004). The scaling of frontal cortex in primates and carnivores. *Proceedings of the National Academy of Sciences, USA, 101*, 3962–3966.

Bushman, B. J., & Baumeister, R. F. (1998). Threatened egotism, narcissism, self-esteem, and direct and displaced aggression: Does self-love or self-hate lead to violence? *Journal of Personality and Social Psychology, 75*, 219–229.

Bushman, B. J., & Huesmann, L. R. (2001). Effects of televised violence on aggression. In D. G. Singer & J. L. Singer (Eds.), *Handbook of children and the media* (pp. 223–254). Thousand Oaks, CA: Sage.

Buss, A. H., & Plomin, R. (1984). *Temperament: Early developing personality traits.* Hillsdale, NJ: Erlbaum.

Buss, D. M. (1989). Sex differences in human mate preferences: Evolutionary hypotheses tested in 37 cultures. *Behavioral and Brain Sciences, 12,* 1–49.

Buss, D. M. (1995). Psychological sex differences: Origins through sexual selection. *American Psychologist, 50,* 164–168. doi: 10.1037/0003-066X.50.3.164

Buss, D. M. (1999). Human nature and individual differences: The evolution of human personality. In L. A. Pervin & O. P. John (Eds.), *Handbook of personality: Theory and research* (pp. 31–56). New York: Guilford Press.

Buss, D. M., & Schmitt, D. P. (1993). Sexual strategies theory: An evolutionary perspective on human mating. *Psychological Review, 100,* 204–232.

Buss, D. M., & Shackelford, T. K. (2008). Attractive women want it all: Good genes, investment, parenting indicators, and commitment. *Evolutionary Psychology, 6,* 134–146.

Butcher, J. N., Mineka, S., & Hooley, J. M. (2007). *Abnormal psychology* (13th ed.). Boston: Allyn and Bacon.

Butler, A. C., Chapman, J. E., Forman, E. M., & Beck, A. T. (2006). The empirical status of cognitive-behavioral therapy: A review of meta-analyses. *Clinical Psychology Review, 26,* 17–31.

Byers-Heinlein, K., Burns, T. C., & Werker, J. F. (2010). The roots of bilingualism in newborns. *Psychological Science, 21,* 343–348.

Cacioppo, J. T., Berntson, G. G., Larsen, J. T., Poehlmann, K. M., & Ito, T. A. (2000). The psychophysiology of emotion. In M. Lewis & R. J. M. Haviland-Jones (Eds.), *The handbook of emotions* (2nd ed., pp. 173–191). New York: Guilford Press.

Cacioppo, J. T., Hughes, M. E., Waite, L. J., Hawkley, L. C., & Thisted, R. A. (2006). Loneliness as a specific risk factor for depressive symptoms: Cross sectional and longitudinal analyses. *Psychology and Aging, 21,* 140–151.

Cacioppo, J. T., & Patrick, W. (2008). *Loneliness: Human nature and the need for social connection.* New York: Norton.

Cahill, L., Haier, R. J., White, N. S., Fallon, J., Kilpatrick, L., Lawrence, C., et al. (2001). Sex-related difference in amygdala activity during emotionally influenced memory storage. *Neurobiology of Learning and Memory, 75,* 1–9.

Cahill, L., Prins, B., Weber, M., & McGaugh, J. L. (1994). Beta-adrenergic activation and memory for emotional events. *Nature, 371,* 702–704.

Cahn, B. R., & Polich, J. (2006). Meditation states and traits: EEG, ERP, and neuroimaging studies. *Psychological Bulletin, 132,* 180–211.

Cairns, R. B., & Cairns, B. D. (1994). *Lifelines and risks: Pathways of youth in our times.* Cambridge, UK: Cambridge University Press.

Campbell, W. K., Bush, C. P., Brunell, A. B., & Shelton, J. (2005). Understanding the social costs of narcissism: The case of tragedy of the commons. *Personality and Social Psychology, 31,* 1358–1368.

Campbell, W. K., Foster, C.A., & Finkel, E. J. (2002). Does self-love lead to love for others? A story of narcissistic game playing. *Journal of Personality and Social Psychology, 83,* 340–354.

Campbell, W. K., & Sedikides, C. (1999). Self-threat magnifies the self-serving bias: A meta-analytic integration. *Review of General Psychology, 3,* 23–43.

Canli, T. (2006). *Biology of personality and individual differences.* New York: Guilford Press.

Cannon, T. D., Cadenhead, K., Cornblatt, B., Woods, S. W., Addington, J., Walker, E., et al. (2008). Prediction of psychosis in youth at high clinical risk: A multisite longitudinal study in North America. *Archives of General Psychiatry, 65,* 28–37.

Cannon, W. B. (1927). The James-Lange theory of emotion: A critical examination and an alternative theory. *American Journal of Psychology 39,* 106–124.

Caporael, L. R. (2001). Evolutionary psychology: Toward a unifying theory and a hybrid science. *Annual Review of Psychology, 52,* 607–628.

Caramaschi, D., de Boer, S. F., & Koolhaus, J. M. (2007). Differential role of the 5-HT receptor in aggressive and non-aggressive mice: An across-strain comparison. *Physiology & Behavior, 90,* 590–601.

Cardeña, E., & Carlson, E. (2011). Acute stress disorder revisited. *Annual Review of Clinical Psychology, 7,* 245–267.

Carey, B. (2011, June 23). Expert on mental illness reveals her own fight. *The New York Times.* Retrieved from http://newyorktimes.com

Carli, L. L., Ganley, R., & Pierce-Otay, A. (1991). Similarity and satisfaction in roommate relationships. *Personality and Social Psychology Bulletin, 17*(4), 419–426. doi:10.1177/0146167291174010

Carmichael, M. (2007, March 26). Stronger, faster, smarter. *Newsweek, 149*(13). Retrieved from http://www.newsweek.com

Carmody, T. P. (1993). Nicotine dependence: Psychological approaches to the prevention of smoking relapse. *Psychology of Addictive Behaviors, 7,* 96–102.

Carnagey, N. L., Anderson, C. A., & Bartholow, B. D. (2007). Media violence and social neuroscience: New questions and new opportunities. *Current Directions in Psychological Science, 16,* 178–182.

Carnagey, N. L., Anderson, C. A., & Bushman, B. J. (2007). The effect of video game violence on physiological desensitization to real-life violence. *Journal of Experimental Social Psychology, 43,* 489–496.

Caro, T. M., & Hauser, M. D. (1992). Is there teaching in nonhuman animals? *Quarterly Journal of Biology, 67,* 151–174.

Carré, J. M., McCormick, C. M., & Hariri, A. R. (2011, in press). The social neuroendocrinology of human aggression. *Psychoneuroendocrinology.*

Carré, J. M., & Putnam, S. K. (2010). Watching a previous victory produces an increase in testosterone among elite hockey players. *Psychoneuroendocrinology, 35,* 475–479.

Carrère, S., Buehlman K. T., Gottman, J. M., Coan, J. A., & Ruckstuhl, L. (2000). Predicting marital stability and divorce in newlywed couples. *Journal of Family Psychology, 14,* 42–58.

Carstensen, L. L. (1995). Evidence for a life-span theory of socioemotional selectivity. *Current Directions in Psychological Science, 4,* 151–156.

Carter, C. S. (2003). Developmental consequences of oxytocin. *Physiology & Behavior, 74,* 383–397.

Caruso, S., Intelisano, G., Farina, M., Di Mari, L., & Agnello, C. (2003). The function of sildenafil on female sexual pathways: A double-blind, cross-over, placebo-controlled study. *European Journal of Obstetrics & Gynecology and Reproductive Biology, 110,* 201–206.

Case, R. (1992). The role of the frontal lobes in development. *Brain and Cognition, 20,* 51–73.

Casey, B. J., Jones, R. M., & Somerville, L. H. (2011). Braking and accelerating of the adolescent brain. *Journal of Research in Adolescence, 21,* 21–33.

Caspi, A. (2000). The child is father of the man: Personality continuities from childhood to adulthood. *Journal of Personality and Social Psychology, 78*, 158–172.

Caspi, A., & Herbener, E. S. (1990). Continuity and change: Assortative marriage and the consistency of personality in adulthood. *Journal of Personality and Social Psychology, 58*, 250–258.

Caspi, A., McClay, J., Moffit, T. E., Mill, J., Martin, J., Craig, I. W., et al. (2002). Role of genotype in the cycle of violence in maltreated children. *Science, 29*, 851–854.

Castellanos, F. X., Giedd, J. N., Eckberg, P., & Marsh, W. L. (1998). Quantitative morphology of the caudate nucleus in attention deficit hyperactivity disorder. *American Journal of Psychiatry, 151*, 1791–1796.

Cattell, R. B. (1965). *The scientific analysis of personality*. London: Penguin.

Cattell, R. B. (1971). *Abilities: Their structure, growth, and action*. Boston: Houghton Mifflin.

Cavanagh, J. O., Carson, A. J., Sharpe, M. M., & Lawrie, S. M. (2003). Psychological autopsy studies of suicide: A systematic review. *Psychological Medicine: A Journal of Research in Psychiatry and the Allied Sciences, 33*(3), 395–405.

Ceci, S. J. (1999). Schooling and intelligence. In S. J. Ceci & W. M. Williams (Eds.), *The nature-nurture debate: The essential readings* (pp. 168–175). Oxford, UK: Blackwell.

CensusScope. (2000). *Multiracial profile: United States*. Retrieved from http://www.censusscope.org/us/chart_multi.html

Centers for Disease Control and Prevention. (1999, November 17). A report of the Surgeon General: Physical activity and health. Retrieved from http://www.cdc.gov/nccdphp/sgr/adults.htm

Centers for Disease Control and Prevention, National Center for Health Statistics. (2002, October 8). *HHS news: Obesity still on the rise, new data show* [Press release.]. Retrieved from http://www.cdc.gov/nchs/PRESSROOM/02news/obesityonrise.htm

Centers for Disease Control and Prevention, National Center on Birth Defects and Developmental Disabilities. (2004, July). *Fetal alcohol syndrome: Guidelines for referral and diagnosis*. Retrieved from http://www.cdc.gov/ncbddd/fas/publications/FAS_guidelines_ accessible.pdf

Centers for Disease Control and Prevention. (2010a). How tobacco smoke causes disease: The biology and behavioral basis for smoking-attributable disease: A Report of the Surgeon General.

Centers for Disease Control and Prevention, National Center for Health Statistics. (2010b). [Table 22, Life expectancy at birth, at 65 years of age, and at 75 years of age, by race and sex: United States, selected years 1900–2007]. *Health, United States, 2010*. Retrieved from http://www.cdc.gov/nchs/data/hus/hus10.pdf#022

Centers for Disease Control and Prevention. (2010c). Accessed at http://www.cdc.gov/HealthyYouth/yrbs/pdf/us_tobacco_combo.pdf

Centers for Disease Control and Prevention. (2011). Mental illness surveillance among adults in the United States. *Morbidity and Mortality Weekly Report, 60*(3), 1–32.

Cepeda, N. J., Pashler, H., Vul, E., Wixted, J. T., & Rohrer, D. (2006). Distributed practice in verbal recall tasks: A review and quantitative synthesis. *Psychological Bulletin, 132*, 354–380.

Chabas, D., Taheri, S., Renier, C., & Mignot, E. (2003). The genetics of narcolepsy. *Annual Review of Genomics & Human Genetics, 4*, 459–483.

Chabris, C. (1999). Prelude or requiem for the "Mozart effect"? *Nature, 400*, 826–827.

Chambers, D. W. (1983). Stereotypic images of the scientist: The draw-a-scientist test. *Science Education, 67*, 255–265.

Chase, V. D. (2006). *Shattered nerves: How science is solving modern medicine's most perplexing problem*. Baltimore: The Johns Hopkins University Press.

Chase, W. G., & Simon, H. A. (1973). Perception in chess. *Cognitive Psychology, 4*, 55–81.

Chassin, L., Presson, C. C., & Sherman, S. J. (1990). Social psychological contributions to the understanding and prevention of adolescent cigarette smoking. *Personality and Social Psychology Bulletin, 16*, 133–151.

Cherry, E. C. (1953). Some experiments on the recognition of speech, with one and two ears. *Journal of the Acoustical Society of America, 25*, 975–979.

Chesher, G., & Greeley, J. (1992). Tolerance to the effects of alcohol. *Alcohol, Drugs, and Driving, 8*, 93–106.

Chess, S., & Thomas, A. (1984). *Origins and evolution of behavior disorders: From infancy to early adult life*. Cambridge, MA: Harvard University Press.

Cheung, F. M., Cheung, S. F., & Leung, F. (2008). Clinical utility of the cross-cultural (Chinese) personality assessment inventory (CPAI-2) in the assessment of substance use disorders among Chinese men. *Psychological Assessment, 20*, 103–113.

Cheung, F. M., Leung, K., Zhang, J. X, Sun, H. F., Gan, Y. G., Song, W. Z, et al. (2001). Indigenous Chinese personality constructs: Is the five-factor model complete? *Journal of Cross-Cultural Psychology, 32*, 407–433.

Chiao, J. Y., Iidaka, T., Gordon, H. L., Nogawa, J., Bar, M., Aminoff, E., et al. (2008). Cultural specificity in amygdala response to fear faces. *Journal of Cognitive Neuroscience, 20*(12), 2167–2174.

Chistyakov, A. V., Kaplan, B., Rubichek, O., Kreinin, I., Koren, D., Feinsod, M., et al. (2004). Antidepressant effects of different schedules of repetitive transcranial magnetic stimulation vs. clomipramine in patients with major depression: Relationship to changes in cortical excitability. *International Journal of Neuropsychopharmacology, 8*, 223–233.

Choi, I., Dalal, R., Kim-Prieto, C., & Park, H. (2003). Culture and judgment of causal relevance. *Journal of Personality and Social Psychology, 84*, 46–59.

Choi, I., Nisbett, R. E., & Norenzayan, A. (1999). Causal attribution across cultures: Variation and universality. *Psychological Bulletin, 125*, 47–63.

Choleris, E., Gustafsson, J. A., Korach, K. S., Muglia, L. J., Pfaff, D. W., & Ogawa, S. (2003). An estrogen-dependent four-gene micronet regulating social recognition: A study with oxytocin and estrogen receptor-alpha and -beta knockout mice. *Proceedings of the National Academy of Sciences, USA, 100*, 6192–6197.

Christakis, N. A., & Fowler, J. H. (2007). The spread of obesity in a large social network over 32 years. *New England Journal of Medicine, 357*, 370–379.

Christianson, S. (1992). Emotional stress and eyewitness memory: A critical review. *Psychological Bulletin, 112*, 284–309.

Chronis, A. M., Jones, H. A., & Raggi, V. L. (2006). Evidence-based psychosocial treatments for children and adolescents with attention-deficit/hyperactivity disorder. *Clinical Psychology Review, 26*, 486–502.

Chun, M. M., Golomb, J. D., & Turk-Browne, N. B. (2011). A taxonomy of external and internal attention. *Annual Review of Psychology, 62*, 73–101.

Cialdini, R. B. (2008). *Influence: Science and prejudice* (5th ed.). Boston: Allyn & Bacon.

Cialdini, R. B., Shaller, M., Houlihan, D., Arps, K., Fultz, J., & Beaman, A. L. (1987). Empathy-based helping: Is it selflessly or selfishly motivated? *Journal of Personality and Social Psychology, 52*, 749–758.

Cicchetti, D., Rogosh, F. A., & Toth, S. (1998). Maternal depressive disorder and contextual risk: Contributions to the development of attachment insecurity and behavior problems in toddlerhood. *Development and Psychopathology, 10*, 283–300.

Clark, L. A. (2007). Assessment and diagnosis of personality disorder: Perennial issues and an emerging reconceptualization. *Annual Review of Psychology, 58*, 227–257.

Clark, R. D., & Hatfield, E. (1989). Gender differences in receptivity to sexual offers. *Journal of Psychology and Human Sexuality, 2*, 39–55.

Clark, S. E., & Wells, G. L. (2008). On the diagnosticity of multiple-witness identifications. *Law and Human Behavior, 32*, 406–422.

Cleckley, H. M. (1941). *The mask of sanity: An attempt to reinterpret the so-called psychopathic personality*. St. Louis: Mosby.

Cloninger, C., Adolfsson, R., & Svrakic, N. (1996). Mapping genes for human personality. *Nature and Genetics, 12*, 3–4.

Cohen, D., Nisbett, R. E., Bowdle, B. F., & Schwarz, N. (1996). Insult, aggression, and the southern culture of honor: An "experimental ethnography." *Journal of Personality and Social Psychology, 70*, 945–960.

Cohen, G. L., Garcia, J., Apfel, N., & Master, A. (2006). Reducing the racial achievement gap: A social-psychological intervention. *Science, 313*, 1307–1310.

Cohen, S., Alper, C. M., Doyle, W. J., Treanor, J. J., & Turner, R. B. (2006). Positive emotional style predicts resistance to illness after experimental exposure to rhinovirus or influenza A virus. *Psychomatic Medicine, 68*, 809–815.

Cohen, S., Doyle, W. J., Skoner, D. P., Rabin, B. S., & Gwaltney, J. M. J. (1997). Social ties and susceptibility to the common cold. *Journal of the American Medical Association, 277*, 1940–1944.

Cohen, S., Janicki-Deverts, D., & Miller, G. E. (2007). Psychological stress and disease. *Journal of the American Medical Assocation, 298*, 1685–1687.

Cohen, S., Kamarck, T., & Mermelstein, R. (1983). A global measure of perceived stress. *Journal of Health and Social Behavior, 24*, 386–396.

Cohen, S., Tyrrell, D. A. J., & Smith, A. P. (1991). Psychological stress and susceptibility to the common cold. *New England Journal of Medicine, 325*, 606–612.

Cohen, S., & Wills, T. A. (1985). Stress, social support, and the buffering hypothesis. *Psychological Bulletin, 98*, 310–357.

Cohn, J. F., & Tronick, E. Z. (1983). Three month old infants' reaction to simulated maternal depression. *Child Development, 54*, 185–193.

Colapinto, J. (2000). *As nature made him: The boy who was raised as a girl*. New York: HarperCollins.

Colcombe, S. J., Erickson, K. I., Scalf, P., Kim, J., Prkash, R., McAuley, E., et al. (2006). Aerobic exercise training increases brain volume in aging humans. *Journal of Gerontology: Medical Sciences, 61A*, 1166–1170.

Compton, W. M., Conway, K. P., Stinson, F. S., Colliver, J. D., & Grant, B. F. (2005). Prevalence, correlates, and comorbidity of DSM-IV antisocial personality syndromes and alcohol and specific drug use disorders in the United States: Results from the national epidemiologic survey on alcohol and related conditions. *Journal of Clinical Psychiatry, 66*, 677–685.

Conn, C., Warden, R., Stuewig, R., Kim, E., Harty, L., Hastings, M., & Tangney, J. P. (2010). Borderline personality disorder among jail inmates: How common and how distinct? *Corrections Compendium, 35*, 6–13.

Conrad, A., Wilhelm, F. H., Roth, W. T., Spiegel, D., & Taylor, C. B. (2008). Circadian affective, cardiopulmonary, and cortisol variability in depressed and nondepressed individuals at risk for cardiovascular disease. *Journal of Psychiatric Research, 42*, 769–777.

Conway, A. R. A., Kane, M. J., Bunting, M. F., Hambrick, D. Z., Wilhelm, O., & Engle, R. W. (2005). Working memory span tasks: A methodological review and user's guide. *Psychonomic Bulletin & Review,* 12, 769–786.

Conway, A. R. A., Kane, M. J., & Engle, R. W. (2003). Working memory capacity and its relation to general intelligence. *Trends in Cognitive Sciences, 7*, 547–552.

Conway, M. A., Anderson, S. J., Larsen, S. F., Donnelly, C. M., McDaniel, M. A., McClelland, A. G. R., et al. (1994). The formation of flashbulb memories. *Memory and Cognition, 22*, 326–343.

Conway, M., & Ross, M. (1984). Getting what you want by revising what you had. *Journal of Personality and Social Psychology, 47*, 738–748.

Cook, G. I., Marsh, R. L., Clark-Foos, A., & Meeks, J. T. (2007, February). Learning is impaired by activated intentions. *Psychonomic Bulletin and Review, 14*, 101–106.

Cook, M., & Mineka, S. (1989). Observational conditioning of fear to fear-relevant versus fear-irrelevant stimuli in rhesus monkeys. *Journal of Abnormal Psychology, 98*, 448–459.

Cooke, S. F., & Bliss, T. V. P. (2006). Plasticity in the human central nervous system. *Brain: A Journal of Neurology, 129*, 1659–1673.

Cooney, J., & Gazzaniga, M. S. (2003). Neurological disorders and the structure of human consciousness. *Trends in Cognitive Sciences, 7*, 161–165.

Cooper, C. R., Denner, J., & Lopez, E. M. (1999). Cultural brokers: Helping Latino children on pathways toward success. *The Future of Children, 9*, 51–57.

Corder, E. H., Saunders, A. M., Strittmatter, W. J., Schmechel, D. E., Gaskell, P. C., Small, G. W., et al. (1993). Gene dose of apolipoprotein E type 4 allele and the risk of Alzheimer's disease in late onset families. *Science, 261*, 921–923.

Coren, S. (1996). Daylight savings time and traffic accidents. *New England Journal of Medicine, 334*, 924.

Correll, C. U., Leucht, S., & Kane, J. M. (2004). Lower risk for tardive dyskinesia associated with second-generation antipsychotics: A systematic review of 1-year studies. *American Journal of Psychiatry, 161*, 414–425.

Correll, J., Park, B., Judd, C. M., Wittenbrink, B., Sadler, M. S., & Keesee, T. (2007). Across the thin blue line: Police officers and racial bias in the decision to shoot. *Journal of Personality and Social Psychology, 92*, 1006–1023.

Cosmides, L., & Tooby, J. (1997). *Evolutionary psychology: A primer*. Retrieved May 24, 2002, from http://www.psych.ucsb.edu/research/cep/primer.html

Cosmides, L., & Tooby, J. (2000). The cognitive neuroscience of social reasoning. In M. S. Gazzaniga (Ed.), *The new cognitive neurosciences* (pp. 1259–1270). Cambridge, MA: MIT Press.

Costa, P. T., & McCrae, R. R. (1992). *Revised NEO Personality Inventory (NEO-PI-R) and NEO Five-Factor Inventory (NEO-FFI) professional manual*. Odessa, FL: Psychological Assessment Resources.

Costa, P. T., Terracciano, A., & McCrae, R. R. (2001). Gender differences in personality traits across cultures: Robust and surprising findings. *Journal of Personality and Social Psychology, 81*, 322–331.

Courchesne, E., Pierce, K., Schumann, C. M., Redcay, E., Buckwalter, J. A., Kennedy, D. P., et al. (2007). Mapping early brain development in autism. *Neuron, 56*, 399–413.

Courchesne, E., Redcay, E., & Kennedy, D. P. (2004). The autistic brain: Birth through adulthood. *Current Opinion in Neurology, 17*, 489–496.

Cowan, C. P., & Cowan, P. A. (1988). Who does what when partners become parents? Implications for men, women, and marriage. In R. Palkovitz & M. B. Sussman (Eds.), *Transitions to parenthood* (pp. 105–132). New York: The Haworth Press.

Cowell, P. E., Turetsky, B. E., Gur, R. C., Grossman, R. I., Shtasel, D. L., & Gur, R. E. (1994). Sex differences in aging of the human frontal and temporal lobes. *Journal of Neuroscience, 14*, 4748–4755.

Craft, L. L., & Perna, F. M. (2004). The benefits of exercise for the clinically depressed. *Journal of Clinical Psychiatry, 6*, 104–111.

Craik, F. I. M., & Lockhart, R. S. (1972). Levels of processing: A framework for memory research. *Journal of Verbal Learning and Verbal Behavior, 11*, 671–684.

Crawford, H. J., Corby, J. C., & Kopell, B. (1996). Auditory event-related potentials while ignoring tone stimuli: Attentional differences reflected in stimulus intensity and latency responses in low and highly hypnotizable persons. *International Journal of Neuroscience, 85*, 57–69.

Crocker, J. (2006, June). *Time for your life and your goals.* Workshop sponsored by the Junior Scholars Professional Development Task Force, presented at the biannual meeting of the Society for the Psychological Study of Social Issues, Long Beach, CA.

Crocker, J., & Major, B. (1989). Social stigma and self-esteem: The self-protective properties of stigma. *Psychological Review, 96*, 608–630.

Crocker, J., Niiya, Y., & Mischkowski, D. (2008). Why does writing about important values reduce defensiveness? Self-affirmation and the role of positive other-directed feelings. *Psychological Science, 19*(7), 740–747. doi:10.1111/j.1467-9280.2008.02150.x

Crocker, J., Olivier, M., & Nuer, N. (2009). Self-image goals and compassionate goals: Costs and benefits. *Self and Identity, 8*(2–3), 251–269. doi:10.1080/15298860802505160

Crosnoe, R., & Elder, G. H., Jr. (2002). Successful adaptation in the later years: A life-course approach to aging. *Social Psychology Quarterly, 65*, 309–328.

Cross, S. E., Bacon, P. L., & Morris, M. L. (2000). The relational-interdependent self-construal and relationships. *Journal of Personality and Social Psychology, 78*(4), 791–808. doi:10.1037/0022-3514.78.4.791

Crowe, R. R. (2000). Molecular genetics of anxiety disorders. In D. S. Charney, E. J. Nestler, & B. S. Bunney (Eds.), *Neurobiology of mental illness* (pp. 451–462). New York: Oxford University Press.

Csikszentmihalyi, M. (1990). *Flow: The psychology of optimal experience.* New York: Harper & Row.

Csikszentmihalyi, M. (1999). If we are so rich, why aren't we happy? *American Psychologist, 54*, 821–827.

Cummings, J. R., & Druss, B. G. (2010). Racial/ethnic differences in mental health service use among adolescents with major depression. *Journal of the American Academy of Child & Adolescent Psychiatry, 50*, 160–170.

Cunningham, M. R., Barbee, A. P., & Druen, P. B. (1996). Social allergens and the reactions they produce: Escalation of annoyance and disgust in love and work. In R. M. Kowalski (Ed.), *Aversive interpersonal behaviors* (pp. 189–214). New York: Plenum Press.

Cunningham, M. R., Roberts, A. R., Barbee, A. P., Druen, P. B., & Wu, C. (1995). Their ideas of beauty are, on the whole, the same as ours: Consistency and variability in the cross-cultural perception of female physical attractiveness. *Journal of Personality and Social Psychology, 68*, 261–279.

Cunningham, W. A., Johnson, M. K., Raye, C. L., Gatenby, J. C., Gore, J. C., & Banaji, M. R. (2004). Separable neural components in the processing of black and white faces. *Psychological Science, 15*, 806–813.

Cupach, W. R., & Metts, S. (1990). Remedial processes in embarrassing predicaments. In J. Anderson (Ed.), *Communication yearbook* (pp. 323–352). Newbury Park, CA: Sage.

Curtiss, S. (1977). *Genie: A psycholinguistic study of a modern day "wild child."* New York: Academic Press.

Cvetkovic-Lopes, V., Bayer, L., Dorsaz, S., Maret, S., Pradervand, S., Dauvilliers, Y., et al. (2010). Elevated Tribbles homolog 2-specific antibody levels in narcolepsy patients. *Journal of Clinical Investigation, 120*, 713–719.

Dabbs, J. M., & Morris, R. (1990). Testosterone, social class, and antisocial behavior in a sample of 4462 men. *Psychological Science, 1*, 209–211.

Dalton, M. A., Bernhardt, A. M., Gibson, J. J., Sargent, J. D., Beach, M. L., Adachi-Mejia, A. M., Titus-Ernstoff, L. T., & Heatherton, T. F. (2005). "Honey, have some smokes." Preschoolers use cigarettes and alcohol while role playing as adults. *Archives of Pediatrics & Adolescent Medicine, 159*, 854–859.

Damasio, A. R. (1994). *Descartes' error.* New York: Avon Books.

Damasio, H., Grabowski, T., Frank, R., Galaburda, A. M., & Damasio, A. R. (1994, May 20). The return of Phineas Gage: Clues about the brain from the skull of a famous patient. *Science, 264*, 1102–1105.

Dapretto, M., Davies, M. S., Pfeifer, J. H., Scott, A. A., Sigman, M., Bookheimer, S. Y., & Iacoboni, M. (2006). Understanding emotions in others: Mirror neuron dysfunction in children with autism spectrum disorders. *Nature Neuroscience, 9*, 28–30.

Darley, J. M., & Batson, C. D. (1973). "From Jerusalem to Jericho": A study of situational and dispositional variables in helping behavior. *Journal of Personality and Social Psychology, 27*, 100–108.

Darwin, C. (1859). *On the origin of species by means of natural selection, or the preservation of favoured races in the struggle for life.* London: John Murray.

Darwin, C. R. (1872). *The expression of the emotions in man and animals.* London: John Murray.

Dasgupta, A. G., & Greenwald, A. G. (2001). Exposure to admired group members reduces automatic intergroup bias. *Journal of Personality and Social Psychology, 81*, 800–814.

Davidson, J. R., Foa, E. B., Huppert, J. D., Keefe, F. J., Franklin, M. E., Compton, J. S., et al. (2004). Fluoxetine, comprehensive cognitive behavioral therapy, and placebo in generalized social phobia. *Archives of General Psychiatry, 61*, 1005–1013.

Davidson, R. J. (2000). Affective style, psychopathology, and resilience: Brain mechanisms and plasticity. *American Psychologist, 55*, 1196–1214.

Davidson, R. J., Pizzagalli, D., Nitschke, J. B., & Putnam, K. M. (2002). Depression: Perspectives from affective neuroscience. *Annual Review of Psychology, 53*, 545–574.

Davidson Ward, S. L., Bautisa, D., Chan, L., Derry, M., Lisbin, A., Durfee, M., et al. (1990). Sudden infant death syndrome in infants of drug abusing mothers. *Journal of Pediatrics, 117*, 876–887.

Davies, M. F. (1997). Belief persistence after evidential discrediting: The impact of generated versus provided explanations on the likelihood of discredited outcomes. *Journal of Experimental Social Psychology, 33*, 561–578.

Davis, K. L., Stewart, D. G., Friedman, J. I., Buchsbaum, M., Harvey, P. D., Hof, P. R., et al. (2003). White matter changes in schizophrenia: Evidence for myelin-related dysfunction. *Archives of General Psychiatry, 60*, 443–456.

Davis, M. (1997). Neurobiology of fear responses: The role of the amygdala. *Journal of Neuropsychological and Clinical Neuroscience, 9*, 382–402.

Deacon, B. J., & Abramowitz, J. S. (2004). Cognitive and behavioral treatments for anxiety disorders: A review of meta-analytic findings. *Journal of Clinical Psychology, 60*, 429–441.

DeAngelis, T. (2008). Psychology's growth careers. *Monitor on Psychology, 39*, 64.

Deary, I. J. (2000). *Looking down on human intelligence*. New York: Oxford University Press.

Deary, I. J. (2001). *Intelligence: A very short introduction*. New York: Oxford University Press.

Deary, I. J., Batty, G. D., Pattie, A., & Gale, C. R. (2008). More intelligent, more dependable children live longer: A 55-year longitudinal study of a representative sample of the Scottish nation. *Psychological Science, 19*, 874–880.

Deary, I. J., & Der, G. (2005). Reaction time explains IQ's association with death. *Psychological Science, 16*, 64–69.

DeCasper, A. J., & Fifer, W. P. (1980, June 6). Of human bonding: Newborns prefer their mothers' voices. *Science, 208*, 1174–1176.

DeCasper, A. J., & Spence, M. J. (1986). Prenatal maternal speech influences newborns' perception of speech sounds. *Infant Behavior and Development, 9*, 133–150.

deCharms, R. C., Maeda, F., Glover, G. H, Ludlow, D., Pauly, J. M., Soneji, D., et al. (2005). Control over brain activation and pain learned by using real-time functional MRI. *Proceedings of the National Academy of Sciences, USA, 102*, 18626–18631.

Deci, E. L., & Ryan, R. M. (1987). The support of autonomy and the control of behavior. *Journal of Personality and Social Psychology, 53*, 1024–1037.

Decyk, B. N. (1994).Using examples to teach concepts. In *Changing college classrooms: New teaching and learning strategies for an increasingly complex world* (pp. 39–63). San Francisco: Jossey Bass.

Dehaene, S., Changeux, J. P., Naccache, L., Sackur, J., & Sergent, C. (2006). Conscious, preconscious, and subliminal processing: A testable taxonomy. *Trends in Cognitive Sciences, 10*, 204–211.

Dejong, W., & Kleck, R. E. (1986). The social psychological effects of overweight. In C. P. Herman, M. P. Zanna, & E. T. Higgins (Eds.), *Physical appearance, stigma and social behavior: The Ontario Symposium* (pp. 65–87). Hillsdale, NJ: Erlbaum.

De Lisi, R., & Staudt, J. (1980). Individual differences in college students' performance on formal operations tasks. *Journal of Applied Developmental Psychology, 1*, 201–208. doi: 10.1016/0193-3973(80)90009-X

DeLong, M. R., & Wichmann, T. (2008). *The expanding potential of deep brain stimulation: The 2008 progress report on brain research*. New York: Dana Foundation.

Demerouti, E. (2006). Job characteristics, flow, and performance: The moderating role of conscientiousness. *Journal of Occupational Health Psychology, 11*(3), 266–280.

Demir, E., & Dickson, B. J. (2005). Fruitless: Splicing specifies male courtship behavior in drosophila. *Cell, 121*, 785–794.

Demos, K. D., Kelley, W. M., Heatherton, T. F. (2011). Dietary restraint violations influence reward responses in the nucleus accumbens and amygdala. *Journal of Cognitive Neuroscience, 23*(8), 1952–1963.

Despues, D., & Friedman, H. S. (2007). Ethnic differences in health behaviors among college students. *Journal of Applied Social Psychology, 37*, 131–142.

Devine, P. G. (1989). Stereotypes and prejudice: Their automatic and controlled components. *Journal of Personality and Social Psychology, 56*, 5–18.

de Wijk, R. A., Schab, F. R., & Cain, W. S. (1995). Odor identification. In F. R. Schab (Ed.), *Memory for odors* (pp. 21–37). Mahwah, NJ: Erlbaum.

DeYoung, C. G. (2010). Personality neuroscience and the biology of traits. *Social and Personality Psychology Compass, 4*, 1165–1180.

DeYoung, C. G., & Gray, J. R. (2009). Personality neuroscience: Explaining individual differences in affect, behavior, and cognition. In P. J. Corr & G. Matthews (Eds.), *The Cambridge handbook of personality psychology* (pp. 323–346). New York: Cambridge University Press.

DeYoung, C. G., Hirsh, J. B., Shane, M. S., Papademetris, X., Rajeevan, N., & Gray, J. R. (2010). Testing predictions from personality neuroscience: Brain structure and the big five. *Psychological Science, 21*, 820–828.

Diamond, D. M., Fleshner, M., Ingersoll, N., & Rose, G. (1996). Psychological stress impairs spatial working memory: Relevance to electro-physiological studies of hippocampal function. *Behavioural Brain Research, 62*, 301–307.

Dickson, P. R., & Vaccarino, F. J. (1994). GRF-induced feeding: Evidence for protein selectivity and opiate involvement. *Peptides, 15*(8), 1343–1352.

Diener, E. (2000). Subjective well-being: The science of happiness and a proposal for a national index. *American Psychologist, 55*, 34–43.

Diener, E., Gohm, C. L., Suh, E., & Oishi, S. (2000). Similarity of the relations between marital status and subjective well-being. *Journal of Cross-Cultural Psychology, 31*, 419–436.

Diener, E., & Wellborn, M. (1976). Effect of self-awareness on antinormative behavior. *Journal of Research in Personality, 10*, 107–111.

Diener, E., Wolsic, B., & Fujita, F. (1995). Physical attractiveness and subjective well-being. *Journal of Personality and Social Psychology, 69*, 120–129.

Dijksterhuis, A. (2004). Think different: The merits of unconscious thought in preference development and decision making. *Journal of Personality and Social Psychology, 87*, 586–598.

Dijksterhuis, A., & Aarts, H. (2010). Goals, attention, and (un)conscious. *Annual Review of Psychology, 61*, 467–490.

Dijksterhuis, A., & Nordgren, L. F. (2006). A theory of unconscious thought. *Perspectives on Psychological Science, 1*, 95–109.

Dijksterhuis, A., & van Knippenberg, A. (1998). The relation between perception and behavior, or how to win a game of Trivial Pursuit. *Journal of Personality and Social Psychology, 74*, 865–877.

Dineley, K. T., Westernman, M., Bui, D., Bell, K., Ashe, K. H., & Sweatt, J. D. (2001). β-amyloid activates the mitogen-activated protein kinase cascade via hippocampal α7 nicotinic acetylcholine receptors: In vitro and in vivo mechanisms related to Alzheimer's Disease. *The Journal of Neuroscience, 21,* 4125–4133.

Dinstein, I., Thomas, C., Humphreys, K., Minshew, N., Behrmann, M., & Heeger, D. J. (2010). Normal movement selectivity in autism. *Neuron, 66,* 461–469.

Dion, K., Berscheid, E., & Walster, E. (1972). What is beautiful is good. *Journal of Personality and Social Psychology, 24,* 285–290.

Diotallevi, M. (2008). Testimonials versus evidence. *Canadian Medical Association Journal, 179,* 449.

Dobbs, D. (2006, August/September). Turning off depression. *Scientific American Mind,* 26–31.

Docherty, N. M. (2005). Cognitive impairments and disordered speech in schizophrenia: Thought disorder, disorganization, and communication failure perspectives. *Journal of Abnormal Psychology, 114,* 269–278.

Dockray, A., & Steptoe, A. (2010). Positive affect and psychobiological process. *Neuroscience and Biobehavioral Reviews, 35,* 69–75.

Dohrenwend, B. P., Shrout, P. E., Link, B. G., Skodol, A. E., & Martin, J. L. (1986). Overview and initial results from a risk factor study of depression and schizophrenia. In J. E. Barrett (Ed.), *Mental disorders in the community: Progress and challenge* (pp. 184–215). New York: Guilford Press.

Dolan, R. J. (2000). Emotion processing in the human brain revealed through functional neuroimaging. In M. S. Gazzaniga (Ed.), *The new cognitive neurosciences* (pp. 115–131). Cambridge, MA: MIT Press.

Domhoff, G. W. (2003). *The scientific study of dreams: Neural networks, cognitive development, and content analysis.* Washington, DC: American Psychological Association.

Domino, M. E., Burns, B. J., Silva, S. G., Kratochvil, C. J., Vitiello, B., Reinecke, M. A., et al. (2008). Cost-effectiveness of treatments for adolescent depression: Results from TADS. *American Journal of Psychiatry, 165,* 588–596.

Domjan, M. (2003). *Principles of learning and behavior* (5th ed.). Belmont, CA: Thomson/Wadsworth.

Donahue, A. B. (2000). Electroconvulsive therapy and memory loss: A personal journey. *Journal of ECT, 16,* 133–143.

Dovidio, J. F., ten Vergert, M., Stewart, T. L., Gaertner, S. L., Johnson, J. D., Esses, V. M., et al. (2004). Perspective and prejudice: Antecedents and mediating mechanisms. *Personality and Social Psychology Bulletin, 30,* 1537–1549.

Doyal, L. (2001). Sex, gender, and health: The need for a new approach. *British Medical Journal, 323,* 1061–1063.

Drews, F. A., Pasupathi, M., & Strayer, D. L. (2008). Passenger and cell phone conversations in simulated driving. *Journal of Experimental Psychology: Applied, 14,* 392–400.

Drosopoulos, S., Schulze, C., Fischer, S., & Born, J. (2007). Sleep's function in the spontaneous recovery and consolidation of memories. *Journal of Experimental Psychology: General 136*(2), 169–183.

Duckworth, A. L., & Seligman, M. E. P. (2005). Self-discipline outdoes IQ in predicting academic performance of adolescents. *Psychological Science, 16,* 939–944.

Dugatkin, L. A. (2004). *Principles of animal behavior.* New York: Norton.

Dunbar, R. I. M., Baron, R., Frangou, A., Pearce, E., van Leeuwen, E. J. C., Stow, J., Partridge, G., MacDonald, I., Barra, V., & van Vugt, M. (2011). Social laughter is correlated with elevated pain threshold. *Proceedings of the Royal Society Biological Sciences.* http://rspb.royalsocietypublishing.org/content/early/2011/09/19/rspb.2011.1373

Duncan, J., Burgess, P., & Emslie, H. (1995). Fluid intelligence after frontal lobe lesions. *Neuropsychologia, 33,* 261–268.

Duncker, K. (1945). On problem solving. *Psychological Monographs, 58*(5, Whole No. 70).

Dunlap, K. (1927). *The role of eye-muscles and mouth-muscles in the expression of the emotions.* Worcester, MA: Clark University Press.

Durante, K. M., Li, N. P., & Haselton, M. G. (2008). Changes in women's choice of dress across the ovulatory cycle: Naturalistic and laboratory task-based evidence. *Personality and Social Psychology Bulletin, 34,* 1451–1460.

Dutton, D. G., & Aron, A. P. (1974). Some evidence for heightened sexual attraction under conditions of high anxiety. *Journal of Personality and Social Psychology, 30,* 510–517.

Duval, S., & Wicklund, R. A. (1972). *A theory of objective self-awareness.* New York: Academic Press.

Dykman, B. M., Horowitz, L. M., Abramson, L. Y., & Usher, M. (1991). Schematic and situational determinants of depressed and nondepressed students' interpretation of feedback. *Journal of Abnormal Psychology, 100,* 45–55.

Eacott, M. J. (1999). Memory for the events of early childhood. *Current Directions in Psychological Science, 8,* 46–49.

Eagly, A. H., Karau, S. J., & Makhijani, M. G. (1995). Gender and the effectiveness of leaders: A meta-analysis. *Psychological Bulletin, 117,* 125–145.

Eaker, E. D., Sullivan, L. M., Kelly-Hayes, M., D'Agostino, R. B., Sr., & Benjamin, E. J. (2004). Anger and hostility predict the development of atrial fibrillation in men in the Framingham Offspring Study. *Circulation, 109,* 1267–1271.

Eberhardt, J. L., Goff, P. A., Purdie, V. J., & Davies, P. G. (2004). Seeing black: Race, crime, and visual processing. *Journal of Personality and Social Psychology, 87,* 876–893.

Ecker, U. K. H., Lewandowsky, S., Oberauer, K., & Chee, A. E. H. (2010). The components of working memory updating: An experimental decomposition and individual differences. *Journal of Experimental Psychology: Learning, Memory, and Cognition, 36,* 170–189.

Egeland, J. A., Gerhard, D. S., Pauls, D. L., Sussex, J. N., Kidd, K. K., Allen, C. R., et al. (1987). Bipolar affective disorders linked to DNA markers on chromosome 11. *Nature, 325,* 783–787.

Eich, J. E., Weingartner, H., Stillman, R. C., & Gillin, J. C. (1975). State-dependent accessibility of retrieval cues in the retention of a categorized list. *Journal of Verbal Learning and Verbal Behavior, 14,* 408–417.

Einstein, G. O., & McDaniel, M. A. (2005). Prospective memory. Multiple retrieval processes. *Current Directions in Psychological Science, 14,* 286–290.

Eisenberg, N. (2000). Emotion, regulation, and moral development. *Annual Review of Psychology, 51,* 665–697.

Eisenberg, N. (2002). Empathy-related emotional responses, altruism, and their socialization. In R. J. Davidson and A. Harrington (Eds.), *Visions of compassion: Western scientists and Tibetan Buddhists examine human nature* (pp. 131–164). New York: Oxford University Press.

Ekelund, J., Lichtermann, D., Jaervelin, M., & Peltonen, L. (1999). Association between novelty seeking and type 4 dopamine receptor gene in a large Finnish cohort sample. *American Journal of Psychiatry, 156*, 1453–1455.

Ekman, P., & Friesen, W. V. (1971). Constants across cultures in the face and emotion. *Journal of Personality and Social Psychology, 17*, 124–129.

Ekman, P., Levenson, R. W., & Friesen, W. V. (1983, September 16). Autonomic nervous system activity distinguishes among emotions. *Science, 221*, 1208–1210.

Ekman, P., Sorenson, E. R., & Friesen, W. V. (1969, April 4). Pan-cultural elements in facial displays of emotions. *Science, 164*, 86–88.

Elfenbein, H. A., & Ambady, N. (2002). On the universality of cultural specificity of emotion recognition: A meta-analysis. *Psychological Bulletin, 128*, 203–235.

Else-Quest, N., Hyde, J. S., Goldsmith, H. H., & Van Hulle, C. A. (2006). Gender differences in temperament: A meta-analysis. *Psychological Bulletin, 132*, 33–72.

Emery, C. F., Kiecolt-Glaser, J. K., Glaser, R., Malarkey, W. B., & Frid, D. J. (2005). Exercise accelerates wound healing among healthy older adults: A preliminary investigation. *Journals of Gerontology, 60A*(11), 1432–1436.

Emslie, G. J., Rush, A. J., Weinberg, W. A., Kowatch, R. A., Hughes, C. W., Carmody, T., et al. (1997). A double-blind, randomized, placebo-controlled trial of fluoxetine in children and adolescents with depression. *Archives of General Psychiatry, 54*, 1031–1037.

Endo, Y., & Meijer, Z. (2004). Autobiographical memory of success and failure experiences. In Y. Kashima, Y. Endo, E. S. Kashima, C. Leung, & J. McClure (Eds.), *Progress in Asian social psychology* (Vol. 4, pp. 67–84). Seoul, Korea: Kyoyook-Kwahak-Sa Publishing.

Engle, R. W., & Kane, M. J. (2004). Executive attention, working memory capacity, and a two-factor theory of cognitive control. In B. Ross (Ed.), *The psychology of learning and motivation* (pp. 145–199). New York: Elsevier.

Engle, R. W., Tuholski, S. W., Laughlin, J. E., & Conway, A. R. A. (1999). Working memory, short-term memory, and general fluid intelligence: A latent variable approach. *Journal of Experimental Psychology: General, 128*, 309–331.

Engwall, M., & Duppils, G. S. (2009). Music as a nursing intervention for postoperative pain: A systematic review. *Journal of Perianesthesia Nursing, 24*, 370–383.

Enns, J. (2005). *The thinking eye, the seeing brain.* New York: Norton.

Epstein, L. H., Robinson, J. L., Roemmich, J. N., Marusewski, A. L., & Roba, L. G. (2010). What constitutes food variety? Stimulus specificity of food. *Appetite, 54*, 23–29.

Era, P., Jokela, J., & Heikkinen, E. (1986). Reaction and movement times in men of different ages: A population study. *Perceptual and Motor Skills, 63*, 111–130.

Erikson, E. H. (1968). *Identity: Youth and crisis.* New York: Norton.

Erikson, E. H. (1980). *Identity and the life cycle.* New York: Norton.

Eriksson, P. S., Perfilieva, E., Bjork-Eriksson, T., Alborn, A. M., Nordborg, C., Peterson, D. A., et al. (1998). Neurogenesis in the adult human hippocampus. *Nature Medicine, 4*, 1313–1317.

Erk, S., Spitzer, M., Wunderlich, A. P., Galley, L., & Walter, H. (2002). Cultural objects modulate reward circuitry. *Neuroreport, 13*(18), 2499–2503.

Eron, L. D. (1987). The development of aggressive behavior from the perspective of a developing behaviorism. *American Psychologist, 42*, 435–442.

Espie, C. A. (2002). Insomnia: Conceptual issues in the development, persistence, and treatment of sleep disorders in adults. *Annual Review of Psychology, 53*, 215–243.

Eysenck, M. W., Mogg, K., May, J., Richards, A., & Matthews, A. (1991). Bias in interpretation of ambiguous sentences related to threat in anxiety. *Journal of Abnormal Psychology, 100*, 144–150.

Fabiano, G. A., Pelham, W. E., Coles, E. K., Gnagy, E. M., Chronis-Tuscano, A., & O'Connor, B. C. (2009). A meta-analysis of behavioral treatments for attention-deficit/hyperactivity disorder. *Clinical Psychology Review, 29*, 129–140.

Fagerström, K. O., & Schneider, N. G. (1989). Measuring nicotine dependence: A review of the Fagerström tolerance questionnaire. *Journal of Behavioral Medicine, 12*, 159–181.

Fallon, A. E., & Rozin, P. (1985). Sex differences in perceptions of desirable body shape. *Journal of Abnormal Psychology, 94*, 102–105.

Fantz, R. L. (1966). Pattern discrimination and selective attention as determinants of perceptual development from birth. In A. H. Kidd & L. J. Rivoire (Eds.), *Perceptual development in children* (pp. 143–173). New York: International Universities Press.

Farah, M. J. (1996). Is face recognition "special"? Evidence from neuropsychology. *Behavioural Brain Research, 76*, 181–189.

Farah, M. J., Betancourt, L., Shera, D. M., Savage, J. H., Giannetta, J. M., Malmud, E. K., et al. (2008). Environmental stimulation, parental nurturance and cognitive development in humans. *Developmental Science, 11*, 793–801.

Farah, M. J., Shera, D. M., Savage, J. H., Betancourt, L., Giannetta, J. M., Brodsky, N. L., et al. (2006). Childhood poverty: Specific associations with neurocognitive development. *Brain Research, 1110*, 166–174.

Farb, N. A., Anderson, A. K., Mayberg, H., Bean, J., McKeon, D., & Segal, Z. V. (2010). Minding one's emotions: Mindfulness training alters the neural expression of sadness. *Emotion, 10*, 25–33.

Farb, N. A., Segal, Z. V., Mayberg, H., Bean, J., McKeon, D., Fatima, Z., et al. (2007). Attending to the present: Mindfulness meditation reveals distinct neural modes of self-reference. *Social Cognitive and Affective Neuroscience, 2*, 313–322.

Farooqi, I. S., Bullmore, E., Keogh, J., Gillard, J., O'Rahilly, S., & Fletcher, P. C. (2007, September 7). Leptin regulates striatal regions and human eating behavior. *Science, 317*, 1355.

Fawcett, J. (1992). Suicide risk factors in depressive disorders and in panic disorders. *Journal of Clinical Psychiatry, 53*, 9–13.

Fazio, R. H. (1995). Attitudes as object-evaluation associations: Determinants, consequences, and correlates of attitude accessibility. In R. E. Petty & J. A. Krosnick (Eds.), *Attitude strength: Antecedents and consequences* (pp. 247–282). Hillsdale, NJ: Erlbaum.

Fazio, R. H., Eisner, J. R., & Shook, N. J. (2004). Attitude formation through exploration: Valence asymmetries. *Journal of Personality and Social Psychology, 87*, 293–311.

Feingold, A. (1992). Good-looking people are not what we think. *Psychological Bulletin, 111*, 304–341.

Feingold, A. (1994). Gender differences in personality: A meta-analysis. *Psychological Bulletin, 116*, 429–456.

Feldman, R., Weller, A., Zagoory-Sharon, O., & Levine, A. (2007). Evidence for a neuroendocrinological foundation of human affiliation: Plasma oxytocin levels across pregnancy and the postpartum period predict mother-infant bonding. *Psychological Science, 18*, 965–970.

Feldman, S. S., & Rosenthal, D. A. (1991). Age expectations of behavioural autonomy in Hong Kong, Australian and American youth: The Influence of family variables and adolescents' values. *International Journal of Psychology, 26*, 1–23.

Feldman Barrett, L., Lane, R. D., Sechrest, L., & Schwartz, G. E. (2000). Sex differences in emotional awareness. *Personality and Social Psychology Bulletin, 26*, 1027–1035.

Fergus, I., & McDowd, J. M. (1987). Age differences in recall and recognition. *Journal of Experimental Psychology: Learning, Memory, and Cognition, 13*, 474–479. doi: 10.1037/0278-7393.13.3.474

Ferguson, J. N., Young, L. J., Hearn, E. F., Matzuk, M. M., Insel, T. R., & Winslow, J. T. (2000). Social amnesia in mice lacking the oxytocin gene. *Nature Neuroscience, 25*, 284–288.

Ferguson, T. J., & Stegge, H. (1995). Emotional states and traits in children: The case of guilt and shame. In J. P. Tangney & K. W. Fischer (Eds.), *Self-conscious emotions* (pp. 174–197). New York: Guilford Press.

Fernald, A. (1989). Intonation and communicative intent in mothers' speech to infants: Is the melody the message? *Child Development, 60*, 1497–1510.

Fernberger, S. W. (1943). Edwin Burket Twitmyer 1873–1943. *Psychological Review 50*(3), 345–349. doi: 10.1037/h0063068

Ferrari, P. F., Gallese, V., Rizzolatti, G., & Fogassi, L. (2003). Mirror neurons responding to the observation of ingestive and communicative mouth actions in the monkey ventral premotor cortex. *European Journal of Neuroscience, 17*, 1703–1714.

Ferrari, P. F., Visalberghi, E., Paukner, A., Fogassi, L., Ruggiero, A., & Suomi, S. (2006). Neonatal imitation in rhesus macaques. *PLoS Biology, 4*, 1501–1508.

Ferry, G. (Writer/Broadcaster). (2002, 12 & 19 November). Hearing colours, eating sounds. *BBC Radio 4, Science*. Retrieved from BBC, http://www.bbc.co.uk/radio4/science/hearingcolours.shtml

Festinger, L. (1954). A theory of social comparison processes. *Human Relations, 7*, 117–140.

Festinger, L. (1987). A personal memory. In N. E. Grunberg, R. E. Nisbett, J. Rodin, & J. E. Singer (Eds.), *A distinctive approach to psychological research: The influence of Stanley Schachter* (pp. 1–9). New York: Erlbaum.

Festinger, L., & Carlsmith, J. M. (1959). Cognitive consequences of forced compliance. *Journal of Abnormal and Social Psychology, 58*, 203–210.

Festinger, L., Riecken, H. W., & Schachter, S. (1956). *When prophecy fails*. Minneapolis: University of Minnesota Press.

Festinger, L., Schachter, S., & Back, K. W. (1950). *Social pressures in informal groups*. New York: Harper.

Fibiger, H. C. (1993). Mesolimbic dopamine: An analysis of its role in motivated behavior. *Seminars in Neuroscience, 5*, 321–327.

Fillipek, P. A., Semrud-Clikeman, M., Steingard, R. J., Renshaw, P. F., Kennedy, D. N., & Biederman, J. (1997). Volumetric MRI analysis comparing subjects having attention-deficit hyperactivity disorder with normal controls. *Neurology, 48*, 589–600.

Finger, S. (1994). *Origins of neuroscience*. Oxford, UK: Oxford University Press.

Fink, M. (2001). Convulsive therapy: A review of the first 55 years. *Journal of Affective Disorders, 63*, 1–15.

Fischer, C., Hatzidimitriou, G., Wlos, J., Katz, J., & Ricaurte, G. (1995). Reorganization of ascending 5-HT axon projections in animals previously exposed to the recreational drug (+/–)3,4-methylene-dioxymethamphetamine (MDMA, "ecstasy"). *Journal of Neuroscience, 15*, 5476–5485.

Fischer, H., Nyberg, L., Karlsson, S., Karisson, P., Brehmer, Y., Rieckmann, A., et al. (2010). Simulating neurocognitive aging: Effects of dopaminergic antagonist on brain activity during working memory. *Biological Psychiatry, 67*, 575–580.

Fischer, K. (1980). A theory of cognitive development: The control and construction of hierarchies of skills. *Psychological Review, 87*, 477–531.

Fisher, H. E., Aron, A., & Brown, L. L. (2006). Romantic love: A mammalian brain system for mate choice. *Philosophical Transactions of the Royal Society of London, 361B*, 2173–2186.

Fitzgerald, P. B., Brown, T. L., Marston, N. A., Daskalakis, Z. J., De Castella, A., & Kulkarni, J. (2003). Transcranial magnetic stimulation in the treatment of depression: A double-blind, placebo-controlled trial. *Archives of General Psychiatry, 60*, 1002–1008.

Fixx, J. F. (1978). *Solve it*. New York: Doubleday.

Flegal, K. M., Carroll, M. D., Ogden, C. L., & Curtin, L. R. (2010). Prevalence and trends in obesity among U.S. adults, 1999–2008. *Journal of the American Medical Association, 303*(3), 235–41.

Flynn, J. R. (1981). The mean IQ of Americans: Massive gains 1932 to 1978. *Psychological Bulletin, 95*, 29–51.

Flynn, J. R. (1987). Massive IQ gains in 14 nations: What IQ tests really measure. *Psychological Bulletin, 101*, 171–191.

Flynn, J. R. (2007, October/November). Solving the IQ puzzle. *Scientific American Mind*, 24–31.

Foa, E. B., Liebowitz, M. R., Kozak, M. J., Davies, S., Campeas, R., Franklin, M. E., et al. (2005). Randomized, placebo-controlled trial of exposure and ritual prevention, clomipramine, and their combination in the treatment of obsessive-compulsive disorder. *American Journal of Psychiatry, 162*, 151–161.

Foer, Joshua. (2011, February 20). Secrets of a mind-gamer: How I trained my brain and became a world-class memory athlete. *The New York Times Magazine*. Retrieved from http://www.nytimes.com

Foley, K. M. (1993). Opioids. *Neurologic Clinics, 11*, 503–522.

Folkman, S., & Lazarus, R. S. (1988). Coping as a mediator of emotion. *Journal of Personality and Social Psychology, 54*, 466–475.

Folkman, S., & Moskowitz, J. T. (2000). Positive affect and the other side of coping. *American Psychologist, 55*, 647–654.

Forgas, J. P. (1998). Asking nicely: Mood effects on responding to more or less polite requests. *Personality and Social Psychology Bulletin, 24*, 173–185.

Fost, N. (1989). Maternal-fetal conflicts: Ethical and legal considerations. *Annals of the New York Academy of Sciences, 56*, 248–254.

Fox, N. A., Henderson, H. A., Marshall, P. J., Nichols, K. E., & Ghera, M. M. (2005). Behavioral inhibition: Linking biology and behavior within a developmental framework. *Annual Review of Psychology, 56*, 235–262.

Fraley, R. C., & Shaver, P. R. (2000). Adult romantic attachment: Theoretical developments, emerging controversies, and unanswered questions. *Review of General Psychology, 4*, 132–154.

Frangou, S., Chitins, X., & Williams, S. C. (2004). Mapping IQ and gray matter density in healthy young people. *Neuroimage, 23*, 800–805.

Frank, C. K., & Temple, E. (2009). Cultural effects on the neural basis of theory of mind. *Progress in Brain Research, 178*, 213–223.

Franken, I. H. A., Muris, P., & Georgieva, I. (2006). Gray's model of personality and addiction. *Addictive Behaviors, 31*, 399–403.

Franken, R. E. (1998). *Human motivation*. Pacific Grove, CA: Brooks Cole.

Frankl, V. E. (1959). *Man's search for meaning*. New York: Simon & Schuster.

Franklin, A. J. (2007). Gender, race and invisibility in psychotherapy with African American men. In J. C. Muran (Ed.), *Dialogues on difference: Studies of diversity in the therapeutic relationship* (pp. 117–131). Washington, DC: American Psychological Association.

Franklin, M. E., & Foa, E. B. (2011, April). Treatment of obsessive compulsive disorder. *Annual Review of Clinical Psychology, 7*, 229–243.

Fratiglioni, L., Paillard-Borg, S., & Winblad, B. (2004). An active and socially integrated lifestyle in late life might protect against dementia. *Lancet Neurology, 3*, 343–353.

Fredrickson, B. L. (2001). The role of positive emotions in positive psychology: The broaden-and-build theory of positive emotions. *American Psychologist, 56*, 218–226.

Freedman, J. L. (1984). Effects of television violence on aggression. *Psychological Bulletin, 96*, 227–246.

Freedman, J. L., & Fraser, S. C. (1966). Compliance without pressure: The foot-in-the-door technique. *Journal of Personality and Social Psychology, 4*, 196–202.

Freud, A. (1936). *The ego and the mechanisms of defense*. New York: International Universities Press.

Friedman, J. M., & Halaas, J. (1998). Leptin and the regulation of body weight in mammals. *Nature, 395*, 763–770.

Frijda, N. H. (1994). Emotions are functional, most of the time. In P. Ekman & R. J. Davidson (Eds.), *The nature of emotion: Fundamental questions, Vol. 4. Series in affective science* (pp. 112–122). New York: Oxford University Press.

Funder, D. C. (1995). On the accuracy of personality judgment: A realistic approach. *Psychological Review, 102*, 652–670.

Funder, D. C. (2001). Personality. *Annual Review of Psychology, 52*, 197–221.

Fung, H. H., & Carstensen, L. L. (2004). Motivational changes in response to blocked goals and foreshortened time: Testing alternatives to socioemotional selectivity theory. *Psychology and Aging, 19*, 68–78.

Fung, M. T., Raine, A., Loeber, R., Lynam, D. R., Steinhauer, S. R., Venables, P. D., et al. (2005). Reduced electrodermal activity in psychopathy-prone adolescents. *Journal of Abnormal Psychology, 114*, 187–196.

Galanter, E. (1962). Contemporary psychophysics. In R. Brown (Ed.), *New directions in psychology*. New York: Holt, Rinehart & Winston.

Galef, B. G., Jr., & Whiskin, E. E. (2000). Social influences on the amount eaten by Norway rats. *Appetite, 34*, 327–332.

Gallup. (1995). *Disciplining children in America: A Gallup poll report*. Princeton, NH: Author.

Gangestad, S. W., Simpson, J. A., Cousins, A. J., Garver-Apgar, C. E., & Christensen, P. N. (2004). Women's preferences for male behavioral displays change across the menstrual cycle. *Psychological Science, 15*, 203–207.

Garcia, J., & Koelling, R. A. (1966). Relation of cue to consequence in avoidance learning. *Psychonomic Science, 4*, 123–124.

Gardner, H. (1983). *Frames of mind: The theory of multiple intelligences*. New York: Basic Books.

Gardner, W. L., Pickett, C. L., Jefferis, V., & Knowles, M. (2005). On the outside looking in: Loneliness and social monitoring. *Personality and Social Psychology Bulletin, 31*, 1549–1560.

Garlick, D. (2002). Understanding the nature of the general factor of intelligence: The role of individual differences in neural plasticity as an explanatory mechanism. *Psychological Review, 109*, 116–136.

Garoff-Eaton, R. J., Slotnick, S. D., & Schacter, D. L. (2006). Not all false memories are created equal: The neural basis of false recognition. *Cerebral Cortex, 16*, 1645–1652.

Garon, N., Bryson, S. E., & Smith, I. M. (2008). Executive function in preschoolers: A review using an integrative framework. *Psychological Bulletin, 134*, 31–60.

Gawryluk, J. R., D'Arcy, R. C., Connolly, J. F., & Weaver, D. F. (2010). Improving the clinical assessment of consciousness with advances in electrophysiological and neuroimaging techniques. *BioMed Central Neurology, 10*(11). doi:10.1186/1471-2377-10-11

Gazzaniga, M. S. (2000). Cerebral specialization and interhemispheric communication: Does the corpus callosum enable the human condition? *Brain, 123*, 1293–1326.

Geddes, J. R., Burgess, S., Hawton, K., Jamison, K., & Goodwin, G. M. (2004). Long-term lithium therapy for bipolar disorder: Systematic review and meta-analysis of randomized controlled trials. *American Journal of Psychiatry, 161*, 217–222.

Geen, R. G. (1984). Preferred stimulation levels in introverts and extraverts: Effects on arousal and performance. *Journal of Personality and Social Psychology, 46*, 1303–1312.

Gentile, D. A., Saleem, M., & Anderson, C. A. (2007). Public policy and the effects of media violence on children. *Social Issues and Policy Review, 1*, 15–51.

George, M. S., Lisanby, S. H., & Sackheim, H. A. (1999). Transcranial magnetic stimulation: Applications in neuropsychiatry. *Archives of General Psychiatry, 56*, 300–311.

George, M. S., Wassermann, E. M., Williams, W. A., Callahan, A., Ketter, T. A., Basser, P., et al. (1995). Daily repetitive transcranial magnetic stimulation (rTMS) improves mood in depression. *Neuroreport, 6*, 1853–1856.

Gergely, G., & Csibra, G. (2003). Teleological reasoning in infancy: The naïve theory of rational action. *Trends in Cognitive Sciences, 7*, 287–292.

Gernsbacher, M. A., Dawson, M., & Goldsmith, H. H. (2005). Three reasons not to believe in an autism epidemic. *Current Directions in Psychological Science, 14*, 55–58.

Gershoff, E. T. (2002). Parental corporal punishment and associated child behaviors and experiences: A meta-analytic and theoretical review. *Psychological Bulletin, 128*, 539–579.

Gershon, E. S., Berrettini, W. H., & Goldin, L. R. (1989). Mood disorders: Genetic aspects. In H. I. Kaplan & B. J. Sadock (Eds.), *Comprehensive textbook of psychiatry* (5th ed.). Baltimore: Williams & Wilkins.

Geula, C., & Mesulam, M. (1994). Cholinergic systems and related neuropathological predilection patterns in Alzheimer disease. In R. D. Terry, R. Katzman, & K. Bick (Eds.), *Alzheimer disease* (pp. 263–291). New York: Raven Press.

Gibbons, M. B. C., Crits-Christoph, P., & Hearon, B. (2008). The empirical status of psychodynamic therapies. *Annual Review of Clinical Psychology, 4*, 93–108.

Gick, M. L., & Holyoak, K. J. (1983). Schema induction and analogical transfer. *Cognitive Psychology, 15*, 1–38.

Giedd, J. N., Castellanos, F. X., Rajapakse, J. C., Vaituzis, A. C., & Rapoport, J. L. (1997). Sexual dimorphism of the developing human brain. *Progress in Neuro-Psychopharmacology & Biological Psychiatry, 21*(8), 1185–1201.

Gigerenzer, G. (2004). Dread risk, September 11, and fatal traffic accidents. *Psychological Science, 15*, 286–287.

Gijsman, H. J., Geddes, J. R., Rendell, J. M., Nolen, W. A., & Goodwin, G. M. (2004). Antidepressants for bipolar depression: A systematic review of randomized, controlled trials. *American Journal of Psychiatry, 161*, 1537–1547.

Gilbert, D. T., Giesler, R. B., & Morris, K. A. (1995). When comparisons arise. *Journal of Personality and Social Psychology, 69*, 227–236.

Gilbert, D. T., Morewedge, C. K., Risen, J. L., & Wilson, T. D. (2004). Looking forward to looking backward: The misprediction of regret. *Psychological Science, 15*, 346–350.

Gilbert, D. T., Pinel, E. C., Wilson, T. D., Blumberg, S. J., & Wheatley, T. (1998). Immune neglect: A source of durability bias in affective forecasting. *Journal of Personality and Social Psychology, 75*, 617–638.

Gilbert, D. T., & Wilson, T. D. (2007, September). Prospection: Experiencing the future. *Science, 317*, 1351–1354.

Gillihan, S. J, & Farah, M. J. (2005). Is self special? A critical review of evidence from experimental psychology and cognitive neuroscience. *Psychological Bulletin, 131*, 76–97.

Gillogley, K. M., Evans, A. T., Hansen, R. L., Samuels, S. J., & Batra, K. K. (1990). The perinatal impact of cocaine, amphetamine, and opiate use detected by universal intrapartum screening. *American Journal of Obstetrics and Gynecology, 163*, 1535–1542.

Gilman, S. R., Iossifov, I., Levy, D., Ronemus, M., Wigler, M., & Vitkup, D. (2011). Rare de novo variants associated with autism implicate a large functional network of genes involved in formation and function of synapses. *Neuron, 70*, 898–907.

Gilovich, T. (1991). *How we know what isn't so: The fallibility of human reason in everyday life*. New York: The Free Press.

Gilpin, E. A., Choi, W. S., Berry, C., & Pierce, J. P. (1999). How many adolescents start smoking each day in the United States? *Journal of Adolescent Health, 25*, 248–255.

Gizewski, E. R., Krause, E., Karama, S., Baars, A., Senf, W., & Forsting, M. (2006). There are differences in cerebral activation between females in distinct menstrual phases during viewing of erotic stimuli: A fMRI study. *Experimental Brain Research, 174*, 101–108.

Gladwell, M. (2005). *Blink: The power of thinking without thinking*. New York: Little, Brown.

Glaser, R. & Kiecolt-Glaser, J. K. (2005). Stress-induced immune dysfunction: Implications for health. *Nature Reviews, 5*, 243–251.

Godden, D. R., & Baddeley, A. D. (1975). Context-dependent memory in two natural environments: On land and underwater. *British Journal of Psychology, 66*, 325–331.

Golby, A. J., Gabrieli, J. D. E., Chiao, J. Y., & Eberhardt, J. L. (2001). Differential responses in the fusiform region to same-race and other-race faces. *Nature Neuroscience, 4*, 845–850.

Goldapple, K., Segal, Z., Garson, C., Lau, M., Bieling, P., Kennedy, S., et al. (2004). Modulation of cortical-limbic pathways in major depression: Treatment-specific effects of cognitive behavior therapy. *Archives of General Psychiatry, 61*, 34–41.

Goldenberg, J. L., McCoy, S. K., Pyszczynski, T., Greenberg, J., & Solomon, S. (2000). The body as a source of self-esteem: The effects of mortality salience on identification with one's body, interest in sex, and appearance monitoring. *Journal of Personality and Social Psychology, 79*, 118–130.

Goldstein, J. (2011, January 18). Life tenure for federal judges raises issues of senility, dementia. *ProPublica: Journalism in the Public Interest.* Retrieved from http://www.propublica.org/article/life-tenure-for-federal-judges-raises-issues-of-senility-dementia

Goldstein, R. Z., Craig, A. D. B., Bechara, A., Garavan, H., Childress, A. R., Paulus, M. P., & Volkow, N. D. (2009). The neurocircuitry of impaired insight in drug addiction. *Trends in Cognitive Science, 13*, 372–380.

Gong, Q., Sluming, V., Mayes, A., Keller, S., Barrick, T., Cezayirli, E., et al. (2005). Voxel-based morphometry and stereology provide convergent evidence of the importance of medial prefrontal cortex for fluid intelligence in healthy adults. *Neuroimage, 25*, 1175–1186.

Gonzales, R., Mooney, L., & Rawson, R. A. (2010). The methamphetamine problem in the United States. *Annual Review of Public Health, 31*, 385–398.

Goodale, M. A., & Milner, A. D. (1992). Separate visual pathways for perception and action. *Trends in Neuroscience, 15*, 22–25.

Goodall, G. (1984). Learning due to the response-shock contingency in signaled punishment. *Quarterly Journal of Experimental Psychology, 36*, 259–279.

Goodman, R., & Stevenson, J. (1989). A twin study of hyperactivity-II. The aetiological role of genes, family relationships, and perinatal adversity. *Journal of Child Psychology and Psychiatry, 30*, 691–709.

Goodman, S. H., & Gotlib, I. H. (1999). Risk for psychopathology in the children of depressed mothers: A developmental model for understanding mechanisms of transmission. *Psychological Review, 106*, 458–490.

Goodwin, D. W., Powell, B., Bremer, D., Hoine, H., & Stern, J. (1969, March 21). Alcohol and recall: State dependent effects in man. *Science, 163*, 1358.

Goodwin, F. K., & Jamison, K. R. (1990). *Manic-depressive illness*. New York: Oxford University Press.

Goodwin, R. D., Lieb, R., Hoefler, M., Pfister, H., Bittner, A., Beesdo, K., et al. (2004). Panic attack as a risk factor for severe psychopathology. *American Journal of Psychiatry, 161*, 2207–2214.

Gopnik, A., & Graf, O. (1988). Knowing how you know: Young children's ability to identify and remember the sources of their beliefs. *Child Development, 59*, 1366–1371.

Gore, J. S., Cross, S. E., & Morris, M. L. (2006). Let's be friends: Relational self-construal and the development of intimacy. *Personal Relationships, 13*(1), 83–102. doi:10.1111/j.1475-6811.2006.00106.x

Gosling, S. D. (1998). Personality dimensions in spotted hyenas (*Crocuta crocuta*). *Journal of Comparative Psychology, 112*, 107–118.

Gosling, S. D. (2001). From mice to men: What can we learn about personality from animal research? *Psychological Bulletin, 127*, 45–86.

Gosling, S. D. (2008). *Snoop: What your stuff says about you.* New York: Basic Books.

Gosling, S. D., & John, O. P. (1999). Personality dimension in non-human animals: A cross-species review. *Current Directions in Psychological Science, 8*, 69–75.

Gosling, S. D., Ko, S. J., Mannarelli, T., & Morris, M. E. (2002). A room with a cue: Judgments of personality based on offices and bedrooms. *Journal of Personality and Social Psychology, 82*, 379–398.

Gosling, S. D., Kwan, V. S. Y., & John, O. P. (2003). A dog's got personality: A cross-species comparative approach to evaluating personality judgments. *Journal of Personality and Social Psychology, 85*, 1161–1169.

Gosselin, P., & Larocque, C. (2000). Facial morphology and children's categorization of facial expressions and emotions: A comparison between Asian and Caucasian faces. *Journal of Genetic Psychology, 161*, 346–358.

Gottesman, I. I. (1991). *Schizophrenia genesis: The origins of madness.* New York: Freeman.

Gottesman, I. I., & Hanson, D. R. (2005). Human development: Biological and genetic processes. *Annual Review of Psychology, 56*, 263–286.

Gottfredson, L. S. (2004a). Intelligence: Is it the epidemiologists' elusive "fundamental cause" of social class inequalities in health? *Journal of Personality and Social Psychology, 86*, 174–199.

Gottfredson, L. S. (2004b, Summer). Schools and the g factor. *The Wilson Quarterly, 28*(3), 35–45.

Gottfredson, L. S., & Deary, I. J. (2004). Intelligence predicts health and longevity: But why? *Current Directions in Psychological Science, 13*, 1–4.

Gottman, J. (1994). *Why marriages succeed or fail . . . and how you can make yours last.* New York: Simon & Schuster.

Gottman, J. M. (1998). Psychology and the study of marital processes. *Annual Review of Psychology, 49*, 169–197.

Gould, E., & Tanapat, P. (1999). Stress and hippocampal neurogenesis. *Biological Psychiatry, 46*, 1472–1479.

Graf, P., & Schacter, D. L. (1985). Implicit and explicit memory for new associations in normal and amnesic subjects. *Journal of Experimental Psychology: Learning, Memory and Cognition, 13*, 45–53.

Graf, P., & Uttl, B. (2001). Prospective memory: A new focus for research. *Consciousness and Cognition, 10*, 437–450.

Grandin, T. (1995). *Thinking in pictures: And other reports from my life with autism.* New York: Doubleday.

Granot, D., & Mayseless, O. (2001). Attachment security and adjustment to school in middle childhood. *International Journal of Behavioral Development*, 25, 530–541. doi: 10.1080/01650250042000366 000

Gray, J. R., & Thompson, P. M. (2004). Neurobiology of intelligence: Science and ethics. *Nature Reviews Neuroscience, 5*, 471–482.

Gray, J. A. (1987). *The psychology of fear and stress* (2nd ed.). Cambridge: Cambridge University Press.

Green, A. E., Munafò, M. R., DeYoung, C. G., Fossella, J. A., Fan, J., & Gray, J. R. (2008). Using genetic data in cognitive neuroscience: From growing pains to genuine insights. *Nature Reviews Neuroscience, 9*, 710–720.

Green, D. M., & Swets, J. A. (1966). *Signal detection theory and psychophysics.* New York: Wiley.

Green, J. J., & Hollander, E. (2010). Autism and oxytocin: New developments in translational approaches to therapeutics. *Neurotherapeutics,* 7, 250–257.

Greenberg, B. D., Gabriels, L. A., Malone, D. A., Jr., Rezai, A. R., Friehs, G. M., Okun, M. S., et al. (2008). Deep brain stimulation of the ventral internal capsule/ventral striatum for obsessive-compulsive disorder: Worldwide experience. *Molecular Psychiatry.* Advance online publication. Retrieved May 20, 2008. doi: 10.1038/mp.2008.55

Greenberg, J. (2008). Understanding the vital human quest for self-esteem. *Perspectives on Psychological Science, 3*, 48–55.

Greenberg, J., Solomon, S., & Pyszczynski, T. (1997). Terror management theory of self-esteem and cultural worldviews: Empirical assessments and conceptual refinements. In M. P. Zanna (Ed.), *Advances in Experimental Social Psychology* (Vol. 29, pp. 61–136). New York: Academic Press.

Greene, B. (2007). How difference makes a difference. In J. C. Muran (Ed.), *Dialogues on difference: Studies of diversity in the therapeutic relationship* (pp. 47–63). Washington, DC: American Psychological Association.

Greenwald, A. G. (1992). New look 3: Reclaiming unconscious cognition. *American Psychologist, 47*, 766–779.

Greenwald, A. G., & Banaji, M. R. (1995). Implicit social cognition: Attitudes, self-esteem, and stereotypes. *Psychological Review, 102*, 4–27.

Greenwald, A. G., McGhee, D., & Schwartz, J. (1998). Measuring individual differences in implicit cognition: The implicit association test. *Journal of Personality and Social Psychology, 74*, 1464–1480.

Greenwald, A. G., Oakes, M. A., & Hoffman, H. (2003). Targets of discrimination: Effects of race on responses to weapons holders. *Journal of Experimental Social Psychology, 39*, 399–405.

Greenwald, A. G., Poehlman, T. A., Uhlmann, E., & Banaji, M. R. (2009). Understanding and using the Implicit Association Test: III. Meta-analysis of predictive validity. *Journal of Personality and Social Psychology, 97*, 17–41.

Greitemeyer, T. (2009). Effects of songs with prosocial lyrics on prosocial behavior: Further evidence and a mediating mechanism. *Personality and Social Psychology Bulletin, 35*(11), 1500–1511.

Grill-Spector, K., Knouf, N., & Kanwisher, N. (2004). The fusiform face area subserves face perception, not generic within-category identification. *Nature Neuroscience,* 7, 555–562.

Groebel, J. (1998). *The UNESCO global study on media violence: A joint project of UNESCO, the world organization of the Scout movement and Utrecht University, the Netherlands. Report Presented to the Director General of UNESCO.* Paris: UNESCO.

Gross, J. J. (1999). Emotion and emotion regulation. In L. A. Pervin & O. P. John (Eds.), *Handbook of personality: Theory and research* (2nd ed., pp. 525–552). New York: Guilford Press.

Grossman, L. (2005, January 24). Grow up? Not so fast. *Time, 165*, 42–53.

Grossman, M., & Wood, W. (1993). Sex differences in intensity of emotional experience: A social role interpretation. *Journal of Personality and Social Psychology, 65*, 1010–1022.

Gruber, S. A., Silveri, M. M., & Yurgelun-Todd, D. A. (2007). Neuropsychological consequences of opiate use. *Neuropsychological Review, 17*, 299–315.

Gruenewald, P. J., Millar, A. B., Treno, A. J., Yang, Z., Ponicki, W. R., & Roeper, P. (1996). The geography of availability and driving after drinking. *Addiction, 91*, 967–983.

Gruzelier, J. H. (2000). Redefining hypnosis:Theory, methods, and integration. *Contemporary Hypnosis, 17*, 51–70.

Guenther, F. H., Brumberg, J. S., Wright, E. J., Nieto-Castanon, A., Tourville, J. A., et al. (2009). A wireless brain-machine interface for real-time speech synthesis. *PLoS ONE, 4*(12), e82128.

Guerin, B. (1994). What do people think about the risks of driving? Implications for traffic safety interventions. *Journal of Applied Social Psychology, 24*, 994–1021.

Guerri, C. (2002). Mechanisms involved in central nervous system dysfunctions induced by prenatal ethanol exposure. *Neurotoxicity Research, 4*(4), 327–335.

Guimond, S. (2008). Psychological similarities and differences between women and men across cultures. *Social and Personality Psychology Compass, 2*, 494–510.

Guimond, S., Branscombe, N. R., Brunot, S., Buunk, A. P., Chatard, A., Desert, M., et al. (2007). Culture, gender, and the self: Variations and impact of social comparison processes. *Journal of Personality and Social Psychology, 92*, 1118–1134.

Gunderson, J. G. (1984). *Borderline personality disorder.* Washington, DC: American Psychiatric Press.

Gur, R. C., & Gur, R. E. (2004). Gender differences in the functional organization of the brain. In M. J. Legato (Ed.), *Principles of gender-specific medicine* (pp. 63–70). Amsterdam: Elsevier.

Haier, R. J., Jung, R. E., Yeo, R. A., Head, K., & Alkire, M. T. (2005). The neuroanatomy of general intelligence: Sex matters. *Neuroimage, 25*, 320–327.

Halligan, P. W., & Marshall, J. C. (1998). Neglect of awareness. *Consciousness and Cognition, 7*, 356–380.

Hallmayer, J., Cleveland, S., Torres, A., Phillips, J., Cohen, B., Torigoe, T., Miller, J., Fedele, A., Collins, J., Smith, K., Lotspeich, L., Croen, L. A., Ozonoff, S., Lajonchere, C., Grether, J. K., & Risch, N. (2011). Genetic heritability and shared environmental factors among twin pairs with autism. *Archives of General Psychiatry*, doi:10.1001/archgenpsychiatry.2011.76, e-pub ahead of print.

Halpern, C. T., Udry, J. R., & Suchindran, C. (1997). Testosterone predicts initiation of coitus in adolescent females. *Psychosomatic Medicine, 59*, 161–171.

Halpern, D. F. (2000). *Sex differences in cognitive abilities* (3rd ed.). Mahwah, NJ: Erlbaum.

Halpern, D. F. (2003). *Thought and knowledge: An introduction to critical thinking* (4th ed.). Mahwah, NJ: Erlbaum.

Halpern, D. F., Benbow, C., Geary, D., Gur, D., Hyde, J., & Gernsbacher, M. A. (2007). The science of sex-differences in science and mathematics. *Psychological Science in the Public Interest, 8*, 1–51.

Hamann, S. B., Ely, T. D., Grafton, D. T., & Kilts, C. D. (1999). Amygdala activity related to enhanced memory for pleasant and aversive stimuli. *Nature Neuroscience, 2*, 289–293.

Hamann, S., Herman, R. A., Nolan, C. L., & Wallen, K. (2004). Men and women differ in amygdala response to visual sexual stimuli. *Nature Neuroscience, 7*, 411–416.

Hambrecht, M., Maurer, K., Hafner, H., & Sartorius, N. (1992). Transnational stability of gender differences in schizophrenia: Recent findings on social skills training and family psychoeducation. *Clinical Psychology Review, 11*, 23–44.

Hamilton, N. A., Gallagher, M. W., Preacher, K. J., Stevens, N., Nelson, C. A., Karlson, C., et al. (2007). Insomnia and well-being. *Journal of Consulting and Clinical Psychology, 75*, 939–946.

Hammen, C. (2005). Stress and depression. *Annual Review of Clinical Psychology, 1*, 293–319.

Hancock, P. J., Bruce, V., & Burton, A. M. (2000). Recognition of unfamiliar faces. *Trends in Cognitive Sciences, 4*, 330–337.

Handleman, J. S., Gill, M. J., & Alessandri, M. (1988). Generalization by severely developmentally disabled children: Issues, advances, and future directions. *Behavior Therapist, 11*, 221–223.

Hanewinkel, R., & Sargent, J. D. (2008). Exposure to smoking in internationally distributed American movies and youth smoking in Germany: A cross-cultural cohort study. *Pediatrics, 121*, 108–117.

Haney, C., Banks, C., & Zimbardo, P. (1973). Interpersonal dynamics in a simulated prison. *International Journal of Criminology and Penology, 1*, 69–97.

Hansen, C. J., Stevens, L. C., & Coast, J. R. (2001). Exercise duration and mood state: How much is enough to feel better? *Health Psychology, 20*, 267–275.

Hansen, W. B., Graham, J. W., Sobel, J. L., Shelton, D. R., Flay, B. R., & Johnson, C. A. (1987). The consistency of peer and parental influences on tobacco, alcohol, and marijuana use among young adolescents. *Journal of Behavioral Medicine, 10*, 559–579.

Haque, A. (2004). Psychology from Islamic perspective: Contributions of early Muslim scholars and challenges to contemporary Muslim psychologists. *Journal of Religion & Health, 43*(4), 357–377.

Harburger, L. L., Nzerem, C. K., & Frick, K. M. (2007). Single enrichment variables differentially reduce age-related memory decline in female mice. *Behavioral Neuroscience, 121*(4), 679–688.

Harding, C. M., Zubin, J., & Strauss, J. S. (1987). Chronicity in schizophrenia: Fact, partial fact, or artifact? *Hospital and Community Psychiatry, 38*, 477–486.

Hare, R. D. (1993). *Without conscience: The disturbing world of the psychopaths among us.* New York: Pocket Books.

Hare, R. D., McPherson, L. M., & Forth, A. E. (1988). Male psychopaths and their criminal careers. *Journal of Consulting and Clinical Psychology, 56*, 710–714.

Hariri, A. R., Mattay, V. S., Tessitore, A., Kolachana, B., Fera, F., Goldman, D., et al. (2002, July 19). Serotonin transporter genetic variation and the response of the human amygdala. *Science, 297*, 400–403.

Harlow, H. F., & Harlow, M. K (1966). Learning to love. *American Scientist, 54*, 244–272.

Harlow, H. F., Harlow, M. K., & Meyer, D. R. (1950). Learning motivated by a manipulation drive. *Journal of Experimental Psychology, 40*, 228–234.

Harpur, T. J., & Hare, R. D. (1994). Assessment of psychopathy as a function of age. *Journal of Abnormal Psychology, 103*, 604–609.

Harris, J. L., Bargh, J. A., & Brownell, K. D. (2009). Priming effects of television food advertising on eating behavior. *Health Psychology, 28*, 404–413.

Hartford, J., Kornstein, S., Liebowitz, M., Pigott, T., Russell, J., Detke, M., et al. (2007). Duloxetine as an SNRI treatment for generalized anxiety disorder: Results from a placebo and active-controlled trial. *International Clinical Psychopharmacology, 22*, 167–174.

Hauk, O., Johnsrude, I., & Pulvermüller, F. (2004). Somatotopic representation of action words in human motor and premotor cortex. *Neuron, 41*, 301–307.

Hawkley, L., & Cacioppo, J. T. (2010). Loneliness matters: A theoretical and empirical review of consequences and mechanisms. *Annals of Behavioral Medicine, 40*, 218–227.

Hayne, H. (2004). Infant memory development: Implications for childhood amnesia. *Developmental Review, 24*, 33–73. doi: 10.1016/j.dr.2003.09.007

Hazan, C., & Shaver, P. R. (1987). Romantic love conceptualized as an attachment process. *Journal of Personality and Social Psychology, 52*, 511–524.

Heatherton, T. F. (2011). Neuroscience of self and self-regulation. *Annual Review of Psychology, 62*, 363–390.

Heatherton, T. F., & Baumeister, R. F. (1991). Binge eating as escape from self-awareness. *Psychological Bulletin, 110*, 86–108.

Heatherton, T. F., Herman, C. P., & Polivy, J. (1991). Effects of physical threat and ego threat on eating behavior. *Journal of Personality and Social Psychology, 60*, 138–143.

Heatherton, T. F., & Vohs, K. D. (2000). Interpersonal evaluations following threats to self: Role of self-esteem. *Journal of Personality and Social Psychology, 78*, 725–736.

Heatherton, T. F., & Weinberger, J. L. (1994). *Can personality change?* Washington, DC: American Psychological Association.

Hebl, M. R., & Heatherton, T. F. (1998). The stigma of obesity in women: The difference is black and white. *Personality and Social Psychology Bulletin, 24*, 417–426.

Heine, S. J. (2003). An exploration of cultural variation in self-enhancing and self-improving motivations. In V. Murphy-Berman & J. J. Berman (Eds.), *Nebraska symposium on motivation: Vol. 49. Cross-cultural differences in perspectives on the self* (pp. 101–128). Lincoln: University of Nebraska Press.

Heine, S. J. (2005). Where is the evidence for pancultural self-enhancement? A reply to Sedikides, Gaertner, & Toguchi. *Journal of Personality and Social Psychology, 89*, 531–538.

Heine, S. J., Buchtel, E., & Norenzayan, A. (2008). What do cross-national comparisons of self-reported personality traits tell us? The case of conscientiousness. *Psychological Science, 19*, 309–313.

Heine, S. J., & Hamamura, T. (2007). In search of East Asian self-enhancement. *Personality and Social Psychology Review, 11*, 4–27.

Heine, S. J., Kitayama, S., & Hamamura, T. (2007). The inclusion of additional studies yields different conclusions: A reply to Sedikides, Gaertner, & Vevea (2005), Journal of Personality and Social Psychology. *Asian Journal of Social Psychology, 10*, 49–58.

Heine, S. J., Lehman, D. R., Markus, H. R., & Kitayama, S. (1999). Is there a universal need for positive self-regard? *Psychological Review, 106*, 766–794.

Heine, S. J., & Lehman, D. R. (1999). Culture, self-discrepancies, and self-satisfaction. *Personality and Social Psychology Bulletin, 25*, 915–925.

Heine, S. J., Lehman, D. R., Markus, H. R., & Kitayama, S. (1999). Is there a universal need for positive self-regard? *Psychological Review, 106*, 766–794.

Heller, D., Watson, D., & Ilies, R. (2004). The role of person versus situation in life satisfaction: A critical examination. *Psychological Bulletin, 130*, 574–600.

Helmreich, R., Aronson, E., & LeFan, J. (1970). To err is humanizing sometimes: Effects of self-esteem, competence, and a pratfall on interpersonal attraction. *Journal of Personality and Social Psychology, 16*, 259–264.

Hendricks, M., Rottenberg, J., & Vingerhoets, A. J. (2007). Can the distress-signal and arousal-reduction views of crying be reconciled? Evidence from the cardiovascular system. *Emotion, 7*, 458–463.

Henrich, J., Heine, S. J., & Norenzayan, A. (2010). The weirdest people in the world? *Behavioral and Brain Sciences, 33*, 61–83, 111–135. doi:10.1017/S0140525X0999152X

Henriques, J. B., & Davidson, R. J. (1990). Regional brain electrical asymmetries discriminate between previously depressed and healthy control subjects. *Journal of Abnormal Psychology, 99*, 22–23.

Herbert, T. B., & Cohen, S. (1993). Stress and immunity in humans: A meta-analytic review. *Psychosomatic Medicine, 55*, 364–379.

Herdener, M., Esposito, F., di Salle, F., Boller, C., Hilti, C. C., et al. (2010). Musical training induces functional plasticity in human hippocampus. *Journal of Neuroscience, 30*(4), 1377–1384.

Hering, E. (1964). *Outlines of a theory of the light sense* (L. M. Hurvich & D. Jameson, Trans.). Cambridge, MA: Harvard University Press. (Original work published 1878).

Herrnstein, R. J., & Murray, C. (1994). *The bell curve: Intelligence and class structure in American life.* New York: Free Press.

Herz, R. S., & Cahill, E. D. (1997). Differential use of sensory information in sexual behavior as a function of gender. *Human Nature, 8*, 275–285.

Hester, R. K., Delaney, H. D., & Campbell, W. (2011). ModerateDrinking.com and moderation management: Outcomes of a randomized clinical trail with non-dependent problem drinkers. *Journal of Consulting and Clinical Psychology, 79*, 215–234.

Hickok, G. (2009). Eight problems for the mirror neuron theory of action understanding in monkeys and humans. *Journal of Cognitive Neuroscience, 21*, 1229–1243.

Higgins, E. T. (1987). Self-discrepancy: A theory relating self and affect. *Psychological Review, 94*, 319–340.

Higgins, L. T., & Zheng, M. (2002). An introduction to Chinese psychology—Its historical roots until the present day. *The Journal of Psychology, 136*(2), 225–239.

Higgins, S. C., Gueorguiev, M., & Korbonits, M. (2007). Ghrelin, the peripheral hunger hormone. *Annals of Medicine, 39*, 116–136.

Higley, J. D., Mehlman, P.T., Higley, S. B., Fernald, B., Vickers, J., Lindell, S. G., et al. (1996). Excessive mortality in young free-ranging male nonhuman primates with low cerebrospinal fluid 5-hydroxyindoleacetic acid concentrations. *Archives of General Psychiatry, 53*, 537–543.

Hilgard, E. R., & Hilgard, J. R. (1975). *Hypnosis in the relief of pain.* Los Altos, CA: Kaufmann.

Hill, S. E., & Durante, K. M. (2009). Do women feel worse to look their best? Testing the relationship between self-esteem and fertility status across the menstrual cycle. *Personality and Social Psychology Bulletin, 35*, 1592–1601.

Hines, T. (2003). *Pseudoscience and the paranormal.* Amherst, NY: Prometheus.

Hirst, W., Phelps, E. A., Buckner, R. L., Budson, A. E., Cuc, A., Gabrieli, J. D. E., et al. (2009). Long-term memory for the terrorist attack of September 11: Flashbulb memories, event memories, and the factors that influence their retention. *Journal of Experimental Psychology: General, 138*, 161–176.

Hirstein, W., & Ramachandran, V. S. (1997). Capgras syndrome: a novel probe for understanding the neural representation of the identity and familiarity of persons. *Proceedings of the Royal Society B (Biological Sciences), 264*, 437–444.

Ho, B. C., Andreasen, N. C., Nopoulos, P., Arndt, S., Magnotta, V., & Flaum, M. (2003). Progressive structural brain abnormalities and their relationship to clinical outcome: A longitudinal magnetic resonance imaging study early in schizophrenia. *Archives of General Psychiatry, 60*, 585–594.

Hobson, J. A. (2009). REM sleep and dreaming: Towards a theory of protoconsciousness. *Nature Reviews Neuroscience, 10*, 803–814.

Hobson, J. A., & McCarley, R. (1977.) The brain as a dream state generator: An activation-synthesis hypothesis of the dream process. *American Journal of Psychiatry, 134*, 1335–1348.

Hobson, J. A., Pace-Schott, E. F., & Stickgold, R. (2000). Consciousness: Its vicissitudes in waking and sleep. In M. S. Gazzaniga (Ed.), *The new cognitive neurosciences* (pp. 1341–1354). Cambridge, MA: MIT Press.

Hockley, W. E. (2008). The effect of environmental context on recognition memory and claims of remembering. *Journal of Experimental Psychology: Learning, Memory, and Cognition, 34,* 1412–1429.

Hofmann, S. G., & Smits, J. A. J. (2008). Cognitive-behavioral therapy for adult anxiety disorders: A meta-analysis of randomized placebo-controlled trials. *Journal of Clinical Psychiatry, 69,* 621–632.

Hogan, M. J., Parker, J. D., Wiener, J., Watters, C., Wood, L. M., & Oke, A. (2010). Academic success in adolescence: Relationships among verbal IQ, social support and emotional intelligence. *Australian Journal of Psychology, 62,* 30–41.

Hoge, M. A., Morris, J. A., Daniels, A. S., Stuart, G. W., Huey, L. Y., & Adams, N. (2007). *An action plan for behavioral health workplace development.* Washington, DC: U.S. Department of Health and Human Services.

Holden, C. (2005, June 10). Sex and the suffering brain. *Science, 308,* 1574.

Holland, P. C. (1977). Conditioned stimulus as a determinant of the form of the Pavlovian conditioned response. *Journal of Experimental Psychology: Animal Behavior Processes, 3,* 77–104.

Hollander, E., Bartz, J., Chaplin, W., Phillips, A., Sumner, J., Soorya, L., et al. (2007). Oxytocin increases retention of social cognition in autism. *Biological Psychiatry, 61,* 498–503.

Hollander, E., Novotny, S., Hanratty, M., Yaffe, R., DeCaria, C. M., Aronowitz, B. R., et al. (2003). Oxytocin infusion reduces repetitive behaviors in adults with autistic and Asperger's disorders. *Neuropsychopharmacology, 28,* 193–198.

Hollis, K. L. (1997). Contemporary research on Pavlovian conditioning: A "new" functional analysis. *American Psychologist, 52,* 956–965.

Hollon, S. D., Stewart, M. O., & Strunk, D. (2006). Enduring effects for cognitive behavior therapy in the treatment of depression and anxiety. *Annual Review of Psychology, 57,* 285–315.

Hollon, S. D., Thase, M. E., & Markowitz, J. C. (2002). Treatment and prevention of depression. *Psychological Science in the Public Interest, 3,* 39–77.

Holmbeck, G. N. (1996). A model of family relational transformations during the transition to adolescence: Parent-adolescent conflict and adaptation. In J. A. Graber, J. Brooks-Gunn, & A. C. Petersen (Eds.), *Transitions through Adolescence* (pp. 67–200). Mahwah, NJ: Lawrence Erlbaum.

Holstein, S. B., & Premack, D. (1965). On the different effects of random reinforcement and presolution reversal on human concept-identification. *Journal of Experimental Psychology, 70*(3), 335–337.

Holtzman, N. S., Vazire, S., & Mehl, M. R. (2010). Sounds like a narcissist: Behavioral manifestations of narcissism in everyday life. *Journal of Research in Personality, 44,* 478–484.

Hooley, J. (2007). Expressed emotion and relapse of psychopathology. *Annual Review of Clinical Psychology, 3,* 329–352.

Hooley, J. M., & Gotlib, I. H. (2000). A diathesis-stress conceptualization of expressed emotion and clinical outcome. *Applied and Preventive Psychology, 9,* 135–152.

Horn, J. L. (1968). Organization of abilities and the development of intelligence. *Psychological Review, 75,* 242–259.

Horn, J. L., & Hofer, S. M. (1992). Major abilities and development in the adult period. In R. J. Sternberg & C. A. Berg (Eds.), *Intellectual development* (pp. 44–99). New York: Cambridge University Press.

Horn, J. L., & McArdle, J. J. (2007). Understanding human intelligence since Spearman. In R. Cudeck & R. C. MacCallum (Eds.), *Factor analysis at 100: Historical developments and future directions* (pp. 205–247). Mahwah, NJ: Erlbaum.

Hoshino, Y., Kumashiro, H., Yashima, Y., Tachibana, R., Watanabe, M., & Furukawa, H. (1980). Early symptoms of autism in children and their diagnostic significance. *Japanese Journal of Child and Adolescent Psychiatry, 21,* 284–299.

Hothersall, D. (1995). *History of psychology.* New York: McGraw-Hill.

House, J. S., Landis, K. R., & Umberson, D. (1988, July 29). Social relationships and health. *Science, 241,* 540–545.

Hovland, C. I., Janis, I. L., & Kelley, H. H. (1953). *Communication and persuasion: Psychological studies of opinion change.* New Haven, CT: Yale University Press.

Howlin, P., Mawhood, L., & Rutter, M. (2000). Autism and developmental receptive language disorder—A follow-up comparison in early adult life. II: Social, behavioural, and psychiatric outcomes. *Journal of Child Psychology and Psychiatry and Allied Disciplines, 41,* 561–578.

Hubel, D. H., & Wiesel, T. N. (1962). Receptive fields, binocular interaction, and functional architecture in the cat's visual cortex. *Journal of Physiology* (London), *160,* 106–154.

Huesmann, L. R. (1998). The role of social information processing and cognitive schemas in the acquisition and maintenance of habitual aggressive behavior. In R. G. Geen & E. Donnerstein (Eds.), *Human aggression: Theories, research, and implications for policy* (pp. 73–109). New York: Academic Press.

Hughes, H. C. (1999). *Sensory exotica.* Cambridge, MA: MIT Press.

Hull, C. L. (1943). *Principles of behavior: An introduction to behavior theory.* New York: D. Appleton-Century.

Hull, J. G., & Bond, C. F. (1986). Social and behavioral consequences of alcohol consumption and expectancy: A meta-analysis. *Psychological Bulletin, 99,* 347–360.

Hulse, G. K., Milne, E., English, D. R., & Holman, C. D. J. (1998). Assessing the relationship between maternal opiate use and ante-partum haemorrhage. *Addiction, 93,* 1553–1558.

Hunsley, J., & Mash, E. J. (2007). Evidence-based assessment. *Annual Review of Clinical Psychology, 3,* 29–51.

Hyde, J. S. (2005). The gender similarities hypothesis. *American Psychologist, 60,* 581–592. doi: 10.1037/0003-066X.60.6.581

Hyman, I. E., & Pentland, J. (1996). The role of mental imagery in the creation of false childhood memories. *Journal of Memory and Languages, 35,* 101–117.

Hyman, S. E. (2008). A glimmer of light for neuropsychiatric disorders. *Nature, 455,* 890–893.

Ikier, S., Tekcan, A. I., Gülgöz, S., & Küntay, A. (2003). Whose life is it anyway? Adoption of each other's autobiographical memories by twins. *Applied Cognitive Psychology, 17,* 237–247.

Ilan, A. B., Smith, M. E., & Gevins, A. (2004). Effects of marijuana on neurophysiological signals of working and episodic memory. *Psychopharmacology, 176,* 214–222.

Insel, T. R., & Young, L. J. (2001). The neurobiology of attachment. *Nature Reviews Neurosicence, 2,* 129–136.

Insel, T. R., & Charney, D. S. (2003). Research on major depression. *Journal of the American Medical Association, 289,* 3167–3168.

Isen, A. M. (1993). Positive affect and decision making. In M. Lewis & J. M. Haviland (Eds.), *Handbook of emotions* (pp. 261–277). New York: Guilford Press.

Ishigami, Y., & Klein, R. M. (2009). Is a handsfree phone safer than a handheld phone? *Journal of Safety Research, 40*, 157–164.

Ivanovic, D. M., Leiva, B. P., Perez, H. T., Olivares, M. G., Diaz, N. S., Urrutia, M. S., et al. (2004). Head size and intelligence, learning, nutritional status and brain development: Head, IQ, learning, nutrition and brain. *Neuropsychologia, 42*, 1118–1131.

Iyengar, S. S., & Lepper, M. R. (2000). When choice is demotivating: Can one desire too much of a good thing? *Journal of Personality and Social Psychology, 79*, 995–1006.

Izard, C. E., & Malatesta, C. Z. (1987). Perspectives on emotional development. In J. Osofsky (Ed.), *Handbook of infant development* (pp. 494–554). New York: Wiley.

Jablensky, A. (1989). Epidemiology and cross-cultural aspects of schizophrenia. *Psychiatric Annals, 19*, 516–524.

Jackson, B., Kubzansky, L. D., Cohen, S., Jacobs, D. R., Jr., & Wright, R. J. (2007). Does harboring hostility hurt? Associations between hostility and pulmonary function in the coronary artery risk development in (young) adults (CARDIA) Study. *Health Psychology, 26*(3), 333–340.

Jackson, S. A., Thomas, P. R., Marsh, H. W., & Smethurst, C. J. (2001). Relationships between flow, self-concept, psychological skills, and performance. *Journal of Applied Sport Psychology, 13*, 129–153.

Jacoby, L. L., Kelley, C., Brown, J., & Jasechko, J. (1989). Becoming famous overnight: Limits on the ability to avoid unconscious influences of the past. *Journal of Personality and Social Psychology, 56*, 326–338.

Jacoby, L. L., & Witherspoon, D. (1982). Remembering without awareness. *Canadian Journal of Psychology, 32*, 300–324.

James, William. (1884). What is an emotion? *Mind, 9*, 188–205.

James, W. (1890). *The principles of psychology*. New York: Henry Holt.

Jamieson, G. A. (2007). *Hypnosis and conscious states: The cognitive neuroscience perspective*. New York: Oxford University Press.

Jamison, K. R. (1993). *Touched with fire: Manic-depressive illness and the artistic temperament*. New York: Simon & Schuster.

Jamison, K. R. (1995). *An unquiet mind*. New York: Vintage Books.

Janata, P. (2009). The neural architecture of music-evoked autobiographical memories. *Cerebral Cortex, 19*, 2579–2594.

Jang, K. L., Hu, S., Livesly, W. J., Angleitner, A., Riemann, R., Ando, J., et al. (2001). Covariance structure of neuroticism and agreeableness: A twin and molecular genetic analysis of the role of the serotonin transporter gene. *Journal of Personality and Social Psychology, 81*, 295–304.

Janssen, E., Carpenter, D., & Graham, C. A. (2003). Selecting films for sex research: Gender differences in erotic film preference. *Archives of Sexual Behavior, 32*, 243–251.

Jencks, C. (1979). *Who gets ahead? The determinants of economic success in America*. New York: Basic Books.

Jensen, A. R. (1998). *The g factor: The science of mental ability*. Westport, CT: Praeger.

Jensen, P. S., Arnold, L. E., Swanson, J. M., Vitiello, B., Abikoff, H. B., Greenhill, L. L., et al. (2007). 3-year follow-up of the NIMH MTA study. *Journal of the American Academy of Child and Adolescent Psychiatry, 46*, 989–1002.

Jensen, P. S., Garcia, J. A., Glied, S., Crowe, M., Foster, M., Schlander, M., et al. (2005). Cost-effectiveness of ADHD treatments: Findings from the multimodal treatment study of children with ADHD. *American Journal of Psychiatry, 162*, 1628–1636.

Jensen, P. S., Hinshaw, S. P., Swanson, J. M., Greenhill, L. L., Conners, C. K., Arnold, L. E., et al. (2001). Findings from the NIMH multimodal treatment study of ADHD (MTA): Implications and applications for primary care providers. *Journal of Developmental and Behavioral Pediatrics, 22*, 60–73.

Jiang, Y., Sheikh, K., & Bullock, C. (2006). Is there a sex or race difference in stroke mortality? *Journal of Stroke and Cerebrovascular Disease 15*(5), 179–186.

John, O. P. (1990). The "Big Five" factor taxonomy: Dimensions of personality in the natural language and in questionnaires. In L. A. Pervin & O. P. John (Eds.), *Handbook of personality: Theory and research* (pp. 66–100). New York: Guilford Press.

John, O. P., & Srivastava, S. (1999). The Big Five trait taxonomy: History, measurement, and theoretical perspectives. In L. A. Pervin & O. P. John (Eds.), *Handbook of personality: Theory and research* (2nd ed., pp. 102–138). New York: Guilford Press.

Johns, F., Schmader, T., & Martens, A. (2005). Knowing is half the battle—Teaching stereotype threat as a means of improving women's math performance. *Psychological Science, 16*, 175–179.

Johnson, D. L., Wiebe, J. S., Gold, S. M., Andreasen, N. C., Hichwa, R. D., Watkins, G. L., et al. (1999). Cerebral blood flow and personality: A positron emission tomography study. *American Journal of Psychiatry, 156*, 252–257.

Johnson, K. L., Gill, S., Reichman, V., & Tassinary, L. G. (2007). Swagger, sway, and sexuality: Judging sexual orientation from body motion and morphology. *Journal of Personality and Social Psychology, 93*, 321–334.

Johnson, W., Jung, R. E., Colom, R., & Haier, R. J. (2008). Cognitive abilities independent of IQ correlate with regional brain structure. *Intelligence, 36*, 18–28.

Johnston, L. D., O'Malley, P. M., Bachman, J. G., & Schulenberg, J. E. (2011). *Monitoring the future national results on adolescent drug use: Overview of key findings, 2010*. Ann Arbor: Institute for Social Research, University of Michigan.

Joiner, T. E. (2005). *Why people die by suicide*. Cambridge, MA: Harvard University Press.

Joiner, T. E., Coyne, J. C., & Blalock, J. (1999). On the interpersonal nature of depression: Overview and synthesis. In T. E. Joiner & J. C. Coyne (Eds.), *The interactional nature of depression: Advances in interpersonal approaches* (pp. 3–19). Washington, DC: American Psychological Association.

Joiner, T. E., Jr., Walker, R. L., Pettit, J. W., Perez, M., & Cukrowicz, K. C. (2005). Evidence-based assessment of depression in adults. *Psychological Assessment, 17*, 267–277.

Jokela, M., Elovainio, M., Kivimaki, M., & Keltikangas-Jarvinen, L. (2008). Temperament and migration patterns in Finland. *Psychological Science, 19*, 831–837.

Jokela, M., Elovainio, M., Singh-Manoux, A., & Kivimäki, M. (2009). IQ, socioeconomic status, and early death. *Psychosomatic Medicine, 71*, 322–328.

Jones, M. C. (1924). A laboratory study of fear: The case of Peter. *The Pedagogical Seminary, 31*, 308–315.

Jones, S. S., Collins, K., & Hong, H. (1991). An audience effect on smile production in 10-month-old infants. *Psychological Science, 2*, 45–49.

Jope, R. S. (1999). Anti-bipolar therapy: Mechanism of action of lithium. *Molecular Psychiatry, 4*, 117–128.

Jorm, A. F. (2000). Does old age reduce the risk of anxiety and depression?: A review of epidemiological studies across the adult life span. *Psychological Medicine, 30*, 3011–3022. doi: 10.1017/S0033291799001452

Jureidini, J. N., Doecke, C. J., Mansfield, P. R., Haby, M., Menkes, D. B., & Tonkin, A. L. (2004). Efficacy and safety of antidepressants for children and adolescents. *British Medical Journal, 328*, 879–883.

Kagan, J. (2011). Three lessons learned. *Perspectives in Psychological Science, 6*, 107–113.

Kagan, J., & Snidman, N. (1991). Infant predictors of inhibited and uninhibited profiles. *Psychological Science, 2*, 40–44.

Kahneman, D. (2007, July 20–22). *A short course in thinking about thinking. A master class by Danny Kahneman.* [Online video.] Retrieved from *Edge, The Third Culture,* at http://www.edge.org/3rd_culture/kahneman07/kahneman07_index.html/

Kahneman, D., & Tversky, A. (1972). Subjective probability: A study of representativeness. *Cognitive Psychology, 3*, 430–454.

Kahneman, D., & Tversky, A. (1984). Choices, values, and frames. *American Psychologist, 39*, 341–350.

Kalechstein, A. D., De La Garza II, R., Mahoney III, J. J., Fantegrossi, W. E., & Newton, T. F. (2007). MDMA use and neurocognition: A meta-analytic review. *Psychopharmacology, 189*, 531–537.

Kallio, S., & Revonsuo, A. (2003). Hypnotic phenomena and altered states of consciousness: A multi-level framework of description and explanation. *Contemporary Hypnosis, 20*, 111–164.

Kamara, S., Colom, R., Johnson, W., Deary, I., Haier, R., Waber, D., et al., and the Brain Development Cooperative Groups. (2011). Cortical thickness correlates of specific cognitive performance accounted for by the general factor of intelligence in healthy children aged 6 to 18. *Neuroimage, 55*(4), 1443–1453. doi:10.1016/j.neuroimage.2011.01.016

Kanayama, G., Pope, H. G., Cohane, G., & Hudson, J. L. (2003). Risk factors for anabolic-steroid use among weightlifters: A case-control study. *Drug and Alcohol Dependence, 71,* 77–86.

Kanazawa, S. (2004). General intelligence as a domain-specific adaptation. *Psychological Review, 111*, 512–523.

Kandall, S. R., & Gaines, J. (1991). Maternal substance use and subsequent sudden infant death syndrome (SIDS) in offspring. *Neurotoxicology and Teratology, 13*, 235–240.

Kandel, E. R. (1998). A new intellectual framework for psychiatry. *American Journal of Psychiatry, 155*, 457–469.

Kandel, E. R., Schwartz, J. H., & Jessell, T. M. (1995). *Essentials of neural science and behavior.* Norwalk, CT: Appleton & Lange.

Kane, M. J., Hambrick, D. Z., & Conway, A. R. (2005). Working memory capacity and fluid intelligence are strongly related constructs: Comment on Ackerman, Beier, and Boyle (2005). *Psychological Bulletin, 131*, 66–71.

Kang, D. H., Coe, C. L., McCarthy, D. O., & Ershler, W. B. (1997). Immune responses to final exams in healthy and asthmatic adolescents. *Nursing Research, 46*, 12–19.

Kanwisher, N., Tong, F., & Nakayama, K. (1998). The effect of face inversion on the human fusiform face area. *Cognition, 68*, 1–11.

Kaplan, R. M. (2007). Should Medicare reimburse providers for weight loss interventions? *American Psychologist, 62*, 217–219.

Kappenberg, E. S., & Halpern, D. F. (2006). Kinship center attachment questionnaire: Development of a caregiver-completed attachment measure for children under six years of age. *Educational and Psychological Measurement, 66*, 852–873.

Kapur, S. E., Craik, F. I. M., Tulving, E., Wilson, A. A., Houle, S., & Brown, G. R. (1994). Neuroanatomical correlates of encoding in episodic memory: Levels of processing effects. *Proceedings of the National Academy of Sciences, USA, 91*, 2008–2011.

Karasek, R. A., & Theorell, T. (1990). *Healthy work: Stress, productivity, and the reconstruction of working life.* New York: Basic Books.

Karney, B. R., & Bradbury, T. N. (1995). The longitudinal course of marital quality and stability: A review of theory, methods, and research. *Psychological Bulletin, 118*, 3–34.

Karpas, A. (2009). Mysterious tears: The phenomenon of crying from the perspective of social neuroscience. In T. Fögen (Ed.), *Tears in the Graeco-Roman world* (pp. 419–437). Berlin, Germany: De Gruyter.

Karpicke, J. D., & Blunt, J. R. (2011). Retrieval practice produces more learning than elaborative studying with concept mapping. *Science, 331*, 772–775.

Kasari, C., Paparella, T., Freeman, S., & Jahromi, L. B. (2008). Language outcomes in autism: Randomized comparison of joint attention and play interventions. *Journal of Counseling and Clinical Psychology, 76*, 125–137.

Kawachi, I., Kennedy, B., & Glass, R. (1999). Social capital and self-rated health: A contextual analysis. *American Journal of Public Health, 89*(8), 1187–1193.

Kawakami, K., Dovidio, J. F., Moll, J., Hermsen, S., & Russin, A. (2000). Just say no (to stereotyping): Effects of training in the negation of stereotypic associations on stereotype activation. *Journal of Personality and Social Psychology, 78*, 871–888.

Kawakami, K., Dovidio, J. F., & van Kamp, S. (2005). Kicking the habit: Effects of nonstereotypic association training and correction processes on hiring decisions. *Journal of Experimental Social Psychology, 41*, 68–75.

Kawas, C., Gray, S., Brookmeyer, R., Fozard, J., & Zonderman, A. (2000). Age-specific incidence rates of Alzheimer's disease: The Baltimore longitudinal study of aging, *Neurology, 54*, 2072–2077.

Kay, K. N., Naselaris, T., Prenger, R. J., & Gallant, J. L. (2008). Identifying natural images from human brain activity. *Nature, 452*, 352–355.

Kazak, A., Simms, S., & Rourke, M. (2002). Family systems practice in pediatric psychology. *Journal of Pediatric Psychology, 27*, 133–143.

Kazdin, A. E. (1994). Methodology, design, and evaluation in psychotherapy research. In A. E. Bergin & S. L. Garfield (Eds.), *International handbook of behavior modification and behavior change* (4th ed., pp. 19–71). New York: Wiley.

Kazdin, A. E. (2008). Evidence-based treatment and practice: New opportunities to bridge clinical research and practice, enhance the knowledge base, and improve patient care. *American Psychologist, 63*, 146–159.

Kazdin, A. E., & Benjet, C. (2003). Spanking children: Evidence and issues. *Current Directions in Psychological Science, 12*, 99–103.

Kazdin, A. E., & Blase, S. L. (2011). Rebooting psychotherapy research and practice to reduce the burden of mental illness. *Perspectives in Psychological Science, 6*, 21–37.

Keane, M. (1987). On retrieving analogues when solving problems. *Quarterly Journal of Experimental Psychology, 39A*, 29–41.

Keel, P. K., Baxter, M. G., Heatherton, T. F., & Joiner, T. E. (2007). A 20-year longitudinal study of body weight, dieting, and eating disorder symptoms. *Journal of Abnormal Psychology, 116*, 422–432.

Keel, P. K., & Mitchell, J. E. (1997). Outcome in bulimia nervosa. *American Journal of Psychiatry, 154*, 313–321.

Keller, J., & Bless, H. (2008). Flow and regulatory compatibility: An experimental approach to the flow model of intrinsic motivation. *Personality and Social Psychology Bulletin, 34*, 196–209.

Keller, M. B., & Baker, L. A. (1991). Bipolar disorder: Epidemiology, course, diagnosis, and treatment. *Bulletin of the Menninger Clinic, 55*, 172–181.

Keller, M. B., McCullough, J. P., Klein, D. N., Arnow, B., Dunner, D. L., Gelenberg, A. J., et al. (2000). A comparison of nefazodone, a cognitive behavioral analysis system of psychotherapy, and their combination for the treatment of chronic depression. *New England Journal of Medicine, 342*, 1462–1470.

Kelley, W. T., Macrae, C. N., Wyland, C., Caglar, S., Inati, S., & Heatherton, T. F. (2002). Finding the self? An event-related fMRI study. *Journal of Cognitive Neuroscience, 14*, 785–794.

Kellman, P. J., Spelke, E. S., & Short, K. R. (1986). Infant perception of object unity from translatory motion in depth and vertical translation. *Child Development, 57*, 72–86.

Kelly, D. J., Quinn, P. C., Slater, A., Lee, K., Ge, L., & Pascalis, O. (2007). The other-race effect develops during infancy: Evidence of perceptual narrowing. *Psychological Science, 18*, 1084–1089.

Kelly, G. A. (1955). *The psychology of personal constructs*. New York: Norton.

Keltner, D., & Anderson, C. (2000). Saving face for Darwin: The functions and uses of embarrassment. *Current Directions in Psychological Science, 9*, 187–192.

Keltner, D., & Bonanno, G. A. (1997). A study of laughter and dissociation: Distinct correlates of laughter and smiling during bereavement. *Journal of Personality and Social Psychology, 73*, 687–702.

Keltner, D., Young, R. C., Heerey, E. A., Oemig, C., & Monarch, N. D. (1998). Teasing in hierarchical and intimate relations. *Journal of Personality and Social Psychology, 75*, 1231–1247.

Kendler, K. S., Prescott, C. A., Myers, J., & Neale, M. C. (2003). The structure of genetic and environmental risk factors for common psychiatric and substance use disorders in men and women. *Archives of General Psychiatry, 60*, 929–937.

Kennedy, Q., Mather, M., & Carstensen, L. L. (2004). The role of motivation in the age-related positivity effect in autobiographical memory. *Psychological Science, 15*, 208–214.

Kennedy, S. H., Giacobbe, P., Rizvi, S., Placenza, F. M., Nishikawa, Y., Mayberg, H. S., & Lozano, A. M. (2011). Deep brain stimulation for treatment-resistant depression: Follow-up after 3 to 6 years. *American Journal of Psychiatry, 168*, 502–510.

Kenrick, D. T., & Funder, D. C. (1991). The person-situation debate: Do personality traits really exist? In V. J. Derlega, B. A. Winstead, & W. H. Jones (Eds.), *Personality: Contemporary theory and research* (pp. 149–174). Chicago: Nelson Hall.

Kenrick, D. T., Montello, D. R., Gutierres, S. E., & Trost, M. R. (1993). Effects of physical attractiveness on affect and perceptual judgments: When social comparison overrides social reinforcement. *Personality and Social Psychology Bulletin, 19*, 195–199.

Kessler, R. C., Adler, L., Barkley, R., Biederman, J., Conners, C. K., Demler, O., et al. (2006). The prevalence and correlates of adult ADHD in the United States: Results from the national comorbidity survey replication. *American Journal of Psychiatry, 163*, 716–723.

Kessler, R. C., Berglund, P., Demler, O., Jin, R., Koretz, D., Merikangas, K., et al. (2003). The epidemiology of major depressive disorder: Results from the national comorbidity survey replication (NCS-R). *Journal of the American Medical Association, 289*, 3095–3105.

Kessler, R. C., Chiu, W. T., Demler, O., & Walters, E. E. (2005a). Prevalence, severity, and comorbidity of twelve-month DSM-IV disorders in the national comorbidity survey replication (NCS-R). *Archives of General Psychiatry, 62*, 617–627.

Kessler, R. C., Demler, O., Frank, R. G., Olfson, M., Pincus, M. A., Walters, E. E., et al. (2005b). Prevalence and treatment of mental disorders, 1990 to 2003. *New England Journal of Medicine, 352*, 2515–2523.

Kessler, R. C., McGonagle, K. A., Zhao, S., Nelson, C. B., Hugh, M., Eshleman, S., et al. (1994). Lifetime and 12-month prevalence of DSM-III-R psychiatric disorders in the United States: Results from the national comorbidity study. *Archives of General Psychiatry, 51*, 8–19.

Kessler, R. C., Merikangas, K. R., & Wang, P. S. (2007). Prevalence, comorbidity, and service utilization for mood disorders in the United States at the beginning of the twenty-first century. In S. NolenHoeksema, T. Cannon, & T. Widiger (Eds.), *Annual review of clinical psychology: Vol. 3* (pp. 137–158). Palo Alto, CA: Annual Reviews.

Kessler, R. C., Sonnega, A., Bromet, E., Hughes, M., & Nelson, C. B. (1995). Posttraumatic stress disorder in the national comorbidity survey. *Archives of General Psychiatry, 52*, 1048–1060.

Kessler, R. C., & Wang, P. S. (2008). The descriptive epidemiology of commonly occurring mental disorders in the United States. *Annual Review of Public Health, 29*, 115–129.

Keyes, Daniel. (1981). *The minds of Billy Milligan*. New York: Random House.

Keys, A., Brozek, J., Henschel, A. L., Mickelsen, O., & Taylor, H. L. (1950). *The biology of human starvation*. Minneapolis: University of Minnesota Press.

Khan, M. M. (2005). Suicide prevention and developing countries. *Journal of the Royal Society of Medicine, 98*, 459–463.

Kiecolt-Glaser, J. K., & Glaser, R. I. (1988). Immunological competence. In E. A. Blechman & K. D. Brownell (Eds.), *Handbook of behavioral medicine for women* (pp. 195–205). Elmsford, NY: Pergamon Press.

Kiecolt-Glaser, J. K., & Glaser, R. I (1991). Stress and immune function in humans. In Ader, R., Felten, D., and Cohen, N. (Eds.), *Psychoneuroimmunology II* (pp. 849–867). San Diego: Academic Press.

Kiecolt-Glaser, J. K., Malarkey, W. B., Chee, M., & Newton, T. (1993). Negative behavior during marital conflict is associated with immunological down-regulation. *Psychosomatic Medicine, 55*, 395–409.

Kiecolt-Glaser, J. K., Page, G. G., Marucha, P. T., MacCullum, R. C., & Glaser, R. (1998). Psychological influences on surgical recovery: Perspectives from psychoneuroimmunology. *American Psychologist, 53*, 1209–1218.

Kihlstrom, J. F. (1985). Hypnosis. *Annual Review of Psychology, 36*, 385–418.

Kihlstrom, J. F. (2005). Dissociative disorder. *Annual Review of Clinical Psychology, 1*, 227–253.

Kihlstrom, J. F., & Eich, E. (1994). Altering states of consciousness. In D. Druckman & R. A. Bjork (Eds.), *Learning, remembering, and believing: Enhancing performance* (pp. 207–248). Washington, DC: National Academy Press.

Kilbride, J. E., Robbins, M. C., & Kilbride, P. L. (1970). The comparative motor development of Bagandan, American white, and American black infants. *American Anthropologist, 72*, 1422–1428.

Kim, J. B., Zaehres, H., Wu, G., Gentile, L., Ko, K., Sebastiano, V., et al. (2008). Pluripotent stem cells induced from adult neural stem cells by reprogramming with two factors. *Nature, 454*, 646–650.

Kim, J. J., & Jung, M. W. (2006). Neural circuits and mechanisms involved in Pavlovian fear conditioning: A critical review. *Neuroscience & Biobehavioral Reviews, 30*(2), 188–202.

Kim, S. J., Lyoo, I. K., Hwang, J., Chung, A., Hoon Sung, Y., Kim, J., et al. (2006). Prefrontal grey-matter changes in short-term and long-term abstinent methamphetamine abusers. *The International Journal of Neuropsychopharmacology, 9*, 221–228.

Kimura, D. (1999). *Sex and Cognition*. Cambridge, MA: MIT Press.

Kirsch, I. (2011, June). The placebo effect has come of age. *The Journal of Mind-Body Regulation, 1*(2), 106–109.

Kirsch, I., Deacon, B. J., Huedo-Medina, T. B., Scoboria, A., Moore, T. J., & Johnson, B. T. (2008). Initial severity and antidepressant benefits: A metaanalysis of data submitted to the Food and Drug Administration. *PLoS Medicine, 5*: e45. doi:10.1371

Kirsch, I., & Lynn, S. J. (1995). The altered state of hypnosis: Changes in the theoretical landscape. *American Psychologist, 10*, 846–858.

Klatsky, A. (2009). Alcohol and cardiovascular health. *Physiology and Behavior, 100*, 76–81.

Klauer, M. H., Musch, J., & Naumer, B. (2000). On belief bias in syllogistic reasoning. *Psychological Review, 107*, 852–884.

Klin, A., Jones, W., Schultz, R., & Volkmar, F. (2003). The enactive mind, or from actions to cognition: Lessons from autism. *Philosophical Transactions of the Royal Society of London, 358B*, 345–360.

Klump, K. L., & Culbert, K. M. (2007). Molecular genetic studies of eating disorders: Current status and future directions. *Current Directions in Psychological Science, 16*, 37–41.

Kluver, H., & Bucy, P. C. (1937). Psychic blindness and other symptoms following bilateral temporal lobectomy in rhesus monkeys. *American Journal of Physiology, 119*, 352–353.

Knight, R. (1953). Borderline states. *Bulletin of the Menninger Clinic, 17*, 1–12.

Knox, S. S., Weidner, G., Adelman, A., Stoney, C. M., & Ellison, R. C. (2004). Hostility and physiological risk in the national heart, lung, and blood institute family heart study. *Archives of Internal Medicine, 164*, 2442–2447.

Knutson, B., Fong, G. W., Adams, C. M., Varner, J. L., & Hommer, D. (2001). Dissociation of reward anticipation and outcome with event-related fMRI. *NeuroReport, 12*, 3683–3687.

Knutson, B., Wolkowitz, O. M., Cole, S. W., Chan, T., Moore, E. A., Johnson, R. C., et al. (1998). Selective alteration of personality and social behavior by serotonergic intervention. *American Journal of Psychiatry, 155*, 373–379.

Kobasa, S. C. (1979). Personality and resistance to illness. *American Journal of Community Psychology, 7*, 413–423.

Koch, J. L. (1891). *Die psychopathischen Minderwertigkeiten*. Ravensburg, Germany: Maier.

Kocsis, J. H., Rush, A. J., Markowitz, J. C., Borian, F. E., Dunner, D. L., Koran, L. M., et al. (2003). Continuation treatment of chronic depression: A comparison of nefazodone, cognitive behavioral analysis system of psychotherapy, and their combination. *Psychopharmacology Bulletin, 37*, 73–87.

Koelsch, S., Offermanns, K., & Franzke, P. (2010). Music in the treatment of affective disorders: A new method for music-therapeutic research. *Music Perception, 27*(4), 307–316.

Koh, K., Joiner, W. J., Wu, M. N., Yue, Z., Smith, C. J., Sehgal, A. (2008). Identification of SLEEPLESS, a sleep-promoting factor. *Science, 321*, 372–376.

Kohlberg, L. (1984). *Essays on moral development: Vol. 2. The psychology of moral development*. San Francisco: Harper & Row.

Köhler, W. (1925). *The mentality of apes*. New York: Harcourt Brace.

Kohn, D. (2008, March 11). Cases without borders: Psychotherapy for all. *The New York Times*. Retrieved from http://www.nytimes.com

Kolar, D. W., Funder, D. C., & Colvin, C. R. (1996). Comparing the accuracy of personality judgments by the self and knowledgeable others. *Journal of Personality, 64*, 311–337.

Kontsevich, L. L., & Tyler, C. W. (2004). What makes Mona Lisa smile? *Vision Research, 44*, 1493–1498.

Koole, S. L., Dijksterhuis, A., & van Knippenberg, A. (2001). What's in a name: Implicit self-esteem and the automatic self. *Journal of Personality and Social Psychology, 80*, 669–685.

Korn, M. L., Kotler, M., Molcho, A., Botsis, A. J., Grosz, D., Chen, C., et al. (1992). Suicide and violence associated with panic attacks. *Biological Psychiatry, 31*, 607–612.

Kosslyn, S. M. (2007). *Clear and to the point: 8 principles for compelling PowerPoint presentations*. New York: Oxford University Press.

Kosslyn, S. M., & Koenig, O. (1995). *Wet mind: The new cognitive neuroscience*. New York: Free Press.

Kosslyn, S. M., Thompson, W. L., Constantine-Ferrando, M. F., Alpert, N. M., & Spiegel, D. (2000). Hypnotic visual illusion alters color processing in the brain. *American Journal of Psychiatry, 157*, 1279–1284.

Kosslyn, S. M., Thompson, W. L., Kim, I. J., & Alpert, N. M. (1995). Topographical representations of mental images in primary visual cortex. *Nature, 378*, 496–493.

Kowalski, P., & Taylor, A. K. (2004). Ability and critical thinking as predictors of change in students' psychological misconceptions. *Journal of Instructional Psychology, 31*, 297.

Kozorovitskiy, Y., & Gould, E. (2004). Dominance hierarchy influences adult neurogenesis in the dentate gyrus. *Journal of Neuroscience, 24*, 6755–6759.

Kramer, M. S., Aboud, F., Mironova, E., Vanilovich, I., Platt, R. W., & Matush, L., et al. (2008). Breastfeeding and child cognitive development: New evidence from a large randomized trial. *Archives of General Psychiatry, 65*, 578–584.

Krantz, D. S., & McCeney, M. K. (2002). Effects of psychological and social factors on organic disease: A critical assessment of research on coronary heart disease. *Annual Review of Psychology, 53*, 341–369.

Krendl, A. C., Richeson, J. A., Kelley, W. M., & Heatherton, T. F. (2008). The negative consequences of threat: An fMRI investigation of the neural mechanisms underlying women's underperformance in math. *Psychological Science, 19*, 168–175.

Kringelbach, M. L., & Berridge, K. C. (2009). Toward a functional neuroanatomy of pleasure and happiness. *Trends in Cognitive Sciences, 13*, 479–487.

Krueger, R. F. (1999). The structure of common mental disorders. *Archives of General Psychiatry, 56*, 921–926.

Krueger, R. F., & Markon, K. E. (2006). Understanding psychopathology: Melding behavior genetics, personality, and quantitative psychology to develop an empirically based model. *Current Directions in Psychological Science, 15*, 113–117.

Kruesi, M. J., Hibbs, E. D., Zahn, T. P., Keysor, C. S., Hamburger, S. D., Bartko, J. J., et al. (1992). A 2-year prospective follow-up study of children and adolescents with disruptive behavior disorders. Prediction by cerebrospinal fluid 5-hydroxyindoleacetic acid, homovanillic acid, and autonomic measures. *Archives of General Psychiatry, 49*, 429–435.

Krulwich, R. (2007). Sweet, sour, salty, bitter . . . and umami. *NPR: Krulwich on Science.* Retrieved November 14, 2008, from http://www.npr.org/templates/story/story.php?storyId=15819485

Kuhl, P. K. (2004). Early language acquisition: Cracking the speech code. *Nature Reviews Neuroscience, 5*, 831–843.

Kuhl, P. K. (2006). Is speech learning "gated" by the social brain? *Developmental Science, 10*, 110–120.

Kuhl, P. K., Stevens, E., Hayashi, A., Deguchi, T., Kiritani, S., & Iverson, P. (2006). Infants show a facilitation effect for native language phonetic perception between 6 and 12 months. *Developmental Science, 9*, F13–F21.

Kuhl, P. K., Tsao, F. M., & Liu, H. M. (2003). Foreign-language experience in infancy: effects of short-term exposure and social interaction on phonetic learning. *Proceedings of the National Academy of Sciences, USA, 100*, 9096–9101.

Kuhn, C., Swartzwelder, S., & Wilson, W. (2003). *Buzzed: The straight facts about the most used and abused drugs from alcohol to ecstasy* (2nd ed.). New York: Norton.

Kulhara, P., & Chakrabarti, S. (2001). Culture and schizophrenia and other psychotic disorders. *Psychiatric Clinics of North America, 24*, 449–464.

Kuncel, N. R., Hezlett, S. A., & Ones, D. S. (2004). Academic performance, career potential, creativity, and job performance: Can one construct predict them all? *Journal of Personality and Social Psychology, 86*, 148–161.

Kunda, Z., & Spencer, S. J. (2003). When do stereotypes come to mind and when do they color judgment? A goal-based theoretical framework for stereotype activation and application. *Psychological Bulletin, 129*, 522–544.

Kyllonen, P. C., & Christal, R. E. (1990). Reasoning ability is (little more than) working-memory capacity?! *Intelligence, 14*, 389–433.

LaFrance, M. L., & Banaji, M. (1992). Toward a reconsideration of the gender-emotion relationship. In M. Clarke (Ed.), *Review of personality and social psychology* (pp. 178–201). Beverly Hills, CA: Sage.

Lager, A., Bremberg, S., & Vågerö, D. (2009). The association of early IQ and education with mortality: 65 year longitudinal study in Malmö, Sweden. *British Medical Journal, 339*(b5282). doi:10.1136/bmj.b582.

Laird, J. D. (1974). Self-attribution of emotion: The effects of expressive behavior on the quality of emotional experience. *Journal of Perspectives in Social Psychology,* 29, 475–486.

Lambert, T. J., Fernandez, S. M., & Frick, K. M. (2005). Different types of environmental enrichment have discrepant effects on spatial memory and synaptophysin levels in female mice. *Neurobiology of Learning and Memory, 83*, 206–216.

Lamm, C., Batson, C. D., & Decety, J. (2007). The neural substrate of human empathy: Effects of perspective-taking and cognitive appraisal. *Journal of Cognitive Neuroscience, 19*, 42–58.

Landa, R., Holman, K., & Garrett-Mayer, E. (2007). Social and communication development in toddlers with early and later diagnosis of autism spectrum disorders. *Archives of General Psychiatry, 64*, 853–864.

Langlois, J. H., Kalakanis, L., Rubenstein, A. J., Larson, A., Hallam, M., & Smoot, M. (2000). Maxims or myths of beauty? A meta-analytic and theoretical review. *Psychological Bulletin, 126*, 390–423.

Langlois, J. H., Ritter, J. M., Casey, R. J., & Sawin, D. B. (1995). Infant attractiveness predicts maternal behaviors and attitudes. *Developmental Psychology, 31*, 464–472.

Langlois, J. H., & Roggman, L. A. (1990). Attractive faces are only average. *Psychological Science, 1*, 115–121.

Larsen, J. T., McGraw, A. P., & Cacioppo, J. T. (2001). Can people feel happy and sad at the same time? *Journal of Personality and Social Psychology, 81*, 684–696.

Larson, E. B., Wang, L., Bowen, J. D., McCormick, W. C., Teri, L., Crane, P., & Kukull, W. (2006). Exercise is associated with reduced risk for incident dementia among persons 65 years of age and older. *Annals of Internal Medicine, 144*, 73–81.

Latané, B., & Darley, J. M. (1968). Group inhibition of bystander intervention in emergencies. *Journal of Personality and Social Psychology, 10*, 215–221.

Latané, B., Williams, K., & Harkins, S. G. (1979). Many hands make light the work: The causes and consequences of social loafing. *Journal of Personality and Social Psychology, 37*, 822–832.

Laureys, S. (2007, May). Eyes open, brain shut. *Scientific American, 296*, 84–89.

Lautenschlager, N. T., Cox, K. L., Flicker, L., Foster, J. K., van Bockxmeer, F. M., Xiao, J., et al. (2008). Effect of physical exercise on cognitive function in older adults at risk for Alzheimer disease. *Journal of the American Medical Association, 300*, 1027–1037.

Layton, M. (1995, May/June). Emerging from the shadows. *Family Therapy Networker*, 35–41.

Lazarus, R. S. (1993). From psychological stress to the emotions: A history of changing outlooks. *Annual Review of Psychology, 44*, 1–21.

Leary, M. R. (2004). The function of self-esteem in terror management theory and sociometer theory: Comment on Pyszczynski et al. *Psychological Bulletin, 130*, 478–482.

Leary, M. R., & MacDonald, G. (2003). Individual differences in self-esteem: A review and theoretical integration. In M. R. Leary & J. P. Tangney (Eds.), *Handbook of self and identity* (pp. 401–418). New York: Guilford Press.

Leary, M. R., Tambor, E. S., Terdal, S. K., & Downs, D. L. (1995). Self-esteem as an interpersonal monitor: The sociometer hypothesis. *Journal of Personality and Social Psychology, 68*, 518–530.

Leckman, J. F., Elliott, G. R., Bromet, E. J., Campbell, M., Cicchetti, D., Cohen, D. J., et al. (1995). Report card on the national plan for research on child and adolescent mental disorders: The midway point. *Archives of General Psychiatry, 34*, 715–723.

LeDoux, J. E. (1996). *The emotional brain: The mysterious underpinnings of emotional life.* New York: Simon & Schuster.

LeDoux, J. E. (2000). Emotion circuits in the brain. *Annual Review of Neuroscience, 23*, 155–184.

LeDoux, J. E. (2002). *Synaptic self.* New York: Viking.

LeDoux, J. E. (2007). The amygdala. *Current Biology, 17*, R868–R874.

Lee, P. A. (1980). Normal ages of pubertal events among American males and females. *Journal of Adolescent Health Care, 1*, 26–29. doi: 10.1016/S0197-0070(80)80005-2.

Leff, J., Sartorius, N., Jablensky, A., Korten, A., & Ernberg, G. (1992). The international pilot study of schizophrenia: Five-year follow-up findings. *Psychological Medicine, 22*, 131–145.

Lehrner, J. P. (1993). Gender differences in long-term odor recognition memory: Verbal versus sensory influences and the consistency of label use. *Chemical Senses, 18*, 17–26.

Leichsenring, F., Rabung, S., & Leibing, E. (2004). The efficacy of short-term psychodynamic psychotherapy in specific psychiatric disorders: A meta-analysis. *Archives of General Psychiatry, 61*, 1208–1216.

Leigh, B. C., & Schafer, J. C. (1993). Heavy drinking occasions and the occurrence of sexual activity. *Psychology of Addictive Behaviors, 7*, 197–200.

Leigh, B. C., & Stacy, A. W. (2004). Alcohol expectancies and drinking in different age groups. *Addiction, 99*, 215–217.

Lenzenweger, M. F., Lane, M. C., Loranger, A. W., & Kessler, R. C. (2007). DSM-IV personality disorders in the national comorbidity survey replication. *Biological Psychiatry, 62*, 553–564.

Lepper, M. R., Greene, D., & Nisbett, R. E. (1973). Undermining children's intrinsic interest with extrinsic reward: A test of the "overjustification" hypothesis. *Journal of Personality and Social Psychology, 28*, 129–137.

Lesniak, K. T., & Dubbert, P. M. (2001). Exercise and hypertension. *Current Opinion in Cardiology, 16*, 356–359.

Leuchter, A. F., Cook, I. A., Witte, E. A., Morgan, M., & Abrams, M. (2002). Changes in brain function of depressed subjects during treatment with placebo. *American Journal of Psychiatry, 159*, 122–129.

LeVay, S. (1991, August 30). A difference in hypothalamic structure between heterosexual and homosexual men. *Science, 253*, 1034–1037.

Leventhal, H., & Cleary, P. D. (1980). The smoking problem: A review of research and theory in behavioral risk modification. *Psychological Bulletin, 88*, 370–405.

Levin, J. M., Ross, M. H., Mendelson, J. H., Kaufman, M. J., Lange, N., et al. (1998). Reduction in BOLD fMRI response to primary visual stimulation following alcohol ingestion. *Psychiatry Research, 82*(3), 135–146.

Levinson, D. F. (2006). The genetics of depression: A review. *Biological Psychiatry, 60*, 84–92.

Levitin, D. J. (2006). *This is your brain on music: The science of a human obsession*. New York: Dutton/Penguin.

Levitin, D. J., & Menon, V. (2003). Musical structure in "language" areas of the brain: A possible role for Brodmann Area 47 in temporal coherence. *NeuroImage, 20*, 2142–2152.

Levy, D., Ronemus, M., Yamrom, B., Lee, Y., Leotta, A., Kendall, J., et al. (2011). Rare de novo and transmitted copy-number variation in autistic spectrum disorders. *Neuron, 70*, 886–897.

Lewin, C., & Herlitz, A. (2002). Sex differences in face recognition: Women's faces make the difference. *Brain and Cognition, 50*, 121–128.

Lewinsohn, P. M., Allen, N. B., Seeley, J. R., & Gotlib, I. H. (1999). First onset versus recurrence of depression: Differential processes of psychosocial risk. *Journal of Abnormal Psychology, 108*, 483–489.

Lewinsohn, P. M., Rodhe, P. D., Seeley, J. R., & Hops, H. (1991). Comorbidity of unipolar depression: I. Major depression with dysthymia. *Journal of Abnormal Psychology, 98*, 107–116.

Lewontin, R. C. (1976). Race and intelligence. In N. J. Block & G. Dworkin (Eds.), *The IQ controversy*. New York: Pantheon Books.

Li, N. P., Bailey, J. M., Kenrick, D. T., & Linsenmeier, J. A. W. (2002). The necessities and luxuries of mate preferences: Testing the tradeoffs. *Journal of Personality and Social Psychology, 82*, 947–955.

Lieb, K., Zanarini, M. C., Schmahl, C., Linehan, M. M., & Bohus, M. (2004). Borderline personality disorder. *Lancet, 364*, 453–461.

Lieberman, M. D. (2000). Intuition: A social cognitive neuroscience approach. *Psychological Bulletin, 126*, 109–137.

Lieberman, M. D., Ochsner, K. N., Gilbert, D. T., & Schacter, D. L. (2001). Do amnesiacs exhibit cognitive dissonance reduction? The role of explicit memory and attention in attitude change. *Psychological Science, 121*, 135–140.

Lilienfeld, S. O. (2007). Psychological treatments that cause harm. *Perspectives on Psychological Science, 2*, 53–67.

Limosin, F., Rouillon, F., Payan, C., Cohen, J., & Strub, N. (2003). Prenatal exposure to influenza as a risk factor for adult schizophrenia. *Acta Psychiatrica Scandinavica, 107*, 331–335.

Lindemann, B. (2001). Receptors and transduction in taste. *Nature, 413*, 219–225.

Linehan, M. M. (1987). Dialectical behavior therapy for borderline personality disorder: Theory and method. *Bulletin of the Menninger Clinic, 51*, 261–276.

Linehan, M. M., Armstrong, H. E., Suarez, A., Allmon, D., & Heard, H. (1991). Cognitive behavioral treatment of chronically parasuicidal borderline patients. *Archives of General Psychiatry, 48*, 1060–1064.

Linehan, M. M., Heard, H., & Armstrong, H. E. (1993). Naturalistic follow-up of a behavioral treatment for chronically parasuicidal borderline patients. *Archives of General Psychiatry, 50*, 971–974.

Liu, J., Raine, A., Venables, P. H., & Mednick, S. A. (2004). Malnutrition at age 3 years and externalizing behavior problems at ages 8, 11, and 17 years. *American Journal of Psychiatry, 161*, 2005–2013.

Ljungberg, T., Apicella, P., & Schultz, W. (1992). Responses of monkey dopamine neurons during learning of behavioral reactions. *Journal of Neurophysiology, 67*, 145–163.

Lledo, P. M., Gheusi, G., & Vincent, J. D. (2005). Information processing in the mammalian olfactory system. *Physiological Review, 85*, 281–317.

Locke, E. A., & Latham, G. P. (1990). *A theory of goal setting and task performance*. Englewood Cliffs, NJ: Prentice-Hall.

Lockwood, P., & Kunda, Z. (1997). Superstars and me: Predicting the impact of role models on the self. *Journal of Personality and Social Psychology, 73*, 91–103.

Loehlin, J. C., & Nichols, R. C. (1976). *Heredity, environment, and personality: A study of 850 sets of twins*. Austin: University of Texas Press.

Loewenstein, G. F., Weber, E. U., Hsee, C. K., & Welch, N. (2001). Risk as feelings. *Psychological Bulletin, 127*, 267–286.

Loftus, E. F. (1993). The reality of repressed memories. *American Psychologist, 48*, 518–537.

Loftus, E. F., & Palmer, J. C. (1974). Reconstruction of automobile destruction: An example of the interaction between language and memory. *Journal of Learning and Verbal Behavior, 13*, 585–589.

Loftus, E. F., Miller, D. G., & Burns, H. J. (1978). Semantic integration of verbal information into a visual memory. *Journal of Experimental Psychology: Human Learning and Memory, 4*, 19–31.

Logan, J. M., Sanders, A. L., Snyder, A. Z., Morris, J. C., & Buckner, R. L. (2002). Under-recruitment and nonselective recruitment: Dissociable neural mechanisms associated with aging. *Neuron, 33*, 1–20.

Loggia, M. L., Mogil, J. S., & Bushnell, M. C. (2008). Experimentally induced mood changes preferentially affect pain unpleasantness. *Journal of Pain, 9*, 784–791.

Loo, C. K., & Mitchell, P. B. (2005). A review of the efficacy of transcranial magnetic stimulation (TMS) treatment for depression, and current and future strategies to optimize efficacy. *Journal of Affective Disorders, 88*, 255–267.

Lovaas, O. I. (1987). Behavioral treatment and normal educational and intellectual functioning in young autistic children. *Journal of Consulting and Clinical Psychology, 55*, 3–9.

Lowe, P. (2001, October 12). No prison for Candace's adoptive mom. *Denver Rocky Mountain News*, p. 26A.

Lozano, A. M., Laxton, A. W., Tang-Wai, D. F., McAndrews, M. P., Zumsteg, D., et al. (2010). A phase I trial of deep brain stimulation of memory circuits in Alzheimer's disease. *Annals of Neurology 68*(4), 521–534.

Luauté, J. J., Maucort-Boulch, D. D., Tell, L. L., Quelard, F. F., Sarraf, T. T., Iwaz, J. J., Boisson, D., & Fischer, C. C. (2010). Long-term outcomes of chronic minimally conscious and vegetative states. *Neurology, 75*(3), 246–252. doi:10.1212/WNL.0b013e3181e8e8df

Lubinski, D. (2004). Introduction to the special section on cognitive abilities: 100 years after Spearman's (1904) "'General intelligence,' objectively determined and measured." *Journal of Personality and Social Psychology, 86*, 96–111.

Lubinski, D., & Benbow, C. P. (2000). States of excellence. *American Psychologist, 55*, 137–150.

Luchins, A. S. (1942). Mechanization in problem solving. *Psychological Monographs, 54*, Whole No. 248.

Luria, A. R. (1968). *The mind of a mnemonist*. New York: Avon.

Lykken, D. T. (1957). A study of anxiety in the sociopathic personality. *Journal of Abnormal Social Psychology, 55*, 6–10.

Lykken, D. T. (1995). *The antisocial personalities*. Hillsdale, NJ: Erlbaum.

Lykken, D. T. (2000). The causes and costs of crime and a controversial cure. *Journal of Personality, 68*(3), 560–605.

Lykken, D. T., McGue, M., Tellegen, A., & Bouchard, T. J., Jr. (1992). Emergenesis: Genetic traits that may not run in families. *American Psychologist, 47*, 1565–1577.

Lyubomirsky, S., & Nolen-Hoeksema, S. (1995). Effects of self-focused rumination on negative thinking and interpersonal problem solving. *Journal of Personality and Social Psychology, 69*, 176–190.

Lyubomirsky, S., King, L., & Diener, E. (2005). The benefits of frequent positive affect: Does happiness lead to success? *Psychological Bulletin, 131*, 803–855.

Maccoby, E. E., & Jacklin, C. N. (1974). *The psychology of sex differences*. Stanford, CA: Stanford University Press.

MacDonald, G., & Leary, M. R. (2005). Why does social exclusion hurt? The relationship between social and physical pain. *Psychological Bulletin, 131*, 202–223.

MacKay, D. G. (1973). Aspects of a theory of comprehension, memory and attention. *Quarterly Journal of Experimental Psychology, 25*, 22–40.

Macrae, C. N., Bodenhausen, G. V., & Calvini, G. (1999). Contexts of cryptomnesia: May the source be with you. *Social Cognition, 17*, 273–297.

Macrae, C. N., Moran, J. M., Heatherton, T. F., Banfield, J. F., & Kelley, W. M. (2004). Medial prefrontal activity predicts memory for self. *Cerebral Cortex, 14*, 647–654.

Madden, M., & Lenhart, A. (2006, Mar. 5). Online dating. *Pew Internet & American Life Project*. Retrieved from http://www.pewinternet.org/~/media//Files/Reports/2006/PIP_Online_Dating.pdf.pdf.

Maes, M., Van Gastel, A., Delmeire, L., Kenis, G., Bosmans, E., & Song, C. (2002). Platelet alpha2-adrenoceptor density in humans: Relationships to stress-induced anxiety, psychasthenic constitution, gender and stress-induced changes in the inflammatory response system. *Psychological Medicine, 32*, 919–928.

Magnier, M. (2008, May 26). China quake survivors show signs of post-traumatic stress. *Los Angeles Times*, p. 1.

Maguire, E. A., Spiers, H. J., Good, C. D., Hartley, T., Frackowiak, R. S. J., & Burgess, N. (2003). Navigation expertise and the human hippocampus: A structural brain imaging analysis. *Hippocampus, 13*, 250–259.

Maher, B.A., & Maher, W. R. (1994). Personality and psychopathology: A historical perspective. *Journal of Abnormal Psychology, 103*, 72–77.

Maia, T. V., Cooney, R. E., & Peterson, B. S. (2008). The neural bases of obsessive-compulsive disorder in children and adults. *Developmental Psychopathology, 20*, 1251–1283.

Maier, N. R. F. (1931). Reasoning in humans, II: The solution of a problem and its appearance in consciousness. *Journal of Comparative Psychology, 12*, 181–194.

Malle, B. F., Knobe, J., & Nelson, S. (2007). Actor-observer asymmetries in behavior explanations: New answers to an old question. *Journal of Personality and Social Psychology, 93*, 491–514.

Malle, B. F. (2006). The actor-observer asymmetry in causal attribution: A (surprising) meta-analysis. *Psychological Bulletin, 132*, 895–919.

Malone, D. A., Jr., Dougherty, D. D., Rezai, A. R., Carpenter, L. L., Friehs, G. M., Eskandar, E. N., et al. (2009). Deep brain stimulation of the ventral capsule/ventral striatum for treatment-resistant depression. *Biological Psychiatry, 65*, 267–275.

Maner, J. K., Luce, C. L., Neuberg, S. L., Cialdini, R. B., Brown, S., & Sagarin, B. J. (2002). The effects of perspective taking on motivations for helping: Still no evidence for altruism. *Personality and Social Psychology Bulletin, 28*, 1601–1610.

Manhart, K. (2004, December). The limits of multi-tasking. *Scientific American Mind*, 62–67.

Manning, R., Levine, M., & Collins, A. (2007). The Kitty Genovese murder and the social psychology of helping: The parable of the 38 witnesses. *American Psychologist, 62*, 555–562.

Mannuzza, S., Klein, R. G., Bonagura, N., Malloy, P., Giampino, T. L., & Addalli, K. A. (1991). Hyperactive boys almost grown up. Replications of psychiatric status. *Archives of General Psychiatry, 48*, 77–83.

Mannuzza, S., Klein, R. G., Truong, N. L., Moulton, J. L., III, Roizen, E. R., Howell, K. H., et al. (2008). Age of methylphenidate treatment initiation in children with ADHD and later substance abuse: Prospective follow-up into adulthood. *American Journal of Psychiatry, 165*, 604–609.

March, J. S., Silva, S., Petrycki, S., Curry, J., Wells, K., Fairbank, J., et al. (2007). The Treatment for Adolescents With Depression Study (TADS): Long-term effectiveness and safety outcomes. *Archives of General Psychiatry, 64*, 1132–1143.

Marcus, G. F. (1996). Why do children say "breaked"? *Current Directions in Psychological Science, 5*, 81–85.

Marcus, G. F. (2004). *The birth of the mind*. New York: Basic Books.

Marcus, G. F., Pinker, S., Ullman, M., Hollander, M., Rosen, T. S., & Xu, F. (1992). Overregularization in language acquisition. *Monographs of the Society for Research in Child Development, 57*(4, serial No. 228), 181.

Markon, J. (2001, October 8). Elderly judges handle 20 percent of U. S. caseload. *The Wall Street Journal*, p. A15.

Markowitz, J. C., & Weissman, M. M. (1995). Interpersonal psychotherapy. In E. E. Beckham & W. R. Leber (Eds.), *Handbook of depression* (2nd ed., pp. 376–390). New York: Guilford Press.

Markus, H. R. (1977). Self-schemata and processing information about the self. *Journal of Personality and Social Psychology, 35*, 63–78.

Markus, H. R., & Kitayama, S. (1991). Culture and the self: Implications for cognition, emotion, and motivation. *Psychological Review, 98*, 224–253.

Marlatt, G. A. (1999). Alcohol, the magic elixir? In S. Peele & M. Grant (Eds.), *Alcohol and pleasure: A health perspective* (pp. 233–248). Philadelphia: Brunner/Mazel.

Marsella, A. J., & Yamada, A. M (2007). Culture and psychopathology: Foundations, issues, directions. In S. Kitayama & D. Cohen (Eds.), *Handbook of cultural psychology* (pp. 797–819). New York: Guilford Press.

Marsh, A. A., Finger, E. C., Schechter, J. C., Jurkowitz, I. T. N., Reid, M. E., & Blair, R. J. R. (2011). Adolescents with psychopathic traits report reductions in physiological responses to fear. *Journal of Child Psychology & Psychiatry, 52*(8), 834–841.

Marshall, G. D. J., Agarwal, S. K., Lloyd, C., Cohen, L., Henninger, E. M., & Morris, G. J. (1998). Cytokine dysregulation associated with exam stress in healthy medical students. *Brain, Behavior, and Immunity, 12*, 297–307.

Marsland, A. L., Pressman, S., & Cohen, S. (2007). Positive affect and immune function. *Psychoneuroimmunology, 2*, 761–779.

Martin, L. A., Ashwood, P., Braunschweig, D., Cabanlit, M., Van de Water, J., & Amaral, D. G. (2008). Stereotypes and hyperactivity in rhesus monkeys exposed to IgG from mothers of children with autism. *Brain, Behavior, and Immunity, 22*, 804–805.

Martire, L. M., & Schulz, R. (2007). Involving family in psychosocial interventions for chronic illness. *Current Directions in Psychological Science, 16*, 90–94.

Maruta, T., Colligan, R. C., Malinchoc, M., & Offord, K. P. (2002). Optimism-pessimism assessed in the 1960s and self-reported health status 30 years later. *Mayo Clinic Proceedings, 77*, 748–753.

Maslow, A. (1968). *Toward a psychology of being*. New York: Van Nostrand.

Mather, M., & Carstensen, L. L. (2003). Aging and attentional biases for emotional faces. *Psychological Science, 14*, 409–415.

Mayberg, H. S., Lozano, A. M., Voon, V., McNeely, H. E., Seminowicz, D., Hamani, C., et al (2005). Deep brain stimulation for treatment-resistant depression. *Neuron, 45*, 651–660.

Mayhew, D. R., Brown, S. W., & Simpson, H. M. (2002). *The alcohol-crash problem in Canada: 1999*. Ottawa, Canada: Transport Canada.

Mazur, A., & Booth, A. (1998). Testosterone and dominance in men. *Behavioral and Brain Science, 21*, 353–397.

McAdams, D. P. (1999). Personal narratives and the life story. In L. A. Pervin & O. P. John (Eds.), *Handbook of personality: Theory and research* (2nd ed., pp. 478–500). New York: Guilford Press.

McAdams, D. P. (2001). The psychology of life stories. *Review of General Psychology, 5*, 100–122.

McCabe, D. P., Roediger, H. L., McDaniel, M. A., Balota, D. A., & Hambrick, D. Z. (2010). The relationship between working memory capacity and executive functioning: Evidence for a common executive attention construct. *Neuropsychology, 24*, 222–243.

McCarthy, G., Puce, A., Gore, J. C., & Allison, T. (1997). Face-specific processing in the human fusiform gyrus. *Journal of Cognitive Neuroscience, 9*, 605–610.

McClelland, D. C. (1987). *Human motivation*. New York: Cambridge University Press.

McClelland, D. C., Koestner, R., & Weinberger, J. (1989). How do self-attributed and implicit motives differ? *Psychological Review, 96*, 690–702.

McClintock, M. K. (1971). Menstrual synchrony and suppression. *Nature, 229*, 244–245.

McCrae, R. R., & Costa, P. T., Jr. (1990). *Personality in adulthood*. New York: Guilford Press.

McCrae, R. R., & Costa, P. T., Jr. (1999). A five-factor theory of personality. In L. A. Pervin & O. P. John (Eds.), *Handbook of personality: Theory and research* (2nd ed., pp. 139–153). New York: Guilford Press.

McCrae, R. R., Costa, P. T., Ostendorf, F., Angleitner, A., Hrebickova, M., Avia, M. D., et al. (2000). Nature over nurture: Temperament, personality, and life span development. *Journal of Personality and Social Psychology, 78*, 173–186.

McCullough, J. P. (2000). *Treatment for chronic depression: Cognitive behavioral analysis system of psychotherapy (CBASP)*. New York: Guilford Press.

McDaniel, M. A. (2005). Big-brained people are smarter: A meta-analysis of the relationship between in vivo brain volume and intelligence. *Intelligence, 33*, 337–346.

McDaniel, M. A., & Einstein, G. O. (2000). Strategic and automatic processes in prospective memory retrieval: A multiprocess framework. *Applied Cognitive Psychology, 14*, S127–S144.

McEwen, B. S. (2008). Central effects of stress hormones in health and disease: Understanding the protective and damaging effects of stress and stress mediators. *European Journal of Pharmacology, 583*, 174–185.

McEwen, B. S., & Gianaros, P. J. (2011). Stress- and allostatis-induced brain plasticity. *Annual Review of Medicine, 62*, 431–435.

McGlashan, T. H. (1988). A selective review of recent North American long-term follow-up studies of schizophrenia. *Schizophrenia Bulletin, 14*, 515–542.

McGough, J. J., & Barkley, R. A. (2004). Diagnostic controversies in adult attention deficit hyperactivity disorder. *American Journal of Psychiatry, 161*, 1948–1956.

McGrath, R.W. (2010). Prescriptive authority for psychologists. *Annual Review of Clinical Psychology, 6*, 21–47.

McGue, M., Bacon, S., & Lykken, D. T. (1993). Personality stability and change in early adulthood: A behavioral genetic analysis. *Developmental Psychology, 29*, 96–109.

McInnis, M. G., McMahon, F. J., Chase, G. A., Simpson, S. G., Ross, C. A., & DePaulo, J. R. (1993). Anticipation in bipolar affective disorder. *American Journal of Human Genetics, 53*, 385–390.

McKown, C., & Weinstein, R. S. (2008). Teacher expectations, classroom context, and the achievement gap. *Journal of School Psychology, 46*, 235–261.

McNeely, H. E., Mayberg, H. S., Lozano, A. M., & Kennedy, S. H. (2008). Neuropsychological impact of Cg25 deep brain stimulation for treatment-resistant depression: Preliminary results over 12 months. *The Journal of Nervous and Mental Disease, 196*, 405–410.

McNeil, D. G., Jr. (2006, November 23). For rare few, taste is in the ear of the beholder. *The New York Times*. Retrieved from http://www.nytimes.com

McPheeters, M. L., Warren, Z., Sathe, N., Bruzek, J., Krishnaswami, S., et al. (2011). A systematic review of medical treatments for children with autism spectrum disorders. *Pediatrics* (published online April 4).

Meddis, R. (1977). *The sleep instinct.* London: Routledge & Kegan Paul.

Mednick, S. A., Gabrielli, W. F., & Hutchings, B. (1987). Genetic factors in the etiology of criminal behavior. In S. A. Mednick, T. E. Moffitt, & S. A. Stacks (Eds.), *The causes of crime: New biological approaches* (pp. 267–291). New York: Cambridge University Press.

Mednick, S. A., Huttunen, M. O., & Machon, R. A. (1994). Prenatal influenza infections and adult schizophrenia. *Schizophrenia Bulletin, 20*, 263–267.

Medvec, V. H., Madey, S. F., & Gilovich, T. (1995). When less is more: Counterfactual thinking and satisfaction among Olympic medalists. *Journal of Personality and Social Psychology, 69*, 603–610.

Mehl, M. R., Gosling, S. D., & Pennebaker, J. W. (2006). Personality in its natural habitat: Manifestations and implicit folk theories of personality in daily life. *Journal of Personality and Social Psychology, 90*, 862–877.

Mehl, M. R., Pennebaker, J. W., Crow, M. D., Dabbs, J., & Price, J. H. (2001). The electronically activated recorder (EAR): A device for sampling naturalistic daily activities and conversations. *Behavior Research Methods, Instruments, and Computers, 33*, 517–523.

Mehl, M. R., Vazire, S., Holleran, S. E., & Clark, C. S. (2010). Eavesdropping on happiness: Well-being is related to having less small talk and more substantive conversations. *Psychological Science, 21*, 539–541.

Mehl, M. R., Vazire, S., Ramirez-Esparza, N., Slatcher, R. B., & Pennebaker, J. W. (2007). Are women really more talkative than men? *Science, 317*, 82.

Mehler, J., & Bever, T. G. (1967, October 6). Cognitive capacity of very young children. *Science, 158*, 141–142.

Mehta, P. H., & Beer, J. (2010). Neural mechanisms of the testosterone-aggression relation: The role of orbitofrontal cortex. *Journal of Cognitive Neuroscience, 22*, 2357–2368.

Mehta, P. H., Jones, A. C., & Josephs, R. A. (2008). The social endocrinology of dominance: Basal testosterone predicts cortisol changes and behavior following victory and defeat. *Journal of Personality and Social Psychology, 94*, 1078–1093.

Mehu, M., & Dunbar, R. M. (2008). Naturalistic observations of smiling and laughter in human group interactions. *Behaviour, 145*(12), 1747–1780. doi:10.1163/156853908786279619

Melzack, R., & Wall, P. D. (1965). Pain mechanisms: A new theory. *Science, 150*, 971–979.

Melzack, R., & Wall, P. D. (1982). *The challenge of pain.* New York: Basic Books.

Mendez, I., Viñuela, A., Astradsson, A., Mukhida, K., Hallett, P., Robertson, H., et al. (2008). Dopamine neurons implanted into people with Parkinson's disease survive without pathology for 14 years. *Nature Medicine, 14*, 507–509.

Mennella, J. A., Jagnow, C. P., & Beauchamp, G. K. (2001). Prenatal and postnatal flavor learning by human infants. *Pediatrics, 107*, e88.

Mercer, K. B., Orcutt, H. K., Quinn, J. F., Fitzgerald, C. A., Conneely, K. N., Barfield, R. T., Gillespie, C. F., & Ressler, K. J. (2011). Acute and posttraumatic stress symptoms in a prospective gene x environment study of a university campus shooting. *Archives of General Psychiatry,* doi:10.1001/archgenpsychiatry.2011.109, e-pub ahead of print.

Merikangas, K. R., Burstein, M., Swanson, S. A., Avenevoli, S., Cui, L., Benjet, C., et al. (2010). Lifetime prevalence of mental disorders in U.S. adolescents: Results from the national comorbidity survey replication-adolescent supplement (NCS-A). *Journal of the American Academy of Child and Adolescent Psychiatry, 49*, 980–989.

Merikangas, K., He, J., Burstein, M., Swendsen, J., Avenevoli, S., Case, B., et al. (2011). Service utilization for lifetime mental disorders in U.S. adolescents: Results of the National comorbidity survey–adolescent supplement (NCS-A). *Journal of the American Academy of Child and Adolescent Psychiatry, 50*, 32–45.

Messias, E., Kirkpatrick, B., Bromet, E., Ross, D., Buchanan, R. W., Carpenter, W. T., Jr., et al. (2004). Summer birth and deficit schizophrenia: A pooled analysis from 6 countries. *Archives of General Psychiatry, 61*, 985–989.

Meston, C. M., & Frohlich, P. F. (2000). The neurobiology of sexual function. *Archives of General Psychiatry, 57*, 1012–1030.

Metcalfe, J., & Mischel, W. (1999). A hot/cool-system analysis of delay of gratification: Dynamics of willpower. *Psychological Review, 106*, 3–19.

Mezulis, A. H., Abramson, L. Y., Hyde, J. S., & Hankin, B. L. (2004). Is there a universal positivity bias in attributions? A meta-analytic review of individual, developmental, and culture differences in the self-serving attributional bias. *Psychological Bulletin, 130*, 711–747.

Mickelson, K. D., Kessler, R. C., & Shaver, P. R. (1997). Adult attachment in a nationally representative sample. *Journal of Personality and Social Psychology, 73*, 1092–1106.

Milgram, S. (1974). *Obedience to authority: An experimental view.* New York: Harper & Row.

Mill, J. S. (1843). *A system of logic, ratiocinative and inductive: Being a connected view of the principles of evidence and the methods of scientific investigation.* London: John W. Parker.

Miller, G. (2005, July 1). How are memories stored and retrieved? *Science, 309*, 92–93.

Miller, G. E., Freedland, K. E., Carney, R. M., Stetler, C. A., & Banks, W. A. (2003). Cynical hostility, depressive symptoms, and the expression of inflammatory risk markers for coronary heart disease. *Journal of Behavioral Medicine, 26*, 501–515.

Miller, I. W., Norman, W. H., & Keitner, G. I. (1989). Cognitive-behavioral treatment of depressed inpatients: Six- and twelve-month follow-up. *American Journal of Psychiatry, 146*, 1274–1279.

Miller, L. C., & Fishkin, S. A. (1997). On the dynamics of human bonding and reproductive success: Seeking windows on the adapted-for human-environmental interface. In J. Simpson & D. T. Kenrick (Eds.), *Evolutionary social psychology* (pp. 197–236). Mahwah, NJ: Erlbaum.

Miller, R. S. (1996). *Embarrassment: Poise and peril in everyday life.* New York: Guilford Press.

Miller, R. S. (1997). We always hurt the ones we love: Aversive interactions in close relationships. In R. M. Kowalski (Ed.), *Aversive interpersonal behaviors* (pp. 11–29). New York: Plenum Press.

Miller, W. T. (2000). Rediscovering fire: Small interventions, large effects. *Psychology of Addictive Behaviors, 14*, 6–18.

Milton, J., & Wiseman, R. (2001). Does psi exist? Reply to Storm and Ertel (2001). *Psychological Bulletin, 127*, 434–438.

Mineka, S., Davidson, M., Cook, M., & Keir, R. (1984). Observational conditioning of snake fear in rhesus monkeys. *Journal of Abnormal Psychology, 93*, 355–372.

Miniño, A. M. (2010). Mortality among teenagers aged 12–19 years: United States, 1999–2006. NCHS Data Brief, No. 37. U.S. Department of Health and Human Services.

Minshew, N. J., & Keller, T.A. (2010). The nature of brain dysfunction in autism: Functional brain imaging studies. *Current Opinions in Neurology, 23*, 124–130.

Minshew, N. J., & Williams, D. L. (2007). The new neurobiology of autism: Cortex, connectivity, and neuronal organization. *Archives of Neurology, 64*, 945–950.

Mischel, W., & Shoda, Y. (1995). A cognitive-affective system theory of personality: Reconceptualizing situations, dispositions, dynamics, and invariance in personality structure. *Psychological Review, 102*, 246–268.

Mischel, W., Shoda, Y., & Rodriguez, M. L. (1989, May 26). Delay of gratification in children. *Science, 244*, 933–938.

Mitelman, S. A., Shihabuddin, L., Brickman, A. M., Hazlett, E. A., & Buchsbaum, M. S. (2005). Volume of the cingulate and outcome in schizophrenia. *Schizophrenia Research, 72*, 91–108.

Mittal, V. A., Neumann, C., Saczawa, M., & Walker, E. F. (2008). Longitudinal progression of movement abnormalities in relation to psychotic symptoms in adolescents at high risk of schizophrenia. *Archives of General Psychiatry, 65*, 165–171.

Miyake, K. (1993). Temperament, mother-child interaction, and early development. *The Japanese Journal of Research on Emotions, 1*, 48–55.

Miyamoto, Y., & Kitayama, S. (2002). Cultural variation in correspondence bias: The critical role of attitude diagnosticity of socially constrained behavior. *Journal of Personality and Social Psychology, 83*, 1239–1248.

Mobbs, D., Greicius, M. D., Abdel-Azim, E., Menon, V., & Reiss, A. L. (2003). Humor modulates the mesolimbic reward centers. *Neuron, 40*, 1041–1048.

Moeller, S. J., & Crocker, J. (2009). Drinking and desired self-images: Path models of self-image goals, coping motives, heavy-episodic drinking, and alcohol problems. *Psychology of Addictive Behaviors, 23*(2), 334–340. doi:10.1037/a0015913

Moffitt, T. E., Arseneault, L., Belsky, D., Dickson, N., Hancox, R. J., Harrington, H., et al. (2011). A gradient of childhood self-control predicts health, wealth, and public safety. *Proceedings of the National Academy of Sciences*. Advanced publication: www.pnas.org/cgi/doi/10.1073/pnas.1010076108

Moffitt, T. E., Brammer, G. L., Caspi, A., Fawcett, J. P., Raleigh, M., Yuwiler, A., et al. (1998). Whole blood serotonin relates to violence in an epidemiological study. *Biological Psychiatry, 43*, 446–457.

Moises, H. W., & Gottesman, I. I. (2004). Does glial asthenia predispose to schizophrenia? *Archives of General Psychiatry, 61*, 1170.

Moll, J., & de Oliveira-Souza, R. (2007). Moral judgments, emotions and the utilitarian brain. *Trends in Cognitive Sciences, 11*, 319–321, ISSN 1364-6613. doi: 10.1016/j.tics.2007.06.001

Monroe, S. M., & Simons, A. D. (1991). Diathesis-stress theories in the context of life-stress research: Implications for depressive disorders. *Psychological Bulletin, 110*, 406–425.

Monteith, M. J. (1993). Self-regulation of prejudiced responses: Implications for progress in prejudice reduction efforts. *Journal of Personality and Social Psychology, 65*, 469–485.

Monteith, M. J., Ashburn-Nardo, L., Voils, C. I., & Czopp, A. M. (2002). Putting the brakes on prejudice: On the development and operation of cues for control. *Journal of Personality and Social Psychology, 83*, 1029–1050.

Montepare, J. M., & Vega, C. (1988). Women's vocal reactions to intimate and casual male friends. *Personality and Social Psychology Bulletin, 14*, 103–113.

Montgomery, G. H., DuHamel, K. N., & Redd, W. H. (2000). A meta-analysis of hypnotically induced analgesia: How effective is hypnosis? *International Journal of Clinical and Experimental Hypnosis, 48*, 138–153.

Monti, M. M., Vanhaudenhuyse, A., Coleman, M. R., Boly, M., Pickard, J. D., Tshibanda, L., et al. (2010). Willful modulation of brain activity in disorders of consciousness. *New England Journal of Medicine, 362*, 579–589.

Morgan, R. K. (n.d.) *Information for majors*. Retrieved April 23, 2008, from http://homepages.ius.edu/RMORGAN

Morin, C. M., Vallières, A., Guay, B., Ivers, H., Savard, J., Mérette, C., et al. (2009). Cognitive behavioral therapy, singly and combined with medication, for persistent insomnia: A randomized controlled trial. *Journal of the American Medical Association, 301*, 2005–2015.

Morr Serewicz, M., & Gale, E. (2008). First-date scripts: Gender roles, context, and relationship. *Sex Roles, 58*(3–4), 149–164. doi:10.1007/s11199-007-9283-4

Morris, N. M., Udry, J. R., Khan-Dawood, F., & Dawood, M. Y. (1987). Marital sex frequency and midcycle female testosterone. *Archives of Sexual Behavior, 16*, 27–37.

Morrison, A. B., & Chein, J. M. (2011). Does working memory training work? The promise and challenges of enhancing cognition by training working memory. *Psychonomic Bulletin Review, 18*, 46–60.

Morrison, M. (n.d.) *Sports superstitions*. Retrieved November 11, 2008, from http://www.infoplease.com/spot/superstitions1.html

Mortensen, E. L., & Hogh, P. (2001). A gender difference in the association between APOE genotype and age-related cognitive decline. *Neurology, 57*, 89–95.

Mortensen, E. L., Michaelsen, K. F., Sanders, S. A., & Reinisch, J. M. (2002). The association between duration of breastfeeding and adult intelligence. *Journal of the American Medical Association, 287*, 2365–2371.

Morton, J., & Johnson, M. H. (1991). CONSPEC and CONLERN: A two-process theory of infant face recognition. *Psychological Review, 98*, 164–181.

Moscovitch, M. (1995). Confabulation. In D. L. Schacter (Ed.), *Memory distortions: How minds, brains, and societies reconstruct the past* (pp. 226–251). Cambridge, MA: Harvard University Press.

Moskowitz, A. K. (2004). "Scared stiff": Catatonia as an evolutionary-based fear response. *Psychological Bulletin, 111*, 984–1002.

Moskowitz, H., & Fiorentino, D. A. (2000). *Review of the literature on the effects of low doses of alcohol on driving-related skills*. Washington, DC: National Highway Traffic Safety Administration.

Mowery, P. D., Brick, P. D., & Farrelly, M. (2000). Pathways to established smoking: Results from the 1999 national youth tobacco survey (Legacy First Look Report No. 3). Washington, DC: American Legacy Foundation.

Mroczek, D. K., & Kolarz, C. M.(1998). The effect of age on positive and negative affect: A developmental perspective on happiness. *Journal of Personality and Social Psychology, 75*, 1333–1349.

Mufson, L., Dorta, K. P., Wickramaratne, P., Nomura, Y., Olfson, M., & Weissman, M. M. (2004). A randomized effectiveness trial of interpersonal psychotherapy for depressed adolescents. *Archives of General Psychiatry, 61*, 577–584.

Muhle, R., Trentacoste, S. V., & Rapin, I. (2004). The genetics of autism. *Pediatrics, 113*, 472–486.

Mukherjee, R. A. S., Hollins, S., Abou-Saleh, M. T., & Turk, J. (2005). Low levels of alcohol consumption and the fetus. *British Medical Journal, 330*(7488), 375–385.

Mulder, J., Ter Bogt, T. F. M., Raiijmakers, Q. A. W., Nic Gabhainn, S., et al. (2009). The soundtrack of substance abuse: Music preference and adolescent smoking and drinking. *Substance Use & Misuse 44*(4), 514–531.

Mumford, D. B., Saeed, K., Ahmad, I., Latif, S., & Mubbashar, M. H. (1997). Stress and psychiatric disorder in rural Punjab: A community survey. *British Journal of Psychiatry, 170*, 473–478.

Munson, J. A., McMahon, R. J., & Spieker, S. J. (2001). Structure and variability in the developmental trajectory of children's externalizing problems: Impact of infant attachment, maternal depressive symptomatology, and child sex. *Development and Psychopathology, 13*, 277–296.

Murata, M. (2000). Secular trends in growth and changes in eating patterns of Japanese children. *American Journal of Clinical Nutrition, 72*, 1379–1383.

Murray, H. A. (1943.) *Analysis of the Personality of Adolph Hitler: With Predictions of his Future Behavior and Suggestions for Dealing with Him Now and After Germany's Surrender.* Washington, DC: OSS Archives.

Murray, S. L., Holmes, J. G., & Griffin, D. W. (1996). The benefits of positive illusions: Idealization and the construction of satisfaction in close relationships. *Journal of Personality and Social Psychology, 70*, 79–98.

Mustanski, B. S., Chivers, M. L., & Bailey, J. M. (2002). A critical review of recent biological research on human sexual orientation. *Annual Review of Sex Research, 13*, 89–140.

Myers, D. G. (2000). The funds, friends, and faith of happy people. *American Psychologist, 55*, 56–67.

Myers, D. G., & Lamm, H. (1976). The group polarization phenomenon. *Psychological Bulletin, 83*, 602–627.

Nader, K., & Einarsson, E. O. (2010). Memory reconsolidation: An update. *Annals of the New York Academy of Sciences, 1191*(1), 27–41.

Nader, K., Schafe, G. E., & Le Doux, J. E. (2000). Fear memories require protein synthesis in the amygdala for reconsolidation after retrieval. *Nature, 406*, 722–726.

Nakano, K., & Kitamura, T. (2001). The relation of the anger subcomponent of type A behavior to psychological symptoms in Japanese and foreign students. *Japanese Psychological Research, 43*(1), 50–54.

Ziv, N., & Goshen, M. (2006). The effect of 'sad' and 'happy' background music on the interpretation of a story in 5- to 6-year-old children. *British Journal of Music Education 23*, 303–314.

Naqvi, N. H., Rudrauf, D., Damasio, H., & Bechara, A. (2007, January 27). Damage to the insula disrupts addiction to cigarette smoking. *Science, 315*, 531–534.

Nash, M., & Barnier, A. (2008). *The Oxford handbook of hypnosis.* New York: Oxford University Press.

Nassar, N., Dixon, G., Bourke, J., Bower, C., Glasson, E., de Klerk, N., et al. (2009). Autism spectrum disorders in young children: Effect of changes in diagnostic practices. *International Journal of Epidemiology, 38*, 1245–1254.

National Center for Learning Disabilities (2009). *LD at a glance.* Retrieved from http://www.ncld.org/ld-basics/ld-explained/basic-facts/learning-disabilities-at-a-glance

National Highway Traffic Safety Administration. (2009). An examination of driver distraction as recorded in NHSTA databases. DOT HS 811216. September 2009. Retrieved from http://www-nrd.nhtsa.dot.gov/pubs/811216.pdf

National Human Genome Research Institute. (n.d.). *Learning about sickle cell disease.* Retrieved October 12, 2007, from http://www.genome.gov/10001219

National Institute of Drug Abuse. (2006). *NIDA Research Report: Methamphetamine Abuse and Addiction.* (NIH Publication No. 06–4210). Retrieved from http://www.nida.nih.gov/ResearchReports/methamph/methamph.html

National Institute of Drug Abuse. (2010). *MDMA (Ecstasy)* [Fact sheet]. Retrieved from http://teens.drugabuse.gov/facts/facts_xtc1.php

National Research Council, Committee on Educational Interventions for Children with Autism. (2001). *Educating young children with autism.* Washington, DC: National Academy Press.

Neimeyer, R. A., & Mitchell, K. A. (1988). Similarity and attraction: A longitudinal study. *Journal of Social and Personal Relationships, 5*, 131–148.

Neisser, U. (1967). *Cognitive psychology.* New York: Appleton-Century-Crofts.

Neisser, U., Boodoo, G., Bouchard, T. J., Jr., Boykin, A. W., Brody, N., Ceci, S. J., et al. (1996). Intelligence: Knowns and unknowns. *American Psychologist, 51*, 77–101.

Neisser, U., & Harsch, N. (1993). Phantom flashbulbs: False recollections of hearing the news about Challenger. In E. Winograd & U. Neisser (Eds.), *Affect and accuracy in recall: Studies of "flashbulb" memories* (pp. 9–31). New York: Cambridge University Press.

Nelson, G. (1998, April 29). The observatory: You don't have to be a rocket scientist to think like one. *Minneapolis Star Tribune*, p. 14.

Nelson, R. M., & DeBacker, T. K. (2008). Achievement motivation in adolescents: The role of peer climate and best friends. *Journal of Experimental Education, 76*(2), 170–189.

Newman, M. G., Szkodny, L., Llera, S. J., & Przeworski, A. (2011). A review of technology assisted self-help and minimal contact therapies for drug and alcohol abuse and smoking addiction: Is human contact necessary for therapeutic efficacy? *Clinical Psychology Review, 31*(1), 178–186.

Ng, D. M., & Jeffrey, E. W. (2003). Relationships between perceived stress and health behaviors in a sample of working adults. *Health Psychology, 22*, 638–642.

Nicolini, H., Bakish, D., Duenas, H., Spann, M., Erickson, J., Hallberg, C., et al. (2008). Improvement of psychic and somatic symptoms in adult patients with generalized anxiety disorder: Examination from a duloxetine, venlafaxine extended-release and placebo-controlled trial. *Psychological Medicine, 19*, 1–10.

Nisbett, R. E., Peng, K., Choi, I., & Norenzayan, A. (2001). Culture and systems of thought: Holistic versus analytic cognition. *Psychological Review, 108*, 291–310.

Nisbett, R. E., & Ross, L. (1980). *Human inferences: Strategies and shortcomings of social judgment.* Englewood Cliffs, NJ: Prentice-Hall.

Nisbett, R. E., & Wilson, T. D. (1977). Telling more than we can know: Verbal reports on mental processes. *Psychological Review, 84*, 231–259.

Nishino, S. (2007). Narcolepsy: Pathophysiology and pharmacology. *Journal of Clinical Psychiatry, 68*(Suppl. 13), 9–15.

Noftle, E. E., & Robins, R. W. (2007). Personality predictors of academic outcomes: Big five correlates of GPA and SAT scores. *Journal of Personality and Social Psychology, 93*, 116–130.

Norem, J. K. (1989). Cognitive strategies as personality: Effectiveness, specificity, flexibility and change. In D. M. Buss & N. Cantor (Eds.), *Personality psychology: Recent trends and emerging issues* (pp. 45–60). New York: Springer-Verlag.

Norman, K. A., Polyn, S. M., Detre, G. J., & Haxby, J. V. (2006). Beyond mind-reading: Multi-voxel pattern analysis of fMRI data. *Trends in Cognitive Sciences, 10*, 424–423.

Norton, M. I., Frost, J. A., & Ariely, D. (2007). Less is more: The lure of ambiguity, or why familiarity breeds contempt. *Journal of Personality and Social Psychology, 92*, 97–106.

Nosek, B. A., Hawkins, C. B., & Frazier, R. S. (2011). Implicit social cognition: From measures to mechanisms. *Trends in Cognitive Sciences, 15*, 152–159.

Novotny, S. L., Hollander, E., Allen, A., Aronowitz, B. R., DeCaria, C., Cartwright, C., et al. (2000). Behavioral response to oxytocin challenge in adult autistic disorders. *Biological Psychiatry, 47*, 52.

Noyes, R. (1991). Suicide and panic disorder: A review. *Journal of Affective Disorders, 22*, 1–11.

Nurnberger, J. J., Goldin, L. R., & Gershon, E. S. (1994). Genetics of psychiatric disorders. In G. Winokur & P. M. Clayton (Eds.), *The medical basis of psychiatry* (pp. 459–492). Philadelphia: Saunders.

O'Kane, G. O., Kensinger, E. A., & Corkin, S. (2004). Evidence for semantic learning in profound amnesia: An investigation with the patient H. M. *Hippocampus, 14*, 417–425.

O'Leary, S. G. (1995). Parental discipline mistakes. *Current Directions in Psychological Science, 4*, 11–13.

O'Neal, J. M. (1984). First person account: Finding myself and loving it. *Schizophrenia Bulletin, 10*, 109–110.

O'Neil, J. (2004, December 29). Slow-motion miracle: One boy's journey out of autism's grasp. *The New York Times*, p. B8.

O'Neil, S. (1999). Flow theory and the development of musical performance skills. *Bulletin of the Council for Research in Music Education, 141*, 129–134.

O'Toole, A. J., Jiang, F., Abdi, H., & Haxby, J. V. (2005). Partially distributed representations of objects and faces in ventral temporal cortex. *Journal of Cognitive Neuroscience, 17*, 580–590.

Oberauer, K., Schulze, R., Wilhelm, O., & Süß, H. M. (2005). Working memory and intelligence—Their correlation and their relation: Comment on Ackerman, Beier, and Boyle (2005). *Psychological Bulletin, 131*, 61–65.

Obot, I. S., & Room, R. (2005). *Alcohol, gender and drinking problems: Perspectives from low and middle income countries.* Geneva, Switzerland: World Health Organization.

Ochsner, K. N., Bunge, S. A., Gross, J. J., & Gabrieli, J. D. E. (2002). Rethinking feelings: An fMRI study of the cognitive regulation of emotion. *Journal of Cognitive Neuroscience, 14*, 1215–1299.

Oei, N. Y. L., Everaerd, W. T. A. M., Elzinga, B. M., Van Well, S., & Bermond, B. (2006). Psychosocial stress impairs working memory at high loads: An association with cortisol levels and memory retrieval. *Stress, 9*, 133–141.

Ogbu, J. U. (1994). From cultural differences to differences in cultural frames of reference. In P. M. Greenfield & R. R. Cocking (Eds.), *Cross cultural roots of minority child development* (pp. 365–392). Hillsdale, NJ: Erlbaum.

Ogden, C. L., & Carroll, M. (2010). Prevalence of overweight, obesity, and extreme obesity among adults: United States, trends 1976–1980 through 2007–2008. A report of the National Center for Health Statistics. http://www.cdc.gov/NCHS/data/hestat/obesity_adult_07_08/obesity_adult_07_08.pdf/

Ogletree, S. M., Turner, G., Vieira, A., & Brunotte, J. (2005). College living: Issues related to housecleaning attitudes. *College Student Journal, 39*(4), 729–733.

Olanow, C. W., Goetz, C. G., Kordower, J. H., Stoessl, A. J., Sossi, V., Brin, M. F., et al. (2003). A double-blind controlled trial of bilateral fetal nigral transplantation in Parkinson's disease. *Annals of Neurology, 54*, 403–414.

Olds, J. (1962). Hypothalamic substrates of reward. *Psychological Review, 42*, 554–604.

Olds, J., & Milner, P. (1954). Positive reinforcement produced by electrical stimulation of the septal area and other regions of the rat brain. *Journal of Comparative and Physiological Psychology, 47*, 419–428.

Olfson, M., Marcus, S. C., Druss, B., Elinson, L., Tanielian, T., & Pincus, H. A. (2002). National trends in the outpatient treatment of depression. *Journal of the American Medical Association, 287*, 203–209.

Olfson, M., Shaffer, D., Marcus, S. C., & Greenberg, T. (2003). Relationship between antidepressant medication treatment and suicide in adolescents. *Archives of General Psychiatry, 60*, 978–982.

Olshansky, S. J., Passaro, D. J., Hershow, R. C., Layden, J. C., Bruce, A., Brody, J., .& Ludwig, D. S. (2005). A potential decline in life expectancy in the United States in the 21st century. *Journal of Obstetrical & Gynecological Survey, 60*, 450–452.

Olson, J. M., Vernon, P. A., Harris, J. A., & Jang, K. L. (2001). The heritability of attitudes: A study of twins. *Journal of Personality and Social Psychology, 80*, 845–860.

Olson, R., Hogan, L., & Santos, L. (2006). Illuminating the history of psychology: Tips for teaching students about the Hawthorne studies. *Psychology Learning and Teaching, 5*, 110–118.

Olsson, A., Ebert, J. P., Banaji, M. R., & Phelps, E. A. (2005, July 29). The role of social groups in the persistence of learned fear. *Science, 309*, 785–787.

Olsson, A., Nearing, K. I., & Phelps, E. A. (2007). Learning fears by observing others: The neural systems of social fear transmission. *Social Cognitive and Affective Neuroscience Advance Access, 2*, 3–11.

Olsson, A., & Phelps, E. A. (2007). Social learning of fear. *Nature Neuroscience, 10*, 1095–1102.

Oltmanns, T. F., Martin, M. T., Neale, J. M., & Davison, G. C. (2009). *Case studies in abnormal psychology*. Hoboken, NJ: Wiley.

Onishi, K. H., & Baillargeon, R. (2005, April 8). Do 15-month-old infants understand false beliefs? *Science, 308*, 255–258.

Ortigue, S., Bianchi-Demicheli, F., Hamilton, C., & Grafton, S. T. (2007, July). The neural basis of love as a subliminal prime: An event-related functional magnetic resonance imaging study. *Journal of Cognitive Neuroscience, 19*(7), 1218–1230.

Osterling, J., & Dawson, G. (1994). Early recognition of children with autism: A study of first birthday home videotapes. *Journal of Autism and Developmental Disorders, 24*, 247–257.

Ottieger, A. E., Tressell, P. A., Inciardi, J. A., & Rosales, T. A. (1992). Cocaine use patterns and overdose. *Journal of Psychoactive Drugs, 24*, 399–410.

Owen, A. M., Coleman, M. R., Boly, M., Davis, M. H., Laureys, S., & Pickard, J. D. (2006). Detecting awareness in the vegetative state. *Science, 313*, 1402.

Owen, A. M., Hampshire, A., Grahn, J. A., Stenton, R., Dajani, S., Burns, A. S., Howard, R. J., & Ballard, C. G. (2010). Putting brain training to the test. *Nature, 465*(7299), 775–778 doi:10.1038/nature09042

Pack, A.I., & Pien, G.W. (2011). Update on sleep and its disorders. *Annual Review of Medicine, 62*, 447–460.

Padberg, F., & George, M. S. (2009). Repetitive transcranial magnetic stimulation of the prefrontal cortex in depression. *Experimental Neurology, 219*, 2–13.

Pagnoni, G., & Cekic, M. (2007). Age effects on gray matter volume and attentional performance in Zen meditation. *Neurobiology of Aging, 28*, 1623–1627.

Panksepp, J. (1992). Oxytocin effects on emotional processes: Separation distress, social bonding, and relationships to psychiatric disorders. *Annals of the New York Academy of Sciences, 652*, 243–252.

Papadimitriou, G. N., Zervas, I. M., & Papakostas, Y. G. (2001). Unilateral ECT for prophylaxis in affective illness. *Journal of ECT, 17*, 229–231.

Paquette, V., Levesque, J., Mensour, B., Leroux, J. M., Beaudoin, G., Bourgouin, P., et al. (2003). "Change the mind and you change the brain": Effects of cognitive-behavioral therapy on the neural correlates of spider phobia. *Neuroimage, 18*, 401–409.

Pascual-Leone, A., Catala, M. D., & Pascual-Leone, P. A. (1996). Lateralized effect of rapid-rate transcranial magnetic stimulation of the prefrontal cortex on mood. *Neurology, 46*, 499–502.

Pasupathi, M., & Carstensen, L. L. (2003). Age and emotional experience during mutual reminiscing. *Psychology and Aging, 18*, 430–442.

Patterson, B. W. (2004). The "tyranny of the eyewitness." *Law & Psychology Review, 28*, 195–203.

Patterson, C. M., & Newman, J. P. (1993). Reflectivity and learning from aversive events: Toward a psychological mechanism for the syndromes of disinhibition. *Psychological Review, 100*, 716–736.

Patterson, D., & Jensen, M. (2003). Hypnosis and clinical pain. *Psychological Bulletin, 129*(4), 495–521.

Paul-Labrador, M., Polk, D., Dwyer, J. H., Velasquez, I., Nidich, S., Rainforth, M., et al. (2006). Effects of a randomized controlled trial of transcendental meditation on components of the metabolic syndrome in subjects with coronary heart disease. *Archives of Internal Medicine, 166*, 1218–1224.

Pauls, D. L. (2008). The genetics of obsessive compulsive disorder: A review of the evidence. *American Journal of Medical Genetics, 148C*, 133–139.

Paunonen, S. V., & Ashton, M. C. (2001). Big five factors and facets and the prediction of behavior. *Journal of Personality and Social Psychology, 81*, 524–539.

Pavlov, I. P. (1927). *Conditioned reflexes: An investigation of the physiological activity of the cerebral cortex.* (Translated and edited by G. V. Anrep.) London: Oxford University Press; Humphrey Milford.

Pavot, W., & Diener, E. (1993). Review of the satisfaction with life scale. *Psychological Assessment, 5*, 164–172.

Paykel, E. S. (2003). Life events and affective disorders. *Acta Psychiatrica Scandinavica, 108*, 61–66.

Payne, B. K. (2001). Prejudice and perception: The role of automatic and controlled processes in misperceiving a weapon. *Journal of Personality and Social Psychology, 81*, 181–192.

Payne, B. K., Krosnick, J. A., Pasek, J., Lelkes, Y., Akhtar, O., & Tompson, T. (2010) Implicit and explicit prejudice in the 2008 American presidential election. *Journal of Experimental Social Psychology, 46*, 367–374.

Paz-Elizur, T., Krupsky, M., Blumenstein, S., Elinger, D., Schechtman, E., & Livneh, Z. (2003). DNA repair activity for oxidative damage and risk of lung cancer. *Journal of the National Cancer Institute, 95*, 1312–1331.

Pegna, A. J., Khateb, A., Lazeyras, F., & Seghier, M. L. (2005). Discriminating emotional faces without primary visual cortices involves the right amygdala. *Nature Neuroscience, 8*, 24–25.

Pelham, W. E., McBurnett, K., Harper, G. W., Milich, R., Murphy, D. A., Clinton, J., et al. (1990). Methylphenidate and baseball playing in ADHD children: Who's on first? *Journal of Consulting and Clinical Psychology, 58*, 130–133.

Penacoli, J. (2011). "Extra's" Jerry Penacoli to Michael Douglas: Your story inspired me. Retrieved from http://extratv.warnerbros.com/2011/01/extras_jerry_penacoli_to_michael_douglas_your_story_inspired_me.php

Penfield, W., & Jasper, H. (1954). *Epilepsy and the functional anatomy of the human brain.* Boston: Little, Brown.

Pennebaker, J. W. (1990). *Opening up: The healing power of confiding in others.* New York: Morrow.

Pennebaker, J. W. (1995). *Emotion, disclosure, & health.* Washington, DC: American Psychological Association.

Pennebaker, J. W., Barger, S. D., & Tiebout, J. (1989). Disclosure of traumas and health among Holocaust survivors. *Psychosomatic Medicine, 51*(5), 577–589.

Pennebaker, J. W., & Beall, S. K. (1986). Confronting a traumatic event: Toward an understanding of inhibition and disease. *Journal of Abnormal Psychology, 95*, 274–281.

Pennebaker, J. W., Mayne, T. J., & Francis, M. E. (1997). Linguistic predictors of adaptive bereavement. *Journal of Personality and Social Psychology, 72*, 863–871.

Pennisi, E. (2007, December 21). Breakthrough of the year. Human genetic variation. *Science, 318*, 1842–1843.

Penton-Voak, I. S., Perrett, D. I., Castles, D., Burt, M., Koyabashi, T., & Murray, L. K. (1999). Female preference for male faces changes cyclically. *Nature, 399*, 741–742.

Peretz, I. (1996). Can we lose memory for music? A case of music agnosia in a nonmusician. *Journal of Cognitive Neuroscience, 8*, 481–496.

Peretz, I., & Zatorre, R. J. (2005). Brain organization for music processing. *Annual Review of Psychology, 56*, 89–114.

Perez-Stable, E. J., Marin, G., & Marin, B. V. (1994). Behavioral risk factors: Comparison of Latinos and non-Latino whites in San Francisco. *American Journal of Public Health, 84*, 971–976.

Perkins, W. J. (2007, February/March). How does anesthesia work? *Scientific American Mind*, 84.

Perrett, D. I., May, K. A., & Yoshikawa, S. (1994). Facial shape and judgments of female attractiveness. *Nature, 368*, 239–242.

Perry, B. D. (2002). Childhood experience and the expression of genetic potential: What childhood neglect tells us about nature and nurture. *Brain and Mind, 3*, 79–100.

Pessiglione, M., Schmidt, L., Draganski, B., Kalisch, R., Lau, H., Dolan, R. J., et al. (2007, May 11). How the brain translates money into force: A neuroimaging study of subliminal motivation. *Science, 316*, 904–906.

Petitto, L. A. (2000). On the biological foundations of human language. In H. Lane & K. Emmorey (Eds.), *The signs of language revisited* (pp. 447–471). Mahwah, NJ: Erlbaum.

Petitto, L. A., & Seidenberg, M. S. (1979). On the evidence for linguistic abilities in signing apes. *Brain and Language, 8*, 162–183.

Petrie, K. J., Fontanilla, I., Thomas, M. G., Booth, R. J., & Pennebaker, J. W. (2004). Effect of written emotional expression on immune function in patients with human immunodeficiency virus infection: A randomized trial. *Psychosomatic Medicine, 66*, 272–275.

Petronis, A., & Kennedy, J. L. (1995). Unstable genes—Unstable mind? *American Journal of Psychiatry, 152*, 164–172.

Petty, R. E., & Cacioppo, J. T. (1986). *Communication and persuasion: Central and peripheral routes to attitude change.* New York: Springer-Verlag.

Petty, R. E., & Wegener, D. T. (1998). Attitude change: Multiple roles for persuasion variables. In D. T. Gilbert, S. T. Fiske, & G. Lindzey (Eds.), *The handbook of social psychology* (4th ed., pp. 323–390). Boston: McGraw-Hill.

Pezdek, K., & Hodge, D. (1999). Planting false childhood memories in children: The role of event plausibility. *Child Development, 70*, 887–895.

Pfaus, J. G. (2009). Pathways of sexual desire. *Journal of Sex Medicine, 6*, 1506–1533.

Phelan, J. (2006). Foreword. In A. Ziv, *Breeding between the lines: Why inter-racial people are healthier and more attractive.* Lanham, MD: National Book Network.

Phelps, E. A. (2004). Human emotion and memory: Interactions of the amygdala and hippocampal complex. *Current Opinion in Neurobiology, 14*, 198–202.

Phelps, E. A. (2006). Emotion and cognition: Insights from studies of the human amygdala. *Annual Review of Psychology, 57*, 27–53.

Phelps, E. A., Ling, S., & Carrasco, M. (2006). Emotion facilitates perception and potentiates the perceptual benefits of attention. *Psychological Science, 17*, 292–299.

Phinney, J. S. (1990). Ethnic identity in adolescents and adults: Review of research. *Psychological Bulletin, 108*, 499–514.

Piet, J., & Hougaard E. (2011). The effect of mindfulness-based cognitive therapy for prevention of relapse in recurrent major depressive disorder: A systematic review and meta-analysis. *Clinical Psychology Review, 31*(6), 1032–1040. doi 10.1016/j.cpr.2011.05.002

Pilcher, J. J., & Huffcutt, A. I. (1996). Effects of sleep deprivation on performance: A meta-analysis. *Sleep, 19*(4), 318–326.

Pinker, S. (1984). *Language learnability and language development.* Cambridge, MA: Harvard University Press.

Pinker, S. (1994). *The language instinct.* New York: Morrow.

Pinto, D., Pagnamenta, A. T., Klei, L., Anney, R., Merico, D., Regan, R., et al. (2010). Functional impact of global rare copy number variation in autism spectrum disorders. *Nature.* Published online June 9, 2010. doi:10.1038/nature09146

Pitman, R., Sanders, K., Zusman, R., Healy, A., Cheema, F., Lasko, N., et al. (2002). Pilot study of secondary prevention of posttraumatic stress disorder with propranolol. *Biological Psychiatry, 51*, 189–192.

Plakun, E. M., Burkhardt, P. E., & Muller, A. P. (1985). Fourteen-year follow-up of borderline and schizotypal personality disorders. *Comprehensive Psychiatry, 26*, 448–455.

Plant, E. A., Hyde, J. S., Keltner, D., & Devine, P. G. (2000). The gender stereotyping of emotions. *Psychology of Women Quarterly, 24*, 81–92.

Plant, E. A., & Peruche, M. (2005). The consequences of race for police officers' responses to criminal suspects. *Psychological Science, 16*, 180–183.

Plomin, R., & Caspi, A. (1999). Behavioral genetics and personality. In L. A. Pervin & O. P. John (Eds.), *Handbook of personality: Theory and research* (2nd ed., pp. 251–276). New York: Guilford Press.

Plomin, R., & Spinath, F. M. (2004). Intelligence: Genetics, genes, and genomics. *Journal of Personality and Social Psychology, 86*, 112–129.

Polivy, J., & Herman, C. P. (1985). Dieting and bingeing: A causal analysis. *American Psychologist, 40*, 193–201.

Polivy, J., & Herman, C. P. (2002). Causes of eating disorders. *Annual Review of Psychology, 53*, 187–213.

Pollock, K. M. (2004). Exercise in treating depression: Broadening the psychotherapist's role. *Journal of Clinical Psychology, 57*, 1289–1300.

Poma, P. A. (1983). Hispanic cultural influences on medical practice. *Journal of the National Medical Association, 75*, 941–946.

Pope, H. G., Jr., Kouri, E. M., & Hudson, J. I. (2000). Effects of supraphysiologic doses of testosterone on mood and aggression in normal men: A randomized controlled trial. *Archives of General Psychiatry, 57*, 133–140.

Posner, M. I., & DiGirolamo, G. J. (2000). Cognitive neuroscience: Origins and promise. *Psychological Bulletin, 126*, 873–889.

Premack, D. (1959). Toward empirical behavior laws: 1. Positive reinforcement. *Psychological Review, 66*(4), 219-233.

Premack, D. (1970). Mechanisms of self-control. In W. A. Hunt (Ed.), *Learning mechanisms in smoking* (pp. 107–123). Chicago: Aldine.

Prentiss, D., Power, R., Balmas, G., Tzuang, G., & Israelski, D. (2004). Patterns of marijuana use among patients with HIV/AIDS followed in a public health care setting. *Journal of Acquired Immune Deficiency Syndromes, 35*(1), 38–45.

Press, C., Cook, J., Blakemore, S. J., & Kilner, J. (2011). Dynamic properties of the perception-action matching system. *Journal of Neuroscience, 31*, 2792–2800.

Price, D. D., Harkins, S. W., & Baker, C. (1987). Sensory-affective relationships among different types of clinical and experimental pain. *Pain, 28*, 297–307.

Program on International Policy Attitudes (PIPA)/Knowledge Networks Poll. (2004, October 21). *Bush supporters still believe Iraq had WMD or major program, supported al Qaeda* [Press release]. Retrieved from http://www.pipa.org/OnlineReports/Iraq/IraqRealities_Oct04/IraqRealitiesOct04rpt.pdf

Provencher, V., Polivy, J., & Herman, C. P. (2009). Perceived healthiness of food: If it's healthy, you can eat more! *Appetite 2009, 52*, 340–344.

*Psychological Review, 88*, 354–364. doi: 10.1037/0033-295X.88.4.354

Pyszczynski, T., Greenberg, J., Solomon, S., Arndt, J., & Schimel, J. (2004). Why do people need self-esteem? A theoretical and empirical review. *Psychological Bulletin, 130*, 435–468.

Raesaenen, S., Pakaslahti, A., Syvaelahti, E., Jones, P. B., & Isohanni, M. (2000). Sex differences in schizophrenia: A review. *Nordic Journal of Psychiatry, 54*, 37–45.

Raine, A. (1989). Evoked potentials and psychopathy. *International Journal of Psychopathology, 8*, 1–16.

Raine, A., Mellingen, K., Liu, J., Venables, P., & Mednick, S. A. (2003). Effects of environmental enrichment at ages 3–5 years on schizotypal personality and antisocial behavior at ages 17 and 23 years. *American Journal of Psychiatry, 160*, 1627–1635.

Rainville, P., Duncan, G. H., Price, D. D., Carrier, B., & Bushnell, M. C. (1997, August 15). Pain affect encoded in human anterior cingulate but not somatosensory cortex. *Science, 277*, 968–971.

Rainville, P., Hofbauer, R. K., Bushnell, M. C., Duncan, G. H., & Price, D. D. (2002). Hypnosis modulates activity in brain structures involved in the regulation of consciousness. *Journal of Cognitive Neuroscience, 14*, 887–901.

Raleigh, M. J., McGuire, M. T., Brammer, G. L., Pollack, D. B., & Yuwiler, A. (1991). Serotonergic mechanisms promote dominance in adult male vervet monkeys. *Brain Research, 559*, 181–190.

Ram, S., Seirawan, H., Kumar, S.K., & Clark, G.T. (2010). Prevalence and impact of sleep disorders and sleep habits in the United States. *Sleep Breath, 14*, 63–70.

Ramachandran, V. S., & Hirstein, W. (1998). The perception of phantom limbs: The D. O. Hebb lecture. *Brain, 121*, 1603–1630.

Ramachandran, V. S., & Hubbard, E. M. (2001). Psychophysical investigations into the neural basis of synaesthesia. *Proceedings of the Royal Society of London, 268B*, 979–983.

Ramachandran, V. S., & Hubbard, E. M. (2003, May). Hearing colors, tasting shapes: Color-coded world. *Scientific American, 288*(5), 42–49.

Rampon, C., Jiang, C. H., Dong, H., Tang, Y., Lockhart, D. J., Schultz, P. G., et al. (2000). Effects of environmental enrichment on gene expression in the brain. *Proceedings of the National Academy of Sciences, USA, 97*, 12880–12884.

Ramsden, S. R., & Hubbard, J. A. (2002). Family expressiveness and family emotion coaching: Their role in children's emotion regulation and aggression. *Journal of Abnormal Child Psychology, 30*, 657–667. doi: 10.1023/A:1020819915881

Rapoport, J. L. (1989, March). The biology of obsessions and compulsions. *Scientific American, 260*, 83–89.

Rapoport, J. L. (1990). *The boy who couldn't stop washing: The experience and treatment of obsessive-compulsive disorder.* New York: Penguin.

Rapoport, J. L. (1991). Recent advances in obsessive-compulsive disorder. *Neuropsychopharmacology, 5*, 1–10.

Rapport, M. D., & Moffitt, C. (2002). Attention-deficit/hyperactivity disorder and methylphenidate: A review of the height/weight, cardiovascular, and somatic complaint side effects. *Clinical Psychology Review, 22*, 1107–1131.

Rauch, S. L., van der Kolk, B. A., Fisler, R. E., & Alpert, N. M. (1996). A symptom provocation study of posttraumatic stress disorder using positron emission tomography and script-driven imagery. *Archives of General Psychiatry, 53*, 380–387.

Rauscher, F. H., Shaw, G. L., & Ky, K. N. (1993). Music and spatial task performance. *Nature, 365*, 611.

Raynor, H. A., & Epstein, L. H. (2001). Dietary variety, energy regulation, and obesity. *Psychological Bulletin, 127*, 325–341.

Raz, A., Fan, J., & Posner, M. I. (2005). Hypnotic suggestion reduces conflict in the human brain. *Proceedings of the National Academy of Sciences, USA, 102*, 9978–9983.

Raz, A., Shapiro, T., Fan, J., & Posner, M. I. (2002, December). Hypnotic suggestion and the modulation of Stroop interference. *Archives of General Psychiatry, 59*, 1155–1161.

Read, J. P., & Brown, R. A. (2003). The role of exercise in alcoholism treatment and recovery. *Professional Psychology: Research and Practice, 34*, 49–56.

Reddy, L., Tsuchiya, N., & Serre, T. (2010). Reading the mind's eye: Decoding category information during mental information. *Neuroimage, 50*, 818–825.

Reeves, L. M., & Weisberg, R. W. (1994). The role of content and abstract information in analogical transfer. *Psychological Bulletin, 115*, 381–400.

Regard, M., & Landis, T. (1997). "Gourmand syndrome": Eating passion associated with right anterior lesions. *Neurology, 48*, 1185–1190.

Reichenberg, A., & Harvey, P. D. (2007). Neuropsychological impairments in schizophrenia: Integration of performance-based and brain imaging findings. *Psychological Bulletin, 133*, 833–858.

Reinders, A. A., Nijenhuis, E. R., Paans, A. M., Korf, J., Willemsen, A. T., & den Boer, J. A. (2003). One brain, two selves. *Neuroimage, 20*, 2119–2125.

Reis, D. L., Brackett, M. A., Shamosh, N. A., Kiehl, K. A., Salovey, P., & Gray, J. R. (2007). Emotional intelligence predicts individual differences in social exchange reasoning. *Neuroimage, 35*, 1385–1391.

Reis, H. X, Wheeler, L., Spiegel, N., Kernis, M. H., Nezlek, J., & Perri, M. (1982). Physical attractiveness in social interaction: II. Why does appearance affect social experience? *Journal of Personality and Social Psychology, 43*, 979–996.

Renfrow, P. J., & Gosling, S. D. (2003). The do re mi's of everyday life: The structure and personality correlates of music preferences. *Journal of Personality and Social Psychology, 84*, 1236–1256.

Rescorla, R. (1966). Predictability and number of pairings in Pavlovian fear conditioning. *Psychonomic Science, 4*, 383–384.

Rescorla, R. A., & Wagner, A. R. (1972). A theory of Pavlovian conditioning: Variations in the effectiveness of reinforcement and non-reinforcement. In A. H. Black & W. F. Prokosy (Eds.), *Classical conditioning II: Current research and theory* (pp. 64–99). New York: Appleton-Century-Crofts.

Ressler, K. J., & Mayberg, H. S. (2007). Targeting abnormal neural circuits in mood and anxiety disorders: From the laboratory to the clinic. *Nature Neuroscience, 10*, 1116–1124.

Revonsuo, A. (2000). *Prospects for a scientific research program on consciousness—Neural correlates of consciousness.* Cambridge, MA: MIT Press.

Reyna, C., Brandt, M., & Viki, G. T. (2009). Blame it on hip-hop: Anti-rap attitudes as a proxy for prejudice. *Group Process and Intergroup Relations, 12*, 361–380.

Rhodewalt, F., & Morf, C. C. (1998). On self-aggrandizement and anger: A temporal analysis of narcissism and affective reactions to success and failure. *Journal of Personality and Social Psychology, 74*, 672–685.

Richman, L. S., Kubzansky, L., Maselko, J., Kawachi, I., Choo, P., & Bauer, M. (2005). Positive emotion and health: Going beyond the negative. *Health Psychology, 24*(4), 422–429.

Ridley, M. (2003). *Nature versus nurture: Genes, experience, and what makes us human.* New York: HarperCollins.

Rifkin, A., & Rifkin, W. (2004). Adolescents with depression. *Journal of the American Medical Association, 292*, 2577–2578.

Rinck, M., Reinecke, A., Ellwart, T., Heuer, K., & Becker, E. S. (2005). Speeded detection and increased distraction in fear of spiders: Evidence from eye movements. *Journal of Abnormal Psychology, 114*, 235–248.

Rizzolatti, G., & Arbib, M. A. (1998). Language within our grasp. *Trends in Neuroscience, 21*, 188–194.

Rizzolatti, G., & Craighero, L. (2004). The mirror-neuron system. *Annual Reviews in Neuroscience, 27*, 169–192.

Rizzolatti, G., & Fabbri-Destro, M. (2010). Mirror neurons: From discovery to autism. *Experimental Brain Research, 200*, 223–237.

Rizzolatti, G., Fadiga, L., Gallese, V., & Fogassi, L. (1996). Premotor cortex and the recognition of motor actions. *Cognitive Brain Research, 3*, 131–141.

Roberts, B. W., & Friend-DelVecchio, W. (2000). The rank-order consistency of personality traits from childhood to old age: A quantitative review of longitudinal studies. *Psychological Bulletin, 126*, 3–25.

Roberts, B. W., Walton, K. E., & Viechtbauer, W. (2006). Patterns of mean-level change in personality traits across the life course: A meta-analysis of longitudinal studies. *Psychological Bulletin, 132*, 3–21.

Roberts, D. F. (2000). Media and youth: Access, exposure, and privatization. *Journal of Adolescent Health 27*(Suppl.), 8–14.

Roberts, S. (2006, November 15). A neuroscientist's life's work: Analyzing brains to study structure and cognition. *The New York Times*. Retrieved from http://www.nytimes.com

Robins, L. N., & Regier, D. A. (1991). *Psychiatric disorders in America: The epidemiological catchment areas study*. New York: Free Press.

Robins, L. N., Helzer, J. E., & Davis, D. H. (1975). Narcotic use in Southeast Asia and afterward: An interview study of 898 Vietnam returnees. *Archives of General Psychiatry, 32*, 955–961.

Robinson, T. E., & Berridge, K. C. (1993). The neural basis of drug craving: An incentive-sensitization theory of addiction. *Brain Research Reviews, 18*, 247–291.

Robles, T. F., & Kiecolt-Glaser, J. K. (2003). The physiology of marriage: Pathways to health. *Physiology & Behavior, 79*, 409–416.

Rock, I. (1984). *Perception*. New York: Scientific American Books.

Roediger, H. L., III, & Karpicke, J. D. (2006). The power of testing memory: Basic research and implications for educational practice. *Psychological Science, 1*, 181–210.

Roethlisberger, F. J., & Dickson, W. J. (1939). *Management and the worker: An account of a research program conducted by the Western Electric Company, Hawthorne Works, Chicago*. Cambridge, MA: Harvard University Press.

Rogan, M. T., Stäubli, U. V., & LeDoux, J. E. (1997). Fear conditioning induces associative long-term potentiation in the amygdala. *Nature, 390*, 604–607.

Rogers, T. B., Kuiper, N. A., & Kirker, W. S. (1977). Self-reference and the encoding of personal information. *Journal of Personality and Social Psychology, 35*, 677–688.

Roisman, G. I., Clausell, E., Holland, A., Fortuna, K., & Elieff, C. (2008). Adult romantic relationships as contexts of human development: A multimethod comparison of same-sex couples with opposite-sex dating, engaged, and married dyads. *Developmental Psychology, 44*, 91–101.

Rolls, B. J., Roe, L. S., & Meengs, J. S. (2007). The effect of large portion sizes on energy intake is sustained for 11 days. *Obesity Research, 15*, 1535–1543.

Rolls, E. T. (2007). Sensory processing in the brain related to the control of food intake. *Proceedings of the Nutritional Society, 66*, 96–112.

Rolls, E. T., Burton, M. J., & Mora, F. (1980). Neurophysiological analysis of brain-stimulation reward in the monkey. *Brain Research, 194*, 339–357.

Roscoe, W. (2000). *Changing ones: Third and fourth genders in native North America*. New York: St. Martins Griffin.

Rosenman, R. H., Brand, R. J., Jenkins, C. D., Friedman, M., Straus, R., & Wurm, M. (1975). Coronary heart disease in the Western Collaborative Group Study: Final follow-up experience of 8½ years. *Journal of the American Medical Association, 233*, 872–877.

Rosenman, R. H., Friedman, M., Straus, R., Wurm, M., Kositchek, R., Hahn, W., et al. (1964). A predictive study of heart disease. *Journal of the American Medical Association, 189*(1), 15–22.

Rosenstein, D., & Oster, H. (1988). Differential facial responses to four basic tastes in newborns. *Child Development, 59*, 1555–1568.

Rosenthal, R., & Fode, K. L. (1963). The effect of experimenter bias on the performance of the albino rat. Behavioral Science, 8, 183–189.

Rosenzweig, M. R., Bennett, E. L., & Diamond, M. C. (1972, February). Brain changes in response to experience. *Scientific American, 226*, 22–29.

Ross, H. E., & Young, L. J. (2009). Oxytocin and the neural mechanisms regulating social cognition and affiliative behavior. *Frontiers in Neuroendocrinology, 30*, 534–547.

Rothbaum, B. O., Hodges, L., Alarcon, R., Ready, D., Shahar, F., Graap, K., et al. (1999). Virtual reality exposure therapy for PTSD Vietnam veterans: A case study. *Journal of Traumatic Stress, 12*, 263–271.

Rothemund, Y., Preuschhof, C., Bohner, G., Bauknecht, H. C., Klingebiel, R., Flor, H., et al. (2007). Differential activation of the dorsal striatum by high-calorie visual food stimuli in obese individuals. *Neuroimage, 37*, 410–421.

Rotter, J. B. (1954). *Social learning and clinical psychology*. New York: Prentice-Hall.

Rovee-Collier, C. (1999). The development of infant memory. *Current Directions in Psychological Science, 8*, 80–85.

Rowe, D. C., Chassin, L., Presson, C., & Sherman, S. J. (1996). Parental smoking and the "epidemic" spread of cigarette smoking. *Journal of Applied Social Psychology, 26*, 437–445.

Roy, A. (1992). Are there genetic factors in suicide? *International Review of Psychiatry, 4*, 169–175.

Rozin, P. (1996). Sociocultural influences on human food selection. In E. D. Capaldi (Ed.), *Why we eat what we eat: The psychology of eating* (pp. 233–263). Washington, DC: American Psychological Association.

Rubenstein, A. J., Kalakanis, L., & Langlois, J. H. (1999). Infant preferences for attractive faces: A cognitive explanation. *Developmental Psychology, 35*, 848–855.

Rudman, L. A., & Goodwin, S. A. (2004). Gender differences in automatic in-group bias: Why do women like women more than men like men? *Journal of Personality and Social Psychology, 87*, 494–509.

Rupp, H. A., James, T. W., Ketterson, E. D., Sengelaub, D. R., Janssen, E., & Heiman, J. R. (2009). Neural activation in the orbitofrontal cortex in response to male faces increases during the follicular phase. *Hormones and Behavior, 56*, 66–72.

Rusbult, C. E., & Buunk, B. D. Commitment processes in close relationships: An interdependence analysis. *Journal of Social and Personal Relationships, 10*, 175–204.

Rusbult, C. E., & Van Lange, P. A. M. (1996). Interdependence processes. In E. T. Higgins & A. Kruglanski (Eds.), *Social psychology: Handbook of basic principles* (pp. 564–596). New York: Guilford Press.

Ruscio, A. M., Brown, T. A., Chiu, W. T., Sareen, J., Stein, M. B., & Kessler, R. C. (2008). Social fears and social phobia in the USA: Results from the national comorbidity survey replication. *Psychological Medicine, 35*, 15–28.

Russell, C. A., Clapp, J. D., & Dejong, W. (2005). Done 4: Analysis of a failed social norms marketing campaign. *Health Communication, 17*(1), 57–65.

Russell, J. A. (1980). A circumplex model of affect. *Journal of Personality and Social Psychology, 39*, 1161–1178.

Russell, J. A. (1994). Is there universal recognition of emotion from facial expressions? A review of the cross-cultural studies. *Psychological Bulletin, 115*, 102–141.

Russell, M. A. H. (1990). The nicotine trap: A 40-year sentence for four cigarettes. *British Journal of Addiction, 85*, 293–300.

Russo, N.F., & Denmark, F. L. (1987). Contributions of women to psychology. *Annual Review of Psychology, 38*, 279–298.

Rutgers, A. H., Bakermans-Kranenburg, M. J., van Ijzendoorn, M. H., & van Berckelaer-Onnes, I. A. (2004). Autism and attachment: A meta-analytic review. *Journal of Child Psychology and Psychiatry, 45*, 1123–1134. doi: 10.1111/j.1469-7610.2004.t01-1-00305.x

Rutter, M. (2005). Incidence of autism disorders: Changes over time and their meaning. *Acta Paediatrica, 94*, 2–15.

Rymer, R. (1993). *Genie: A scientific tragedy*. New York: HarperCollins.

Sabol, S. Z., Nelson, M. L., Fisher, C., Gunzerath, L., Brody, C. L., Hu, S., et al. (1999). A genetic association for cigarette smoking behavior. *Health Psychology, 18*, 7–13.

Sacks, O. (1995). *An anthropologist on Mars: Seven paradoxical tales*. New York: Knopf.

Saha, S., Chant, D. C., Welham, J. L., & McGrath, J. J. (2006). The incidence and prevalence of schizophrenia varies with latitude. *Acta Psychiatrica Scandinavica, 114*, 36–39.

Salimpoor, V. N., Benovoy, M., Larcher, K., Dagher, A., & Zatorre, R.J. (2011). Anatomically distinct dopamine release during anticipation and experience of peak emotion to music. *Nature Neuroscience, 14*, 257–262. *doi*:10.1038/nn.2726

Salovey, P., & Grewel, D. (2005). The science of emotional intelligence. *Current Directions in Psychological Science, 14*, 281–286.

Salovey, P., & Mayer, J. D. (1990). Emotional intelligence. *Imagination, Cognition, and Personality, 9*, 185–211.

Salthouse, T. (1992). The information-processing perspective on cognitive aging. In R. Sternberg & C. Berg (Eds.), *Intellectual development* (pp. 261–277). Cambridge, UK: Cambridge University Press.

Salum, G. A., Polanczyk, G. V., Miguel, E. C., & Rohde, L. A. (2010). Effects of childhood development on late-life mental disorders. *Current Opinion in Psychiatry, 23*, 498–503.

SAMHSA (2011). Major depressive episode and treatment among adolescents: 2009. *National Survey on Drug Use and Health*. Accessed at http://www.oas.samhsa.gov/2k11/009/AdolescentDepression.htm

Sanderson, W. C., & Barlow, D. H. (1990). A description of patients diagnosed with DSM-III-R generalized anxiety disorder. *The Journal of Nervous and Mental Disease, 178*, 588–591.

Sapolsky, R. M. (1994). *Why zebras don't get ulcers*. New York: Freeman.

Sargent, J. D., Beach, M. L., Adachi-Mejia, A. M., Gibson, J. J., Titus-Ernstoff, L. T., Carusi, C. P., et al. (2005). Exposure to movie smoking: Its relation to smoking initiation among US adolescents. *Pediatrics, 116*, 1183–1191.

Savic, I., Berglund, H., & Lindström, P. (2005). Brain responses to putative pheromones in homosexual men. *Proceedings of the National Academy of Sciences, USA, 102*, 7356–7361.

Savitz, D. A., Schwingle, P. J., & Keels, M. A. (1991). Influences of paternal age, smoking, and alcohol consumption on congenital anomalies. *Teratology, 44*, 429–440.

Sayette, M. A. (1993). An appraisal-disruption model of alcohol's effects on stress responses in social drinkers. *Psychological Bulletin, 114*, 459–476.

Scarr, S., & McCarthy, K. (1983). How people make their own environments: A theory of genotype l environment effects. *Child Development, 54*, 424–435.

Schab, F. R. (1991). Odor memory: Taking stock. *Psychological Bulletin, 109*, 242–251.

Schachter, H. M., Pham, B., King, J., Langford, S., & Moher, D. (2001). How efficacious and safe is short-acting methylphenidate for the treatment of attention-deficit hyperactivity disorder in children and adolescents? A meta-analysis. *Canadian Medical Association Journal, 165*, 1475–1488.

Schachter, S. (1951). Deviation, rejection, and communication. *Journal of Abnormal Psychology, 46*, 190–207.

Schachter, S. (1959). *The psychology of affiliation*. Stanford, CA: Stanford University Press.

Schachter, S., & Singer, J. (1962). Cognitive, social, and physiological determinants of emotional state. *Psychological Review, 69*, 379–399.

Schacter, D. L. (1996). *Searching for memory: The brain, the mind, and the past*. New York: Basic Books.

Schacter, D. L. (1999). The seven sins of memory: Insights from psychology and cognitive neuroscience. *American Psychologist, 54*, 182–203.

Schacter, D. L. (2001). *The seven sins of memory: How the mind forgets and remembers*. Boston: Houghton Mifflin.

Schacter, D. L., & Tulving, E. (1994). What are the memory systems of 1994? In D. L. Schacter & E. Tulving (Eds.), *Memory systems 1994* (pp. 1–38). Cambridge, MA: MIT Press.

Schaie, K. W. (1990). Intellectual development in adulthood. In J. E. Birren & K. W. Schaie (Eds.), *Handbook of the psychology of aging* (3rd ed., pp. 291–319). New York: Van Nostrand Reinhold.

Schank, R. C., & Abelson, R. P. (1977). *Scripts, plans, goals, and understanding*. Hillsdale, NJ: Erlbaum.

Scheerer, M. (1963). Problem-solving. *Scientific American, 208*, 118–128.

Schiffman, J., Walker, E., Ekstrom, M., Schulsinger, F., Sorensen, H., & Mednick, S. (2004). Childhood videotaped social and neuromotor precursors of schizophrenia: A prospective investigation. *American Journal of Psychiatry, 161*, 2021–2027.

Schiller, D., Monfils, M., Raio, C., Johnson, D., LeDoux, J. E., & Phelps, E. A. (2010). Preventing the return of fear in humans using reconsolidation update mechanisms. *Nature, 463*, 49–54.

Schimel, J., Hayes, J., Williams, T. J., & Jahrig, J. (2007). Is death really the worm at the core? Converging evidence that worldview threat increases death-thought accessibility. *Journal of Personality and Social Psychology, 92*, 789–803.

Schmader, T. (2010). Stereotype threat deconstructed. *Current Directions in Psychological Science, 19*, 14–18.

Schmader, T., Johns, M., & Forbes, C. (2008). An integrated process model of stereotype threat effects on performance. *Psychological Review, 115*, 336–356.

Schmajuk, N. A., Lamoureux, J. A., & Holland, P. C. (1998). Occasion setting: A neural network approach. *Psychological Review, 105*, 3–32.

Schmidt, F. L., & Hunter, J. (2004). General mental ability in the world of work: Occupational attainment and job performance. *Journal of Personality and Social Psychology, 96*, 162–173.

Schmidt, N. B., & Keough, M. E. (2011). Treatment of panic. *Annual Review of Clinical Psychology, 6*, 241–256.

Schmitt, D. P., Alcalay, L., Allik, J., Angleitner, A., Ault, L., Austers, I., et al. (2003). Universal sex differences in the desire for sexual variety: Tests from 52 nations, 6 continents, and 13 islands. *Journal of Personality and Social Psychology, 85*, 85–104.

Schmitt, D. P., Allik, J., McCrae, R. R., & Benet-Martinez, V. (2007). The geographic distribution of big five personality traits: Patterns and profiles of human self-description across 56 nations. *Journal of Cross-Cultural Psychology, 38*, 173–212.

Schmitt, D. P., Realo, A., Voracek, M., & Allik, J. (2008). Why can't a man be more like a woman? *Journal of Personality and Social Psychology, 94*, 168–182.

Schmitz, T. W., De Rosa, E., & Anderson, A. K. (2009). Opposing influences of affective state valence in visual cortical encoding. *Journal of Neuroscience, 29*, 7199–7207.

Schneider, B., & Csikszentmihalyi, M. (2000). *Becoming adult: How teenagers prepare for the world of work.* New York: Basic Books.

Schoenemann, P. T., Sheehan, M. J., & Glotzer, L. D. (2005). Prefrontal white matter volume is disproportionately larger in humans than in other primates. *Nature Neuroscience, 8*, 242–252.

Schreiber, F. R. (1974). *Sybil: The true story of a woman possessed by sixteen personalities.* London: Penguin.

Schultz, P. W., Nolan, J. M., Cialdini, R. B., Goldstein, N. J., & Griskevicius, V. (2007). The constructive, destructive, and reconstructive power of social norms. *Psychological Science, 18*, 429–434.

Schultz, W. (2010). Dopamine signals for reward value and risk: Basic and recent data. *Behavioral and Brain Functions, 6*(24): 1–9.

Schulz, K. P., Fan, J., Tang, C. Y., Newcorn, J. H., Buchsbaum, M. S., Cheung, A. M., et al. (2004). Response inhibition in adolescents diagnosed with attention deficit hyperactivity disorder during childhood: An event-related fMRI study. *American Journal of Psychiatry, 161*, 1650–1657.

Schuur, Diane. (1999, June 14). Heroes and icons: Helen Keller. *Time.* Retrieved from http://www.time.com/time/time100/heroes/profile/keller01.html

Schwartz, B. (2004). *The paradox of choice: Why more is less.* New York: Ecco.

Schwartz, C. E., Wright, C. I., Shin, L. M., Kagan, J., & Rauch, S. L. (2003, June 20). Inhibited and uninhibited infants "grown up": Adult amygdalar response to novelty. *Science, 300*, 1952–1953.

Schwartz, J. M., Stoessel, P. W., Baxter, L. R., Martin, K. M., & Phelps, M. E. (1996). Systematic changes in cerebral glucose metabolic rate after successful behavior modification treatment of obsessive-compulsive disorder. *Archives of General Psychiatry, 53*, 109–113.

Schwartz, S., & Maquet, P. (2002). Sleep imaging and the neuropsychological assessment of dreams. *Trends in Cognitive Sciences, 6*, 23–30.

Schwarz, N., & Clore, G. L. (1983). Mood, misattribution, and judgments of well-being: Informative and directive functions of affective states. *Journal of Personality and Social Psychology, 45*, 513–523.

Scislowska, M. (2007, June 4). Man wakes from 19-year coma to "prettier" Poland. Railway worker is shocked at radical changes. *Associated Press.* Retrieved from http://www.associatedpress.com

Sclafani, A., & Springer, D. (1976). Dietary obesity in adult rats: Similarities to hypothalamic and human obesity syndromes. *Physiology and Behavior, 17*, 461–471.

Sedikides, C., Gaertner, L., & Toguchi, Y. (2003). Pancultural self-enhancement. *Journal of Personality and Social Psychology, 84*, 60–79.

Sedikides, C., & Gregg, A. (2008). Self-enhancement: Food for thought. *Perspectives on Psychological Science, 3*, 102–116.

Sedlmeier, P., & Gigerenzer, G. (1997). Intuitions about sample size: The empirical law of large numbers. *Journal of Behavioral Decision Making, 10*, 33–51.

Seegmiller, J. K., Watson, J. M., & Strayer, D. L. (2011, February 7). Individual differences in susceptibility to inattentional blindness. *Journal of Experimental Psychology: Learning, Memory, and Cognition.* Advance online publication. doi: 10.1037/a0022474

Segerstrom, S. C., & Miller, G. E. (2004). Psychological stress and the human immune system: A meta-analytic study of 30 years of inquiry. *Psychological Bulletin, 130*, 601–630.

Seguin, J. R. (2004). Neurocognitive elements of antisocial behavior: Relevance of an orbitofrontal cortex account. *Brain and Cognition, 55*, 185–197.

Seligman, M. E. P. (1970). On the generality of the laws of learning. *Psychological Review, 77*, 406–418.

Seligman, M. E. P. (1974). Depression and learned helplessness. In R. J. Friedman & M. M. Katz (Eds.), *The psychology of depression: Contemporary theory and research* (pp. 83–113). Washington, DC: V. H. Winston.

Seligman, M. E. P. (1975). *Helplessness: On depression, development, and death.* San Francisco: Freeman.

Seligman, M. E. P. (2011). *Flourish.* New York: Simon & Schuster.

Seligman, M. E. P., & Csikszentmihalyi, M. (2000). Positive psychology: An introduction. *American Psychologist, 55*, 5–14.

Seligman, M. E. P., Steen, T. A., Park, N., & Peterson, C. (2005). Positive psychology progress: Empirical validation of interventions. *American Psychologist, 60*, 410–421.

Seligman, M. E. P., Walker, E. F., & Rosenhan, D. L. (2001). *Abnormal psychology.* New York: Norton.

Shah, R. S., Chang, S., Min, H., Cho, Z., Blaha, C., & Lee, K. H. (2010). Deep brain stimulation: Technology at the cutting edge. *Journal of Clinical Neurology, 6*, 167–182.

Shallice, T., & Warrington, E. (1969). Independent functioning of verbal memory stores. *Quarterly Journal of Experimental Psychology, 22*, 261–273.

Shapiro, A. F., Gottman, J. M., & Carrère, S. (2000). The baby and the marriage: Identifying factors that buffer against decline in marital satisfaction after the first baby arrives. *Journal of Family Psychology, 14*, 59–70. doi: 10.1037/0893-3200.14.1.59

Shedler, J. (2010). The efficacy of psychodynamic psychotherapy. *American Psychologist, 65*, 98–109.

Shedler, J., & Block, J. (1990). Adolescent drug use and psychological health: A longitudinal inquiry. *American Psychologist, 45*, 612–630.

Sheese, B. E., Brown, E. L., & Graziano, W. G. (2004). Emotional expression in cyberspace: Searching for moderators of the Pennebaker disclosure effect via e-mail. *Health Psychology, 23*, 457–464.

Shenkin, S. D., Starr, J. M., & Deary, I. J. (2004). Birth weight and cognitive ability in childhood: A systematic review. *Psychological Bulletin, 130*, 989–1013.

Shephard, R. J. (1997). *Aging, physical activity, and health.* Champaign, IL: Human Kinetics Publishers.

Sher, L. (2000). Sociopolitical events and technical innovations may affect the content of delusions and the course of psychotic disorders. *Medical Hypotheses, 55*, 507–509.

Sherif, M., Harvey, O. J., White, B. J., Hood, W. R., & Sherif, C. W. (1961). *Intergroup cooperation and competition: The Robbers Cave experiment.* Norman, OK: University Book Exchange.

Sherman, D. K., McGue, M. K., & Iacono, W. G. (1997). Twin concordance for attention deficit hyperactivity disorder: A comparison of teacher's and mother's reports. *American Journal of Psychiatry, 154*, 532–535.

Sherman, S. J., Presson, C., Chassin, L., Corty, E., & Olshavsky, R. (1983). The false consensus effect in estimates of smoking prevalence: Underlying mechanisms. *Personality and Social Psychology Bulletin, 9*, 197–207.

Sherwin, B. B. (1988). A comparative analysis of the role of androgen in human male and female sexual behavior: Behavioral specificity, critical thresholds, and sensitivity. *Psychobiology, 16*, 416–425.

Sherwin, B. B. (1994). Sex hormones and psychological functioning in postmenopausal women. *Experimental Gerontology, 29*, 423–430.

Sherwin, B. B. (2008). Hormones, the brain, and me. *Canadian Psychology, 49*, 42–48.

Sherwood, R. A., Keating, J., Kavvadia, V., Greenough, A., & Peters, T. J. (1999). Substance misuse in early pregnancy and relationship to fetal outcome. *European Journal of Pediatrics, 158*, 488–492.

Shettleworth, S. J. (2001). Animal cognition and animal behaviour. *Animal Behaviour, 61*, 277–286.

Shih, M., Pittinsky, T. L., & Ambady, N. (1999). Stereotype susceptibility: Identity salience and shifts in quantitative performance. *Psychological Science, 10*, 80–83.

Siegel, J. M. (2008). Do all animals sleep? *Trends in Neuroscience, 31*, 208–213.

Siegel, S. (1984). Pavlovian conditioning and heroin overdose: Reports by overdose victims. *Bulletin of the Psychonomic Society, 22*, 428–430.

Siegel, S. (2005). Drug tolerance, drug addiction, and drug anticipation. *Current Directions in Psychological Science, 14*(6), 296–300.

Siegel, S., Baptista, M. A. S., Kim, J. A., McDonald, R. V., & Weise-Kelly, L. (2000). Pavlovian psychopharmacology: The associative basis of tolerance. *Experimental and Clinical Psychopharmacology, 8*, 276–293.

Siegel, S., Hinson, R. E., Krank, M. D., & McCully, J. (1982). Heroin "overdose" death: Contribution of drug-associated environmental cues. *Science, 216*, 436–437.

Siegler, I. C., Costa, P. T., Brummett, B. H., Helms, M. J., Barefoot, J. C., Williams, R., et al. (2003). Patterns of change in hostility from college to midlife in the UNC alumni heart study predict high-risk status. *Psychosomatic Medicine, 65*, 738–745.

Sigurdsson, T., Doyère, V., Cain, C. K., & LeDoux, J. E. (2007). Long-term potentiation in the amygdala: A cellular mechanism of fear learning and memory. *Neuropharmacology, 52*, 215–227.

Silber, M., Ancoli-Israel, S., Bonnet, M., Chokroverty, S., Grigg-Damberger, M., Hirshkowitz, M., et al. (2007). The visual scoring of sleep in adults. *Journal of Clinical Sleep Medicine, 3*, 121–131.

Silbersweig, D., Clarkin, J. F., Goldstein, M., Kernberg, O. F., Tuescher, O., Levy, K. N., et al. (2007). Failure of frontolimbic inhibitory function in the context of negative emotion in borderline personality disorder. *American Journal of Psychiatry, 64*, 1832–1841.

Silva, C. E., & Kirsch, I. (1992). Interpretive sets, expectancy, fantasy proneness, and dissociation as predictors of hypnotic response. *Journal of Personality and Social Psychology, 63*, 847–856.

Simner, J., Mulvenna, C., Sagiv, N., Tsakanikos, E., Witherby, S. A., Fraser, C., et al. (2006). Synaesthesia: The prevalence of atypical cross-modal experiences. *Perception, 35*, 1024–1033.

Simon, T. (2003). Photographer's foreword to *The Innocents.* [Electronic version]. Retrieved from http://www.pbs.org/wgbh/pages/frontline/shows/burden/innocents/

Simons, D. J., & Ambinder, M. S. (2005). Change blindness: Theory and consequences. *Current Directions in Psychological Science, 14*, 44–48.

Simons, D. J., & Levin, D. T. (1998). Failure to detect changes to people during a real-world interaction. *Psychonomic Bulletin and Review, 5*, 644–649.

Simpson, H. B., Foa, E. B., Liebowitz, M. R., Ledley, D. R., Huppert, J. D., Cahill, S., et al. (2008). A randomized, controlled trial of cognitive-behavioral therapy for augmenting pharmacotherapy in obsessive-compulsive disorder. *American Journal of Psychiatry, 165*, 621–630.

Simpson, J. A., Collins, A., Tran, S., & Haydon, K. C. (2007). Attachment and the experience and expression of emotions in romantic relationships: A developmental perspective. *Journal of Personality and Social Psychology, 92*, 355–367.

Sims, H. E. A., Goldman, R. F., Gluck, C. M., Horton, E., Kelleher, P., & Rowe, D. (1968). Experimental obesity in man. *Transactions of the Association of American Physicians, 81*, 153–170.

Singer, T., Seymour, B., O'Doherty, J., Kaube, H., Dolan, R. J., & Frith, C. D. (2004, February 20). Empathy for pain involves the affective but not sensory components of pain. *Science, 303*, 1157–1162.

Sirois, B. C., & Burg, M. M. (2003). Negative emotion and coronary heart disease: A review. *Behavior Modification, 27*, 83–102.

Six most feared but least likely causes of death. (2005, July 13). *Be Safe, Live Long & Prosper* [E-newsletter]. Retrieved from http://www.sixwise.com/newsletters/05/07/13/the_six_most_feared_but_least_likely_causes_of_death.htm

Skinner, B. F. (1948). *Walden two.* Indianapolis: Hackett.

Skinner, B. F. (1971). *Beyond freedom and dignity.* New York: Wiley.

Skodol, A. E., Siever, L. J., Livesley, W. J., Gunderson, J. G., Pfohl, B., & Widiger, T. A. (2002). The borderline diagnosis II: Biology, genetics, and clinical course. *Biological Psychiatry, 51*, 951–963.

Slovic, P., Finucane, M., Peters, E., & MacGregor, D. (2002). The affect heuristic. In T. Gilovich, D. Griffin, & D. Kahneman (Eds.), *Heuristics and biases: The psychology of intuitive judgment* (pp. 397–420). New York: Cambridge University Press.

Smith, C., & Lapp, L. (1991). Increases in number of REMs and REM density in humans following an intensive learning period. *Sleep, 14*, 325–330.

Smith, D. M., Langa, K. M., Kabeto, M. U., & Ubel, P. A. (2005). Health, wealth, and happiness: Financial resources buffer subjective well-being after the onset of a disability. *Psychological Science, 16*, 663–664.

Smith, L. B., & Thelen, E. (August, 2003). Development as a dynamic system. *Trends in Cognitive Sciences, 7*, 343–348.

Smith, S. M., Glenberg, A. M., & Bjork, R. A. (1978). Environmental context and human memory. *Memory and Cognition, 6*, 342–353.

Smith, T. W., Orleans, C. T., & Jenkins, C. D. (2004). Prevention and health promotion: Decades of progress, new challenges, and an emerging agenda. *Health Psychology, 23*, 126–131.

Snider, L. A., & Swedo, S. E. (2004). PANDAS: Current status and directions for research. *Molecular Psychiatry, 9*, 900–907.

Snyder, E. E., Walts, B. M., Chagnon, Y. C., Pérusse, L., Weisnagel, S. J., Chagnon, Y. C., et al. (2004). The human obesity gene map: The 2003 update. *Obesity Research, 12*, 369–438.

Snyder, M., & Cantor, N. (1998). Understanding personality and personal behavior: A functionalist strategy. In D. T. Gilbert, S. T. Fiske, & G. Lindzey (Eds.), *Handbook of social psychology* (pp. 635–679). New York: McGraw-Hill.

Snyder, M., Tanke, E. D., & Berscheid, E. (1977). Social perception and interpersonal behavior: On the self-fulfilling nature of social stereotypes. *Journal of Personality and Social Psychology, 35*, 656–666.

Solms, M. (2000). Dreaming and REM sleep are controlled by different brain mechanisms. *Behavioral and Brain Sciences, 23*, 793.

Somerville, L. H., Kim, H., Johnstone, T., Alexander, A. L., & Whalen, P. J. (2004). Human amygdala responses during presentation of happy and neutral faces: Correlations with state anxiety. *Biological Psychiatry, 55*, 897–903.

Sommerville, J. A., & Woodward, A. L. (2005). Pulling out the intentional structure of action: The relation between action processing and action production in infancy. *Cognition, 95*, 1–30.

Sorensen, T., Holst, C., Stunkard, A. J., & Skovgaard, L. T. (1992). Correlations of body mass index of adult adoptees and their biological and adoptive relatives. *International Journal of Obesity and Related Metabolic Disorders, 16*, 227–236.

Southgate, V., & Hamilton, A. F. (2008). Unbroken mirrors: Challenging a theory of autism. *Trends in Cognitive Science, 12*, 225–229.

Spanos, N. P., & Coe, W. C. (1992). A social-psychological approach to hypnosis. In E. Fromm & M. Nash (Eds.), *Contemporary hypnosis research* (pp. 102–130). New York: Guilford Press.

Spearman, C. (1904). "General intelligence," objectively determined and measured. *American Journal of Psychology, 15*, 201–293.

Spencer, M. B., Fegley, S. G., & Harpalani, V. (2003). A theoretical and empirical examination of identity as coping: Linking coping resources to the self processes of African American youth. *Applied Developmental Science, 7*, 181–188.

Spencer, S. J., Steele, C. M., & Quinn, D. M. (1999). Stereotype threat and women's math performance. *Journal of Experimental Social Psychology, 35*, 4–28.

Sperling, G. (1960). The information available in brief visual presentations. *Psychological Monographs, 74*, 1–29.

Spitzer, R. L., Skodol, A. E., Gibbon, M., & Williams, J. B. W. (1983). *Psychopathology, a case book.* New York: McGraw-Hill.

Spitzer, R. L., Williams, J. B., Gibbon, M., & First, M. B. (1992). The structured clinical interview for DSM-III-R (SCID). I: History, rationale, and description. *Archives of General Psychiatry, 49*, 624–629.

Spurr, K. F., Graven, M. A., & Gilbert, R. W. (2008). Prevalence of unspecified sleep apnea and the use of continuous positive airway pressure in hospitalized patients, 2004 national hospital discharge survey. *Sleep and Breathing, 12*, 229–234.

Squire, L. R., & Moore, R. Y. (1979). Dorsal thalamic lesion in a noted case of human memory dysfunction. *Annals of Neurology, 6*, 503–506.

Squire, L. R., Stark, C. E. L., & Clark, R. E. (2004). The medial temporal lobe. *Annual Review of Neuroscience, 27*(27), 279–306.

Srivastava, S., John, O. P., Gosling, S. D., & Potter, J. (2003). Development of personality in early and middle adulthood: Set like plaster or persistent change? *Journal of Personality and Social Psychology, 84*, 1041–1053.

Srivastava, S., McGonigal, K. M., Richards, J. M., Butler, E. A., & Gross, J. J. (2006). Optimism in close relationships: How seeing things in a positive light makes them so. *Personality Processes and Individual Differences, 91*(1), 143–153.

Starcevic, V., Linden, M., Uhlenhuth, E. H., Kolar, D., & Latas, M. (2004). Treatment of panic disorder with agoraphobia in an anxiety disorders clinic: Factors influencing psychiatrists' treatment choices. *Psychiatry Research, 125*, 41–52.

Stark, S. (2000, December 22)."Cast Away" lets Hanks fend for himself. *The Detroit News*. Retrieved from http://www.detnews.com

Steele, C. M., & Aronson, J. (1995). Stereotype threat and the intellectual test performance of African-Americans. *Journal of Personality and Social Psychology, 69*(5), 797–811.

Steeves, J. K., Culham, J. C., Duchaine, B. C., Pratesi, C. C., Valyear, K. F., Schindler, I., et al. (2006). The fusiform face area is not sufficient for face recognition: Evidence from a patient with dense prosopagnosia and no occipital face area. *Neuropsychologia, 4*, 594–609.

Steffenburg, S., Gillberg, C., Helgren, L., Anderson, L., Gillberg, L., Jakobsson, G., et al. (1989). A twin study of autism in Denmark, Finland, Iceland, Norway, and Sweden. *Journal of Child Psychological Psychiatry, 30*, 405–416.

Stein, J., & Richardson, A. (1999). Cognitive disorders: A question of misattribution. *Current Biology, 9*, R374–R376.

Stein, M. B., & Stein, D. J. (2008). Social anxiety disorder. *Lancet, 371*, 1115–1125.

Steinberg, L. (2001). We know some things: Parent–adolescent relationships in retrospect and prospect. *Journal of Research on Adolescence, 11*, 1–19.

Steinberg, L., & Sheffield, A. M. (2001). Adolescent development. *Journal of Cognitive Education and Psychology, 2*, 55–87.

Steiner, J. E. (1977). Facial expressions of the neonate infant indicating the hedonics of food-related chemical stimuli. In J. M. Weiffenbach (Ed.), *Taste and development* (pp. 173–189). Bethesda, MD: National Institutes of Health.

Stellar, J. R., Kelley, A. E., & Corbett, D. (1983). Effects of peripheral and central dopamine blockade on lateral hypothalamic self-stimulation: Evidence for both reward and motor deficits. *Pharmacology, Biochemistry, and Behavior, 18*, 433–442.

Steriade, M. (1992). Basic mechanisms of sleep generation. *Neurology, 42*(Suppl. 6), 9–18.

Sternberg, R. J. (1986). A triangular theory of love. *Psychological Review, 93*, 119–135.

Sternberg, R. J. (1999). The theory of successful intelligence. *Review of General Psychology, 3*, 292–316.

Stewart, J. L., Coan, J. A., Towers, D. N., & Allen, J. J. B. (2011). Frontal EEG asymmetry during emotional challenge differentiates individuals with and without major depressive disorder. *Journal of Affective Disorders, 129*, 167–174.

Stewart, J. Y. (2007, June 4). Bettye Travis, 55; activist for the overweight [Obituary.]. *Los Angeles Times*, p. B7.

Stice, E. (2002). Risk and maintenance factors for eating pathology: A meta-analytic review. *Psychological Bulletin, 128*, 825–848.

Stickgold, R., Whidbee, D., Schirmer, B., Patel, V., & Hobson, J. A. (2000). Visual discrimination task improvement: A multi-step process occurring during sleep. *Journal of Cognitive Neuroscience, 12*, 246–254.

Stokes, M., Thompson, R., Cusack, R., & Duncan, J. (2009). Top-down activation of shape-specific population codes in visual cortex during mental imagery. *Journal of Neuroscience, 29*, 1565–1572.

Stokstad, E. (2001, October 5). New hints into the biological basis of autism. *Science, 294*, 34–37.

Stoleru, S., Gregoire, M. C., Gerard, D., Decety, J., Lafarge, E., Cinotti, L., et al. (1999). Neuroanatomical correlates of visually evoked sexual arousal in human males. *Archives of Sexual Behavior, 28*, 1–21.

Stone, A. A., Neale, J. M., Cox, D. S., Napoli, A., Valdimardottir, H., & Kennedy-Moore, E. (1994). Daily events are associated with a secretory immune response to an oral antigen in men. *Health Psychology, 13*, 440–446.

Stone, M. H., Stone, D. K., & Hurt, S. W. (1987). The natural history of borderline patients treated by intensive hospitalization. *Psychiatric Clinics of North America, 10*, 185–206.

Stone, V. E., Baron-Cohen, S., & Knight, R. T. (1998). Frontal lobe contributions to theory of mind. *Journal of Cognitive Neuroscience, 10*, 640–656.

Strahan, E. J., Spencer, S. J., & Zanna, M. P. (2002). Subliminal priming and persuasion: Striking while the iron is hot. *Journal of Experimental Social Psychology, 38*, 556–568.

Strayer, D. L., & Drews, F. A. (2007). Cell-phone-induced driver distraction. *Current Directions in Psychological Science, 16*, 128–131.

Strayer, D. L., Drews, F. A., & Johnston, W. A. (2003). Cell phone-induced failures of visual attention during simulated driving. *Journal of Experimental Psychology: Applied, 9*, 23–32.

Strentz, T., & Auerbach, S. M. (1988). Adjustment to the stress of simulated captivity: Effects of emotion-focused versus problem-focused preparation on hostages differing in locus of control. *Journal of Personality and Social Psychology, 55*, 652–660.

Striegel-Moore, R. H., & Franko, D. L. (2008). Should binge eating disorder be included in the DSM-V? A critical review of the state of the evidence. *Annual Review of Clinical Psychology, 4*, 305–324.

Stunkard, A. J. (1996). Current views on obesity. *American Journal of Medicine, 100*, 230–236.

Stuss, D. T. (1991). Self, awareness, and the frontal lobes: A neuropsychological perspective. In J. Strauss & G. R. Goethals (Eds.), *The self: Interdisciplinary approaches* (pp. 255–278). New York: Springer-Verlag.

Stuss, D. T., Gow, C. A., & Hetherington, C. R. (1992). "No longer Gage": Frontal lobe dysfunction and emotional changes. *Journal of Consulting and Clinical Psychology, 60*, 349–359.

Süß, H. M., Oberauer, K., Wittman, W. W., Wilhelm, O., & Schulze, R. (2002). Working-memory capacity explains reasoning ability—and a little bit more. *Intelligence, 30*, 261–288.

Sulin, R. A., & Dooling, D. J. (1974). Intrusion of a thematic idea in retention of prose. *Journal of Experimental Psychology, 103*, 255–262.

Sullivan, M. J. L., Thorn, B., Haythornthwaite, J. A., Keefe, F., Martin, M., Bradley, L. A., et al. (2001). Theoretical perspectives on the relation between catastrophizing and pain. *Clinical Journal of Pain, 17*, 52–64.

Super, C. M. (1976). Environmental effects on motor development: The case of African precocity. *Developmental Medicine and Child Neurology, 18*, 561–567.

Surian, L., Caldi, S., & Sperber, D. (2007). Attribution of beliefs by 13-month-old infants. *Psychological Science, 18*, 580–586.

Svenson, O. (1981). Are we all less risky and more skillful than our fellow drivers? *Acta Psychologica, 47*, 143–148.

Swaab, D. F. (2004). Sexual differentiation of the human brain: Relevance for gender identity, transsexualism and sexual orientation. *Gynecological Endocrinology, 19*, 301–312.

Swartz, M. S., Blazer, D., George, L., & Winfield, I. (1990). Estimating the prevalence of borderline personality disorder in the community. *Journal of Personality Disorders, 4*, 257–272.

Tajfel, H., & Turner, J. C. (1979). An integrative theory of intergroup conflict. In W. G. Austin & S. Worchel (Eds.), *The social psychology of intergroup relations* (pp. 33–47). Monterey, CA: Brooks/Cole.

Talarico, J. M., & Rubin, D. C. (2003). Confidence, not consistency, characterizes flashbulb memories. *Psychological Science, 14*, 455–461.

Talley, P. R., Strupp, H. H., & Morey, L. C. (1990). Matchmaking in psychotherapy: Patient-therapist dimensions and their impact on outcome. *Journal of Consulting and Clinical Psychology, 58*, 182–188.

Tandon, R., Keshavan, M. S., & Nasrallah, H. A. (2008). Schizophrenia, "Just the facts." What we know in 2008. 2. Epidemiology and etiology. *Schizophrenia Research, 102*, 1–18.

Tang, Y. P., Wang, H., Feng, R., Kyin, M., Tsien, J. Z. (2001). Differential effects of enrichment on learning and memory function in NR2B transgenic mice. *Neuropharmacology, 41*, 779–790.

Tang, Y. Y., Ma, Y. H., Wang, J. H., Fan, Y. X., Feng, S. G., Lu, Q. L., et al. (2007). Short-term meditation training improves attention and self-regulation. *Proceedings of the National Academy of Sciences, USA, 104*, 17152–17156.

Tangney, J. P., Stuewig, J., & Mashek, D. J. (2007). Moral emotions and moral behavior. *Annual Review of Psychology, 58*, 345–372. doi: 10.1146/annurev.psych.56.091103.070145

Tateyama, M., Asai, M., Kamisada, M., Hashimoto, M., Bartels, M., & Heimann, H. (1993). Comparison of schizophrenic delusions between Japan and Germany. *Psychopathology, 26*, 151–158.

Taylor, S. E. (2006). Tend and befriend: Biobehavioral bases of affiliation under stress. *Current Directions in Psychological Science, 15*, 273–277.

Taylor, S. E., & Brown, J. D. (1988). Illusion and well-being: A social psychological perspective on mental health. *Psychological Bulletin, 103*, 193–210.

Taylor, S. E., Lewis, B. P., Gruenewald, T. L., Gurung, R. A. R., Updegraff, J. A., & Klein, L. C. (2002). Sex differences in biobehavioral responses to threat: Reply to Geary and Flinn. *Psychological Review, 109*, 751–753.

Taylor, S. E., Saphire-Bernstein, S., & Seeman, T. E. (2010). Are plasma oxytocin in women and plasma vasopressin in men biomarkers of distressed pair-bond relationships? *Psychological Science, 21*, 3–7.

Teasdale, J. D., Segal, Z. V., Williams, J. M. G., Ridgeway, V. A., Soulsby, J. M., & Lau, M. A. (2000). Prevention of relapse/recurrence in major depression by mindfulness-based cognitive therapy. *Journal of Consulting and Clinical Psychology, 68*, 615–623.

Teller, D. Y., Morse, R., Borton, R., & Regal, C. (1974). Visual acuity for vertical and diagonal gratings in human infants. *Vision Research, 14*, 1433–1439.

Terracciano, A., Abdel-Khalek, A. M., Ádám, N., Adamovová, L., Ahn, C. K., Ahn, H. N., et al. (2005, October 7). National character does not reflect mean personality trait levels in 49 cultures. *Science, 310*, 96–100.

Tesser, A. (1988). Toward a self-evaluation maintenance model of social behavior. *Advances in Experimental Social Psychology, 21*, 181–227.

Tesser, A. (1993). The importance of heritability: The case of attitudes. *Psychological Review, 100*, 129–142.

Tessler, L. G. (1997). *How college students with learning disabilities can advocate for themselves.* Retrieved from http://www.ldanatl.org/aboutld/adults/post_secondary/print_college.asp

Tettamanti, M., Buccino, G., Saccuman, M. C., Gallese, V., Danna, M., Scifo, P., et al. (2005). Listening to action-related sentences activates fronto-parietal motor circuits. *Journal of Cognitive Neuroscience, 17*, 273–281.

Thigpen, C. H., & Cleckley, H. (1954). A case of multiple personality. *Journal of Abnormal Psychology, 49*, 135–151.

Thoits, P. A. (2010) Stress and health: Major findings and policy implications. *Journal of Health and Social Behavior, 51*, 41–53.

Thompson, P. (1980). Margaret Thatcher: A new illusion. *Perception, 9*, 483–484.

Thompson, P. M., Hayashi, K. M., Simon, S. L., Geaga, J. A., Hong, M. S., Sui, Y., et al. (2004). Structural abnormalities in the brains of human subjects who use methamphetamine. *Journal of Neuroscience, 24*, 6028–6036.

Thompson, W. F., Schellenberg, E. G., & Husain, G. (2001). Arousal, mood, and the Mozart effect. *Psychological Science, 12*, 248–251.

Thorgeirsson, T. E., Geller, F., Sulem, P., Rafnar, T., Wiste, A., Magnusson, K. P., et al. (2008). A variant associated with nicotine dependence, lung cancer and peripheral arterial disease. *Nature, 452*, 638–642.

Tickle, J. J., Sargent, J. D., Dalton, M. A., Beach, M. L., & Heatherton, T. F. (2001). Favorite movie stars, their tobacco use in contemporary movies and its association with adolescent smoking. *Tobacco Control, 10*, 16–22.

Tienari, P., Lahti, I., Sorri, A., Naarala, M., Moring, J., Kaleva, M., et al. (1990). Adopted-away offspring of schizophrenics and controls: The Finnish adoptive family study of schizophrenia. In L. Robins & M. Rutter (Eds.), *Straight and devious pathways from childhood to adulthood* (pp. 365–379). New York: Cambridge University Press.

Tienari, P., Wynne, L. C., Moring, J., Lahti, I., Naarala, M., Sorri, A., et al. (1994). The Finnish adoptive family study of schizophrenia: Implications for family research. *British Journal of Psychiatry, 23*(Suppl.), 20–26.

Tienari, P., Wynne, L. C., Sorri, A., Lahti, I., Laksy, K., Moring, J., et al. (2004). Genotype-environment interaction in schizophrenia spectrum disorder. *British Journal of Psychiatry, 184*, 216–222.

Tiggermann, M., & McGill, B. (2004). The role of social comparison in the effect of magazine advertisements on women's mood and body dissatisfaction. *Journal of Social and Clinical Psychology, 23*, 23–44.

Tipper, C. M., Handy, T. C., Giesbrecht, B., & Kingstone, A. F. (2008). Brain responses to biological relevance. *Journal of Cognitive Neuroscience, 20*, 879–891.

Tollesfson, G. D. (1995). Selective serotonin reuptake inhibitors. In A. F. Schatzberg & C. B. Nemeroff (Eds.), *The American Psychiatric Press textbook of psychopharmacology* (1st ed., pp. 161–182). Washington, DC: American Psychiatric Press.

Tolman, E. C., & Honzik, C. H. (1930). Introduction and removal of reward, and maze performance in rats. *University of California Publications in Psychology, 4*, 257–275.

Tomasello, M. (1999). *The cultural origins of human cognition.* Cambridge, MA: Harvard University Press.

Tombs, S., & Silverman, I. (2004). Pupillometry: A sexual selection approach. *Evolution and Human Behavior, 25*, 221–228.

Tomkins, S. S. (1963). *Affect imagery consciousness: Vol. 2. The negative affects.* New York: Tavistock/Routledge.

Tong, F., Nakayama, K., Vaughan, J. T., & Kanwisher, N. (1998). Binocular rivalry and visual awareness in human extrastriate cortex. *Neuron, 21*, 753–759.

Torgersen, S., Kringlen, E., & Cramer, V. (2001). The prevalence of personality disorders in a community sample. *Archives of General Psychiatry, 58*, 590–596.

Torrey, E. F. (1999). Epidemiological comparison of schizophrenia and bipolar disorder. *Schizophrenia Research, 39*, 101–106.

Torrey, E. F., Torrey, B. B., & Peterson, M. R. (1977). Seasonality of schizophrenic births in the United States. *Archives of General Psychiatry, 34*, 1065–1070.

Tracy, J. L., & Matsumoto, D. (2008). The spontaneous display of pride and shame: Evidence for biologically innate nonverbal displays. *Proceedings of the National Academy of Sciences, USA, 105*, 11655–11660.

Tracy, J. L., & Robins, R. W. (2008). The nonverbal expression of pride: Evidence for cross-cultural recognition. *Journal of Personality and Social Psychology, 94*, 516–530.

Treatment for Adolescents with Depression Study (TADS) Team. (2004). Fluoxetine, cognitive-behavioral therapy, and their combination for adolescents with depression: Treatment for adolescents with depression study (TADS) randomized controlled trial. *Journal of the American Medical Association, 292*, 807–820.

Treffert, D. A., & Christensen, D. D. (2006, June/July). Inside the mind of a savant. *Scientific American Mind*, 50–55.

Treisman, A., & Gelade, G. (1980). A feature-integration theory of attention. *Cognitive Psychology, 12*, 97–136.

Tremblay, P. F., Graham, K., & Wells, S. (2008). Severity of physical aggression reported by university students: A test of the interaction between trait aggression and alcohol consumption. *Personality and Individual Differences, 45*(1), 3–9.

Triandis, H. C. (1989). The self and social behavior in differing cultural contexts. *Psychological Review, 96*, 506–520.

Trivers, R. L. (1971). The evolution of reciprocal altruism. *Quarterly Review of Biology, 46*, 35–57.

Tryon, W. W., & Tryon, G. S. (2011). No ownership of common factors. *American Psychologist, 66*, 151–152.

Trzesniewski, K. H., Donnellan, M. B., & Roberts, R. W. (2008). Is "generation me" really more narcissistic than previous generations? *Journal of Personality, 76*, 903–918.

Tsien, J. Z. (2000, April). Building a brainier mouse. *Scientific American, 282*, 62–68.

Tugade, M. M., & Fredrickson, B. L. (2004). Resilient individuals use positive emotions to bounce back from negative emotional experiences. *Journal of Personality and Social Psychology, 86*, 320–333.

Turner, E. H., Matthews, A. M., Linardatos, B. S., Tell, R. A., & Rosenthal, R. (2008). Selective publication of antidepressant trials and its influence on apparent efficacy. *New England Journal of Medicine, 358*, 252–260.

Twenge, J. M., & Campbell, W. K. (2003). "Isn't it fun to get the respect that we're going to deserve?" Narcissism, social rejection, and aggression. *Personality and Social Psychology Bulletin, 29*, 261–272.

Twenge, J. M., Konrath, S., Foster, J. D., Campbell, K. W., & Bushman, B. J. (2008). Egos inflating over time: A cross-temporal meta-analysis of the narcissistic personality inventory. *Journal of Personality, 76*, 875–902.

U.S. Bureau of Labor Statistics, U.S. Department of Labor. (2009). *Occupational outlook handbook, 2008–2009 edition: psychologists*. Retrieved from http://www.bls.gov/oco/ocos056.htm

Ungerleider, L. G., & Mishkin, M. (1982). Two cortical visual systems. In D. J. Ingle, Mansfield, R. J. W., & M. S. Goodale (Eds.), *The analysis of visual behavior* (pp. 549–586). Cambridge, MA: MIT Press.

United Nations Office on Drugs and Crime. (2009). *World Drug Report 2009*. Vienna, Austria: Author. Retrieved from http://www.unodc.org/unodc/en/data-and-analysis/WDR-2009.html

United Nations Office on Drugs and Crime. (n.d.). Homicide statistics, criminal justice sources—Latest available year (2003–2009). [Data from the Eleventh United Nations Survey of Crime Trends and Operations of Criminal Justice Systems (UN-CTS), 2007–2008]. Retrieved from http://www.unodc.org/unodc/en/data-and-analysis/homicide.html

United States Census Bureau. (2011, September 27). 2012 Statistical abstract: Deaths. Retrieved from http://www.census.gov/compendia/statab/cats/births_deaths_marriages_divorces/deaths.html

United States Department of Health and Human Services. (2001, 8 January). *Preventing disease and death from tobacco use* [Press release]. Retrieved from http://archive.hhs.gov/news/press/2001pres/01fstbco.html

United States Department of Health and Human Services, Office of the Surgeon General (2004, May 27). *The health consequences of smoking: A report of the Surgeon General*. Available from http://www.surgeongeneral.gov/library/smokingconsequences

United States Government. (1990). *Americans with Disabilities Act of 1990, as amended*. Retrieved from http://www.ada.gov/pubs/adastatute08.htm

Upton, N. (1994). Mechanisms of action of new antiepileptic drugs: Rational design and serendipitous findings. *Trends in Pharmacological Sciences, 15*, 456–463.

Urberg, K. A., Degirmencioglue, S. M., Tolson, J. M., & Halliday-Scher, K. (1995). The structure of adolescent peer networks. *Developmental Psychology, 31*, 540–547. doi: 10.1037/0012-1649.31.4.540

Ustün, T. B., Ayuso-Mateos, J. L., Chatterji, S., Mathers, C., & Murray, C. J. (2004). Global burden of depressive disorders in the year 2000. *British Journal of Psychiatry, 184*, 386–392.

Uvnas-Moberg, K. (1998). Oxytocin may mediate the benefits of positive social interaction and emotions. *Psychoneuroendocrinology, 23*, 819–835.

Vallabha, G. K., McClelland, J. L., Pons, F., Werker, J. F., & Amano, S. (2007). Unsupervised learning of vowel categories from infant-directed speech. *Proceedings of the National Academy of Sciences, USA, 104*, 13273–13278.

Van der Oord, S., Prins, P. J. M., Oosterlaan, J., & Emmelkamp, P. M. G. (2008). Efficacy of methylphenidate, psychosocial treatments and their combination in school-aged children with ADHD: A meta-analysis. *Clinical Psychology Review, 28*, 783–800.

van Haren, N. E., Schnack, H. G., Cahn, W., van den Heuvel, M. P., Lepage, C., Collins, L., Evans, A. C., Hulshoff Pol, H. E., & Kahn, R. S. (2011). Changes in cortical thickness during the course of illness in schizophrenia. *Archives of General Psychiatry, 68*, 871–880.

Vargas-Reighley, R. V. (2005). *Bicultural competence and academic resilience among immigrants*. El Paso, TX: LFB Scholarly Publishing.

Vargha-Khadem, F., Gadian, D. G., Watkins, K. E., Connelly, A., Van Paesschen, W., & Mishkin, M. (1997, July 18). Differential effects of early hippocampal pathology on episodic and semantic memory. *Science, 277*, 376–380.

Vazire, S. (2010). Who knows what about a person? The self-other knowledge asymmetry (SOKA) model. *Journal of Personality and Social Psychology, 98*, 281–300.

Vazire, S., & Carlson, E. N. (2011). Others sometimes know us better than we know ourselves. *Current Directions in Psychological Science, 20*, 104–108.

Vazire, S., & Gosling, S. D. (2004). e-perceptions: Personality impressions based on personal websites. *Journal of Personality and Social Psychology, 87*, 123–132.

Vazire, S., & Mehl, M. R. (2008). Knowing me, knowing you: The accuracy and unique predictive validity of self and other ratings of daily behavior. *Journal of Personality and Social Psychology, 95*, 1202–1216.

Ventura, P., Pattamadilok, C., & Fernandes, T. (2008). Schooling in Western culture promotes context-free processing. *Journal of Experimental Child Psychology, 100*(2), 79–88.

Vernon, P. A., Wickett, J. C., Bazana, P. G., Stelmack, R. M., & Sternberg, R. J. (2000). The neuropsychology and psychophysiology of human intelligence. In R. J. Sternberg (Ed.), *Handbook of intelligence* (pp. 245–264). Cambridge, UK: Cambridge University Press.

Vingerhoets, A. J., Bylsma, L. M., & Rottenberg, J. (2009). Crying: A biopsychosocial phenomenon. In T. Fögen (Ed.), *Tears in the Graeco-Roman world* (pp. 439–474). Berlin, Germany: De Gruyter.

Vismera, L., & Rogers, S. (2010). Behavioral treatments in autism spectrum disorders: What do we know? *Annual Review of Clinical Psychology, 6*, 447–468.

Vohs, K. D., & Heatherton, T. F. (2004). Ego threat elicits different social comparison processes among high and low self-esteem people: Implications for interpersonal perceptions. *Social Cognition, 22*, 168–190.

Volkmar, F., Chawarska, K., & Klin, A. (2005). Autism in infancy and early childhood. *Annual Review of Psychology, 56*, 1–21.

Volkow, N. D. (2007, September). This is your brain on food. Interview by Kristin Leutwyler-Ozelli. *Scientific American, 297*, 84–85.

Volkow, N. D., Wang, G. J., & Baler, R. D. (2011). Reward, dopamine, and the control of food intake: Implications for obesity. *Trends in Cognitive Science, 15*, 37–46.

Volkow, N. D., Wang, G. J., Telang, F., Fowler, J. S., Logan, J., Childress, A. R., et al. (2008). Dopamine increases in striatum do not elicit craving in cocaine abusers unless they are coupled with cocaine cues. *Neuroimage, 39*, 1266–1273.

von Neumann, J., & Morgenstern, O. (1947). *Theory of games and economic behavior*. Princeton, NJ: Princeton University Press.

von Restorff, H. (1933). Uber die wirkung von bereichsbildungen im spurenfeld [On the effect of spheres' formations in the trace field]. *Psychologische Forschung, 18*, 299–342.

Vygotsky, L. S. (1978). *Mind in society*. Cambridge, MA: Harvard University Press.

Vytal, K., & Hamann, S. (2010). Neuroimaging support for discrete neural correlates of basic emotions: A voxel-based meta-analysis. *Journal of Cognitive Neuroscience, 22*, 2864–2885.

Wadhwa, P. D., Sandman, C. A., & Garite, T. J. (2001). The neurobiology of stress in human pregnancy: Implications for prematurity and development of the fetal central nervous system. *Progress in Brain Research, 133*, 131–142.

Wager, T. D. (2005). Placebo effects in the brain: Linking mental and physiological processes. *Brain, Behavior, and Immunity, 19*(4), 281–282.

Wagner, D. D., Dal Cin, S., Sargent, J. D., Kelley, W. M., & Heatherton, T. F. (2011). Spontaneous action representation in smokers when watching movie characters smoke. *Journal of Neuroscience,* 31, 894–898.

Waite, L. J. (1995). Does marriage matter? *Demography 32*, 483–507.

Walker, E., Kestler, L., Bollini, A., & Hochman, K. M. (2004). Schizophrenia: Etiology and course. *Annual Review of Psychology, 55*, 401–430.

Walker, M. P., & Stickgold, R. (2006). Sleep, memory, and plasticity. *Annual Review of Psychology, 57*, 139–166.

Walsh, T., McClellan, J. M., McCarthy, S. E., Addington, A. M., Pierce, S. B., Cooper, G. M., et al. (2008, March 27). Rare structural variants disrupt multiple genes in neurodevelopmental pathways in schizophrenia. *Science, 320*, 539–543.

Walton, G. M., & Spencer, S. J. (2009). Latent ability: Grades and test scores systematically underestimate the intellectual ability of negatively stereotyped students. *Psychological Science, 20*, 1132–1139.

Waltrip, R. W., Buchanan, R. W., Carpenter, W. T., Kirkpatrick, B., Summerfelt, A., Breier, A., et al. (1997). Borna disease virus antibodies and the deficit syndrome of schizophrenia. *Schizophrenia Research, 23*, 253–257.

Wamsley, E. J., Tucker, M., Payne, J. D., Benavides, J. A., & Stickgold, R. (2010). Dreaming of a learning task is associated with enhanced sleep-dependent memory consolidation. *Current Biology, 20*(9), 850–855. doi:10.1016/j.cub.2010.03.027

Wardle, J., Carnell, S., Haworth, C. M., & Plomin, R. (2008). Evidence for a strong genetic influence on childhood adiposity despite the force of the obesogenic environment. *American Journal of Clinical Nutrition, 87*, 398–404.

Warren, Z., McPheeters, M., Sathe, N., et al. (2011). A systematic review of early intensive intervention for autism spectrum disorders. *Pediatrics, 127*, e1303–1311.

Watson, D., & Clark, L. A. (1997). Extraversion and its positive emotional core. In R. Hogan, J. Johnson, & S. Briggs (Eds.), *Handbook of personality psychology* (pp. 767–793). San Diego, CA: Academic Press.

Watson, D., Wiese, D., Vaidya, J., & Tellegen, A. (1999). The two general activation systems of affect: Structural findings, evolutionary considerations, and psychobiological evidence. *Journal of Personality and Social Psychology, 76*, 820–838.

Watson, J. B. (1924). *Behaviorism.* New York: Norton.

Watson, J. B., & Rayner, R. (1920). Conditioned emotional reactions. *Journal of Experimental Psychology, 3*, 1–14.

Waugh, C. E., Wager, T. D., Fredrickson, B. L., Noll, D. N., & Taylor, S. F. (2008). The neural correlates of trait resilience when anticipating and recovering from threat. *Social Cognitive and Affective Neuroscience, 3*, 322–332.

Weber, N., & Brewer, N. (2004). Confidence-accuracy calibration in absolute and relative face recognition judgments. *Journal of Experimental Psychology: Applied, 10*, 156–172.

Wegner, D., Shortt, J., Blake, A., & Page, M. (1990). The suppression of exciting thoughts. *Journal of Personality and Social Psychology, 58*, 409–418.

Weiner, B. (1974). *Achievement motivation and attribution theory.* Morristown, NJ: General Learning Press.

Weiss, A., Bates, T. C., & Luciano, M. (2008). Happiness is a personal(ity) thing: The genetics of personality and well-being in a representative sample. *Psychological Science, 19*, 205–210.

Weissman, M. M., Bland, R. C., Canino, G. J., Greenwald, S., Hwu, H. G., Lee, C. K., et al. (1994). The cross national epidemiology of obsessive compulsive disorder. The cross national collaborative group. *Journal of Clinical Psychiatry, 55*, 5–10.

Wells, G. L. (2008). Field experiments on eyewitness identification: Towards a better understanding of pitfalls and prospects. *Law and Human Behavior, 32*, 6–10.

Wells, G. L., Small, M., Penrod, S., Malpass, R. S., Fulero, S. M., & Brimacombe, C. A. E. (1998). Eyewitness identification procedures: Recommendations for lineups and photospreads. *Law and Human Behavior, 22*, 603–647.

Werker, J. F., Gilbert, J. H., Humphrey, K., & Tees, R. C. (1981). Developmental aspects of cross-language speech perception. *Child Development, 52*, 349–355.

West, G. L., Anderson, A. A., Ferber, S., & Pratt, J. (2011, in press). Electrophysiological evidence for biased competition in V1 for fear expressions. *Journal of Cognitive Neuroscience.* doi:10.1162/jocn.2011.21605

West, G., Anderson, A., & Pratt, J. (2009). Motivationally significant stimuli show visual prior entry: Direct evidence for attentional capture. *Journal of Experimental Psychology: Human Perception and Performance, 35*, 1032–1042.

Westen, D. (1998). The scientific legacy of Sigmund Freud: Toward a psychodynamically informed psychological science. *Psychological Bulletin, 124*, 333–371.

Westen, D., Novotny, C. M., & Thompson-Brenner, H. (2004). The empirical status of empirically supported psychotherapies: Assumptions, findings, and reporting in controlled clinical trials. *Psychological Bulletin, 130*, 631–663.

Weyandt, L. L., Janusis, G., Wilson, K., Verdi, G., Paquin, G., Lopes, J., Varejao, M., & Dussault, C. (2009). Nonmedical prescription stimulant use among a sample of college students: Relationships with psychological variables. *Journal of Attention Disorders, 13*, 284-296.

Whalen, C. K. (1989). Attention deficit and hyperactivity disorders. In T. H. Ollendick & M. Herson (Eds.), *Handbook of child psychopathology* (2nd ed., pp. 131–169). New York: Plenum Press.

Whalen, P. J., Rauch, S. L., Etcoff, N. L., McInerney, N. L., Lee, M. B., & Jenike, M. A. (1998). Masked presentations of emotional facial expressions modulate amygdala activity without explicit knowledge. *Journal of Neuroscience, 18*, 411–418.

Whalen, P. J., Shin, L. M., McInerney, S. C. L., Fischer, H., Wright, C. I., & Rauch, S. L. (2001). A functional MRI study of human amygdala responses to facial expressions of fear versus anger. *Emotion, 1*, 70–83.

Wheatley, T., & Haidt, J. (2005). Hypnotic disgust makes moral judgments more severe. *Psychological Science, 16*, 780–784.

Whiteside, S. P., Port, J. D., & Abramowitz, J. S. (2004). A meta-analysis of functional neuroimaging in obsessive-compulsive disorder. *Psychiatry Research, 15*, 69–79.

Widiger, T. A., & Corbitt, E. M. (1995). Are personality disorders well-classified in DSM-IV? In W. J. Livesly (Ed.), *The DSM-IV personality disorders* (pp. 103–126). New York: Guilford Press.

Widom, C. S. (1978). A methodology for studying noninstitutionalized psychopaths. In R. D. Hare & D. A. Schalling (Eds.), *Psychopathic behavior: Approaches to research* (pp. 72ff). Chichester, UK: Wiley.

Wierson, M., Long, P. J., & Forehand, R. L. (1993). Toward a new understanding of early menarche: The role of environmental stress in pubertal timing. *Adolescence, 28*, 913–924.

Wiesel, T. N., & Hubel, D. H. (1963). Single-cell responses in striate cortex of kittens deprived of vision in one eye. *Journal of Neurophysiology, 26*, 1003–1017.

Wilens, T. E., Faraone, S. V., & Biederman, J. (2004). Attention-deficit/hyperactivity disorder in adults. *Journal of the American Medical Association, 292*, 619–623.

Wilfley, D. E., Bishop, M., Wilson, G. T., & Agras, W. S. (2007). Classification of eating disorders: Toward DSM-V. *International Journal of Eating Disorders, 40(suppl)*, S123–S129.

Wilke, M., Sohn, J. H., Byars, A. W., & Holland, S. K. (2003). Bright spots: Correlations of gray matter volume with IQ in a normal pediatric population. *Neuroimage, 20*, 202–215

Williams, K., Harkins, S. G., & Latané, B. (1981). Identifiability as a deterrent to social loafing: Two cheering experiments. *Journal of Personality and Social Psychology, 40*, 303–311.

Williams, L. E., & Bargh, J. A. (2008, October 24). Experiences of physical warmth influence interpersonal warmth. *Science, 322*, 606–607.

Williams, R. B., Jr. (1987). Refining the type A hypothesis: Emergence of the hostility complex. *American Journal of Cardiology, 60*, 27J–32J.

Wills, T. A., DuHamel, K., & Vaccaro, D. (1995). Activity and mood temperament as predictors of adolescent substance use: Test of a self-regulation mediational model. *Journal of Personality and Social Psychology, 68*, 901–916.

Wilsnack, R. W., Wilsnack, S. C., & Obot, I. S. (2005). Why study gender, alcohol and culture? In I. S. Obot & R. Room (Eds.), *Alcohol, gender and drinking problems: Perspectives from low and middle income countries* (pp. 1–23). Geneva, Switzerland: World Health Organization.

Wilson, M. A., & McNaughton, B. L. (1994). Reactivation of hippocampal ensemble memories during sleep. *Science, 265*(5172), 676–679.

Wilson, A. E., & Ross, M. (2001). From chump to champ: People's appraisals of their earlier and present selves. *Journal of Personality and Social Psychology, 80*, 572–584.

Wilson, F. A., & Stimpson, J. P. (2010). Trends in fatalities from distracted driving in the United States, 1999 to 2008. *American Journal of Public Health, 100*, 2213–2219.

Wilson, M. A., & McNaughton, B. L. (1994, July 29). Reactivation of hippocampal ensemble memories during sleep. *Science, 265*, 676–679.

Wilson, T. D., & Gilbert, D. T. (2003). Affective forecasting. In M. Zanna (Ed.), *Advances in experimental social psychology* (Vol. 35, pp. 345–411). New York: Elsevier.

Wilson, T. D., & Schooler, J. W. (1991). Thinking too much: Introspection can reduce the quality of preferences and decisions. *Journal of Personality and Social Psychology 60*, 181–192.

Winberg, J., & Porter, R. H. (1998). Olfaction and human neonatal behaviour: Clinical implications. *Acta Paediatrica, 87*, 6–10.

Winfried, R., & Hofmann, S. G. (2008). The missing data problem in meta-analyses. *Archives of General Psychiatry, 65*, 238.

Wise, R. A., & Rompre, P. P. (1989). Brain dopamine and reward. *Annual Review of Psychology, 40*, 191–225.

Wiseman, C. V., Harris, W. A., & Halmi, K. A. (1998). Eating disorders. *Medical Clinics of North America, 82*, 145–159.

Wolfe, J. M., & Horowitz, T. S. (2004). What attributes guide the deployment of visual attention and how do they do it? *Nature Reviews Neuroscience, 5*, 495–501.

Wolford, G. L., Miller, M. B., & Gazzaniga, M. (2000). The left hemisphere's role in hypothesis formation. *Journal of Neuroscience, 20*, 1–4.

Woller, K. M., Buboltz, W. C. J., & Loveland, J. M. (2007). Psychological reactance: Examination across age, ethnicity, and gender. *American Journal of Psychology, 120*(1), 15–24.

Wolpe, J. (1997). Thirty years of behavior therapy. *Behavior Therapy, 28*, 633–635.

Wolraich, M. L., Wilson, D. B., & White, J. W. (1995). The effects of sugar on behavior or cognition in children: A meta-analysis. *Journal of the American Medical Association, 274*, 1617–1621.

Wood, J. M., Garb, H. N., Lilienfeld, S. O., & Nezworski, M. T. (2002). Clinical assessment. *Annual Review of Psychology, 53*, 519–543.

Woodworth, M., & Porter, S. (2002). In cold blood: Characteristics of criminal homicides as a function of psychopathy. *Journal of Abnormal Psychology, 111*, 436–445.

World Health Organization. (2008). *WHO Report on the global tobacco epidemic.* Retrieved from http://www.who.int/tobacco/mpower/en/

World Health Organization. (2011). *The top ten causes of death* [Fact sheet]. Retrieved from http://www.who.int/mediacentre/factsheets/fs310/en/index.html

Worley, H. (2006, June). *Depression: A leading contributor to global burden of disease: Myriad obstacles—particularly stigma—block better treatment in developing countries.* Retrieved November 10, 2008, from http://www.prb.org/Articles/2006/DepressionaLeadingContributortoGlobalBurdenofDisease.aspx

Wright, S. C., & Tropp, L. R. (2005). Language and intergroup contact: Investigating the impact of bilingual instruction on children's intergroup attitudes. *Group Processes and Intergroup Relations, 8*, 309–328.

Xu, J., Kochanek, K. D., Murphy, S. L., & Tejada-Vera, B. (2010). Deaths: Final data for 2007. *National Vital Statistics Reports, 58,* Number 19. U.S. Department of Health and Human Services.

Xu, J., & Roberts, R. E. (2010). The power of positive emotions: It's a matter of life or death—subjective well-being and longevity in a general population. *Health Psychology, 29*, 9–19.

Yamagata, S., Suzuki, A., Ando, J., Ono, Y., Kijima, N., Yoshimura, K., et al. (2006). Is the genetic structure of human personality universal? A cross-cultural twin study from North America, Europe, and Asia. *Journal of Personality and Social Psychology, 90*, 987–998.

Yamaguchi, S., Greenwald, A. G., Banaji, M. R., Murakami, F., Chen, D., Shiomura, K., et al. (2007). Apparent universality of positive implicit self-esteem. *Psychological Science, 18*, 498–500.

Yates, W. R., Perry, P., & Murray, S. (1992). Aggression and hostility in anabolic steroid users. *Biological Psychiatry, 31*, 1232–1234.

Yerkes, R. M., & Dodson, J. D. (1908). The relation of strength of stimulus to rapidity of habit formation. *Journal of Comparative Neurology & Psychology, 18*, 459–482.

Yeshurun, Y., & Sobel, N. (2010). An odor is not worth a thousand words: From multidimensional odors to unidimensional odor objects. *Annual Review of Psychology, 61*, 219–41.

Yoo, S. S., Hu, P. T., Gujar, N., Jolesz, F. A., & Walker, M. P. (2007). A deficit in the ability to form new human memories without sleep. *Nature Neuroscience, 10*, 385–392.

Yucel, M., Harrison, B. J., Wood, S. J., Fornito, A., Wellard, R. M., Pujol, J., et al. (2007). Functional and biochemical alterations of the medial frontal cortex in obsessive-compulsive disorder. *Archives of General Psychiatry, 64*, 946–955.

Yuille, J. C., & Cutshall, J. L. (1986). A case study of eyewitness memory of a crime. *Journal of Applied Psychology, 71*, 291–301.

Zahn-Waxler, C., & Radke-Yarrow, M. (1990). The origins of empathic concern. *Motivation and Emotion, 14*, 107–130.

Zahn-Waxler, C., & Robinson, J. (1995). Empathy and guilt: Early origins of feelings of responsibility. In J. P. Tangney & K. W. Fischer (Eds.), *Self-conscious emotions: The psychology of shame, guilt, embarrassment, and pride* (pp. 143–173). New York: Guilford Press.

Zajonc, R. B. (1965, July 15). Social facilitation. *Science, 149*, 269–274.

Zajonc, R. B. (1968). Attitudinal effects of mere exposure. *Journal of Personality and Social Psychology Monographs, 9*, 1–27.

Zajonc, R. B. (1980). Feeling and thinking: Preferences need no inferences. *American Psychologist, 35*, 151–175.

Zajonc, R. B. (2001). Mere exposure: A gateway to the subliminal. *Current Directions in Psychological Science 10*, 224–228.

Zak, P. J., Kurzban, R., & Matzner, W. T. (2005). Oxytocin is associated with human trustworthiness. *Hormones and Behavior, 48*(5), 522–527.

Zametkin, A. J., Nordahl, T. E., Gross, M., King, A. C., Stemple, W. E., Rumsey, J., et al. (1990). Cerebral glucose metabolism in adults with hyperactivity of childhood onset. *New England Journal of Medicine, 323*, 1361–1366.

Zebian, S., Alamuddin, R., Mallouf, M., & Chatila, Y. (2007). Developing an appropriate psychology through culturally sensitive research practices in the Arab-speaking world: A content analysis of psychological research published between 1950 and 2004. *Journal of Cross-Cultural Psychology, 38*, 91–122.

Zentall, S. S., Sutton, J. E., & Sherburne, L. M. (1996). True imitative learning in pigeons. *Psychological Science, 7*, 343–346.

Zihl, J., von Cramon, D., & Mai, N. (1983). Selective disturbance of movement vision after bilateral brain damage. *Brain, 106*, 313–340.

Zimbardo, P. G. (1990). *Shyness: What it is, what to do about it.* Reading, MA: Addison-Wesley.

Zorrilla, E. P., Iwasaki, S., Moss, J. A., Chang, J., Otsuji, J., Inoue, K., et al. (2006). Vaccination against weight gain. *Proceedings of the National Academy of Sciences, USA, 103*, 13226–13231.

Zuckerman, M. (2007). *Sensation seeking and risky behavior.* Washington, DC: American Psychological Association.

# ANSWER KEY FOR CAPTION QUESTIONS AND FOR PRACTICE TESTS

*For additional Practice Tests and other review materials, visit StudySpace at http://wwnorton.com/studyspace*

## CHAPTER 1

### Caption Question, p. 4

**Answer:** In evaluating science-related announcements, most of us first rely on common sense. When news reports pass the common sense test, we might then do research: asking someone with related knowledge, reading a professionally prepared and acknowledged source. One *unreliable* method would be to do a Web search and simply believe whatever information comes up.

### Caption Question, p. 5

**Answer:** Answers will vary. One example: The multimillion-dollar "brain training" industry claims computer mind games improve cognitive function, yet these claims lack empirical support. Improvement seems to be task specific and results from training and practice, not general overall improvement (Owen et al., 2010).

### Caption Question, p. 18

**Answer:** The precise amount of influence that biology exerts on behavior cannot be determined. In a sense, since we cannot separate biology from who we are, every choice we make or action we take is biological. However, as emphasized throughout this book, environment (nurture) is continuously interacting with biology (nature) in making us who we are.

### Caption Question, p. 20

**Answer:** Answers will vary. When considering our ancestors' early evolution, you might think about the development of very basic survival behaviors. When considering more-recent evolution, you might think about the increasing size and complexity of the frontal cortex. This development brought about additional means of survival, namely the greater complexity of humans and of their intelligence.

### Practice Test, p. 27

1. **Answer:** c. "I think you'll be surprised by the range of questions psychologists ask about the mind, the brain, and behavior, not to mention the methods they use to answer these questions."
2. **Answers:** a. adaptations; b. survival of the fittest; c. natural selection.
3. **Answers:** a. social; b. biological; c. cultural; d. individual.
4. **Answers:** a. Titchener, Wundt; b. Dewey, James; c. Kohler, Wertheimer; d. Skinner, Watson; e. Köhler, Miller, Tolman; f. Lewin.
5. **Answers:** a. introspection; b. dualism; c. localization; d. stream of consciousness; e. information processing theory.
6. **Answer:** c. "That's great! Psychologists do research to figure out which interventions are most helpful for people with different concerns."

## CHAPTER 2

### Caption Question, p. 47

**Answer:** This small sample shows women clustered on the beach. Another small sample might show men clustered. Yet another small sample might show an unrepresentative mixing of women and men. In other words, the smallness of the sample might distort the information available in it. The larger the sample, the greater the chance that the ratio of women to men in the sample will be representative of the beach. In studying the beachgoing ways of women and men, of course, you would want to study more than one beach. The larger your sample of beachgoers, the greater the number of beaches you study, the more likely it will be that your results will be generalizable.

### Caption Questions, p. 67

**Answer for Figure 2.22:** The mean is the most valuable number. Because it is the arithmetic average of all the results, it provides the most generalizable sense of the effect of alcohol on balance. By contrast, the range is based on only the highest and lowest numbers. Therefore it provides the vaguest sense of the results for all the study participants. Note that for any set of data, the mean is always more meaningful when reported with the standard deviation, which expresses the variation in the scores. Note, too, that for this set of data, the mode is not really useful because the frequency is based on only two values (i.e., one more than each individual value). Here the median turns out to be close to the mean, but the median is based on the placement of values rather than their combination.

**Answer for Figure 2.23:** In general, this relationship is a negative correlation: the greater the level of intoxication, the less ability to balance.

### Practice Test, p. 71

1. **Answer:** c. replication.
2. **Answer:** b, because it offers a specific prediction.
3. **Answer:** a, because it is random.
4. **Answer:** c, because it includes experimental and control groups.
5. **Answer:** a, because it uses random assignment.

## CHAPTER 3

### Caption Question, p. 84

**Answer:** Answers will vary.

### Caption Question, p. 112

**Answer:** In addition to genetics (nature), environment (nurture) needs to be considered as a factor in the similarities between twins raised apart. What type of environment was each twin raised in, and how might that environment have affected the twin's characteristics? For example, the twins might have been raised apart in highly similar environments. Adoption agencies might tend to place particular kinds of children with particular kinds of parents. Those parents and the communities they live in might tend to have similar values and similar emphases (such as on the merit of being a firefighter). In addition, whether the twins were in similar or different environments, each twin's temperament and physical appearance, both genetically based, might have elicited similar responses from people.

### Practice Test, p. 129

1. **Answer:** c. bricks, walls.
2. **Answers:** Choices a, b, and c are true.
3. **Answers:** b. sensory neuron, e. afferent neuron.
4. **Answer:** a. someone who plays computer games requiring the exploration of complex virtual worlds.

## CHAPTER 4

### Caption Question, p. 137

**Answer:** Answers will vary about the adjustment time. Kinds of constant stimulation that people must adjust to include flashing lights, machinery noises, and cooking smells. By the way, olfaction appears to have the fastest rate of adaptation.

### Caption Question, p. 156

**Answer:** (a) The blue on the left is brighter because its color is more saturated. The blue on the right is paler because its color is less saturated. (b) The central squares of each pair look different because each square is surrounded by a different color. The brightness of the surrounding color influences your perception of the lightness of the central square.

### Caption Question, p. 167

**Answer:** Context here is the meaning of each word: Your reading of "THE" enables you to see its middle character as an "H." Your reading of "CAT" enables you to see its middle character as an "A." Without the context, each middle character would look the same to you.

### Caption Question, p. 170

**Answer:** Answers will vary. Note that some people are so dominant in one eye that this "crossing" does not occur easily.

### Caption Question, p. 171

**Answer:**

**Occlusion:** The tree blocks the building behind it.

**Relative size:** The people at the front of the picture are larger than the people toward the middle and back of the picture.

**Familiar size:** We know the relative height of men, and we do not assume that the single dark figure is especially small relative to the man in front. Therefore the dark figure must be farther away.

**Linear perspective:** The lines of the street and of the buildings converge toward the horizon.

**Texture gradient:** Textures in the foreground are more distinguishable. In the background, as the buildings recede into the distance, textures get denser and blur together.

**Position relative to horizon:** The figures positioned higher on the page, near the horizon, appear farther away.

### Caption Question, p. 175

**Answer:** When you look at each image, the eye simply collects information about the size of the bearded man. Perspective causes the brain to treat that information differently each time. In (a), the man is farther away, so the brain adjusts his size to make him human size. In (b), the bearded man is on the same frontal plane as the man in the red sweater. Thus the brain does not correct for the bearded man's size. As far as the brain can tell, the bearded man is tiny compared with the man in the sweater.

### Practice Test, p. 179

1. **Answer:** a. specialized receptors, thalamus, cortex.
2. **Answer:** c. You can decipher qualitative differences among the instruments because of the involvement of specific sensory receptors, whereas you can make quantitative distinctions—recognizing variations in the notes' intensity—due to the rate of firing of your sensory neurons.
3. **Answer:** b. The intensity of the auditory stimulation does not exceed the minimum threshold needed for you to detect a sensation.
4. **Answers:** a. activated by chemical changes in tissue; e. nonmyelinated axons; f. slow fibers.
5. **Answer:** d. Directing the girl's hand on a quick touching tour of the nearby environment and saying things such as "Feel this tree's rough bark. Touch the grass; it tickles. Feel how smooth this rock is!"

## CHAPTER 5

### Caption Question, p. 185

**Answer:** Since this question asks you to imaginatively project yourself into the experience of regaining full consciousness, answers will vary. Note that the few people who emerge from a minimally conscious state do so with severe disabilities (Luauté et al., 2010).

### Caption Question, p. 205

**Answer:** Since this question asks you to evaluate the evidence in the text, answers will vary.

### Caption Question, p. 210

**Answer:** Answers will vary. A case could be made that video games improve eye/hand coordination and even sharpen perception. An opposing case could be made that video games dull perception through sensory overload and that they interfere with person-to-person social interaction.

### Caption Question, p. 217

**Answer:** (a) Patrons such as this woman are physically addicted to smoking. They do not want to step outside the restaurant to smoke, but they are willing to stick their heads and arms through padded holes in the wall. (b) Casinos encourage patrons' "addiction" to gambling through enclosed spaces, bright lights, stimulating sounds, and control of information from the outside environment.

### Practice Test, p. 221

1. **Answer:** c. The person in the minimally conscious state shows some degree of brain activity, whereas the person in the persistent vegetative state shows no brain activity.
2. **Answer:** b. Participants in Condition A will be more friendly toward the stranger than will participants in Condition B.
3. **Answer:** a. The participant will say he saw a tire and will draw a car.
4. **Answers:** a. narcolepsy; b. somnambulism; c. insomnia; d. apnea.
5. **Answers:** b. All animals sleep.; c. It is impossible to resist indefinitely the urge to sleep.; e. Animals die when deprived of sleep for extended periods.
6. **Answer:** d. "It's pretty cool that a hypnotist could help those people enter an altered state of consciousness."
7. **Answer:** b. "Lying on your back, rest your hands gently on your abdomen. As you breathe in and out, focus attention on your breath. Notice the rhythmic rise and fall of your abdomen and the slow, deep movement of your chest."

## CHAPTER 6

### Caption Question, p. 224

**Answer:** Though answers will vary, today's parenting styles are very different from those of Skinner's time, and people today tend to balk even more at this type of approach.

### Caption Question, p. 234

**Answer:** When an animal learns to avoid food that makes it sick, the animal has a greater chance of surviving. An increased chance of survival gives the animal a greater chance of passing on its genes than the chance of an animal that dies from eating the wrong thing. As the genes of "wiser" and healthier animals are passed along, the species evolves as that much "wiser" and healthier.

### Caption Question, p. 236

**Answer:** The potential misfortunes are unlikely to be supernatural. For example, if you and the cat are in the middle of the road, you might be hit by a car. Or if you try to pet the cat, it might scratch you. If the ladder is not positioned securely, it might fall and hit you. Or you might be so distracted by the ladder that you miss some other peril.

### Caption Question, p. 241

**Answer:** Answers will vary. For example, you might use shaping to teach yourself how to cook an elaborate gourmet meal. How would you begin? Perhaps you need to start with basic skills, such as boiling water to prepare rice. Your next step might be to buy, clean, and slice fresh vegetables. If your recipes call for sauces on those vegetables, you might need to develop sauce-making techniques. Cooking meat or seafood can require specific methods. In learning and layering these abilities, you would be working up to the day when you can put them in the proper order to create a feast.

### Caption Question, p. 251

**Answer:** Answers will vary. However, answers should reflect the fact that memes are units of cultural evolution, influenced in their creation and selection by biological evolution. Biological evolution is slow, and cultural transmission (always predicated on biology) is quick. Macaques learned to enjoy gritless, slightly salty sweet potatoes and passed on this "cultural" food choice. Likewise, we shape and select many behaviors, and those behaviors shape us. For example, the human preference for sweet food has an evolutionary component that then translates into culture-specific representations of candy. Consider Swiss chocolate versus Indonesian durian coconut candy. Milk chocolate may not make as much sense in the hot, humid climate of Indonesia as a candy made from durian fruit and coconut, and durian coconut candy might not taste good to a non-Indonesian Swiss. The human shapes the culture, and the culture shapes the human.

### Practice Test, p. 265

1. **Answers:** US is food, UR is going to the food dish to eat the food, CS is the program's theme song, CR is going to the food dish to eat the food when the theme song plays.
2. **Answers:** US is lemon, UR is a pucker, CS is a blue dot, CR is a pucker at the sight of the blue dot.
3. **Answer:** c. The students will experience puckering responses, because of stimulus generalization.
4. **Answer:** b. Eating a box of raisins and experiencing extreme nausea a few hours later.
5. **Answers:** a. positive reinforcement; b. positive punishment; c. negative reinforcement; d. negative punishment (removal of affection).

## CHAPTER 7

### Caption Question, p. 269

**Answer:** Computer memory stores whatever information is correctly put into it. Unless the computer is instructed by the user to perform some function on the stored information, the information will remain in the stored form. By contrast, human memory changes the nature of the material it stores. Even without conscious intervention by the rememberer, human memory involves incompleteness, bias, and distortion. And in humans, memory retrieval is sometimes consciously deliberate and other times seemingly random.

### Caption Question, p. 272

**Answer:** Answers will vary. Each of us will have different reasons for wanting to lose or keep particular memories. Eliminating painful parts of the past might make life easier to bear. However, losing a bad memory might end up changing some positive aspect of your personality that is connected to the memory. Losing a bad memory might also cause you to make a related mistake more than once.

### Caption Question, p. 274

**Answer:** At the center of the photo, the woman is looking up, wearing glasses, and wearing a red jacket.

### Caption Question, p. 283

**Answer:** Answers will vary. Successful strategies for remembering might include chunking (e.g., remembering your student ID number in chunks) or mnemonics (e.g., knowing the difference between afferent and efferent neurons by remembering that efferent starts with "e" and so does the word *exit,* so these neurons carry messages away from the CNS).

### Practice Test, p. 316

1. **Answer:** a. conjunction task; effortful.
2. **Answer:** d. Anna should use Sarah's name in a sentence.

## CHAPTER 8

### Caption Question, p. 335

**Answer:** Answer will vary. It could be that evolution biases us toward gains of resources or toward representations of success. Therefore we perceive loss more acutely as failure to be successful in the acquisition and maintenance of resources.

### Caption Question, p. 337

**Answer:** Answers will vary and may concern job performance, athletics, musical performances, grades, and so on. Your expectations of success or failure may have a direct relationship with your feelings about the outcome of an effort.

### Caption Question, p. 338

**Answer:** Schwartz would recommend that, in making a noncrucial decision such as which variety of Spam to buy, you should not seek to make the absolutely right choice. Instead, you should aim for a reasonable choice that will meet your needs, then focus on the positive aspects of your choice.

### Caption Question, p. 347

**Answer:** Answers will vary. If you agree that the test is not culturally biased, you might argue that the shapes and colors have no cultural meanings in and of themselves. If you disagree, you might argue that, since these colored shapes do not necessarily appear in nature (i.e., without human intervention), their unfamiliarity to some people in some parts of the world might constitute cultural bias. In addition, the type of thinking required to solve a puzzle like this might be emphasized in some cultures more than others and thus give some people a problem-solving advantage.

### Caption Question, p. 354

**Answer:** As the text notes, the overall size and weight of Einstein's brain are unremarkable. Thus the smartest people do not necessarily have the largest brains. The size of Einstein's parietal lobe was larger than average. This finding supports the idea that different kinds of intelligence are related to the sizes of particular brain regions.

### Practice Test, p. 363

1. **Answers:** a. All attributes of a category are equally salient.; b. All members of a category fit equally well into that category.; e. Membership within a category is on an all-or-none basis.
2. **Answers:** Option a is most likely; option c is least likely.
3. **Answer:** a. Students will settle into their seats and perhaps glance over the handout. People who already know each other might converse, but they most likely will not discuss the questions.
4. **Answers:** a. inductive; b. deductive; c. deductive; d. inductive; e. inductive.
5. **Answers:** a. framing effect; b. availability heuristic; c. representativeness heuristic.
6. **Answer:** a. achievement, aptitude.

## CHAPTER 9

### Caption Question, p. 368

**Answer:** The brain on the right is smaller than the brain on the left and perhaps a bit misshapen, the folds of its cerebral cortex are less elaborate, and its color is different. FAS might have contributed to these aspects of the appearance of the brain on the right.

### Caption Question, p. 375

**Answer:** Imprinting is a biologically timed, biologically determined, and species-specific adaptive process. The ducks are programmed to follow what moves. Attachment is far more complex. Infants develop attachment, but it varies qualitatively based on the interactive dynamic of the infant and mother.

### Caption Question, p. 382

**Answer:** The preferential-looking technique is being used in this test.

### Caption Question, p. 391

**Answer:** Children who like to eat M&M's will tend to be motivated when it comes to determining the number of M&M's. That is, knowing which row has more candies increases the chance that the child will get to eat more candies.

### Caption Question, p. 413

**Answer:** Answers will vary. You might argue that rock music was created as a celebration of youth and that "rocking" requires youthful energy. Alternatively, you might argue that rock is all about spirit and that the Stones still have the spirit of youthful rockers. Then the question is what qualifies a person as elderly—is it chronological age or attitude?

### Caption Question, p. 416

**Answer:** By exercising, socializing, and laughing, these women are increasing their chances of feeling well physically and mentally. Eating right and not consuming harmful things will improve their chances, as will maintaining appropriate weights for their individual body types. In addition, the women should remain mentally active, such as by reading, paying attention to current events, solving problems, and taking in the arts. Since development is always a matter of nature *and* nurture, however, there are biological factors beyond the women's control. Genetics may play a major role in the women's health and longevity.

### Practice Test, p. 419

1. **Answers:** a. differentiate between sweet and nonsweet tastes; c. grasp a caregiver's finger; e. orient toward loud sounds; i. turn his or her head toward the smell of the mother's breast milk; j. turn toward a nipple near his or her mouth.
2. **Answer:** c. Contact with comforting "mothers" promoted a sense of security.
3. **Answer:** d. The infant will stare at the three remaining cubes for a relatively long time.
4. **Answers:** a—preconventional; b—postconventional; c—conventional.

## CHAPTER 10

### Caption Question, p. 423

**Answer:** Answers will of course vary, but the authors hope your valence and activation are somewhere on the right side of the map.

### Caption Question, p. 425

**Answer:** The woman on the left is more likely to report feeling happy, because she is holding the pen in a way that makes her mouth curve into a smile. The woman on the right is holding the pencil in a way that makes her mouth pucker. Your responses are likely to reflect the ways in which you hold your pen or pencil.

### Caption Question, p. 446

**Answer:** "BUY 1 GET 1 FREE" can be a very attractive offer, especially if you really want the item to begin with. However, "LAST CHANCE TO BUY" conveys special urgency because we are averse to loss. "BUY 1 GET 1 FREE" indicates that the item is in great enough supply that it will be around for a while. "LAST CHANCE TO BUY" indicates that the supply is limited and perhaps running out.

### Caption Question, p. 447

**Answer:** In each case, the person delays gratification by turning his or her attention away from the desired item. Thinking of the item as something similar but undesired turns the thought of the item from hot to cold. Simply ignoring the item, if successful, can remove the hot thought. Self-distraction provides a block between the conscious mind and the hot thought.

### Caption Question, p. 452

**Answer:** Answers will vary, but you might consider factors such as your emotional state, the presence of other people, and the occasion for eating (a special occasion? a celebration? a routine meal?).

### Caption Question, p. 453

**Answer:** Answers will vary, depending on factors such as your palate and adventurousness.

### Practice Test, p. 467

1. **Answer:** b. Sonya is somewhat anxious about this presentation. She knows her stuff but recognizes how much is riding on the quality of this presentation. This anxious energy motivates her to polish her slides and practice her talk.
2. **Answer:** b. GABA.

## CHAPTER 11

### Caption Question, p. 473

**Answer:** If you study as usual, you are likely to get a grade closer to your usual grades. Regression to the mean is the principle behind this result. The hypnotist might contribute to the result, if you are susceptible to hypnosis and the hypnosis session helps calm your anxiety.

### Caption Question, p. 477

**Answer:** Some of our coping strategies involve solving the problem that has created the stress (e.g., coming up with a plan and schedule for getting a paper done on time). At other times, we try to simply mask the stress by engaging in behaviors that change how we feel (e.g., going to a party instead of studying).

### Caption Question, p. 485

**Answer:** It may be nearly impossible to imagine yourself in that situation. Still, consider that some of the passengers clearly engaged in a secondary appraisal process to develop a plan. They focused on the problem to change the outcome (i.e., not allowing their plane to crash in Washington, D.C.). Could you have done this under the circumstances?

### Caption Question, p. 503

**Answer:** As this chapter emphasizes, a positive attitude can contribute to one's health and well-being. Laughter can be a sign of positivity, but is it, by itself, a means of improving a person's state of mind and physical shape? Psychologists interested in this question have performed experiments to test the effects of laughter. The benefits of laughter are numerous and have an adaptive basis (Dunbar et al., 2011; Mehu & Dunbar, 2008).

### Practice Test, p. 511

1. **Answer:** d. Genetic predispositions to some illnesses exist. But living healthily can help reduce the chance of developing a disease.
2. **Answer:** b. biopsychosocial model.
3. **Answer:** a. "Well, I figured I couldn't stay in that funk forever. Things eventually had to start looking up again."
4. **Answers:** a. are committed to daily activities; e. see challenges as opportunities for growth; f. see themselves as able to control their own lives.
5. **Answer:** All the choices are true.

## CHAPTER 12

### Caption Questions, p. 514

**Answers:** For (a) and (b), answers will of course vary, depending on each reader's view of the situations, the results, and people.

### Caption Question, p. 515

**Answer:** Body language indicates that the couple is having a disagreement. The woman's right hand is on her hip in a "holding the line" pose. Her left hand is raised in an "oh, please, do not try to make me believe that" gesture. Her upwardly tilted head also indicates disbelief, and she does not seem to be meeting the man's gaze. The man, meanwhile, is stretching out his hands in a gesture of entreaty: "Hey, come on, believe me!" His legs are bent in a way that angles his body toward the woman. His expression suggests mental focus on the matter at hand. At the same time, there is the suggestion of playfulness in both of these people's appearances. Their disagreement might not mean the end of the relationship.

### Caption Question, p. 518

**Answer:** As a critical thinker, you probably would avoid stereotyping all Canadians as hockey fans. After all, is there a country in which *every* person shares an interest? Still, selection bias is on display in this photo: Because it is a photo of hockey fans at an international event, enthusiasm for a particular sport is unmistakably associated with a country's flag and major symbol (hockey = Canada = red maple leaf). This imagery conveys the impression that the sport has particular significance for the national identity. So while you might not stereotype all Canadians as liking hockey, you might associate Canadians with hockey and with patriotism. By contrast, what would the photo of an individual tell you about national identity? You would be on unsteady ground if you were to assert that all Canadians, all Canadian women, all Canadian singers—all anything—share the attributes of Céline Dion. In other words, when you consider the implications of imagery, you need to consider the sample size on display, just as you would consider the sample size in evaluating scientific findings.

### Caption Question, p. 532

**Answer:** If the pledges' behavior matched that of people generally, they justified the hazing as a necessary means of attaining the important goal of joining the fraternity. To justify the importance of that goal, of course, the pledges might have overestimated the importance of belonging to the fraternity.

### Caption Question, p. 538

**Answer:** By uniting the individual with a group, deindividuation can lead to a feeling of belonging. Of course, some groups might be more worth belonging to than other groups are. At its most negative, deindividuation could lead the individual to go along with the group to the point of engaging in behaviors that the individual will regret, such as behaviors that are harmful to the individual or others.

### Caption Question, p. 553

**Answer:** So far, the story might lead you to believe that Genovese was the victim of bystander apathy. After all, how could so many witnesses fail to report the attack? But read on for a fuller understanding of the situation.

### Practice Test, p. 565

1. **Answers:** a. ingroup favoritism; b. illusory correlation; c. outgroup homogeneity.
2. **Answer:** d. "We can hold an all-campus competition, where teams of dorms would compete for prizes. Dorm A and Dorm B could be on one team; Dorm C and Dorm D could be on the other team."

## CHAPTER 13

### Caption Question, p. 574

**Answer:** The student's thoughts might be something like, "Okay, which is it, stay in and study or go to the party? On the one hand, if I study, I might do better on this test than I did on that last one! On the other hand, if I study, I might miss out on a great time. Chances are good that it'll be a fun party. So, which is more important to me, improving my chances of getting a good grade in this course or having fun tonight? I might hate to admit this, even to myself, but I want to do well in college. Time to study." In this inner monologue, positive reinforcement comes in the form of potential success: a better grade on a test, thus a better grade in the course, thus a better GPA, thus a better chance for success down the line.

### Caption Question, p. 575

**Answer:** The CAPS model indicates that cognitive-social influences can better predict behavior than personality traits can. According to this model, one's response to a situation depends on one's perception of the situation, one's emotional reaction to it, one's relevant skills, and one's anticipation of the outcome. Personality might inform each of those factors, but personality itself does not determine response.

### Caption Question, p. 581

**Answer:** By responding to these statements, you are experiencing one of the ways personality is measured. There are no right responses, as personality varies from person to person.

### Caption Question, p. 590

**Answer:** If dogs have personalities, then it is possible that any answer would have to take into account both the tendency of the particular breeds and individual variation. In other words, do not let these "anecdotal" photos bias your response as to which type of dog is friendlier! Golden retrievers might tend to be friendlier than rottweilers, but an individual golden retriever might be unfriendly and an individual rottweiler might be friendly. Nature and nurture both come into play. To test your hypothesis, you might set up an experiment that would involve safely coming into contact with a number of golden retrievers and a number of rottweilers. You would have to act the same way in the presence of each dog and measure what you would consider the dog's friendliness.

### Practice Test, p. 615

1. **Answers:** a. type and trait; b. learning and cognition; c. psychodynamic; d. humanistic.
2. **Answer:** a. idiographic; projective.
3. **Answers:** b. Predictions of our own behaviors may be biased in favor of our subjective perceptions (how we *think* we act) rather than our objective behaviors (how we *do* act).; c. We tend to pay more attention to others than to ourselves and thus fail to notice our own behavior; others notice how we behave and are better able to predict our future behaviors.

## CHAPTER 14

### Caption Question, p. 622

**Answer:** A clinician might note that a person at point A is currently not experiencing anxiety, a person at point B is somewhat anxious or intermittently anxious, and a person at point C is currently very anxious. States of anxiety vary from person to person and from time to time, and their evaluation is always a judgment call on the part of the individual and the clinician. In much the same way, psychological disorders involve continuums: They are generally not all-or-nothing, yes-or-no matters. Evaluation of a patient's symptoms and whether the patient has a particular disorder always involves some investigative work and judgment.

### Caption Question, p. 626

**Answer:** In this model, nature is represented by genetic predisposition, and nurture is represented by childhood trauma. Each of these factors, separately and in combination, can contribute to a person's vulnerability to mental disorder.

### Practice Test, p. 671

1. **Answers:** a. Does the behavior deviate from cultural norms?; b. Is the behavior causing the individual personal distress?; c. Is the behavior maladaptive?
2. **Answer:** c. internalizing, females; externalizing, males.

## CHAPTER 15

### Caption Question, p. 676

**Answer:** The potential benefits come from the client's position. Because the client is not forced to meet the therapist's gaze, the client might feel less under scrutiny and therefore freer to be honest. Reclining on a presumably soft couch, rather than sitting upright in a comparably harder chair, might also encourage the client to open up about his or her circumstances, feelings, perceptions, and symptoms. One potential drawback is that the position will encourage the client to feel so free that the client drifts into fantasy or drama rather than honesty. Or the client might perceive the therapist as a distant, cut-off authority figure rather than an impartial listener. Too, the therapist might feel distant and cut off rather than able to fully observe the client's facial expressions during their interaction.

### Caption Question, p. 679

**Answer:** Cognitive therapy focuses on distorted thought patterns and how those thought patterns help produce maladaptive behaviors and emotions. By employing cognitive restructuring, the therapist aims to help the client change the thought patterns and thus change the behaviors and emotions. According to this approach, the more realistic and positive the client's thinking, the healthier the client's behaviors and emotions.

### Caption Question, p. 712

**Answer:** As discussed in the paragraphs below, possible contributing factors are a reduction in biological drives during middle age, the patient's gaining of insight into his or her self-defeating behaviors, and the patient's getting too worn out to continue his or her manipulative ways.

### Caption Question, p. 716

**Answer:** In considering the decrease in suicide rates, if we view medication (i.e., the altering of biology) as representing nature, then we also have to ask how nurture might be related. For example, was there an increase in public awareness of teenage suicide, so that young people received more support from their communities? Were the economic conditions at the time on an upturn, so that young people were feeling more upbeat and less stressed out?

### Practice Test, p. 725

1. **Answers:** Choices a, b, and e are true.
2. **Answers:** a. Treatments should be based on evidence of their effectiveness.; b. Treatments should be appropriate for the particular disorders.; c. Specific techniques for treatment should be developed in the laboratory by psychologists.
3. **Answer:** The correct order is c, a, b.
4. **Answer:** c. Joshua's tendency to get into fistfights.
5. **Answers:** Choices a, b, and d are likely true.

# PERMISSIONS ACKNOWLEDGMENTS

Every effort has been made to contact the copyright holders of the material used in *Psychological Science*. Rights holders of any material not credited should contact Permissions Department, W. W. Norton & Company, Inc., 500 Fifth Avenue, New York, NY 10110 for a correction to be made in the next reprinting of our work.

## CHAPTER 1

**Opener:** Ann Summa/Workbook Stock/Getty Images.

**Fig. 1.1:** *Time*, January 29, 2007.

**Fig. 1.3:** © 2010, *Weekly World News*, Bat Boy LLC, All rights reserved.

**Fig. 1.4:** Hermann J. Knippertz/AP.

**Fig. 1.5:** Rischgitz/Getty Images.

**Fig. 1.6:** The Granger Collection, New York.

**Fig. 1.7:** Imagno/Getty Images.

**Fig. 1.8:** Bettmann/Corbis.

**Fig. 1.9:** Archives of the History of American Psychology, University of Akron.

**Fig. 1.10:** Wikimedia Commons.

**Fig. 1.11:** From *American Journal of Psychology*. © 1974 by the Board of Trustees of the University of Illinois. Used with permission of the University of Illinois Press.

**Fig. 1.12:** From *Mind Sights* by Roger N. Shepard. © 1990 by Roger N. Shepard. Henry Holt and Company, LLC.

**Fig. 1.13:** Archives of the History of American Psychology, University of Akron.

**Fig. 1.14:** Department of Psychology Archives/McMicken College of Arts and Sciences.

**Fig. 1.15:** Scott Squire.

**Fig. 1.16:** Bettmann/Corbis.

**Fig. 1.17:** Archives of the History of American Psychology, University of Akron.

**Fig. 1.18:** Courtesy George Miller, Princeton University, © 2001, Pryde Brown Photographs, Princeton, NJ.

**Fig. 1.19:** Archives of the History of American Psychology, University of Akron.

**Fig. 1.20:** *Time,* January 28, 2008, cover.

**Fig. 1.21:** Courtesy Professor Joseph J. Campos, University of California, Berkeley.

**Fig. 1.22:** *Newsweek,* March 19, 2007.

**Fig. 1.23a:** Rick Gomez/Corbis.

**Fig. 1.23b:** Luke Duggleby/OnAsia.

**Fig. 1.24(i):** SIU/Peter Arnold Images.

**Fig. 1.24(ii):** © Stockbyte/Alamy.

**Fig. 1.24(iii):** © Somos Images LLC/Alamy.

**Fig. 1.24(iv):** Bruno De Hogues/Getty Images.

**Fig. 1.25:** Levitin, D. J., and Menon, V. (2003).

**Cartoon 1.1:** © The *New Yorker* Collection 1998/Sam Gross from cartoonbank.com. All Rights Reserved.

**Cartoon 1.2:** *The Far Side* ® by Gary Larson © 1982 FarWorks, Inc. All Rights Reserved. Used with permission.

## CHAPTER 2

**Opener:** Laura Burke/Corbis.

**Fig. 2.1a:** Pearl Gabel/*New York Daily News*.

**Fig. 2.1b:** Jesse Ward/*New York Daily News*.

**Fig. 2.3a:** Ocean/Corbis.

**Fig. 2.3b:** Steve Skjold/Photo Edit.

**Fig. 2.3c:** Ace Stock Limited/Alamy.

**Fig. 2.3e:** Christy Varonfakis Johnson/Alamy.

**Fig. 2.4a:** Karl Ammann/Corbis.

**Fig. 2.4b:** Lawrence S. Sugiyama/University of Oregon.

**Fig. 2.5:** Courtesy of First Run Features.

**Fig. 2.6a:** Ocean/Corbis.

**Fig. 2.6b:** Pauline St. Denis/Corbis.

**Fig. 2.8:** Peter Arnold, Inc./Alamy.

**Fig. 2.11:** Corbis/SuperStock.

**Fig. 2.12a–b:** © Peter Menzel/www.menzelphoto.com.

**Fig. 2.13a–b:** Roethlisberger, F. J., & Dickson, W. J. (1939). *Management and the worker: An account of a research program conducted by the Western Electric Company, Hawthorne Works, Chicago*. Cambridge, MA: Harvard University Press.

**Fig. 2.14a:** Richard B. Levine/Newscom.

**Fig. 2.14b:** Charles Dharapak/AP.

**Fig. 2.15a:** Janine Wiedel Photolibrary/Alamy.

**Fig. 2.15b:** John Birdsall/The Image Works.

**Fig. 2.15c:** JUPITERIMAGES/Creatas/Alamy.

**Fig. 2.18a:** Mark Burnett/Alamy.

**Fig. 2.18b:** Richard T. Nowitz/Photo Researchers.

**Fig. 2.18c:** AJPhoto/Photo Researchers.

**Fig. 2.18d:** James Cavallini/Photo Researchers.

**Fig. 2.18e:** Michael Ventura/Alamy.

**Fig. 2.18f:** WDCN/Univ. College London/Photo Researchers.

**Fig. 2.18g:** Charles Thatcher/Getty Images.

**Fig. 2.18i:** Mark Harmel/Alamy.

**Fig. 2.18j:** Courtesy of Psych Central.

**Fig. 2.18k:** Marcello Massimini/University of Wisconsin–Madison.

**Fig. 2.18l:** Dr. K. Singh, Liverpool University/Dr. S. Hamdy & Dr. Q. Aziz, Manchester University.

**Fig. 2.19:** LOVETTE/REYNOLDS/NIKITIN/SIPA.

**Cartoon 2.1:** ScienceCartoonsPlus.com.

**Cartoon 2.2:** Sydney Harris.

**Cartoon 2.3:** Src. 2005 Sidney Harris from cartoonbanks.com.

## CHAPTER 3

**Opener:** Martin Adolfsson/Gallery Stock.

**Fig. 3.2a:** © SF Palm/StageImage/The Image Works.

**Fig. 3.2b:** Brigitte Engl/Redferns/Getty Images.

**Fig. 3.3:** James Cavallini/Photo Researchers.

**Fig. 3.10:** Newscom.

**Fig. 3.11:** Mendez et al. "Simultaneous intrastriatal and intranigral fetal dopaminergic grafts in patients with Parkinson disease: A pilot study, Report of three cases," *J. Neurosurg.*/Volume 96/March 2002.

**Fig. 3.12:** Philippe Lopez/AFP/Getty Images.

**Fig. 3.14a:** From Spurzheim, J. (1825). Phrenology, or, the doctrine of the mind and the relations between its manifestations and the body, etc.

**Fig. 3.14b:** Bettmann/Corbis.

**Fig. 3.15a(i):** *Nature Reviews Neuroscience 5,* 812–819 (October 2004).

**Fig. 3.21b–c:** From Penfield, Wilder (1958), *The excitable cortex in conscious man.* Liverpool University Press.

**Fig. 3.22:** Ramachandran, V. S., and Blakeslee, S., Fig. 6.1, drawing made by a neglect patient, from *Phantoms in the brain.* Copyright © 1998 by V. S. Ramachandran and Sandra Blakeslee. Reprinted by permission of HarperCollins Publishers Inc.

**Fig. 3.23a:** Collection of Jack and Beverly Wilgus.

**Fig. 3.23b:** www.hbs.deakin.edu.au/gagepage/pgage.htm.

**Fig. 3.23c:** Hanna Damasio, © 2004 Massachusetts Medical Society.

**Fig. 3.24:** Bettmann/Corbis.

**Fig. 3.28:** Mark Wilson/Getty Images.

**Fig. 3.29a:** Martin Adolfsson/Gallery Stock.

**Fig. 3.29b:** Dr. Dennis Kunkel/Getty Images.

**Fig. 3.29c:** CNRI/Science Photo Library Researchers, Inc.

**Fig. 3.30:** Ron Edmonds/AP.

**Fig. 3.31:** CNRI/Science Photo Library Researchers.

**Fig. 3.33a–h:** Harry B. Clay, Jr.

**Fig. 3.34a:** David Fox/Oxford Scientific/Photolibrary.

**Fig. 3.34b:** Dr. David M. Phillips/Visuals Unlimited/Getty Images.

**Fig. 3.35a:** Tony Freeman/PhotoEdit.

**Fig. 3.35b:** Bob Sacha.

**Fig. 3.36a:** © Bob Daemmrich/The Image Works.

**Fig. 3.36b:** Binda, C., Newton-Vinson, P., Hubalek, F., Edmondson, D. E., Mattevi, A. (2002).

**Fig. 3.36c:** Robin Nelson/PhotoEdit.

**Fig. 3.37:** Philippe Garo/Photo Researchers, Inc.

**Fig. 3.39:** Joan Y. Chiao, Tetsuya Iidaka, Heather L. Gordon, Junpei Nogawa, Moshe Bar, Elissa Aminoff, Norihiro Sadato, and Nalini Ambady, "Cultural Specificity in Amygdala Response to Fear Faces" from *Journal of Cognitive Neuroscience*, 20:12 (December 2008), pp. 2167–2174. Copyright © 2008 by the Massachusetts Institute of Technology. **Photos 3.39a–d:** Courtesy of Ekman & Matsumoto. **Photo 3.39e:** Courtesy of Dr. Joan Chiao.

**Fig. 3.41:** David Emmite/WORKBOOK.

**Fig. 3.42:** From Vilayanur S. Ramachandran and Edward M. Hubbard, "Hearing Colors, Tasting Shapes." *Scientific American*, May 2003. Copyright © 2003 Scientific American, Inc. Reproduced with permission. All rights reserved.

**Fig. 3.43a–b:** Indiana University School of Medicine.

**Fig. 3.44:** AP Photo.

**Cartoon 3.1:** Cartoonstock.com.

**Cartoon 3.2:** © The *New Yorker* Collection 1999/William Haefeli from cartoonbank.com. All Rights Reserved.

## CHAPTER 4

**Opener:** John-Francis Bourke/Getty Images.

**Fig. 4.1:** Photo courtesy of the New England Historic Genealogical Society (Boston, Mass.).

**Fig. 4.6:** Jonathan Olley/Getty Images.

**Fig. 4.7:** George Pimentel/WireImage/Getty Images.

**Fig. 4.8:** Marcy Maloy/Getty Images.

**Fig. 4.9:** John-Francis Bourke/Getty Images.

**Fig. 4.10a:** Steven Errico/Digital Vision/Getty Images.

**Fig. 4.10b:** Jose Luis Pelaez Inc./Blend Images/Getty Images.

**Fig. 4.11:** Jochen Sand/agefotostock.

**Fig. 4.12:** John Bazemore/AP.

**Fig. 4.14:** Marcos Welsh/agefotostock.

**Fig. 4.15:** James King-Holmes/Photo Researchers.

**Fig. 4.16(ii):** Cheyenne Rouse/Getty Images.

**Fig. 4.20a–b:** © Bjørn Rørslett/NN.

**Fig. 4.21b:** Figure "Color contrast and color appearance: Brightness constancy and color" from *Vision and Visual Perception*, ed. C.H. Graham (New York: Wiley, 1965). We have made diligent efforts to contact the copyright holder to obtain permission to reprint this selection. If you have information that would help us, please write to us at the address given above.

**Fig. 4.25a:** Stephen Dalton/NHPA.

**Fig. 4.26a:** Olveczky et al., 2003, Segregation of Object and Background Motion in Retina. *Nature, 423*, 401–408.

**Fig. 4.26b:** From Celeste McCollough, "Color adaptation of edge detectors in the human visual system," *Science 149*:1115 (9/3/1965). Reprinted with permission from AAAS.

**Fig. 4.26c:** Kitaoka, A. "Light of Sweden illusion." Reprinted by permission of Akiyoshi Kitaoka.

**Fig. 4.27a–b:** Figure 8.4 (a) and (b) from p. 280 of *Psychology* by Peter Gray. © 1991, 1994, 1999 by Worth Publishers. Used with permission.

**Fig. 4.27e(i):** Figure from Varin, D., "Fenomeni di contrasto e diffusione cromatica," *Rivista di Psicologia 65* (1970).

**Fig. 4.27e(ii):** Kanizsa, G. "Subjective Contours" from *Scientific American 234*. Copyright © 1976. Reprinted by permission of Jerome Kuhl.

**Fig. 4.28:** Selfridge, Oliver, "Pattern Recognition and Modern Computers" from *Proceedings of the Western Computer Conference*. Copyright © 1955 by the Association for Computing Machinery, Inc. Reprinted with permission.

**Fig. 4.29:** A Hawthorne/Arctic Photo.

**Fig. 4.30a–b(ii):** From McCarthy, G., Price, A., Allison, T. (1997). Face specific processing in the human fusiform gyrus. *Journal of Cognitive Neuroscience, 9I*, 605–610, etc.

**Fig. 4.31:** Courtesy Peter Thompson, University of York.

**Fig. 4.34:** Munch, Edvard (1863–1944) © ARS, NY/Scala/Art Resource, NY.

**Fig. 4.35:** Sartore/Getty Images/*National Geographic*.

**Fig. 4.36:** Courtesy of Todd Heatherton.

**Fig. 4.37a–b:** © Exploratorium, www.exploratorium.edu.

**Fig. 4.40:** Figure from *The Art Pack* by Christopher Frayling, Helen Frayling, and Ron Van der Meer, copyright © 1992 by Singram Company Ltd. The Art Pack copyright © 1992 by Van der Meer Paper Design Ltd. Text copyright © 1992 by Christopher & Helen Frayling. Copyright © 1992 by The Art Pack. Used by permission of Alfred A. Knopf, a division of Random House, Inc.

**Fig. 4.41a–b:** From *Psychology,* 6th Edition, by Henry Gleitman, Alan J. Fridlund, Daniel Reisberg. Copyright © 2004 by W. W. Norton, etc.

**Fig. 4.42:** Illustration "Turning Tables" illusion from *Mind Sights* by Roger N. Shepard. Copyright © 1990 by Roger N. Shepard. Reprinted by permission of Henry Holt and Company, LLC.

**Cartoon 4.1:** © The *New Yorker* Collection, Pat Byrnes from Cartoonbank.com.

**Cartoon 4.2:** © *Social Signal* 2010. Reprinted by permission. Original cartoon at RobCottingham.com.

## CHAPTER 5

**Opener:** Peter Augustine/Gallery Stock.

**Fig. 5.1:** Courtesy of Eddie and Erik Ramsey.

**Fig. 5.2:** Sidney Harris.

**Fig. 5.4a:** Courtesy Michael Schiavo.

**Fig. 5.4b:** Bogdan Hrywniak/AFP/Getty Images.

**Fig. 5.11:** The Photo Works.

**Fig. 5.13b:** James King-Holmes/Photo Researchers.

**Fig. 5.15:** PHOTOTAKE Inc./Alamy.

**Fig. 5.16:** Blickwinkel/Alamy.

**Fig. 5.17:** Chris Rout/Alamy.

**Fig. 5.19:** Newscom.

**Fig. 5.20:** Courtesy Steve G. Jones, Ed.D., Clinical Hypnotherapist.

**Fig. 5.21:** David Young-Wolff/Getty Images.

**Fig. 5.22a–b:** "Minding one's emotions" by Farb, Norman A. S.; Anderson, Adam K.; Mayberg, Helen; Bean, Jim; McKeon, Deborah; Segal, Zindel V. *Emotion*. Vol. 10(2), Apr. 2010.

**Fig. 5.23:** Nathan Benn/Alamy.

**Fig. 5.24:** Eckehard Schulz/AP.

**Fig. 5.26:** Kim, S. J., Lyoo, I. K., Hwang, J., Chung, A., Hoon Sung, Y., Kim, J., Kwon, D. H., Chang, K. H., & Renshaw, P. F. (2006).

**Fig. 5.27:** Multnomah County Sheriff's Office.

**Fig. 5.28a–b:** 5th edition of the textbook *Biological Psychology: An Introduction to Behavioral, Cognitive, and Clinical Neuroscience,* by Breedlove, Rosenzweig, and Watson (Sinauer Associates).

**Fig. 5.30a:** Newscom.

**Fig. 5.30b:** Peter Treanor/Alamy.

**Fig. 5.32a:** Robert Altman/The Image Works.

**Fig. 5.32b:** Bettmann/Corbis.

**Cartoon 5.1:** © Sidney Harris, cartoonbank.com.

**Cartoon 5.2:** © Sidney Harris.

**Cartoon 5.3:** 2005 Robert Mankoff, cartoonbank.com. All Rights Reserved.

## CHAPTER 6

**Opener:** Brian Sokol.

**Fig. 6.1:** Bettmann/Corbis.

**Fig. 6.2a:** Bettmann/Corbis.

**Fig. 6.7a:** Psychology Archives—The University of Akron.

**Fig. 6.7b:** Benjamin Harris, University of New Hampshire

**Fig. 6.8:** Childress, A. R., Mozey, P. D., McElgin, W., Fitzgerald, J., Revich, M., O'Brien, C. P. (1999).

**Fig. 6.9a–b:** Lincoln P. Bower.

**Fig. 6.10a:** Pegaz/Alamy.

**Fig. 6.10b:** Jonathan Storey/Getty Images.

**Fig. 6.12a:** Yerkes, Robert M. Manuscripts & Archives, Yale University.

**Fig. 6.14a:** Nina Leen/*Time*/Pix Images.

**Fig. 6.15:** AP/Wide World Photos.

**Fig. 6.18:** Image Source/Getty Images.

**Fig. 6.19:** Lynn M. Stone/naturepl.com.

**Fig. 6.21:** F. B. M. deWaal.

**Fig. 6.22:** Albert Bandura, Dept. of Psychology, Stanford University.

**Fig. 6.23:** D. Hurst/Alamy.

**Fig. 6.24:** Susan Mineka, Northwestern University.

**Fig. 6.25:** Geri Engberg/The Image Works.

**Fig. 6.26:** © IFC Films/Courtesy Everett Collection.

**Fig. 6.27:** Courtesy Daniel Miller, Dpt. of Neurology, Carthage College.

**Fig. 6.29:** Biophoto Associates/Photo Researchers, Inc.

**Fig. 6.31:** AP/Wide World Photos.

**Cartoon 6.1:** © The *New Yorker* Collection 1993/Tom Cheney from cartoonbank.com.

## CHAPTER 7

**Opener:** Paul Elledge.

**Fig. 7.2:** Copyright © Suzanne Corkin, used with permission of The Wylie Agency LLC.

**Fig. 7.5:** From Wheeler, M. E., Petersen, S. E., & Buckner, R. L. (2000). Memory's echo: Vivid remembering reactivates sensory specific cortex. *Proceedings of the National Academy of Sciences, 97,* 11125–11129.

**Fig. 7.6:** Photofest.

**Fig. 7.7b:** Alamy.

**Fig. 7.10a–c:** Courtesy Daniel J. Simons.

**Fig. 7.13:** Newscom.

**Fig. 7.18a:** Bjorn Svensson/Alamy.

**Fig. 7.18c:** Chris A. Crumley/Alamy.

**Fig. 7.19a:** David Turnley/Getty Images.

**Fig. 7.19b:** Newscom.

**Fig. 7.20:** Michael Blann/Getty Images.

**Fig. 7.21:** © Asia Images/SuperStock.

**Fig. 7.23:** Robert E. Klein/AP.

**Fig. 7.24a:** John Froschauer/AP.

**Fig. 7.24b:** Photofest.

**Fig. 7.25a:** Charla Jones/Getstock.com.

**Fig. 7.25b:** Kennedy Space Center/NASA.

**Fig. 7.26:** Joe Raedle/Getty Images.

**Fig. 7.26c:** Tom Stoddart/Getty Images.

**Fig. 7.27a–b:** AP/Wide World Photos.

**Fig. 7.28a–b:** From Loftus, Miller, & Burns, 1978. Courtesy Elizabeth Loftus.

**Fig. 7.29:** Tony Gutierrez/AP.

**Fig. 7.32a–b:** Peter DaSilva/AP.

**Cartoon 7.1:** © The *New Yorker* Collection 1998/Mick Stevens from cartoonbank.com.

## CHAPTER 8

**Opener:** Jon Feingersh Photography Inc./Blend Images/Corbis.

**Fig. 8.1:** Ed Andrieski/AP/Wide World Photos.

**Fig. 8.2a:** Carmen Taylor/AP.

**Fig. 8.2b:** Rick Bowmer/AP.

**Fig. 8.6:** Eysenck, M. W., Figure 8.3, *Cognitive psychology: A student's handbook,* 2nd Edition, Lawrence Erlbaum Associates. Copyright 1990. Reprinted by permission.

**Fig. 8.8a:** Imagebroker/Alamy.

**Fig. 8.8b:** Steven Vidler/Eurasia Press/Corbis.

**Fig. 8.8c:** Warner Bros./Photofest.

**Fig. 8.8d:** Artisan Entertainment/Photofest.

**Fig. 8.9:** © Peter Arnold, Inc./Alamy.

**Fig. 8.10a:** Mario Tama/Getty Images.

**Fig. 8.10b:** Agencia Estado via AP Images/Wide World Photos.

**Fig. 8.11a:** © AKG-images/The Image Works.

**Fig. 8.11b:** Alamy.

**Fig. 8.12a:** Jeff Greenberg/PhotoEdit.

**Fig. 8.12b:** Erik Dreyer/Getty Images.

**Fig. 8.12c:** Corbis.

**Fig. 8.13:** Dalton, M. A., Bernhardt, A. M., Gibson, J. J., Sargent, J. D., Beach, M. L., Adachi-Mejia, A. M., Titus-Ernstoff, L. T., & Heatherton, T. F. (2005). *Archives of Pediatrics & Adolescent Medicine, 159,* 854–859.

**Fig. 8.14a:** Imageshop/Alamy.

**Fig. 8.14b:** © Cultura Limited/SuperStock.

**Fig. 8.14c:** Alamy.

**Fig. 8.14d:** © PhotoAlto/SuperStock.

**Fig. 8.14e:** Glowimages/Getty Images.

**Fig. 8.14f:** Photodisc/Alamy.

**Fig. 8.14g:** Photodisc/Getty Images.

**Fig. 8.14h:** Agency Design Pics Inc./Alamy.

**Fig. 8.18a:** Mandel Ngan/AFP/Getty Images.

**Fig. 8.18b:** Mike Coppola/Getty Images.

**Fig. 8.19:** Adam Butler/AP.

**Fig. 8.20a–b:** Courtesy Sheena Iyengar. Iyengar, S. S., & Lepper, M. R. (2000). *Journal of Personality and Social Psychology, 79,* 995–1006.

**Fig. 8.21:** Alamy.

**Fig. 8.26:** The Granger Collection, New York.

**Fig. 8.30a:** Reuters New Media Inc./Corbis.

**Fig. 8.30b:** Duomo/Corbis.

**Fig. 8.31a–b:** AP/Wide World Photos.

**Fig. 8.34:** Jim Ross for *The New York Times*.

**Fig. 8.35:** Dan Kitwood/Getty Images.

**Fig. 8.38:** From Kristensen and Bjerkedal, "Explaining the relation between birth order and intelligence," *Science 316*:1717 (6/22/2007). Reprinted with permission from AAAS.

**Fig. 8.39:** Phelan M. Ebenhack/AP.

**Cartoon 8.1:** © The *New Yorker* Collection 2005/Leo Cullum from cartoonbank.com. All Rights Reserved.

**Cartoon 8.2:** © The *New Yorker* by Leo Cullum, November 30, 1998. www.cartoonbank.com. All Rights Reserved.

**Cartoon 8.3:** © The *New Yorker* Collection 2001/David Sipress. www.cartoonbank.com. All Rights Reserved

## CHAPTER 9

**Opener:** Dennis Manarchy/Gallery Stock.

**Fig. 9.1:** Bettmann/Corbis.

**Fig. 9.2a:** Dr. Yorgos Nikas/Phototake.

**Fig. 9.2b:** Petit Format/Photo Researchers.

**Fig. 9.2c:** Biophoto Associates/Photo Researchers, Inc.

**Fig. 9.3:** © Bettmann/Corbis.

**Fig. 9.4a–b:** Courtesy of Sterling K. Clarren, M.D., Clinical Professor of Pediatrics, University of British Columbia Faculty of Medicine.

**Fig. 9.6a:** Sergio Pitamitz/Marka/agefotostock.

**Fig. 9.6b:** Panos Pictures.

**Fig. 9.6c:** Larry Mayer/Billings Gazette/AP.

**Fig. 9.6d:** Monica Almeida/*The New York Times*/Redux.

**Fig. 9.7:** From studies conducted by researchers from The ChildTrauma Academy (www.ChildTrauma.org) led by Bruce D. Perry, M.D., Ph.D.

**Fig. 9.8:** Nina Leen/TimePix/Getty Images.

**Fig. 9.9a–b:** Nina Leen/Time Life Pictures/Getty Images.

**Fig. 9.11:** Stock Boston, LLC/Spencer Grant.

**Fig. 9.12:** Courtesy Velma Dobson, University of Arizona.

**Fig. 9.13a–b:** Dr. Carolyn Rovee-Collier, Director, Rutgers Early Learning Project.

**Fig. 9.14:** Bettman/Corbis.

**Fig. 9.15a:** Sally and Richard Greenhill/Alamy.

**Fig. 9.15b:** Tom Mareschal/Alamy.

**Fig. 9.15c:** Alamy.

**Fig. 9.15d:** Jon Feingersh/Getty Images.

**Fig. 9.16a–c:** Michael Newman/PhotoEdit.

**Fig. 9.20:** Alamy.

**Fig. 9.21:** Ellen Senisi/The Image Works.

**Fig. 9.22:** Christina Kennedy/Alamy.

**Fig. 9.23:** Tomas Munita/*The New York Times*/Redux.

**Fig. 9.24:** Courtesy of Laura-Ann Petitto.

**Fig. 9.27:** Photo courtesy David Reimer. From Colapinto, John, *As nature made him: The boy who was raised as a girl* (2000), HarperCollins Publishers Inc.

**Fig. 9.28:** Reuters Newsmedia Inc./Corbis.

**Fig. 9.29:** Bruno Morandi/Getty Images.

**Fig. 9.30:** Gale Zucker/Getty Images.

**Fig. 9.31:** © Peter Turnley/Corbis.

**Fig. 9.32:** © Heather Bragman/Syracuse Newspapers/The Image Works.

**Fig. 9.33a:** Alamy.

**Fig. 9.33b:** R. Matina/agefotostock.

**Fig. 9.33c:** Alamy.

**Fig. 9.34:** Chris McGrath/Getty Images.

**Fig. 9.35:** Stephanie Maze/Corbis.

**Fig. 9.36:** Corbis.

**Fig. 9.37:** Getty Images.

**Cartoon 9.1:** © The *New Yorker* Collection 2003/Donald Reilly from cartoonbank.com. All Rights Reserved.

**Cartoon 9.2:** © The *New Yorker* Collection 2001/Edward Koren from cartoonbank.com. All Rights Reserved.

**Cartoon 9.3:** © The *New Yorker* Collection 1994/Sidney Harris from cartoonbank.com. All Rights Reserved.

## CHAPTER 10

**Opener:** Scott Thomas/Corbis.

**Fig. 10.1:** Bulsara et al., *Neurosurg Focus 13*(4) Article 5, 2002, Figure 1.

**Fig. 10.4(i):** Courtesy of W. W. Norton & Co., Inc.

**Fig. 10.4(ii):** Courtesy of W. W. Norton & Co., Inc.

**Fig. 10.10:** Chris Lisle/Corbis.

**Fig. 10.11a–b:** Aviezer, H., Hassin, R. R., Ryan, J., Grady, C., Susskind, J., Anderson, A., Moscovitch, M. & Bentin, S.

**Fig. 10.12a–d:** Ekman (1972–2004).

**Fig. 10.13a–b:** Tracy & Matsumoto (2008)/Courtesy of Jessica Tracy.

**Fig. 10.15:** Courtesy of Dacher Keltner.

**Fig. 10.20a–o:** Jacob E. Steiner, Ph.D., Laboratory of Oral Physiology, The Hebrew University.

**Fig. 10.21a–b:** Alamy.

**Fig. 10.23:** Saxpix.com/agefotostock.

**Fig. 10.25:** Jeff Greenberg/Alamy.

**Fig. 10.26:** Bob Daemmrich/The Image Works.

**Fig. 10.27:** Reuters/Corbis.

**Fig. 10.29:** Simone van den Berg/FeaturePics.

**Fig. 10.31:** Alex Mares-Manton/agefotostock.

**Fig. 10.31b:** Seishiro Akiyama/Getty Images.

**Fig. 10.31c:** Alex Mares-Manton/agefotostock.

**Fig. 10.33:** Brent Sims, Joseph Taravella, Eva Olielska, and Pail Zei.

**Cartoon 10.1:** Copyright 205 Bob Zahn from cartoonbank.com.

**Cartoon 10.2:** © The *New Yorker* collection 1997/Barbara Smaller from cartoonbank.com. All Rights Reserved.

## CHAPTER 11

**Opener:** Laurie Swope/Aurora Photos.

**Fig. 11.1:** Jim Mahoney/*Dallas Morning News*.

**Fig. 11.4:** Adam Gault/Photo Researchers.

**Fig. 11.5a:** Alaska Stock LLC/Alamy.

**Fig. 11.5b:** Alamy.

**Fig. 11.7:** Park Street/Photo Edit.

**Fig. 11.8:** Janine Wiedel Photolibrary/Alamy.

**Fig. 11.11:** American Heart Association.

**Fig. 11.12:** The Kobal Collection.

**Fig. 11.13:** From Sheldon Cohen, Tom Kamarck, and Robin Mermelstein, "A Global Measure of Perceived Stress." *Journal of Health and Social Behavior*, Vol. 24, No. 4 (Dec. 1983), Appendix A. Reprinted by permission of The American Sociological Association.

**Fig. 11.17a:** Douglas Peebles/photolibrary.

**Fig. 11.17b:** Eric Johnson/*The New York Times*.

**Fig. 11.17c:** Stephane Cardinale/People Avenue/Corbis.

**Fig. 11.18a:** Keith Morris/Alamy.

**Fig. 11.18b:** nobleIMAGES/Alamy.

**Fig. 11.19a:** Teh Eng Koon/AFP/Getty Images.

**Fig. 11.19b:** Travel Ink/Getty Images.

**Fig. 11.21:** The Granger Collection.

**Fig. 11.22:** © AMC/Courtesy Everett Collection.

**Fig. 11.23:** Ana Nance/Redux.

**Fig. 11.26:** AFP/Getty Images.

**Fig. 11.29:** Alamy.

**Cartoon 11.1:** The *New Yorker* Collection 1987/Donald Reilly from cartoonbank.com. All Rights Reserved.

**Cartoon 11.02:** © Peanuts Worldwide LLC.

## CHAPTER 12

**Opener:** Glenn Glasser/Gallery Stock.

**Fig. 12.1a:** AP.

**Fig. 12.1b:** Copyright Philip G. Zimbardo, Ph.D.

**Fig. 12.2:** Image Source Pink/Alamy.

**Fig. 12.4:** King World Productions/Photofest.

**Fig. 12.5a:** Ryan Remorz/The Canadian Press.

**Fig. 12.5b:** Michel Linssen/Redferns/Getty Images.

**Fig. 12.6:** Ronald Zak/AP.

**Fig. 12.7(i):** SAE.

**Fig. 12.7(ii):** Courtesy Keith Pyne, Washington University.

**Fig. 12.7(iii):** Courtesy Keith Pyne, Washington University.

**Fig. 12.8:** Ramon Espinosa/AP.

**Fig. 12.9(ii–v):** Intergroup Conflict and Cooperation: The Robbers Cave Experiment by Muzafer Sherif, et al. 1961, University of Oklahoma.

**Fig. 12.10 (i):** Morry Gash/AP.

**Fig. 12.11:** IAT Corp., Project Implicit, Inc.

**Fig. 12.12:** © 1982 Karen Zbuion, Courtesy New School Public Relations Dept.

**Fig. 12.14:** Photo courtesy of *Terp Weekly Edition.*

**Fig. 12.18:** June Frantz-Hunt/Icon SMI.

**Fig. 12.20a–c:** Photos by William Vandivert.

**Fig. 12.21:** Courtesy Alexandra Milgram.

**Fig. 12.23a–c:** Courtesy Alexandra Milgram.

**Fig. 12.25:** Bob Daemmrich/The Image Works.

**Fig. 12.28:** Courtesy of the Everett Collection.

**Fig. 12.29:** *New York Times* Pictures.

**Fig. 12.31a–e:** From Langlois, J. H., & Ruggerman, L. A. (1990). Attractive faces are only average. *Psychological Science 1*, 115–121. Photographs courtesy Judith Hall Langlois, UT Austin.

**Fig. 12.32a–c:** From Perrett, D. I., May, K. A., Yoshikawa, S. (1994). Facial shape and judgments of female attractiveness. Reprinted by permission from *Nature,* 1994, vol. 386, 238–242. Copyright 2002 Macmillan Publishers Ltd. Images courtesy D.I. Perrett, University of St. Andrews.

**Fig. 12.33a:** Davi Russo/© The Weinstein Company/courtesy Everett Collection.

**Fig. 12.33b:** David James/TM and © Twentieth Century Fox Film Corporation. All rights reserved. Courtesy Everett Collection.

**Fig. 12.34a:** Eddie Arrossi/Alamy.

**Fig. 12.34b:** Tetra Images/Alamy.

**Cartoon 12.1:** Copyright *New Yorker* Collection 1996/Tom Cheney from cartoonbank.com. All Rights Reserved.

## CHAPTER 13

**Opener:** Glenn Glasser/Gallery Stock.

**Fig. 13.2:** Bettman/Corbis.

**Fig. 13.4:** Imagno/Getty Images.

**Fig. 13.5:** Courtesy Carl Rogers Memorial Library.

**Fig. 13.6:** agefotostock/SuperStock.

**Fig. 13.8:** Hulton Archive/Getty Images.

**Fig. 13.11:** Hulton-Deutsch Collection/Corbis.

**Fig. 13.12:** Lewis J. Merrim/Photo Researchers, Inc.

**Fig. 13.13:** Courtesy David Funder, University of California, Riverside. © The Photo Works.

**Fig. 13.15a:** Alamy.

**Fig. 13.15b:** Martin Thomas Photography/Alamy.

**Fig. 13.17:** Courtesy Dr. Christine Drea.

**Fig. 13.18a:** Royalty-Free/Corbis.

**Fig. 13.18b:** Ralph A. Clavenger/Corbis.

**Fig. 13.26:** Urban Zintel/Getty Images.

**Fig. 13.28:** Kelley et al. 2002, Figure 4, p. 789.

**Fig. 13.31:** Georgina Bowater/Corbis.

**Fig. 13.35a:** Walter Hodges/Getty Images.

**Fig. 13.35b:** Kyodo via AP Images.

**Cartoon 13.1:** The *New Yorker* Collection 1996/J. B. Handelsman from cartoonbank.com. All Rights Reserved.

**Cartoon 13.2:** The *New Yorker* Collection 1999/Barbara Smaller from cartoonbank.com. All Rights Reserved.

## CHAPTER 14

**Opener:** Joshua Sheldon/Getty Images.

**Fig. 14.1:** Zuma Press/Newscom.

**Fig. 14.2:** The Granger Collection, New York.

**Fig. 14.5:** Southern Illinois University.

**Fig. 14.8:** Joe McNally.

**Fig. 14.9:** David Hoffman/Photo Library/Alamy.

**Fig. 14.12:** Amy Toensing/Getty Images.

**Fig. 14.14:** Charles Eshelman/FilmMagic/Getty Images.

**Fig. 14.16(i):** Christina Kennedy/PhotoEdit.

**Fig. 14.16(ii):** Carl E. Schwartz et al., *Science 300,* 1952 (2003); DOI: 10.1126/science.1083703.

**Fig. 14.18:** *The New York Times*/Redux.

**Fig. 14.19:** Thomas Traill.

**Fig. 14.21:** Reprinted by permission of the publisher from *Why People Die by Suicide* by Thomas Joiner, p. 138, Cambridge, Mass.: Harvard University Press, Copyright © 2005 by the President and Fellows of Harvard College. All rights reserved.

**Fig. 14.22a–c:** *Abnormal Psychology,* 4th ed., by Seligman, Walker, and Rosenhan. Copyright W. W. Norton & Company, Inc. Used by permission of W. W. Norton & Company, Inc.

**Fig. 14.23:** Universal Pictures/Photofest.

**Fig. 14.26:** Peter Aprahamian/Corbis.

**Fig. 14.27:** Courtesy of Everett Collection.

**Fig. 14.28a–b:** From Osterlin, J., & Dawson, G. (1994). Early recognition of children with autism. A study of first birthday home videotapes. *Journal of Autism and Developmental Disorders, 24*, 247–257. Photographs courtesy Geraldine Dawson.

**Fig. 14.29(i–ii):** Courtesy of Dr. Ami Klin. (2003). The enactive mind from actions to cognition: Lessons from autism. *Philosophical Transactions of the Royal Society*.

**Fig. 14.30(i–ii):** From Zametkin, A. J., Nordhal, T. E., Gross, M., et al. (1990). Cerebral glucose metabolism in adults with hyperactivity of childhood onset. *New England Journal of Medicine, 323*(0), 1361–1366. Images courtesy of Alan Zametkin, NIH.

**Fig. 14.31:** JULI/LEONARD/MCT/Landov.

**Cartoon 14.1:** © The *New Yorker* Collection 2003/Michael Shaw from cartoonbank.com. All Rights Reserved.

## CHAPTER 15

**Opener:** Alex Telfer/Gallery Stock.

**Fig. 15.1:** Israel Images/Alamy.

**Fig. 15.2:** Bettmann/Corbis.

**Fig. 15.3:** Jack Guez/AFP/Getty Images.

**Fig. 15.4:** Courtesy Barbara A. Marinelli.

**Fig. 15.6a–e:** © 1983 Erika Stone.

**Fig. 15.7:** Nancy Sheehan/PhotoEdit.

**Fig. 15.8:** Barbara Davidson/*Los Angeles Times*.

**Fig. 15.10:** Daniele Pellegrini/Photo Researchers, Inc.

**Fig. 15.11:** Will McIntyre/Photo Researchers, Inc.

**Fig. 15.14:** Harry Goodwin/Rex Features.

**Fig. 15.15:** Alamy.

**Fig. 15.16:** Alain Jocard/AFP/Getty Images.

**Fig. 15.17:** Stockbyte Photography/Veer.

**Fig. 15.19:** The Advertising Archives.

**Fig. 15.22:** Pascal Goetheluck/Science Photo Library/Photo Researchers, Inc.

**Fig. 15.23:** *Scientific American Mind*, p. 31, courtesy of Helen Mayberg, M.D., Professor, Psychiatry and Behavioral Sciences.

**Fig. 15.24a:** Wide World Photos/AP.

**Fig. 15.24b:** Ulf Andersen/Getty Images.

**Fig. 15.27:** Peter Yates/*The New York Times*/REDUX.

**Fig. 15.30(i):** Najlah Feanny/Corbis.

**Fig. 15.30(ii):** Michael Newman/PhotoEdit.

**Fig. 15.32(i):** DMAC/Alamy.

**Fig. 15.32(ii):** Mary Kate Denny/PhotoEdit.

**Fig. 15.33:** The Lovaas Institute for Early Intervention.

**Fig. 15.34:** Kasari, C., Paparella, T., Freeman, S., & Jahromi, L. B. (2008). Language outcomes in autism: Randomized comparison of joint attention and play interventions. *Journal of Counseling and Clinical Psychology, 76*, 125–137.

**Fig. 15.35:** Richard Perry/*The New York Times*.

**Cartoon 15.1:** © The *New Yorker* Collection 1989/Danny Shanahan from cartoonbank.com. All Rights Reserved.

**Cartoon 15.2:** © The *New Yorker* Collection 1993/Lee Lorenz from cartoonbank.com. All Rights Reserved.

# NAME INDEX

Page numbers in *italics* refer to illustrations.

# SUBJECT INDEX

Page numbers in *italics* refer to figures.